SCIENCE AND HEALTH

WITH KEY TO THE SCRIPTURES

Writings by Mary Baker Eddy

Science and Health with Key to the Scriptures

Retrospection and Introspection

Miscellaneous Writings 1883-1896

Rudimental Divine Science

The People's Idea of God — Its Effect on Health and Christianity

Christian Healing

No and Yes

Unity of Good

Poems

Christ and Christmas

Christian Science versus Pantheism

Pulpit and Press

The First Church of Christ, Scientist, and Miscellany

Manual of The Mother Church

Message to The Mother Church, 1900

Message to The Mother Church, 1901

Message to The Mother Church, 1902

SCIENCE AND HEALTH

WITH KEY TO THE SCRIPTURES

BY MARY BAKER EDDY

Marcas Registradas

President of Massachusetts Metaphysical College and
Pastor Emeritus of The First Church of Christ, Scientist
Boston, Massachusetts

THE WRITINGS OF | MaryBakerEddy

BOSTON

ISBN 0-87952-260-7 hardcover

ISBN 0-87952-262-3 leather

Library of Congress Catalog Card Number 00-105023

Printed in the United States of America

Ye shall know the truth,
and the truth shall make you free. — JOHN viii. 32

There is nothing either good or bad,
but thinking makes it so. — SHAKESPEARE

Oh! Thou hast heard my prayer;
And I am blest!
This is Thy high behest: —
Thou here, and **everywhere***.* — MARY BAKER G. EDDY

Contents

Preface

1   **T**o those leaning on the sustaining infinite, to-day is big with blessings. The wakeful shepherd beholds
3 the first faint morning beams, ere cometh the full radiance of a risen day. So shone the pale star to the prophet-shepherds; yet it traversed the night, and came where, in
6 cradled obscurity, lay the Bethlehem babe, the human herald of Christ, Truth, who would make plain to benighted understanding the way of salvation through Christ
9 Jesus, till across a night of error should dawn the morning beams and shine the guiding star of being. The Wisemen were led to behold and to follow this daystar of
12 divine Science, lighting the way to eternal harmony.

     The time for thinkers has come. Truth, independent of doctrines and time-honored systems, knocks at the
15 portal of humanity. Contentment with the past and the cold conventionality of materialism are crumbling away. Ignorance of God is no longer the stepping-
18 stone to faith. The only guarantee of obedience is a right apprehension of Him whom to know aright is Life eternal. Though empires fall, "the Lord shall
21 reign forever."

     A book introduces new thoughts, but it cannot make them speedily understood. It is the task of the sturdy
24 pioneer to hew the tall oak and to cut the rough granite. Future ages must declare what the pioneer has accomplished.
27   Since the author's discovery of the might of Truth in

the treatment of disease as well as of sin, her system has   1
been fully tested and has not been found wanting; but
to reach the heights of Christian Science, man must live   3
in obedience to its divine Principle. To develop the full
might of this Science, the discords of corporeal sense
must yield to the harmony of spiritual sense, even as the   6
science of music corrects false tones and gives sweet concord to sound.

Theology and physics teach that both Spirit and   9
matter are real and good, whereas the fact is that
Spirit is good and real, and matter is Spirit's opposite. The question, What is Truth, is answered by   12
demonstration, — by healing both disease and sin; and
this demonstration shows that Christian healing confers the most health and makes the best men. On this   15
basis Christian Science will have a fair fight. Sickness
has been combated for centuries by doctors using material remedies; but the question arises, Is there less   18
sickness because of these practitioners? A vigorous
"No" is the response deducible from two connate
facts, — the reputed longevity of the Antediluvians,   21
and the rapid multiplication and increased violence of
diseases since the flood.

In the author's work, RETROSPECTION AND INTROSPEC-   24
TION, may be found a biographical sketch, narrating
experiences which led her, in the year 1866, to the discovery of the system that she denominated Christian   27
Science. As early as 1862 she began to write down and
give to friends the results of her Scriptural study, for
the Bible was her sole teacher; but these compositions   30
were crude, — the first steps of a child in the newly discovered world of Spirit.

1 She also began to jot down her thoughts on the
main subject, but these jottings were only infantile
3 lispings of Truth. A child drinks in the outward world
through the eyes and rejoices in the draught. He is
as sure of the world's existence as he is of his own; yet
6 he cannot describe the world. He finds a few words,
and with these he stammeringly attempts to convey his
feeling. Later, the tongue voices the more definite
9 thought, though still imperfectly.

So was it with the author. As a certain poet says of
himself, she "lisped in numbers, for the numbers
12 came." Certain essays written at that early date are
still in circulation among her first pupils; but they are
feeble attempts to state the Principle and practice of
15 Christian healing, and are not complete nor satisfactory expositions of Truth. To-day, though rejoicing
in some progress, she still finds herself a willing dis-
18 ciple at the heavenly gate, waiting for the Mind of
Christ.

Her first pamphlet on Christian Science was copy-
21 righted in 1870; but it did not appear in print until
1876, as she had learned that this Science must be
demonstrated by healing, before a work on the subject
24 could be profitably studied. From 1867 until 1875,
copies were, however, in friendly circulation.

Before writing this work, SCIENCE AND HEALTH, she
27 made copious notes of Scriptural exposition, which
have never been published. This was during the years
1867 and 1868. These efforts show her comparative
30 ignorance of the stupendous Life-problem up to that
time, and the degrees by which she came at length
to its solution; but she values them as a parent

may treasure the memorials of a child's growth, and   1
she would not have them changed.

The first edition of SCIENCE AND HEALTH was pub-   3
lished in 1875. Various books on mental healing have
since been issued, most of them incorrect in theory
and filled with plagiarisms from SCIENCE AND HEALTH.   6
They regard the human mind as a healing agent,
whereas this mind is not a factor in the Principle of
Christian Science. A few books, however, which are   9
based on this book, are useful.

The author has not compromised conscience to suit
the general drift of thought, but has bluntly and hon-   12
estly given the text of Truth. She has made no effort
to embellish, elaborate, or treat in full detail so infinite a theme. By thousands of well-authenticated   15
cases of healing, she and her students have proved the
worth of her teachings. These cases for the most part
have been abandoned as hopeless by regular medical   18
attendants. Few invalids will turn to God till all
physical supports have failed, because there is so little
faith in His disposition and power to heal disease.   21

The divine Principle of healing is proved in the
personal experience of any sincere seeker of Truth. Its
purpose is good, and its practice is safer and more po-   24
tent than that of any other sanitary method. The un-
biased Christian thought is soonest touched by Truth,
and convinced of it. Only those quarrel with her   27
method who do not understand her meaning, or discerning the truth, come not to the light lest their
works be reproved. No intellectual proficiency is req-   30
uisite in the learner, but sound morals are most desirable.

1   Many imagine that the phenomena of physical healing in Christian Science present only a phase of the
3   action of the human mind, which action in some unexplained way results in the cure of disease. On the contrary, Christian Science rationally explains that all
6   other pathological methods are the fruits of human
faith in matter, — faith in the workings, not of Spirit,
but of the fleshly mind which must yield to Science.

9   The physical healing of Christian Science results
now, as in Jesus' time, from the operation of divine
Principle, before which sin and disease lose their real-
12   ity in human consciousness and disappear as naturally
and as necessarily as darkness gives place to light and
sin to reformation. Now, as then, these mighty works
15   are not supernatural, but supremely natural. They are
the sign of Immanuel, or "God with us," — a divine
influence ever present in human consciousness and re-
18   peating itself, coming now as was promised aforetime,

> To preach deliverance to the captives [of sense],
> And recovering of sight to the blind,
21   > To set at liberty them that are bruised.

      When God called the author to proclaim His Gospel
to this age, there came also the charge to plant and
24   water His vineyard.

      The first school of Christian Science Mind-healing
was started by the author with only one student in
27   Lynn, Massachusetts, about the year 1867. In 1881,
she opened the Massachusetts Metaphysical College in
Boston, under the seal of the Commonwealth, a law
30   relative to colleges having been passed, which enabled
her to get this institution chartered for medical pur-

poses. No charters were granted to Christian Scien-   1
tists for such institutions after 1883, and up to that
date, hers was the only College of this character which   3
had been established in the United States, where
Christian Science was first introduced.

During seven years over four thousand students   6
were taught by the author in this College. Meanwhile
she was pastor of the first established Church of
Christ, Scientist; President of the first Christian Sci-   9
entist Association, convening monthly; publisher of
her own works; and (for a portion of this time) sole
editor and publisher of the Christian Science Journal,   12
the first periodical issued by Christian Scientists. She
closed her College, October 29, 1889, in the height of
its prosperity with a deep-lying conviction that the   15
next two years of her life should be given to the preparation of the revision of SCIENCE AND HEALTH, which
was published in 1891. She retained her charter, and   18
as its President, reopened the College in 1899 as auxil-
iary to her church. Until June 10, 1907, she had never
read this book throughout consecutively in order to elu-   21
cidate her idealism.

In the spirit of Christ's charity, — as one who "hopeth
all things, endureth all things," and is joyful to bear   24
consolation to the sorrowing and healing to the sick, —
she commits these pages to honest seekers for Truth.

MARY BAKER EDDY

SCIENCE AND HEALTH

Chapter 1

Prayer

For verily I say unto you,
That whosoever shall say unto this mountain,
Be thou removed, and be thou cast into the sea;
and shall not doubt in his heart, but shall believe that
those things which he saith shall come to pass;
he shall have whatsoever he saith.
Therefore I say unto you, What things soever ye desire
when ye pray, believe that ye receive them,
and ye shall have them.

Your Father knoweth what things ye have need of,
before ye ask Him. — CHRIST JESUS.

1   The prayer that reforms the sinner and heals the
sick is an absolute faith that all things are
3 possible to God, — a spiritual understanding of Him,
an unselfed love. Regardless of what another may say
or think on this subject, I speak from experience.
6 Prayer, watching, and working, combined with self-immolation, are God's gracious means for accomplishing
whatever has been successfully done for the Christian-
9 ization and health of mankind.

    Thoughts unspoken are not unknown to the divine
Mind. Desire is prayer; and no loss can occur from
12 trusting God with our desires, that they may be
moulded and exalted before they take form in words
and in deeds.

1

What are the motives for prayer? Do we pray to   1
make ourselves better or to benefit those who hear us,

**Right
motives**
to enlighten the infinite or to be heard of   3
men? Are we benefited by praying? Yes,
the desire which goes forth hungering after righteousness is blessed of our Father, and it does not return   6
unto us void.

God is not moved by the breath of praise to do more
than He has already done, nor can the infinite do less   9

**Deity
unchangeable**
than bestow all good, since He is unchanging wisdom and Love. We can do more for
ourselves by humble fervent petitions, but the All-lov-   12
ing does not grant them simply on the ground of lip-
service, for He already knows all.

Prayer cannot change the Science of being, but it   15
tends to bring us into harmony with it. Goodness at-
tains the demonstration of Truth. A request that
God will save us is not all that is required. The mere   18
habit of pleading with the divine Mind, as one pleads
with a human being, perpetuates the belief in God as
humanly circumscribed, — an error which impedes spirit-   21
ual growth.

God is Love. Can we ask Him to be more? God is
intelligence. Can we inform the infinite Mind of any-   24

**God's
standard**
thing He does not already comprehend?
Do we expect to change perfection? Shall
we plead for more at the open fount, which is pour-   27
ing forth more than we accept? The unspoken desire
does bring us nearer the source of all existence and
blessedness.   30

Asking God to *be* God is a vain repetition. God is
"the same yesterday, and to-day, and forever;" and

1 He who is immutably right will do right without being
reminded of His province. The wisdom of man is not
3 sufficient to warrant him in advising God.

Who would stand before a blackboard, and pray the
principle of mathematics to solve the problem? The
6 rule is already established, and it is our   The spiritual
task to work out the solution. Shall we   mathematics
ask the divine Principle of all goodness to do His own
9 work? His work is done, and we have only to avail
ourselves of God's rule in order to receive His blessing, which enables us to work out our own salvation.

12 The Divine Being must be reflected by man, — else
man is not the image and likeness of the patient,
tender, and true, the One "altogether lovely;" but to
15 understand God is the work of eternity, and demands
absolute consecration of thought, energy, and desire.

How empty are our conceptions of Deity! We admit
18 theoretically that God is good, omnipotent, omnipresent, infinite, and then we try to give   Prayerful
information to this infinite Mind. We plead   ingratitude
21 for unmerited pardon and for a liberal outpouring of
benefactions. Are we really grateful for the good
already received? Then we shall avail ourselves of the
24 blessings we have, and thus be fitted to receive more.
Gratitude is much more than a verbal expression of
thanks. Action expresses more gratitude than speech.
27 If we are ungrateful for Life, Truth, and Love, and
yet return thanks to God for all blessings, we are insincere and incur the sharp censure our Master pro-
30 nounces on hypocrites. In such a case, the only
acceptable prayer is to put the finger on the lips and
remember our blessings. While the heart is far from

divine Truth and Love, we cannot conceal the ingrati-   1
tude of barren lives.

What we most need is the prayer of fervent desire   3
for growth in grace, expressed in patience, meekness,

love, and good deeds. To keep the commandments of our Master and follow his   6
example, is our proper debt to him and the only
worthy evidence of our gratitude for all that he has
done. Outward worship is not of itself sufficient to   9
express loyal and heartfelt gratitude, since he has
said: "If ye love me, keep my commandments."

The habitual struggle to be always good is unceas-   12
ing prayer. Its motives are made manifest in the
blessings they bring, — blessings which, even if not
acknowledged in audible words, attest our worthiness   15
to be partakers of Love.

Simply asking that we may love God will never
make us love Him; but the longing to be better   18

and holier, expressed in daily watchfulness and in striving to assimilate more of
the divine character, will mould and fashion us   21
anew, until we awake in His likeness. We reach the
Science of Christianity through demonstration of the
divine nature; but in this wicked world goodness   24
will "be evil spoken of," and patience must bring
experience.

Audible prayer can never do the works of spiritual   27
understanding, which regenerates; but silent prayer,

watchfulness, and devout obedience enable
us to follow Jesus' example. Long prayers,   30
superstition, and creeds clip the strong pinions of love,
and clothe religion in human forms. Whatever mate-

1 rializes worship hinders man's spiritual growth and keeps
him from demonstrating his power over error.

3 Sorrow for wrong-doing is but one step towards reform
and the very easiest step. The next and great step required by wisdom is the test of our sincerity, Sorrow and
6 — namely, reformation. To this end we are reformation
placed under the stress of circumstances. Temptation
bids us repeat the offence, and woe comes in return for
9 what is done. So it will ever be, till we learn that there
is no discount in the law of justice and that we must pay
"the uttermost farthing." The measure ye mete "shall
12 be measured to you again," and it will be full "and running over."

Saints and sinners get their full award, but not always
15 in this world. The followers of Christ drank his cup.
Ingratitude and persecution filled it to the brim; but God
pours the riches of His love into the understanding and
18 affections, giving us strength according to our day. Sinners flourish "like a green bay tree;" but, looking farther,
the Psalmist could see their end, — the destruction of sin
21 through suffering.

Prayer is not to be used as a confessional to cancel sin.
Such an error would impede true religion. Sin is forgiven
24 only as it is destroyed by Christ, — Truth and Cancellation
Life. If prayer nourishes the belief that sin is of human sin
cancelled, and that man is made better merely by praying,
27 prayer is an evil. He grows worse who continues in sin
because he fancies himself forgiven.

An apostle says that the Son of God [Christ] came to
30 "destroy the *works* of the devil." We should Diabolism
follow our divine Exemplar, and seek the de- destroyed
struction of all evil works, error and disease included.

We cannot escape the penalty due for sin. The Scrip-   1
tures say, that if we deny Christ, "he also will deny us."

Divine Love corrects and governs man. Men may   3
pardon, but this divine Principle alone reforms the

Pardon and amendment sinner. God is not separate from the wisdom He bestows. The talents He gives we   6
must improve. Calling on Him to forgive our work
badly done or left undone, implies the vain supposition
that we have nothing to do but to ask pardon, and   9
that afterwards we shall be free to repeat the offence.

To cause suffering as the result of sin, is the means
of destroying sin. Every supposed pleasure in sin   12
will furnish more than its equivalent of pain, until belief in material life and sin is destroyed. To reach
heaven, the harmony of being, we must understand   15
the divine Principle of being.

"God is Love." More than this we cannot ask,
higher we cannot look, farther we cannot go. To   18

Mercy without partiality suppose that God forgives or punishes sin
according as His mercy is sought or un-
sought, is to misunderstand Love and to make prayer   21
the safety-valve for wrong-doing.

Jesus uncovered and rebuked sin before he cast it
out. Of a sick woman he said that Satan had bound   24

Divine severity her, and to Peter he said, "Thou art an offence unto me." He came teaching and
showing men how to destroy sin, sickness, and death.   27
He said of the fruitless tree, "[It] is hewn down."

It is believed by many that a certain magistrate,
who lived in the time of Jesus, left this record: "His   30
rebuke is fearful." The strong language of our Master confirms this description.

1   The only civil sentence which he had for error was,
"Get thee behind me, Satan." Still stronger evidence
3   that Jesus' reproof was pointed and pungent is found
in his own words, — showing the necessity for such
forcible utterance, when he cast out devils and healed
6   the sick and sinning. The relinquishment of error de-
prives material sense of its false claims.

    Audible prayer is impressive; it gives momentary
9   solemnity and elevation to thought. But does it produce any lasting benefit? Looking deeply
into these things, we find that "a zeal . . .
12 not according to knowledge" gives occasion for reaction unfavorable to spiritual growth, sober resolve, and
wholesome perception of God's requirements. The mo-
15 tives for verbal prayer may embrace too much love of
applause to induce or encourage Christian sentiment.

Audible praying

    Physical sensation, not Soul, produces material ec-
18 stasy and emotion. If spiritual sense always guided
men, there would grow out of ecstatic moments a higher experience and a better life
21 with more devout self-abnegation and purity. A self-
satisfied ventilation of fervent sentiments never makes
a Christian. God is not influenced by man. The "di-
24 vine ear" is not an auditory nerve. It is the all-hearing
and all-knowing Mind, to whom each need of man is
always known and by whom it will be supplied.

Emotional utterances

27   The danger from prayer is that it may lead us into temptation. By it we may become involuntary hypocrites, uttering desires which are not real and consoling
30 ourselves in the midst of sin with the recollection
that we have prayed over it or mean to ask forgiveness at some later day. Hypocrisy is fatal to religion.

Danger from audible prayer

A wordy prayer may afford a quiet sense of self-
justification, though it makes the sinner a hypocrite.
We never need to despair of an honest heart; but
there is little hope for those who come only spasmodi-
cally face to face with their wickedness and then seek to
hide it. Their prayers are indexes which do not correspond
with their character. They hold secret fellowship with
sin, and such externals are spoken of by Jesus as "like
unto whited sepulchres . . . full . . . of all uncleanness."

If a man, though apparently fervent and prayerful,
is impure and therefore insincere, what must be the
Aspiration and love comment upon him? If he reached the
loftiness of his prayer, there would be no
occasion for comment. If we feel the aspiration, humility, gratitude, and love which our words express, —
this God accepts; and it is wise not to try to deceive
ourselves or others, for "there is nothing covered that
shall not be revealed." Professions and audible prayers are like charity in one respect, — they "cover the
multitude of sins." Praying for humility with whatever fervency of expression does not always mean a
desire for it. If we turn away from the poor, we are
not ready to receive the reward of Him who blesses
the poor. We confess to having a very wicked heart
and ask that it may be laid bare before us, but do
we not already know more of this heart than we are
willing to have our neighbor see?

We should examine ourselves and learn what is the
affection and purpose of the heart, for in this way
Searching the heart only can we learn what we honestly are. If a
friend informs us of a fault, do we listen pa-
tiently to the rebuke and credit what is said? Do we not

1 rather give thanks that we are "not as other men"?
During many years the author has been most grateful
3 for merited rebuke. The wrong lies in unmerited censure, — in the falsehood which does no one any good.

The test of all prayer lies in the answer to these
6 questions: Do we love our neighbor better because of
this asking? Do we pursue the old selfishness, satisfied with having prayed for some-

*Summit of
aspiration*

9 thing better, though we give no evidence of the sincerity of our requests by living consistently with our
prayer? If selfishness has given place to kindness,
12 we shall regard our neighbor unselfishly, and bless
them that curse us; but we shall never meet this great
duty simply by asking that it may be done. There is
15 a cross to be taken up before we can enjoy the fruition
of our hope and faith.

Dost thou "love the Lord thy God with all thy
18 heart, and with all thy soul, and with all thy mind"?
This command includes much, even the sur-
render of all merely material sensation, affec-

*Practical
religion*

21 tion, and worship. This is the El Dorado of Christianity.
It involves the Science of Life, and recognizes only the
divine control of Spirit, in which Soul is our master,
24 and material sense and human will have no place.

Are you willing to leave all for Christ, for Truth, and
so be counted among sinners? No! Do you really desire
27 to attain this point? No! Then why make long
prayers about it and ask to be Christians,

*The chalice
sacrificial*

since you do not care to tread in the footsteps of our
30 dear Master? If unwilling to follow his example, why
pray with the lips that you may be partakers of his
nature? Consistent prayer is the desire to do right.

Prayer means that we desire to walk and will walk in   1
the light so far as we receive it, even though with bleeding footsteps, and that waiting patiently on the Lord,   3
we will leave our real desires to be rewarded by Him.

The world must grow to the spiritual understanding
of prayer. If good enough to profit by Jesus' cup of   6
earthly sorrows, God will sustain us under these sorrows. Until we are thus divinely qualified and are
willing to drink his cup, millions of vain repetitions   9
will never pour into prayer the unction of Spirit in
demonstration of power and "with signs following."
Christian Science reveals a necessity for overcoming the   12
world, the flesh, and evil, and thus destroying all error.

Seeking is not sufficient. It is striving that enables
us to enter. Spiritual attainments open the door to a   15
higher understanding of the divine Life.

One of the forms of worship in Thibet is to carry a
praying-machine through the streets, and stop at the   18

Perfunctory prayers

doors to earn a penny by grinding out a
prayer. But the advance guard of progress has
paid for the privilege of prayer the price of persecution.   21

Experience teaches us that we do not always receive
the blessings we ask for in prayer. There is some misapprehension of the source and means of   24

Asking amiss

all goodness and blessedness, or we should
certainly receive that for which we ask. The Scriptures say: "Ye ask, and receive not, because ye ask   27
amiss, that ye may consume it upon your lusts." That
which we desire and for which we ask, it is not always
best for us to receive. In this case infinite Love will   30
not grant the request. Do you ask wisdom to be merciful and not to punish sin? Then "ye ask amiss."

1   Without punishment, sin would multiply. Jesus' prayer, "Forgive us our debts," specified also the terms of
3   forgiveness. When forgiving the adulterous woman he said, "Go, and sin no more."

   A magistrate sometimes remits the penalty, but this
6   may be no moral benefit to the criminal, and at best, it only saves the criminal from one form of **Remission**
punishment. The moral law, which has the **of penalty**
9   right to acquit or condemn, always demands restitution before mortals can "go up higher." Broken law brings penalty in order to compel this progress.

12   Mere legal pardon (and there is no other, for divine Principle never pardons our sins or mistakes till they are corrected) leaves the offender free to re- **Truth**
15   peat the offence, if indeed, he has not already **annihilates**
suffered sufficiently from vice to make him turn from it **error**
with loathing. Truth bestows no pardon upon error, but
18   wipes it out in the most effectual manner. Jesus suffered for our sins, not to annul the divine sentence for an individual's sin, but because sin brings inevitable suffering.

21   Petitions bring to mortals only the results of mortals' own faith. We know that a desire for holiness is requisite in order to gain holiness; but if we **Desire for**
24   desire holiness above all else, we shall sac- **holiness**
rifice everything for it. We must be willing to do this, that we may walk securely in the only practical road
27   to holiness. Prayer cannot change the unalterable Truth, nor can prayer alone give us an understanding of Truth; but prayer, coupled with a fervent habitual
30   desire to know and do the will of God, will bring us into all Truth. Such a desire has little need of audible expression. It is best expressed in thought and in life.

"The prayer of faith shall save the sick," says the Scripture. What is this healing prayer? A mere request that God will heal the sick has no power to gain more of the divine presence than is always at hand. The beneficial effect of such prayer for the sick is on the human mind, making it act more powerfully on the body through a blind faith in God. This, however, is one belief casting out another, — a belief in the unknown casting out a belief in sickness. It is neither Science nor Truth which acts through blind belief, nor is it the human understanding of the divine healing Principle as manifested in Jesus, whose humble prayers were deep and conscientious protests of Truth, — of man's likeness to God and of man's unity with Truth and Love.

Prayer to a corporeal God affects the sick like a drug, which has no efficacy of its own but borrows its power from human faith and belief. The drug does nothing, because it has no intelligence. It is a mortal belief, not divine Principle or Love, which causes a drug to be apparently either poisonous or sanative.

The common custom of praying for the recovery of the sick finds help in blind belief, whereas help should come from the enlightened understanding. Changes in belief may go on indefinitely, but they are the merchandise of human thought and not the outgrowth of divine Science.

Does Deity interpose in behalf of one worshipper, and not help another who offers the same measure of prayer? If the sick recover because they pray or are prayed for audibly, only petitioners (*per se* or by proxy) should get well. In divine Science, where prayers are mental, *all* may avail them-

1

3

6

9

12

15

18

21

24

27

30

selves of God as "a very present help in trouble."
Love is impartial and universal in its adaptation and
bestowals. It is the open fount which cries, "Ho,
every one that thirsteth, come ye to the waters."

In public prayer we often go beyond our convictions,
beyond the honest standpoint of fervent desire. If we
are not secretly yearning and openly striving for the accomplishment of all we ask,
our prayers are "vain repetitions," such as the heathen
use. If our petitions are sincere, we labor for what we
ask; and our Father, who seeth in secret, will reward
us openly. Can the mere public expression of our desires increase them? Do we gain the omnipotent ear
sooner by words than by thoughts? Even if prayer is
sincere, God knows our need before we tell Him or our
fellow-beings about it. If we cherish the desire honestly and silently and humbly, God will bless it, and
we shall incur less risk of overwhelming our real
wishes with a torrent of words.

If we pray to God as a corporeal person, this will
prevent us from relinquishing the human doubts and
fears which attend such a belief, and so we
cannot grasp the wonders wrought by infi-
nite, incorporeal Love, to whom all things are possible.
Because of human ignorance of the divine Principle,
Love, the Father of all is represented as a corporeal
creator; hence men recognize themselves as merely
physical, and are ignorant of man as God's image or reflection and of man's eternal incorporeal existence. The
world of error is ignorant of the world of Truth, — blind
to the reality of man's existence, — for the world of sensation is not cognizant of life in Soul, not in body.

Public exaggerations

Corporeal ignorance

If we are sensibly with the body and regard omnipo-   1
tence as a corporeal, material person, whose ear we
would gain, we are not "absent from the   3

**Bodily
presence**

body" and "present with the Lord" in the
demonstration of Spirit. We cannot "serve two masters." To be "present with the Lord" is to have, not   6
mere emotional ecstasy or faith, but the actual demonstration and understanding of Life as revealed in
Christian Science. To be "with the Lord" is to be in   9
obedience to the law of God, to be absolutely governed
by divine Love, — by Spirit, not by matter.

Become conscious for a single moment that Life and   12
intelligence are purely spiritual, — neither in nor of

**Spiritualized
consciousness**

matter, — and the body will then utter no
complaints. If suffering from a belief in   15
sickness, you will find yourself suddenly well. Sorrow
is turned into joy when the body is controlled by spiritual Life, Truth, and Love. Hence the hope of the   18
promise Jesus bestows: "He that believeth on me,
the works that I do shall he do also; . . . because I
go unto my Father," — [because the Ego is absent from   21
the body, and present with Truth and Love.] The
Lord's Prayer is the prayer of Soul, not of material
sense.   24

Entirely separate from the belief and dream of material living, is the Life divine, revealing spiritual understanding and the consciousness of man's dominion   27
over the whole earth. This understanding casts out
error and heals the sick, and with it you can speak
"as one having authority."   30

"When thou prayest, enter into thy closet, and,
when thou hast shut thy door, pray to thy Father

1 which is in secret; and thy Father, which seeth in secret, shall reward thee openly."

3 So spake Jesus. The closet typifies the sanctuary of Spirit, the door of which shuts out sinful sense but lets in Truth, Life, and Love. Closed to

6 error, it is open to Truth, and *vice versa*.

Spiritual sanctuary

The Father in secret is unseen to the physical senses, but He knows all things and rewards according to

9 motives, not according to speech. To enter into the heart of prayer, the door of the erring senses must be closed. Lips must be mute and materialism silent,

12 that man may have audience with Spirit, the divine Principle, Love, which destroys all error.

In order to pray aright, we must enter into the

15 closet and shut the door. We must close the lips and silence the material senses. In the quiet sanctuary of earnest longings, we must

Effectual invocation

18 deny sin and plead God's allness. We must resolve to take up the cross, and go forth with honest hearts to work and watch for wisdom, Truth, and Love. We

21 must "pray without ceasing." Such prayer is answered, in so far as we put our desires into practice. The Master's injunction is, that we pray in secret and

24 let our lives attest our sincerity.

Christians rejoice in secret beauty and bounty, hidden from the world, but known to God. Self-forgetfulness,

27 purity, and affection are constant prayers. Practice not profession, understanding not belief, gain the ear and right hand of omnipotence and

Trustworthy beneficence

30 they assuredly call down infinite blessings. Trustworthiness is the foundation of enlightened faith. Without a fitness for holiness, we cannot receive holiness.

Loftiest
adoration

A great sacrifice of material things must precede this
advanced spiritual understanding. The highest prayer
is not one of faith merely; it is demonstration. Such prayer heals sickness, and must
destroy sin and death. It distinguishes between Truth
that is sinless and the falsity of sinful sense.

Our Master taught his disciples one brief prayer,
which we name after him the Lord's Prayer. Our Mas-
The prayer of
Jesus Christ
ter said, "After this manner therefore pray
ye," and then he gave that prayer which
covers all human needs. There is indeed some doubt
among Bible scholars, whether the last line is not an
addition to the prayer by a later copyist; but this does
not affect the meaning of the prayer itself.

In the phrase, "Deliver us from evil," the original
properly reads, "Deliver us from the evil one." This
reading strengthens our scientific apprehension of the peti-
tion, for Christian Science teaches us that "the evil one," or
one evil, is but another name for the first lie and all liars.

Only as we rise above all material sensuousness and
sin, can we reach the heaven-born aspiration and spiritual consciousness, which is indicated in the Lord's
Prayer and which instantaneously heals the sick.

Here let me give what I understand to be the spiritual sense of the Lord's Prayer:

Our Father which art in heaven,
  Our Father-Mother God, all-harmonious,

Hallowed be Thy name.
  Adorable One.

Thy kingdom come.
  Thy kingdom is come; Thou art ever-present.

1   Thy will be done in earth, as it is in heaven.

Enable us to know, — as in heaven, so on earth, — God is
3   *omnipotent, supreme.*

Give us this day our daily bread;

Give us grace for to-day; feed the famished affections;

6   And forgive us our debts, as we forgive our debtors.

And Love is reflected in love;

And lead us not into temptation, but deliver us from
9   evil;

*And God leadeth us not into temptation, but delivereth
us from sin, disease, and death.*

12   For Thine is the kingdom, and the power, and the
glory, forever.

For God is infinite, all-power, all Life, Truth, Love, over
15   *all, and All.*

Chapter 2

Atonement and Eucharist

And they that are Christ's have crucified the flesh
with the affections and lusts. — PAUL.

For Christ sent me not to baptize,
but to preach the gospel. — PAUL.

For I say unto you,
I will not drink of the fruit of the vine,
until the kingdom of God shall come. — JESUS.

A tonement is the exemplification of man's unity   1
with God, whereby man reflects divine Truth, Life,
and Love. Jesus of Nazareth taught and demonstrated   3
man's oneness with the Father, and for this we owe him
endless homage. His mission was both in-

Divine oneness   dividual and collective. He did life's work   6
aright not only in justice to himself, but in mercy to
mortals, — to show them how to do theirs, but not to do
it for them nor to relieve them of a single responsibility.   9
Jesus acted boldly, against the accredited evidence of the
senses, against Pharisaical creeds and practices, and he
refuted all opponents with his healing power.   12

The atonement of Christ reconciles man to God, not
God to man; for the divine Principle of Christ is God,

Human reconciliation   and how can God propitiate Himself? Christ   15
is Truth, which reaches no higher than itself.
The fountain can rise no higher than its source. Christ,
Truth, could conciliate no nature above his own, derived   18

18

1   from the eternal Love. It was therefore Christ's purpose
to reconcile man to God, not God to man. Love and

3   Truth are not at war with God's image and likeness.
Man cannot exceed divine Love, and so atone for himself. Even Christ cannot reconcile Truth to error, for

6   Truth and error are irreconcilable. Jesus aided in recon-
ciling man to God by giving man a truer sense of Love,
the divine Principle of Jesus' teachings, and this truer

9   sense of Love redeems man from the law of matter,
sin, and death by the law of Spirit, — the law of divine
Love.

12   The Master forbore not to speak the whole truth, declaring precisely what would destroy sickness, sin, and
death, although his teaching set households at variance,

15   and brought to material beliefs not peace, but a
sword.

Every pang of repentance and suffering, every effort

18   for reform, every good thought and deed, will help us to
understand Jesus' atonement for sin and aid   **Efficacious**
its efficacy; but if the sinner continues to pray   **repentance**

21   and repent, sin and be sorry, he has little part in the atonement, — in the *at-one-ment* with God, — for he lacks the
practical repentance, which reforms the heart and enables

24   man to do the will of wisdom. Those who cannot demonstrate, at least in part, the divine Principle of the teachings and practice of our Master have no part in God. If

27   living in disobedience to Him, we ought to feel no security, although God is good.

Jesus urged the commandment, "Thou shalt have no

30   other gods before me," which may be ren-   **Jesus'**
dered: Thou shalt have no belief of Life as   **sinless career**
mortal; thou shalt not know evil, for there is one Life, —

even God, good. He rendered "unto Cæsar the things   1
which are Cæsar's; and unto God the things that are
God's." He at last paid no homage to forms of doctrine   3
or to theories of man, but acted and spake as he was moved,
not by spirits but by Spirit.

To the ritualistic priest and hypocritical Pharisee   6
Jesus said, "The publicans and the harlots go into the
kingdom of God before you." Jesus' history made a
new calendar, which we call the Christian era; but he   9
established no ritualistic worship. He knew that men
can be baptized, partake of the Eucharist, support the
clergy, observe the Sabbath, make long prayers, and yet   12
be sensual and sinful.

Jesus bore our infirmities; he knew the error of mortal
belief, and "with his stripes [the rejection of error] we are   15
Perfect healed." "Despised and rejected of men,"
example returning blessing for cursing, he taught mortals the opposite of themselves, even the nature of God;   18
and when error felt the power of Truth, the scourge and
the cross awaited the great Teacher. Yet he swerved not,
well knowing that to obey the divine order and trust God,   21
saves retracing and traversing anew the path from sin to
holiness.

Material belief is slow to acknowledge what the   24
spiritual fact implies. The truth is the centre of all
Behest of religion. It commands sure entrance into
the cross the realm of Love. St. Paul wrote, "Let us   27
lay aside every weight, and the sin which doth so
easily beset us, and let us run with patience the race that
is set before us;" that is, let us put aside material self   30
and sense, and seek the divine Principle and Science of
all healing.

1   If Truth is overcoming error in your daily walk and
conversation, you can finally say, "I have fought a
3   good fight . . . I have kept the faith," be-   **Moral**
cause you are a better man. This is having   **victory**
our part in the at-one-ment with Truth and Love.
6   Christians do not continue to labor and pray, expecting
because of another's goodness, suffering, and triumph,
that they shall reach his harmony and reward.
9   If the disciple is advancing spiritually, he is striving to enter in. He constantly turns away from material sense, and looks towards the imperishable things
12 of Spirit. If honest, he will be in earnest from the
start, and gain a little each day in the right direction,
till at last he finishes his course with joy.
15   If my friends are going to Europe, while I am *en
route* for California, we are not journeying together.
We have separate time-tables to consult,   **Inharmonious**
18 different routes to pursue. Our paths have   **travellers**
diverged at the very outset, and we have little opportunity to help each other. On the contrary, if my
21 friends pursue my course, we have the same railroad
guides, and our mutual interests are identical; or, if I
take up their line of travel, they help me on, and our
24 companionship may continue.
    Being in sympathy with matter, the worldly man is at
the beck and call of error, and will be attracted thither-
27 ward. He is like a traveller going westward   **Zigzag**
for a pleasure-trip. The company is alluring   **course**
and the pleasures exciting. After following the sun for
30 six days, he turns east on the seventh, satisfied if he can
only imagine himself drifting in the right direction. By-
and-by, ashamed of his zigzag course, he would borrow

Science and Health

the passport of some wiser pilgrim, thinking with the aid 1
of this to find and follow the right road.

Vibrating like a pendulum between sin and the hope 3
of forgiveness, — selfishness and sensuality causing constant retrogression, — our moral progress will
be slow. Waking to Christ's demand, mortals 6
experience suffering. This causes them, even as drowning men, to make vigorous efforts to save themselves; and
through Christ's precious love these efforts are crowned 9
with success.

**Moral
retrogression**

"Work out your own salvation," is the demand of
Life and Love, for to this end God worketh with you. 12
"Occupy till I come!" Wait for your re-
ward, and "be not weary in well doing." If
your endeavors are beset by fearful odds, and you receive 15
no present reward, go not back to error, nor become a
sluggard in the race.

**Wait for
reward**

When the smoke of battle clears away, you will dis- 18
cern the good you have done, and receive according to
your deserving. Love is not hasty to deliver us from
temptation, for Love means that we shall be tried and 21
purified.

Final deliverance from error, whereby we rejoice in
immortality, boundless freedom, and sinless sense, is not 24
reached through paths of flowers nor by pinning
one's faith without works to another's vicarious
effort. Whosoever believeth that wrath is righteous or 27
that divinity is appeased by human suffering, does not
understand God.

**Deliverance
not vicarious**

Justice requires reformation of the sinner. Mercy 30
cancels the debt only when justice approves. Revenge
is inadmissible. Wrath which is only appeased is not

destroyed, but partially indulged. Wisdom and Love
may require many sacrifices of self to save us from sin.
One sacrifice, however great, is insufficient to
pay the debt of sin. The atonement requires
constant self-immolation on the sinner's part. That
God's wrath should be vented upon His beloved Son, is
divinely unnatural. Such a theory is man-made. The
atonement is a hard problem in theology, but its scientific explanation is, that suffering is an error of sinful sense
which Truth destroys, and that eventually both sin and suffering will fall at the feet of everlasting Love.

Rabbinical lore said: "He that taketh one doctrine,
firm in faith, has the Holy Ghost dwelling in him."
This preaching receives a strong rebuke in
the Scripture, "Faith without works is dead."
Faith, if it be mere belief, is as a pendulum swinging between nothing and something, having no fixity. Faith,
advanced to spiritual understanding, is the evidence gained
from Spirit, which rebukes sin of every kind and establishes the claims of God.

In Hebrew, Greek, Latin, and English, *faith* and the
words corresponding thereto have these two definitions, *trustfulness* and *trustworthiness*. One
kind of faith trusts one's welfare to others.
Another kind of faith understands divine Love and how
to work out one's "own salvation, with fear and trembling." "Lord, I believe; help thou mine unbelief!"
expresses the helplessness of a blind faith; whereas the
injunction, "Believe . . . and thou shalt be saved!"
demands self-reliant trustworthiness, which includes spiritual understanding and confides all to God.

The Hebrew verb *to believe* means also *to be firm* or

Marginal headings:

Justice and substitution

Doctrines and faith

Self-reliance and confidence

Line numbers: 1, 3, 6, 9, 12, 15, 18, 21, 24, 27, 30

to be constant. This certainly applies to Truth and Love   1
understood and practised. Firmness in error will never
save from sin, disease, and death.   3

Acquaintance with the original texts, and willingness
to give up human beliefs (established by hierarchies, and
instigated sometimes by the worst passions of   6
men), open the way for Christian Science to be
understood, and make the Bible the chart of life, where
the buoys and healing currents of Truth are pointed   9
out.

He to whom "the arm of the Lord" is revealed will
believe our report, and rise into newness of life with re-   12
generation. This is having part in the atone-
ment; this is the understanding, in which
Jesus suffered and triumphed. The time is not distant   15
when the ordinary theological views of atonement will
undergo a great change, — a change as radical as that
which has come over popular opinions in regard to pre-   18
destination and future punishment.

Does erudite theology regard the crucifixion of Jesus
chiefly as providing a ready pardon for all sinners who   21
ask for it and are willing to be forgiven?
Does spiritualism find Jesus' death necessary
only for the presentation, after death, of the material   24
Jesus, as a proof that spirits can return to earth? Then
we must differ from them both.

The efficacy of the crucifixion lay in the practical af-   27
fection and goodness it demonstrated for mankind. The
truth had been lived among men; but until they saw that
it enabled their Master to triumph over the grave, his own   30
disciples could not admit such an event to be possible.
After the resurrection, even the unbelieving Thomas was

Margin notes:

Life's healing currents

Radical changes

Purpose of crucifixion

1   forced to acknowledge how complete was the great proof of
Truth and Love.

3   The spiritual essence of blood is sacrifice. The efficacy of Jesus' spiritual offering is infinitely greater than
can be expressed by our sense of human

True flesh
and blood

6   blood. The material blood of Jesus was no
more efficacious to cleanse from sin when it was shed
upon "the accursed tree," than when it was flowing in

9   his veins as he went daily about his Father's business.
His true flesh and blood were his Life; and they truly eat
his flesh and drink his blood, who partake of that divine

12   Life.

       Jesus taught the way of Life by demonstration, that
we may understand how this divine Principle heals

15   the sick, casts out error, and triumphs over
death. Jesus presented the ideal of God better

Effective
triumph

than could any man whose origin was less spiritual. By

18   his obedience to God, he demonstrated more spiritually than all others the Principle of being. Hence the
force of his admonition, "If ye love me, keep my com-

21   mandments."

       Though demonstrating his control over sin and disease,
the great Teacher by no means relieved others from giving

24   the requisite proofs of their own piety. He worked for
their guidance, that they might demonstrate this power as
he did and understand its divine Principle. Implicit faith

27   in the Teacher and all the emotional love we can bestow
on him, will never alone make us imitators of him. We
must go and do likewise, else we are not improving the

30   great blessings which our Master worked and suffered to
bestow upon us. The divinity of the Christ was made
manifest in the humanity of Jesus.

While we adore Jesus, and the heart overflows with
gratitude for what he did for mortals, — treading alone

**Individual
experience**
his loving pathway up to the throne of
glory, in speechless agony exploring the way
for us, — yet Jesus spares us not one individual experience, if we follow his commands faithfully; and all
have the cup of sorrowful effort to drink in proportion
to their demonstration of his love, till all are redeemed
through divine Love.

The Christ was the Spirit which Jesus implied in his
own statements: "I am the way, the truth, and the life;"

**Christ's
demonstration**
"I and my Father are one." This Christ,
or divinity of the man Jesus, was his divine
nature, the godliness which animated him. Divine Truth,
Life, and Love gave Jesus authority over sin, sickness,
and death. His mission was to reveal the Science of
celestial being, to prove what God is and what He does
for man.

A musician demonstrates the beauty of the music he
teaches in order to show the learner the way by prac-

**Proof in
practice**
tice as well as precept. Jesus' teaching and
practice of Truth involved such a sacrifice
as makes us admit its Principle to be Love. This was
the precious import of our Master's sinless career and
of his demonstration of power over death. He proved
by his deeds that Christian Science destroys sickness, sin,
and death.

Our Master taught no mere theory, doctrine, or belief.
It was the divine Principle of all real being which he
taught and practised. His proof of Christianity was no
form or system of religion and worship, but Christian
Science, working out the harmony of Life and Love.

1   Jesus sent a message to John the Baptist, which was intended to prove beyond a question that the Christ had
3   come: "Go your way, and tell John what things ye have
seen and heard; how that the blind see, the lame walk,
the lepers are cleansed, the deaf hear, the dead are raised,
6   to the poor the gospel is preached." In other words:
Tell John what the demonstration of divine power is,
and he will at once perceive that God is the power in
9   the Messianic work.

    That Life is God, Jesus proved by his reappearance
after the crucifixion in strict accordance with his scien-
12   tific statement: "Destroy this temple [body],   **Living**
and in three days I [Spirit] will raise it up."   **temple**
It is as if he had said: The I — the Life, substance,
15   and intelligence of the universe — is not in matter to
be destroyed.

    Jesus' parables explain Life as never mingling with
18   sin and death. He laid the axe of Science at the root
of material knowledge, that it might be ready to cut
down the false doctrine of pantheism, — that God, or
21   Life, is in or of matter.

    Jesus sent forth seventy students at one time, but only
eleven left a desirable historic record. Tradition credits
24   him with two or three hundred other disciples   **Recreant**
who have left no name. "Many are called,   **disciples**
but few are chosen." They fell away from grace because
27   they never truly understood their Master's instruction.

    Why do those who profess to follow Christ reject the
essential religion he came to establish? Jesus' persecu-
30   tors made their strongest attack upon this very point.
They endeavored to hold him at the mercy of matter and
to kill him according to certain assumed material laws.

The Pharisees claimed to know and to teach the divine will, but they only hindered the success of Jesus'
mission. Even many of his students stood
in his way. If the Master had not taken a
student and taught the unseen verities of God, he would
not have been crucified. The determination to hold Spirit
in the grasp of matter is the persecutor of Truth and
Love.

Help and hindrance

While respecting all that is good in the Church or out
of it, one's consecration to Christ is more on the ground
of demonstration than of profession. In conscience, we
cannot hold to beliefs outgrown; and by understanding
more of the divine Principle of the deathless Christ, we
are enabled to heal the sick and to triumph over sin.

Neither the origin, the character, nor the work of
Jesus was generally understood. Not a single component part of his nature did the material
world measure aright. Even his righteousness and purity did not hinder men from saying: He
is a glutton and a friend of the impure, and Beelzebub is
his patron.

Misleading conceptions

Remember, thou Christian martyr, it is enough if
thou art found worthy to unloose the sandals of thy
Master's feet! To suppose that persecution
for righteousness' sake belongs to the past,
and that Christianity to-day is at peace with the world
because it is honored by sects and societies, is to mistake the very nature of religion. Error repeats itself.
The trials encountered by prophet, disciple, and apostle,
"of whom the world was not worthy," await, in some
form, every pioneer of truth.

Persecution prolonged

There is too much animal courage in society and not

1 sufficient moral courage. Christians must take up arms
against error at home and abroad. They must grapple
3 with sin in themselves and in others, and   **Christian**
continue this warfare until they have finished   **warfare**
their course. If they keep the faith, they will have the
6 crown of rejoicing.

Christian experience teaches faith in the right and disbelief in the wrong. It bids us work the more earnestly
9 in times of persecution, because then our labor is more
needed. Great is the reward of self-sacrifice, though we
may never receive it in this world.

12 There is a tradition that Publius Lentulus wrote to
the authorities at Rome: "The disciples of Jesus believe him the Son of God." Those instructed   **The Father-**
15 in Christian Science have reached the glori-   **hood of God**
ous perception that God is the only author of man.
The Virgin-mother conceived this idea of God, and
18 gave to her ideal the name of Jesus — that is, Joshua,
or Saviour.

The illumination of Mary's spiritual sense put to
21 silence material law and its order of generation, and
brought forth her child by the revelation of   **Spiritual**
Truth, demonstrating God as the Father of   **conception**
24 men. The Holy Ghost, or divine Spirit, overshadowed
the pure sense of the Virgin-mother with the full recognition that being is Spirit. The Christ dwelt forever
27 an idea in the bosom of God, the divine Principle of the
man Jesus, and woman perceived this spiritual idea,
though at first faintly developed.

30 Man as the offspring of God, as the idea of Spirit,
is the immortal evidence that Spirit is harmonious and
man eternal. Jesus was the offspring of Mary's self-

conscious communion with God. Hence he could give
a more spiritual idea of life than other men, and could
demonstrate the Science of Love — his Father or divine
Principle.

Born of a woman, Jesus' advent in the flesh partook
partly of Mary's earthly condition, although he was endowed with the Christ, the divine Spirit, without measure. This accounts for his struggles
in Gethsemane and on Calvary, and this enabled him to
be the mediator, or *way-shower*, between God and men.
Had his origin and birth been wholly apart from mortal
usage, Jesus would not have been appreciable to mortal
mind as "the way."

Jesus the way-shower

Rabbi and priest taught the Mosaic law, which said:
"An eye for an eye," and "Whoso sheddeth man's blood,
by man shall his blood be shed." Not so did Jesus, the
new executor for God, present the divine law of Love,
which blesses even those that curse it.

As the individual ideal of Truth, Christ Jesus came to
rebuke rabbinical error and all sin, sickness, and death, —
to point out the way of Truth and Life. This
ideal was demonstrated throughout the whole
earthly career of Jesus, showing the difference between
the offspring of Soul and of material sense, of Truth and
of error.

Rebukes helpful

If we have triumphed sufficiently over the errors of
material sense to allow Soul to hold the control, we
shall loathe sin and rebuke it under every mask. Only
in this way can we bless our enemies, though they
may not so construe our words. We cannot choose for
ourselves, but must work out our salvation in the way
Jesus taught. In meekness and might, he was found

1

3

6

9

12

15

18

21

24

27

30

1   preaching the gospel to the poor. Pride and fear are unfit
to bear the standard of Truth, and God will never place
3   it in such hands.

    Jesus acknowledged no ties of the flesh. He said: "Call
no man your father upon the earth: for one is your Father,
6   which is in heaven." Again he asked: "Who   **Fleshly ties**
is my mother, and who are my brethren," im-   **temporal**
plying that it is they who do the will of his Father. We
9   have no record of his calling any man by the name of
father. He recognized Spirit, God, as the only creator, and
therefore as the Father of all.

12   First in the list of Christian duties, he taught his followers the healing power of Truth and Love. He attached
no importance to dead ceremonies. It is the   **Healing**
15   living Christ, the practical Truth, which makes   **primary**
Jesus "the resurrection and the life" to all who follow him
in deed. Obeying his precious precepts, — following his
18   demonstration so far as we apprehend it, — we drink of
his cup, partake of his bread, are baptized with his purity; and at last we shall rest, sit down with him, in a full
21   understanding of the divine Principle which triumphs
over death. For what says Paul? "As often as ye eat
this bread, and drink this cup, ye do show the Lord's
24   death till he come."

    Referring to the materiality of the age, Jesus said:
"The hour cometh, and now is, when the true wor-
27   shippers shall worship the Father in spirit   **Painful**
and in truth." Again, foreseeing the perse-   **prospect**
cution which would attend the Science of Spirit, Jesus
30   said: "They shall put you out of the synagogues; yea,
the time cometh, that whosoever killeth you will think
that he doeth God service; and these things will they

do unto you, because they have not known the Father 1
nor me."

In ancient Rome a soldier was required to swear 3
allegiance to his general. The Latin word for this oath
was *sacramentum*, and our English word
sacrament is derived from it. Among the 6
Jews it was an ancient custom for the master of a
feast to pass each guest a cup of wine. But the
Eucharist does not commemorate a Roman soldier's 9
oath, nor was the wine, used on convivial occasions and
in Jewish rites, the cup of our Lord. The cup shows
forth his bitter experience, — the cup which he prayed 12
might pass from him, though he bowed in holy submission to the divine decree.

"As they were eating, Jesus took bread, and blessed 15
it and brake it, and gave it to the disciples, and said,
Take, eat; this is my body. And he took the cup, and
gave thanks, and gave it to them saying, Drink ye all 18
of it."

The true sense is spiritually lost, if the sacrament is
confined to the use of bread and wine. The disciples 21
had eaten, yet Jesus prayed and gave them
bread. This would have been foolish in a
literal sense; but in its spiritual signification, it was nat- 24
ural and beautiful. Jesus prayed; he withdrew from the
material senses to refresh his heart with brighter, with
spiritual views. 27

The Passover, which Jesus ate with his disciples in
the month Nisan on the night before his crucifixion,
was a mournful occasion, a sad supper taken 30
at the close of day, in the twilight of a
glorious career with shadows fast falling around; and

1 this supper closed forever Jesus' ritualism or concessions
to matter.

3   His followers, sorrowful and silent, anticipating the hour
of their Master's betrayal, partook of the heavenly manna,
which of old had fed in the wilderness the

Heavenly supplies

6 persecuted followers of Truth. Their bread
indeed came down from heaven. It was the great truth
of spiritual being, healing the sick and casting out error.

9 Their Master had explained it all before, and now this
bread was feeding and sustaining them. They had borne
this bread from house to house, *breaking* (explaining) it to

12 others, and now it comforted themselves.

For this truth of spiritual being, their Master was about
to suffer violence and drain to the dregs his cup of sorrow.

15 He must leave them. With the great glory of an everlasting victory overshadowing him, he gave thanks and said,
"Drink ye all of it."

18   When the human element in him struggled with the
divine, our great Teacher said: "Not my will, but
Thine, be done!" — that is, Let not the flesh,

The holy struggle

21 but the Spirit, be represented in me. This
is the new understanding of spiritual Love. It gives all
for Christ, or Truth. It blesses its enemies, heals the

24 sick, casts out error, raises the dead from trespasses
and sins, and preaches the gospel to the poor, the meek
in heart.

27   Christians, are you drinking his cup? Have you
shared the blood of the New Covenant, the persecutions
which attend a new and higher understand-

Incisive questions

30 ing of God? If not, can you then say that
you have commemorated Jesus in his cup? Are all
who eat bread and drink wine in memory of Jesus willing

truly to drink his cup, take his cross, and leave all for   1
the Christ-principle? Then why ascribe this inspiration to a dead rite, instead of showing, by casting out   3
error and making the body "holy, acceptable unto God,"
that Truth has come to the understanding? If Christ,
Truth, has come to us in demonstration, no other com-   6
memoration is requisite, for demonstration is Immanuel,
or *God with us;* and if a friend be with us, why need we
memorials of that friend?   9

If all who ever partook of the sacrament had really
commemorated the sufferings of Jesus and drunk of

Millennial glory

his cup, they would have revolutionized the   12
world. If all who seek his commemoration
through material symbols will take up the cross, heal
the sick, cast out evils, and preach Christ, or Truth,   15
to the poor, — the receptive thought, — they will bring
in the millennium.

Through all the disciples experienced, they became more   18
spiritual and understood better what the Master had

Fellowship with Christ

taught. His resurrection was also their resurrection. It helped them to raise themselves and   21
others from spiritual dulness and blind belief in God into
the perception of infinite possibilities. They needed this
quickening, for soon their dear Master would rise again   24
in the spiritual realm of reality, and ascend far above
their apprehension. As the reward for his faithfulness,
he would disappear to material sense in that change which   27
has since been called the ascension.

What a contrast between our Lord's last supper and

The last breakfast

his last spiritual breakfast with his disciples   30
in the bright morning hours at the joyful
meeting on the shore of the Galilean Sea! His gloom

1   had passed into glory, and his disciples' grief into repent-
     ance, — hearts chastened and pride rebuked. Convinced
3   of the fruitlessness of their toil in the dark and wakened
     by their Master's voice, they changed their methods, turned
     away from material things, and cast their net on the right
6   side. Discerning Christ, Truth, anew on the shore of
     time, they were enabled to rise somewhat from mortal
     sensuousness, or the burial of mind in matter, into new-
9   ness of life as Spirit.

     This spiritual meeting with our Lord in the dawn of a
     new light is the morning meal which Christian Scientists
12   commemorate. They bow before Christ, Truth, to re-
     ceive more of his reappearing and silently to commune
     with the divine Principle, Love. They celebrate their
15   Lord's victory over death, his probation in the flesh
     after death, its exemplification of human probation, and
     his spiritual and final ascension above matter, or the flesh,
18   when he rose out of material sight.

     Our baptism is a purification from all error. Our
     church is built on the divine Principle, Love. We can
21   unite with this church only as we are new-   Spiritual
     born of Spirit, as we reach the Life which   Eucharist
     is Truth and the Truth which is Life by bringing forth
24   the fruits of Love, — casting out error and healing the
     sick. Our Eucharist is spiritual communion with the one
     God. Our bread, "which cometh down from heaven,"
27   is Truth. Our cup is the cross. Our wine the inspira-
     tion of Love, the draught our Master drank and com-
     mended to his followers.

30   The design of Love is to reform the sinner. If the
     sinner's punishment here has been insufficient to re-
     form him, the good man's heaven would be a hell to

the sinner. They, who know not purity and affection by   1
experience, can never find bliss in the blessed company of

Final purpose Truth and Love simply through translation   3
into another sphere. Divine Science reveals
the necessity of sufficient suffering, either before or after
death, to quench the love of sin. To remit the penalty   6
due for sin, would be for Truth to pardon error. Escape
from punishment is not in accordance with God's government, since justice is the handmaid of mercy.   9

Jesus endured the shame, that he might pour his
dear-bought bounty into barren lives. What was his
earthly reward? He was forsaken by all save John,   12
the beloved disciple, and a few women who bowed in
silent woe beneath the shadow of his cross. The earthly
price of spirituality in a material age and the great moral   15
distance between Christianity and sensualism preclude
Christian Science from finding favor with the worldly-
minded.   18

A selfish and limited mind may be unjust, but the unlimited and divine Mind is the immortal law of justice as

Righteous retribution well as of mercy. It is quite as impossible for   21
sinners to receive their full punishment this
side of the grave as for this world to bestow on the righteous their full reward. It is useless to suppose that the   24
wicked can gloat over their offences to the last moment
and then be suddenly pardoned and pushed into heaven,
or that the hand of Love is satisfied with giving us only   27
toil, sacrifice, cross-bearing, multiplied trials, and mockery of our motives in return for our efforts at well doing.

Vicarious suffering Religious history repeats itself in the suf-   30
fering of the just for the unjust. Can God
therefore overlook the law of righteousness which de-

stroys the belief called sin? Does not Science show that
sin brings suffering as much to-day as yesterday? They
who sin must suffer. "With what measure ye mete, it
shall be measured to you again."

History is full of records of suffering. "The blood of
the martyrs is the seed of the Church." Mortals try in
vain to slay Truth with the steel or the stake,
but error falls only before the sword of Spirit.
Martyrs are the human links which connect one stage with
another in the history of religion. They are earth's lumi-
naries, which serve to cleanse and rarefy the atmosphere of
material sense and to permeate humanity with purer ideals.
Consciousness of right-doing brings its own reward; but
not amid the smoke of battle is merit seen and appreciated
by lookers-on.

Martyrs inevitable

When will Jesus' professed followers learn to emulate
him in *all* his ways and to imitate his mighty works?
Those who procured the martyrdom of that
righteous man would gladly have turned his
sacred career into a mutilated doctrinal platform. May
the Christians of to-day take up the more practical import of that career! It is possible, — yea, it is the duty
and privilege of every child, man, and woman, — to follow
in some degree the example of the Master by the demonstration of Truth and Life, of health and holiness. Christians claim to be his followers, but do they follow him in
the way that he commanded? Hear these imperative commands: "Be ye therefore perfect, even as your Father
which is in heaven is perfect!" "Go ye into all the world,
and preach the gospel to every creature!" *"Heal the
sick!"*

Complete emulation

Why has this Christian demand so little inspiration

to stir mankind to Christian effort? Because men are   1
assured that this command was intended only for a par-

Jesus' teaching belittled
ticular period and for a select number of fol-   3
lowers. This teaching is even more pernicious
than the old doctrine of foreordination, — the election of a
few to be saved, while the rest are damned; and so it will   6
be considered, when the lethargy of mortals, produced
by man-made doctrines, is broken by the demands of
divine Science.   9

Jesus said: "These signs shall follow them that believe; . . . they shall lay hands on the sick, and they
shall recover." Who believes him? He was addressing   12
his disciples, yet he did not say, "These signs shall follow
you," but *them* — "them that believe" in all time to come.
Here the word *hands* is used metaphorically, as in the text,   15
"The right hand of the Lord is exalted." It expresses
spiritual power; otherwise the healing could not have
been done spiritually. At another time Jesus prayed, not   18
for the twelve only, but for as many as should believe
"through their word."

Jesus experienced few of the pleasures of the physical   21
senses, but his sufferings were the fruits of other peo-

Material pleasures
ple's sins, not of his own. The eternal Christ,
his spiritual selfhood, never suffered. Jesus   24
mapped out the path for others. He unveiled the Christ,
the spiritual idea of divine Love. To those buried in the
belief of sin and self, living only for pleasure or the grati-   27
fication of the senses, he said in substance: Having eyes
ye see not, and having ears ye hear not; lest ye should understand and be converted, and I might heal you. He   30
taught that the material senses shut out Truth and its
healing power.

1   Meekly our Master met the mockery of his unrecog-
nized grandeur. Such indignities as he received, his fol-
3 lowers will endure until Christianity's last **Mockery**
triumph. He won eternal honors. He over- **of truth**
came the world, the flesh, and all error, thus proving
6 their nothingness. He wrought a full salvation from sin,
sickness, and death. We need "Christ, and him crucified." We must have trials and self-denials, as well as
9 joys and victories, until all error is destroyed.

    The educated belief that Soul is in the body causes
mortals to regard death as a friend, as a stepping-stone
12 out of mortality into immortality and bliss. **A belief**
The Bible calls death an enemy, and Jesus **suicidal**
overcame death and the grave instead of yielding to them.
15 He was "the way." To him, therefore, death was not
the threshold over which he must pass into living
glory.

18   "*Now*," cried the apostle, "is the accepted time; behold, *now* is the day of salvation," — meaning, not that
now men must prepare for a future-world salva- **Present**
21 tion, or safety, but that now is the time in which **salvation**
to experience that salvation in spirit and in life. Now is
the time for so-called material pains and material pleas-
24 ures to pass away, for both are unreal, because impossible
in Science. To break this earthly spell, mortals must get
the true idea and divine Principle of all that really exists
27 and governs the universe harmoniously. This thought is
apprehended slowly, and the interval before its attainment is attended with doubts and defeats as well as
30 triumphs.

    Who will stop the practice of sin so long as he believes
in the pleasures of sin? When mortals once admit that

Sin and penalty

evil confers no pleasure, they turn from it. Remove error   1
from thought, and it will not appear in effect. The advanced thinker and devout Christian, perceiv-   3
ing the scope and tendency of Christian healing
and its Science, will support them. Another will say:
"Go thy way for this time; when I have a convenient   6
season I will call for thee."

Divine Science adjusts the balance as Jesus adjusted
it. Science removes the penalty only by first removing   9
the sin which incurs the penalty. This is my sense of
divine pardon, which I understand to mean God's method
of destroying sin. If the saying is true, "While there's   12
life there's hope," its opposite is also true, While there's
sin there's doom. Another's suffering cannot lessen our
own liability. Did the martyrdom of Savonarola make   15
the crimes of his implacable enemies less criminal?

Was it just for Jesus to suffer? No; but it was
inevitable, for not otherwise could he show us the way   18

Suffering inevitable

and the power of Truth. If a career so great
and good as that of Jesus could not avert a
felon's fate, lesser apostles of Truth may endure human   21
brutality without murmuring, rejoicing to enter into
fellowship with him through the triumphal arch of
Truth and Love.   24

Our heavenly Father, divine Love, demands that all
men should follow the example of our Master and his

Service and worship

apostles and not merely worship his personal-   27
ity. It is sad that the phrase *divine service*
has come so generally to mean public worship instead of
daily deeds.   30

The nature of Christianity is peaceful and blessed,
but in order to enter into the kingdom, the anchor of

1   hope must be cast beyond the veil of matter into the
Shekinah into which Jesus has passed before us; and

3   this advance beyond matter must come
through the joys and triumphs of the righteous as well as through their sorrows and afflictions.

6   Like our Master, we must depart from material sense
into the spiritual sense of being.

Within
the veil

     The God-inspired walk calmly on though it be with

9   bleeding footprints, and in the hereafter they will reap
what they now sow. The pampered hypo-
crite may have a flowery pathway here, but

12   he cannot forever break the Golden Rule and escape the
penalty due.

The thorns
and flowers

     The proofs of Truth, Life, and Love, which Jesus gave

15   by casting out error and healing the sick, completed his
earthly mission; but in the Christian Church
this demonstration of healing was early lost,

18   about three centuries after the crucifixion. No ancient
school of philosophy, *materia medica,* or scholastic theology ever taught or demonstrated the divine healing of

21   absolute Science.

Healing
early lost

     Jesus foresaw the reception Christian Science would have
before it was understood, but this foreknowledge hindered

24   him not. He fulfilled his God-mission, and
then sat down at the right hand of the Father.
Persecuted from city to city, his apostles still went about

27   doing good deeds, for which they were maligned and
stoned. The truth taught by Jesus, the elders scoffed at.
Why? Because it demanded more than they were willing

30   to practise. It was enough for them to believe in a national
Deity; but that belief, from their time to ours, has never
made a disciple who could cast out evils and heal the sick.

Immortal
achieval

Jesus' life proved, divinely and scientifically, that God
is Love, whereas priest and rabbi affirmed God to be a
mighty potentate, who loves and hates. The Jewish theology gave no hint of the unchanging love of God.

The universal belief in death is of no advantage. It
cannot make Life or Truth apparent. Death

A belief
in death

will be found at length to be a mortal dream,
which comes in darkness and disappears with the light.

The "man of sorrows" was in no peril from salary or
popularity. Though entitled to the homage of the world

Cruel
desertion

and endorsed pre-eminently by the approval
of God, his brief triumphal entry into Jerusalem was followed by the desertion of all save a few friends,
who sadly followed him to the foot of the cross.

The resurrection of the great demonstrator of God's
power was the proof of his final triumph over body

Death
outdone

and matter, and gave full evidence of divine
Science, — evidence so important to mortals.
The belief that man has existence or mind separate from
God is a dying error. This error Jesus met with divine
Science and proved its nothingness. Because of the won-
drous glory which God bestowed on His anointed, temptation, sin, sickness, and death had no terror for Jesus.
Let men think they had killed the body! Afterwards he
would show it to them unchanged. This demonstrates
that in Christian Science the true man is governed by
God — by good, not evil — and is therefore not a mortal
but an immortal. Jesus had taught his disciples the
Science of this proof. He was here to enable them to
test his still uncomprehended saying, "He that believeth on me, the works that I do shall he do also." They
must understand more fully his Life-principle by casting

1   out error, healing the sick, and raising the dead, even as
    they did understand it after his bodily departure.

3   The magnitude of Jesus' work, his material disappear-
    ance before their eyes and his reappearance, all enabled
    the disciples to understand what Jesus had   **Pentecost**
6   said. Heretofore they had only believed;   **repeated**
    now they understood. The advent of this understanding
    is what is meant by the descent of the Holy Ghost, — that
9   influx of divine Science which so illuminated the Pentecos-
    tal Day and is now repeating its ancient history.
        Jesus' last proof was the highest, the most convincing,
12 the most profitable to his students. The malignity of
    brutal persecutors, the treason and suicide of   **Convincing**
    his betrayer, were overruled by divine Love to   **evidence**
15 the glorification of the man and of the true idea of God,
    which Jesus' persecutors had mocked and tried to slay.
    The final demonstration of the truth which Jesus taught,
18 and for which he was crucified, opened a new era for the
    world. Those who slew him to stay his influence perpetu-
    ated and extended it.
21   Jesus rose higher in demonstration because of the cup
    of bitterness he drank. Human law had condemned
    him, but he was demonstrating divine Science.   **Divine**
24 Out of reach of the barbarity of his enemies,   **victory**
    he was acting under spiritual law in defiance of mat-
    ter and mortality, and that spiritual law sustained him.
27 The divine must overcome the human at every point.
    The Science Jesus taught and lived must triumph over
    all material beliefs about life, substance, and intelli-
30 gence, and the multitudinous errors growing from such
    beliefs.
        Love must triumph over hate. Truth and Life must

seal the victory over error and death, before the thorns   1
can be laid aside for a crown, the benediction follow,
"Well done, good and faithful servant," and the suprem-   3
acy of Spirit be demonstrated.

The lonely precincts of the tomb gave Jesus a refuge
from his foes, a place in which to solve the great   6

Jesus in the tomb

problem of being. His three days' work in
the sepulchre set the seal of eternity on time.
He proved Life to be deathless and Love to be the mas-   9
ter of hate. He met and mastered on the basis of Christian Science, the power of Mind over matter, all the claims
of medicine, surgery, and hygiene.   12

He took no drugs to allay inflammation. He did not
depend upon food or pure air to resuscitate wasted
energies. He did not require the skill of a surgeon to   15
heal the torn palms and bind up the wounded side and
lacerated feet, that he might use those hands to remove
the napkin and winding-sheet, and that he might employ   18
his feet as before.

Could it be called supernatural for the God of nature
to sustain Jesus in his proof of man's truly derived power? 21

The deific naturalism

It was a method of surgery beyond material
art, but it was not a supernatural act. On
the contrary, it was a divinely natural act, whereby divinity 24
brought to humanity the understanding of the Christ-
healing and revealed a method infinitely above that of
human invention.   27

His disciples believed Jesus to be dead while he was
hidden in the sepulchre, whereas he was alive, demon-

Obstacles overcome

strating within the narrow tomb the power   30
of Spirit to overrule mortal, material sense.
There were rock-ribbed walls in the way, and a great

stone must be rolled from the cave's mouth; but Jesus
vanquished every material obstacle, overcame every law
of matter, and stepped forth from his gloomy resting-place,
crowned with the glory of a sublime success, an everlasting
victory.

Our Master fully and finally demonstrated divine Science in his victory over death and the grave. Jesus'
deed was for the enlightenment of men and
for the salvation of the whole world from sin,
sickness, and death. Paul writes: "For if, when we were
enemies, we were reconciled to God by the [seeming] death
of His Son, much more, being reconciled, we shall be saved
by his life." Three days after his bodily burial he talked
with his disciples. The persecutors had failed to hide immortal Truth and Love in a sepulchre.

Victory over the grave

Glory be to God, and peace to the struggling hearts!
Christ hath rolled away the stone from the door of human hope and faith, and through the revelation and demonstration of life in God, hath
elevated them to possible at-one-ment with the spiritual
idea of man and his divine Principle, Love.

The stone rolled away

They who earliest saw Jesus after the resurrection
and beheld the final proof of all that he had taught,
misconstrued that event. Even his disciples
at first called him a spirit, ghost, or spectre,
for they believed his body to be dead. His reply was:
"Spirit hath not flesh and bones, as ye see me have."
The reappearing of Jesus was not the return of a spirit.
He presented the same body that he had before his crucifixion, and so glorified the supremacy of Mind over
matter.

After the resurrection

Jesus' students, not sufficiently advanced fully to un-

derstand their Master's triumph, did not perform many   1
wonderful works, until they saw him after his crucifixion
and learned that he had not died. This convinced them   3
of the truthfulness of all that he had taught.

In the walk to Emmaus, Jesus was known to his friends
by the words, which made their hearts burn within them,   6

Spiritual
interpretation

and by the breaking of bread. The divine
Spirit, which identified Jesus thus centuries
ago, has spoken through the inspired Word and will speak   9
through it in every age and clime. It is revealed to the
receptive heart, and is again seen casting out evil and
healing the sick.   12

The Master said plainly that physique was not Spirit,
and after his resurrection he proved to the physical senses

Corporeality
and Spirit

that his body was not changed until he himself   15
ascended, — or, in other words, rose even
higher in the understanding of Spirit, God. To convince
Thomas of this, Jesus caused him to examine the nail-   18
prints and the spear-wound.

Jesus' unchanged physical condition after what seemed
to be death was followed by his exaltation above all ma-   21

Spiritual
ascension

terial conditions; and this exaltation explained
his ascension, and revealed unmistakably a
probationary and progressive state beyond the grave.   24
Jesus was "the way;" that is, he marked the way for
all men. In his final demonstration, called the ascension, which closed the earthly record of Jesus, he rose   27
above the physical knowledge of his disciples, and the
material senses saw him no more.

His students then received the Holy Ghost. By this is   30
meant, that by all they had witnessed and suffered, they
were roused to an enlarged understanding of divine Sci-

1 ence, even to the spiritual interpretation and discernment
of Jesus' teachings and demonstrations, which gave them
3 a faint conception of the Life which is God.
They no longer measured man by material
sense. After gaining the true idea of their glorified Master,
6 they became better healers, leaning no longer on matter,
but on the divine Principle of their work. The influx of
light was sudden. It was sometimes an overwhelming
9 power as on the Day of Pentecost.

Pentecostal power

Judas conspired against Jesus. The world's ingratitude
and hatred towards that just man effected his betrayal.
12 The traitor's price was thirty pieces of silver
and the smiles of the Pharisees. He chose his
time, when the people were in doubt concerning Jesus'
15 teachings.

The traitor's conspiracy

A period was approaching which would reveal the infinite distance between Judas and his Master. Judas
18 Iscariot knew this. He knew that the great goodness of
that Master placed a gulf between Jesus and his betrayer,
and this spiritual distance inflamed Judas' envy. The
21 greed for gold strengthened his ingratitude, and for a time
quieted his remorse. He knew that the world generally
loves a lie better than Truth; and so he plotted the be-
24 trayal of Jesus in order to raise himself in popular esti-
mation. His dark plot fell to the ground, and the
traitor fell with it.

27 The disciples' desertion of their Master in his last
earthly struggle was punished; each one came to a violent death except St. John, of whose death we have no
30 record.

During his night of gloom and glory in the garden,
Jesus realized the utter error of a belief in any possi-

ble material intelligence. The pangs of neglect and the
staves of bigoted ignorance smote him sorely. His stu-

Gethsemane
glorified

dents slept. He said unto them: "Could ye
not watch with me one hour?" Could they
not watch with him who, waiting and struggling in voice-
less agony, held uncomplaining guard over a world?
There was no response to that human yearning, and so
Jesus turned forever away from earth to heaven, from
sense to Soul.

Remembering the sweat of agony which fell in holy
benediction on the grass of Gethsemane, shall the hum-
blest or mightiest disciple murmur when he drinks from the
same cup, and think, or even wish, to escape the exalting ordeal of sin's revenge on its destroyer? Truth and
Love bestow few palms until the consummation of a
life-work.

Judas had the world's weapons. Jesus had not one
of them, and chose not the world's means of defence.

Defensive
weapons

"He opened not his mouth." The great demonstrator of Truth and Love was silent before
envy and hate. Peter would have smitten the enemies of
his Master, but Jesus forbade him, thus rebuking re-
sentment or animal courage. He said: "Put up thy
sword."

Pale in the presence of his own momentous question,
"What is Truth," Pilate was drawn into acquiescence

Pilate's
question

with the demands of Jesus' enemies. Pilate
was ignorant of the consequences of his awful
decision against human rights and divine Love, knowing
not that he was hastening the final demonstration of what
life is and of what the true knowledge of God can do for
man.

1   The women at the cross could have answered Pilate's
question. They knew what had inspired their devotion,
3   winged their faith, opened the eyes of their understanding, healed the sick, cast out evil, and caused the disciples
to say to their Master: "Even the devils are subject
6   unto us through thy name."

     Where were the seventy whom Jesus sent forth? Were
all conspirators save eleven? Had they forgotten the
9   great exponent of God? Had they so soon lost *Students'* / *ingratitude*
sight of his mighty works, his toils, privations,
sacrifices, his divine patience, sublime courage, and unre-
12   quited affection? O, why did they not gratify his last
human yearning with one sign of fidelity?

     The meek demonstrator of good, the highest instruc-
15   tor and friend of man, met his earthly fate alone with
God. No human eye was there to pity, no *Heaven's* / *sentinel*
arm to save. Forsaken by all whom he had
18   blessed, this faithful sentinel of God at the highest
post of power, charged with the grandest trust of
heaven, was ready to be transformed by the renewing
21   of the infinite Spirit. He was to prove that the Christ
is not subject to material conditions, but is above the
reach of human wrath, and is able, through Truth,
24   Life, and Love, to triumph over sin, sickness, death, and
the grave.

     The priests and rabbis, before whom he had meekly
27   walked, and those to whom he had given the highest
proofs of divine power, mocked him on the *Cruel* / *contumely*
cross, saying derisively, "He saved others;
30   himself he cannot save." These scoffers, who turned
"aside the right of a man before the face of the Most
High," esteemed Jesus as "stricken, smitten of God."

"He is brought as a lamb to the slaughter, and as a sheep before her shearers is dumb, so he openeth not his mouth." "Who shall declare his generation?" Who shall decide what truth and love are?

The last supreme moment of mockery, desertion, torture, added to an overwhelming sense of the magnitude of his work, wrung from Jesus' lips the awful cry, "My God, why hast Thou forsaken me?"

A cry of despair

This despairing appeal, if made to a human parent, would impugn the justice and love of a father who could withhold a clear token of his presence to sustain and bless so faithful a son. The appeal of Jesus was made both to his divine Principle, the God who is Love, and to himself, Love's pure idea. Had Life, Truth, and Love forsaken him in his highest demonstration? This was a startling question. No! They must abide in him and he in them, or that hour would be shorn of its mighty blessing for the human race.

If his full recognition of eternal Life had for a moment given way before the evidence of the bodily senses, what would his accusers have said? Even what they did say, — that Jesus' teachings were false, and that all evidence of their correctness was destroyed by his death. But this saying could not make it so.

Divine Science misunderstood

The burden of that hour was terrible beyond human conception. The distrust of mortal minds, disbelieving the purpose of his mission, was a million times sharper than the thorns which pierced his flesh. The real cross, which Jesus bore up the hill of grief, was the world's hatred of Truth and Love. Not the spear nor the material cross wrung from his faithful

The real pillory

1 lips the plaintive cry, *"Eloi, Eloi, lama sabachthani?"* It
was the possible loss of something more important than
3 human life which moved him, — the possible misapprehension of the sublimest influence of his career. This
dread added the drop of gall to his cup.

6 Jesus could have withdrawn himself from his enemies.
He had power to lay down a human sense of life for his
spiritual identity in the likeness of the divine;

Life-power indestructible

9 but he allowed men to attempt the destruction of the mortal body in order that he might furnish
the proof of immortal life. Nothing could kill this Life
12 of man. Jesus could give his temporal life into his
enemies' hands; but when his earth-mission was accomplished, his spiritual life, indestructible and eternal,
15 was found forever the same. He knew that matter had
no life and that real Life is God; therefore he could no
more be separated from his spiritual Life than God could
18 be extinguished.

  His consummate example was for the salvation of us
all, but only through doing the works which he did and
21 taught others to do. His purpose in healing

Example for our salvation

was not alone to restore health, but to demonstrate his divine Principle. He was inspired by God, by
24 Truth and Love, in all that he said and did. The motives
of his persecutors were pride, envy, cruelty, and vengeance,
inflicted on the physical Jesus, but aimed at the divine Prin-
27 ciple, Love, which rebuked their sensuality.

  Jesus was unselfish. His spirituality separated him
from sensuousness, and caused the selfish materialist
30 to hate him; but it was this spirituality which enabled
Jesus to heal the sick, cast out evil, and raise the
dead.

From early boyhood he was about his "Father's business." His pursuits lay far apart from theirs. His master was Spirit; their master was matter. He
served God; they served mammon. His affections were pure; theirs were carnal. His senses drank in
the spiritual evidence of health, holiness, and life; their
senses testified oppositely, and absorbed the material evidence of sin, sickness, and death.

Their imperfections and impurity felt the ever-present
rebuke of his perfection and purity. Hence the world's
hatred of the just and perfect Jesus, and the
prophet's foresight of the reception error would
give him. "Despised and rejected of men," was Isaiah's
graphic word concerning the coming Prince of Peace.
Herod and Pilate laid aside old feuds in order to unite
in putting to shame and death the best man that ever
trod the globe. To-day, as of old, error and evil again
make common cause against the exponents of truth.

The "man of sorrows" best understood the nothingness of material life and intelligence and the mighty actuality of all-inclusive God, good. These were
the two cardinal points of Mind-healing, or
Christian Science, which armed him with Love. The highest earthly representative of God, speaking of human
ability to reflect divine power, prophetically said to his
disciples, speaking not for their day only but for all time:
"He that believeth on me, the works that I do shall he do
also;" and "These signs shall follow them that believe."

The accusations of the Pharisees were as self-contradictory as their religion. The bigot, the deb-
auchee, the hypocrite, called Jesus a glutton
and a wine-bibber. They said: "He casteth out devils

through Beelzebub," and is the "friend of publicans and sinners." The latter accusation was true, but not in their meaning. Jesus was no ascetic. He did not fast as did the Baptist's disciples; yet there never lived a man so far removed from appetites and passions as the Nazarene. He rebuked sinners pointedly and unflinchingly, because he was their friend; hence the cup he drank.

The reputation of Jesus was the very opposite of his character. Why? Because the divine Principle and practice of Jesus were misunderstood. He was at work in divine Science. His words and works were unknown to the world because above and contrary to the world's religious sense. Mortals believed in God as humanly mighty, rather than as divine, infinite Love.

Reputation and character

The world could not interpret aright the discomfort which Jesus inspired and the spiritual blessings which might flow from such discomfort. Science shows the cause of the shock so often produced by the truth, — namely, that this shock arises from the great distance between the individual and Truth. Like Peter, we should weep over the warning, instead of denying the truth or mocking the lifelong sacrifice which goodness makes for the destruction of evil.

Inspiring discontent

Jesus bore our sins in his body. He knew the mortal errors which constitute the material body, and could destroy those errors; but at the time when Jesus felt our infirmities, he had not conquered all the beliefs of the flesh or his sense of material life, nor had he risen to his final demonstration of spiritual power.

Bearing our sins

Had he shared the sinful beliefs of others, he would

have been less sensitive to those beliefs. Through the   1
magnitude of his human life, he demonstrated the divine
Life. Out of the amplitude of his pure affection, he de-   3
fined Love. With the affluence of Truth, he vanquished
error. The world acknowledged not his righteousness,
seeing it not; but earth received the harmony his glorified   6
example introduced.

Who is ready to follow his teaching and example? All
must sooner or later plant themselves in Christ, the true   9

idea of God. That he might liberally pour
his dear-bought treasures into empty or sin-
filled human storehouses, was the inspiration of Jesus'   12
intense human sacrifice. In witness of his divine commission, he presented the proof that Life, Truth, and
Love heal the sick and the sinning, and triumph over   15
death through Mind, not matter. This was the highest
proof he could have offered of divine Love. His hearers
understood neither his words nor his works. They   18
would not accept his meek interpretation of life nor
follow his example.

His earthly cup of bitterness was drained to the   21
dregs. There adhered to him only a few unpretentious

Spiritual
friendship

friends, whose religion was something more
than a name. It was so vital, that it en-   24
abled them to understand the Nazarene and to share
the glory of eternal life. He said that those who followed him should drink of his cup, and history has con-   27
firmed the prediction.

If that Godlike and glorified man were physically on

Injustice to
the Saviour

earth to-day, would not some, who now pro-   30
fess to love him, reject him? Would they
not deny him even the rights of humanity, if he enter-

1 tained any other sense of being and religion than theirs?
The advancing century, from a deadened sense of the
3 invisible God, to-day subjects to unchristian comment and
usage the idea of Christian healing enjoined by Jesus; but
this does not affect the invincible facts.

6 Perhaps the early Christian era did Jesus no more
injustice than the later centuries have bestowed upon
the healing Christ and spiritual idea of being. Now
9 that the gospel of healing is again preached by the
wayside, does not the pulpit sometimes scorn it? But
that curative mission, which presents the Saviour in a
12 clearer light than mere words can possibly do, cannot be
left out of Christianity, although it is again ruled out of
the synagogue.

15 Truth's immortal idea is sweeping down the centuries,
gathering beneath its wings the sick and sinning. My
weary hope tries to realize that happy day, when man shall
18 recognize the Science of Christ and love his neighbor as
himself, — when he shall realize God's omnipotence and
the healing power of the divine Love in what it has done
21 and is doing for mankind. The promises will be fulfilled. The time for the reappearing of the divine healing
is throughout all time; and whosoever layeth his earthly
24 all on the altar of divine Science, drinketh of Christ's
cup now, and is endued with the spirit and power of
Christian healing.

27 In the words of St. John: "He shall give you another
Comforter, that he may abide with you *forever.*" This
Comforter I understand to be Divine Science.

Chapter 3

Marriage

What therefore God hath joined together,
let not man put asunder.

In the resurrection they neither marry,
nor are given in marriage,
but are as the angels of God in heaven. — JESUS.

When our great Teacher came to him for baptism, 1
John was astounded. Reading his thoughts, Jesus
added: "Suffer it to be so now: for thus it becometh us 3
to fulfil all righteousness." Jesus' concessions (in certain
cases) to material methods were for the advancement of
spiritual good. 6

Marriage is the legal and moral provision for generation among human kind. Until the spiritual creation
Marriage is discerned intact, is apprehended and under- 9
temporal stood, and His kingdom is come as in the vision
of the Apocalypse, — where the corporeal sense of creation was cast out, and its spiritual sense was revealed from 12
heaven, — marriage will continue, subject to such moral
regulations as will secure increasing virtue.

Infidelity to the marriage covenant is the social scourge 15
of all races, "the pestilence that walketh in darkness,
Fidelity . . . the destruction that wasteth at noonday."
required The commandment, "Thou shalt not com- 18
mit adultery," is no less imperative than the one, "Thou
shalt not kill."

56

1   Chastity is the cement of civilization and progress. Without it there is no stability in society, and without it

3 one cannot attain the Science of Life.

    Union of the masculine and feminine qualities constitutes completeness. The masculine mind reaches a

6 higher tone through certain elements of the feminine, while the feminine mind gains courage and strength through masculine qualities. These

9 different elements conjoin naturally with each other, and their true harmony is in spiritual oneness. Both sexes should be loving, pure, tender, and strong. The attrac

12 tion between native qualities will be perpetual only as it is pure and true, bringing sweet seasons of renewal like the returning spring.

15   Beauty, wealth, or fame is incompetent to meet the demands of the affections, and should never weigh against the better claims of intellect, good

18 ness, and virtue. Happiness is spiritual, born of Truth and Love. It is unselfish; therefore it cannot exist alone, but requires all mankind to

21 share it.

    Human affection is not poured forth vainly, even though it meet no return. Love enriches the nature, en

24 larging, purifying, and elevating it. The wintry blasts of earth may uproot the flowers of affection, and scatter them to the winds; but this severance

27 of fleshly ties serves to unite thought more closely to God, for Love supports the struggling heart until it ceases to sigh over the world and begins to unfold its wings for

30 heaven.

    Marriage is unblest or blest, according to the disappointments it involves or the hopes it fulfils. To happify

Mental elements

Affection's demands

Help and discipline

existence by constant intercourse with those adapted to   1
elevate it, should be the motive of society. Unity of
spirit gives new pinions to joy, or else joy's drooping   3
wings trail in dust.

Ill-arranged notes produce discord. Tones of the
human mind may be different, but they should be con-   6
Chord and   cordant in order to blend properly. Unselfish
discord   ambition, noble life-motives, and purity, —
these constituents of thought, mingling, constitute in-   9
dividually and collectively true happiness, strength, and
permanence.

There is moral freedom in Soul. Never contract the   12
horizon of a worthy outlook by the selfish exaction of
Mutual   all another's time and thoughts. With ad-
freedom   ditional joys, benevolence should grow more   15
diffusive. The narrowness and jealousy, which would
confine a wife or a husband forever within four walls, will
not promote the sweet interchange of confidence and love;   18
but on the other hand, a wandering desire for incessant
amusement outside the home circle is a poor augury for
the happiness of wedlock. Home is the dearest spot on   21
earth, and it should be the centre, though not the boundary, of the affections.

Said the peasant bride to her lover: "Two eat no more   24
together than they eat separately." This is a hint that
A useful   a wife ought not to court vulgar extravagance
suggestion   or stupid ease, because another supplies her   27
wants. Wealth may obviate the necessity for toil or the
chance for ill-nature in the marriage relation, but nothing can abolish the cares of marriage.   30

"She that is married careth . . . how she may please
her husband," says the Bible; and this is the pleasantest

thing to do. Matrimony should never be entered into without a full recognition of its enduring obligations on both sides. There should be the most tender solicitude for each other's happiness, and mutual attention and approbation should wait on all the years of married life.

Mutual compromises will often maintain a compact which might otherwise become unbearable. Man should not be required to participate in all the annoyances and cares of domestic economy, nor should woman be expected to understand political economy. Fulfilling the different demands of their united spheres, their sympathies should blend in sweet confidence and cheer, each partner sustaining the other, — thus hallowing the union of interests and affections, in which the heart finds peace and home.

Tender words and unselfish care in what promotes the welfare and happiness of your wife will prove more salutary in prolonging her health and smiles than stolid indifference or jealousy. Husbands, hear this and remember how slight a word or deed may renew the old trysting-times.

After marriage, it is too late to grumble over incompatibility of disposition. A mutual understanding should exist before this union and continue ever after, for deception is fatal to happiness.

The nuptial vow should never be annulled, so long as its moral obligations are kept intact; but the frequency of divorce shows that the sacredness of this relationship is losing its influence, and that fatal mistakes are undermining its foundations. Separation never should take place, and it never would, if both

husband and wife were genuine Christian Scientists.   1
Science inevitably lifts one's being higher in the scale of
harmony and happiness.   3

Kindred tastes, motives, and aspirations are necessary
to the formation of a happy and permanent companion-

Permanent affection ship. The beautiful in character is also the   6
good, welding indissolubly the links of affec-
tion. A mother's affection cannot be weaned from her
child, because the mother-love includes purity and con-   9
stancy, both of which are immortal. Therefore maternal
affection lives on under whatever difficulties.

From the logic of events we learn that selfishness   12
and impurity alone are fleeting, and that wisdom will
ultimately put asunder what she hath not joined
together.   15

Marriage should improve the human species, becoming
a barrier against vice, a protection to woman, strength to

Centre for affections man, and a centre for the affections. This,   18
however, in a majority of cases, is not its
present tendency, and why? Because the education of
the higher nature is neglected, and other considerations,   21
— passion, frivolous amusements, personal adornment,
display, and pride, — occupy thought.

An ill-attuned ear calls discord harmony, not appreciat-   24
ing concord. So physical sense, not discerning the true

Spiritual concord happiness of being, places it on a false basis.
Science will correct the discord, and teach us   27
life's sweeter harmonies.

Soul has infinite resources with which to bless mankind,
and happiness would be more readily attained and would   30
be more secure in our keeping, if sought in Soul. Higher
enjoyments alone can satisfy the cravings of immortal

1   man. We cannot circumscribe happiness within the
limits of personal sense. The senses confer no real
3   enjoyment.

The good in human affections must have ascendency
over the evil and the spiritual over the animal, or happi-
6   ness will never be won. The attainment of   **Ascendency**
this celestial condition would improve our   **of good**
progeny, diminish crime, and give higher aims to ambi-
9   tion. Every valley of sin must be exalted, and every
mountain of selfishness be brought low, that the highway
of our God may be prepared in Science. The offspring
12   of heavenly-minded parents inherit more intellect, better
balanced minds, and sounder constitutions.

If some fortuitous circumstance places promising chil-
15   dren in the arms of gross parents, often these beautiful
children early droop and die, like tropical   **Propensities**
flowers born amid Alpine snows. If perchance   **inherited**
18   they live to become parents in their turn, they may reproduce in their own helpless little ones the grosser traits
of their ancestors. What hope of happiness, what noble
21   ambition, can inspire the child who inherits propensities
that must either be overcome or reduce him to a loathsome wreck?

24   Is not the propagation of the human species a greater
responsibility, a more solemn charge, than the culture of
your garden or the raising of stock to increase your flocks
27   and herds? Nothing unworthy of perpetuity should be
transmitted to children.

The formation of mortals must greatly improve to
30   advance mankind. The scientific *morale* of marriage is
spiritual unity. If the propagation of a higher human
species is requisite to reach this goal, then its material con-

ditions can only be permitted for the purpose of gener-   1
ating. The fœtus must be kept mentally pure and the
period of gestation have the sanctity of virginity.   3

The entire education of children should be such as to
form habits of obedience to the moral and spiritual law,
with which the child can meet and master the belief in so-   6
called physical laws, a belief which breeds disease.

If parents create in their babes a desire for incessant
amusement, to be always fed, rocked, tossed, or talked   9

Inheritance heeded to, those parents should not, in after years,
complain of their children's fretfulness or fri-
volity, which the parents themselves have occasioned.   12
Taking less "thought for your life, what ye shall eat, or
what ye shall drink"; less thought "for your body what
ye shall put on," will do much more for the health of the   15
rising generation than you dream. Children should be
allowed to remain children in knowledge, and should
become men and women only through growth in the   18
understanding of man's higher nature.

We must not attribute more and more intelligence
to matter, but less and less, if we would be wise and   21

The Mind creative healthy. The divine Mind, which forms the
bud and blossom, will care for the human
body, even as it clothes the lily; but let no mortal inter-   24
fere with God's government by thrusting in the laws of
erring, human concepts.

The higher nature of man is not governed by the lower;   27
if it were, the order of wisdom would be reversed.

Superior law of Soul Our false views of life hide eternal harmony,
and produce the ills of which we complain.   30
Because mortals believe in material laws and reject the
Science of Mind, this does not make materiality first and

the superior law of Soul last. You would never think
that flannel was better for warding off pulmonary disease
than the controlling Mind, if you understood the Science
of being.

In Science man is the offspring of Spirit. The beautiful, good, and pure constitute his ancestry. His origin is
not, like that of mortals, in brute instinct, nor
does he pass through material conditions prior
to reaching intelligence. Spirit is his primitive and ultimate source of being; God is his Father, and Life is the
law of his being.

Spiritual
origin

Civil law establishes very unfair differences between the
rights of the two sexes. Christian Science furnishes no
precedent for such injustice, and civilization
mitigates it in some measure. Still, it is a
marvel why usage should accord woman less rights than
does either Christian Science or civilization.

The rights
of woman

Our laws are not impartial, to say the least, in their
discrimination as to the person, property, and parental
claims of the two sexes. If the elective fran-
chise for women will remedy the evil with-
out encouraging difficulties of greater magnitude, let us
hope it will be granted. A feasible as well as rational
means of improvement at present is the elevation of
society in general and the achievement of a nobler
race for legislation, — a race having higher aims and
motives.

Unfair
discrimination

If a dissolute husband deserts his wife, certainly the
wronged, and perchance impoverished, woman should be
allowed to collect her own wages, enter into business
agreements, hold real estate, deposit funds, and own her
children free from interference.

Want of uniform justice is a crying evil caused by the   1
selfishness and inhumanity of man. Our forefathers
exercised their faith in the direction taught by the Apostle   3
James, when he said: "Pure religion and undefiled before
God and the Father, is this, To visit the fatherless and
widows in their affliction, and to keep himself unspotted   6
from the world."

Pride, envy, or jealousy seems on most occasions to
be the master of ceremonies, ruling out primitive Chris-   9

Benevolence hindered

tianity. When a man lends a helping hand
to some noble woman, struggling alone with
adversity, his wife should not say, "It is never well to   12
interfere with your neighbor's business." A wife is
sometimes debarred by a covetous domestic tyrant from
giving the ready aid her sympathy and charity would   15
afford.

Marriage should signify a union of hearts. Further-
more, the time cometh of which Jesus spake, when he   18

Progressive development

declared that in the resurrection there should
be no more marrying nor giving in marriage,
but man would be as the angels. Then shall Soul re-   21
joice in its own, in which passion has no part. Then
white-robed purity will unite in one person masculine wisdom and feminine love, spiritual understanding and per-   24
petual peace.

Until it is learned that God is the Father of all, marriage will continue. Let not mortals permit a disregard   27
of law which might lead to a worse state of society than
now exists. Honesty and virtue ensure the stability of
the marriage covenant. Spirit will ultimately claim its   30
own, — all that really is, — and the voices of physical
sense will be forever hushed.

Experience should be the school of virtue, and human
happiness should proceed from man's highest nature.
May Christ, Truth, be present at every bridal

Blessing
of Christ

altar to turn the water into wine and to give to
human life an inspiration by which man's spiritual and
eternal existence may be discerned.

If the foundations of human affection are consistent
with progress, they will be strong and enduring. Divorces
should warn the age of some fundamental error

Righteous
foundations

in the marriage state. The union of the sexes
suffers fearful discord. To gain Christian Science and its
harmony, life should be more metaphysically regarded.

The broadcast powers of evil so conspicuous to-day
show themselves in the materialism and sensualism of
the age, struggling against the advancing

Powerless
promises

spiritual era. Beholding the world's lack of
Christianity and the powerlessness of vows to make home
happy, the human mind will at length demand a higher
affection.

There will ensue a fermentation over this as over many
other reforms, until we get at last the clear straining of
truth, and impurity and error are left among

Transition
and reform

the lees. The fermentation even of fluids is
not pleasant. An unsettled, transitional stage is never
desirable on its own account. Matrimony, which was once
a fixed fact among us, must lose its present slippery foot-
ing, and man must find permanence and peace in a more
spiritual adherence.

The mental chemicalization, which has brought conjugal infidelity to the surface, will assuredly throw off
this evil, and marriage will become purer when the scum
is gone.

Thou art right, immortal Shakespeare, great poet of humanity:

> Sweet are the uses of adversity;
> Which, like the toad, ugly and venomous,
> Wears yet a precious jewel in his head.

Trials teach mortals not to lean on a material staff, — a broken reed, which pierces the heart. We do not

Salutary sorrow

half remember this in the sunshine of joy and prosperity. Sorrow is salutary. Through great tribulation we enter the kingdom. Trials are proofs of God's care. Spiritual development germinates not from seed sown in the soil of material hopes, but when these decay, Love propagates anew the higher joys of Spirit, which have no taint of earth. Each successive stage of experience unfolds new views of divine goodness and love.

Amidst gratitude for conjugal felicity, it is well to remember how fleeting are human joys. Amidst conjugal infelicity, it is well to hope, pray, and wait patiently on divine wisdom to point out the path.

Husbands and wives should never separate if there is no Christian demand for it. It is better to await the

Patience is wisdom

logic of events than for a wife precipitately to leave her husband or for a husband to leave his wife. If one is better than the other, as must always be the case, the other pre-eminently needs good company. Socrates considered patience salutary under such circumstances, making his Xantippe a discipline for his philosophy.

The gold and dross

Sorrow has its reward. It never leaves us where it found us. The furnace separates the gold from the dross that the precious metal may be graven with the image of God. The cup our Father hath given, shall we not drink it and learn the lessons He teaches?

When the ocean is stirred by a storm, then the clouds lower, the wind shrieks through the tightened shrouds, and the waves lift themselves into mountains. We ask the helmsman: "Do you know your course? Can you steer safely amid the storm?" He answers bravely, but even the dauntless seaman is not sure of his safety; nautical science is not equal to the Science of Mind. Yet, acting up to his highest understanding, firm at the post of duty, the mariner works on and awaits the issue. Thus should we deport ourselves on the seething ocean of sorrow. Hoping and working, one should stick to the wreck, until an irresistible propulsion precipitates his doom or sunshine gladdens the troubled sea.

Weathering the storm

The notion that animal natures can possibly give force to character is too absurd for consideration, when we remember that through spiritual ascendency our Lord and Master healed the sick, raised the dead, and commanded even the winds and waves to obey him. Grace and Truth are potent beyond all other means and methods.

Spiritual power

The lack of spiritual power in the limited demonstration of popular Christianity does not put to silence the labor of centuries. Spiritual, not corporeal, consciousness is needed. Man delivered from sin, disease, and death presents the true likeness or spiritual ideal.

Systems of religion and medicine treat of physical pains and pleasures, but Jesus rebuked the suffering from any such cause or effect. The epoch approaches when the

understanding of the truth of being will be the basis of   1
true religion. At present mortals progress slowly for

Basis of true religion

fear of being thought ridiculous. They are   3
slaves to fashion, pride, and sense. Sometime we shall learn how Spirit, the great architect, has
created men and women in Science. We ought to weary   6
of the fleeting and false and to cherish nothing which
hinders our highest selfhood.

Jealousy is the grave of affection. The presence of   9
mistrust, where confidence is due, withers the flowers
of Eden and scatters love's petals to decay. Be not
in haste to take the vow "until death do us part."   12
Consider its obligations, its responsibilities, its relations to your growth and to your influence on other
lives.   15

I never knew more than one individual who believed
in agamogenesis; she was unmarried, a lovely charac-

Insanity and agamogenesis

ter, was suffering from incipient insanity, and   18
a Christian Scientist cured her. I have named
her case to individuals, when casting my bread upon
the waters, and it may have caused the good to ponder   21
and the evil to hatch their silly innuendoes and lies, since
salutary causes sometimes incur these effects. The per-
petuation of the floral species by bud or cell-division is   24
evident, but I discredit the belief that agamogenesis
applies to the human species.

Christian Science presents unfoldment, not accretion;   27
it manifests no material growth from molecule to mind,

God's creation intact

but an impartation of the divine Mind to man
and the universe. Proportionately as human   30
generation ceases, the unbroken links of eternal, harmonious being will be spiritually discerned; and man,

1 not of the earth earthly but coexistent with God, will
appear. The scientific fact that man and the universe
3 are evolved from Spirit, and so are spiritual, is as fixed in
divine Science as is the proof that mortals gain the sense
of health only as they lose the sense of sin and disease.
6 Mortals can never understand God's creation while believing that man is a creator. God's children already created
will be cognized only as man finds the truth of being.
9 Thus it is that the real, ideal man appears in proportion
as the false and material disappears. No longer to marry
or to be "given in marriage" neither closes man's con-
12 tinuity nor his sense of increasing number in God's infinite plan. Spiritually to understand that there is but
one creator, God, unfolds all creation, confirms the Scrip-
15 tures, brings the sweet assurance of no parting, no pain,
and of man deathless and perfect and eternal.

If Christian Scientists educate their own offspring
18 spiritually, they can educate others spiritually and not
conflict with the scientific sense of God's creation. Some
day the child will ask his parent: "Do you keep the First
21 Commandment? Do you have one God and creator, or
is man a creator?" If the father replies, "God creates
man through man," the child may ask, "Do you teach
24 that Spirit creates materially, or do you declare that
Spirit is infinite, therefore matter is out of the question?" Jesus said, "The children of this world marry,
27 and are given in marriage: But they which shall be accounted worthy to obtain that world, and the resurrection from the dead, neither marry, nor are given in
30 marriage."

Chapter 4

Christian Science versus Spiritualism

And when they shall say unto you,
Seek unto them that have familiar spirits,
And unto wizards that peep and that mutter;
Should not a people seek unto their God? — ISAIAH.

Verily, verily, I say unto you,
If a man keep my saying, he shall never see death.
Then said the Jews unto him,
Now we know that thou hast a devil. — JOHN.

Mortal existence is an enigma. Every day is a   1
mystery. The testimony of the corporeal senses
cannot inform us what is real and what is delusive, but   3
the revelations of Christian Science unlock the treasures
of Truth. Whatever is false or sinful can

The infinite one Spirit

never enter the atmosphere of Spirit. There   6
is but one Spirit. Man is never God, but spiritual man,
made in God's likeness, reflects God. In this scientific
reflection the Ego and the Father are inseparable. The   9
supposition that corporeal beings are spirits, or that there
are good and evil spirits, is a mistake.

    The divine Mind maintains all identities, from a blade   12
of grass to a star, as distinct and eternal. The

Real and unreal identity

questions are: What are God's identities?
What is Soul? Does life or soul exist in the thing   15
formed?

70

Nothing is real and eternal, — nothing is Spirit, — but
God and His idea. Evil has no reality. It is neither
person, place, nor thing, but is simply a belief, an illusion
of material sense.

The identity, or idea, of all reality continues forever;
but Spirit, or the divine Principle of all, is not *in* Spirit's
formations. Soul is synonymous with Spirit, God, the
creative, governing, infinite Principle outside of finite form,
which forms only reflect.

Close your eyes, and you may dream that you see a
flower, — that you touch and smell it. Thus you learn
that the flower is a product of the so-called
mind, a formation of thought rather than of
matter. Close your eyes again, and you may see land-
scapes, men, and women. Thus you learn that these
also are images, which mortal mind holds and evolves
and which simulate mind, life, and intelligence. From
dreams also you learn that neither mortal mind nor
matter is the image or likeness of God, and that immortal Mind is not in matter.

Dream-lessons

When the Science of Mind is understood, spiritualism
will be found mainly erroneous, having no scientific basis
nor origin, no proof nor power outside of
human testimony. It is the offspring of the
physical senses. There is no sensuality in Spirit. I never
could believe in spiritualism.

Found wanting

The basis and structure of spiritualism are alike material and physical. Its spirits are so many corporealities,
limited and finite in character and quality. Spiritualism
therefore presupposes Spirit, which is ever infinite, to be
a corporeal being, a finite form, — a theory contrary to
Christian Science.

There is but one spiritual existence, — the Life of
which corporeal sense can take no cognizance. The
divine Principle of man speaks through immortal sense.
If a material body — in other words, mortal, material
sense — were permeated by Spirit, that body would
disappear to mortal sense, would be deathless. A condition precedent to communion with Spirit is the gain of
spiritual life.

So-called *spirits* are but corporeal communicators. As
light destroys darkness and in the place of darkness all
is light, so (in absolute Science) Soul, or God,
is the only truth-giver to man. Truth destroys mortality, and brings to light immortality. Mortal
belief (the material sense of life) and immortal Truth
(the spiritual sense) are the tares and the wheat, which
are not united by progress, but separated.

Perfection is not expressed through imperfection.
Spirit is not made manifest through matter, the antipode of Spirit. Error is not a convenient sieve through
which truth can be strained.

God, good, being ever present, it follows in divine
logic that evil, the suppositional opposite of good, is never
present. In Science, individual good derived
from God, the infinite All-in-all, may flow
from the departed to mortals; but evil is neither communicable nor scientific. A sinning, earthly mortal is
not the reality of Life nor the medium through which
truth passes to earth. The joy of intercourse becomes
the jest of sin, when evil and suffering are communicable.
Not personal intercommunion but divine law is the communicator of truth, health, and harmony to earth and
humanity. As readily can you mingle fire and frost as

Spirits
obsolete

Scientific
phenomena

1

3

6

9

12

15

18

21

24

27

30

1   Spirit and matter. In either case, one does not support
the other.

3   Spiritualism calls one person, living in this world, *material*, but another, who has died to-day a sinner and supposedly will return to earth to-morrow, it terms a *spirit*.

6   The fact is that neither the one nor the other is infinite
Spirit, for Spirit is God, and man is His likeness.

        The belief that one man, as spirit, can control an-

9   other man, as matter, upsets both the individuality and
the Science of man, for man is image. God
controls man, and God is the only Spirit. Any

12 other control or attraction of so-called spirit is a mortal
belief, which ought to be known by its fruit, — the repetition of evil.

15   If Spirit, or God, communed with mortals or controlled
them through electricity or any other form of matter, the
divine order and the Science of omnipotent, omnipresent

18 Spirit would be destroyed.

        The belief that material bodies return to dust, hereafter
to rise up as spiritual bodies with material sensations and

21 desires, is incorrect. Equally incorrect is the
belief that spirit is confined in a finite, material body, from which it is freed by death, and that, when

24 it is freed from the material body, spirit retains the sensations belonging to that body.

        It is a grave mistake to suppose that matter is any part

27 of the reality of intelligent existence, or that Spirit and
matter, intelligence and non-intelligence, can
commune together. This error Science will

30 destroy. The sensual cannot be made the mouthpiece of
the spiritual, nor can the finite become the channel of
the infinite. There is no communication between so-

Marginal notes:

One
government

Incorrect
theories

No
mediumship

called material existence and spiritual life which is not   1
subject to death.

To be on communicable terms with Spirit, persons must   3
be free from organic bodies; and their return to a material condition, after having once left it, would

be as impossible as would be the restoration   6
to its original condition of the acorn, already absorbed
into a sprout which has risen above the soil. The seed
which has germinated has a new form and state of exist-   9
ence. When here or hereafter the belief of life in matter
is extinct, the error which has held the belief dissolves
with the belief, and never returns to the old condition.   12
No correspondence nor communion can exist between
persons in such opposite dreams as the belief of having
died and left a material body and the belief of still living   15
in an organic, material body.

The caterpillar, transformed into a beautiful insect,
is no longer a worm, nor does the insect return to   18

fraternize with or control the worm. Such
a backward transformation is impossible in
Science. Darkness and light, infancy and manhood,   21
sickness and health, are opposites, — different beliefs,
which never blend. Who will say that infancy can utter
the ideas of manhood, that darkness can represent light,   24
that we are in Europe when we are in the opposite hemi-
sphere? There is no bridge across the gulf which divides
two such opposite conditions as the spiritual, or incor-   27
poreal, and the physical, or corporeal.

In Christian Science there is never a retrograde step,
never a return to positions outgrown. The so-called dead   30
and living cannot commune together, for they are in
separate states of existence, or consciousness.

1   This simple truth lays bare the mistaken assumption
that man dies as matter but comes to life as spirit. The
3   so-called dead, in order to reappear to those
still in the existence cognized by the physical
senses, would need to be tangible and material, — to have
6   a material investiture, — or the material senses could take
no cognizance of the so-called dead.

Unscientific investiture

    Spiritualism would transfer men from the spiritual sense
9   of existence back into its material sense. This gross materialism is scientifically impossible, since to infinite Spirit
there can be no matter.

12   Jesus said of Lazarus: "Our friend Lazarus sleepeth;
but I go, that I may awake him out of sleep." Jesus
restored Lazarus by the understanding that
15   Lazarus had never died, not by an admission that his body had died and then lived again. Had
Jesus believed that Lazarus had lived or died in his
18   body, the Master would have stood on the same plane of
belief as those who buried the body, and he could not have
resuscitated it.

Raising the dead

21   When you can waken yourself or others out of the belief
that all must die, you can then exercise Jesus' spiritual
power to reproduce the presence of those who have thought
24   they died, — but not otherwise.

    There is one possible moment, when those living on the
earth and those called dead, can commune together, and
27   that is the moment previous to the transition,
— the moment when the link between their opposite beliefs is being sundered. In the vestibule through
30   which we pass from one dream to another dream, or
when we awake from earth's sleep to the grand verities
of Life, the departing may hear the glad welcome of those

Vision of the dying

who have gone before. The ones departing may whisper   1
this vision, name the face that smiles on them and the
hand which beckons them, as one at Niagara, with eyes   3
open only to that wonder, forgets all else and breathes
aloud his rapture.

When being is understood, Life will be recognized as   6
neither material nor finite, but as infinite, — as God,

**Real Life
is God**

universal good; and the belief that life, or
mind, was ever in a finite form, or good in   9
evil, will be destroyed. Then it will be understood that
Spirit never entered matter and was therefore never
raised from matter. When advanced to spiritual being   12
and the understanding of God, man can no longer commune with matter; neither can he return to it, any more
than a tree can return to its seed. Neither will man seem   15
to be corporeal, but he will be an individual consciousness, characterized by the divine Spirit as idea, not matter.

Suffering, sinning, dying beliefs are unreal. When   18
divine Science is universally understood, they will have
no power over man, for man is immortal and lives by
divine authority.   21

The sinless joy, — the perfect harmony and immortality
of Life, possessing unlimited divine beauty and goodness

**Immaterial
pleasure**

without a single bodily pleasure or pain, —   24
constitutes the only veritable, indestructible
man, whose being is spiritual. This state of existence
is scientific and intact, — a perfection discernible only   27
by those who have the final understanding of Christ in
divine Science. Death can never hasten this state of
existence, for death must be overcome, not submitted to,   30
before immortality appears.

The recognition of Spirit and of infinity comes not

suddenly here or hereafter. The pious Polycarp said:
"I cannot turn at once from good to evil." Neither do
other mortals accomplish the change from error to truth
at a single bound.

Existence continues to be a belief of corporeal sense
until the Science of being is reached. Error brings its
own self-destruction both here and hereafter, for mortal mind creates its own physical conditions. Death will occur on the next plane of existence as on this, until the spiritual understanding of Life is reached. Then, and not until then, will it be demonstrated that "the second death hath no power."

Second death

The period required for this dream of material life, embracing its so-called pleasures and pains, to vanish from consciousness, "knoweth no man . . . neither the Son, but the Father." This period will be of longer or shorter duration according to the tenacity of error. Of what advantage, then, would it be to us, or to the departed, to prolong the material state and so prolong the illusion either of a soul inert or of a sinning, suffering sense, — a so-called mind fettered to matter.

A dream vanishing

Even if communications from spirits to mortal consciousness were possible, such communications would grow beautifully less with every advanced stage of existence. The departed would gradually rise above ignorance and materiality, and Spiritualists would outgrow their beliefs in material spiritualism. Spiritism consigns the so-called dead to a state resembling that of blighted buds, — to a wretched purgatory, where the chances of the departed for improvement narrow into nothing and they return to their old standpoints of matter.

Progress and purgatory

The decaying flower, the blighted bud, the gnarled oak, 1
the ferocious beast, — like the discords of disease, sin,

and death, — are unnatural. They are the fal- 3
sities of sense, the changing deflections of mortal mind; they are not the eternal realities of Mind.

How unreasonable is the belief that we are wearing 6
out life and hastening to death, and that at the same

time we are communing with immortality!
If the departed are in rapport with mor- 9
tality, or matter, they are not spiritual, but must still
be mortal, sinning, suffering, and dying. Then why
look to them — even were communication possible — for 12
proofs of immortality, and accept them as oracles? Communications gathered from ignorance are pernicious in
tendency. 15

Spiritualism with its material accompaniments would
destroy the supremacy of Spirit. If Spirit pervades all
space, it needs no material method for the transmission 18
of messages. Spirit needs no wires nor electricity in order
to be omnipresent.

Spirit is not materially tangible. How then can it 21
communicate with man through electric, material effects?

How can the majesty and omnipotence of
Spirit be lost? God is not in the medley 24
where matter cares for matter, where spiritism makes
many gods, and hypnotism and electricity are claimed
to be the agents of God's government. 27

Spirit blesses man, but man cannot "tell whence
it cometh." By it the sick are healed, the sorrowing are
comforted, and the sinning are reformed. These are the 30
effects of one universal God, the invisible good dwelling
in eternal Science.

The act of describing disease — its symptoms, locality, and fatality — is not scientific. Warning people against death is an error that tends to frighten into death those who are ignorant of Life as God. Thousands of instances could be cited of health restored by changing the patient's thoughts regarding death.

Thought regarding death

A scientific mental method is more sanitary than the use of drugs, and such a mental method produces permanent health. Science must go over the whole ground, and dig up every seed of error's sowing. Spiritualism relies upon human beliefs and hypotheses. Christian Science removes these beliefs and hypotheses through the higher understanding of God, for Christian Science, resting on divine Principle, not on material personalities, in its revelation of immortality, introduces the harmony of being.

Fallacious hypotheses

Jesus cast out evil spirits, or false beliefs. The Apostle Paul bade men have the Mind that was in the Christ. Jesus did his own work by the one Spirit. He said: "My Father worketh hitherto, and I work." He never described disease, so far as can be learned from the Gospels, but he healed disease.

The unscientific practitioner says: "You are ill. Your brain is overtaxed, and you must rest. Your body is weak, and it must be strengthened. You have nervous prostration, and must be treated for it." Science objects to all this, contending for the rights of intelligence and asserting that Mind controls body and brain.

Mistaken methods

Mind-science teaches that mortals need "not be weary in well doing." It dissipates fatigue in doing good. Giving does not impoverish us in the service of our Maker, neither does withholding enrich us.

Divine strength

We have strength in proportion to our apprehension of 1
the truth, and our strength is not lessened by giving
utterance to truth. A cup of coffee or tea is not the equal 3
of truth, whether for the inspiration of a sermon or for
the support of bodily endurance.

A communication purporting to come from the late 6
Theodore Parker reads as follows: "There never was,

A denial of
immortality

and there never will be, an immortal spirit."
Yet the very periodical containing this sen- 9
tence repeats weekly the assertion that spirit-communica-
tions are our only proofs of immortality.

I entertain no doubt of the humanity and philanthropy 12
of many Spiritualists, but I cannot coincide with their

Mysticism
unscientific

views. It is mysticism which gives spiritualism its force. Science dispels mystery and 15
explains extraordinary phenomena; but Science never
removes phenomena from the domain of reason into the
realm of mysticism. 18

It should not seem mysterious that mind, without the
aid of hands, can move a table, when we already know

Physical
falsities

that it is mind-power which moves both table 21
and hand. Even planchette — the French toy
which years ago pleased so many people — attested the control of mortal mind over its substratum, called matter. 24

It is mortal mind which convulses its substratum, matter.
These movements arise from the volition of human belief,
but they are neither scientific nor rational. Mortal mind 27
produces table-tipping as certainly as table-setting, and
believes that this wonder emanates from spirits and electricity. This belief rests on the common conviction that 30
mind and matter cooperate both visibly and invisibly,
hence that matter is intelligent.

1   There is not so much evidence to prove intercommuni-
cation between the so-called dead and the living, as there
3   is to show the sick that matter suffers and has   Poor
post-mortem
evidence
sensation; yet this latter evidence is destroyed by
Mind-science. If Spiritualists understood the
6   Science of being, their belief in mediumship would vanish.

At the very best and on its own theories, spiritualism
can only prove that certain individuals have a continued
9   existence after death and maintain their affili-   **No proof of
immortality**
ation with mortal flesh; but this fact affords
no certainty of everlasting life. A man's assertion that
12   he is immortal no more proves him to be so, than the opposite assertion, that he is mortal, would prove immortality a lie. Nor is the case improved when alleged spirits
15   teach immortality. Life, Love, Truth, is the only proof
of immortality.

Man in the likeness of God as revealed in Science can-
18   not help being immortal. Though the grass seemeth to
wither and the flower to fade, they reappear.
Erase the figures which express number, silence   **Mind's
manifestations
immortal**
21   the tones of music, give to the worms the body
called man, and yet the producing, governing, divine
Principle lives on, — in the case of man as truly as in
24   the case of numbers and of music, — despite the so-called
laws of matter, which define man as mortal. Though
the inharmony resulting from material sense hides the
27   harmony of Science, inharmony cannot destroy the divine
Principle of Science. In Science, man's immortality depends upon that of God, good, and follows as a necessary
30   consequence of the immortality of good.

That somebody, somewhere, must have known the
deceased person, supposed to be the communicator, is

evident, and it is as easy to read distant thoughts as near.   1
We think of an absent friend as easily as we do of one
present. It is no more difficult to read the   3
absent mind than it is to read the present.

Chaucer wrote centuries ago, yet we still read his thought
in his verse. What is classic study, but discernment of   6
the minds of Homer and Virgil, of whose personal existence we may be in doubt?

If spiritual life has been won by the departed, they   9
cannot return to material existence, because different
states of consciousness are involved, and one

person cannot exist in two different states of   12
consciousness at the same time. In sleep we
do not communicate with the dreamer by our side despite
his physical proximity, because both of us are either un-   15
conscious or are wandering in our dreams through different mazes of consciousness.

In like manner it would follow, even if our departed   18
friends were near us and were in as conscious a state of
existence as before the change we call death, that their
state of consciousness must be different from ours. We   21
are not in their state, nor are they in the mental realm
in which we dwell. Communion between them and
ourselves would be prevented by this difference. The   24
mental states are so unlike, that intercommunion is as
impossible as it would be between a mole and a human
being. Different dreams and different awakenings be-   27
token a differing consciousness. When wandering in
Australia, do we look for help to the Esquimaux in their
snow huts?   30

In a world of sin and sensuality hastening to a
greater development of power, it is wise earnestly to

1 consider whether it is the human mind or the divine
Mind which is influencing one. What the prophets of
3 Jehovah did, the worshippers of Baal failed to do; yet
artifice and delusion claimed that they could equal the
work of wisdom.

6 Science only can explain the incredible good and evil
elements now coming to the surface. Mortals must find
refuge in Truth in order to escape the error of these latter
9 days. Nothing is more antagonistic to Christian Science
than a blind belief without understanding, for such a
belief hides Truth and builds on error.

12 Miracles are impossible in Science, and here Science
takes issue with popular religions. The scientific manifestation of power is from the divine nature

Natural wonders

15 and is not supernatural, since Science is an
explication of nature. The belief that the universe, including man, is governed in general by material laws, but
18 that occasionally Spirit sets aside these laws, — this belief belittles omnipotent wisdom, and gives to matter the
precedence over Spirit.

21 It is contrary to Christian Science to suppose that life
is either material or organically spiritual. Between
Christian Science and all forms of superstition

Conflicting standpoints

24 a great gulf is fixed, as impassable as that between Dives and Lazarus. There is mortal mind-reading
and immortal Mind-reading. The latter is a revelation
27 of divine purpose through spiritual understanding, by
which man gains the divine Principle and explanation of
all things. Mortal mind-reading and immortal Mind-
30 reading are distinctly opposite standpoints, from which
cause and effect are interpreted. The act of reading
mortal mind investigates and touches only human beliefs.

Science is immortal and coordinate neither with the 1
premises nor with the conclusions of mortal beliefs.

The ancient prophets gained their foresight from a 3
spiritual, incorporeal standpoint, not by foreshadowing

evil and mistaking fact for fiction, — predicting the future from a groundwork of corpo- 6
reality and human belief. When sufficiently advanced
in Science to be in harmony with the truth of being, men
become seers and prophets involuntarily, controlled not 9
by demons, spirits, or demigods, but by the one Spirit.
It is the prerogative of the ever-present, divine Mind, and
of thought which is in rapport with this Mind, to know 12
the past, the present, and the future.

Acquaintance with the Science of being enables us to
commune more largely with the divine Mind, to foresee 15
and foretell events which concern the universal welfare,
to be divinely inspired, — yea, to reach the range of fetter-
less Mind. 18

To understand that Mind is infinite, not bounded by
corporeality, not dependent upon the ear and eye for

sound or sight nor upon muscles and bones 21
for locomotion, is a step towards the Mind-
science by which we discern man's nature and existence.
This true conception of being destroys the belief of spirit- 24
ualism at its very inception, for without the concession of
material personalities called spirits, spiritualism has no
basis upon which to build. 27

All we correctly know of Spirit comes from God, divine
Principle, and is learned through Christ and Christian

Science. If this Science has been thoroughly 30
learned and properly digested, we can know
the truth more accurately than the astronomer can read

1 the stars or calculate an eclipse. This Mind-reading
is the opposite of clairvoyance. It is the illumination of
3 the spiritual understanding which demonstrates the capacity of Soul, not of material sense. This Soul-sense
comes to the human mind when the latter yields to the
6 divine Mind.

Such intuitions reveal whatever constitutes and perpetuates harmony, enabling one to do good, but not
9 evil. You will reach the perfect Science of
healing when you are able to read the human
mind after this manner and discern the error you would
12 destroy. The Samaritan woman said: "Come, see a
man, which told me all things that ever I did: is not this
the Christ?"

Value of intuition

15 It is recorded that Jesus, as he once journeyed with his
students, "knew their thoughts," — read them scientifically. In like manner he discerned disease and healed
18 the sick. After the same method, events of great moment were foretold by the Hebrew prophets. Our
Master rebuked the lack of this power when he said:
21 "O ye hypocrites! ye can discern the face of the sky;
but can ye not discern the signs of the times?"

Both Jew and Gentile may have had acute corporeal
24 senses, but mortals need spiritual sense. Jesus knew the
generation to be wicked and adulterous, seek-
ing the material more than the spiritual. His
27 thrusts at materialism were sharp, but needed. He never
spared hypocrisy the sternest condemnation. He said:
"These ought ye to have done, and not to leave the other
30 undone." The great Teacher knew both cause and
effect, knew that truth communicates itself but never
imparts error.

Hypocrisy condemned

Jesus once asked, "Who touched me?" Supposing this inquiry to be occasioned by physical contact alone,

Mental
contact

his disciples answered, "The multitude throng thee." Jesus knew, as others did not, that it was not matter, but mortal mind, whose touch called for aid. Repeating his inquiry, he was answered by the faith of a sick woman. His quick apprehension of this mental call illustrated his spirituality. The disciples' misconception of it uncovered their materiality. Jesus possessed more spiritual susceptibility than the disciples. Opposites come from contrary directions, and produce unlike results.

Mortals evolve images of thought. These may appear to the ignorant to be apparitions; but they are myste-

Images of
thought

rious only because it is unusual to see thoughts, though we can always feel their influence. Haunted houses, ghostly voices, unusual noises, and apparitions brought out in dark seances either involve feats by tricksters, or they are images and sounds evolved involuntarily by mortal mind. Seeing is no less a quality of physical sense than feeling. Then why is it more difficult to see a thought than to feel one? Education alone determines the difference. In reality there is none.

Portraits, landscape-paintings, fac-similes of penman-ship, peculiarities of expression, recollected sentences,

Phenomena
explained

can all be taken from pictorial thought and memory as readily as from objects cognizable by the senses. Mortal mind sees what it believes as certainly as it believes what it sees. It feels, hears, and sees its own thoughts. Pictures are mentally formed before the artist can convey them to canvas. So is it

1

3

6

9

12

15

18

21

24

27

30

1 with all material conceptions. Mind-readers perceive
these pictures of thought. They copy or reproduce
3 them, even when they are lost to the memory of the mind
in which they are discoverable.

It is needless for the thought or for the person hold-
6 ing the transferred picture to be individually and consciously present. Though individuals have

Mental environment

passed away, their mental environment re-
9 mains to be discerned, described, and transmitted. Though
bodies are leagues apart and their associations forgotten,
their associations float in the general atmosphere of human
12 mind.

The Scotch call such vision "second sight," when
really it is first sight instead of second, for it presents
15 primal facts to mortal mind. Science enables

Second sight

one to read the human mind, but not as a
clairvoyant. It enables one to heal through Mind, but
18 not as a mesmerist.

The mine knows naught of the emeralds within its
rocks; the sea is ignorant of the gems within its caverns,
21 of the corals, of its sharp reefs, of the tall ships

Buried secrets

that float on its bosom, or of the bodies which
lie buried in its sands: yet these are all there. Do not
24 suppose that any mental concept is gone because you do
not think of it. The true concept is never lost. The
strong impressions produced on mortal mind by friend-
27 ship or by any intense feeling are lasting, and mind-
readers can perceive and reproduce these impressions.

Memory may reproduce voices long ago silent. We
30 have but to close the eyes, and forms rise

Recollected friends

before us, which are thousands of miles away
or altogether gone from physical sight and sense, and

this not in dreamy sleep. In our day-dreams we can   1
recall that for which the poet Tennyson expressed the
heart's desire, —   3

> the touch of a vanished hand,
> And the sound of a voice that is still.

The mind may even be cognizant of a present flavor and   6
odor, when no viand touches the palate and no scent
salutes the nostrils.

How are veritable ideas to be distinguished from il-   9
lusions? By learning the origin of each. Ideas are

Illusions
not ideas

emanations from the divine Mind. Thoughts,
proceeding from the brain or from matter, are   12
offshoots of mortal mind; they are mortal material beliefs. Ideas are spiritual, harmonious, and eternal. Beliefs
proceed from the so-called material senses, which at one 15
time are supposed to be substance-matter and at another
are called spirits.

To love one's neighbor as one's self, is a divine idea;   18
but this idea can never be seen, felt, nor understood
through the physical senses. Excite the organ of ven-
eration or religious faith, and the individual manifests 21
profound adoration. Excite the opposite development,
and he blasphemes. These effects, however, do not proceed from Christianity, nor are they spiritual phenomena, 24
for both arise from mortal belief.

Eloquence re-echoes the strains of Truth and Love.
It is due to inspiration rather than to erudition. It shows 27

Trance
speaking
illusion

the possibilities derived from divine Mind,
though it is said to be a gift whose endowment
is obtained from books or received from the   30
impulsion of departed spirits. When eloquence proceeds
from the belief that a departed spirit is speaking, who

1   can tell what the unaided medium is incapable of knowing or uttering? This phenomenon only shows that the
3   beliefs of mortal mind are loosed. Forgetting her ignorance in the belief that another mind is speaking through
her, the devotee may become unwontedly eloquent. Hav-
6   ing more faith in others than in herself, and believing
that somebody else possesses her tongue and mind, she
talks freely.

9   Destroy her belief in outside aid, and her eloquence
disappears. The former limits of her belief return. She
says, "I am incapable of words that glow, for I am un-
12   educated." This familiar instance reaffirms the Scriptural word concerning a man, "As he thinketh in his heart,
so is he." If one believes that he cannot be an orator with-
15   out study or a superinduced condition, the body responds
to this belief, and the tongue grows mute which before
was eloquent.

18   Mind is not necessarily dependent upon educational
processes. It possesses of itself all beauty and poetry,
and the power of expressing them. Spirit,   **Scientific**
21   God, is heard when the senses are silent. We   **improvisation**
are all capable of more than we do. The influence or
action of Soul confers a freedom, which explains the phe-
24   nomena of improvisation and the fervor of untutored lips.

      Matter is neither intelligent nor creative. The tree is
not the author of itself. Sound is not the originator of
27   music, and man is not the father of man. Cain   **Divine**
very naturally concluded that if life was in the   **origination**
body, and man gave it, man had the right to take it away.
30   This incident shows that the belief of life in matter was
"a murderer from the beginning."

      If seed is necessary to produce wheat, and wheat to

produce flour, or if one animal can originate another,   1
how then can we account for their primal origin? How
were the loaves and fishes multiplied on the shores of   3
Galilee, — and that, too, without meal or monad from
which loaf or fish could come?

The earth's orbit and the imaginary line called the   6
equator are not substance. The earth's motion and

Mind is substance position are sustained by Mind alone. Divest
yourself of the thought that there can be sub-   9
stance in matter, and the movements and transitions now
possible for mortal mind will be found to be equally
possible for the body. Then being will be recognized   12
as spiritual, and death will be obsolete, though now
some insist that death is the necessary prelude to
immortality.   15

In dreams we fly to Europe and meet a far-off friend.
The looker-on sees the body in bed, but the supposed

Mortal delusions inhabitant of that body carries it through   18
the air and over the ocean. This shows the
possibilities of thought. Opium and hashish eaters mentally travel far and work wonders, yet their bodies stay   21
in one place. This shows what mortal mentality and
knowledge are.

The admission to one's self that man is God's own like-   24
ness sets man free to master the infinite idea. This con-

Scientific finalities viction shuts the door on death, and opens it
wide towards immortality. The understanding   27
and recognition of Spirit must finally come, and we may
as well improve our time in solving the mysteries of being
through an apprehension of divine Principle. At present   30
we know not what man is, but we certainly shall know
this when man reflects God.

1 The Revelator tells us of "a new heaven and a
new earth." Have you ever pictured this heaven and
3 earth, inhabited by beings under the control of supreme
wisdom?

Let us rid ourselves of the belief that man is separated
6 from God, and obey only the divine Principle, Life and
Love. Here is the great point of departure for all true
spiritual growth.

9 It is difficult for the sinner to accept divine Science,
because Science exposes his nothingness; but the sooner
error is reduced to its native nothingness, the
12 sooner man's great reality will appear and his
genuine being will be understood. The destruction of
error is by no means the destruction of Truth or Life, but
15 is the acknowledgment of them.

Man's genuine being

Absorbed in material selfhood we discern and reflect
but faintly the substance of Life or Mind. The denial of
18 material selfhood aids the discernment of man's spiritual and eternal individuality, and destroys the erroneous
knowledge gained from matter or through what are termed
21 the material senses.

Certain erroneous postulates should be here considered
in order that the spiritual facts may be better
24 apprehended.

Erroneous postulates

The first erroneous postulate of belief is, that substance,
life, and intelligence are something apart from God.

27 The second erroneous postulate is, that man is both
mental and material.

The third erroneous postulate is, that mind is both evil
30 and good; whereas the real Mind cannot be evil nor the
medium of evil, for Mind is God.

The fourth erroneous postulate is, that matter is in-

telligent, and that man has a material body which is part   1
of himself.

The fifth erroneous postulate is, that matter holds in   3
itself the issues of life and death, — that matter is not
only capable of experiencing pleasure and pain, but also
capable of imparting these sensations. From the illusion   6
implied in this last postulate arises the decomposition of
mortal bodies in what is termed death.

Mind is not an entity within the cranium with the power   9
of sinning now and forever.

In old Scriptural pictures we see a serpent coiled around
the tree of knowledge and speaking to Adam and Eve.   12

Knowledge of good and evil   This represents the serpent in the act of
commending to our first parents the knowl-
edge of good and evil, a knowledge gained from matter,   15
or evil, instead of from Spirit. The portrayal is still
graphically accurate, for the common conception of mortal man — a burlesque of God's man — is an outgrowth   18
of human knowledge or sensuality, a mere offshoot of
material sense.

Uncover error, and it turns the lie upon you. Until   21
the fact concerning error — namely, its nothingness —

Opposing power   appears, the moral demand will not be met,
and the ability to make nothing of error will   24
be wanting. We should blush to call that real which is
only a mistake. The foundation of evil is laid on a belief
in something besides God. This belief tends to support   27
two opposite powers, instead of urging the claims of Truth
alone. The mistake of thinking that error can be real,
when it is merely the absence of truth, leads to belief in   30
the superiority of error.

Do you say the time has not yet come in which to

recognize Soul as substantial and able to control the
body? Remember Jesus, who nearly nineteen centuries
ago demonstrated the power of Spirit and said,
"He that believeth on me, the works that I
do shall he do also," and who also said, "But the hour
cometh, and *now is,* when the true worshippers shall
worship the Father in spirit and in truth." "Behold,
now is the accepted time; behold, *now* is the day of salvation," said Paul.

Divine logic and revelation coincide. If we believe
otherwise, we may be sure that either our
logic is at fault or that we have misinterpreted
revelation. Good never causes evil, nor creates aught
that can cause evil.

Good does not create a mind susceptible of causing
evil, for evil is the opposing error and not the truth of
creation. Destructive electricity is not the offspring of infinite good. Whatever contradicts the real nature of the
divine *Esse,* though human faith may clothe it with angelic
vestments, is without foundation.

The belief that Spirit is finite as well as infinite has
darkened all history. In Christian Science, Spirit, as a
proper noun, is the name of the Supreme Being.
It means quantity and quality, and applies ex-
clusively to God. The modifying derivatives of the word
spirit refer only to quality, not to God. Man is spiritual.
He is not God, Spirit. If man were Spirit, then men
would be spirits, gods. Finite spirit would be mortal,
and this is the error embodied in the belief that the infinite can be contained in the finite. This belief tends to
becloud our apprehension of the kingdom of heaven and
of the reign of harmony in the Science of being.

Jesus taught but one God, one Spirit, who makes man 1
in the image and likeness of Himself, — of Spirit, not of

Scientific man   matter. Man reflects infinite Truth, Life, and 3
Love. The nature of man, thus understood,
includes all that is implied by the terms "image" and
"likeness" as used in Scripture. The truly Christian 6
and scientific statement of personality and of the relation
of man to God, with the demonstration which accompanied it, incensed the rabbis, and they said: "Crucify him, 9
crucify him . . . by our law he ought to die, because he
made himself the Son of God."

The eastern empires and nations owe their false gov- 12
ernment to the misconceptions of Deity there prevalent.
Tyranny, intolerance, and bloodshed, wherever found,
arise from the belief that the infinite is formed after the 15
pattern of mortal personality, passion, and impulse.

The progress of truth confirms its claims, and our
Master confirmed his words by his works. His healing- 18

Ingratitude and denial   power evoked denial, ingratitude, and betrayal, arising from sensuality. Of the ten
lepers whom Jesus healed, but one returned to give God 21
thanks, — that is, to acknowledge the divine Principle
which had healed him.

Our Master easily read the thoughts of mankind, and 24
this insight better enabled him to direct those thoughts
aright; but what would be said at this period of an infidel blasphemer who should hint that Jesus used his in- 27
cisive power injuriously? Our Master read mortal mind
on a scientific basis, that of the omnipresence of Mind.
An approximation of this discernment indicates spiritual 30
growth and union with the infinite capacities of the one
Mind. Jesus could injure no one by his Mind-reading.

1   The effect of his Mind was always to heal and to save,
and this is the only genuine Science of reading mortal
3   mind. His holy motives and aims were tra-   Spiritual
duced by the sinners of that period, as they   insight
would be to-day if Jesus were personally present. Paul
6   said, "To be spiritually minded is life." We approach
God, or Life, in proportion to our spirituality, our fidelity to Truth and Love; and in that ratio we know all
9   human need and are able to discern the thought of the
sick and the sinning for the purpose of healing them.
Error of any kind cannot hide from the law of God.
12   Whoever reaches this point of moral culture and goodness cannot injure others, and must do them good. The
greater or lesser ability of a Christian Scientist to discern
15   thought scientifically, depends upon his genuine spirituality. This kind of mind-reading is not clairvoyance,
but it is important to success in healing, and is one of the
18   special characteristics thereof.
We welcome the increase of knowledge and the end
of error, because even human invention must have its
21   day, and we want that day to be succeeded   Christ's
by Christian Science, by divine reality. Mid-   reappearance
night foretells the dawn. Led by a solitary star amid
24   the darkness, the Magi of old foretold the Messiahship
of Truth. Is the wise man of to-day believed, when he
beholds the light which heralds Christ's eternal dawn
27   and describes its effulgence?
Lulled by stupefying illusions, the world is asleep
in the cradle of infancy, dreaming away the hours.
30   Material sense does not unfold the facts of   Spiritual
existence; but spiritual sense lifts human   awakening
consciousness into eternal Truth. Humanity advances

slowly out of sinning sense into spiritual understanding;   1
unwillingness to learn all things rightly, binds Christendom with chains.   3

Love will finally mark the hour of harmony, and spiritualization will follow, for Love is Spirit. Before error

The darkest
hours of all
is wholly destroyed, there will be interrup-   6
tions of the general material routine. Earth
will become dreary and desolate, but summer and winter,
seedtime and harvest (though in changed forms), will   9
continue unto the end, — until the final spiritualization of
all things. "The darkest hour precedes the dawn."

This material world is even now becoming the arena   12
for conflicting forces. On one side there will be discord

Arena of
contest
and dismay; on the other side there will be
Science and peace. The breaking up of mate-   15
rial beliefs may seem to be famine and pestilence, want
and woe, sin, sickness, and death, which assume new
phases until their nothingness appears. These disturb-   18
ances will continue until the end of error, when all
discord will be swallowed up in spiritual Truth.

Mortal error will vanish in a moral chemicalization.   21
This mental fermentation has begun, and will continue
until all errors of belief yield to understanding. Belief is
changeable, but spiritual understanding is changeless.   24

As this consummation draws nearer, he who has
shaped his course in accordance with divine Science

Millennial
glory
will endure to the end. As material knowl-   27
edge diminishes and spiritual understanding
increases, real objects will be apprehended mentally
instead of materially.   30

During this final conflict, wicked minds will endeavor
to find means by which to accomplish more evil; but

those who discern Christian Science will hold crime in
check. They will aid in the ejection of error. They
will maintain law and order, and cheerfully await the
certainty of ultimate perfection.

In reality, the more closely error simulates truth and
so-called matter resembles its essence, mortal mind, the
more impotent error becomes as a belief. According to human belief, the lightning is fierce

**Dangerous
resemblances**

and the electric current swift, yet in Christian Science
the flight of one and the blow of the other will become
harmless. The more destructive matter becomes, the
more its nothingness will appear, until matter reaches
its mortal zenith in illusion and forever disappears. The
nearer a false belief approaches truth without passing
the boundary where, having been destroyed by divine
Love, it ceases to be even an illusion, the riper it becomes
for destruction. The more material the belief, the more
obvious its error, until divine Spirit, supreme in its domain, dominates all matter, and man is found in the likeness of Spirit, his original being.

The broadest facts array the most falsities against
themselves, for they bring error from under cover. It
requires courage to utter truth; for the higher Truth
lifts her voice, the louder will error scream, until its in-
articulate sound is forever silenced in oblivion.

"He uttered His voice, the earth melted." This Scripture indicates that all matter will disappear before the
supremacy of Spirit.

Christianity is again demonstrating the Life that is
Truth, and the Truth that is Life, by the apostolic work of casting out error and healing the

**Christianity
still rejected**

sick. Earth has no repayment for the persecutions which

attend a new step in Christianity; but the spiritual recom-   1
pense of the persecuted is assured in the elevation of existence above mortal discord and in the gift of divine Love.   3

The prophet of to-day beholds in the mental horizon
the signs of these times, the reappearance of the Chris-

**Spiritual fore-
shadowings**

tianity which heals the sick and destroys error,   6
and no other sign shall be given. Body cannot be saved except through Mind. The Science of Christianity is misinterpreted by a material age, for it is the   9
healing influence of Spirit (not *spirits*) which the material
senses cannot comprehend, — which can only be spiritually discerned. Creeds, doctrines, and human hypotheses   12
do not express Christian Science; much less can they
demonstrate it.

Beyond the frail premises of human beliefs, above the   15
loosening grasp of creeds, the demonstration of Christian

**Revelation
of Science**

Mind-healing stands a revealed and practical
Science. It is imperious throughout all ages   18
as Christ's revelation of Truth, of Life, and of Love, which
remains inviolate for every man to understand and to
practise.   21

For centuries — yea, always — natural science has not
been considered a part of any religion, Christianity not

**Science as
foreign to
all religion**

excepted. Even now multitudes consider that   24
which they call *science* has no proper connection with faith and piety. Mystery does
not enshroud Christ's teachings, and they are not theo-   27
retical and fragmentary, but practical and complete; and
being practical and complete, they are not deprived of
their essential vitality.   30

The way through which immortality and life are learned
is not ecclesiastical but Christian, not human but divine,

not physical but metaphysical, not material but scientifically spiritual. Human philosophy, ethics, and superstition afford no demonstrable divine Principle
by which mortals can escape from sin; yet
to escape from sin, is what the Bible demands. "Work
out your own salvation with fear and trembling," says
the apostle, and he straightway adds: "for it is God
which worketh in you both to will and to do of His good
pleasure" (Philippians ii. 12, 13). Truth has furnished
the key to the kingdom, and with this key Christian Science has opened the door of the human understanding.
None may pick the lock nor enter by some other door.
The ordinary teachings are material and not spiritual.
Christian Science teaches only that which is spiritual and
divine, and not human. Christian Science is unerring
and Divine; the human sense of things errs because it
is human.

Those individuals, who adopt theosophy, spiritualism,
or hypnotism, may possess natures above some others
who eschew their false beliefs. Therefore my contest is
not with the individual, but with the false system. I
love mankind, and shall continue to labor and to endure.

The calm, strong currents of true spirituality, the
manifestations of which are health, purity, and self-
immolation, must deepen human experience, until the
beliefs of material existence are seen to be a bald imposi-
tion, and sin, disease, and death give everlasting place
to the scientific demonstration of divine Spirit and to
God's spiritual, perfect man.

Key to the kingdom

Chapter 5

Animal Magnetism Unmasked

For out of the heart proceed evil thoughts,
murders, adulteries, fornications,
thefts, false witness, blasphemies:
these are the things which defile a man. — JESUS.

M esmerism or animal magnetism was first brought 1
into notice by Mesmer in Germany in 1775. According to the American Cyclopædia, he regarded this 3
so-called force, which he said could be ex-
erted by one living organism over another, as
a means of alleviating disease. His propositions were 6
as follows:

"There exists a mutual influence between the celestial
bodies, the earth, and animated things. Animal bodies 9
are susceptible to the influence of this agent, disseminat-
ing itself through the substance of the nerves."

In 1784, the French government ordered the medical 12
faculty of Paris to investigate Mesmer's theory and to
report upon it. Under this order a commission was
appointed, and Benjamin Franklin was one of the com- 15
missioners. This commission reported to the government as follows:

"In regard to the existence and utility of animal mag- 18
netism, we have come to the unanimous conclusions that
there is no proof of the existence of the animal magnetic

1   fluid; that the violent effects, which are observed in
      the public practice of magnetism, are due to manipula-
3   tions, or to the excitement of the imagination and the
      impressions made upon the senses; and that there is one
      more fact to be recorded in the history of the errors of
6   the human mind, and an important experiment upon
      the power of the imagination."

      In 1837, a committee of nine persons was appointed,
9   among whom were Roux, Bouillaud, and Clo-   Clairvoyance,
      quet, which tested during several sessions the   magnetism
      phenomena exhibited by a reputed clairvoyant. Their
12   report stated the results as follows:

      "The facts which had been promised by Monsieur
      Berna [the magnetizer] as conclusive, and as adapted to
15   throw light on physiological and therapeutical questions,
      are certainly not conclusive in favor of the doctrine of
      animal magnetism, and have nothing in common with
18   either physiology or therapeutics."

      This report was adopted by the Royal Academy of
      Medicine in Paris.

21   The author's own observations of the workings of
      animal magnetism convince her that it is not   Personal
      a remedial agent, and that its effects upon   conclusions
24   those who practise it, and upon their subjects who do
      not resist it, lead to moral and to physical death.

      If animal magnetism seems to alleviate or to cure dis-
27   ease, this appearance is deceptive, since error cannot
      remove the effects of error. Discomfort under error is
      preferable to comfort. In no instance is the effect of
30   animal magnetism, recently called hypnotism, other
      than the effect of illusion. Any seeming benefit derived
      from it is proportional to one's faith in esoteric magic.

Mere
negation

Animal magnetism has no scientific foundation, for   1
God governs all that is real, harmonious, and eternal, and
His power is neither animal nor human. Its   3
basis being a belief and this belief animal, in
Science animal magnetism, mesmerism, or hypnotism is
a mere negation, possessing neither intelligence, power,   6
nor reality, and in sense it is an unreal concept of the so-
called mortal mind.

There is but one real attraction, that of Spirit. The   9
pointing of the needle to the pole symbolizes this all-
embracing power or the attraction of God, divine Mind.

The planets have no more power over man than over   12
his Maker, since God governs the universe; but man,
reflecting God's power, has dominion over all the earth
and its hosts.   15

The mild forms of animal magnetism are disappearing, and its aggressive features are coming to the front.

Hidden
agents

The looms of crime, hidden in the dark re-   18
cesses of mortal thought, are every hour weav-
ing webs more complicated and subtle. So secret are the
present methods of animal magnetism that they ensnare   21
the age into indolence, and produce the very apathy on
the subject which the criminal desires. The following
is an extract from the Boston Herald: 24

"Mesmerism is a problem not lending itself to an easy
explanation and development. It implies the exercise
of despotic control, and is much more likely to be abused   27
by its possessor, than otherwise employed, for the individual or society."

Mankind must learn that evil is not power. Its so-   30
called despotism is but a phase of nothingness. Christian
Science despoils the kingdom of evil, and pre-eminently

1 promotes affection and virtue in families and therefore
in the community. The Apostle Paul refers to the
3 personification of evil as "the god of this
world," and further defines it as dishonesty
and craftiness. Sin was the Assyrian moon-god.

6   The destruction of the claims of mortal mind through
Science, by which man can escape from sin
and mortality, blesses the whole human fam-
9 ily. As in the beginning, however, this liberation does not scientifically show itself in a knowledge of
both good and evil, for the latter is unreal.

12   On the other hand, Mind-science is wholly separate
from any half-way impertinent knowledge, because Mind-
science is of God and demonstrates the divine Principle,
15 working out the purposes of good only. The maximum
of good is the infinite God and His idea, the All-in-all.
Evil is a suppositional lie.

18   As named in Christian Science, animal magnetism or
hypnotism is the specific term for error, or mortal mind.
It is the false belief that mind is in matter, and
21 is both evil and good; that evil is as real as
good and more powerful. This belief has not one quality of Truth. It is either ignorant or malicious. The
24 malicious form of hypnotism ultimates in moral idiocy.
The truths of immortal Mind sustain man, and they annihilate the fables of mortal mind, whose flimsy and gaudy
27 pretensions, like silly moths, singe their own wings and
fall into dust.

   In reality there is no *mortal* mind, and conse-
30 quently no transference of mortal thought
and will-power. Life and being are of
God. In Christian Science, man can do no harm, for

scientific thoughts are true thoughts, passing from God   1
to man.

When Christian Science and animal magnetism are   3
both comprehended, as they will be at no distant date,
it will be seen why the author of this book has been
so unjustly persecuted and belied by wolves in sheep's   6
clothing.

Agassiz, the celebrated naturalist and author, has
wisely said: "Every great scientific truth goes through   9
three stages. First, people say it conflicts with the Bible.
Next, they say it has been discovered before. Lastly,
they say they have always believed it."   12

Christian Science goes to the bottom of mental action,
and reveals the theodicy which indicates the rightness of

Perfection
of divine
government
all divine action, as the emanation of divine   15
Mind, and the consequent wrongness of the
opposite so-called action, — evil, occultism,
necromancy, mesmerism, animal magnetism, hypnotism.   18

The medicine of Science is divine Mind; and dishonesty,
sensuality, falsehood, revenge, malice, are animal pro-

Adulteration
of Truth
pensities and by no means the mental quali-   21
ties which heal the sick. The hypnotizer
employs one error to destroy another. If he heals sickness through a belief, and a belief originally caused the   24
sickness, it is a case of the greater error overcoming the
lesser. This greater error thereafter occupies the ground,
leaving the case worse than before it was grasped by the   27
stronger error.

Our courts recognize evidence to prove the motive as

Motives
considered
well as the commission of a crime. Is it not   30
clear that the human mind must move the
body to a wicked act? Is not mortal mind the mur-

1 derer? The hands, without mortal mind to direct them, could not commit a murder.

3 Courts and juries judge and sentence mortals in order to restrain crime, to prevent deeds of violence or to punish them. To say that these tribunals have no

6 jurisdiction over the carnal or mortal mind, would be to contradict precedent and to admit that the power of human law is restricted to matter, while mortal

9 mind, evil, which is the real outlaw, defies justice and is recommended to mercy. Can matter commit a crime? Can matter be punished? Can you separate the men-

12 tality from the body over which courts hold jurisdiction? Mortal mind, not matter, is the criminal in every case; and human law rightly estimates crime, and courts rea-

15 sonably pass sentence, according to the motive.

When our laws eventually take cognizance of mental crime and no longer apply legal rulings wholly to physical

18 offences, these words of Judge Parmenter of Boston will become historic: "I see no reason why metaphysics is not as important to medicine as to

21 mechanics or mathematics."

Whoever uses his developed mental powers like an escaped felon to commit fresh atrocities as opportunity oc-

24 curs is never safe. God will arrest him. Divine justice will manacle him. His sins will be millstones about his neck, weighing him down to the

27 depths of ignominy and death. The aggravation of error foretells its doom, and confirms the ancient axiom: "Whom the gods would destroy, they first make mad."

30 The distance from ordinary medical practice to Christian Science is full many a league in the line of light; but to go in healing from the use of

Mental crimes

Important decision

Evil let loose

The misuse of mental power

inanimate drugs to the criminal misuse of human will-   1
power, is to drop from the platform of common manhood
into the very mire of iniquity, to work against the free   3
course of honesty and justice, and to push vainly against
the current running heavenward.

Like our nation, Christian Science has its Declaration   6
of Independence. God has endowed man with inalien-

Proper self-
government
able rights, among which are self-government,
reason, and conscience. Man is properly self-   9
governed only when he is guided rightly and governed by
his Maker, divine Truth and Love.

Man's rights are invaded when the divine order is in-   12
terfered with, and the mental trespasser incurs the divine
penalty due this crime.

Let this age, which sits in judgment on Christian   15
Science, sanction only such methods as are demonstrable

Right
methods
in Truth and known by their fruit, and classify
all others as did St. Paul in his great epistle   18
to the Galatians, when he wrote as follows:

"Now the works of the flesh are manifest, which are
these; Adultery, fornication, uncleanness, lasciviousness,   21
idolatry, *witchcraft,* hatred, variance, emulations, wrath,
strife, seditions, heresies, envyings, murders, drunkenness,
revellings and such like: of the which I tell you before,   24
as I have also told you in time past, that they which do
such things shall not inherit the kingdom of God. But
the fruit of the Spirit is love, joy, peace, longsuffering,   27
gentleness, goodness, faith, meekness, temperance: against
such there is no law."

Chapter 6

Science, Theology, Medicine

But I certify you, brethren,
that the gospel which was preached of me is not after man.
For I neither received it of man, neither was I taught it,
but by the revelation of Jesus Christ. — PAUL.

The kingdom of heaven is like unto leaven, which a woman took,
and hid in three measures of meal, till the whole was leavened. — JESUS.

1 In the year 1866, I discovered the Christ Science or divine laws of Life, Truth, and Love, and
3 named my discovery Christian Science. God had been graciously preparing me during many years for the reception of this final revelation of the absolute divine Principle of scientific mental healing.

Christian Science discovered

This apodictical Principle points to the revelation of Immanuel, "God with us," — the sovereign ever-pres-
9 ence, delivering the children of men from every ill "that flesh is heir to." Through Christian Science, religion and medicine are
12 inspired with a diviner nature and essence; fresh pinions are given to faith and understanding, and thoughts acquaint themselves intelligently with God.

Mission of Christian Science

15 Feeling so perpetually the false consciousness that life inheres in the body, yet remembering that in reality God is our Life, we may well tremble
18 in the prospect of those days in which we must say, "I have no pleasure in them."

Discontent with life

Whence came to me this heavenly conviction, — a con-   1
viction antagonistic to the testimony of the physical senses?
According to St. Paul, it was "the gift of the grace of   3
God given unto me by the effectual working of His power."
It was the divine law of Life and Love, unfolding to me
the demonstrable fact that matter possesses neither sen-   6
sation nor life; that human experiences show the falsity
of all material things; and that immortal cravings, "the
price of learning love," establish the truism that the   9
only sufferer is mortal mind, for the divine Mind cannot
suffer.

My conclusions were reached by allowing the evidence   12
of this revelation to multiply with mathematical certainty

Demonstrable
evidence
and the lesser demonstration to prove the
greater, as the product of three multiplied by   15
three, equalling nine, proves conclusively that three times
three duodecillions must be nine duodecillions, — not
a fraction more, not a unit less.   18

When apparently near the confines of mortal existence,
standing already within the shadow of the death-valley,

Light shining
in darkness
I learned these truths in divine Science: that   21
all real being is in God, the divine Mind, and
that Life, Truth, and Love are all-powerful and ever-
present; that the opposite of Truth, — called error, sin,   24
sickness, disease, death, — is the false testimony of false
material sense, of mind in matter; that this false sense
evolves, in belief, a subjective state of mortal mind which   27
this same so-called mind names *matter*, thereby shutting
out the true sense of Spirit.

New lines
of thought
My discovery, that erring, mortal, misnamed   30
mind produces all the organism and action of
the mortal body, set my thoughts to work in new channels,

1   and led up to my demonstration of the proposition that
Mind is All and matter is naught as the leading factor in
3   Mind-science.

    • Christian Science reveals incontrovertibly that Mind
is All-in-all, that the only realities are the divine Mind
6   and idea. This great fact is not, however, seen   **Scientific**
to be supported by sensible evidence, until its   **evidence**
divine Principle is demonstrated by healing the sick and
9   thus proved absolute and divine. This proof once seen,
no other conclusion can be reached.

    For three years after my discovery, I sought the solu-
12   tion of this problem of Mind-healing, searched the Scriptures and read little else, kept aloof from so-   **Solitary**
ciety, and devoted time and energies to dis-   **research**
15   covering a positive rule. The search was sweet, calm, and
buoyant with hope, not selfish nor depressing. I knew
the Principle of all harmonious Mind-action to be God,
18   and that cures were produced in primitive Christian
healing by holy, uplifting faith; but I must know the
Science of this healing, and I won my way to absolute
21   conclusions through divine revelation, reason, and demonstration. The revelation of Truth in the understanding came to me gradually and apparently through divine
24   power. When a new spiritual idea is borne to earth, the
prophetic Scripture of Isaiah is renewedly fulfilled:
"Unto us a child is born, . . . and his name shall be
27   called Wonderful."

    Jesus once said of his lessons: "My doctrine is not
mine, but His that sent me. If any man will do His will,
30   he shall know of the doctrine, whether it be of God, or
whether I speak of myself." (John vii. 16, 17.)

    The three great verities of Spirit, omnipotence, omnipresence, omniscience, — Spirit possessing all power, filling all space, constituting all Science, — contradict forever the belief that matter can be actual. These eternal verities reveal primeval existence as the radiant reality of God's creation, in which all that He has made is pronounced by His wisdom good.

Thus it was that I beheld, as never before, the awful unreality called evil. The equipollence of God brought to light another glorious proposition, — man's perfectibility and the establishment of the kingdom of heaven on earth.

In following these leadings of scientific revelation, the Bible was my only textbook. The Scriptures were illumined; reason and revelation were reconciled, and afterwards the truth of Christian Science was demonstrated. No human pen nor tongue taught me the Science contained in this book, SCIENCE AND HEALTH; and neither tongue nor pen can overthrow it. This book may be distorted by shallow criticism or by careless or malicious students, and its ideas may be temporarily abused and misrepresented; but the Science and truth therein will forever remain to be discerned and demonstrated.

Jesus demonstrated the power of Christian Science to heal mortal minds and bodies. But this power was lost sight of, and must again be spiritually discerned, taught, and demonstrated according to Christ's command, with "signs following." Its Science must be apprehended by as many as believe on Christ and spiritually understand Truth.

No analogy exists between the vague hypotheses of

1   agnosticism, pantheism, theosophy, spiritualism, or
millenarianism and the demonstrable truths of Chris-
3   tian Science; and I find the will, or sensuous
reason of the human mind, to be opposed to
the divine Mind as expressed through divine Science.

Mystical antagonists

6   Christian Science is natural, but not physical. The
Science of God and man is no more supernatural than
is the science of numbers, though departing
9   from the realm of the physical, as the Science
of God, Spirit, must, some may deny its right to
the name of Science. The Principle of divine metaphysics
12   is God; the practice of divine metaphysics is the utiliza-
tion of the power of Truth over error; its rules demonstrate its Science. Divine metaphysics reverses perverted
15   and physical hypotheses as to Deity, even as the explanation of optics rejects the incidental or inverted
image and shows what this inverted image is meant to
18   represent.

Optical illustration of Science

      A prize of one hundred pounds, offered in Oxford Uni-
versity, England, for the best essay on Natural Science,
21   — an essay calculated to offset the tendency of
the age to attribute physical effects to physical
causes rather than to a final spiritual cause, — is one of
24   many incidents which show that Christian Science meets
a yearning of the human race for spirituality.

Pertinent proposal

      After a lengthy examination of my discovery and its
27   demonstration in healing the sick, this fact became evident to me, — that Mind governs the body,
not partially but wholly. I submitted my
30   metaphysical system of treating disease to the broadest practical tests. Since then this system has gradually
gained ground, and has proved itself, whenever scien-

Confirmatory tests

tifically employed, to be the most effective curative agent   1
in medical practice.

Is there more than one school of Christian Science?   3
Christian Science is demonstrable. There can, therefore, be but one method in its teaching. Those who de-

**One school
of Truth**

part from this method forfeit their claims to   6
belong to its school, and they become adher-
ents of the Socratic, the Platonic, the Spencerian, or some
other school. By this is meant that they adopt and ad-   9
here to some particular system of human opinions. Although these opinions may have occasional gleams of
divinity, borrowed from that truly divine Science which   12
eschews man-made systems, they nevertheless remain
wholly human in their origin and tendency and are not
scientifically Christian.   15

From the infinite One in Christian Science comes one
Principle and its infinite idea, and with this infinitude

**Unchanging
Principle**

come spiritual rules, laws, and their demon-   18
stration, which, like the great Giver, are "the
same yesterday, and to-day, and forever;" for thus are
the divine Principle of healing and the Christ-idea charac-   21
terized in the epistle to the Hebrews.

Any theory of Christian Science, which departs from
what has already been stated and proved to be true, af-   24

**On sandy
foundations**

fords no foundation upon which to establish
a genuine school of this Science. Also, if any
so-called new school claims to be Christian Science, and   27
yet uses another author's discoveries without giving that
author proper credit, such a school is erroneous, for it
inculcates a breach of that divine commandment in the   30
Hebrew Decalogue, "Thou shalt not steal."

God is the Principle of divine metaphysics. As there

1   is but one God, there can be but one divine Principle of
all Science; and there must be fixed rules for the demon-
3   stration of this divine Principle. The letter
of Science plentifully reaches humanity to-day,
but its spirit comes only in small degrees. The vital part,
6   the heart and soul of Christian Science, is Love. Without this, the letter is but the dead body of Science, —
pulseless, cold, inanimate.

9   The fundamental propositions of divine metaphysics
are summarized in the four following, to me, *self-evident*
propositions. Even if reversed, these proposi-
12   tions will be found to agree in statement and
proof, showing mathematically their exact relation to
Truth. De Quincey says mathematics has not a foot to
15   stand upon which is not purely metaphysical.

    1. God is All-in-all.

    2. God is good. Good is Mind.

18   3. God, Spirit, being all, nothing is matter.

    4. Life, God, omnipotent good, deny death, evil, sin,
disease. — Disease, sin, evil, death, deny good, omnipo-
21   tent God, Life.

Which of the denials in proposition four is true? Both
are not, cannot be, true. According to the Scripture,
24   I find that God is true, "but every [mortal] man a
liar."

The divine metaphysics of Christian Science, like the
27   method in mathematics, proves the rule by inversion.
For example: There is no pain in Truth, and
no truth in pain; no nerve in Mind, and no

30   mind in nerve; no matter in Mind, and no mind in matter; no matter in Life, and no life in matter; no matter
in good, and no good in matter.

**Definition of
mortal mind**

Usage classes both evil and good together as *mind;*   1
therefore, to be understood, the author calls sick and sinful humanity *mortal mind,* — meaning by this   3
term the flesh opposed to Spirit, the human
mind and evil in contradistinction to the divine Mind, or
Truth and good. The spiritually unscientific definition   6
of mind is based on the evidence of the physical senses,
which makes minds many and calls *mind* both human and
divine.   9

In Science, Mind is *one,* including noumenon and phenomena, God and His thoughts.

Mortal mind is a solecism in language, and involves an   12
improper use of the word *mind.* As Mind is immortal,

**Imperfect
terminology**

the phrase *mortal mind* implies something untrue and therefore unreal; and as the phrase   15
is used in teaching Christian Science, it is meant to
designate that which has no real existence. Indeed, if
a better word or phrase could be suggested, it would   18
be used; but in expressing the new tongue we must
sometimes recur to the old and imperfect, and the new
wine of the Spirit has to be poured into the old bottles of   21
the letter.

Christian Science explains all cause and effect as mental, not physical. It lifts the veil of mystery from Soul and   24

**Causation
mental**

body. It shows the scientific relation of man
to God, disentangles the interlaced ambiguities
of being, and sets free the imprisoned thought. In divine   27
Science, the universe, including man, is spiritual, harmonious, and eternal. Science shows that what is termed *mat-*
ter is but the subjective state of what is termed by the   30
author *mortal mind.*

Apart from the usual opposition to everything new,

1   the one great obstacle to the reception of that spirituality, through which the understanding of Mind-science
3   comes, is the inadequacy of material terms for
metaphysical statements, and the consequent
difficulty of so expressing metaphysical ideas as to make
6   them comprehensible to any reader, who has not personally demonstrated Christian Science as brought forth in
my discovery. Job says: "The ear trieth words, as the
9   mouth tasteth meat." The great difficulty is to give the
right impression, when translating material terms back
into the original spiritual tongue.

Philological inadequacy

12   SCIENTIFIC TRANSLATION OF IMMORTAL MIND

     GOD: Divine Principle, Life, Truth, Love,
         Soul, Spirit, Mind.

Divine synonyms

15   MAN: God's spiritual idea, individual, per-
         fect, eternal.

Divine image

     IDEA: An image in Mind; the immediate
18   object of understanding. — *Webster.*

Divine reflection

SCIENTIFIC TRANSLATION OF MORTAL MIND

First Degree: Depravity.

21   PHYSICAL. Evil beliefs, passions and appetites, fear,
         depraved will, self-justification, pride, envy, de-
         ceit, hatred, revenge, sin, sickness, disease,
24   death.

Unreality

Second Degree: Evil beliefs disappearing.

     MORAL. Humanity, honesty, affection, com-
27   passion, hope, faith, meekness, temperance.

Transitional qualities

Third Degree: Understanding.   1

SPIRITUAL. Wisdom, purity, spiritual understanding,

Reality   spiritual power, love, health, holiness.   3

In the third degree mortal mind disappears, and man as
God's image appears. Science so reverses the evidence

Spiritual   before the corporeal human senses, as to make   6
universe   this Scriptural testimony true in our hearts,
"The last shall be first, and the first last," so that God
and His idea may be to us what divinity really is and   9
must of necessity be, — all-inclusive.

A correct view of Christian Science and of its adaptation to healing includes vastly more than is at first seen.   12

Aim of   Works on metaphysics leave the grand point
Science   untouched. They never crown the power of
Mind as the Messiah, nor do they carry the day against   15
physical enemies, — even to the extinction of all belief in
matter, evil, disease, and death, — nor insist upon the fact
that God is all, therefore that matter is nothing beyond an   18
image in mortal mind.

Christian Science strongly emphasizes the thought that

Divine   God is not *corporeal,* but *incorporeal,* — that is,   21
personality   bodiless. Mortals are corporeal, but God is
incorporeal.

As the words *person* and *personal* are commonly and   24
ignorantly employed, they often lead, when applied to
Deity, to confused and erroneous conceptions of divinity
and its distinction from humanity. If the term personality,   27
as applied to God, means infinite personality, then God *is*
infinite *Person,* — in the sense of infinite personality, but
not in the lower sense. An infinite Mind in a finite form   30
is an absolute impossibility.

The term *individuality* is also open to objections, because an individual may be one of a series, one of many, as an individual man, an individual horse; whereas God is *One*, — not one of a series, but one alone and without an equal.

God is Spirit; therefore the language of Spirit must be, and is, spiritual. Christian Science attaches no physical nature and significance to the Supreme Being or His manifestation; mortals alone do this. God's essential language is spoken of in the last chapter of Mark's Gospel as the new tongue, the spiritual meaning of which is attained through "signs following."

Spiritual language

Ear hath not heard, nor hath lip spoken, the pure language of Spirit. Our Master taught spirituality by similitudes and parables. As a divine student he unfolded God to man, illustrating and demonstrating Life and Truth in himself and by his power over the sick and sinning. Human theories are inadequate to interpret the divine Principle involved in the miracles (marvels) wrought by Jesus and especially in his mighty, crowning, unparalleled, and triumphant exit from the flesh.

The miracles of Jesus

Evidence drawn from the five physical senses relates solely to human reason; and because of opacity to the true light, human reason dimly reflects and feebly transmits Jesus' works and words. Truth is a revelation.

Opacity of the senses

Jesus bade his disciples beware of the leaven of the Pharisees and of the Sadducees, which he defined as human doctrines. His parable of the "leaven, which a woman took, and hid in three measures

Leaven of Truth

of meal, till the whole was leavened," impels the infer- 1
ence that the spiritual leaven signifies the Science of Christ
and its spiritual interpretation, — an inference far above 3
the merely ecclesiastical and formal applications of the
illustration.

Did not this parable point a moral with a prophecy, 6
foretelling the second appearing in the flesh of the
Christ, Truth, hidden in sacred secrecy from the visible world? 9

Ages pass, but this leaven of Truth is ever at work. It
must destroy the entire mass of error, and so be eternally
glorified in man's spiritual freedom. 12

In their spiritual significance, Science, Theology, and
Medicine are means of divine thought, which include spirit-

The divine and human contrasted

ual laws emanating from the invisible and in- 15
finite power and grace. The parable may
import that these spiritual laws, perverted by
a perverse material sense of law, are metaphysically pre- 18
sented as three measures of meal, — that is, three modes
of mortal thought. In all mortal forms of thought, dust
is dignified as the natural status of men and things, and 21
modes of material motion are honored with the name of
laws. This continues until the leaven of Spirit changes
the whole of mortal thought, as yeast changes the chemical 24
properties of meal.

The definitions of material law, as given by natural
science, represent a kingdom necessarily divided against 27

Certain contradictions

itself, because these definitions portray law as
physical, not spiritual. Therefore they contradict the divine decrees and violate the law of Love, in 30
which nature and God are one and the natural order of
heaven comes down to earth.

1   When we endow matter with vague spiritual power, —
that is, when we do so in our theories, for of course we

Unescapable
dilemma

3 cannot really endow matter with what it does
not and cannot possess, — we disown the Almighty, for such theories lead to one of two things. They

6 either presuppose the self-evolution and self-government
of matter, or else they assume that matter is the product
of Spirit. To seize the first horn of this dilemma and con-

9 sider matter as a power in and of itself, is to leave the creator out of His own universe; while to grasp the other
horn of the dilemma and regard God as the creator of

12 matter, is not only to make Him responsible for all disas-
ters, physical and moral, but to announce Him as their
source, thereby making Him guilty of maintaining perpet-

15 ual misrule in the form and under the name of natural
law.

     In one sense God is identical with nature, but this na-

18 ture is spiritual and is not expressed in matter. The lawgiver, whose lightning palsies or prostrates in
death the child at prayer, is not the divine ideal

God and
nature

21 of omnipresent Love. God is natural good, and is represented only by the idea of goodness; while evil should be
regarded as unnatural, because it is opposed to the nature

24 of Spirit, God.

     In viewing the sunrise, one finds that it contradicts
the evidence before the senses to believe that the earth

27 is in motion and the sun at rest. As astronomy reverses the human perception of the
movement of the solar system, so Christian Science re-

The sun
and Soul

30 verses the seeming relation of Soul and body and makes
body tributary to Mind. Thus it is with man, who
is but the humble servant of the restful Mind, though it

seems otherwise to finite sense. But we shall never under- 1
stand this while we admit that soul is in body or mind in
matter, and that man is included in non-intelligence. 3
Soul, or Spirit, is God, unchangeable and eternal; and
man coexists with and reflects Soul, God, for man is God's
image. 6

Science reverses the false testimony of the physical
senses, and by this reversal mortals arrive at the funda-

Reversal of mental facts of being. Then the question in- 9
testimony evitably arises: Is a man sick if the material
senses indicate that he is in good health? No! for matter
can make no conditions for man. And is he well if the 12
senses say he is sick? Yes, he is well in Science in which
health is normal and disease is abnormal.

Health is not a condition of matter, but of Mind; nor 15
can the material senses bear reliable testimony on the sub-
Health and ject of health. The Science of Mind-healing
the senses shows it to be impossible for aught but Mind 18
to testify truly or to exhibit the real status of man. Therefore the divine Principle of Science, reversing the testimony of the physical senses, reveals man as harmoniously 21
existent in Truth, which is the only basis of health; and
thus Science denies all disease, heals the sick, overthrows
false evidence, and refutes materialistic logic. 24

Any conclusion *pro* or *con*, deduced from supposed sensation in matter or from matter's supposed consciousness
of health or disease, instead of reversing the testimony of 27
the physical senses, confirms that testimony as legitimate
and so leads to disease.

Historic When Columbus gave freer breath to the 30
illustrations globe, ignorance and superstition chained the
limbs of the brave old navigator, and disgrace and star-

1   vation stared him in the face; but sterner still would have
been his fate, if his discovery had undermined the favor-
3   ite inclinations of a sensuous philosophy.

Copernicus mapped out the stellar system, and before
he spake, astrography was chaotic, and the heavenly fields
6   were incorrectly explored.

The Chaldean Wisemen read in the stars the fate of
empires and the fortunes of men. Though no higher
9   revelation than the horoscope was to them dis-   **Perennial**
played upon the empyrean, earth and heaven   **beauty**
were bright, and bird and blossom were glad in God's
12   perennial and happy sunshine, golden with Truth. So
we have goodness and beauty to gladden the heart; but
man, left to the hypotheses of material sense unexplained
15   by Science, is as the wandering comet or the desolate
star — "a weary searcher for a viewless home."

The earth's diurnal rotation is invisible to the physical
18   eye, and the sun seems to move from east to west, instead
of the earth from west to east. Until rebuked   **Astronomic**
by clearer views of the everlasting facts, this   **unfoldings**
21   false testimony of the eye deluded the judgment and in-
duced false conclusions. Science shows appearances often
to be erroneous, and corrects these errors by the simple
24   rule that the greater controls the lesser. The sun is the
central stillness, so far as our solar system is concerned,
and the earth revolves about the sun once a year, besides
27   turning daily on its own axis.

As thus indicated, astronomical order imitates the
action of divine Principle; and the universe, the reflec-
30   tion of God, is thus brought nearer the spiritual fact, and
is allied to divine Science as displayed in the everlasting
government of the universe.

The evidence of the physical senses often reverses the real Science of being, and so creates a reign of discord, —

assigning seeming power to sin, sickness, and death; but the great facts of Life, rightly understood, defeat this triad of errors, contradict their false witnesses, and reveal the kingdom of heaven, — the actual reign of harmony on earth. The material senses' reversal of the Science of Soul was practically exposed nineteen hundred years ago by the demonstrations of Jesus; yet these so-called senses still make mortal mind tributary to mortal body, and ordain certain sections of matter, such as brain and nerves, as the seats of pain and pleasure, from which matter reports to this so-called mind its status of happiness or misery.

The optical focus is another proof of the illusion of material sense. On the eye's retina, sky and tree-tops

apparently join hands, clouds and ocean meet and mingle. The barometer, — that little prophet of storm and sunshine, denying the testimony of the senses, — points to fair weather in the midst of murky clouds and drenching rain. Experience is full of instances of similar illusions, which every thinker can recall for himself.

To material sense, the severance of the jugular vein

takes away life; but to spiritual sense and in Science, Life goes on unchanged and being is eternal. Temporal life is a false sense of existence.

Our theories make the same mistake regarding Soul and body that Ptolemy made regarding the solar system. They insist that soul is in body and mind therefore tributary to matter. Astronomical science has destroyed the

1   false theory as to the relations of the celestial bodies, and
    Christian Science will surely destroy the greater error as
3   to our terrestrial bodies. The true idea and   **Ptolemaic**
    Principle of man will then appear. The Ptole-   **and psychical**
    maic blunder could not affect the harmony of   **error**
6   being as does the error relating to soul and body, which
    reverses the order of Science and assigns to matter the
    power and prerogative of Spirit, so that man becomes
9   the most absolutely weak and inharmonious creature in
    the universe.

    The verity of Mind shows conclusively how it is that
12 matter seems to be, but is not. Divine Science,   **Seeming**
    rising above physical theories, excludes matter,   **and being**
    resolves *things* into *thoughts,* and replaces the objects of
15 material sense with spiritual ideas.

    The term CHRISTIAN SCIENCE was introduced by
    the author to designate the scientific system of divine
18 healing.

    The revelation consists of two parts:

    1. The discovery of this divine Science of Mind-
21 healing, through a spiritual sense of the Scriptures and
    through the teachings of the Comforter, as promised by
    the Master.

24 2. The proof, by present demonstration, that the so-
    called miracles of Jesus did not specially belong to a
    dispensation now ended, but that they illustrated an
27 ever-operative divine Principle. The operation of this
    Principle indicates the eternality of the scientific order
    and continuity of being.

30 Christian Science differs from material sci-   **Scientific**
    ence, but not on that account is it less scien-   **basis**
    tific. On the contrary, Christian Science is pre-emi-

nently scientific, being based on Truth, the Principle of   1
all science.

Physical science (so-called) is human knowledge, — a   3
law of mortal mind, a blind belief, a Samson shorn of his

Physical
science a
blind belief

strength. When this human belief lacks organizations to support it, its foundations are gone.   6
Having neither moral might, spiritual basis,
nor holy Principle of its own, this belief mistakes effect
for cause and seeks to find life and intelligence in matter,   9
thus limiting Life and holding fast to discord and death.
In a word, human belief is a blind conclusion from material
reasoning. This is a mortal, finite sense of things, which   12
immortal Spirit silences forever.

The universe, like man, is to be interpreted by Science
from its divine Principle, God, and then it can be under-   15
stood; but when explained on the basis of

Right
interpretation

physical sense and represented as subject to
growth, maturity, and decay, the universe, like man, is,   18
and must continue to be, an enigma.

Adhesion, cohesion, and attraction are properties of
Mind. They belong to divine Principle, and support   21
the equipoise of that thought-force, which

All force
mental

launched the earth in its orbit and said to the
proud wave, "Thus far and no farther."   24

Spirit is the life, substance, and continuity of all
things. We tread on forces. Withdraw them, and
creation must collapse. Human knowledge calls them   27
forces of matter; but divine Science declares that they
belong wholly to divine Mind, are inherent in this
Mind, and so restores them to their rightful home and   30
classification.

The elements and functions of the physical body and

1 of the physical world will change as mortal mind changes
its beliefs. What is now considered the best condition
3 for organic and functional health in the human
body may no longer be found indispensable
to health. Moral conditions will be found always har-
6 monious and health-giving. Neither organic inaction
nor overaction is beyond God's control; and man will
be found normal and natural to changed mortal thought,
9 and therefore more harmonious in his manifestations than
he was in the prior states which human belief created and
sanctioned.

Corporeal changes

12 As human thought changes from one stage to another of conscious pain and painlessness, sorrow and
joy, — from fear to hope and from faith to understand-
15 ing, — the visible manifestation will at last be man governed by Soul, not by material sense. Reflecting God's
government, man is self-governed. When subordinate
18 to the divine Spirit, man cannot be controlled by sin or
death, thus proving our material theories about laws of
health to be valueless.

21 The seasons will come and go with changes of time and
tide, cold and heat, latitude and longitude. The agriculturist will find that these changes cannot
24 affect his crops. "As a vesture shalt Thou
change them and they shall be changed." The mariner
will have dominion over the atmosphere and the great
27 deep, over the fish of the sea and the fowls of the air.
The astronomer will no longer look up to the stars, —
he will look out from them upon the universe; and the
30 florist will find his flower before its seed.

The time and tide

Thus matter will finally be proved nothing more
than a mortal belief, wholly inadequate to affect a man

through its supposed organic action or supposed exist-   1
ence. Error will be no longer used in stating truth. The

problem of nothingness, or "dust to dust," will   3
be solved, and mortal mind will be without
form and void, for mortality will cease when man beholds
himself God's reflection, even as man sees his reflection   6
in a glass.

All Science is divine. Human thought never pro-
jected the least portion of true being. Human belief   9

has sought and interpreted in its own way
the echo of Spirit, and so seems to have
reversed it and repeated it materially; but the human   12
mind never produced a real tone nor sent forth a positive
sound.

The point at issue between Christian Science on the   15
one hand and popular theology on the other is this: Shall

Science explain cause and effect as being
both natural and spiritual? Or shall all that   18
is beyond the cognizance of the material senses be called
supernatural, and be left to the mercy of speculative
hypotheses?   21

I have set forth Christian Science and its application
to the treatment of disease just as I have discovered them.

I have demonstrated through Mind the effects   24
of Truth on the health, longevity, and morals
of men; and I have found nothing in ancient or in modern
systems on which to found my own, except the teachings   27
and demonstrations of our great Master and the lives of
prophets and apostles. The Bible has been my only authority. I have had no other guide in "the straight and   30
narrow way" of Truth.

If Christendom resists the author's application of the

1   word Science to Christianity, or questions her use of the
   word Science, she will not therefore lose faith in Chris-

3   tianity, nor will Christianity lose its hold upon   **Science and**
   her. If God, the All-in-all, be the creator of   **Christianity**
   the spiritual universe, including man, then everything

6   entitled to a classification as truth, or Science, must be
   comprised in a knowledge or understanding of God, for
   there can be nothing beyond illimitable divinity.

9   The terms Divine Science, Spiritual Science, Christ
   Science or Christian Science, or Science alone, she employs interchangeably, according to the re-   **Scientific**

12   quirements of the context. These synony-   **terms**
   mous terms stand for everything relating to God, the infinite, supreme, eternal Mind. It may be said, however,

15   that the term Christian Science relates especially to
   Science as applied to humanity. Christian Science reveals God, not as the author of sin, sickness, and death,

18   but as divine Principle, Supreme Being, Mind, exempt
   from all evil. It teaches that matter is the falsity, not
   the fact, of existence; that nerves, brain, stomach, lungs,

21   and so forth, have — as matter — no intelligence, life, nor
   sensation.
      There is no physical science, inasmuch as all truth

24   proceeds from the divine Mind. Therefore truth is not
   human, and is not a law of matter, for matter   **No physical**
   is not a lawgiver. Science is an emanation of   **science**

27   divine Mind, and is alone able to interpret God aright.
   It has a spiritual, and not a material origin. It is a divine
   utterance, — the Comforter which leadeth into all truth.

30   Christian Science eschews what is called natural science,
   in so far as this is built on the false hypotheses that matter
   is its own lawgiver, that law is founded on material con-

ditions, and that these are final and overrule the might of   1
divine Mind. Good is natural and primitive. It is not
miraculous to itself.   3

The term Science, properly understood, refers only to
the laws of God and to His government of the universe,

Practical   inclusive of man. From this it follows that   6
Science   business men and cultured scholars have found
that Christian Science enhances their endurance and
mental powers, enlarges their perception of character,   9
gives them acuteness and comprehensiveness and an
ability to exceed their ordinary capacity. The human
mind, imbued with this spiritual understanding, becomes   12
more elastic, is capable of greater endurance, escapes
somewhat from itself, and requires less repose. A knowledge of the Science of being develops the latent abilities   15
and possibilities of man. It extends the atmosphere of
thought, giving mortals access to broader and higher
realms. It raises the thinker into his native air of insight 18
and perspicacity.

An odor becomes beneficent and agreeable only in proportion to its escape into the surrounding atmosphere.   21
So it is with our knowledge of Truth. If one would
not quarrel with his fellow-man for waking him from
a cataleptic nightmare, he should not resist Truth, which   24
banishes — yea, forever destroys with the higher testimony of Spirit — the so-called evidence of matter.

Science relates to Mind, not matter. It rests on fixed   27
Principle and not upon the judgment of false sensation.

Mathematics   The addition of two sums in mathematics must
and scientific always bring the same result. So is it with   30
logic   logic. If both the major and the minor propositions of a syllogism are correct, the conclusion, if properly

1   drawn, cannot be false. So in Christian Science there
are no discords nor contradictions, because its logic is as
3   harmonious as the reasoning of an accurately stated syllogism or of a properly computed sum in arithmetic.
Truth is ever truthful, and can tolerate no error in
6   premise or conclusion.

If you wish to know the spiritual fact, you can dis-
cover it by reversing the material fable, be the   **Truth by**
9   fable *pro* or *con,* — be it in accord with your   **inversion**
preconceptions or utterly contrary to them.

Pantheism may be defined as a belief in the intelli-
12   gence of matter, — a belief which Science overthrows.
In those days there will be "great tribulation   **Antagonistic**
such as was not since the beginning of the   **theories**
15   world;" and earth will echo the cry, "Art thou [Truth]
come hither to torment us before the time?" Animal
magnetism, hypnotism, spiritualism, theosophy, agnos-
18   ticism, pantheism, and infidelity are antagonistic to true
being and fatal to its demonstration; and so are some
other systems.

21   We must abandon pharmaceutics, and take up ontology, — "the science of real being." We must look deep
into realism instead of accepting only the out-   **Ontology**
24   ward sense of things. Can we gather peaches   **needed**
from a pine-tree, or learn from discord the concord of
being? Yet quite as rational are some of the leading
27   illusions along the path which Science must tread in its
reformatory mission among mortals. The very name,
illusion, points to nothingness.

30   The generous liver may object to the author's small
estimate of the pleasures of the table. The sinner sees,
in the system taught in this book, that the demands of

God must be met. The petty intellect is alarmed by con-   1
stant appeals to Mind. The licentious disposition is dis-

Reluctant guests   couraged over its slight spiritual prospects.   3
When all men are bidden to the feast, the ex-
cuses come. One has a farm, another has merchandise,
and therefore they cannot accept.   6

    It is vain to speak dishonestly of divine Science, which

Excuses for ignorance   destroys all discord, when you can demonstrate
the actuality of Science. It is unwise to doubt   9
if reality is in perfect harmony with God, divine Principle,
— if Science, when understood and demonstrated, will
destroy all discord, — since you admit that God is om-   12
nipotent; for from this premise it follows that good and
its sweet concords have all-power.

    Christian Science, properly understood, would dis-   15
abuse the human mind of material beliefs which war

Children and adults   against spiritual facts; and these material
beliefs must be denied and cast out to make   18
place for truth. You cannot add to the contents of a
vessel already full. Laboring long to shake the adult's
faith in matter and to inculcate a grain of faith in God, —   21
an inkling of the ability of Spirit to make the body harmonious, — the author has often remembered our Master's
love for little children, and understood how truly such as   24
they belong to the heavenly kingdom.

    If thought is startled at the strong claim of Science
for the supremacy of God, or Truth, and doubts the su-   27

All evil unnatural   premacy of good, ought we not, contrari-
wise, to be astounded at the vigorous claims
of evil and doubt them, and no longer think it natural to   30
love sin and unnatural to forsake it, — no longer imagine
evil to be ever-present and good absent? Truth should

1   not seem so surprising and unnatural as error, and error
should not seem so real as truth. Sickness should not seem
3   so real as health. There is no error in Science, and our
lives must be governed by reality in order to be in harmony with God, the divine Principle of all being.

6   When once destroyed by divine Science, the false evidence before the corporeal senses disappears. Hence the
opposition of sensuous man to the Science of   **The error of**
9   Soul and the significance of the Scripture, "The   **carnality**
carnal mind is enmity against God." The central fact of
the Bible is the superiority of spiritual over physical power.

12   THEOLOGY

Must Christian Science come through the Christian
churches as some persons insist? This Science has come
15   already, after the manner of God's appoint-   **Churchly**
ing, but the churches seem not ready to re-   **neglect**
ceive it, according to the Scriptural saying, "He came
18   unto his own, and his own received him not." Jesus once
said: "I thank Thee, O Father, Lord of heaven and
earth, that Thou hast hid these things from the wise
21   and prudent, and hast revealed them unto babes: even
so, Father, for so it seemed good in Thy sight." As aforetime, the spirit of the Christ, which taketh away the cere-
24   monies and doctrines of men, is not accepted until the
hearts of men are made ready for it.

The mission of Jesus confirmed prophecy, and ex-
27   plained the so-called miracles of olden time as natural
demonstrations of the divine power, demonstra-   **John**
tions which were not understood. Jesus' works   **the Baptist,**
                                                    and the
30   established his claim to the Messiahship. In   **Messiah**
reply to John's inquiry, "Art thou he that should come,"

Jesus returned an affirmative reply, recounting his works   1
instead of referring to his doctrine, confident that this
exhibition of the divine power to heal would fully an-   3
swer the question. Hence his reply: "Go and show
John again those things which ye do hear and see: the
blind receive their sight and the lame walk, the lepers   6
are cleansed, and the deaf hear, the dead are raised up,
and the poor have the gospel preached to them. And
blessed is he, whosoever shall not be offended in me." In   9
other words, he gave his benediction to any one who
should not deny that such effects, coming from divine
Mind, prove the unity of God, — the divine Principle   12
which brings out all harmony.

The Pharisees of old thrust the spiritual idea and the
man who lived it out of their synagogues, and retained   15

**Christ
rejected**

their materialistic beliefs about God. Jesus'
system of healing received no aid nor approval
from other sanitary or religious systems, from doctrines   18
of physics or of divinity; and it has not yet been generally accepted. To-day, as of yore, unconscious of the
reappearing of the spiritual idea, blind belief shuts the   21
door upon it, and condemns the cure of the sick and sinning if it is wrought on any but a material and a doctrinal
theory. Anticipating this rejection of idealism, of the   24
true idea of God, — this salvation from all error, physical and mental, — Jesus asked, "When the Son of man
cometh, shall he find faith on the earth?"   27

Did the doctrines of John the Baptist confer healing
power upon him, or endow him with the truest concep-

**John's
misgivings**

tion of the Christ? This righteous preacher   30
once pointed his disciples to Jesus as "the
Lamb of God;" yet afterwards he seriously questioned

1
the signs of the Messianic appearing, and sent the inquiry
to Jesus, "Art thou he that should come?"

3   Was John's faith greater than that of the Samaritan
woman, who said, "Is not this the Christ?"

Faith
according
to works

There was also a certain centurion of whose
6   faith Jesus himself declared, "I have not found so great
faith, no, not in Israel."

In Egypt, it was Mind which saved the Israelites from
9   belief in the plagues. In the wilderness, streams flowed
from the rock, and manna fell from the sky. The Israelites
looked upon the brazen serpent, and straightway believed
12   that they were healed of the poisonous stings of vipers.
In national prosperity, miracles attended the successes of
the Hebrews; but when they departed from the true
15   idea, their demoralization began. Even in captivity
among foreign nations, the divine Principle wrought
wonders for the people of God in the fiery furnace and
18   in kings' palaces.

Judaism was the antithesis of Christianity, because
Judaism engendered the limited form of a national or
21   tribal religion. It was a finite and material

Judaism
antipathetic

system, carried out in special theories concerning God, man, sanitary methods, and a religious cultus.
24   That he made "himself equal with God," was one of the
Jewish accusations against him who planted Christianity
on the foundation of Spirit, who taught as he was in-
27   spired by the Father and would recognize no life, intelligence, nor substance outside of God.

The Jewish conception of God, as Yawah, Jehovah,
30   or only a mighty hero and king, has not quite

Priestly
learning

given place to the true knowledge of God.
Creeds and rituals have not cleansed their hands of

rabbinical lore. To-day the cry of bygone ages is re-   1
peated, "Crucify him!" At every advancing step, truth
is still opposed with sword and spear.   3

The word *martyr*, from the Greek, means *witness*; but
those who testified for Truth were so often persecuted

unto death, that at length the word *martyr*   6
was narrowed in its significance and so has
come always to mean one who suffers for his convictions.
The new faith in the Christ, Truth, so roused the hatred   9
of the opponents of Christianity, that the followers of
Christ were burned, crucified, and otherwise persecuted;
and so it came about that human rights were hallowed   12
by the gallows and the cross.

Man-made doctrines are waning. They have not waxed
strong in times of trouble. Devoid of the Christ-power,   15

how can they illustrate the doctrines of Christ
or the miracles of grace? Denial of the possi-
bility of Christian healing robs Christianity of the very   18
element, which gave it divine force and its astonishing and
unequalled success in the first century.

The true Logos is demonstrably Christian Science, the   21
natural law of harmony which overcomes discord, — not

because this Science is supernatural or pre-
ternatural, nor because it is an infraction of   24
divine law, but because it is the immutable law of God,
good. Jesus said: "I knew that Thou hearest me always;" and he raised Lazarus from the dead, stilled the   27
tempest, healed the sick, walked on the water. There
is divine authority for believing in the superiority of
spiritual power over material resistance.   30

A miracle fulfils God's law, but does not violate that
law. This fact at present seems more mysterious than

the miracle itself. The Psalmist sang: "What ailed
thee, O thou sea, that thou fleddest? Thou Jordan,
that thou wast driven back? Ye mountains,
that ye skipped like rams, and ye little hills,
like lambs? Tremble, thou earth, at the presence of the
Lord, at the presence of the God of Jacob." The miracle
introduces no disorder, but unfolds the primal order,
establishing the Science of God's unchangeable law.
Spiritual evolution alone is worthy of the exercise of
divine power.

Lawful
wonders

The same power which heals sin heals also sickness.
This is "the beauty of holiness," that when Truth heals
the sick, it casts out evils, and when Truth
casts out the evil called disease, it heals the
sick. When Christ cast out the devil of
dumbness, "it came to pass, when the devil was gone out,
the dumb spake." There is to-day danger of repeating
the offence of the Jews by limiting the Holy One of Israel
and asking: "Can God furnish a table in the wilderness?"
What cannot God do?

Fear and
sickness
identical

It has been said, and truly, that Christianity must be
Science, and Science must be Christianity, else one or the
other is false and useless; but neither is unim-
portant or untrue, and they are alike in demonstration. This proves the one to be identical
with the other. Christianity as Jesus taught it was not
a creed, nor a system of ceremonies, nor a special gift
from a ritualistic Jehovah; but it was the demonstration
of divine Love casting out error and healing the sick,
not merely in the *name* of Christ, or Truth, but in demonstration of Truth, as must be the case in the cycles of
divine light.

The unity of
Science and
Christianity

The
Christ-mission

Jesus established his church and maintained his mission   1
on a spiritual foundation of Christ-healing. He taught
his followers that his religion had a divine   3
Principle, which would cast out error and heal
both the sick and the sinning. He claimed no intelligence, action, nor life separate from God. Despite the   6
persecution this brought upon him, he used his divine
power to save men both bodily and spiritually.

The question then as now was, How did Jesus heal the   9
sick? His answer to this question the world rejected.

Ancient
spiritualism

He appealed to his students: "Whom do
men say that I, the Son of man, am?" That   12
is: Who or what is it that is thus identified with casting
out evils and healing the sick? They replied, "Some
say that thou art John the Baptist; some, Elias; and   15
others, Jeremias, or one of the prophets." These prophets
were considered dead, and this reply may indicate that
some of the people believed that Jesus was a medium,   18
controlled by the spirit of John or of Elias.

This ghostly fancy was repeated by Herod himself.
That a wicked king and debauched husband should have   21
no high appreciation of divine Science and the great work
of the Master, was not surprising; for how could such
a sinner comprehend what the disciples did not fully   24
understand? But even Herod doubted if Jesus was controlled by the sainted preacher. Hence Herod's assertion: "John have I beheaded: but who is this?" No   27
wonder Herod desired to see the new Teacher.

The disciples apprehended their Master better than

Doubting
disciples

did others; but they did not comprehend all   30
that he said and did, or they would not have
questioned him so often. Jesus patiently persisted in

1   teaching and demonstrating the truth of being. His students saw this power of Truth heal the sick, cast out evil,
3   raise the dead; but the ultimate of this wonderful work
was not spiritually discerned, even by them, until after the
crucifixion, when their immaculate Teacher stood before
6   them, the victor over sickness, sin, disease, death, and
the grave.

    Yearning to be understood, the Master repeated,
9   "But whom say *ye* that I am?" This renewed inquiry
meant: Who or what is it that is able to do the work, so
mysterious to the popular mind? In his rejection of the
12   answer already given and his renewal of the question,
it is plain that Jesus completely eschewed the narrow
opinion implied in their citation of the common report
15   about him.

    With his usual impetuosity, Simon replied for his
brethren, and his reply set forth a great fact: "Thou
18   art the Christ, the Son of the living God!"   **A divine**
That is: The Messiah is what thou hast de-   **response**
clared, — Christ, the spirit of God, of Truth, Life, and
21   Love, which heals mentally. This assertion elicited from
Jesus the benediction, "Blessed art thou, Simon Bar-
jona: for flesh and blood hath not revealed it unto thee,
24   but my Father which is in heaven;" that is, Love hath
shown thee the way of Life!

    Before this the impetuous disciple had been called
27   only by his common names, Simon Bar-jona, or son of
Jona; but now the Master gave him a spir-   **The true and**
itual name in these words: "And I say also   **living rock**
30   unto thee, That thou art Peter; and upon this rock [the
meaning of the Greek word *petros*, or *stone*] I will build
my church; and the gates of hell [*hades*, the *under-*

world, or the *grave*] shall not prevail against it." In   1
other words, Jesus purposed founding his society, not
on the personal Peter as a mortal, but on the God-   3
power which lay behind Peter's confession of the true
Messiah.

It was now evident to Peter that divine Life, Truth, and   6
Love, and not a human personality, was the healer of the

Sublime
summary

sick and a rock, a firm foundation in the realm
of harmony. On this spiritually scientific basis   9
Jesus explained his cures, which appeared miraculous to
outsiders. He showed that diseases were cast out neither
by corporeality, by *materia medica,* nor by hygiene, but by   12
the divine Spirit, casting out the errors of mortal mind.
The supremacy of Spirit was the foundation on which
Jesus built. His sublime summary points to the religion   15
of Love.

Jesus established in the Christian era the precedent for
all Christianity, theology, and healing. Christians are   18
under as direct orders now, as they were then,

New era
in Jesus

to be Christlike, to possess the Christ-spirit, to
follow the Christ-example, and to heal the sick as well as   21
the sinning. It is easier for Christianity to cast out sickness than sin, for the sick are more willing to part with
pain than are sinners to give up the sinful, so-called pleas-   24
ure of the senses. The Christian can prove this to-day as
readily as it was proved centuries ago.

Our Master said to every follower: "Go ye into all the   27
world, and preach the gospel to every creature! . . .

Healthful
theology

Heal the sick! . . . Love thy neighbor as
thyself!" It was this theology of Jesus which   30
healed the sick and the sinning. It is his theology in this
book and the spiritual meaning of this theology, which

1   heals the sick and causes the wicked to "forsake his way,
    and the unrighteous man his thoughts." It was our Mas-
3   ter's theology which the impious sought to destroy.
        From beginning to end, the Scriptures are full of
    accounts of the triumph of Spirit, Mind, over matter.
6   Moses proved the power of Mind by what men   Marvels and
    called miracles; so did Joshua, Elijah, and   reformations
    Elisha. The Christian era was ushered in with signs and
9   wonders. Reforms have commonly been attended with
    bloodshed and persecution, even when the end has been
    brightness and peace; but the present new, yet old, re-
12 form in religious faith will teach men patiently and wisely
    to stem the tide of sectarian bitterness, whenever it flows
    inward.
15   The decisions by vote of Church Councils as to what
    should and should not be considered Holy Writ; the man-
    ifest mistakes in the ancient versions; the   Science
18 thirty thousand different readings in the Old   obscured
    Testament, and the three hundred thousand in the New,
    — these facts show how a mortal and material sense stole
21 into the divine record, with its own hue darkening to some
    extent the inspired pages. But mistakes could neither
    wholly obscure the divine Science of the Scriptures seen
24 from Genesis to Revelation, mar the demonstration of
    Jesus, nor annul the healing by the prophets, who foresaw
    that "the stone which the builders rejected" would be-
27 come "the head of the corner."
        Atheism, pantheism, theosophy, and agnosticism are
    opposed to Christian Science, as they are to ordinary re-
30 ligion; but it does not follow that the profane   Opponents
    or atheistic invalid cannot be healed by Chris-   benefited
    tian Science. The moral condition of such a man de-

mands the remedy of Truth more than it is needed in most   1
cases; and Science is more than usually effectual in the
treatment of moral ailments.   3

That God is a corporeal being, nobody can truly affirm.
The Bible represents Him as saying: "Thou canst not
see My face; for there shall no man see Me,   6
and live." Not materially but spiritually we
know Him as divine Mind, as Life, Truth, and Love. We
shall obey and adore in proportion as we apprehend the   9
divine nature and love Him understandingly, warring no
more over the corporeality, but rejoicing in the affluence
of our God. Religion will then be of the heart and not of   12
the head. Mankind will no longer be tyrannical and pro-
scriptive from lack of love, — straining out gnats and
swallowing camels.   15

We worship spiritually, only as we cease to worship
materially. Spiritual devoutness is the soul of Christianity. Worshipping through the medium of   18
matter is paganism. Judaic and other rituals
are but types and shadows of true worship. "The true
worshippers shall worship the Father in spirit and in   21
truth."

The Jewish tribal Jehovah was a man-projected God,
liable to wrath, repentance, and human changeableness.   24
The Christian Science God is universal, eter-
nal, divine Love, which changeth not and caus-
eth no evil, disease, nor death. It is indeed mournfully   27
true that the older Scripture is reversed. In the beginning God created man in His, God's, image; but mortals would procreate man, and make God in their own   30
human image. What is the god of a mortal, but a mortal
magnified?

God invisible to the senses

The true worship

Anthropo-morphism

1   This indicates the distance between the theological and
ritualistic religion of the ages and the truth preached by
3 Jesus. More than profession is requisite for
Christian demonstration. Few understand or
adhere to Jesus' divine precepts for living and
6 healing. Why? Because his precepts require the disciple to cut off the right hand and pluck out the right eye,
— that is, to set aside even the most cherished beliefs
9 and practices, to leave all for Christ.

More than profession required

     All revelation (such is the popular thought!) must come
from the schools and along the line of scholarly and eccle-
12 siastical descent, as kings are crowned from a
royal dynasty. In healing the sick and sinning,
Jesus elaborated the fact that the healing effect
15 followed the understanding of the divine Principle and
of the Christ-spirit which governed the corporeal Jesus.
For this Principle there is no dynasty, no ecclesiastical
18 monopoly. Its only crowned head is immortal sovereignty. Its only priest is the spiritualized man. The
Bible declares that all believers are made "kings and
21 priests unto God." The outsiders did not then, and
do not now, understand this ruling of the Christ; therefore they cannot demonstrate God's healing power.
24 Neither can this manifestation of Christ be comprehended, until its divine Principle is scientifically
understood.

No ecclesiastical monopoly

27   The adoption of scientific religion and of divine healing will ameliorate sin, sickness, and death. Let our
pulpits do justice to Christian Science. Let
30 it have fair representation by the press. Give
to it the place in our institutions of learning now occupied by scholastic theology and physiology, and it will

A change demanded

eradicate sickness and sin in less time than the old systems, 1
devised for subduing them, have required for self-estab-
lishment and propagation. 3

Anciently the followers of Christ, or Truth, measured
Christianity by its power over sickness, sin, and death;

Two claims omitted

but modern religions generally omit all but one 6
of these powers, — the power over sin. We
must seek the undivided garment, the whole Christ, as our
first proof of Christianity, for Christ, Truth, alone can 9
furnish us with absolute evidence.

If the soft palm, upturned to a lordly salary, and archi-
tectural skill, making dome and spire tremulous with 12
beauty, turn the poor and the stranger from the

Selfishness and loss

gate, they at the same time shut the door on
progress. In vain do the manger and the cross tell their 15
story to pride and fustian. Sensuality palsies the right
hand, and causes the left to let go its grasp on the divine.

As in Jesus' time, so to-day, tyranny and pride need to 18
be whipped out of the temple, and humility and divine Sci-

Temple cleansed

ence to be welcomed in. The strong cords of
scientific demonstration, as twisted and wielded 21
by Jesus, are still needed to purge the temples of their
vain traffic in worldly worship and to make them meet
dwelling-places for the Most High. 24

MEDICINE

Which was first, Mind or medicine? If Mind was
first and self-existent, then Mind, not matter, must have 27

Question of precedence

been the first medicine. God being All-in-
all, He made medicine; but that medicine was
Mind. It could not have been matter, which departs 30
from the nature and character of Mind, God. Truth

1 is God's remedy for error of every kind, and Truth destroys only what is untrue. Hence the fact that, to-day,
3 as yesterday, Christ casts out evils and heals the
sick.

It is plain that God does not employ drugs or hygiene,
6 nor provide them for human use; else Jesus would have
recommended and employed them in his healing. The sick are more deplorably lost than
9 the sinning, if the sick cannot rely on God for help and
the sinning can. The divine Mind never called matter
medicine, and matter required a material and human be-
12 lief before it could be considered as medicine.

Methods rejected

Sometimes the human mind uses one error to medicine another. Driven to choose between two difficulties,
15 the human mind takes the lesser to relieve the
greater. On this basis it saves from starvation by theft, and quiets pain with anodynes. You
18 admit that mind influences the body somewhat, but
you conclude that the stomach, blood, nerves, bones,
etc., hold the preponderance of power. Controlled by
21 this belief, you continue in the old routine. You lean on
the inert and unintelligent, never discerning how this de-
prives you of the available superiority of divine Mind.
24 The body is not controlled scientifically by a negative
mind.

Error not curative

Mind is the grand creator, and there can be no power
27 except that which is derived from Mind. If Mind was
first chronologically, is first potentially, and
must be first eternally, then give to Mind the
30 glory, honor, dominion, and power everlastingly due its
holy name. Inferior and unspiritual methods of healing
may try to make Mind and drugs coalesce, but the two will

Impossible coalescence

not mingle scientifically. Why should we wish to make   1
them do so, since no good can come of it?

If Mind is foremost and superior, let us rely upon Mind,   3
which needs no cooperation from lower powers, even if
these so-called powers are real.

> Naught is the squire, when the king is nigh;   6
> Withdraws the star, when dawns the sun's brave light.

The various mortal beliefs formulated in human philosophy, physiology, hygiene, are mainly predicated of matter,   9
and afford faint gleams of God, or Truth.

**Soul and
sense**

The more material a belief, the more obstinately
tenacious its error; the stronger are the manifestations of   12
the corporeal senses, the weaker the indications of Soul.

Human will-power is not Science. Human will belongs
to the so-called material senses, and its use is to be con-   15
demned. Willing the sick to recover is not the
metaphysical practice of Christian Science, but

**Will-power
detrimental**

is sheer animal magnetism. Human will-power may in-   18
fringe the rights of man. It produces evil continually,
and is not a factor in the realism of being. Truth, and
not corporeal will, is the divine power which says to   21
disease, "Peace, be still."

Because divine Science wars with so-called physical
science, even as Truth wars with error, the old schools   24
still oppose it. Ignorance, pride, or prejudice
closes the door to whatever is not stereotyped.

**Conservative
antagonism**

When the Science of being is universally understood,   27
every man will be his own physician, and Truth will be
the universal panacea.

It is a question to-day, whether the ancient inspired   30
healers understood the Science of Christian healing, or

1 whether they caught its sweet tones, as the natural
musician catches the tones of harmony, without being
3 able to explain them. So divinely imbued
were they with the spirit of Science, that the
lack of the letter could not hinder their work; and that
6 letter, without the spirit, would have made void their
practice.

Ancient healers

The struggle for the recovery of invalids goes on, not
9 between material methods, but between mortal minds
and immortal Mind. The victory will be on
the patient's side only as immortal Mind
12 through Christ, Truth, subdues the human belief in
disease. It matters not what material method one may
adopt, whether faith in drugs, trust in hygiene, or reliance
15 on some other minor curative.

The struggle and victory

Scientific healing has this advantage over other methods, — that in it Truth controls error. From this fact
18 arise its ethical as well as its physical effects. Indeed, its ethical and physical effects
are indissolubly connected. If there is any mystery
21 in Christian healing, it is the mystery which godliness
always presents to the ungodly, — the mystery always
arising from ignorance of the laws of eternal and unerr-
24 ing Mind.

Mystery of godliness

Other methods undertake to oppose error with error,
and thus they increase the antagonism of one form of
27 matter towards other forms of matter or error,
and the warfare between Spirit and the flesh
goes on. By this antagonism mortal mind must con-
30 tinually weaken its own assumed power.

Matter versus matter

The theology of Christian Science includes healing
the sick. Our Master's first article of faith propounded

to his students was healing, and he proved his faith by   1
his works. The ancient Christians were healers. Why

has this element of Christianity been lost?   3
Because our systems of religion are governed
more or less by our systems of medicine. The first idolatry was faith in matter. The schools have rendered   6
faith in drugs the fashion, rather than faith in Deity. By
trusting matter to destroy its own discord, health and
harmony have been sacrificed. Such systems are barren   9
of the vitality of spiritual power, by which material sense
is made the servant of Science and religion becomes
Christlike.   12

Material medicine substitutes drugs for the power of
God — even the might of Mind — to heal the body.

Scholasticism clings for salvation to the per-   15
son, instead of to the divine Principle, of the
man Jesus; and his Science, the curative agent of God,
is silenced. Why? Because truth divests material drugs   18
of their imaginary power, and clothes Spirit with supremacy. Science is the "stranger that is within thy gates,"
remembered not, even when its elevating effects prac-   21
tically prove its divine origin and efficacy.

Divine Science derives its sanction from the Bible,
and the divine origin of Science is demonstrated through   24

the holy influence of Truth in healing sickness and sin. This healing power of Truth
must have been far anterior to the period in   27
which Jesus lived. It is as ancient as "the Ancient of
days." It lives through all Life, and extends throughout
all space.   30

Divine metaphysics is now reduced to a system, to a
form comprehensible by and adapted to the thought of

1   the age in which we live. This system enables the
learner to demonstrate the divine Principle,
3   upon which Jesus' healing was based, and
the sacred rules for its present application to the cure of
disease.

6   Late in the nineteenth century I demonstrated the divine
rules of Christian Science. They were submitted to the
broadest practical test, and everywhere, when honestly ap-
9   plied under circumstances where demonstration was humanly possible, this Science showed that Truth had lost
none of its divine and healing efficacy, even though cen-
12   turies had passed away since Jesus practised these rules
on the hills of Judæa and in the valleys of Galilee.

     Although this volume contains the complete Science of
15   Mind-healing, never believe that you can absorb the whole
meaning of the Science by a simple *perusal*
of this book. The book needs to be *studied,*
18   and the demonstration of the rules of scientific healing
will plant you firmly on the spiritual groundwork of
Christian Science. This proof lifts you high above the
21   perishing fossils of theories already antiquated, and enables you to grasp the spiritual facts of being hitherto
unattained and seemingly dim.

24   Our Master healed the sick, practised Christian healing, and taught the generalities of its divine Principle to
his students; but he left no definite rule for
27   demonstrating this Principle of healing and
preventing disease. This rule remained to be discovered
in Christian Science. A pure affection takes form in good-
30   ness, but Science alone reveals the divine Principle of
goodness and demonstrates its rules.

     Jesus never spoke of disease as dangerous or as difficult

Marginal headings:
Reduction to system

Perusal and practice

A definite rule discovered

to heal. When his students brought to him a case they
had failed to heal, he said to them, "O faithless generation," implying that the requisite power
to heal was in Mind. He prescribed no drugs,
urged no obedience to material laws, but acted in direct
disobedience to them.

Jesus' own
practice

Neither anatomy nor theology has ever described man
as created by Spirit, — as God's man. The former explains the men of *men,* or the "children of
men," as created corporeally instead of spiritually and as emerging from the lowest, instead of from the highest, conception of being. Both
anatomy and theology define man as both physical and
mental, and place mind at the mercy of matter for every
function, formation, and manifestation. Anatomy takes
up man at all points materially. It loses Spirit, drops the
true tone, and accepts the discord. Anatomy and theology reject the divine Principle which produces harmonious man, and deal — the one wholly, the other primarily
— with matter, calling that *man* which is not the counter-
part, but the counterfeit, of God's man. Then theology
tries to explain how to make this man a Christian, — how
from this basis of division and discord to produce the concord and unity of Spirit and His likeness.

The man of
anatomy and
of theology

Physiology exalts matter, dethrones Mind, and claims
to rule man by material law, instead of spiritual. When
physiology fails to give health or life by this
process, it ignores the divine Spirit as unable
or unwilling to render help in time of physical need.
When mortals sin, this ruling of the schools leaves them
to the guidance of a theology which admits God to be
the healer of sin but not of sickness, although our great

Physiology
deficient

1   Master demonstrated that Truth could save from sickness as well as from sin.

3   Mind as far outweighs drugs in the cure of disease as in the cure of sin. The more excellent way is divine Science in every case. Is *materia medica* a

Blunders and blunderers

6 science or a bundle of speculative human theories? The prescription which succeeds in one instance fails in another, and this is owing to the different

9 mental states of the patient. These states are not comprehended, and they are left without explanation except in Christian Science. The rule and its perfection of opera-

12 tion never vary in Science. If you fail to succeed in any case, it is because you have not demonstrated the life of Christ, Truth, more in your own life, — because you have

15 not obeyed the rule and proved the Principle of divine Science.

    A physician of the old school remarked with great

18 gravity: "We know that mind affects the body somewhat, and advise our patients to be hopeful and cheerful and to take as little medicine as

Old-school physician

21 possible; but mind can never cure organic difficulties." The logic is lame, and facts contradict it. The author has cured what is termed organic disease as readily as she

24 has cured purely functional disease, and with no power but the divine Mind.

    Since God, divine Mind, governs all, not partially but

27 supremely, predicting disease does not dignify therapeutics. Whatever guides thought spiritually benefits mind and body. We need to understand the

Tests in our day

30 affirmations of divine Science, dismiss superstition, and demonstrate truth according to Christ. To-day there is hardly a city, village, or hamlet, in which are not to

be found living witnesses and monuments to the virtue	1
and power of Truth, as applied through this Christian
system of healing disease.	3

To-day the healing power of Truth is widely demonstrated as an immanent, eternal Science, instead of a

The main	phenomenal exhibition. Its appearing is the	6
purpose	coming anew of the gospel of "on earth peace,
good-will toward men." This coming, as was promised
by the Master, is for its establishment as a permanent	9
dispensation among men; but the mission of Christian
Science now, as in the time of its earlier demonstration,
is not primarily one of physical healing. Now, as then,	12
signs and wonders are wrought in the metaphysical healing of physical disease; but these signs are only to demon-
strate its divine origin, — to attest the reality of the higher	15
mission of the Christ-power to take away the sins of the
world.

The science (so-called) of physics would have one be-	18
lieve that both matter and mind are subject to disease,

Exploded	and that, too, in spite of the individual's pro-
doctrine	test and contrary to the law of divine Mind.	21
This human view infringes man's free moral agency; and
it is as evidently erroneous to the author, and will be to
all others at some future day, as the practically rejected	24
doctrine of the predestination of souls to damnation or
salvation. The doctrine that man's harmony is gov-
erned by physical conditions all his earthly days, and that	27
he is then thrust out of his own body by the operation of
matter, — even the doctrine of the superiority of matter
over Mind, — is fading out.	30

The hosts of Æsculapius are flooding the world with
diseases, because they are ignorant that the human mind

1 and body are myths. To be sure, they sometimes treat
the sick as if there was but one factor in the case; but
3 this one factor they represent to be body, not Disease mental
mind. Infinite Mind could not possibly create
a remedy outside of itself, but erring, finite, human mind
6 has an absolute need of something beyond itself for its
redemption and healing.

Great respect is due the motives and philanthropy of
9 the higher class of physicians. We know that if they understood the Science of Mind-healing, and were Intentions respected
in possession of the enlarged power it confers
12 to benefit the race physically and spiritually, they would
rejoice with us. Even this one reform in medicine would
ultimately deliver mankind from the awful and oppres-
15 sive bondage now enforced by false theories, from which
multitudes would gladly escape.

Mortal belief says that death has been occasioned by
18 fright. Fear never stopped being and its action. The
blood, heart, lungs, brain, etc., have nothing Man governed by Mind
to do with Life, God. Every function of the
21 real man is governed by the divine Mind. The human
mind has no power to kill or to cure, and it has no control over God's man. The divine Mind that made man
24 maintains His own image and likeness. The human
mind is opposed to God and must be put off, as St. Paul
declares. All that really exists is the divine Mind and
27 its idea, and in this Mind the entire being is found harmonious and eternal. The straight and narrow way is to
see and acknowledge this fact, yield to this power, and
30 follow the leadings of truth.

That mortal mind claims to govern every organ of the
mortal body, we have overwhelming proof. But this so-

called mind is a myth, and must by its own consent yield 1
to Truth. It would wield the sceptre of a monarch, but

Mortal mind dethroned
it is powerless. The immortal divine Mind 3
takes away all its supposed sovereignty, and
saves mortal mind from itself. The author has endeavored
to make this book the Æsculapius of mind as well as of 6
body, that it may give hope to the sick and heal them,
although they know not how the work is done. Truth
has a healing effect, even when not fully understood. 9

Anatomy describes muscular action as produced by
mind in one instance and not in another. Such errors

All activity from thought
beset every material theory, in which one 12
statement contradicts another over and over
again. It is related that Sir Humphry Davy once apparently cured a case of paralysis simply by introducing 15
a thermometer into the patient's mouth. This he did
merely to ascertain the temperature of the patient's body;
but the sick man supposed this ceremony was intended 18
to heal him, and he recovered accordingly. Such a fact
illustrates our theories.

The author's medical researches and experiments had 21
prepared her thought for the metaphysics of Christian

The author's experiments in medicine
Science. Every material dependence had
failed her in her search for truth; and she can 24
now understand why, and can see the means
by which mortals are divinely driven to a spiritual source
for health and happiness. 27

Her experiments in homœopathy had made her skep-
tical as to material curative methods. Jahr, from

Homœopathic attenuations
Aconitum to *Zincum oxydatum*, enumerates 30
the general symptoms, the characteristic
signs, which demand different remedies; but the drug

is frequently attenuated to such a degree that not a vestige of it remains. Thus we learn that it is not the drug which expels the disease or changes one of the symptoms of disease.

The author has attenuated *Natrum muriaticum* (common table-salt) until there was not a single saline property left. The salt had "lost his savour;" and yet, with one drop of that attenuation in a goblet of water, and a teaspoonful of the water administered at intervals of three hours, she has cured a patient sinking in the last stage of typhoid fever. The highest attenuation of homœopathy and the most potent rises above matter into mind. This discovery leads to more light. From it may be learned that either human faith or the divine Mind is the healer and that there is no efficacy in a drug.

Only salt and water

You say a boil is painful; but that is impossible, for matter without mind is not painful. The boil simply manifests, through inflammation and swelling, a belief in pain, and this belief is called a boil. Now administer mentally to your patient a high attenuation of truth, and it will soon cure the boil. The fact that pain cannot exist where there is no mortal mind to feel it is a proof that this so-called mind makes its own pain — that is, its own *belief* in pain.

Origin of pain

We weep because others weep, we yawn because they yawn, and we have smallpox because others have it; but mortal mind, not matter, contains and carries the infection. When this mental contagion is understood, we shall be more careful of our mental conditions, and we shall avoid loquacious tattling about disease, as we would avoid advocating crime. Neither sympathy nor society should ever tempt us to cherish

Source of contagion

error in any form, and certainly we should not be error's   1
advocate.

Disease arises, like other mental conditions, from as-   3
sociation. Since it is a law of mortal mind that certain
diseases should be regarded as contagious, this law obtains credit through association, — calling up the fear that   6
creates the image of disease and its consequent manifestation in the body.

This fact in metaphysics is illustrated by the following   9
incident: A man was made to believe that he occupied a

Imaginary
cholera
bed where a cholera patient had died. Immediately the symptoms of this disease appeared,   12
and the man died. The fact was, that he had not caught
the cholera by material contact, because no cholera patient
had been in that bed.   15

If a child is exposed to contagion or infection, the
mother is frightened and says, "My child will be sick."

Children's
ailments
The law of mortal mind and her own fears gov-   18
ern her child more than the child's mind governs itself, and they produce the very results which might
have been prevented through the opposite understanding.   21
Then it is believed that exposure to the contagion wrought
the mischief.

That mother is not a Christian Scientist, and her affec-   24
tions need better guidance, who says to her child: "You
look sick," "You look tired," "You need rest," or "You
need medicine."   27

Such a mother runs to her little one, who thinks she has
hurt her face by falling on the carpet, and says, moaning
more childishly than her child, "Mamma knows you are   30
hurt." The better and more successful method for any
mother to adopt is to say: "Oh, never mind! You're not

1   hurt, so don't think you are." Presently the child forgets
all about the accident, and is at play.

3   When the sick recover by the use of drugs, it is the law
of a general belief, culminating in individual faith, which
heals; and according to this faith will the effect

Drug-power mental

6   be. Even when you take away the individual
confidence in the drug, you have not yet divorced the drug
from the general faith. The chemist, the botanist, the

9   druggist, the doctor, and the nurse equip the medicine
with their faith, and the beliefs which are in the majority
rule. When the general belief endorses the inanimate

12   drug as doing this or that, individual dissent or faith, unless it rests on Science, is but a belief held by a minority,
and such a belief is governed by the majority.

15   The universal belief in physics weighs against the high
and mighty truths of Christian metaphysics. This erroneous general belief, which sustains medicine and

Belief in physics

18   produces all medical results, works against
Christian Science; and the percentage of power on the
side of this Science must mightily outweigh the power of

21   popular belief in order to heal a single case of disease. The
human mind acts more powerfully to offset the discords
of matter and the ills of flesh, in proportion as it puts less

24   weight into the material or fleshly scale and more weight
into the spiritual scale. Homœopathy diminishes the
drug, but the potency of the medicine increases as the

27   drug disappears.

      Vegetarianism, homœopathy, and hydropathy have
diminished drugging; but if drugs are an antidote to

Nature of drugs

30   disease, why lessen the antidote? If drugs
are good things, is it safe to say that the
less in quantity you have of them the better? If drugs

possess intrinsic virtues or intelligent curative qualities, 1
these qualities must be mental. Who named drugs, and
what made them good or bad for mortals, beneficial or 3
injurious?

A case of dropsy, given up by the faculty, fell into
my hands. It was a terrible case. Tapping had been 6

employed, and yet, as she lay in her bed, the
patient looked like a barrel. I prescribed
the fourth attenuation of *Argentum nitratum* with occa- 9
sional doses of a high attenuation of *Sulphuris.* She improved perceptibly. Believing then somewhat in the
ordinary theories of medical practice, and learning that 12
her former physician had prescribed these remedies, I
began to fear an aggravation of symptoms from their
prolonged use, and told the patient so; but she was 15
unwilling to give up the medicine while she was recovering. It then occurred to me to give her unmedicated pellets and watch the result. I did so, and 18
she continued to gain. Finally she said that she would
give up her medicine for one day, and risk the
effects. After trying this, she informed me that she 21
could get along two days without globules; but on
the third day she again suffered, and was relieved by
taking them. She went on in this way, taking the 24
unmedicated pellets, — and receiving occasional visits
from me, — but employing no other means, and she was
cured. 27

Metaphysics, as taught in Christian Science, is the
next stately step beyond homœopathy. In metaphysics,

matter disappears from the remedy entirely, 30
and Mind takes its rightful and supreme
place. Homœopathy takes mental symptoms largely

1 into consideration in its diagnosis of disease. Christian
Science deals wholly with the mental cause in judging and
3 destroying disease. It succeeds where homœopathy fails,
solely because its one recognized Principle of healing is
Mind, and the whole force of the mental element is em-
6 ployed through the Science of Mind, which never shares
its rights with inanimate matter.

Christian Science exterminates the drug, and rests on
9 Mind alone as the curative Principle, acknowledging that
the divine Mind has all power. Homœopathy
mentalizes a drug with such repetition of
12 thought-attenuations, that the drug becomes
more like the human mind than the substratum of this so-
called mind, which we call matter; and the drug's power
15 of action is proportionately increased.

The modus of homœopathy

If drugs are part of God's creation, which (according
to the narrative in Genesis) He pronounced *good*, then
18 drugs cannot be poisonous. If He could create drugs intrinsically bad, then they should
never be used. If He creates drugs at all and designs
21 them for medical use, why did Jesus not employ them
and recommend them for the treatment of disease?
Matter is not self-creative, for it is unintelligent. Erring
24 mortal mind confers the power which the drug seems to
possess.

Drugging unchristian

Narcotics quiet mortal mind, and so relieve the body;
27 but they leave both mind and body worse for this submission. Christian Science impresses the entire corporeality, — namely, mind and body, — and brings out the
30 proof that Life is continuous and harmonious. Science
both neutralizes error and destroys it. Mankind is the
better for this spiritual and profound pathology.

Mythology
and materia
medica

It is recorded that the profession of medicine originated   1
in idolatry with pagan priests, who besought the gods to
heal the sick and designated Apollo as "the god   3
of medicine." He was supposed to have dic-
tated the first prescription, according to the
"History of Four Thousand Years of Medicine." It is   6
here noticeable that Apollo was also regarded as the sender
of disease, "the god of pestilence." Hippocrates turned
from image-gods to vegetable and mineral drugs for heal-   9
ing. This was deemed progress in medicine; but
what we need is the truth which heals both mind and
body. The future history of material medicine may   12
correspond with that of its material god, Apollo, who was
banished from heaven and endured great sufferings
upon earth.   15

Footsteps to
intemperance

Drugs, cataplasms, and whiskey are stupid substitutes
for the dignity and potency of divine Mind and its efficacy to heal. It is pitiful to lead men into   18
temptation through the byways of this wilderness world, — to victimize the race with intoxicating
prescriptions for the sick, until mortal mind acquires an   21
educated appetite for strong drink, and men and women
become loathsome sots.

Evidences of progress and of spiritualization greet us   24
on every hand. Drug-systems are quitting their hold on

Advancing
degrees

matter and so letting in matter's higher stratum, mortal mind. Homœopathy, a step in   27
advance of allopathy, is doing this. Matter is going out
of medicine; and mortal mind, of a higher attenuation
than the drug, is governing the pellet.   30

A woman in the city of Lynn, Massachusetts, was
etherized and died in consequence, although her physi-

cians insisted that it would be unsafe to perform a needed surgical operation without the ether. After the autopsy, her sister testified that the deceased protested against inhaling the ether and said it would kill her, but that she was compelled by her physicians to take it. Her hands were held, and she was forced into submission. The case was brought to trial. The evidence was found to be conclusive, and a verdict was returned that death was occasioned, not by the ether, but by fear of inhaling it.

Effects of fear

Is it skilful or scientific surgery to take no heed of mental conditions and to treat the patient as if she were so much mindless matter, and as if matter were the only factor to be consulted? Had these unscientific surgeons understood metaphysics, they would have considered the woman's state of mind, and not have risked such treatment. They would either have allayed her fear or would have performed the operation without ether.

Mental conditions to be heeded

The sequel proved that this Lynn woman died from effects produced by mortal mind, and not from the disease or the operation.

The medical schools would learn the state of man from matter instead of from Mind. They examine the lungs, tongue, and pulse to ascertain how much harmony, or health, matter is permitting to matter, — how much pain or pleasure, action or stagnation, one form of matter is allowing another form of matter.

False source of knowledge

Ignorant of the fact that a man's belief produces disease and all its symptoms, the ordinary physician is liable to increase disease with his own mind, when he

should address himself to the work of destroying it through   1
the power of the divine Mind.

The systems of physics act against metaphysics, and   3
vice versa. When mortals forsake the material for the
spiritual basis of action, drugs lose their healing force,
for they have no innate power. Unsupported by the   6
faith reposed in it, the inanimate drug becomes
powerless.

The motion of the arm is no more dependent upon the   9
direction of mortal mind, than are the organic action and

Obedient muscles

secretion of the viscera. When this so-called
mind quits the body, the heart becomes as tor-   12
pid as the hand.

Anatomy finds a necessity for nerves to convey the mandate of mind to muscle and so cause action; but what does   15

Anatomy and mind

anatomy say when the cords contract and become immovable? Has mortal mind ceased
speaking to them, or has it bidden them to be impotent?   18
Can muscles, bones, blood, and nerves rebel against mind
in one instance and not in another, and become cramped
despite the mental protest?   21

Unless muscles are self-acting at all times, they are
never so, — never capable of acting contrary to mental
direction. If muscles can cease to act and become rigid   24
of their own preference, — be deformed or symmetrical,
as they please or as disease directs, — they must be self-
directing. Why then consult anatomy to learn how mor-   27
tal mind governs muscle, if we are only to learn from
anatomy that muscle is not so governed?

Mind over matter

Is man a material fungus without Mind   30
to help him? Is a stiff joint or a contracted
muscle as much a result of law as the supple and

elastic condition of the healthy limb, and is God the lawgiver?

You say, "*I have burned my finger.*" This is an exact statement, more exact than you suppose; for mortal mind, and not matter, burns it. Holy inspiration has created states of mind which have been able to nullify the action of the flames, as in the Bible case of the three young Hebrew captives, cast into the Babylonian furnace; while an opposite mental state might produce spontaneous combustion.

In 1880, Massachusetts put her foot on a proposed tyrannical law, restricting the practice of medicine. If her sister States follow this example in harmony with our Constitution and Bill of Rights, they will do less violence to that immortal sentiment of the Declaration, "Man is endowed by his Maker with certain inalienable rights, among which are life, liberty, and the pursuit of happiness."

Restrictive regulations

The oppressive state statutes touching medicine remind one of the words of the famous Madame Roland, as she knelt before a statue of Liberty, erected near the guillotine: "Liberty, what crimes are committed in thy name!"

The ordinary practitioner, examining bodily symptoms, telling the patient that he is sick, and treating the case according to his physical diagnosis, would naturally induce the very disease he is trying to cure, even if it were not already determined by mortal mind. Such unconscious mistakes would not occur, if this old class of philanthropists looked as deeply for cause and effect into mind as into matter. The physician agrees with his "adversary quickly," but upon different terms

Metaphysics challenges physics

than does the metaphysician; for the matter-physician   1
agrees with the disease, while the metaphysician agrees
only with health and challenges disease.   3

Christian Science brings to the body the sunlight of
Truth, which invigorates and purifies. Christian Science

acts as an alterative, neutralizing error with   6
Truth. It changes the secretions, expels humors, dissolves tumors, relaxes rigid muscles, restores
carious bones to soundness. The effect of this Science is   9
to stir the human mind to a change of base, on which it
may yield to the harmony of the divine Mind.

Experiments have favored the fact that Mind governs   12
the body, not in one instance, but in every instance. The

indestructible faculties of Spirit exist without
the conditions of matter and also without the   15
false beliefs of a so-called material existence. Working
out the rules of Science in practice, the author has restored health in cases of both acute and chronic disease in   18
their severest forms. Secretions have been changed, the
structure has been renewed, shortened limbs have been
elongated, ankylosed joints have been made supple, and   21
carious bones have been restored to healthy conditions. I
have restored what is called the lost substance of lungs, and
healthy organizations have been established where disease   24
was organic. Christian Science heals organic disease as
surely as it heals what is called functional, for it requires
only a fuller understanding of the divine Principle of   27
Christian Science to demonstrate the higher rule.

With due respect for the faculty, I kindly
quote from Dr. Benjamin Rush, the famous   30
Philadelphia teacher of medical practice. He
declared that "it is impossible to calculate the mischief

which Hippocrates has done, by first marking Nature
with his name, and afterward letting her loose upon sick
people."

Dr. Benjamin Waterhouse, Professor in Harvard University, declared himself "sick of learned quackery."

Dr. James Johnson, Surgeon to William IV, King of
England, said:

"I declare my conscientious opinion, founded on long
observation and reflection, that if there were not a single
physician, surgeon, apothecary, man-midwife, chemist,
druggist, or drug on the face of the earth, there would be
less sickness and less mortality."

Dr. Mason Good, a learned Professor in London,
said:

"The effects of medicine on the human system are in
the highest degree uncertain; except, indeed, that it has
already destroyed more lives than war, pestilence, and
famine, all combined."

Dr. Chapman, Professor of the Institutes and Practice
of Physic in the University of Pennsylvania, in a published
essay said:

"Consulting the records of our science, we cannot
help being disgusted with the multitude of hypotheses
obtruded upon us at different times. Nowhere is the
imagination displayed to a greater extent; and perhaps
so ample an exhibition of human invention might gratify
our vanity, if it were not more than compensated by the
humiliating view of so much absurdity, contradiction,
and falsehood. To harmonize the contrarieties of medical doctrines is indeed a task as impracticable as to
arrange the fleeting vapors around us, or to reconcile the
fixed and repulsive antipathies of nature. Dark and

perplexed, our devious career resembles the groping of   1
Homer's Cyclops around his cave."

Sir John Forbes, M.D., F.R.S., Fellow of the Royal   3
College of Physicians, London, said:

"No systematic or theoretical classification of diseases
or of therapeutic agents, ever yet promulgated, is true, or   6
anything like the truth, and none can be adopted as a safe
guidance in practice."

It is just to say that generally the cultured class of medi-   9
cal practitioners are grand men and women, therefore
they are more scientific than are false claimants to Christian Science. But all human systems based on material   12
premises are minus the unction of divine Science. Much
yet remains to be said and done before all mankind is
saved and all the mental microbes of sin and all diseased   15
thought-germs are exterminated.

If you or I should appear to die, we should not be
dead. The seeming decease, caused by a majority of   18
human beliefs that man must die, or produced by mental
assassins, does not in the least disprove Christian Science;
rather does it evidence the truth of its basic proposition   21
that mortal thoughts in belief rule the materiality miscalled life in the body or in matter. But the forever fact
remains paramount that Life, Truth, and Love save from   24
sin, disease, and death. "When this corruptible shall have
put on incorruption, and this mortal shall have put on
immortality [divine Science], then shall be brought to pass   27
the saying that is written, Death is swallowed up in
victory" (St. Paul).

Chapter 7

Physiology

Therefore I say unto you,
Take no thought for your life,
what ye shall eat, or what ye shall drink;
nor yet for your body, what ye shall put on.
Is not the life more than meat,
and the body than raiment? — JESUS.

He sent His word, and healed them,
and delivered them from their destructions. — PSALMS.

1   Physiology is one of the apples from "the tree
of knowledge." Evil declared that eating this fruit
3   would open man's eyes and make him as a god. Instead
of so doing, it closed the eyes of mortals to man's God-
given dominion over the earth.

6   To measure intellectual capacity by the size of the
brain and strength by the exercise of muscle, is to
subjugate intelligence, to make mind mor-   **Man not**
9   tal, and to place this so-called mind at the   **structural**
mercy of material organization and non-intelligent
matter.

12   Obedience to the so-called physical laws of health has
not checked sickness. Diseases have multiplied, since
man-made material theories took the place of spiritual
15   truth.

You say that indigestion, fatigue, sleeplessness, cause
distressed stomachs and aching heads. Then   **Causes of**
18   you consult your brain in order to remember   **sickness**
what has hurt you, when your remedy lies in forgetting

the whole thing; for matter has no sensation of its own,   1
and the human mind is all that can produce pain.

As a man thinketh, so is he. Mind is all that feels,   3
acts, or impedes action. Ignorant of this, or shrinking
from its implied responsibility, the healing effort is made
on the wrong side, and thus the conscious control over the   6
body is lost.

The Mohammedan believes in a pilgrimage to Mecca
for the salvation of his soul. The popular doctor believes   9

**Delusions
pagan and
medical**

in his prescription, and the pharmacist believes
in the power of his drugs to save a man's
life. The Mohammedan's belief is a religious   12
delusion; the doctor's and pharmacist's is a medical
mistake.

The erring human mind is inharmonious in itself.   15
From it arises the inharmonious body. To ignore

**Health from
reliance on
spirituality**

God as of little use in sickness is a mistake.
Instead of thrusting Him aside in times of   18
bodily trouble, and waiting for the hour of
strength in which to acknowledge Him, we should learn
that He can do all things for us in sickness as in   21
health.

Failing to recover health through adherence to physiology and hygiene, the despairing invalid often drops   24
them, and in his extremity and only as a last resort, turns
to God. The invalid's faith in the divine Mind is less
than in drugs, air, and exercise, or he would have resorted   27
to Mind first. The balance of power is conceded to be
with matter by most of the medical systems; but when
Mind at last asserts its mastery over sin, disease, and   30
death, then is man found to be harmonious and
immortal.

Should we implore a corporeal God to heal the sick
out of His personal volition, or should we understand the
infinite divine Principle which heals? If we rise no higher
than blind faith, the Science of healing is not attained, and
Soul-existence, in the place of sense-existence, is not comprehended. We apprehend Life in divine Science only
as we live above corporeal sense and correct it. Our pro-
portionate admission of the claims of good or of evil determines the harmony of our existence, — our health, our
longevity, and our Christianity.

We cannot serve two masters nor perceive divine Science with the material senses. Drugs and hygiene cannot
successfully usurp the place and power of the   *The two*
divine source of all health and perfection. If   *masters*
God made man both good and evil, man must remain
thus. What can improve God's work? Again, an error
in the premise must appear in the conclusion. To have
one God and avail yourself of the power of Spirit, you
must love God supremely.

The "flesh lusteth against the Spirit." The flesh and
Spirit can no more unite in action, than good can coincide with evil. It is not wise to take a halt-   *Half-way*
ing and half-way position or to expect to work   *success*
equally with Spirit and matter, Truth and error. There
is but one way — namely, God and His idea — which
leads to spiritual being. The scientific government of the
body must be attained through the divine Mind. It is impossible to gain control over the body in any other way.
On this fundamental point, timid conservatism is absolutely inadmissible. Only through radical reliance on
Truth can scientific healing power be realized.

Substituting good words for a good life, fair seeming

for straightforward character, is a poor shift for the weak   1
and worldly, who think the standard of Christian Science
too high for them.   3

If the scales are evenly adjusted, the removal of a single
weight from either scale gives preponderance to the oppo-

Belief on the wrong side   site. Whatever influence you cast on the side   6
of matter, you take away from Mind, which
would otherwise outweigh all else. Your belief militates
against your health, when it ought to be enlisted on the   9
side of health. When sick (according to belief) you rush
after drugs, search out the material so-called laws of
health, and depend upon them to heal you, though you   12
have already brought yourself into the slough of disease
through just this false belief.

Because man-made systems insist that man becomes   15
sick and useless, suffers and dies, all in consonance with

The divine authority   the laws of God, are we to believe it? Are
we to believe an authority which denies God's   18
spiritual command relating to perfection, — an authority
which Jesus proved to be false? He did the will of the
Father. He healed sickness in defiance of what is called   21
material law, but in accordance with God's law, the law
of Mind.

I have discerned disease in the human mind, and rec-   24
ognized the patient's fear of it, months before the so-called

Disease foreseen   disease made its appearance in the body. Disease being a belief, a latent illusion of mortal   27
mind, the sensation would not appear if the error of belief
was met and destroyed by truth.

Changed mentality   Here let a word be noticed which will be   30
better understood hereafter, — *chemicalization.*
By chemicalization I mean the process which mortal

1 mind and body undergo in the change of belief from a
material to a spiritual basis.

3 Whenever an aggravation of symptoms has occurred
through mental chemicalization, I have seen the mental
signs, assuring me that danger was over, before

Scientific foresight

6 the patient felt the change; and I have said
to the patient, "You are healed," — sometimes to his dis-
comfiture, when he was incredulous. But it always came

9 about as I had foretold.

I name these facts to show that disease has a mental,
mortal origin, — that faith in rules of health or in drugs

12 begets and fosters disease by attracting the mind to the
subject of sickness, by exciting fear of disease, and by dos-
ing the body in order to avoid it. The faith reposed in

15 these things should find stronger supports and a higher
home. If we understood the control of Mind over body,
we should put no faith in material means.

18 Science not only reveals the origin of all disease as
mental, but it also declares that all disease is cured by
divine Mind. There can be no healing ex-

Mind the only healer

21 cept by this Mind, however much we trust
a drug or any other means towards which human faith
or endeavor is directed. It is mortal mind, not mat-

24 ter, which brings to the sick whatever good they may
seem to receive from materiality. But the sick are never
really healed except by means of the divine power.

27 Only the action of Truth, Life, and Love can give
harmony.

Whatever teaches man to have other laws and to

30 acknowledge other powers than the divine
Mind, is anti-Christian. The good that a
poisonous drug seems to do is evil, for it robs man of

Modes of matter

reliance on God, omnipotent Mind, and according to be- 1
lief, poisons the human system. Truth is not the basis of
theogony. Modes of matter form neither a moral nor a 3
spiritual system. The discord which calls for material
methods is the result of the exercise of faith in material
modes, — faith in matter instead of in Spirit. 6

Did Jesus understand the economy of man less than
Graham or Cutter? Christian ideas certainly present

**Physiology
unscientific**
what human theories exclude — the Principle 9
of man's harmony. The text, "Whosoever
liveth and believeth in me shall never die," not only contradicts human systems, but points to the self-sustaining 12
and eternal Truth.

The demands of Truth are spiritual, and reach the
body through Mind. The best interpreter of man's needs 15
said: "Take no thought for your life, what ye shall eat,
or what ye shall drink."

If there are material laws which prevent disease, what 18
then causes it? Not divine law, for Jesus healed the
sick and cast out error, always in opposition, never in
obedience, to physics. 21

Spiritual causation is the one question to be considered,
for more than all others spiritual causation relates to

**Causation
considered**
human progress. The age seems ready to 24
approach this subject, to ponder somewhat
the supremacy of Spirit, and at least to touch the hem
of Truth's garment. 27

The description of man as purely physical, or as both
material and spiritual, — but in either case dependent
upon his physical organization, — is the Pandora box, 30
from which all ills have gone forth, especially despair.
Matter, which takes divine power into its own hands and

1 claims to be a creator, is a fiction, in which paganism and
   lust are so sanctioned by society that mankind has caught
3 their moral contagion.

Through discernment of the spiritual opposite of materiality, even the way through Christ, Truth, man will
6 reopen with the key of divine Science the gates   **Paradise**
of Paradise which human beliefs have closed,   **regained**
and will find himself unfallen, upright, pure, and free,
9 not needing to consult almanacs for the probabilities either
of his life or of the weather, not needing to study brainology to learn how much of a man he is.

12 Mind's control over the universe, including man, is
no longer an open question, but is demonstrable Science.
Jesus illustrated the divine Principle and the   **A closed**
15 power of immortal Mind by healing sickness   **question**
and sin and destroying the foundations of death.

Mistaking his origin and nature, man believes himself to
18 be combined matter and Spirit. He believes that Spirit
is sifted through matter, carried on a nerve, ex-   **Matter**
posed to ejection by the operation of matter.   *versus* **Spirit**
21 The intellectual, the moral, the spiritual, — yea, the image
of infinite Mind, — subject to non-intelligence!

No more sympathy exists between the flesh and Spirit
24 than between Belial and Christ.

The so-called laws of matter are nothing but false beliefs that intelligence and life are present where Mind
27 is not. These false beliefs are the procuring cause of all
sin and disease. The opposite truth, that intelligence and
life are spiritual, never material, destroys sin, sickness,
30 and death.

The fundamental error lies in the supposition that man
is a material outgrowth and that the cognizance of good

or evil, which he has through the bodily senses, con-   1
stitutes his happiness or misery.

Theorizing about man's development from mushrooms   3

Godless
evolution
to monkeys and from monkeys into men
amounts to nothing in the right direction and
very much in the wrong.   6

Materialism grades the human species as rising from
matter upward. How then is the material species maintained, if man passes through what we call death and   9
death is the Rubicon of spirituality? Spirit can form
no real link in this supposed chain of material being.
But divine Science reveals the eternal chain of existence   12
as uninterrupted and wholly spiritual; yet this can be
realized only as the false sense of being disappears.

If man was first a material being, he must have passed   15
through all the forms of matter in order to become man.

Degrees of
development
If the material body is man, he is a portion of
matter, or dust. On the contrary, man is the   18
image and likeness of Spirit; and the belief that there is
Soul in sense or Life in matter obtains in mortals, *alias*
mortal mind, to which the apostle refers when he says   21
that we must "put off the old man."

What is man? Brain, heart, blood, bones, etc., the
material structure? If the real man is in the material   24

Identity
not lost
body, you take away a portion of the man when
you amputate a limb; the surgeon destroys
manhood, and worms annihilate it. But the loss of a limb   27
or injury to a tissue is sometimes the quickener of manli-
ness; and the unfortunate cripple may present more no-
bility than the statuesque athlete, — teaching us by his   30
very deprivations, that "a man's a man, for a' that."

When we admit that matter (heart, blood, brain, acting

1 through the five physical senses) constitutes man, we fail
to see how anatomy can distinguish between

When man
is man

3 humanity and the brute, or determine when
man is really *man* and has progressed farther than his
animal progenitors.

6 When the supposition, that Spirit is within what it
creates and the potter is subject to the clay,
is individualized, Truth is reduced to the level

Individu-
alization

9 of error, and the sensible is required to be made manifest
through the insensible.

What is termed matter manifests nothing but a material

12 mentality. Neither the substance nor the manifestation
of Spirit is obtainable through matter. Spirit is positive.
Matter is Spirit's contrary, the absence of Spirit. For

15 positive Spirit to pass through a negative condition
would be Spirit's destruction.

Anatomy declares man to be structural. Physiology

18 continues this explanation, measuring human
strength by bones and sinews, and human life

Man not
structural

by material law. Man is spiritual, individual, and eter-

21 nal; material structure is mortal.

Phrenology makes man knavish or honest according to
the development of the cranium; but anatomy, physiology,

24 phrenology, do not define the image of God, the real immortal man.

Human reason and religion come slowly to the recogni-

27 tion of spiritual facts, and so continue to call upon
matter to remove the error which the human mind alone
has created.

30 The idols of civilization are far more fatal to health
and longevity than are the idols of barbarism. The idols
of civilization call into action less faith than Buddhism

in a supreme governing intelligence. The Esquimaux   1
restore health by incantations as consciously as do civi-
lized practitioners by their more studied methods.   3

Is civilization only a higher form of idolatry, that
man should bow down to a flesh-brush, to flannels, to
baths, diet, exercise, and air? Nothing save divine   6
power is capable of doing so much for man as he can
do for himself.

The footsteps of thought, rising above material stand-   9
points, are slow, and portend a long night to the traveller;

Rise of
thought
but the angels of His presence — the spiritual
intuitions that tell us when "the night is far   12
spent, the day is at hand" — are our guardians in the
gloom. Whoever opens the way in Christian Science is
a pilgrim and stranger, marking out the path for gen-   15
erations yet unborn.

The thunder of Sinai and the Sermon on the Mount
are pursuing and will overtake the ages, rebuking in   18
their course all error and proclaiming the kingdom of
heaven on earth. Truth is revealed. It needs only to
be practised.   21

Mortal belief is all that enables a drug to cure mortal
ailments. Anatomy admits that mind is somewhere in

Medical
errors
man, though out of sight. Then, if an indi-   24
vidual is sick, why treat the body alone and
administer a dose of despair to the mind? Why declare
that the body is diseased, and picture this disease to the   27
mind, rolling it under the tongue as a sweet morsel and
holding it before the thought of both physician and patient? We should understand that the cause of disease   30
obtains in the mortal human mind, and its cure comes
from the immortal divine Mind. We should prevent the

images of disease from taking form in thought, and we
should efface the outlines of disease already formulated in
the minds of mortals.

When there are fewer prescriptions, and less thought is
given to sanitary subjects, there will be better
constitutions and less disease. In old times
who ever heard of dyspepsia, cerebro-spinal meningitis,
hay-fever, and rose-cold?

What an abuse of natural beauty to say that a rose,
the smile of God, can produce suffering! The joy of its
presence, its beauty and fragrance, should uplift the
thought, and dissuade any sense of fear or fever. It is
profane to fancy that the perfume of clover and the breath
of new-mown hay can cause glandular inflammation,
sneezing, and nasal pangs.

If a random thought, calling itself dyspepsia, had
tried to tyrannize over our forefathers, it would have
been routed by their independence and in-
dustry. Then people had less time for selfishness, coddling, and sickly after-dinner talk. The exact amount of food the stomach could digest was not
discussed according to Cutter nor referred to sanitary
laws. A man's belief in those days was not so severe
upon the gastric juices. Beaumont's "Medical Experiments" did not govern the digestion.

Damp atmosphere and freezing snow empurpled the
plump cheeks of our ancestors, but they never indulged
in the refinement of inflamed bronchial tubes.
They were as innocent as Adam, before he ate
the fruit of false knowledge, of the existence of tubercles
and troches, lungs and lozenges.

"Where ignorance is bliss, 'tis folly to be wise," says

Novel diseases

No ancestral dyspepsia

Pulmonary misbeliefs

the English poet, and there is truth in his sentiment. The   1
action of mortal mind on the body was not so injurious

Our modern
Eves

before inquisitive modern Eves took up the   3
study of medical works and unmanly Adams
attributed their own downfall and the fate of their offspring to the weakness of their wives.   6

The primitive custom of taking no thought about
food left the stomach and bowels free to act in obedience to nature, and gave the gospel a chance to be seen   9
in its glorious effects upon the body. A ghastly array of
diseases was not paraded before the imagination. There
were fewer books on digestion and more "sermons in   12
stones, and good in everything." When the mechanism
of the human mind gives place to the divine Mind, selfishness and sin, disease and death, will lose their   15
foothold.

Human fear of miasma would load with disease the
air of Eden, and weigh down mankind with superimposed   18
and conjectural evils. Mortal mind is the worst foe of
the body, while divine Mind is its best friend.

Should all cases of organic disease be treated by a   21
regular practitioner, and the Christian Scientist try

Diseases
not to be
classified

truth only in cases of hysteria, hypochon-
dria, and hallucination? One disease is no   24
more real than another. All disease is the
result of education, and disease can carry its ill-effects
no farther than mortal mind maps out the way. The   27
human mind, not matter, is supposed to feel, suffer, enjoy. Hence decided types of acute disease are quite as
ready to yield to Truth as the less distinct type and chronic 30
form of disease. Truth handles the most malignant contagion with perfect assurance.

1   Human mind produces what is termed organic disease as certainly as it produces hysteria, and it must re-
3 linquish all its errors, sicknesses, and sins.   **One basis for**
I have demonstrated this beyond all cavil.   **all sickness**
The evidence of divine Mind's healing power and abso-
6 lute control is to me as certain as the evidence of my own
existence.

   Mortal mind and body are one. Neither exists without
9 the other, and both must be destroyed by immortal Mind.
Matter, or body, is but a false concept of mor-   **Mental and**
tal mind. This so-called mind builds its own   **physical**
12 superstructure, of which the material body is   **oneness**
the grosser portion; but from first to last, the body is a
sensuous, human concept.

15   In the Scriptural allegory of the material creation,
Adam or error, which represents the erroneous theory
of life and intelligence in matter, had the   **The effect**
18 naming of all that was material. These names   **of names**
indicated matter's properties, qualities, and forms. But
a lie, the opposite of Truth, cannot name the qualities and
21 effects of what is termed matter, and create the so-called
laws of the flesh, nor can a lie hold the preponderance
of power in any direction against God, Spirit and
24 Truth.

   If a dose of poison is swallowed through mistake, and
the patient dies even though physician and   **Poison**
27 patient are expecting favorable results, does   **defined**
human belief, you ask, cause this death? Even   **mentally**
so, and as directly as if the poison had been intentionally
30 taken.

   In such cases a few persons believe the potion swallowed by the patient to be harmless, but the vast ma-

jority of mankind, though they know nothing of this par-   1
ticular case and this special person, believe the arsenic,
the strychnine, or whatever the drug used, to be poi-   3
sonous, for it is set down as a poison by mortal mind.
Consequently, the result is controlled by the majority of
opinions, not by the infinitesimal minority of opinions in   6
the sick-chamber.

Heredity is not a law. The remote cause or belief
of disease is not dangerous because of its priority and   9
the connection of past mortal thoughts with present.
The predisposing cause and the exciting cause are
mental.   12

Perhaps an adult has a deformity produced prior to his
birth by the fright of his mother. When wrested from
human belief and based on Science or the divine Mind, to   15
which all things are possible, that chronic case is not
difficult to cure.

Mortal mind, acting from the basis of sensation in   18
matter, is animal magnetism; but this so-called mind,

Animal magnetism destroyed
from which comes all evil, contradicts itself,
and must finally yield to the eternal Truth, or   21
the divine Mind, expressed in Science. In proportion to our understanding of Christian Science, we are
freed from the belief of heredity, of mind in matter or ani-   24
mal magnetism; and we disarm sin of its imaginary power
in proportion to our spiritual understanding of the status
of immortal being.   27

Ignorant of the methods and the basis of metaphysical
healing, you may attempt to unite with it hypnotism,
spiritualism, electricity; but none of these methods can   30
be mingled with metaphysical healing.

Whoever reaches the understanding of Christian Science

1   in its proper signification will perform the sudden cures
     of which it is capable; but this can be done only by
3   taking up the cross and following Christ in the daily
     life.

     Science can heal the sick, who are absent from their
6   healers, as well as those present, since space is no ob-
     stacle to Mind. Immortal Mind heals what eye   **Absent**
     hath not seen; but the spiritual capacity to ap-   **patients**
9   prehend thought and to heal by the Truth-power, is won
     only as man is found, not in self-righteousness, but re-
     flecting the divine nature.

12   Every medical method has its advocates. The prefer-
     ence of mortal mind for a certain method creates a demand
     for that method, and the body then seems to re-   **Horses**
15   quire such treatment. You can even educate a   **mistaught**
     healthy horse so far in physiology that he will take cold
     without his blanket, whereas the wild animal, left to his
18   instincts, sniffs the wind with delight. The epizoötic is
     a humanly evolved ailment, which a wild horse might
     never have.

21   Treatises on anatomy, physiology, and health, sustained
     by what is termed material law, are the pro-   **Medical works**
     moters of sickness and disease. It should not   **objectionable**
24   be proverbial, that so long as you read medical works you
     will be sick.

     The sedulous matron — studying her Jahr with homœ-
27   opathic pellet and powder in hand, ready to put you
     into a sweat, to move the bowels, or to produce sleep —
     is unwittingly sowing the seeds of reliance on matter,
30   and her household may erelong reap the effect of this
     mistake.

     Descriptions of disease given by physicians and adver-

tisements of quackery are both prolific sources of sickness.   1
As mortal mind is the husbandman of error, it should be
taught to do the body no harm and to uproot its false   3
sowing.

The patient sufferer tries to be satisfied when he sees
his would-be healers busy, and his faith in their efforts is   6

The invalid's
outlook
somewhat helpful to them and to himself; but
in Science one must understand the resusci-
tating law of Life. This is the seed within itself bearing   9
fruit after its kind, spoken of in Genesis.

Physicians should not deport themselves as if Mind
were non-existent, nor take the ground that all causation   12
is matter, instead of Mind. Ignorant that the human
mind governs the body, its phenomenon, the invalid may
unwittingly add more fear to the mental reservoir already   15
overflowing with that emotion.

Doctors should not implant disease in the thoughts of
their patients, as they so frequently do, by declaring dis-   18

Wrong and
right way
ease to be a fixed fact, even before they go to
work to eradicate the disease through the material faith which they inspire. Instead of furnishing   21
thought with fear, they should try to correct this turbulent
element of mortal mind by the influence of divine Love
which casteth out fear.   24

When man is governed by God, the ever-present
Mind who understands all things, man knows that with
God all things are possible. The only way to this   27
living Truth, which heals the sick, is found in the Science
of divine Mind as taught and demonstrated by Christ
Jesus.   30

To reduce inflammation, dissolve a tumor, or cure organic disease, I have found divine Truth more potent than

1   all lower remedies. And why not, since Mind, God, is
the source and condition of all existence? Before decid-

3   ing that the body, matter, is disordered, one **The important decision**
should ask, "Who art thou that repliest to
Spirit? Can matter speak for itself, or does

6   it hold the issues of life?" Matter, which can neither
suffer nor enjoy, has no partnership with pain and pleasure, but mortal belief has such a partnership.

9   When you manipulate patients, you trust in electricity
and magnetism more than in Truth; and for **Manipulation unscientific**
that reason, you employ matter rather than

12   Mind. You weaken or destroy your power when you resort to any except spiritual means.

It is foolish to declare that you manipulate patients but

15   that you lay no stress on manipulation. If this be so, why
manipulate? In reality you manipulate because you are
ignorant of the baneful effects of magnetism, or are not

18   sufficiently spiritual to depend on Spirit. In either case
you must improve your mental condition till you finally
attain the understanding of Christian Science.

21   If you are too material to love the Science of Mind and
are satisfied with good words instead of effects, if you
adhere to error and are afraid to trust Truth, **Not words but deeds**

24   the question then recurs, "Adam, where art
thou?" It is unnecessary to resort to aught besides
Mind in order to satisfy the sick that you are doing some-

27   thing for them, for if they are cured, they generally know
it and are satisfied.

"Where your treasure is, there will your heart be also."

30   If you have more faith in drugs than in Truth, this faith
will incline you to the side of matter and error. Any
hypnotic power you may exercise will diminish your

ability to become a Scientist, and *vice versa.* The act 1
of healing the sick through divine Mind alone, of casting
out error with Truth, shows your position as a Christian 3
Scientist.

The demands of God appeal to thought only; but the
claims of mortality, and what are termed laws of nature, 6

**Physiology
or Spirit**

appertain to matter. Which, then, are we to
accept as legitimate and capable of producing
the highest human good? We cannot obey both physi- 9
ology and Spirit, for one absolutely destroys the other,
and one or the other must be supreme in the affections.
It is impossible to work from two standpoints. If we 12
attempt it, we shall presently "hold to the one, and
despise the other."

The hypotheses of mortals are antagonistic to Science 15
and cannot mix with it. This is clear to those who heal
the sick on the basis of Science.

Mind's government of the body must supersede the so- 18
called laws of matter. Obedience to material law pre-

**No material
law**

vents full obedience to spiritual law, — the law
which overcomes material conditions and puts 21
matter under the feet of Mind. Mortals entreat the divine Mind to heal the sick, and forthwith shut out the aid
of Mind by using material means, thus working against 24
themselves and their prayers and denying man's God-
given ability to demonstrate Mind's sacred power. Pleas
for drugs and laws of health come from some sad incident, 27
or else from ignorance of Christian Science and its transcendent power.

To admit that sickness is a condition over which God 30
has no control, is to presuppose that omnipotent power
is powerless on some occasions. The law of Christ, or

1   Truth, makes all things possible to Spirit; but the so-
called laws of matter would render Spirit of no avail, and
3   demand obedience to materialistic codes, thus departing
from the basis of one God, one lawmaker. To suppose
that God constitutes laws of inharmony is a mistake; dis-
6   cords have no support from nature or divine law, however
much is said to the contrary.

Can the agriculturist, according to belief, produce a
9   crop without sowing the seed and awaiting its germina-
tion according to the laws of nature? The answer is no,
and yet the Scriptures inform us that sin, or error, first
12   caused the condemnation of man to till the ground, and
indicate that obedience to God will remove this necessity.
Truth never made error necessary, nor devised a law to
15   perpetuate error.

The supposed laws which result in weariness and disease are not His laws, for the legitimate and only possible
18   action of Truth is the production of harmony.   **Laws of**
Laws of nature are laws of Spirit; but mortals   **nature**
commonly recognize as law that which hides the power of **spiritual**
21   Spirit. Divine Mind rightly demands man's entire obedience, affection, and strength. No reservation is made
for any lesser loyalty. Obedience to Truth gives man
24   power and strength. Submission to error superinduces
loss of power.

Truth casts out all evils and materialistic methods
27   with the actual spiritual law, — the law which gives
sight to the blind, hearing to the deaf, voice   **Belief and**
to the dumb, feet to the lame. If Christian   **understanding**
30   Science dishonors human belief, it honors spir-
itual understanding; and the one Mind only is entitled to
honor.

The so-called laws of health are simply laws of mortal   1
belief. The premises being erroneous, the conclusions
are wrong. Truth makes no laws to regulate sickness,   3
sin, and death, for these are unknown to Truth and should
not be recognized as reality.

Belief produces the results of belief, and the penal-   6
ties it affixes last so long as the belief and are inseparable from it. The remedy consists in probing the trouble
to the bottom, in finding and casting out by denial the   9
error of belief which produces a mortal disorder, never
honoring erroneous belief with the title of law nor yielding obedience to it. Truth, Life, and Love are the only   12
legitimate and eternal demands on man, and they are
spiritual lawgivers, enforcing obedience through divine
statutes.   15

Controlled by the divine intelligence, man is harmonious and eternal. Whatever is governed by a false belief
Laws of   is discordant and mortal. We say man suffers   18
human belief   from the effects of cold, heat, fatigue. This
is human belief, not the truth of being, for matter cannot
suffer. Mortal mind alone suffers, — not because a law   21
of matter has been transgressed, but because a law of this
so-called mind has been disobeyed. I have demonstrated
this as a rule of divine Science by destroying the delusion   24
of suffering from what is termed a fatally broken physical
law.

A woman, whom I cured of consumption, always   27
breathed with great difficulty when the wind was from
the east. I sat silently by her side a few moments. Her
breath came gently. The inspirations were deep and nat-   30
ural. I then requested her to look at the weather-vane.
She looked and saw that it pointed due east. The wind

had not changed, but her thought of it had and so her difficulty in breathing had gone. The wind had not produced the difficulty. My metaphysical treatment changed the action of her belief on the lungs, and she never suffered again from east winds, but was restored to health.

No system of hygiene but Christian Science is purely mental. Before this book was published, other books were in circulation, which discussed "mental medicine" and "mind-cure," operating through the power of the earth's magnetic currents to regulate life and health. Such theories and such systems of so-called mind-cure, which have sprung up, are as material as the prevailing systems of medicine. They have their birth in mortal mind, which puts forth a human conception in the name of Science to match the divine Science of immortal Mind, even as the necromancers of Egypt strove to emulate the wonders wrought by Moses. Such theories have no relationship to Christian Science, which rests on the conception of God as the only Life, substance, and intelligence, and excludes the human mind as a spiritual factor in the healing work.

A so-called mind-cure

Jesus cast out evil and healed the sick, not only without drugs, but without hypnotism, which is the reverse of ethical and pathological Truth-power.

Jesus and hypnotism

Erroneous mental practice may seem for a time to benefit the sick, but the recovery is not permanent. This is because erroneous methods act on and through the material stratum of the human mind, called brain, which is but a mortal consolidation of material mentality and its suppositional activities.

A patient under the influence of mortal mind is healed

only by removing the influence on him of this mind, by   1
emptying his thought of the false stimulus
and reaction of will-power and filling it with   3
the divine energies of Truth.

Christian Science destroys material beliefs through the
understanding of Spirit, and the thoroughness of this work   6
determines health. Erring human mind-forces can work
only evil under whatever name or pretence they are employed; for Spirit and matter, good and evil, light and   9
darkness, cannot mingle.

Evil is a negation, because it is the absence of truth.
It is nothing, because it is the absence of something. It   12

is unreal, because it presupposes the absence
of God, the omnipotent and omnipresent.
Every mortal must learn that there is neither   15
power nor reality in evil.

Evil is self-assertive. It says: "I am a real entity, over-
mastering good." This falsehood should strip evil of all   18
pretensions. The only power of evil is to destroy itself. It
can never destroy one iota of good. Every attempt of evil
to destroy good is a failure, and only aids in peremptorily   21
punishing the evil-doer. If we concede the same reality to
discord as to harmony, discord has as lasting a claim upon
us as has harmony. If evil is as real as good, evil is also as   24
immortal. If death is as real as Life, immortality is a myth.
If pain is as real as the absence of pain, both must be immortal; and if so, harmony cannot be the law of being.   27

Mortal mind is ignorant of self, or it could never be
self-deceived. If mortal mind knew how to be better, it

would be better. Since it must believe in some-   30
thing besides itself, it enthrones matter as deity.
The human mind has been an idolater from the beginning,

1   having other gods and believing in more than the one
Mind.

3   As mortals do not comprehend even mortal existence,
how ignorant must they be of the all-knowing Mind and
of His creations.

6   Here you may see how so-called material sense creates
its own forms of thought, gives them material names, and
then worships and fears them. With pagan blindness,

9   it attributes to some material god or medicine an ability
beyond itself. The beliefs of the human mind rob and
enslave it, and then impute this result to another illusive

12   personification, named Satan.

The valves of the heart, opening and closing for the passage of the blood, obey the mandate of mor-
                                          Action of

15   tal mind as directly as does the hand, ad-   **mortal mind**
mittedly moved by the will. Anatomy allows the mental
cause of the latter action, but not of the former.

18   We say, "My hand hath done it." What is this *my* but
mortal mind, the cause of all materialistic action? All
voluntary, as well as miscalled *involuntary*, action of the

21   mortal body is governed by this so-called mind, not by
matter. There is no involuntary action. The divine Mind
includes all action and volition, and man in Science is gov-

24   erned by this Mind. The human mind tries to classify
action as voluntary and involuntary, and suffers from the
attempt.

27   If you take away this erring mind, the mortal material
body loses all appearance of life or action, and this so-
called mind then calls itself dead; but the hu-   **Death and**

30   man mind still holds in belief a body, through   **the body**
which it acts and which appears to the human mind to
live, — a body like the one it had before death. This body

is put off only as the mortal, erring mind yields to God,   1
immortal Mind, and man is found in His image.

What is termed disease does not exist. It is neither   3
mind nor matter. The belief of sin, which has grown
terrible in strength and influence, is an uncon-

Embryonic
sinful
thoughts
scious error in the beginning, — an embryonic   6
thought without motive; but afterwards it
governs the so-called man. Passion, depraved appetites,
dishonesty, envy, hatred, revenge ripen into action, only to   9
pass from shame and woe to their final punishment.

Mortal existence is a dream of pain and pleasure in
matter, a dream of sin, sickness, and death; and it is like   12

Disease
a dream
the dream we have in sleep, in which every one
recognizes his condition to be wholly a state of
mind. In both the waking and the sleeping dream, the   15
dreamer thinks that his body is material and the suffering
is in that body.

The smile of the sleeper indicates the sensation pro-   18
duced physically by the pleasure of a dream. In the
same way pain and pleasure, sickness and care, are
traced upon mortals by unmistakable signs.   21

Sickness is a growth of error, springing from mortal
ignorance or fear. Error rehearses error. What causes
disease cannot cure it. The soil of disease is mortal   24
mind, and you have an abundant or scanty crop of disease,
according to the seedlings of fear. Sin and the fear of
disease must be uprooted and cast out.   27

When darkness comes over the earth, the physical

Sense yields to
understanding
senses have no immediate evidence of a sun.
The human eye knows not where the orb of   30
day is, nor if it exists. Astronomy gives the
desired information regarding the sun. The human or

material senses yield to the authority of this science, and they are willing to leave with astronomy the explanation of the sun's influence over the earth. If the eyes see no sun for a week, we still believe that there is solar light and heat. Science (in this instance named natural) raises the human thought above the cruder theories of the human mind, and casts out a fear.

In like manner mortals should no more deny the power of Christian Science to establish harmony and to explain the effect of mortal mind on the body, though the cause be unseen, than they should deny the existence of the sunlight when the orb of day disappears, or doubt that the sun will reappear. The sins of others should not make good men suffer.

We call the body material; but it is as truly mortal mind, according to its degree, as is the material brain which is supposed to furnish the evidence of all mortal thought or things. The human mortal mind, by an inevitable perversion, makes all things start from the lowest instead of from the highest mortal thought. The reverse is the case with all the formations of the immortal divine Mind. They proceed from the divine source; and so, in tracing them, we constantly ascend in infinite being.

Ascending the scale

From mortal mind comes the reproduction of the species, — first the belief of inanimate, and then of animate matter. According to mortal thought, the development of embryonic mortal mind commences in the lower, basal portion of the brain, and goes on in an ascending scale by evolution, keeping always in the direct line of matter, for matter is the subjective condition of mortal mind.

Human reproduction

Next we have the formation of so-called embryonic
mortal mind, afterwards mortal men or mortals, — all this
while matter is a belief, ignorant of itself, ignorant of what
it is supposed to produce. The mortal says that an inanimate unconscious seedling is producing mortals, both body
and mind; and yet neither a mortal mind nor the immortal
Mind is found in brain or elsewhere in matter or in mortals.

Human stature

This embryonic and materialistic human belief called
mortal man in turn fills itself with thoughts
of pain and pleasure, of life and death, and
arranges itself into five so-called senses, which presently
measure mind by the size of a brain and the bulk of a
body, called man.

Human frailty

Human birth, growth, maturity, and decay are as the
grass springing from the soil with beautiful green blades,
afterwards to wither and return to its native
nothingness. This mortal seeming is temporal;
it never merges into immortal being, but finally disappears, and immortal man, spiritual and eternal, is found
to be the real man.

The Hebrew bard, swayed by mortal thoughts, thus
swept his lyre with saddening strains on human existence:

> As for man, his days are as grass:
> As a flower of the field, so he flourisheth.
> For the wind passeth over it, and it is gone;
> And the place thereof shall know it no more.

When hope rose higher in the human heart, he sang:

> As for me, I will behold Thy face in righteousness:
> I shall be satisfied, when I awake, with Thy likeness.
> .   .   .   .
> For with Thee is the fountain of life;
> In Thy light shall we see light.

1   The brain can give no idea of God's man. It can take
no cognizance of Mind. Matter is not the organ of infi-
3   nite Mind.

As mortals give up the delusion that there is more than
one Mind, more than one God, man in God's likeness will
6   appear, and this eternal man will include in that likeness
no material element.

As a material, theoretical life-basis is found to be a
9   misapprehension of existence, the spiritual and divine
Principle of man dawns upon human thought,   **The immortal**
and leads it to "where the young child was,"   **birth**
12 — even to the birth of a new-old idea, to the spiritual
sense of being and of what Life includes. Thus the whole
earth will be transformed by Truth on its pinions of light,
15 chasing away the darkness of error.

The human thought must free itself from self-imposed
materiality and bondage. It should no longer   **Spiritual**
18 ask of the head, heart, or lungs: What are   **freedom**
man's prospects for life? Mind is not helpless. Intelligence is not mute before non-intelligence.

21 By its own volition, not a blade of grass springs up, not
a spray buds within the vale, not a leaf unfolds its fair
outlines, not a flower starts from its cloistered cell.

24 The Science of being reveals man and immortality as
based on Spirit. Physical sense defines mortal man as
based on matter, and from this premise infers the mor-
27 tality of the body.

The illusive senses may fancy affinities with their opposites; but in Christian Science, Truth never mingles
30 with error. Mind has no affinity with matter,   **No physical**
and therefore Truth is able to cast out the ills   **affinity**
of the flesh. Mind, God, sends forth the aroma of Spirit,

the atmosphere of intelligence. The belief that a pulpy   1
substance under the skull is mind is a mockery of intelligence, a mimicry of Mind.   3

    We are Christian Scientists, only as we quit our reliance
upon that which is false and grasp the true. We are not
Christian Scientists until we leave all for Christ. Human   6
opinions are not spiritual. They come from the hearing
of the ear, from corporeality instead of from Principle,
and from the mortal instead of from the immortal. Spirit   9
is not separate from God. Spirit *is* God.

    Erring power is a material belief, a blind miscalled force,
the offspring of will and not of wisdom, of the mortal mind   12

**Human power
a blind force**

and not of the immortal. It is the headlong
cataract, the devouring flame, the tempest's
breath. It is lightning and hurricane, all that is selfish,   15
wicked, dishonest, and impure.

    Moral and spiritual might belong to Spirit, who holds
the "wind in His fists;" and this teaching accords with   18

**The one
real power**

Science and harmony. In Science, you can
have no power opposed to God, and the physi-
cal senses must give up their false testimony. Your in-   21
fluence for good depends upon the weight you throw into
the right scale. The good you do and embody gives you
the only power obtainable. Evil is not power. It is a   24
mockery of strength, which erelong betrays its weakness
and falls, never to rise.

    We walk in the footsteps of Truth and Love by follow-   27
ing the example of our Master in the understanding of
divine metaphysics. Christianity is the basis of true healing. Whatever holds human thought in line with unselfed   30
love, receives directly the divine power.

    I was called to visit Mr. Clark in Lynn, who had been

confined to his bed six months with hip-disease, caused by a fall upon a wooden spike when quite a boy. On entering the house I met his physician, who said that the patient was dying. The physician had just probed the ulcer on the hip, and said the bone was carious for several inches. He even showed me the probe, which had on it the evidence of this condition of the bone. The doctor went out. Mr. Clark lay with his eyes fixed and sightless. The dew of death was on his brow. I went to his bedside. In a few moments his face changed; its death-pallor gave place to a natural hue. The eyelids closed gently and the breathing became natural; he was asleep. In about ten minutes he opened his eyes and said: "I feel like a new man. My suffering is all gone." It was between three and four o'clock in the afternoon when this took place.

I told him to rise, dress himself, and take supper with his family. He did so. The next day I saw him in the yard. Since then I have not seen him, but am informed that he went to work in two weeks. The discharge from the sore stopped, and the sore was healed. The diseased condition had continued there ever since the injury was received in boyhood.

Since his recovery I have been informed that his physician claims to have cured him, and that his mother has been threatened with incarceration in an insane asylum for saying: "It was none other than God and that woman who healed him." I cannot attest the truth of that report, but what I saw and did for that man, and what his physician said of the case, occurred just as I have narrated.

It has been demonstrated to me that Life is God

**Mind cures
hip-disease**

and that the might of omnipotent Spirit shares not its   1
strength with matter or with human will. Review-
ing this brief experience, I cannot fail to discern the   3
coincidence of the spiritual idea of man with the divine
Mind.

A change in human belief changes all the physical symp-   6
Change of   toms, and determines a case for better or for
belief   worse. When one's false belief is corrected,
Truth sends a report of health over the body.   9

Destruction of the auditory nerve and paralysis of the
optic nerve are not necessary to ensure deafness and blindness; for if mortal mind says, "I am deaf and blind," it   12
will be so without an injured nerve. Every theory opposed to this fact (as I learned in metaphysics) would
presuppose man, who is immortal in spiritual under-   15
standing, a mortal in material belief.

The authentic history of Kaspar Hauser is a useful hint
as to the frailty and inadequacy of mortal mind. It   18
Power of   proves beyond a doubt that education consti-
habit   tutes this so-called mind, and that, in turn,
mortal mind manifests itself in the body by the false   21
sense it imparts. Incarcerated in a dungeon, where
neither sight nor sound could reach him, at the age of
seventeen Kaspar was still a mental infant, crying and   24
chattering with no more intelligence than a babe, and
realizing Tennyson's description:

> An infant crying in the night,   27
> An infant crying for the light,
> And with no language but a cry.

His case proves material sense to be but a belief formed   30
by education alone. The light which affords us joy gave

him a belief of intense pain. His eyes were inflamed by
the light. After the babbling boy had been taught to
speak a few words, he asked to be taken back to his dungeon, and said that he should never be happy elsewhere.
Outside of dismal darkness and cold silence he found no
peace. Every sound convulsed him with anguish. All
that he ate, except his black crust, produced violent
retchings. All that gives pleasure to our educated senses
gave him pain through those very senses, trained in an
opposite direction.

The point for each one to decide is, whether it is mortal
mind or immortal Mind that is causative. We
should forsake the basis of matter for metaphysical Science and its divine Principle.

Useful knowledge

Whatever furnishes the semblance of an idea governed
by its Principle, furnishes food for thought. Through astronomy, natural history, chemistry, music, mathematics,
thought passes naturally from effect back to cause.

Academics of the right sort are requisite. Observation, invention, study, and original thought are expansive
and should promote the growth of mortal mind out of itself, out of all that is mortal.

It is the tangled barbarisms of learning which we
deplore, — the mere dogma, the speculative theory, the
nauseous fiction. Novels, remarkable only for their
exaggerated pictures, impossible ideals, and specimens
of depravity, fill our young readers with wrong tastes
and sentiments. Literary commercialism is lowering the
intellectual standard to accommodate the purse and to
meet a frivolous demand for amusement instead of for
improvement. Incorrect views lower the standard of
truth.

If materialistic knowledge is power, it is not wisdom. $\quad$ 1
It is but a blind force. Man has "sought out many inventions," but he has not yet found it true that knowledge can $\quad$ 3
save him from the dire effects of knowledge. The power
of mortal mind over its own body is little understood.

Better the suffering which awakens mortal mind from $\quad$ 6

Sin destroyed through suffering

its fleshly dream, than the false pleasures
which tend to perpetuate this dream. Sin
alone brings death, for sin is the only element $\quad$ 9
of destruction.

"Fear him which is able to destroy both soul and body
in hell," said Jesus. A careful study of this text shows $\quad$ 12
that here the word *soul* means a false sense or material
consciousness. The command was a warning to beware,
not of Rome, Satan, nor of God, but of sin. Sickness, $\quad$ 15
sin, and death are not concomitants of Life or Truth.
No law supports them. They have no relation to God
wherewith to establish their power. Sin makes its own $\quad$ 18
hell, and goodness its own heaven.

Such books as will rule disease out of mortal mind, —

Dangerous shoals avoided

and so efface the images and thoughts of dis- $\quad$ 21
ease, instead of impressing them with forcible
descriptions and medical details, — will help
to abate sickness and to destroy it. $\quad$ 24

Many a hopeless case of disease is induced by a single
post mortem examination, — not from infection nor from
contact with material virus, but from the fear of the $\quad$ 27
disease and from the image brought before the mind; it
is a mental state, which is afterwards outlined on the
body. $\quad$ 30

The press unwittingly sends forth many sorrows and
diseases among the human family. It does this by giv-

ing names to diseases and by printing long descriptions which mirror images of disease distinctly in thought. A new name for an ailment affects people like a Parisian name for a novel garment. Every one hastens to get it. A minutely described dis-ease costs many a man his earthly days of comfort. What a price for human knowledge! But the price does not exceed the original cost. God said of the tree of knowledge, which bears the fruit of sin, disease, and death, "In the day that thou eatest thereof thou shalt surely die."

Pangs caused by the press

The less that is said of physical structure and laws, and the more that is thought and said about moral and spiritual law, the higher will be the standard of living and the farther mortals will be removed from imbecility or disease.

Higher standard for mortals

We should master fear, instead of cultivating it. It was the ignorance of our forefathers in the departments of knowledge now broadcast in the earth, that made them hardier than our trained physiologists, more honest than our sleek politicians.

We are told that the simple food our forefathers ate helped to make them healthy, but that is a mistake. Their diet would not cure dyspepsia at this period. With rules of health in the head and the most digestible food in the stomach, there would still be dyspeptics. Many of the effeminate constitutions of our time will never grow robust until individual opinions improve and mortal belief loses some portion of its error.

Diet and dyspepsia

The doctor's mind reaches that of his patient. The doctor should suppress his fear of disease, else his belief in its reality and fatality will harm his patients even more

than his calomel and morphine, for the higher stratum of   1
mortal mind has in belief more power to harm man than
the substratum, matter. A patient hears the   3
doctor's verdict as a criminal hears his death-
sentence. The patient may seem calm under it, but he is
not. His fortitude may sustain him, but his fear, which   6
has already developed the disease that is gaining the
mastery, is increased by the physician's words.

The materialistic doctor, though humane, is an art-   9
ist who outlines his thought relative to disease, and then
fills in his delineations with sketches from text-
books. It is better to prevent disease from   12
forming in mortal mind afterwards to appear on the
body; but to do this requires attention. The thought of
disease is formed before one sees a doctor and before   15
the doctor undertakes to dispel it by a counter-irritant,
— perhaps by a blister, by the application of caustic or
croton oil, or by a surgical operation. Again, giving an-   18
other direction to faith, the physician prescribes drugs,
until the elasticity of mortal thought haply causes a
vigorous reaction upon itself, and reproduces a picture   21
of healthy and harmonious formations.

A patient's belief is more or less moulded and formed
by his doctor's belief in the case, even though the doctor   24
says nothing to support his theory. His thoughts and his
patient's commingle, and the stronger thoughts rule the
weaker. Hence the importance that doctors be Christian   27
Scientists.

Because the muscles of the blacksmith's arm are
strongly developed, it does not follow that   30
exercise has produced this result or that a
less used arm must be weak. If matter were the cause

of action, and if muscles, without volition of mortal
mind, could lift the hammer and strike the anvil, it
might be thought true that hammering would enlarge
the muscles. The trip-hammer is not increased in size
by exercise. Why not, since muscles are as material as
wood and iron? Because nobody believes that mind is
producing such a result on the hammer.

Muscles are not self-acting. If mind does not move
them, they are motionless. Hence the great fact that
Mind alone enlarges and empowers man through its
mandate, — by reason of its demand for and supply of
power. Not because of muscular exercise, but by reason of the blacksmith's faith in exercise, his arm becomes
stronger.

Mortals develop their own bodies or make them sick,
according as they influence them through mortal mind.
To know whether this development is produced

Latent fear
subdued

consciously or unconsciously, is of less importance than a knowledge of the fact. The feats of the gym-
nast prove that latent mental fears are subdued by him.
The devotion of thought to an honest achievement makes
the achievement possible. Exceptions only confirm this
rule, proving that failure is occasioned by a too feeble
faith.

Had Blondin believed it impossible to walk the rope
over Niagara's abyss of waters, he could never have
done it. His belief that he could do it gave his thought-
forces, called muscles, their flexibility and power which
the unscientific might attribute to a lubricating oil. His
fear must have disappeared before his power of putting
resolve into action could appear.

When Homer sang of the Grecian gods, Olympus was

Homer and Moses

dark, but through his verse the gods became alive in a nation's belief. Pagan worship began with muscularity, but the law of Sinai lifted thought into the song of David. Moses advanced a nation to the worship of God in Spirit instead of matter, and illustrated the grand human capacities of being bestowed by immortal Mind.

A mortal not man

Whoever is incompetent to explain Soul would be wise not to undertake the explanation of body. Life is, always has been, and ever will be independent of matter; for Life is God, and man is the idea of God, not formed materially but spiritually, and not subject to decay and dust. The Psalmist said: "Thou madest him to have dominion over the works of Thy hands. Thou hast put all things under his feet."

The great truth in the Science of being, that the real man was, is, and ever shall be perfect, is incontrovertible; for if man is the image, reflection, of God, he is neither inverted nor subverted, but upright and Godlike.

The suppositional antipode of divine infinite Spirit is the so-called human soul or spirit, in other words the five senses, — the flesh that warreth against Spirit. These so-called material senses must yield to the infinite Spirit, named God.

St. Paul said: "For I determined not to know anything among you, save Jesus Christ, and him crucified." (I Cor. ii. 2.) Christian Science says: I am determined not to know anything among you, save Jesus Christ, and him glorified.

Footsteps of Truth

Remember, Lord, the reproach of Thy servants;
how I do bear in my bosom the reproach of all the mighty people;
wherewith Thine enemies have reproached, O Lord;
wherewith they have reproached the footsteps of Thine anointed. — PSALMS.

1   The best sermon ever preached is Truth practised
   and demonstrated by the destruction of sin, sickness,
3 and death. Knowing this and knowing too
that one affection would be supreme in us and
take the lead in our lives, Jesus said, "No man can serve
6 two masters."

    We cannot build safely on false foundations. Truth
makes a new creature, in whom old things pass away
9 and "all things are become new." Passions, selfishness,
false appetites, hatred, fear, all sensuality, yield to spirituality, and the superabundance of being is on the side
12 of God, good.

    We cannot fill vessels already full. They must first be
emptied. Let us disrobe error. Then, when
15 the winds of God blow, we shall not hug our
tatters close about us.

    The way to extract error from mortal mind is to pour
18 in truth through flood-tides of Love. Christian perfection is won on no other basis.

    Grafting holiness upon unholiness, supposing that sin

Practical preaching

The uses of truth

201

can be forgiven when it is not forsaken, is as foolish as   1
straining out gnats and swallowing camels.

The scientific unity which exists between God and man   3
must be wrought out in life-practice, and God's will must
be universally done.

If men would bring to bear upon the study of the   6
Science of Mind half the faith they bestow upon the so-

Divine
called pains and pleasures of material sense,
study
they would not go on from bad to worse,   9
until disciplined by the prison and the scaffold; but
the whole human family would be redeemed through
the merits of Christ, — through the perception and ac-   12
ceptance of Truth. For this glorious result Christian
Science lights the torch of spiritual understanding.

Outside of this Science all is mutable; but immortal   15
man, in accord with the divine Principle of his being,

Harmonious
God, neither sins, suffers, nor dies. The days
life-work
of our pilgrimage will multiply instead of di-   18
minish, when God's kingdom comes on earth; for the
true way leads to Life instead of to death, and earthly
experience discloses the finity of error and the infinite   21
capacities of Truth, in which God gives man dominion
over all the earth.

Our beliefs about a Supreme Being contradict the   24
practice growing out of them. Error abounds where

Belief and
Truth should "much more abound." We
practice
admit that God has almighty power, is "a   27
very present help in trouble;" and yet we rely on a drug
or hypnotism to heal disease, as if senseless matter or erring mortal mind had more power than omnipotent Spirit.   30

Common opinion admits that a man may take cold in
the act of doing good, and that this cold may produce

1   fatal pulmonary disease; as though evil could overbear
the law of Love, and check the reward for do-

Sure reward of
righteousness

3   ing good. In the Science of Christianity, Mind
— omnipotence — has all-power, assigns sure
rewards to righteousness, and shows that matter can

6   neither heal nor make sick, create nor destroy.

     If God were understood instead of being merely be-
lieved, this understanding would establish health. The

9   accusation of the rabbis, "He made himself
the Son of God," was really the justification
of Jesus, for to the Christian the only true

Our belief
and
understanding

12   spirit is Godlike. This thought incites to a more exalted
worship and self-abnegation. Spiritual perception brings
out the possibilities of being, destroys reliance on aught

15   but God, and so makes man the image of his Maker in
deed and in truth.

     We are prone to believe either in more than one Su-

18   preme Ruler or in some power less than God. We imagine that Mind can be imprisoned in a sensuous body.
When the material body has gone to ruin, when evil has

21   overtaxed the belief of life in matter and destroyed it,
then mortals believe that the deathless Principle, or
Soul, escapes from matter and lives on; but this is not

24   true. Death is not a stepping-stone to Life, immortality,
and bliss. The so-called sinner is a suicide.
Sin kills the sinner and will continue to kill

Suicide
and sin

27   him so long as he sins. The foam and fury of illegitimate living and of fearful and doleful dying should
disappear on the shore of time; then the waves of sin,

30   sorrow, and death beat in vain.

     God, divine good, does not kill a man in order to give
him eternal Life, for God alone is man's life. God is at

once the centre and circumference of being. It is evil 1
that dies; good dies not.

All forms of error support the false conclusions that 3
there is more than one Life; that material history is as
real and living as spiritual history; that mortal
error is as conclusively mental as immortal 6
Truth; and that there are two separate, antagonistic entities and beings, two powers, — namely,
Spirit and matter, — resulting in a third person (mortal 9
man) who carries out the delusions of sin, sickness, and
death.

Spirit the only intelligence and substance

The first power is admitted to be good, an intelligence or 12
Mind called God. The so-called second power, evil, is the
unlikeness of good. It cannot therefore be mind, though
so called. The third power, mortal man, is a supposed 15
mixture of the first and second antagonistic powers, intelligence and non-intelligence, of Spirit and matter.

Such theories are evidently erroneous. They can never 18
stand the test of Science. Judging them by their fruits,
they are corrupt. When will the ages understand the Ego, and realize only one God, one 21
Mind or intelligence?

Unscientific theories

False and self-assertive theories have given sinners the
notion that they can create what God cannot, — namely, 24
sinful mortals in God's image, thus usurping the name
without the nature of the image or reflection of divine
Mind; but in Science it can never be said that man 27
has a mind of his own, distinct from God, the *all*
Mind.

The belief that God lives in matter is pantheistic. The 30
error, which says that Soul is in body, Mind is in matter,
and good is in evil, must unsay it and cease from such

utterances; else God will continue to be hidden from humanity, and mortals will sin without knowing that they are sinning, will lean on matter instead of Spirit, stumble with lameness, drop with drunkenness, consume with disease, — all because of their blindness, their false sense concerning God and man.

When will the error of believing that there is life in matter, and that sin, sickness, and death are creations of God, be unmasked? When will it be understood that matter has neither intelligence, life, nor sensation, and that the opposite belief is the prolific source of all suffering? God created all through Mind, and made all perfect and eternal. Where then is the necessity for recreation or procreation?

Creation perfect

Befogged in error (the error of believing that matter can be intelligent for good or evil), we can catch clear glimpses of God only as the mists disperse, or as they melt into such thinness that we perceive the divine image in some word or deed which indicates the true idea, — the supremacy and reality of good, the nothingness and unreality of evil.

Perceiving the divine image

When we realize that there is one Mind, the divine law of loving our neighbor as ourselves is unfolded; whereas a belief in many ruling minds hinders man's normal drift towards the one Mind, one God, and leads human thought into opposite channels where selfishness reigns.

Redemption from selfishness

Selfishness tips the beam of human existence towards the side of error, not towards Truth. Denial of the oneness of Mind throws our weight into the scale, not of Spirit, God, good, but of matter.

When we fully understand our relation to the Divine,

we can have no other Mind but His, — no other Love, wisdom, or Truth, no other sense of Life, and no consciousness of the existence of matter or error.

Will-power unrighteous

The power of the human will should be exercised only in subordination to Truth; else it will misguide the judgment and free the lower propensities. It is the province of spiritual sense to govern man. Material, erring, human thought acts injuriously both upon the body and through it.

Will-power is capable of all evil. It can never heal the sick, for it is the prayer of the unrighteous; while the exercise of the sentiments — hope, faith, love — is the prayer of the righteous. This prayer, governed by Science instead of the senses, heals the sick.

In the scientific relation of God to man, we find that whatever blesses one blesses all, as Jesus showed with the loaves and the fishes, — Spirit, not matter, being the source of supply.

Birth and death unreal

Does God send sickness, giving the mother her child for the brief space of a few years and then taking it away by death? Is God creating anew what He has already created? The Scriptures are definite on this point, declaring that His work was *finished*, nothing is new to God, and that it was *good*.

Can there be any birth or death for man, the spiritual image and likeness of God? Instead of God sending sickness and death, He destroys them, and brings to light immortality. Omnipotent and infinite Mind made all and includes all. This Mind does not make mistakes and subsequently correct them. God does not cause man to sin, to be sick, or to die.

There are evil beliefs, often called evil spirits; but

these evils are not Spirit, for there is no evil in Spirit. Because God is Spirit, evil becomes more apparent and obnoxious proportionately as we advance spiritually, until it disappears from our lives.

This fact proves our position, for every scientific statement in Christianity has its proof. Error of statement leads to error in action.

God is not the creator of an evil mind. Indeed, evil is not Mind. We must learn that evil is the awful deception and unreality of existence. Evil is not supreme; good is not helpless; nor are the so-called laws of matter primary, and the law of Spirit secondary. Without this lesson, we lose sight of the perfect Father, or the divine Principle of man.

Body is not first and Soul last, nor is evil mightier than good. The Science of being repudiates self-evident impossibilities, such as the amalgamation of Truth and error in cause or effect. Science separates the tares and wheat in time of harvest.

There is but one primal cause. Therefore there can be no effect from any other cause, and there can be no reality in aught which does not proceed from this great and only cause. Sin, sickness, disease, and death belong not to the Science of being. They are the errors, which presuppose the absence of Truth, Life, or Love.

The spiritual reality is the scientific fact in all things. The spiritual fact, repeated in the action of man and the whole universe, is harmonious and is the ideal of Truth. Spiritual facts are not inverted; the opposite discord, which bears no resemblance to spirituality, is not real. The only evidence of this inversion is obtained from

suppositional error, which affords no proof of God,   1
Spirit, or of the spiritual creation. Material sense defines all things materially, and has a finite sense of the   3
infinite.

The Scriptures say, "In Him we live, and move, and
have our being." What then is this seeming power, in-   6

Seemingly
independent
authority
dependent of God, which causes disease and
cures it? What is it but an error of belief, —
a law of mortal mind, wrong in every sense,   9
embracing sin, sickness, and death? It is the very antipode of immortal Mind, of Truth, and of spiritual law.
It is not in accordance with the goodness of God's char-   12
acter that He should make man sick, then leave man to
heal himself; it is absurd to suppose that matter can both
cause and cure disease, or that Spirit, God, produces   15
disease and leaves the remedy to matter.

John Young of Edinburgh writes: "God is the father
of mind, and of nothing else." Such an utterance is   18
"the voice of one crying in the wilderness" of human
beliefs and preparing the way of Science. Let us learn
of the real and eternal, and prepare for the reign of   21
Spirit, the kingdom of heaven, — the reign and rule of
universal harmony, which cannot be lost nor remain
forever unseen.   24

Mind, not matter, is causation. A material body
only expresses a material and mortal mind. A mortal

Sickness as
only thought
man possesses this body, and he makes it   27
harmonious or discordant according to the
images of thought impressed upon it. You embrace
your body in your thought, and you should delineate   30
upon it thoughts of health, not of sickness. You should
banish all thoughts of disease and sin and of other beliefs

1   included in matter. Man, being immortal, has a perfect
indestructible life. It is the mortal belief which makes
3   the body discordant and diseased in proportion as ignorance, *fear,* or human will governs mortals.

     Mind, supreme over all its formations and governing
6   them all, is the central sun of its own systems of ideas,
the life and light of all its own vast creation;
and man is tributary to divine Mind. The
9   material and mortal body or mind is not the man.

Allness of
Truth

     The world would collapse without Mind, without the in-
telligence which holds the winds in its grasp. Neither
12   philosophy nor skepticism can hinder the march of the
Science which reveals the supremacy of Mind. The immanent sense of Mind-power enhances the glory of Mind.
15   Nearness, not distance, lends enchantment to this view.

     The compounded minerals or aggregated substances
composing the earth, the relations which constituent
18   masses hold to each other, the magnitudes,
distances, and revolutions of the celestial
bodies, are of no real importance, when we remember
21   that they all must give place to the spiritual fact by the
translation of man and the universe back into Spirit. In
proportion as this is done, man and the universe will be
24   found harmonious and eternal.

Spiritual
translation

     Material substances or mundane formations, astro-
nomical calculations, and all the paraphernalia of specu-
27   lative theories, based on the hypothesis of material law
or life and intelligence resident in matter, will ultimately vanish, swallowed up in the infinite calculus of
30   Spirit.

     Spiritual sense is a conscious, constant capacity to un-
derstand God. It shows the superiority of faith by works

over faith in words. Its ideas are expressed only in "new   1
tongues;" and these are interpreted by the translation of
the spiritual original into the language which human   3
thought can comprehend.

The Principle and proof of Christianity are discerned
by spiritual sense. They are set forth in Jesus' demon-   6

Jesus'
disregard
of matter

strations, which show — by his healing the
sick, casting out evils, and destroying death,
"the last enemy that shall be destroyed," —   9
his disregard of matter and its so-called laws.

Knowing that Soul and its attributes were forever
manifested through man, the Master healed the sick,   12
gave sight to the blind, hearing to the deaf, feet to the
lame, thus bringing to light the scientific action of the
divine Mind on human minds and bodies and giving   15
a better understanding of Soul and salvation. Jesus
healed sickness and sin by one and the same metaphysical
process.   18

The expression *mortal mind* is really a solecism, for
Mind is immortal, and Truth pierces the error of mortality

Mind not
mortal

as a sunbeam penetrates the cloud. Because,   21
in obedience to the immutable law of Spirit,
this so-called mind is self-destructive, I name it mortal.
Error soweth the wind and reapeth the whirlwind.   24

What is termed matter, being unintelligent, cannot say,
"I suffer, I die, I am sick, or I am well." It is the so-

Matter
mindless

called mortal mind which voices this and ap-   27
pears to itself to make good its claim. To
mortal sense, sin and suffering are real, but immortal
sense includes no evil nor pestilence. Because immortal   30
sense has no error of sense, it has no sense of error; therefore it is without a destructive element.

1   If brain, nerves, stomach, are intelligent, — if they talk to us, tell us their condition, and report how they feel, —

3   then Spirit and matter, Truth and error, commingle and produce sickness and health, good and evil, life and death; and who shall say whether Truth or error is the

6   greater?

The sensations of the body must either be the sensations of a so-called mortal mind or of matter. Nerves

9   are not mind. Is it not provable that Mind is not *mortal* and that matter has no sensation? Is it not equally true that matter does not appear in the

12   spiritual understanding of being?

Matter sensationless

The sensation of sickness and the impulse to sin seem to obtain in mortal mind. When a tear starts, does not

15   this so-called mind produce the effect seen in the lachrymal gland? Without mortal mind, the tear could not appear; and this action shows the nature of all so-called

18   material cause and effect.

It should no longer be said in Israel that "the fathers have eaten sour grapes, and the children's teeth are set

21   on edge." Sympathy with error should disappear. The transfer of the thoughts of one erring mind to another, Science renders impossible.

24   If it is true that nerves have sensation, that matter has intelligence, that the material organism causes the eyes to see and the ears to hear, then, when the body

Nerves painless

27   is dematerialized, these faculties must be lost, for their immortality is not in Spirit; whereas the fact is that only through dematerialization and spiritualiza-

30   tion of thought can these faculties be conceived of as immortal.

Nerves are not the source of pain or pleasure. We

suffer or enjoy in our dreams, but this pain or pleasure   1
is not communicated through a nerve. A tooth which has
been extracted sometimes aches again in belief, and the   3
pain seems to be in its old place. A limb which has been
amputated has continued in belief to pain the owner. If
the sensation of pain in the limb can return, can be pro-   6
longed, why cannot the limb reappear?

Why need pain, rather than pleasure, come to this mortal sense? Because the memory of pain is more vivid   9
than the memory of pleasure. I have seen an unwitting
attempt to scratch the end of a finger which had been cut
off for months. When the nerve is gone, which we say   12
was the occasion of pain, and the pain still remains, it
proves sensation to be in the mortal mind, not in matter.
Reverse the process; take away this so-called mind instead   15
of a piece of the flesh, and the nerves have no sensation.

Mortals have a modus of their own, undirected and unsustained by God. They produce a rose through seed and   18
Human falsities | soil, and bring the rose into contact with the
olfactory nerves that they may smell it. In
legerdemain and credulous frenzy, mortals believe that   21
unseen spirits produce the flowers. God alone makes
and clothes the lilies of the field, and this He does by
means of Mind, not matter.   24

Because all the methods of Mind are not understood,
we say the lips or hands must move in order to convey
No miracles in Mind-methods | thought, that the undulations of the air convey   27
sound, and possibly that other methods involve
so-called miracles. The realities of being, its
normal action, and the origin of all things are unseen to   30
mortal sense; whereas the unreal and imitative movements of mortal belief, which would reverse the immortal

1   modus and action, are styled the real. Whoever contradicts this mortal mind supposition of reality is called
3   a deceiver, or is said to be deceived. Of a man it has
been said, "As he thinketh in his heart, so is he;" hence
as a man spiritually *understandeth*, so is he in truth.

6   Mortal mind conceives of something as either liquid
or solid, and then classifies it materially. Immortal and
spiritual facts exist apart from this mortal and
9   material conception. God, good, is self-exist-   **Good**
ent and self-expressed, though indefinable as a whole.   **indefinable**
Every step towards goodness is a departure from materi-
12   ality, and is a tendency towards God, Spirit. Material
theories partially paralyze this attraction towards infinite
and eternal good by an opposite attraction towards the
15   finite, temporary, and discordant.

       Sound is a mental impression made on mortal belief.
The ear does not really hear. Divine Science reveals
18   sound as communicated through the senses of Soul —
through spiritual understanding.

       Mozart experienced more than he expressed. The
21   rapture of his grandest symphonies was never heard. He
was a musician beyond what the world knew.   **Music,**
This was even more strikingly true of Bee-   **rhythm of**
                                          head and
24   thoven, who was so long hopelessly deaf. Men-   **heart**
tal melodies and strains of sweetest music supersede conscious sound. Music is the rhythm of head and heart.
27   Mortal mind is the harp of many strings, discoursing
either discord or harmony according as the hand, which
sweeps over it, is human or divine.

30   Before human knowledge dipped to its depths into a
false sense of things, — into belief in material origins
which discard the one Mind and true source of being, —

it is possible that the impressions from Truth were as   1
distinct as sound, and that they came as sound to the
primitive prophets. If the medium of hearing is wholly   3
spiritual, it is normal and indestructible.

If Enoch's perception had been confined to the evidence
before his material senses, he could never have "walked   6
with God," nor been guided into the demonstration of
life eternal.

Adam, represented in the Scriptures as formed from   9
dust, is an object-lesson for the human mind. The mate-

**Adam and
the senses**

rial senses, like Adam, originate in matter and
return to dust, — are proved non-intelligent.   12
They go out as they came in, for they are still the error,
not the truth of being. When it is learned that the spiritual sense, and not the material, conveys the impressions   15
of Mind to man, then being will be understood and found
to be harmonious.

We bow down to matter, and entertain finite thoughts   18
of God like the pagan idolater. Mortals are inclined to

**Idolatrous
illusions**

fear and to obey what they consider a material
body more than they do a spiritual God. All   21
material knowledge, like the original "tree of knowledge,"
multiplies their pains, for mortal illusions would rob God,
slay man, and meanwhile would spread their table with   24
cannibal tidbits and give thanks.

How transient a sense is mortal sight, when a wound on
the retina may end the power of light and lens! But the   27

**The senses
of Soul**

real sight or sense is not lost. Neither age nor
accident can interfere with the senses of Soul,
and there are no other real senses. It is evident that the   30
body as matter has no sensation of its own, and there is no
oblivion for Soul and its faculties. Spirit's senses are with-

1   out pain, and they are forever at peace. Nothing can hide
    from them the harmony of all things and the might and
3   permanence of Truth.

If Spirit, Soul, could sin or be lost, then being and immortality would be lost, together with all the faculties of
6   Mind; but being cannot be lost while God ex-   **Real being**
    ists. Soul and matter are at variance from the   **never lost**
    very necessity of their opposite natures. Mortals are
9   unacquainted with the reality of existence, because matter
    and mortality do not reflect the facts of Spirit.

Spiritual vision is not subordinate to geometric alti-
12 tudes. Whatever is governed by God, is never for an
    instant deprived of the light and might of intelligence
    and Life.

15 We are sometimes led to believe that darkness is as real
    as light; but Science affirms darkness to be only a mortal
    sense of the absence of light, at the coming of   **Light and**
18 which darkness loses the appearance of reality.   **darkness**
    So sin and sorrow, disease and death, are the suppositional
    absence of Life, God, and flee as phantoms of error before
21 truth and love.

With its divine proof, Science reverses the evidence of
material sense. Every quality and condition of mortality
24 is lost, swallowed up in immortality. Mortal man is the
    antipode of immortal man in origin, in existence, and in his
    relation to God.

27 Because he understood the superiority and immor-
    tality of good, Socrates feared not the hemlock poison.
    Even the faith of his philosophy spurned phys-   **Faith of**
30 ical timidity. Having sought man's spiritual   **Socrates**
    state, he recognized the immortality of man. The igno-
    rance and malice of the age would have killed the vener-

able philosopher because of his faith in Soul and his in- 1
difference to the body.

Who shall say that man is alive to-day, but may be dead 3
to-morrow? What has touched Life, God, to such

strange issues? Here theories cease, and Science unveils the mystery and solves the prob- 6
lem of man. Error bites the heel of truth, but cannot kill
truth. Truth bruises the head of error — destroys error.
Spirituality lays open siege to materialism. On which 9
side are we fighting?

The understanding that the Ego is Mind, and that
there is but one Mind or intelligence, begins at once to 12
destroy the errors of mortal sense and to supply
the truth of immortal sense. This understanding makes the body harmonious; it makes the nerves, 15
bones, brain, etc., servants, instead of masters. If man
is governed by the law of divine Mind, his body is in submission to everlasting Life and Truth and Love. The 18
great mistake of mortals is to suppose that man, God's
image and likeness, is both matter and Spirit, both good
and evil. 21

If the decision were left to the corporeal senses, evil
would appear to be the master of good, and sickness to
be the rule of existence, while health would seem the 24
exception, death the inevitable, and life a paradox. Paul
asked: "What concord hath Christ with Belial?" (2 Corinthians vi. 15.) 27

When you say, "Man's body is material," I say with
Paul: Be "willing rather to be absent from the body,
and to be present with the Lord." Give up 30
your material belief of mind in matter, and
have but one Mind, even God; for this Mind forms its

1   own likeness. The loss of man's identity through the
    understanding which Science confers is impossible; and
3   the notion of such a possibility is more absurd than to
    conclude that individual musical tones are lost in the
    origin of harmony.

6   Medical schools may inform us that the healing work
    of Christian Science and Paul's peculiar Christian con-
    version and experience, — which prove Mind   **Paul's**
9   to be scientifically distinct from matter, — are   **experience**
    indications of unnatural mental and bodily conditions,
    even of catalepsy and hysteria; yet if we turn to the Scrip-
12 tures, what do we read? Why, this: "If a man keep my
    saying, he shall never see death!" and "Henceforth know
    we no man after the flesh!"

15   That scientific methods are superior to others, is
    seen by their effects. When you have once conquered
    a diseased condition of the body through   **Fatigue is**
18 Mind, that condition never recurs, and you   **mental**
    have won a point in Science. When mentality gives
    rest to the body, the next toil will fatigue you less, for
21 you are working out the problem of being in divine meta-
    physics; and in proportion as you understand the con-
    trol which Mind has over so-called matter, you will be
24 able to demonstrate this control. The scientific and
    permanent remedy for fatigue is to learn the power of
    Mind over the body or any illusion of physical weariness,
27 and so destroy this illusion, for matter cannot be weary
    and heavy-laden.
        You say, "Toil fatigues me." But what is this *me?*
30 Is it muscle or mind? Which is tired and so speaks?
    Without mind, could the muscles be tired? Do the
    muscles talk, or do you talk for them? Matter is non-

intelligent. Mortal mind does the false talking, and that
which affirms weariness, made that weariness.

You do not say a wheel is fatigued; and yet the body
is as material as the wheel. If it were not for what the
human mind says of the body, the body, like
the inanimate wheel, would never be weary.
The consciousness of Truth rests us more than hours of
repose in unconsciousness.

Mind never weary

The body is supposed to say, "I am ill." The reports
of sickness may form a coalition with the reports of sin,
and say, "I am malice, lust, appetite, envy,
hate." What renders both sin and sickness
difficult of cure is, that the human mind is the
sinner, disinclined to self-correction, and believing that
the body can be sick independently of mortal mind and
that the divine Mind has no jurisdiction over the body.

Coalition of sin and sickness

Why pray for the recovery of the sick, if you are without faith in God's willingness and ability to heal them?
If you do believe in God, why do you sub-
stitute drugs for the Almighty's power, and
employ means which lead only into material ways of
obtaining help, instead of turning in time of need to
God, divine Love, who is an ever-present help?

Sickness akin to sin

Treat a belief in sickness as you would sin, with sudden
dismissal. Resist the temptation to believe in matter as
intelligent, as having sensation or power.

The Scriptures say, "They that wait upon the Lord
. . . shall run, and not be weary; and they shall walk,
and not faint." The meaning of that passage is not
perverted by applying it literally to moments of fatigue,
for the moral and physical are as one in their results.
When we wake to the truth of being, all disease,

1   pain, weakness, weariness, sorrow, sin, death, will be
unknown, and the mortal dream will forever cease. My
3   method of treating fatigue applies to all bodily ailments,
since Mind should be, and is, supreme, absolute, and
final.

6   In mathematics, we do not multiply when we should
subtract, and then say the product is correct. No more
can we say in Science that muscles give strength,   **Affirmation**
9   that nerves give pain or pleasure, or that matter   **and result**
governs, and then expect that the result will be harmony.
Not muscles, nerves, nor bones, but mortal mind makes
12   the whole body "sick, and the whole heart faint;" whereas
divine Mind heals.

When this is understood, we shall never affirm concern-
15   ing the body what we do not wish to have manifested. We
shall not call the body weak, if we would have it strong;
for the belief in feebleness must obtain in the human
18   mind before it can be made manifest on the body, and
the destruction of the belief will be the removal of its
effects. Science includes no rule of discord, but governs
21   harmoniously. "The wish," says the poet, "is ever father
to the thought."

We may hear a sweet melody, and yet misunderstand
24   the science that governs it. Those who are healed
through metaphysical Science, not compre-   **Scientific**
hending the Principle of the cure, may misun-   **beginning**
27   derstand it, and impute their recovery to change of air or
diet, not rendering to God the honor due to Him alone.
Entire immunity from the belief in sin, suffering, and
30   death may not be reached at this period, but we may look
for an abatement of these evils; and this scientific beginning is in the right direction.

We hear it said: "I exercise daily in the open air. I
take cold baths, in order to overcome a predisposition to
take cold; and yet I have continual colds,
catarrh, and cough." Such admissions ought
to open people's eyes to the inefficacy of material hygiene,
and induce sufferers to look in other directions for cause
and cure.

Instinct is better than misguided reason, as even nature declares. The violet lifts her blue eye to greet the
early spring. The leaves clap their hands as nature's
untired worshippers. The snowbird sings and soars
amid the blasts; he has no catarrh from wet feet, and
procures a summer residence with more ease than a na-
bob. The atmosphere of the earth, kinder than the atmosphere of mortal mind, leaves catarrh to the latter.
Colds, coughs, and contagion are engendered solely by
human theories.

Mortal mind produces its own phenomena, and then
charges them to something else, — like a kitten
glancing into the mirror at itself and thinking
it sees another kitten.

A clergyman once adopted a diet of bread and water
to increase his spirituality. Finding his health failing,
he gave up his abstinence, and advised others never to
try dietetics for growth in grace.

The belief that either fasting or feasting makes men
better morally or physically is one of the fruits of "the
tree of the knowledge of good and evil," con-

cerning which God said, "Thou shalt not eat
of it." Mortal mind forms all conditions of the mortal
body, and controls the stomach, bones, lungs, heart, blood,
etc., as directly as the volition or will moves the hand.

1   I knew a person who when quite a child adopted the
Graham system to cure dyspepsia. For many years, he
3 ate only bread and vegetables, and drank noth-   **Starvation**
ing but water. His dyspepsia increasing, he   **and**
decided that his diet should be more rigid, and   **dyspepsia**
6 thereafter he partook of but one meal in twenty-four
hours, this meal consisting of only a thin slice of bread
without water. His physician also recommended that
9 he should not wet his parched throat until three hours
after eating. He passed many weary years in hunger
and weakness, almost in starvation, and finally made up
12 his mind to die, having exhausted the skill of the doctors,
who kindly informed him that death was indeed his only
alternative. At this point Christian Science saved him,
15 and he is now in perfect health without a vestige of the
old complaint.
He learned that suffering and disease were the self-
18 imposed beliefs of mortals, and not the facts of being;
that God never decreed disease, — never ordained a law
that fasting should be a means of health. Hence semi-
21 starvation is not acceptable to wisdom, and it is equally
far from Science, in which being is sustained by God, Mind.
These truths, opening his eyes, relieved his stomach, and
24 he ate without suffering, "giving God thanks;" but he
never enjoyed his food as he had imagined he would
when, still the slave of matter, he thought of the flesh-
27 pots of Egypt, feeling childhood's hunger and undisci-
plined by self-denial and divine Science.
This new-born understanding, that neither food nor
30 the stomach, without the consent of mortal   **Mind and**
mind, can make one suffer, brings with it an-   **stomach**
other lesson, — that gluttony is a sensual illusion, and

that this phantasm of mortal mind disappears as we better   1
apprehend our spiritual existence and ascend the ladder
of life.   3

This person learned that food affects the body only
as mortal mind has its material methods of working, one
of which is to believe that proper food supplies nutriment   6
and strength to the human system. He learned also that
mortal mind makes a mortal body, whereas Truth regenerates this fleshly mind and feeds thought with the   9
bread of Life.

Food had less power to help or to hurt him after he
had availed himself of the fact that Mind governs man,   12
and he also had less faith in the so-called pleasures and
pains of matter. Taking less thought about what he
should eat or drink, consulting the stomach less about   15
the economy of living and God more, he recovered
strength and flesh rapidly. For many years he had
been kept alive, as was believed, only by the strictest ad-   18
herence to hygiene and drugs, and yet he continued ill
all the while. Now he dropped drugs and material
hygiene, and was well.   21

He learned that a dyspeptic was very far from being
the image and likeness of God, — far from having "dominion over the fish of the sea, and over the fowl of the   24
air, and over the cattle," if eating a bit of animal flesh
could overpower him. He finally concluded that God
never made a dyspeptic, while fear, hygiene, physiology,   27
and physics had made him one, contrary to His commands.

In seeking a cure for dyspepsia consult matter not at

**Life only
in Spirit**   all, and eat what is set before you, "asking   30
no question for conscience sake." We must
destroy the false belief that life and intelligence are in

1 matter, and plant ourselves upon what is pure and perfect. Paul said, "Walk in the Spirit, and ye shall not
3 fulfil the lust of the flesh." Sooner or later we shall learn
that the fetters of man's finite capacity are forged by the
illusion that he lives in body instead of in Soul, in matter
6 instead of in Spirit.

Matter does not express Spirit. God is infinite omnipresent Spirit. If Spirit is *all* and is everywhere, what
9 and where is matter? Remember that truth
is greater than error, and we cannot put the
greater into the less. Soul is Spirit, and Spirit is greater
12 than body. If Spirit were once within the body, Spirit
would be finite, and therefore could not be Spirit.

Soul greater
than body

The question, "What is Truth," convulses the world.
15 Many are ready to meet this inquiry with the assurance
which comes of understanding; but more are
blinded by their old illusions, and try to "give
18 it pause." "If the blind lead the blind, both shall fall into
the ditch."

The question
of the ages

The efforts of error to answer this question by some
21 *ology* are vain. Spiritual rationality and free thought accompany approaching Science, and cannot be put down.
They will emancipate humanity, and supplant unscientific
24 means and so-called laws.

Peals that should startle the slumbering thought from
its erroneous dream are partially unheeded; but the last
27 trump has not sounded, or this would not be
so. Marvels, calamities, and sin will much
more abound as truth urges upon mortals its resisted
30 claims; but the awful daring of sin destroys sin, and
foreshadows the triumph of truth. God will over-
turn, until "He come whose right it is." Longevity

Heralds of
Science

is increasing and the power of sin diminishing, for the   1
world feels the alterative effect of truth through every
pore.   3

As the crude footprints of the past disappear from the
dissolving paths of the present, we shall better understand
the Science which governs these changes, and shall plant   6
our feet on firmer ground. Every sensuous pleasure or
pain is self-destroyed through suffering. There should
be painless progress, attended by life and peace instead   9
of discord and death.

In the record of nineteen centuries, there are sects
many but not enough Christianity. Centuries ago re-   12

**Sectarianism
and
opposition**

ligionists were ready to hail an anthropomorphic God, and array His vicegerent with pomp
and splendor; but this was not the manner   15
of truth's appearing. Of old the cross was truth's central sign, and it is to-day. The modern lash is less
material than the Roman scourge, but it is equally as   18
cutting. Cold disdain, stubborn resistance, opposition
from church, state laws, and the press, are still the har-
bingers of truth's full-orbed appearing.   21

A higher and more practical Christianity, demonstrating justice and meeting the needs of mortals in sickness
and in health, stands at the door of this age, knocking   24
for admission. Will you open or close the door upon this
angel visitant, who cometh in the quiet of meekness, as he
came of old to the patriarch at noonday?   27

Truth brings the elements of liberty. On its banner
is the Soul-inspired motto, "Slavery is abolished." The

**Mental
emancipation**

power of God brings deliverance to the cap-   30
tive. No power can withstand divine Love.
What is this supposed power, which opposes itself to God?

Whence cometh it? What is it that binds man with iron
shackles to sin, sickness, and death? Whatever enslaves
man is opposed to the divine government. Truth makes
man free.

You may know when first Truth leads by the few-
ness and faithfulness of its followers. Thus it is that
the march of time bears onward freedom's
banner. The powers of this world will fight,
and will command their sentinels not to let truth pass
the guard until it subscribes to their systems; but Science,
heeding not the pointed bayonet, marches on. There is
always some tumult, but there is a rallying to truth's
standard.

Truth's
ordeal

The history of our country, like all history, illustrates
the might of Mind, and shows human power to be propor-
tionate to its embodiment of right thinking. A
few immortal sentences, breathing the omnipotence of divine justice, have been potent to break despotic
fetters and abolish the whipping-post and slave market;
but oppression neither went down in blood, nor did the
breath of freedom come from the cannon's mouth. Love
is the liberator.

Immortal
sentences

Legally to abolish unpaid servitude in the United
States was hard; but the abolition of mental slavery is
a more difficult task. The despotic tendencies, inherent in mortal mind and always germinating in new forms of tyranny, must be rooted out
through the action of the divine Mind.

Slavery
abolished

Men and women of all climes and races are still in
bondage to material sense, ignorant how to obtain their
freedom. The rights of man were vindicated in a single
section and on the lowest plane of human life, when Afri-

can slavery was abolished in our land. That was only   1
prophetic of further steps towards the banishment of a
world-wide slavery, found on higher planes of existence   3
and under more subtle and depraving forms.

The voice of God in behalf of the African slave was
still echoing in our land, when the voice of the herald of   6

**Liberty's
crusade**

this new crusade sounded the keynote of universal freedom, asking a fuller acknowledg-
ment of the rights of man as a Son of God, demanding   9
that the fetters of sin, sickness, and death be stricken
from the human mind and that its freedom be won, not
through human warfare, not with bayonet and blood, but   12
through Christ's divine Science.

God has built a higher platform of human rights, and
He has built it on diviner claims. These claims are not   15

**Cramping
systems**

made through code or creed, but in demonstration of "on earth peace, good-will toward men."
Human codes, scholastic theology, material medicine and   18
hygiene, fetter faith and spiritual understanding. Divine
Science rends asunder these fetters, and man's birthright
of sole allegiance to his Maker asserts itself.   21

I saw before me the sick, wearing out years of servitude to an unreal master in the belief that the body governed them, rather than Mind.   24

The lame, the deaf, the dumb, the blind, the sick, the
sensual, the sinner, I wished to save from the slavery of

**House of
bondage**

their own beliefs and from the educational   27
systems of the Pharaohs, who to-day, as of
yore, hold the children of Israel in bondage. I saw before me the awful conflict, the Red Sea and the wilder-   30
ness; but I pressed on through faith in God, trusting
Truth, the strong deliverer, to guide me into the land

1 of Christian Science, where fetters fall and the rights of
man are fully known and acknowledged.

3 I saw that the law of mortal belief included all error,
and that, even as oppressive laws are disputed and mortals are taught their right to freedom, so the
6 claims of the enslaving senses must be denied and superseded. The law of the divine Mind must
end human bondage, or mortals will continue unaware
9 of man's inalienable rights and in subjection to hopeless slavery, because some public teachers permit
an ignorance of divine power, — an ignorance that
12 is the foundation of continued bondage and of human
suffering.

*Higher law
ends bondage*

Discerning the rights of man, we cannot fail to fore-
15 see the doom of all oppression. Slavery is not the legitimate state of man. God made man free.
Paul said, "I was free born." All men should
18 be free. "Where the Spirit of the Lord is, there is liberty." Love and Truth make free, but evil and error
lead into captivity.

*Native
freedom*

21 Christian Science raises the standard of liberty and
cries: "Follow me! Escape from the bondage of sickness, sin, and death!" Jesus marked out the
24 way. Citizens of the world, accept the "glorious liberty of the children of God," and be free! This
is your divine right. The illusion of material sense, not
27 divine law, has bound you, entangled your free limbs,
crippled your capacities, enfeebled your body, and de-
faced the tablet of your being.

*Standard
of liberty*

30 If God had instituted material laws to govern man,
disobedience to which would have made man ill, Jesus
would not have disregarded those laws by healing in

direct opposition to them and in defiance of all material   1
conditions.

The transmission of disease or of certain idiosyncra-   3
sies of mortal mind would be impossible if this great fact

No fleshly
heredity

of being were learned, — namely, that nothing
inharmonious can enter being, for Life *is* God.   6
Heredity is a prolific subject for mortal belief to pin theories upon; but if we learn that nothing is real but the
right, we shall have no dangerous inheritances, and fleshly   9
ills will disappear.

The enslavement of man is not legitimate. It will
cease when man enters into his heritage of freedom, his   12

God-given
dominion

God-given dominion over the material senses.
Mortals will some day assert their freedom in
the name of Almighty God. Then they will control their   15
own bodies through the understanding of divine Science.
Dropping their present beliefs, they will recognize harmony as the spiritual reality and discord as the material   18
unreality.

If we follow the command of our Master, "Take no
thought for your life," we shall never depend on bodily   21
conditions, structure, or economy, but we shall be masters
of the body, dictate its terms, and form and control it with
Truth.   24

There is no power apart from God. Omnipotence has
all-power, and to acknowledge any other power is to dis-

Priestly pride
humbled

honor God. The humble Nazarene overthrew   27
the supposition that sin, sickness, and death
have power. He proved them powerless. It should have
humbled the pride of the priests, when they saw the dem-   30
onstration of Christianity excel the influence of their dead
faith and ceremonies.

1   If Mind is not the master of sin, sickness, and death,
they are immortal, for it is already proved that mat-
3   ter has not destroyed them, but is their basis and
support.

    We should hesitate to say that Jehovah sins or suffers;
6   but if sin and suffering are realities of being, whence did
they emanate? God made all that was made,   **No union of**
and Mind signifies God, — infinity, not finity.   **opposites**
9   Not far removed from infidelity is the belief which
unites such opposites as sickness and health, holiness
and unholiness, calls both the offspring of spirit, and
12   at the same time admits that Spirit is God, — virtually declaring Him good in one instance and evil in
another.

15   By universal consent, mortal belief has constituted
itself a law to bind mortals to sickness, sin, and death.
This customary belief is misnamed material   **Self-**
18   law, and the individual who upholds it is mis-   **constituted**
taken in theory and in practice. The so-called law of   **law**
mortal mind, conjectural and speculative, is made void
21   by the law of immortal Mind, and false law should be
trampled under foot.

    If God causes man to be sick, sickness must be good,
24   and its opposite, health, must be evil, for all that He
makes is good and will stand forever. If the   **Sickness from**
transgression of God's law produces sickness, it   **mortal mind**
27   is right to be sick; and we cannot if we would, and should
not if we could, annul the decrees of wisdom. It is the
transgression of a belief of mortal mind, not of a law of
30   matter nor of divine Mind, which causes the belief of sickness. The remedy is Truth, not matter, — the truth that
disease is *unreal.*

If sickness is real, it belongs to immortality; if true,   1
it is a part of Truth. Would you attempt with drugs,
or without, to destroy a quality or condition of Truth?   3
But if sickness and sin are illusions, the awakening from
this mortal dream, or illusion, will bring us into health,
holiness, and immortality. This awakening is the for-   6
ever coming of Christ, the advanced appearing of Truth,
which casts out error and heals the sick. This is the salvation which comes through God, the divine Principle,   9
Love, as demonstrated by Jesus.

It would be contrary to our highest ideas of God to
suppose Him capable of first arranging law and causation   12
so as to bring about certain evil results, and

God never inconsistent

then punishing the helpless victims of His volition for doing what they could not avoid doing. Good   15
is not, cannot be, the author of experimental sins. God,
good, can no more produce sickness than goodness can
cause evil and health occasion disease.   18

Does wisdom make blunders which must afterwards
be rectified by man? Does a law of God produce sick-

Mental narcotics

ness, and can man put that law under his feet   21
by healing sickness? According to Holy Writ,
the sick are never really healed by drugs, hygiene, or any
material method. These merely evade the question.   24
They are soothing syrups to put children to sleep, satisfy
mortal belief, and quiet fear.

We think that we are healed when a disease disap-   27
pears, though it is liable to reappear; but we are never

The true healing

thoroughly healed until the liability to be
ill is removed. So-called mortal mind or the   30
mind of mortals being the remote, predisposing, and
the exciting cause of all suffering, the cause of disease

1   must be obliterated through Christ in divine Science, or
the so-called physical senses will get the victory.

3   Unless an ill is rightly met and fairly overcome by
Truth, the ill is never conquered. If God destroys not
sin, sickness, and death, they are not de-

Destruction of all evil

6   stroyed in the mind of mortals, but seem to
this so-called mind to be immortal. What God cannot
do, man need not attempt. If God heals not the sick,

9   they are not healed, for no lesser power equals the infinite
All-power; but God, Truth, Life, Love, does heal the
sick through the prayer of the righteous.

12   If God makes sin, if good produces evil, if truth results
in error, then Science and Christianity are helpless; but
there are no antagonistic powers nor laws, spiritual or

15   material, creating and governing man through perpetual
warfare. God is not the author of mortal discords.
Therefore we accept the conclusion that discords have

18   only a fabulous existence, are mortal beliefs which divine
Truth and Love destroy.

      To hold yourself superior to sin, because God made

21   you superior to it and governs man, is true wisdom. To
fear sin is to misunderstand the power of Love
and the divine Science of being in man's rela-

Superiority to sickness and sin

24   tion to God, — to doubt His government and
distrust His omnipotent care. To hold yourself superior
to sickness and death is equally wise, and is in accordance

27   with divine Science. To fear them is impossible, when
you fully apprehend God and know that they are no part
of His creation.

30   Man, governed by his Maker, having no other Mind, —
planted on the Evangelist's statement that "all things
were made by Him [the Word of God]; and without

Him was not anything made that was made," — can   1
triumph over sin, sickness, and death.

Many theories relative to God and man neither make   3
man harmonious nor God lovable. The beliefs we com-

monly entertain about happiness and life
afford no scatheless and permanent evidence   6
of either. Security for the claims of harmonious and
eternal being is found only in divine Science.

Scripture informs us that "with God all things are   9
possible," — all good is possible to Spirit; but our prevalent theories practically deny this, and make healing
possible only through matter. These theories must be   12
untrue, for the Scripture is true. Christianity is not
false, but religions which contradict its Principle are
false.   15

In our age Christianity is again demonstrating the
power of divine Principle, as it did over nineteen hundred years ago, by healing the sick and triumphing over   18
death. Jesus never taught that drugs, food, air, and exercise could make a man healthy, or that they could destroy human life; nor did he illustrate these errors by his   21
practice. He referred man's harmony to Mind, not to
matter, and never tried to make of none effect the sentence of God, which sealed God's condemnation of sin,   24
sickness, and death.

In the sacred sanctuary of Truth are voices of solemn import, but we heed them not. It is only when the   27

so-called pleasures and pains of sense pass
away in our lives, that we find unquestion-
able signs of the burial of error and the resurrection to   30
spiritual life.

There is neither place nor opportunity in Science for error

1   of any sort. Every day makes its demands upon us for
     higher proofs rather than professions of Christian power.
3   These proofs consist solely in the destruction   *Profession*
and proof
     of sin, sickness, and death by the power of
     Spirit, as Jesus destroyed them. This is an element of
6   progress, and progress is the law of God, whose law de-
     mands of us only what we can certainly fulfil.

     In the midst of imperfection, perfection is seen and
9   acknowledged only by degrees. The ages must slowly
     work up to perfection. How long it must be   *Perfection*
     before we arrive at the demonstration of scien-   *gained*
12   tific being, no man knoweth, — not even "the   *slowly*
     Son but the Father;" but the false claim of error con-
     tinues its delusions until the goal of goodness is assidu-
15   ously earned and won.

     Already the shadow of His right hand rests upon the
     hour. Ye who can discern the face of the sky, — the
18   sign material, — how much more should ye   *Christ's*
     discern the sign mental, and compass the de-   *mission*
     struction of sin and sickness by overcoming the thoughts
21   which produce them, and by understanding the spiritual
     idea which corrects and destroys them. To reveal this
     truth was our Master's mission to all mankind, including
24   the hearts which rejected him.

     When numbers have been divided according to a fixed
     rule, the quotient is not more unquestionable than the
27   scientific tests I have made of the effects of   *Efficacy*
     truth upon the sick. The counter fact rela-   *of truth*
     tive to any disease is required to cure it. The utterance
30   of truth is designed to rebuke and destroy error. Why
     should truth not be efficient in sickness, which is solely
     the result of inharmony?

Spiritual draughts heal, while material lotions interfere   1
with truth, even as ritualism and creed hamper spirituality. If we trust matter, we distrust Spirit.   3

Whatever inspires with wisdom, Truth, or Love — be
it song, sermon, or Science — blesses the human family

Crumbs of comfort

with crumbs of comfort from Christ's table,   6
feeding the hungry and giving living waters to
the thirsty.

We should become more familiar with good than with   9
evil, and guard against false beliefs as watchfully as we

Hospitality to health and good

bar our doors against the approach of thieves
and murderers. We should love our enemies   12
and help them on the basis of the Golden
Rule; but avoid casting pearls before those who trample
them under foot, thereby robbing both themselves and   15
others.

If mortals would keep proper ward over mortal mind,
the brood of evils which infest it would be cleared out.   18

Cleansing the mind

We must begin with this so-called mind and
empty it of sin and sickness, or sin and sickness will never cease. The present codes of human   21
systems disappoint the weary searcher after a divine
theology, adequate to the right education of human
thought.   24

Sin and disease must be thought before they can be
manifested. You must control evil thoughts in the first
instance, or they will control you in the second. Jesus   27
declared that to look with desire on forbidden objects was
to break a moral precept. He laid great stress on the
action of the human mind, unseen to the senses.   30

Evil thoughts and aims reach no farther and do no more
harm than one's belief permits. Evil thoughts, lusts, and

malicious purposes cannot go forth, like wandering pollen, from one human mind to another, finding unsuspected
3 lodgment, if virtue and truth build a strong defence. Better suffer a doctor infected with smallpox to attend you than to be treated mentally by one who does not obey
6 the requirements of divine Science.

The teachers of schools and the readers in churches should be selected with as direct reference to their
9 morals as to their learning or their correct reading. Nurseries of character should be strongly garrisoned with virtue. School-examinations are
12 one-sided; it is not so much academic education, as a moral and spiritual culture, which lifts one higher. The pure and uplifting thoughts of the teacher, constantly
15 imparted to pupils, will reach higher than the heavens of astronomy; while the debased and unscrupulous mind, though adorned with gems of scholarly attainment, will
18 degrade the characters it should inform and elevate.

Teachers' functions

Physicians, whom the sick employ in their helplessness, should be models of virtue. They should be wise spir-
21 itual guides to health and hope. To the trem- blers on the brink of death, who understand not the divine Truth which is Life and perpetuates being,
24 physicians should be able to teach it. Then when the soul is willing and the flesh weak, the patient's feet may be planted on the rock Christ Jesus, the true idea of spiritual
27 power.

Physicians' privilege

Clergymen, occupying the watchtowers of the world, should uplift the standard of Truth. They should so raise
30 their hearers spiritually, that their listeners will love to grapple with a new, right idea and broaden their concepts. Love of Christianity, rather

Clergymen's duty

than love of popularity, should stimulate clerical labor   1
and progress. Truth should emanate from the pulpit,
but never be strangled there. A special privilege is vested   3
in the ministry. How shall it be used? Sacredly, in the
interests of humanity, not of sect.

Is it not professional reputation and emolument rather   6
than the dignity of God's laws, which many leaders seek?
Do not inferior motives induce the infuriated attacks on
individuals, who reiterate Christ's teachings in support   9
of his proof by example that the divine Mind heals sickness as well as sin?

A mother is the strongest educator, either for or   12
against crime. Her thoughts form the embryo of another mortal mind, and unconsciously mould

A mother's
responsibility

it, either after a model odious to herself or   15
through divine influence, "according to the pattern
showed to thee in the mount." Hence the importance
of Christian Science, from which we learn of the one   18
Mind and of the availability of good as the remedy for
every woe.

Children should obey their parents; insubordination   21
is an evil, blighting the buddings of self-government.

Children's
tractability

Parents should teach their children at the
earliest possible period the truths of health   24
and holiness. Children are more tractable than adults,
and learn more readily to love the simple verities that will
make them happy and good.   27

Jesus loved little children because of their freedom
from wrong and their receptiveness of right. While
age is halting between two opinions or battling with   30
false beliefs, youth makes easy and rapid strides towards
Truth.

1 A little girl, who had occasionally listened to my explanations, badly wounded her finger. She seemed not
3 to notice it. On being questioned about it she answered
ingenuously, "There is no sensation in matter." Bound-
ing off with laughing eyes, she presently added, "Mamma,
6 my finger is not a bit sore."

It might have been months or years before her parents
would have laid aside their drugs, or reached the mental
9 height their little daughter so naturally attained. The more stubborn beliefs and theories of parents often choke the good seed in the minds of
12 themselves and their offspring. Superstition, like "the
fowls of the air," snatches away the good seed before it
has sprouted.

Soil and seed

15 Children should be taught the Truth-cure, Christian
Science, among their first lessons, and kept from discussing or entertaining theories or thoughts about
18 sickness. To prevent the experience of error
and its sufferings, keep out of the minds of your children
either sinful or diseased thoughts. The latter should
21 be excluded on the same principle as the former. This
makes Christian Science early available.

Teaching children

Some invalids are unwilling to know the facts or to
24 hear about the fallacy of matter and its supposed laws.
They devote themselves a little longer to their
material gods, cling to a belief in the life and
27 intelligence of matter, and expect this error to do more
for them than they are willing to admit the only living and
true God can do. Impatient at your explanation, unwill-
30 ing to investigate the Science of Mind which would rid
them of their complaints, they hug false beliefs and suffer
the delusive consequences.

Deluded invalids

Motives and acts are not rightly valued before they are   1
understood. It is well to wait till those whom you would
benefit are ready for the blessing, for Science   3
is working changes in personal character as
well as in the material universe.

To obey the Scriptural command, "Come out from   6
among them, and be ye separate," is to incur society's
frown; but this frown, more than flatteries, enables one
to be Christian. Losing her crucifix, the Roman Catholic   9
girl said, "I have nothing left but Christ." "If God be
for us, who can be against us?"

To fall away from Truth in times of persecution, shows   12
that we never understood Truth. From out the bridal
chamber of wisdom there will come the warn-

ing, "I know you not." Unimproved op-   15
portunities will rebuke us when we attempt to claim the
benefits of an experience we have not made our own, try
to reap the harvest we have not sown, and wish to enter   18
unlawfully into the labors of others. Truth often remains
unsought, until we seek this remedy for human woe because we suffer severely from error.   21

Attempts to conciliate society and so gain dominion over
mankind, arise from worldly weakness. He who leaves
all for Christ forsakes popularity and gains Christianity.   24

Society is a foolish juror, listening only to one side of
the case. Justice often comes too late to secure a verdict.

People with mental work before them have   27
no time for gossip about false law or testimony.
To reconstruct timid justice and place the fact above the
falsehood, is the work of time.   30

The cross is the central emblem of history. It is the
lodestar in the demonstration of Christian healing, — the

1 demonstration by which sin and sickness are destroyed.
The sects, which endured the lash of their predecessors,
3 in their turn lay it upon those who are in advance of
creeds.

Take away wealth, fame, and social organizations,
6 which weigh not one jot in the balance of God, and we
get clearer views of Principle. Break up   Right views
cliques, level wealth with honesty, let worth   of humanity
9 be judged according to wisdom, and we get better views
of humanity.

The wicked man is not the ruler of his upright
12 neighbor. Let it be understood that success in error is
defeat in Truth. The watchword of Christian Science
is Scriptural: "Let the wicked forsake his way, and the
15 unrighteous man his thoughts."

To ascertain our progress, we must learn where our
affections are placed and whom we acknowledge and
18 obey as God. If divine Love is becoming   Standpoint
nearer, dearer, and more real to us, matter is   revealed
then submitting to Spirit. The objects we pursue and
21 the spirit we manifest reveal our standpoint, and show
what we are winning.

Mortal mind is the acknowledged seat of human mo-
24 tives. It forms material concepts and produces every
discordant action of the body. If action pro-   Antagonistic
ceeds from the divine Mind, action is harmo-   sources
27 nious. If it comes from erring mortal mind, it is discordant and ends in sin, sickness, death. Those two opposite
sources never mingle in fount or stream. The perfect
30 Mind sends forth perfection, for God is Mind. Imperfect mortal mind sends forth its own resemblances, of
which the wise man said, "All is vanity."

Nature voices natural, spiritual law and divine Love,   1
but human belief misinterprets nature. Arctic regions,
sunny tropics, giant hills, winged winds,   3
mighty billows, verdant vales, festive flowers,
and glorious heavens, — all point to Mind, the spiritual
intelligence they reflect. The floral apostles are hiero-   6
glyphs of Deity. Suns and planets teach grand lessons.
The stars make night beautiful, and the leaflet turns naturally towards the light.   9

In the order of Science, in which the Principle is above
what it reflects, all is one grand concord. Change this

statement, suppose Mind to be governed by   12
matter or Soul in body, and you lose the keynote of being, and there is continual discord. Mind is
perpetual motion. Its symbol is the sphere. The rota-   15
tions and revolutions of the universe of Mind go on
eternally.

Mortals move onward towards good or evil as time   18
glides on. If mortals are not progressive, past failures
will be repeated until all wrong work is ef-

faced or rectified. If at present satisfied with   21
wrong-doing, we must learn to loathe it. If at present
content with idleness, we must become dissatisfied with
it. Remember that mankind must sooner or later, either   24
by suffering or by Science, be convinced of the error that
is to be overcome.

In trying to undo the errors of sense one must pay fully   27
and fairly the utmost farthing, until all error is finally
brought into subjection to Truth. The divine method
of paying sin's wages involves unwinding one's snarls,   30
and learning from experience how to divide between sense
and Soul.

1   "Whom the Lord loveth He chasteneth." He, who
knows God's will or the demands of divine Science and
3   obeys them, incurs the hostility of envy; and he who
refuses obedience to God, is chastened by Love.

Sensual treasures are laid up "where moth and rust
6   doth corrupt." Mortality is their doom. Sin breaks in
upon them, and carries off their fleeting joys.   **The doom**
The sensualist's affections are as imaginary,   **of sin**
9   whimsical, and unreal as his pleasures. Falsehood, envy,
hypocrisy, malice, hate, revenge, and so forth, steal away
the treasures of Truth. Stripped of its coverings, what
12 a mocking spectacle is sin!

The Bible teaches transformation of the body by the
renewal of Spirit. Take away the spiritual signification
15 of Scripture, and that compilation can do no   **Spirit**
more for mortals than can moonbeams to melt   **transforms**
a river of ice. The error of the ages is preaching without
18 practice.

The substance of all devotion is the reflection and
demonstration of divine Love, healing sickness and
21 destroying sin. Our Master said, "If ye love me, keep
my commandments."

One's aim, a point beyond faith, should be to find the
24 footsteps of Truth, the way to health and holiness. We
should strive to reach the Horeb height where God is revealed; and the corner-stone of all spiritual building is
27 purity. The baptism of Spirit, washing the body of all
the impurities of flesh, signifies that the pure in heart
see God and are approaching spiritual Life and its
30 demonstration.

It is "easier for a camel to go through the eye of a
needle," than for sinful beliefs to enter the kingdom of

heaven, eternal harmony. Through repentance, spiritual   1
baptism, and regeneration, mortals put off their material

Spiritual baptism

beliefs and false individuality. It is only a   3
question of time when "they shall all know
Me [God], from the least of them unto the greatest."
Denial of the claims of matter is a great step towards   6
the joys of Spirit, towards human freedom and the final
triumph over the body.

There is but one way to heaven, harmony, and Christ   9
in divine Science shows us this way. It is to know no

The one only way

other reality — to have no other consciousness of life — than good, God and His reflec-   12
tion, and to rise superior to the so-called pain and pleasure
of the senses.

Self-love is more opaque than a solid body. In pa-   15
tient obedience to a patient God, let us labor to dissolve with the universal solvent of Love the adamant
of error, — self-will, self-justification, and self-love, —   18
which wars against spirituality and is the law of sin
and death.

The vesture of Life is Truth. According to the Bible,   21
the facts of being are commonly misconstrued, for it is

Divided vestments

written: "They parted my raiment among
them, and for my vesture they did cast lots."   24
The divine Science of man is woven into one web of
consistency without seam or rent. Mere speculation or
superstition appropriates no part of the divine vesture,   27
while inspiration restores every part of the Christly garment of righteousness.

The finger-posts of divine Science show the way our   30
Master trod, and require of Christians the proof which
he gave, instead of mere profession. We may hide

1 spiritual ignorance from the world, but we can never
succeed in the Science and demonstration of spiritual
3 good through ignorance or hypocrisy.

The divine Love, which made harmless the poisonous
viper, which delivered men from the boiling oil, from
6 the fiery furnace, from the jaws of the lion,   **Ancient**
can heal the sick in every age and triumph   **and modern**
over sin and death. It crowned the demon-   **miracles**
9 strations of Jesus with unsurpassed power and love. But
the same "Mind . . . which was also in Christ Jesus"
must always accompany the letter of Science in order to
12 confirm and repeat the ancient demonstrations of prophets
and apostles. That those wonders are not more commonly repeated to-day, arises not so much from lack of
15 desire as from lack of spiritual growth.

The clay cannot reply to the potter. The head, heart,
lungs, and limbs do not inform us that they are dizzy,
18 diseased, consumptive, or lame. If this in-   **Mental**
formation is conveyed, mortal mind conveys   **telegraphy**
it. Neither immortal and unerring Mind nor matter,
21 the inanimate substratum of mortal mind, can carry
on such telegraphy; for God is "of purer eyes than
to behold evil," and matter has neither intelligence nor
24 sensation.

Truth has no consciousness of error. Love has no
sense of hatred. Life has no partnership   **Annihilation**
27 with death. Truth, Life, and Love are a law   **of error**
of annihilation to everything unlike themselves, because
they declare nothing except God.
30 Sickness, sin, and death are not the fruits of Life.
They are inharmonies which Truth destroys. Perfection
does not animate imperfection. Inasmuch as God is

good and the fount of all being, He does not produce
moral or physical deformity; therefore such deformity is
not real, but is illusion, the mirage of error.
Divine Science reveals these grand facts. On
their basis Jesus demonstrated Life, never
fearing nor obeying error in any form.

Deformity and perfection

If we were to derive all our conceptions of man from
what is seen between the cradle and the grave, happiness and goodness would have no abiding-place in man,
and the worms would rob him of the flesh; but Paul
writes: "The law of the Spirit of life in Christ Jesus hath
made me free from the law of sin and death."

Man undergoing birth, maturity, and decay is like the
beasts and vegetables, — subject to laws of decay. If
man were dust in his earliest stage of existence, we might admit the hypothesis that he
returns eventually to his primitive condition;
but man was never more nor less than man.

Man never less than man

If man flickers out in death or springs from matter into
being, there must be an instant when God is without His
entire manifestation, — when there is no full reflection
of the infinite Mind.

Man in Science is neither young nor old. He has
neither birth nor death. He is not a beast, a vegetable,
nor a migratory mind. He does not pass from
matter to Mind, from the mortal to the immortal, from evil to good, or from good to evil. Such
admissions cast us headlong into darkness and dogma.
Even Shakespeare's poetry pictures age as infancy, as
helplessness and decadence, instead of assigning to man
the everlasting grandeur and immortality of development,
power, and prestige.

Man not evolved

1
3
6
9
12
15
18
21
24
27
30

1   The error of thinking that we are growing old, and the
benefits of destroying that illusion, are illustrated in a
3   sketch from the history of an English woman, published
in the London medical magazine called The Lancet.

    Disappointed in love in her early years, she became
6   insane and lost all account of time. Believing that she
was still living in the same hour which parted   **Perpetual**
her from her lover, taking no note of years,   **youth**
9   she stood daily before the window watching for her
lover's coming. In this mental state she remained young.
Having no consciousness of time, she literally grew no
12   older. Some American travellers saw her when she was
seventy-four, and supposed her to be a young woman.
She had no care-lined face, no wrinkles nor gray hair, but
15   youth sat gently on cheek and brow. Asked to guess her
age, those unacquainted with her history conjectured that
she must be under twenty.

18   This instance of youth preserved furnishes a useful
hint, upon which a Franklin might work with more certainty than when he coaxed the enamoured lightning
21   from the clouds. Years had not made her old, because
she had taken no cognizance of passing time nor thought
of herself as growing old. The bodily results of her belief
24   that she was young manifested the influence of such a belief. She could not age while believing herself young, for
the mental state governed the physical.

27   Impossibilities never occur. One instance like the
foregoing proves it possible to be young at seventy-four;
and the primary of that illustration makes it plain that
30   decrepitude is not according to law, nor is it a necessity of
nature, but an illusion.

    The infinite never began nor will it ever end. Mind

and its formations can never be annihilated. Man is not
a pendulum, swinging between evil and good, joy and
sorrow, sickness and health, life and death.

Life and its faculties are not measured by
calendars. The perfect and immortal are the eternal
likeness of their Maker. Man is by no means a material
germ rising from the imperfect and endeavoring to reach
Spirit above his origin. The stream rises no higher than
its source.

The measurement of life by solar years robs youth and
gives ugliness to age. The radiant sun of virtue and truth
coexists with being. Manhood is its eternal noon, un-
dimmed by a declining sun. As the physical and material, the transient sense of beauty fades, the radiance of
Spirit should dawn upon the enraptured sense with bright
and imperishable glories.

Never record ages. Chronological data are no part
of the vast forever. Time-tables of birth and death are

so many conspiracies against manhood and
womanhood. Except for the error of measuring and limiting all that is good and beautiful, man
would enjoy more than threescore years and ten and
still maintain his vigor, freshness, and promise. Man,
governed by immortal Mind, is always beautiful and
grand. Each succeeding year unfolds wisdom, beauty,
and holiness.

Life is eternal. We should find this out, and begin the
demonstration thereof. Life and goodness are immortal.

Let us then shape our views of existence into
loveliness, freshness, and continuity, rather
than into age and blight.

Acute and chronic beliefs reproduce their own types.

1   The acute belief of physical life comes on at a remote
period, and is not so disastrous as the chronic belief.

3   I have seen age regain two of the elements it had lost,
sight and teeth. A woman of eighty-five, whom I knew,
had a return of sight. Another woman at

Eyes
and teeth
renewed

6   ninety had new teeth, incisors, cuspids, bi-
cuspids, and one molar. One man at sixty
had retained his full set of upper and lower teeth without

9   a decaying cavity.

     Beauty, as well as truth, is eternal; but the beauty
of material things passes away, fading and fleeting as

12   mortal belief. Custom, education, and fashion
form the transient standards of mortals. Immortality, exempt from age or decay, has a glory of its

Eternal
beauty

15   own, — the radiance of Soul. Immortal men and women
are models of spiritual sense, drawn by perfect Mind
and reflecting those higher conceptions of loveliness

18   which transcend all material sense.

     Comeliness and grace are independent of matter. Be-
ing possesses its qualities before they are perceived hu-

21   manly. Beauty is a thing of life, which
dwells forever in the eternal Mind and reflects the charms of His goodness in expression, form,

The divine
loveliness

24   outline, and color. It is Love which paints the petal
with myriad hues, glances in the warm sunbeam, arches
the cloud with the bow of beauty, blazons the night with

27   starry gems, and covers earth with loveliness.

     The embellishments of the person are poor substitutes
for the charms of being, shining resplendent and eternal

30   over age and decay.

     The recipe for beauty is to have less illusion and
more Soul, to retreat from the belief of pain or pleasure

in the body into the unchanging calm and glorious free- 1
dom of spiritual harmony.

Love never loses sight of loveliness. Its halo rests upon 3
its object. One marvels that a friend can ever seem less
than beautiful. Men and women of riper

years and larger lessons ought to ripen into 6
health and immortality, instead of lapsing into darkness
or gloom. Immortal Mind feeds the body with supernal
freshness and fairness, supplying it with beautiful images 9
of thought and destroying the woes of sense which each
day brings to a nearer tomb.

The sculptor turns from the marble to his model in 12
order to perfect his conception. We are all sculptors,
working at various forms, moulding and chisel-

ing thought. What is the model before mortal 15
mind? Is it imperfection, joy, sorrow, sin, suffering?
Have you accepted the mortal model? Are you reproducing it? Then you are haunted in your work by vicious 18
sculptors and hideous forms. Do you not hear from all
mankind of the imperfect model? The world is holding
it before your gaze continually. The result is that you 21
are liable to follow those lower patterns, limit your life-
work, and adopt into your experience the angular outline
and deformity of matter models. 24

To remedy this, we must first turn our gaze in the right
direction, and then walk that way. We must form perfect

models in thought and look at them continually, 27
or we shall never carve them out in grand and
noble lives. Let unselfishness, goodness, mercy, justice,
health, holiness, love — the kingdom of heaven — reign 30
within us, and sin, disease, and death will diminish until
they finally disappear.

1   Let us accept Science, relinquish all theories based on
sense-testimony, give up imperfect models and illusive
3   ideals; and so let us have one God, one Mind, and that
one perfect, producing His own models of excellence.
   Let the "male and female" of God's creating appear.
6   Let us feel the divine energy of Spirit, bringing us into
newness of life and recognizing no mortal nor   **Renewed**
material power as able to destroy. Let us re-   **selfhood**
9   joice that we are subject to the divine "powers that be."
Such is the true Science of being. Any other theory of
Life, or God, is delusive and mythological.
12   Mind is not the author of matter, and the creator of
ideas is not the creator of illusions. Either there is no
omnipotence, or omnipotence is the only power. God is
15   the infinite, and infinity never began, will never end, and
includes nothing unlike God. Whence then is soulless
matter?
18   Life is, like Christ, "the same yesterday, and to-day,
and forever." Organization and time have nothing to do
with Life. You say, "I dreamed last night."   **Illusive**
21   What a mistake is that! The I is Spirit. God   **dreams**
never slumbers, and His likeness never dreams. Mortals
are the Adam dreamers.
24   Sleep and apathy are phases of the dream that life, substance, and intelligence are material. The mortal night-
dream is sometimes nearer the fact of being than are the
27   thoughts of mortals when awake. The night-dream has
less matter as its accompaniment. It throws off some
material fetters. It falls short of the skies, but makes its
30   mundane flights quite ethereal.
   Man is the reflection of Soul. He is the direct opposite of material sensation, and there is but one Ego. We

run into error when we divide Soul into souls, multiply   1
Mind into minds and suppose error to be mind, then mind

to be in matter and matter to be a lawgiver,   3
unintelligence to act like intelligence, and mortality to be the matrix of immortality.

Mortal existence is a dream; mortal existence has no   6
real entity, but saith "It is I." Spirit is the Ego which

never dreams, but understands all things;
which never errs, and is ever conscious; which   9
never believes, but knows; which is never born and
never dies. Spiritual man is the likeness of this Ego.
Man is not God, but like a ray of light which comes from   12
the sun, man, the outcome of God, reflects God.

Mortal body and mind are one, and that one is called
man; but a mortal is not man, for man is immortal. A   15

mortal may be weary or pained, enjoy or suffer,
according to the dream he entertains in sleep.
When that dream vanishes, the mortal finds himself   18
experiencing none of these dream-sensations. To the
observer, the body lies listless, undisturbed, and sensationless, and the mind seems to be absent.   21

Now I ask, Is there any more reality in the waking
dream of mortal existence than in the sleeping dream?
There cannot be, since whatever appears to be a mortal   24
man is a mortal dream. Take away the mortal mind,
and matter has no more sense as a man than it has as
a tree. But the spiritual, real man is immortal.   27

Upon this stage of existence goes on the dance of mortal
mind. Mortal thoughts chase one another like snowflakes,
and drift to the ground. Science reveals Life as not being   30
at the mercy of death, nor will Science admit that happiness is ever the sport of circumstance.

Error is not real, hence it is not more imperative
as it hastens towards self-destruction. The so-called
belief of mortal mind apparent as an abscess
should not grow more painful before it suppu-
rates, neither should a fever become more severe before
it ends.

Error
self-destroyed

Fright is so great at certain stages of mortal belief
as to drive belief into new paths. In the illusion of
death, mortals wake to the knowledge of two
facts: (1) that they are not dead; (2) that
they have but passed the portals of a new belief. Truth
works out the nothingness of error in just these ways.
Sickness, as well as sin, is an error that Christ, Truth,
alone can destroy.

Illusion
of death

We must learn how mankind govern the body, —
whether through faith in hygiene, in drugs, or in will-
power. We should learn whether they govern
the body through a belief in the necessity of
sickness and death, sin and pardon, or govern
it from the higher understanding that the divine Mind
makes perfect, acts upon the so-called human mind
through truth, leads the human mind to relinquish all
error, to find the divine Mind to be the only Mind,
and the healer of sin, disease, death. This process of
higher spiritual understanding improves mankind until
error disappears, and nothing is left which deserves to
perish or to be punished.

Mortal mind's
disappearance

Ignorance, like intentional wrong, is not Science.
Ignorance must be seen and corrected before we can attain harmony. Inharmonious beliefs, which
rob Mind, calling it matter, and deify their
own notions, imprison themselves in what they create.

Spiritual
ignorance

They are at war with Science, and as our Master said, 1
"If a kingdom be divided against itself, that kingdom
cannot stand." 3

Human ignorance of Mind and of the recuperative
energies of Truth occasions the only skepticism regarding the pathology and theology of Christian Science. 6

When false human beliefs learn even a little of their
own falsity, they begin to disappear. A knowledge of

**Eternal man
recognized**

error and of its operations must precede that 9
understanding of Truth which destroys error,
until the entire mortal, material error finally disappears,
and the eternal verity, man created by and of Spirit, 12
is understood and recognized as the true likeness of his
Maker.

The false evidence of material sense contrasts strikingly 15
with the testimony of Spirit. Material sense lifts its voice
with the arrogance of reality and says:

I am wholly dishonest, and no man knoweth it. I can 18
cheat, lie, commit adultery, rob, murder, and I elude
detection by smooth-tongued villainy. Ani-

**Testimony
of sense**

mal in propensity, deceitful in sentiment, 21
fraudulent in purpose, I mean to make my short span
of life one gala day. What a nice thing is sin! How
sin succeeds, where the good purpose waits! The world 24
is my kingdom. I am enthroned in the gorgeousness
of matter. But a touch, an accident, the law of God,
may at any moment annihilate my peace, for all my 27
fancied joys are fatal. Like bursting lava, I expand but
to my own despair, and shine with the resplendency of
consuming fire. 30

Spirit, bearing opposite testimony, saith:
I am Spirit. Man, whose senses are spiritual, is my

1 likeness. He reflects the infinite understanding, for I am
Infinity. The beauty of holiness, the perfection of being,
3 imperishable glory, — all are Mine, for I am
God. I give immortality to man, for I am
Truth. I include and impart all bliss, for I am Love.
6 I give life, without beginning and without end, for I am
Life. I am supreme and give all, for I am Mind. I am
the substance of all, because I AM THAT I AM.

9   I hope, dear reader, I am leading you into the understanding of your divine rights, your heaven-bestowed harmony, — that, as you read, you see there is no
12 cause (outside of erring, mortal, material sense
which is not power) able to make you sick or
sinful; and I hope that you are conquering this false sense.
15 Knowing the falsity of so-called material sense, you can
assert your prerogative to overcome the belief in sin, disease, or death.

18   If you believe in and practise wrong knowingly, you
can at once change your course and do right. Matter can
make no opposition to right endeavors against
21 sin or sickness, for matter is inert, mindless.
Also, if you believe yourself diseased, you can
alter this wrong belief and action without hindrance from
24 the body.

Do not believe in any supposed necessity for sin, disease, or death, knowing (as you ought to know) that God
27 never requires obedience to a so-called material law, for
no such law exists. The belief in sin and death is destroyed by the law of God, which is the law of Life in-
30 stead of death, of harmony instead of discord, of Spirit
instead of the flesh.

The divine demand, "Be ye therefore perfect," is sci-

entific, and the human footsteps leading to perfection are   1
indispensable. Individuals are consistent who, watching
and praying, can "run, and not be weary; . . .   3
walk, and not faint," who gain good rapidly
and hold their position, or attain slowly and
yield not to discouragement. God requires perfection,   6
but not until the battle between Spirit and flesh is fought
and the victory won. To stop eating, drinking, or being
clothed materially before the spiritual facts of existence   9
are gained step by step, is not legitimate. When we wait
patiently on God and seek Truth righteously, He directs
our path. Imperfect mortals grasp the ultimate of spir-   12
itual perfection slowly; but to *begin* aright and to continue the strife of demonstrating the great problem of
being, is doing much.   15

During the sensual ages, absolute Christian Science
may not be achieved prior to the change called death,
for we have not the power to demonstrate what we do   18
not understand. But the human self must be evangel-
ized. This task God demands us to accept lovingly
to-day, and to abandon so fast as practical the material,   21
and to work out the spiritual which determines the outward and actual.

If you venture upon the quiet surface of error and are   24
in sympathy with error, what is there to disturb the waters?
What is there to strip off error's disguise?

If you launch your bark upon the ever-agitated but   27
healthful waters of truth, you will encounter storms.

Your good will be evil spoken of. This is the
cross. Take it up and bear it, for through it   30
you win and wear the crown. Pilgrim on earth, thy home
is heaven; stranger, thou art the guest of God.

Chapter 9

Creation

Thy throne is established of old:
Thou art from everlasting. — PSALMS.

For we know that the whole creation groaneth
and travaileth in pain together until now.
And not only they, but ourselves also,
which have the firstfruits of the Spirit,
even we ourselves groan within ourselves,
waiting for the adoption, to wit,
the redemption of our body. — PAUL.

1 Eternal Truth is changing the universe. As mortals drop off their mental swaddling-clothes, thought
3 expands into expression. "Let there be light,"
is the perpetual demand of Truth and Love,
changing chaos into order and discord into the
6 music of the spheres. The mythical human theories of
creation, anciently classified as the higher criticism, sprang
from cultured scholars in Rome and in Greece, but they
9 afforded no foundation for accurate views of creation by
the divine Mind.

Inadequate theories of creation

Mortal man has made a covenant with his eyes to be-
12 little Deity with human conceptions. In league
with material sense, mortals take limited views
of all things. That God is corporeal or material, no man
15 should affirm.

Finite views of Deity

The human form, or physical finiteness, cannot be
made the basis of any true idea of the infinite Godhead.
18 Eye hath not seen Spirit, nor hath ear heard His voice.

255

Progress takes off human shackles. The finite must 1
yield to the infinite. Advancing to a higher plane of ac-

No material creation tion, thought rises from the material sense to 3
the spiritual, from the scholastic to the in-
spirational, and from the mortal to the immortal. All
things are created spiritually. Mind, not matter, is the 6
creator. Love, the divine Principle, is the Father and
Mother of the universe, including man.

The theory of three persons in one God (that is, a per- 9

Tritheism impossible sonal Trinity or Tri-unity) suggests polythe-
ism, rather than the one ever-present I AM.
"Hear, O Israel: the Lord our God is one Lord." 12

The everlasting I AM is not bounded nor compressed
within the narrow limits of physical humanity, nor can

No divine corporeality He be understood aright through mortal con- 15
cepts. The precise form of God must be of
small importance in comparison with the sublime question, What is infinite Mind or divine Love? 18

Who is it that demands our obedience? He who, in
the language of Scripture, "doeth according to His will
in the army of heaven, and among the inhabitants of the 21
earth; and none can stay His hand, or say unto Him,
What doest Thou?"

No form nor physical combination is adequate to rep- 24
resent infinite Love. A finite and material sense of God
leads to formalism and narrowness; it chills the spirit of
Christianity. 27

A limitless Mind cannot proceed from physical limita-
tions. Finiteness cannot present the idea or the vast-

Limitless Mind ness of infinity. A mind originating from a 30
finite or material source must be limited and
finite. Infinite Mind is the creator, and creation is the

1 infinite image or idea emanating from this Mind. If
Mind is within and without all things, then all is Mind;
3 and this definition is scientific.

If matter, so-called, is substance, then Spirit, matter's
unlikeness, must be shadow; and shadow cannot produce
6 substance. The theory that Spirit is not the
only substance and creator is pantheistic het-
erodoxy, which ultimates in sickness, sin, and death; it is
9 the belief in a bodily soul and a material mind, a soul
governed by the body and a mind in matter. This belief is shallow pantheism.

Matter is not substance

12 Mind creates His own likeness in ideas, and the substance of an idea is very far from being the supposed substance of non-intelligent matter. Hence the Father Mind
15 is not the father of matter. The material senses and
human conceptions would translate spiritual ideas into
material beliefs, and would say that an anthropomorphic
18 God, instead of infinite Principle, — in other words, divine
Love, — is the father of the rain, "who hath begotten the
drops of dew," who bringeth "forth Mazzaroth in his sea-
21 son," and guideth "Arcturus with his sons."

Finite mind manifests all sorts of errors, and thus
proves the material theory of mind in matter to be the
24 antipode of Mind. Who hath found finite life
or love sufficient to meet the demands of human
want and woe, — to still the desires, to satisfy the aspira-
27 tions? Infinite Mind cannot be limited to a finite form,
or Mind would lose its infinite character as inexhaustible
Love, eternal Life, omnipotent Truth.

Inexhaustible divine Love

30 It would require an infinite form to contain infinite
Mind. Indeed, the phrase *infinite form* involves a contradiction of terms. Finite man cannot be the image and

likeness of the infinite God. A mortal, corporeal, or 1
finite conception of God cannot embrace the glories of

Infinite physique impossible limitless, incorporeal Life and Love. Hence 3
the unsatisfied human craving for something
better, higher, holier, than is afforded by a
material belief in a physical God and man. The insuffi- 6
ciency of this belief to supply the true idea proves the
falsity of material belief.

Man is more than a material form with a mind inside, 9

Infinity's reflection which must escape from its environments in
order to be immortal. Man reflects infinity,
and this reflection is the true idea of God. 12

God expresses in man the infinite idea forever develop-
ing itself, broadening and rising higher and higher from
a boundless basis. Mind manifests all that exists in 15
the infinitude of Truth. We know no more of man as
the true divine image and likeness, than we know of
God. 18

The infinite Principle is reflected by the infinite idea
and spiritual individuality, but the material so-called senses
have no cognizance of either Principle or its idea. The 21
human capacities are enlarged and perfected in proportion as humanity gains the true conception of man and
God. 24

Mortals have a very imperfect sense of the spiritual
man and of the infinite range of his thought. To him

Individual permanency belongs eternal Life. Never born and 27
never dying, it were impossible for man, under
the government of God in eternal Science, to fall from his
high estate. 30

Through spiritual sense you can discern the heart of
divinity, and thus begin to comprehend in Science the

1 generic term *man.* Man is not absorbed in Deity, and
man cannot lose his individuality, for he re-
3 flects eternal Life; nor is he an isolated, solitary idea, for he represents infinite Mind, the sum of all
substance.

6 In divine Science, man is the true image of God. The
divine nature was best expressed in Christ Jesus, who
threw upon mortals the truer reflection of God and lifted
9 their lives higher than their poor thought-models would
allow, — thoughts which presented man as fallen, sick,
sinning, and dying. The Christlike understanding of
12 scientific being and divine healing includes a perfect Principle and idea, — perfect God and perfect man, — as the
basis of thought and demonstration.

15 If man was once perfect but has now lost his perfection,
then mortals have never beheld in man the reflex image
of God. The *lost* image is no image. The
18 true likeness cannot be lost in divine reflection.
Understanding this, Jesus said: "Be ye therefore perfect, even as your Father which is in heaven is
21 perfect."

Mortal thought transmits its own images, and forms
its offspring after human illusions. God, Spirit, works
24 spiritually, not materially. Brain or matter
never formed a human concept. Vibration is
not intelligence; hence it is not a creator. Immortal
27 ideas, pure, perfect, and enduring, are transmitted by
the divine Mind through divine Science, which corrects
error with truth and demands spiritual thoughts, divine
30 concepts, to the end that they may produce harmonious
results.

Deducing one's conclusions as to man from imperfec-

tion instead of perfection, one can no more arrive at the   1
true conception or understanding of man, and make himself like it, than the sculptor can perfect his outlines from   3
an imperfect model, or the painter can depict the form
and face of Jesus, while holding in thought the character
of Judas.   6

Spiritual discovery

The conceptions of mortal, erring thought must give
way to the ideal of all that is perfect and eternal. Through
many generations human beliefs will be attain-   9
ing diviner conceptions, and the immortal and
perfect model of God's creation will finally be seen as
the only true conception of being.   12

Science reveals the possibility of achieving all good,
and sets mortals at work to discover what God has already
done; but distrust of one's ability to gain the goodness   15
desired and to bring out better and higher results, often
hampers the trial of one's wings and ensures failure at the
outset.   18

Requisite change of our ideals

Mortals must change their ideals in order to improve
their models. A sick body is evolved from
sick thoughts. Sickness, disease, and death   21
proceed from fear. Sensualism evolves bad
physical and moral conditions.

Selfishness and sensualism are educated in mortal   24
mind by the thoughts ever recurring to one's self, by
conversation about the body, and by the expectation of
perpetual pleasure or pain from it; and this education   27
is at the expense of spiritual growth. If we array
thought in mortal vestures, it must lose its immortal
nature.   30

If we look to the body for pleasure, we find pain; for
Life, we find death; for Truth, we find error; for Spirit,

we find its opposite, matter. Now reverse this action. Look away from the body into Truth and Love, the Principle of all happiness, harmony, and immortality. Hold thought steadfastly to the enduring, the good, and the true, and you will bring these into your experience proportionably to their occupancy of your thoughts.

The effect of mortal mind on health and happiness is seen in this: If one turns away from the body with such absorbed interest as to forget it, the body experiences no pain. Under the strong impulse of a desire to perform his part, a noted actor was accustomed night after night to go upon the stage and sustain his appointed task, walking about as actively as the youngest member of the company. This old man was so lame that he hobbled every day to the theatre, and sat aching in his chair till his cue was spoken, — a signal which made him as oblivious of physical infirmity as if he had inhaled chloroform, though he was in the full possession of his so-called senses.

Detach sense from the body, or matter, which is only a form of human belief, and you may learn the meaning of God, or good, and the nature of the immutable and immortal. Breaking away from the mutations of time and sense, you will neither lose the solid objects and ends of life nor your own identity. Fixing your gaze on the realities supernal, you will rise to the spiritual consciousness of being, even as the bird which has burst from the egg and preens its wings for a skyward flight.

We should forget our bodies in remembering good and the human race. Good demands of man every hour, in

which to work out the problem of being. Consecration 1
to good does not lessen man's dependence on God, but

heightens it. Neither does consecration di- 3
minish man's obligations to God, but shows
the paramount necessity of meeting them. Christian
Science takes naught from the perfection of God, but it 6
ascribes to Him the entire glory. By putting "off the old
man with his deeds," mortals "put on immortality."

We cannot fathom the nature and quality of God's 9
creation by diving into the shallows of mortal belief. We
must reverse our feeble flutterings — our efforts to find
life and truth in matter — and rise above the testimony 12
of the material senses, above the mortal to the immortal
idea of God. These clearer, higher views inspire the Godlike man to reach the absolute centre and circumference 15
of his being.

Job said: "I have heard of Thee by the hearing of the
ear: but now mine eye seeth Thee." Mortals will echo 18

Job's thought, when the supposed pain and
pleasure of matter cease to predominate. They
will then drop the false estimate of life and happiness, of 21
joy and sorrow, and attain the bliss of loving unselfishly,
working patiently, and conquering all that is unlike God.
Starting from a higher standpoint, one rises spontane- 24
ously, even as light emits light without effort; for "where
your treasure is, there will your heart be also."

The foundation of mortal discord is a false sense of 27
man's origin. To begin rightly is to end rightly. Every

concept which seems to begin with the brain
begins falsely. Divine Mind is the only cause 30
or Principle of existence. Cause does not exist in matter,
in mortal mind, or in physical forms.

Mortals are egotists. They believe themselves to be independent workers, personal authors, and even privileged originators of something which Deity would not or could not create. The creations of mortal mind are material. Immortal spiritual man alone represents the truth of creation.

Human
egotism

When mortal man blends his thoughts of existence with the spiritual and works only as God works, he will no longer grope in the dark and cling to earth because he has not tasted heaven. Carnal beliefs defraud us. They make man an involuntary hypocrite, — producing evil when he would create good, forming deformity when he would outline grace and beauty, injuring those whom he would bless. He becomes a general mis-creator, who believes he is a semi-god. His "touch turns hope to dust, the dust we all have trod." He might say in Bible language: "The good that I would, I do not: but the evil which I would not, *that I do.*"

Mortal man
a mis-creator

There can be but one creator, who has created all. Whatever seems to be a new creation, is but the discovery of some distant idea of Truth; else it is a new multiplication or self-division of mortal thought, as when some finite sense peers from its cloister with amazement and attempts to pattern the infinite.

No new
creation

The multiplication of a human and mortal sense of persons and things is not creation. A sensual thought, like an atom of dust thrown into the face of spiritual immensity, is dense blindness instead of a scientific eternal consciousness of creation.

The fading forms of matter, the mortal body and ma-

terial earth, are the fleeting concepts of the human mind. 1
They have their day before the permanent facts and their

Mind's true camera

perfection in Spirit appear. The crude crea- 3
tions of mortal thought must finally give place
to the glorious forms which we sometimes behold in the
camera of divine Mind, when the mental picture is spir- 6
itual and eternal. Mortals must look beyond fading,
finite forms, if they would gain the true sense of things.
Where shall the gaze rest but in the unsearchable realm 9
of Mind? We must look where we would walk, and we
must act as possessing all power from Him in whom we
have our being. 12

As mortals gain more correct views of God and man,
multitudinous objects of creation, which before were

Self-completeness

invisible, will become visible. When we 15
realize that Life is Spirit, never in nor of
matter, this understanding will expand into self-completeness, finding all in God, good, and needing no other 18
consciousness.

Spirit and its formations are the only realities of being.
Matter disappears under the microscope of Spirit. Sin 21

Spiritual proofs of existence

is unsustained by Truth, and sickness and
death were overcome by Jesus, who proved
them to be forms of error. Spiritual living 24
and blessedness are the only evidences, by which we can
recognize true existence and feel the unspeakable peace
which comes from an all-absorbing spiritual love. 27

When we learn the way in Christian Science and recognize man's spiritual being, we shall behold and understand God's creation, — all the glories of earth and heaven 30
and man.

The universe of Spirit is peopled with spiritual beings,

and its government is divine Science. Man is the offspring, not of the lowest, but of the highest qualities of
Mind. Man understands spiritual existence

in proportion as his treasures of Truth and
Love are enlarged. Mortals must gravitate Godward,
their affections and aims grow spiritual, — they must near
the broader interpretations of being, and gain some proper
sense of the infinite, — in order that sin and mortality
may be put off.

This scientific sense of being, forsaking matter for
Spirit, by no means suggests man's absorption into Deity
and the loss of his identity, but confers upon man enlarged individuality, a wider sphere of thought and action,
a more expansive love, a higher and more permanent
peace.

The senses represent birth as untimely and death as
irresistible, as if man were a weed growing apace or a
flower withered by the sun and nipped by

untimely frosts; but this is true only of a
mortal, not of a man in God's image and likeness. The
truth of being is perennial, and the error is unreal and
obsolete.

Who that has felt the loss of human peace has not gained
stronger desires for spiritual joy? The aspiration after
heavenly good comes even before we discover

what belongs to wisdom and Love. The loss
of earthly hopes and pleasures brightens the ascending
path of many a heart. The pains of sense quickly inform
us that the pleasures of sense are mortal and that joy is
spiritual.

The pains of sense are salutary, if they wrench away
false pleasurable beliefs and transplant the affections

from sense to Soul, where the creations of God are good, 1
"rejoicing the heart." Such is the sword of
Science, with which Truth decapitates error, 3
materiality giving place to man's higher individuality and
destiny.

Decapitation
of error

Would existence without personal friends be to you 6
a blank? Then the time will come when you will be
solitary, left without sympathy; but this
seeming vacuum is already filled with divine 9
Love. When this hour of development comes, even if
you cling to a sense of personal joys, spiritual Love will
force you to accept what best promotes your growth. 12
Friends will betray and enemies will slander, until the
lesson is sufficient to exalt you; for "man's extremity
is God's opportunity." The author has experienced the 15
foregoing prophecy and its blessings. Thus He teaches
mortals to lay down their fleshliness and gain spirituality.
This is done through self-abnegation. Universal Love 18
is the divine way in Christian Science.

Uses of
adversity

The sinner makes his own hell by doing evil, and the
saint his own heaven by doing right. The opposite per- 21
secutions of material sense, aiding evil with evil, would
deceive the very elect.

Mortals must follow Jesus' sayings and his demonstra- 24
tions, which dominate the flesh. Perfect and infinite
Mind enthroned is heaven. The evil beliefs
which originate in mortals are hell. Man is the 27
idea of Spirit; he reflects the beatific presence, illuming
the universe with light. Man is deathless, spiritual. He
is above sin or frailty. He does not cross the barriers 30
of time into the vast forever of Life, but he coexists with
God and the universe.

Beatific
presence

1   Every object in material thought will be destroyed, but
the spiritual idea, whose substance is in Mind, is eternal.

3   The offspring of God start not from matter
or ephemeral dust. They are in and of Spirit,
divine Mind, and so forever continue. God is one. The

6   allness of Deity is His oneness. Generically man is one,
and specifically man means all men.

     It is generally conceded that God is Father, eternal, self-

9   created, infinite. If this is so, the forever Father must
have had children prior to Adam. The great I AM made
all "that was made." Hence man and the spiritual uni-

12 verse coexist with God.

     Christian Scientists understand that, in a religious
sense, they have the same authority for the appellative

15 mother, as for that of brother and sister. Jesus said:
"For whosoever shall do the will of my Father which
is in heaven, the same is my brother, and sister, and

18 mother."

     When examined in the light of divine Science, mortals
present more than is detected upon the surface, since

21 inverted thoughts and erroneous beliefs must
be counterfeits of Truth. Thought is borrowed from a higher source than matter, and

24 by reversal, errors serve as waymarks to the one Mind,
in which all error disappears in celestial Truth. The
robes of Spirit are "white and glistering," like the raiment

27 of Christ. Even in this world, therefore, "let thy garments be always white." "Blessed is the man that endureth [overcometh] temptation: for when he is tried,

30 [proved faithful], he shall receive the crown of life,
which the Lord hath promised to them that love him."
(James i. 12.)

*The infinitude
of God*

*Waymarks
to eternal
Truth*

Chapter 10

Science of Being

That which was from the beginning, which we have heard,
which we have seen with our eyes, which we have looked upon,
and our hands have handled, of the Word of life, . . .
That which we have seen and heard declare we unto you,
that ye also may have fellowship with us:
and truly our fellowship is with the Father,
and with His Son Jesus Christ. — JOHN, First Epistle.

Here I stand. I can do no otherwise;
so help me God! Amen! — MARTIN LUTHER.

I n the material world, thought has brought to light   1
with great rapidity many useful wonders. With
like activity have thought's swift pinions been rising   3
Materialistic towards the realm of the real, to the spiritual
challenge cause of those lower things which give impulse to inquiry. Belief in a material basis, from   6
which may be deduced all rationality, is slowly yielding
to the idea of a metaphysical basis, looking away from
matter to Mind as the cause of every effect. Material-   9
istic hypotheses challenge metaphysics to meet in final
combat. In this revolutionary period, like the shep-
herd-boy with his sling, woman goes forth to battle with   12
Goliath.

   In this final struggle for supremacy, semi-metaphysical systems afford no substantial aid to scientific meta-   15
Confusion physics, for their arguments are based on
confounded the false testimony of the material senses as
well as on the facts of Mind. These semi-metaphysical   18

1   systems are one and all pantheistic, and savor of Pan-
demonium, a house divided against itself.

3   From first to last the supposed coexistence of Mind
and matter and the mingling of good and evil have resulted from the philosophy of the serpent. Jesus' demon-
6   strations sift the chaff from the wheat, and unfold the
unity and the reality of good, the unreality, the nothingness, of evil.

9   Human philosophy has made God manlike. Christian
Science makes man Godlike. The first is error; the latter
is truth. Metaphysics is above physics, and   **Divine**
12   matter does not enter into metaphysical prem-   **metaphysics**
ises or conclusions. The categories of metaphysics rest
on one basis, the divine Mind. Metaphysics resolves
15   things into thoughts, and exchanges the objects of sense
for the ideas of Soul.

   These ideas are perfectly real and tangible to spiritual
18   consciousness, and they have this advantage over the objects and thoughts of material sense, — they are good and
eternal.

21   The testimony of the material senses is neither absolute nor divine. I therefore plant myself unreservedly
on the teachings of Jesus, of his apostles, of   **Biblical**
24   the prophets, and on the testimony of the   **foundations**
Science of Mind. Other foundations there are none.
All other systems — systems based wholly or partly on
27   knowledge gained through the material senses — are reeds
shaken by the wind, not houses built on the rock.

   The theories I combat are these: (1) that all is matter;
30   (2) that matter originates in Mind, and is as   **Rejected**
real as Mind, possessing intelligence and life.   **theories**
The first theory, that matter is everything, is quite as

reasonable as the second, that Mind and matter coexist   1
and cooperate. One only of the following statements can
be true: (1) that everything is matter; (2) that every-   3
thing is Mind. Which one is it?

Matter and Mind are opposites. One is contrary to
the other in its very nature and essence; hence both can-   6
not be real. If one is real, the other must be unreal. Only
by understanding that there is but one power, — not two
powers, matter and Mind, — are scientific and logical   9
conclusions reached. Few deny the hypothesis that intelligence, apart from man and matter, governs the universe; and it is generally admitted that this intelligence   12
is the eternal Mind or divine Principle, Love.

The prophets of old looked for something higher than

**Prophetic
ignorance**
the systems of their times; hence their fore-   15
sight of the new dispensation of Truth. But
they knew not what would be the precise nature of the
teaching and demonstration of God, divine Mind, in His   18
more infinite meanings, — the demonstration which was
to destroy sin, sickness, and death, establish the definition
of omnipotence, and maintain the Science of Spirit.   21

The pride of priesthood is the prince of this world. It
has nothing in Christ. Meekness and charity have divine
authority. Mortals think wickedly; consequently they   24
are wicked. They think sickly thoughts, and so become
sick. If sin makes sinners, Truth and Love alone can
unmake them. If a sense of disease produces suffering   27
and a sense of ease antidotes suffering, disease is mental,
not material. Hence the fact that the human mind alone
suffers, is sick, and that the divine Mind alone heals.   30

The life of Christ Jesus was not miraculous, but it was
indigenous to his spirituality, — the good soil wherein the

seed of Truth springs up and bears much fruit. Christ's Christianity is the chain of scientific being reappearing in all ages, maintaining its obvious correspondence with the Scriptures and uniting all periods in the design of God. Neither emasculation, illusion, nor insubordination exists in divine Science.

Jesus instructed his disciples whereby to heal the sick through Mind instead of matter. He knew that the philosophy, Science, and proof of Christianity were in Truth, casting out all inharmony.

In Latin the word rendered *disciple* signifies student; and the word indicates that the power of healing was not a supernatural gift to those learners, but the result of their cultivated spiritual understanding of the divine Science, which their Master demonstrated by healing the sick and sinning. Hence the universal application of his saying: "Neither pray I for these alone, but for them also which shall believe on me [understand me] through their word."

Studious disciples

Our Master said, "But the Comforter . . . shall teach you all things." When the Science of Christianity appears, it will lead you into all truth. The Sermon on the Mount is the essence of this Science, and the eternal life, not the death of Jesus, is its outcome.

New Testament basis

Those, who are willing to leave their nets or to cast them on the right side for Truth, have the opportunity now, as aforetime, to learn and to practise Christian healing. The Scriptures contain it. The spiritual import of the Word imparts this power. But, as Paul says, "How shall they hear without a preacher? and how shall they preach, except they be

Modern evangel

sent?" If sent, how shall they preach, convert, and heal   1
multitudes, except the people hear?

The spiritual sense of truth must be gained before   3
Truth can be understood. This sense is assimilated only
as we are honest, unselfish, loving, and meek.

Spirituality
of Scripture
In the soil of an "honest and good heart" the   6
seed must be sown; else it beareth not much fruit, for the
swinish element in human nature uproots it. Jesus said:
"Ye do err, not knowing the Scriptures." The spiritual   9
sense of the Scriptures brings out the scientific sense, and
is the new tongue referred to in the last chapter of Mark's
Gospel.   12

Jesus' parable of "the sower" shows the care our
Master took not to impart to dull ears and gross hearts
the spiritual teachings which dulness and grossness could   15
not accept. Reading the thoughts of the people, he said:
"Give not that which is holy unto the dogs, neither cast
ye your pearls before swine."   18

It is the spiritualization of thought and Christianization
of daily life, in contrast with the results of the ghastly farce

Unspiritual
contrasts
of material existence; it is chastity and purity,   21
in contrast with the downward tendencies
and earthward gravitation of sensualism and impurity,
which really attest the divine origin and operation of Chris-   24
tian Science. The triumphs of Christian Science are recorded in the destruction of error and evil, from which are
propagated the dismal beliefs of sin, sickness, and death.   27

The divine Principle of the universe must interpret the
universe. God is the divine Principle of all that repre-

God the
Principle of all
sents Him and of all that really exists. Chris-   30
tian Science, as demonstrated by Jesus, alone
reveals the natural, divine Principle of Science.

Matter and its claims of sin, sickness, and death are contrary to God, and cannot emanate from Him. There is no *material* truth. The physical senses can take no cognizance of God and spiritual Truth. Human belief has sought out many inventions, but not one of them can solve the problem of being without the divine Principle of divine Science. Deductions from material hypotheses are not scientific. They differ from real Science because they are not based on the divine law.

Divine Science reverses the false testimony of the material senses, and thus tears away the foundations of error. Hence the enmity between Science and the senses, and the impossibility of attaining perfect understanding till the errors of sense are eliminated.

Science versus sense

The so-called laws of matter and of medical science have never made mortals whole, harmonious, and immortal. Man is harmonious when governed by Soul. Hence the importance of understanding the truth of being, which reveals the laws of spiritual existence.

God never ordained a material law to annul the spiritual law. If there were such a material law, it would oppose the supremacy of Spirit, God, and impugn the wisdom of the creator. Jesus walked on the waves, fed the multitude, healed the sick, and raised the dead in direct opposition to material laws. His acts were the demonstration of Science, overcoming the false claims of material sense or law.

Spiritual law the only law

Science shows that material, conflicting mortal opinions and beliefs emit the effects of error at all times, but this atmosphere of mortal mind cannot be destructive to morals and health when it is opposed promptly and per-

sistently by Christian Science. Truth and Love antidote   1
this mental miasma, and thus invigorate and sustain ex-

Material
knowledge
illusive
istence. Unnecessary knowledge gained from   3
the five senses is only temporal, — the conception of mortal mind, the offspring of sense, not
of Soul, Spirit, — and symbolizes all that is evil and   6
perishable. *Natural science*, as it is commonly called, is
not really natural nor scientific, because it is deduced from
the evidence of the material senses. Ideas, on the con-   9
trary, are born of Spirit, and are not mere inferences
drawn from material premises.

    The senses of Spirit abide in Love, and they demon-   12
strate Truth and Life. Hence Christianity and the Sci-

Five senses
deceptive
ence which expounds it are based on spiritual
understanding, and they supersede the so-   15
called laws of matter. Jesus demonstrated this great
verity. When what we erroneously term the five physical
senses are misdirected, they are simply the manifested   18
beliefs of mortal mind, which affirm that life, substance,
and intelligence are material, instead of spiritual. These
false beliefs and their products constitute the flesh, and   21
the flesh wars against Spirit.

    Divine Science is absolute, and permits no half-way
position in learning its Principle and rule — establishing   24

Impossible
partnership
it by demonstration. The conventional firm,
called matter and mind, God never formed.
Science and understanding, governed by the unerring and   27
eternal Mind, destroy the imaginary copartnership, matter
and mind, formed only to be destroyed in a manner and
at a period as yet unknown. This suppositional partner-   30
ship is already obsolete, for matter, examined in the light
of divine metaphysics, disappears.

1   Matter has no life to lose, and Spirit never dies. A
partnership of mind with matter would ignore omnipres-
3   ent and omnipotent Mind. This shows that   **Spirit the**
matter did not originate in God, Spirit, and is   **starting-point**
not eternal. Therefore matter is neither substantial, living,
6   nor intelligent. The starting-point of divine Science is
that God, Spirit, is All-in-all, and that there is no other
might nor Mind, — that God is Love, and therefore He
9   is divine Principle.

To grasp the reality and order of being in its Science,
you must begin by reckoning God as the divine Principle
12   of all that really is. Spirit, Life, Truth, Love,   **Divine**
combine as one, — and are the Scriptural names   **synonyms**
for God. All substance, intelligence, wisdom, being, im-
15   mortality, cause, and effect belong to God. These are
His attributes, the eternal manifestations of the infinite
divine Principle, Love. No wisdom is wise but His
18   wisdom; no truth is true, no love is lovely, no life is Life
but the divine; no good is, but the good God bestows.

Divine metaphysics, as revealed to spiritual understand-
21   ing, shows clearly that all is Mind, and that Mind is
God, omnipotence, omnipresence, omniscience,   **The divine**
— that is, all power, all presence, all Science.   **completeness**
24   Hence all is in reality the manifestation of Mind.

Our material human theories are destitute of Science.
The true understanding of God is spiritual. It robs the
27   grave of victory. It destroys the false evidence that mis-
leads thought and points to other gods, or other so-called
powers, such as matter, disease, sin, and death, superior
30   or contrary to the one Spirit.

Truth, spiritually discerned, is scientifically understood.
It casts out error and heals the sick.

Having one God, one Mind, unfolds the power that   1
heals the sick, and fulfils these sayings of Scripture, "I
am the Lord that healeth thee," and "I have   3
found a ransom." When the divine precepts
are understood, they unfold the foundation of fellowship,
in which one mind is not at war with another, but all have   6
one Spirit, God, one intelligent source, in accordance with
the Scriptural command: "Let this Mind be in you,
which was also in Christ Jesus." Man and his Maker   9
are correlated in divine Science, and real consciousness
is cognizant only of the things of God.

The realization that all inharmony is unreal brings   12
objects and thoughts into human view in their true light,
and presents them as beautiful and immortal. Harmony
in man is as real and immortal as in music. Discord is   15
unreal and mortal.

If God is admitted to be the only Mind and Life,
there ceases to be any opportunity for sin and death.   18
When we learn in Science how to be perfect
even as our Father in heaven is perfect,
thought is turned into new and healthy channels, —   21
towards the contemplation of things immortal and away
from materiality to the Principle of the universe, including harmonious man.   24

Material beliefs and spiritual understanding never
mingle. The latter destroys the former. Discord is the
nothingness named error. Harmony is the *somethingness*   27
named Truth.

Nature and revelation inform us that like produces
like. Divine Science does not gather grapes   30
from thorns nor figs from thistles. Intelligence never produces non-intelligence; but matter is

Universal brotherhood *(margin note)*

Perfection requisite *(margin note)*

Like evolving like *(margin note)*

1 ever non-intelligent and therefore cannot spring from
intelligence. To all that is unlike unerring and eternal
3 Mind, this Mind saith, "Thou shalt surely die;" and elsewhere the Scripture says that dust returns to dust. The
non-intelligent relapses into its own unreality. Matter
6 never produces mind. The immortal never produces the
mortal. Good cannot result in evil. As God Himself is
good and is Spirit, goodness and spirituality must be im-
9 mortal. Their opposites, evil and matter, are mortal
error, and error has no creator. If goodness and spirituality are real, evil and materiality are unreal and can-
12 not be the outcome of an infinite God, good.

Natural history presents vegetables and animals as
preserving their original species, — like reproducing like.
15 A mineral is not produced by a vegetable nor the man
by the brute. In reproduction, the order of genus and
species is preserved throughout the entire round of nature.
18 This points to the spiritual truth and Science of being.
Error relies upon a reversal of this order, asserts that
Spirit produces matter and matter produces all the ills
21 of flesh, and therefore that good is the origin of evil.
These suppositions contradict even the order of material
so-called science.

24 The realm of the real is Spirit. The unlikeness of Spirit
is matter, and the opposite of the real is not divine, — it is
a human concept. Matter is an error of state-   **Material**
27 ment. This error in the premise leads to errors   **error**
in the conclusion in every statement into which it enters.
Nothing we can say or believe regarding matter is immor-
30 tal, for matter is temporal and is therefore a mortal phenomenon, a human concept, sometimes beautiful, always
erroneous.

Is Spirit the source or creator of matter? Science re-   1
veals nothing in Spirit out of which to create matter.

Divine metaphysics explains away matter.   3
Spirit is the only substance and consciousness
recognized by divine Science. The material
senses oppose this, but there are no material senses, for   6
matter has no mind. In Spirit there is no matter, even
as in Truth there is no error, and in good no evil. It is
a false supposition, the notion that there is real substance-   9
matter, the opposite of Spirit. Spirit, God, is infinite,
all. Spirit can have no opposite.

That matter is substantial or has life and sensation, is   12
one of the false beliefs of mortals, and exists only in a

supposititious mortal consciousness. Hence,
as we approach Spirit and Truth, we lose the   15
consciousness of matter. The admission that there can
be material substance requires another admission, —
namely, that Spirit is not infinite and that matter is self-   18
creative, self-existent, and eternal. From this it would
follow that there are two eternal causes, warring forever
with each other; and yet we say that Spirit is supreme   21
and all-presence.

The belief of the eternity of matter contradicts the
demonstration of life as Spirit, and leads to the conclu-   24
sion that if man is material, he originated in matter and
must return to dust, — logic which would prove his annihilation.   27

All that we term sin, sickness, and death is a mortal
belief. We define matter as error, because it is the oppo-

site of life, substance, and intelligence. Mat-   30
ter, with its mortality, cannot be substantial
if Spirit is substantial and eternal. Which ought to

1 be substance to us, — the erring, changing, and dying,
the mutable and mortal, or the unerring, immutable,
3 and immortal? A New Testament writer plainly describes faith, a quality of mind, as "the *substance* of things
hoped for."

6 The doom of matter establishes the conclusion that
matter, slime, or protoplasm never originated
in the immortal Mind, and is therefore not
9 eternal. Matter is neither created by Mind nor for the
manifestation and support of Mind.

Material mortality

Ideas are tangible and real to immortal consciousness,
12 and they have the advantage of being eternal.
Spirit and matter can neither coexist nor cooperate, and one can no more create the other than
15 Truth can create error, or *vice versa.*

Spiritual tangibility

In proportion as the belief disappears that life and intelligence are in or of matter, the immortal facts of
18 being are seen, and their only idea or intelligence is
in God. Spirit is reached only through the understanding and demonstration of eternal Life and Truth and
21 Love.

Every system of human philosophy, doctrine, and
medicine is more or less infected with the pantheistic
24 belief that there is mind in matter; but this
belief contradicts alike revelation and right
reasoning. A logical and scientific conclusion is reached
27 only through the knowledge that there are not two
bases of being, matter and mind, but one alone, —
Mind.

Pantheistic tendencies

30 Pantheism, starting from a material sense of God,
seeks cause in effect, Principle in its idea, and life and
intelligence in matter.

In the infinitude of Mind, matter must be unknown.   1
Symbols and elements of discord and decay are not prod-

The things
of God are
beautiful

ucts of the infinite, perfect, and eternal *All*.   3
From Love and from the light and harmony
which are the abode of Spirit, only reflections
of good can come. All things beautiful and harmless are   6
ideas of Mind. Mind creates and multiplies them, and
the product must be mental.

Finite belief can never do justice to Truth in any direc-   9
tion. Finite belief limits all things, and would compress
Mind, which is infinite, beneath a skull bone. Such belief can neither apprehend nor worship the infinite; and   12
to accommodate its finite sense of the divisibility of Soul
and substance, it seeks to divide the one Spirit into persons and souls.   15

Through this error, human belief comes to have "gods
many and lords many." Moses declared as Jehovah's

Belief in
many gods

first command of the Ten: "Thou shalt have   18
no other gods before me!" But behold the
zeal of belief to establish the opposite error of many
minds. The argument of the serpent in the allegory, "Ye   21
shall be as gods," urges through every avenue the belief
that Soul is in body, and that infinite Spirit, and Life, is
in finite forms.   24

Rightly understood, instead of possessing a sentient
material form, man has a sensationless body; and God,

Sensationless
body

the Soul of man and of all existence, being   27
perpetual in His own individuality, harmony,
and immortality, imparts and perpetuates these qualities
in man, — through Mind, not matter. The only excuse   30
for entertaining human opinions and rejecting the Science
of being is our mortal ignorance of Spirit, — ignorance

1 which yields only to the understanding of divine Science,
the understanding by which we enter into the kingdom
3 of Truth on earth and learn that Spirit is infinite and
supreme. Spirit and matter no more commingle than
light and darkness. When one appears, the other dis-
6 appears.

Error presupposes man to be both mind and matter.
Divine Science contradicts the corporeal senses, rebukes
9 mortal belief, and asks: What is the Ego,
whence its origin and what its destiny? The
Ego-man is the reflection of the Ego-God; the Ego-man
12 is the image and likeness of perfect Mind, Spirit, divine
Principle.

God and His image

The one Ego, the one Mind or Spirit called God, is
15 infinite individuality, which supplies all form and come-
liness and which reflects reality and divinity in individual
spiritual man and things.

18 The mind supposed to exist in matter or beneath a
skull bone is a myth, a misconceived sense and false
conception as to man and Mind. When we put off the
21 false sense for the true, and see that sin and mortality
have neither Principle nor permanency, we shall learn
that sin and mortality are without actual origin or right-
24 ful existence. They are native nothingness, out of which
error would simulate creation through a man formed from
dust.

27 Divine Science does not put new wine into old bottles,
Soul into matter, nor the infinite into the finite. Our
false views of matter perish as we grasp
30 the facts of Spirit. The old belief must be
cast out or the new idea will be spilled, and the inspiration, which is to change our standpoint, will be

The true new idea

lost. Now, as of old, Truth casts out evils and heals   1
the sick.

The real Life, or Mind, and its opposite, the so-called   3
material life and mind, are figured by two geometrical

Figures of
being
symbols, a circle or sphere and a straight
line. The circle represents the infinite with-   6
out beginning or end; the straight line represents the
finite, which has both beginning and end. The sphere
represents good, the self-existent and eternal individuality   9
or Mind; the straight line represents evil, a belief in
a self-made and temporary material existence. Eternal
Mind and temporary material existence never unite in   12
figure or in fact.

A straight line finds no abiding-place in a curve, and a
curve finds no adjustment to a straight line. Similarly,   15

Opposite
symbols
matter has no place in Spirit, and Spirit has
no place in matter. Truth has no home in
error, and error has no foothold in Truth. Mind cannot   18
pass into non-intelligence and matter, nor can non-intelligence become Soul. At no point can these opposites
mingle or unite. Even though they seem to touch, one   21
is still a curve and the other a straight line.

There is no inherent power in matter; for all that is
material is a material, human, mortal thought, always   24
governing itself erroneously.

Truth is the intelligence of immortal Mind. Error is
the so-called intelligence of mortal mind.   27

Whatever indicates the fall of man or the opposite of
God or God's absence, is the Adam-dream, which is neither

Truth is not
inverted
Mind nor man, for it is not begotten of the   30
Father. The rule of inversion infers from
error its opposite, Truth; but Truth is the light which

1   dispels error. As mortals begin to understand Spirit,
they give up the belief that there is any true existence
3   apart from God.

     Mind is the source of all movement, and there is no
inertia to retard or check its perpetual and harmonious
6   action. Mind is the same Life, Love, and wisdom "yesterday, and to-day, and forever."
Matter and its effects — sin, sickness, and

Source of all life and action

9   death — are states of mortal mind which act, react, and
then come to a stop. They are not facts of Mind. They
are not ideas, but illusions. Principle is absolute. It
12   admits of no error, but rests upon understanding.

     But what say prevalent theories? They insist that
Life, or God, is one and the same with material life so-
15   called. They speak of both Truth and error as *mind*,
and of good and evil as *spirit*. They claim that to be
life which is but the objective state of material sense, —
18   such as the structural life of the tree and of material
man, — and deem this the manifestation of the one Life,
God.

21   This false belief as to what really constitutes life so
detracts from God's character and nature, that the true
sense of His power is lost to all who cling to

Spiritual structure

24   this falsity. The divine Principle, or Life, cannot be practically demonstrated in length of days, as it
was by the patriarchs, unless its Science be accurately
27   stated. We must receive the divine Principle in the understanding, and live it in daily life; and unless we so do, we
can no more demonstrate Science, than we can teach and
30   illustrate geometry by calling a curve a straight line or a
straight line a sphere.

     Are mentality, immortality, consciousness, resident in

matter? It is not rational to say that Mind is infinite,	1
but dwells in finiteness, — in matter, — or that matter is
infinite and the medium of Mind.	3

If God were limited to man or matter, or if the infinite
could be circumscribed within the finite, God would be

Mind never limited

corporeal, and unlimited Mind would seem	6
to spring from a limited body; but this is an
impossibility. Infinite Mind can have no starting-point,
and can return to no limit. It can never be in bonds,	9
nor be fully manifested through corporeality.

Is God's image or likeness matter, or a mortal, sin,
sickness, and death? Can matter recognize Mind?	12

Material recognition impossible

Can infinite Mind recognize matter? Can the
infinite dwell in the finite or know aught un-
like the infinite? Can Deity be known through	15
the material senses? Can the material senses, which receive no direct evidence of Spirit, give correct testimony
as to spiritual life, truth, and love?	18

The answer to all these questions must forever be in
the negative.

The physical senses can obtain no proof of God. They	21
can neither see Spirit through the eye nor hear it through

Our physical insensibility to Spirit

the ear, nor can they feel, taste, or smell Spirit.
Even the more subtile and misnamed ma-	24
terial elements are beyond the cognizance
of these senses, and are known only by the effects com-
monly attributed to them.	27

According to Christian Science, the only real senses
of man are spiritual, emanating from divine Mind.
Thought passes from God to man, but neither sensation	30
nor report goes from material body to Mind. The in-
tercommunication is always from God to His idea, man.

1 Matter is not sentient and cannot be cognizant of good
or of evil, of pleasure or of pain. Man's individu-
3 ality is not material. This Science of being obtains not
alone hereafter in what men call Paradise, but here
and now; it is the great fact of being for time and
6 eternity.

What, then, is the material personality which suffers,
sins, and dies? It is not man, the image and likeness
9 of God, but man's counterfeit, the inverted   **The human**
likeness, the *unlikeness* called sin, sickness,   **counterfeit**
and death. The unreality of the claim that a mortal is
12 the true image of God is illustrated by the opposite natures of Spirit and matter, Mind and body, for one is
intelligence while the other is non-intelligence.

15 Is God a physical personality? Spirit is not physical.
The belief that a material body is man is a false conception of man. The time has come for a   **Material**
18 finite conception of the infinite and of a ma-   **misconceptions**
terial body as the seat of Mind to give place
to a diviner sense of intelligence and its manifestations, —
21 to the better understanding that Science gives of the
Supreme Being, or divine Principle, and idea.

By interpreting God as a corporeal Saviour but not as
24 the saving Principle, or divine Love, we shall continue
to seek salvation through pardon and not   **Salvation**
through reform, and resort to matter instead   **is through**
    reform
27 of Spirit for the cure of the sick. As mortals
reach, through knowledge of Christian Science, a higher
sense, they will seek to learn, not from matter, but from
30 the divine Principle, God, how to demonstrate the Christ,
Truth, as the healing and saving power.

It is essential to understand, instead of believe, what

relates most nearly to the happiness of being. To seek   1
Truth through belief in a human doctrine is not to understand the infinite. We must not seek the immutable   3
and immortal through the finite, mutable, and mortal,
and so depend upon belief instead of demonstration, for
this is fatal to a knowledge of Science. The understand-   6
ing of Truth gives full faith in Truth, and spiritual understanding is better than all burnt offerings.

The Master said, "No man cometh unto the Father   9
[the divine Principle of being] but by me," Christ,
Life, Truth, Love; for Christ says, "I am the way."
Physical causation was put aside from first to   12
last by this original man, Jesus. He knew that the
divine Principle, Love, creates and governs all that
is real.   15

In the Saxon and twenty other tongues *good* is the term

Goodness
a portion
of God

for God. The Scriptures declare all that He
made to be good, like Himself, — good in   18
Principle and in idea. Therefore the spiritual
universe is good, and reflects God as He is.

God's thoughts are perfect and eternal, are substance   21
and Life. Material and temporal thoughts are human,

Spiritual
thoughts

involving error, and since God, Spirit, is the
only cause, they lack a divine cause. The   24
temporal and material are not then creations of Spirit.
They are but counterfeits of the spiritual and eternal.
Transitory thoughts are the antipodes of everlasting   27
Truth, though (by the supposition of opposite qualities)
error must also say, "I am true." But by this saying
error, the lie, destroys itself.   30

Sin, sickness, and death are comprised in human material belief, and belong not to the divine Mind. They

1   are without a real origin or existence. They have neither
Principle nor permanence, but belong, with all that is

3   material and temporal, to the nothingness of error, which
simulates the creations of Truth. All creations of Spirit
are eternal; but creations of matter must return to dust.

6   Error supposes man to be both mental and material.
Divine Science contradicts this postulate and maintains
man's spiritual identity.

9   We call the absence of Truth, *error.* Truth and error
are unlike. In Science, Truth is divine, and the *infinite*
God can have no unlikeness. Did God, Truth,   **Divine**

12   create error? No! "Doth a fountain send   **allness**
forth at the same place sweet water and bitter?" God
being everywhere and all-inclusive, how can He be absent

15   or suggest the absence of omnipresence and omnipotence?
How can there be more than *all?*

Neither understanding nor truth accompanies error,

18   nor is error the offshoot of Mind. Evil calls itself something, when it is nothing. It saith, "I am man, but I am
not the image and likeness of God;" whereas the Scrip-

21   tures declare that man was made in God's likeness.

Error is false, mortal belief; it is illusion, without spiritual identity or foundation, and it has no real existence.

24   The supposition that life, substance, and in-   **Error**
telligence are *in* matter, or *of* it, is an error.   **unveiled**
Matter is neither a thing nor a person, but merely the

27   objective supposition of Spirit's opposite. The five material senses testify to truth and error as united in a mind
both good and evil. Their false evidence will finally

30   yield to Truth, — to the recognition of Spirit and of the
spiritual creation.

Truth cannot be contaminated by error. The state-

ment that *Truth is real* necessarily includes the correlated   1
statement, that *error, Truth's unlikeness, is unreal.*

The suppositional warfare between truth and error is   3
only the mental conflict between the evidence of the spiritual senses and the testimony of the material

The great
conflict

senses, and this warfare between the Spirit and   6
flesh will settle all questions through faith in and the understanding of divine Love.

Superstition and understanding can never combine.   9
When the final physical and moral effects of Christian
Science are fully apprehended, the conflict between truth
and error, understanding and belief, Science and material   12
sense, foreshadowed by the prophets and inaugurated
by Jesus, will cease, and spiritual harmony reign. The
lightnings and thunderbolts of error may burst and flash   15
till the cloud is cleared and the tumult dies away in the
distance. Then the raindrops of divinity refresh the
earth. As St. Paul says: "There remaineth therefore   18
a rest to the people of God" (of Spirit).

The chief stones in the temple of Christian Science are
to be found in the following postulates: that Life is God,   21

The chief
stones in
the temple

good, and not evil; that Soul is sinless, not
to be found in the body; that Spirit is not, and
cannot be, materialized; that Life is not subject   24
to death; that the spiritual real man has no birth, no material life, and no death.

Science reveals the glorious possibilities of immortal   27

The
Christ-element

man, forever unlimited by the mortal senses.
The Christ-element in the Messiah made him
the Way-shower, Truth and Life.   30

The eternal Truth destroys what mortals seem to have
learned from error, and man's real existence as a child

1   of God comes to light. Truth demonstrated is eternal
life. Mortal man can never rise from the temporal *débris*

3   of error, belief in sin, sickness, and death, until he learns
that God is the only Life. The belief that life and sensation are in the body should be overcome by the under-

6   standing of what constitutes man as the image of God.
Then Spirit will have overcome the flesh.

    A wicked mortal is not the idea of God. He is little

9   else than the expression of error. To suppose that sin,
lust, hatred, envy, hypocrisy, revenge, have life   **Wickedness**
abiding in them, is a terrible mistake. Life   **is not man**

12   and Life's idea, Truth and Truth's idea, never make men
sick, sinful, or mortal.

    The fact that the Christ, or Truth, overcame and still

15   overcomes death proves the "king of terrors" to be but
a mortal belief, or error, which Truth destroys   **Death but**
with the spiritual evidences of Life; and this   **an illusion**

18   shows that what appears to the senses to be death is but a
mortal illusion, for to the real man and the real universe
there is no death-process.

21   The belief that matter has life results, by the universal
law of mortal mind, in a belief in death. So man, tree,
and flower are supposed to die; but the fact remains,

24   that God's universe is spiritual and immortal.

    The spiritual fact and the material belief of things are
contradictions; but the spiritual is true, and therefore the

27   material must be untrue. Life is not in matter.   **Spiritual**
Therefore it cannot be said to pass out of mat-   **offspring**
ter. Matter and death are mortal illusions. Spirit and

30   all things spiritual are the real and eternal.

    Man is not the offspring of flesh, but of Spirit, — of
Life, not of matter. Because Life is God, Life must be

eternal, self-existent. Life is the everlasting I AM, the Be-   1
ing who was and is and shall be, whom nothing can erase.

If the Principle, rule, and demonstration of man's being   3
are not in the least understood before what is termed death

Death no
advantage
overtakes mortals, they will rise no higher spiritually in the scale of existence on account of   6
that single experience, but will remain as material as before the transition, still seeking happiness through a material, instead of through a spiritual sense of life, and from   9
selfish and inferior motives. That Life or Mind is finite
and physical or is manifested through brain and nerves,
is false. Hence Truth comes to destroy this error and   12
its effects, — sickness, sin, and death. To the spiritual
class, relates the Scripture: "On such the second death
hath no power."   15

If the change called *death* destroyed the belief in sin,
sickness, and death, happiness would be won at the mo-

Future
purification
ment of dissolution, and be forever permanent;   18
but this is not so. Perfection is gained only
by perfection. They who are unrighteous shall be unrighteous still, until in divine Science Christ, Truth, re-   21
moves all ignorance and sin.

The sin and error which possess us at the instant of
death do not cease at that moment, but endure until the   24

Sin is
punished
death of these errors. To be wholly spiritual,
man must be sinless, and he becomes thus only
when he reaches perfection. The murderer, though slain   27
in the act, does not thereby forsake sin. He is no more
spiritual for believing that his body died and learning that
his cruel mind died not. His thoughts are no purer until   30
evil is disarmed by good. His body is as material as his
mind, and *vice versa*.

1   The suppositions that sin is pardoned while unfor-
saken, that happiness can be genuine in the midst of
3   sin, that the so-called death of the body frees from sin,
and that God's pardon is aught but the destruction of
sin, — these are grave mistakes. We know that all will
6   be changed "in the twinkling of an eye," when the last
trump shall sound; but this last call of wisdom cannot
come till mortals have already yielded to each lesser call
9   in the growth of Christian character. Mortals need not
fancy that belief in the experience of death will awaken
them to glorified being.

12   Universal salvation rests on progression and probation,
and is unattainable without them. Heaven is not a locality, but a divine state of Mind in which all the

Salvation and probation

15   manifestations of Mind are harmonious and
immortal, because sin is not there and man is
found having no righteousness of his own, but in posses-
18   sion of "the mind of the Lord," as the Scripture says.

"In the place where the tree falleth, there it shall
be." So we read in Ecclesiastes. This text has been
21   transformed into the popular proverb, "As the tree
falls, so it must lie." As man falleth asleep, so shall he
awake. As death findeth mortal man, so shall he be
24   after death, until probation and growth shall effect the
needed change. Mind never becomes dust. No resurrection from the grave awaits Mind or Life, for the grave
27   has no power over either.

No final judgment awaits mortals, for the judgment-
day of wisdom comes hourly and continually,

Day of judgment

30   even the judgment by which mortal man is di-
vested of all material error. As for spiritual error there
is none.

When the last mortal fault is destroyed, then the final   1
trump will sound which will end the battle of Truth with
error and mortality; "but of that day and hour, knoweth   3
no man." Here prophecy pauses. Divine Science alone
can compass the heights and depths of being and reveal
the infinite.   6

Truth will be to us "the resurrection and the life" only
as it destroys all error and the belief that Mind, the only
immortality of man, can be fettered by the   9
body, and Life be controlled by death. A sin-
ful, sick, and dying mortal is not the likeness of God, the
perfect and eternal.   12

Primitive error

Matter is the primitive belief of mortal mind, because
this so-called mind has no cognizance of Spirit. To
mortal mind, matter is substantial, and evil is   15
real. The so-called senses of mortals are material.
Hence the so-called life of mortals is dependent on
matter.   18

Explaining the origin of material man and mortal mind,
Jesus said: "Why do ye not understand my speech?
Even because ye cannot hear my word. Ye are of your   21
father, the devil [evil], and the lusts of your father ye will
do. He was a murderer from the beginning, and abode
not in the truth, because there is no truth in him. When   24
he speaketh a lie, he speaketh of his own: for he is a liar,
and the father of it."

This carnal material mentality, misnamed *mind*, is   27
mortal. Therefore man would be annihilated, were it
not for the spiritual real man's indissoluble
connection with his God, which Jesus brought   30
to light. In his resurrection and ascension, Jesus showed
that a mortal man is not the real essence of manhood, and

Immortal man

1   that this unreal material mortality disappears in presence
of the reality.

3   Electricity is not a vital fluid, but the least material
form of illusive consciousness, — the material mindless-
ness, which forms no link between matter and

                    Elementary electricity

6   Mind, and which destroys itself. Matter and
mortal mind are but different strata of human belief. The
grosser substratum is named matter or body; the more

9   ethereal is called mind. This so-called mind and body
is the illusion called a mortal, a mind in matter. In reality
and in Science, both strata, mortal mind and mortal body,

12   are false representatives of man.

    The material so-called gases and forces are counter-
feits of the spiritual forces of divine Mind, whose potency

15   is Truth, whose attraction is Love, whose adhesion and
cohesion are Life, perpetuating the eternal facts of being.
Electricity is the sharp surplus of materiality which coun-

18   terfeits the true essence of spirituality or truth, — the
great difference being that electricity is not intelligent,
while spiritual truth is Mind.

21   There is no vapid fury of mortal mind — expressed in
earthquake, wind, wave, lightning, fire, bestial ferocity
— and this so-called mind is self-destroyed.

                    The counterfeit forces

24   The manifestations of evil, which counterfeit
divine justice, are called in the Scriptures, "The anger
of the Lord." In reality, they show the self-destruction

27   of error or matter and point to matter's opposite, the
strength and permanency of Spirit. Christian Science
brings to light Truth and its supremacy, universal har-

30   mony, the entireness of God, good, and the nothingness
of evil.

    The five physical senses are the avenues and instru-

ments of human error, and they correspond with error.   1
These senses indicate the common human belief, that life,

substance, and intelligence are a unison of   3
matter with Spirit. This is pantheism, and
carries within itself the seeds of all error.

If man is both mind and matter, the loss of one finger   6
would take away some quality and quantity of the man,
for matter and man would be one.

The belief that matter thinks, sees, or feels is not more   9
real than the belief that matter enjoys and suffers. This

mortal belief, misnamed *man*, is error, saying:
"Matter has intelligence and sensation. Nerves   12
feel. Brain thinks and sins. The stomach can make a
man cross. Injury can cripple and matter can kill man."
This verdict of the so-called material senses victimizes   15
mortals, taught, as they are by physiology and pathology,
to revere false testimony, even the errors that are destroyed
by Truth through spiritual sense and Science.   18

The lines of demarcation between immortal man, representing Spirit, and mortal man, representing the error that

life and intelligence are in matter, show the   21
pleasures and pains of matter to be myths, and
human belief in them to be the father of mythology, in
which matter is represented as divided into intelligent gods.   24
Man's genuine selfhood is recognizable only in what is
good and true. Man is neither self-made nor made by
mortals. God created man.   27

The inebriate believes that there is pleasure in intoxication. The thief believes that he gains something by steal-
ing, and the hypocrite that he is hiding himself. The   30
Science of Mind corrects such mistakes, for Truth demonstrates the falsity of error.

1   The belief that a severed limb is aching in the old location, the sensation seeming to be in nerves which

3   are no longer there, is an added proof of the un-
reliability of physical testimony.
      God creates and governs the universe, including man.
6   The universe is filled with spiritual ideas, which He
evolves, and they are obedient to the Mind
that makes them. Mortal mind would trans-

9   form the spiritual into the material, and then
recover man's original self in order to escape from the
mortality of this error. Mortals are not like immortals,
12   created in God's own image; but infinite Spirit being all,
mortal consciousness will at last yield to the scientific fact
and disappear, and the real sense of being, perfect and
15   forever intact, will appear.
      The manifestation of God through mortals is as light
passing through the window-pane. The light and the
18   glass never mingle, but as matter, the glass
is less opaque than the walls. The mortal

      mind through which Truth appears most vividly is that
21   one which has lost much materiality — much error — in
order to become a better transparency for Truth. Then,
like a cloud melting into thin vapor, it no longer hides
24   the sun.
      All that is called mortal thought is made up of error.
The theoretical mind is matter, named *brain*, or *mate-*
27   *rial consciousness*, the exact opposite of real
Mind, or Spirit. Brainology teaches that

mortals are created to suffer and die. It further
30   teaches that when man is dead, his immortal soul is
resurrected from death and mortality. Thus error the-
orizes that spirit is born of matter and returns to mat-

ter, and that man has a resurrection from dust; whereas   1
Science unfolds the eternal verity, that man is the spiritual,
eternal reflection of God.   3

Progress is born of experience. It is the ripening of
mortal man, through which the mortal is dropped for
Scientific   the immortal. Either here or hereafter, suf-   6
purgation   fering or Science must destroy all illusions
regarding life and mind, and regenerate material sense
and self. The old man with his deeds must be put off.   9
Nothing sensual or sinful is immortal. The death of a
false material sense and of sin, not the death of organic
matter, is what reveals man and Life, harmonious, real,   12
and eternal.

The so-called pleasures and pains of matter perish,
and they must go out under the blaze of Truth, spiritual   15
sense, and the actuality of being. Mortal belief must lose
all satisfaction in error and sin in order to part with
them.   18

Whether mortals will learn this sooner or later, and
how long they will suffer the pangs of destruction, depends upon the tenacity of error.   21

The knowledge obtained from the corporeal senses
leads to sin and death. When the evidence of Spirit
Mixed   and matter, Truth and error, seems to com-   24
testimony   mingle, it rests upon foundations which time
is wearing away. Mortal mind judges by the testimony
of the material senses, until Science obliterates this false   27
testimony. An improved belief is one step out of error,
and aids in taking the next step and in understanding
the situation in Christian Science.   30

Mortal belief is a liar from the beginning, not deserving
power. It says to mortals, "You are wretched!" and they

1 think they are so; and nothing can change this state, until
the belief changes. Mortal belief says, "You are happy!"

3 and mortals are so; and no circumstance can
alter the situation, until the belief on this subject changes. Human belief says to mortals, "You are

6 sick!" and this testimony manifests itself on the body as
sickness. It is as necessary for a health-illusion, as for
an illusion of sickness, to be instructed out of itself into

9 the understanding of what constitutes health; for a change
in either a health-belief or a belief in sickness affects the
physical condition.

Belief an autocrat

12 Erroneous belief is destroyed by truth. Change the
evidence, and that disappears which before seemed real
to this false belief, and the human conscious-

15 ness rises higher. Thus the reality of being
is attained and man found to be immortal. The only
fact concerning any material concept is, that it is neither

18 scientific nor eternal, but subject to change and dissolution.

Self-improvement

Faith is higher and more spiritual than belief. It is

21 a chrysalis state of human thought, in which spiritual
evidence, contradicting the testimony of material sense, begins to appear, and Truth, the

24 ever-present, is becoming understood. Human thoughts
have their degrees of comparison. Some thoughts are
better than others. A belief in Truth is better than a

27 belief in error, but no mortal testimony is founded on the
divine rock. Mortal testimony can be shaken. Until
belief becomes faith, and faith becomes spiritual under-

30 standing, human thought has little relation to the actual
or divine.

Faith higher than belief

A mortal belief fulfils its own conditions. Sickness,

sin, and death are the vague realities of human conclu-   1
sions. Life, Truth, and Love are the realities of divine
Science. They dawn in faith and glow full-orbed in   3
spiritual understanding. As a cloud hides the sun it
cannot extinguish, so false belief silences for a while the
voice of immutable harmony, but false belief cannot de-   6
stroy Science armed with faith, hope, and fruition.

What is termed material sense can report only a mor-
tal temporary sense of things, whereas spiritual sense can   9

Truth's
witness

bear witness only to Truth. To material sense,
the unreal is the real until this sense is corrected
by Christian Science.   12

Spiritual sense, contradicting the material senses, involves intuition, hope, faith, understanding, fruition, reality. Material sense expresses the belief that mind is in   15
matter. This human belief, alternating between a sense
of pleasure and pain, hope and fear, life and death, never
reaches beyond the boundary of the mortal or the unreal.   18
When the real is attained, which is announced by Science,
joy is no longer a trembler, nor is hope a cheat. Spiritual ideas, like numbers and notes, start from Principle,   21
and admit no materialistic beliefs. Spiritual ideas lead
up to their divine origin, God, and to the spiritual sense
of being.   24

Angels are not etherealized human beings, evolving
animal qualities in their wings; but they are celestial

Thought-
angels

visitants, flying on spiritual, not material,   27
pinions. Angels are pure thoughts from God,
winged with Truth and Love, no matter what their indi-
vidualism may be. Human conjecture confers upon angels   30
its own forms of thought, marked with superstitious outlines, making them human creatures with suggestive

feathers; but this is only fancy. It has behind it no more
reality than has the sculptor's thought when he carves
his "Statue of Liberty," which embodies his conception of an unseen quality or condition, but which has
no physical antecedent reality save in the artist's own observation and "chambers of imagery."

My angels are exalted thoughts, appearing at the door
of some sepulchre, in which human belief has buried
its fondest earthly hopes. With white fingers they point upward to a new and glo-
rified trust, to higher ideals of life and its joys. Angels
are God's representatives. These upward-soaring beings
never lead towards self, sin, or materiality, but guide to
the divine Principle of all good, whither every real individuality, image, or likeness of God, gathers. By giving
earnest heed to these spiritual guides they tarry with us,
and we entertain "angels unawares."

Our angelic messengers

Knowledge gained from material sense is figuratively
represented in Scripture as a tree, bearing the fruits of
sin, sickness, and death. Ought we not then
to judge the knowledge thus obtained to be
untrue and dangerous, since "the tree is known by his
fruit"?

Knowledge and Truth

Truth never destroys God's idea. Truth is spiritual,
eternal substance, which cannot destroy the right reflection. Corporeal sense, or error, may seem to hide Truth,
health, harmony, and Science, as the mist obscures the
sun or the mountain; but Science, the sunshine of Truth,
will melt away the shadow and reveal the celestial
peaks.

If man were solely a creature of the material senses,
he would have no eternal Principle and would be mutable

and mortal. Human logic is awry when it attempts   1
to draw correct spiritual conclusions regarding life from

matter. Finite sense has no true apprecia-   3
tion of infinite Principle, God, or of His infinite image or reflection, man. The mirage, which makes
trees and cities seem to be where they are not, illustrates   6
the illusion of material man, who cannot be the image
of God.

So far as the scientific statement as to man is under-   9
stood, it can be proved and will bring to light the true
reflection of God — the real man, or the *new* man (as
St. Paul has it).   12

The temporal and unreal never touch the eternal and
real. The mutable and imperfect never touch the im-

mutable and perfect. The inharmonious and   15
self-destructive never touch the harmonious
and self-existent. These opposite qualities are the tares
and wheat, which never really mingle, though (to mortal   18
sight) they grow side by side until the harvest; then, Science separates the wheat from the tares, through the realization of God as ever present and of man as reflecting   21
the divine likeness.

Spirit is God, Soul; therefore Soul is not in matter. If
Spirit were in matter, God would have no representative,   24

and matter would be identical with God.
The theory that soul, spirit, intelligence, in-
habits matter is taught by the schools. This theory is   27
unscientific. The universe reflects and expresses the divine substance or Mind; therefore God is seen only in the
spiritual universe and spiritual man, as the sun is seen in   30
the ray of light which goes out from it. God is revealed only in that which reflects Life, Truth, Love, —

1 yea, which manifests God's attributes and power, even
as the human likeness thrown upon the mirror, repeats
3 the color, form, and action of the person in front of the
mirror.

Few persons comprehend what Christian Science
6 means by the word *reflection.* To himself, mortal and
material man seems to be substance, but his sense of
substance involves error and therefore is material,
9 temporal.

On the other hand, the immortal, spiritual man is really
substantial, and reflects the eternal substance, or Spirit,
12 which mortals hope for. He reflects the divine, which
constitutes the only real and eternal entity. This reflection
seems to mortal sense transcendental, because the spiritual
15 man's substantiality transcends mortal vision and is revealed only through divine Science.

As God is substance and man is the divine image and
18 likeness, man should wish for, and in reality has, only
the substance of good, the substance of Spirit,
not matter. The belief that man has any other

Inverted
images
and ideas

21 substance, or mind, is not spiritual and breaks
the First Commandment, Thou shalt have one God, one
Mind. Mortal man seems to himself to be material sub-
24 stance, while man is "image" (idea). Delusion, sin, disease, and death arise from the false testimony of material
sense, which, from a supposed standpoint outside the
27 focal distance of infinite Spirit, presents an inverted image
of Mind and substance with everything turned upside
down.

30 This falsity presupposes soul to be an unsubstantial
dweller in material forms, and man to be material instead
of spiritual. Immortality is not bounded by mortality.

Soul is not compassed by finiteness. Principle is not to   1
be found in fragmentary ideas.

The material body and mind are temporal, but the   3
real man is spiritual and eternal. The identity of the

Identity
not lost
real man is not lost, but found through this
explanation; for the conscious infinitude of   6
existence and of all identity is thereby discerned and remains unchanged. It is impossible that man should lose
aught that is real, when God is all and eternally his. The   9
notion that mind is in matter, and that the so-called pleasures and pains, the birth, sin, sickness, and death of
matter, are real, is a mortal belief; and this belief is all   12
that will ever be lost.

Continuing our definition of *man*, let us remember that
harmonious and immortal man has existed forever, and   15

Definition
of man
is always beyond and above the mortal illusion of any life, substance, and intelligence
as existent in matter. This statement is based on fact,   18
not fable. The Science of being reveals man as perfect,
even as the Father is perfect, because the Soul, or Mind,
of the spiritual man is God, the divine Principle of all   21
being, and because this real man is governed by Soul
instead of sense, by the law of Spirit, not by the so-called
laws of matter.   24

God is Love. He is therefore the divine, infinite Principle, called Person or God. Man's true consciousness
is in the mental, not in any bodily or personal likeness   27
to Spirit. Indeed, the body presents no proper likeness
of divinity, though mortal sense would fain have us so
believe.   30

Even in Christian Science, reproduction by Spirit's
individual ideas is but the reflection of the creative power

of the divine Principle of those ideas. The reflection, through mental manifestation, of the multitudinous forms of Mind which people the realm of the real is controlled by Mind, the Principle governing the reflection. Multiplication of God's children comes from no power of propagation in matter, it is the reflection of Spirit.

Mental propagation

The minutiæ of lesser individualities reflect the one divine individuality and are comprehended in and formed by Spirit, not by material sensation. Whatever reflects Mind, Life, Truth, and Love, is spiritually conceived and brought forth; but the statement that man is conceived and evolved both spiritually and materially, or by both God and man, contradicts this eternal truth. All the vanity of the ages can never make both these contraries true. Divine Science lays the axe at the root of the illusion that life, or mind, is formed by or is in the material body, and Science will eventually destroy this illusion through the self-destruction of all error and the beatified understanding of the Science of Life.

The belief that pain and pleasure, life and death, holiness and unholiness, mingle in man, — that mortal, material man is the likeness of God and is himself a creator, — is a fatal error.

Error defined

God, without the image and likeness of Himself, would be a nonentity, or Mind unexpressed. He would be without a witness or proof of His own nature. Spiritual man is the image or idea of God, an idea which cannot be lost nor separated from its divine Principle. When the evidence before the material senses yielded to spiritual sense, the apostle declared that nothing could alienate him from

Man's entity spiritual

God, from the sweet sense and presence of Life and
Truth.

It is ignorance and false belief, based on a material
sense of things, which hide spiritual beauty and good-

Man inseparable from Love

ness. Understanding this, Paul said: "Neither death, nor life, . . . nor things present,
nor things to come, nor height, nor depth, nor
any other creature, shall be able to separate us from
the love of God." This is the doctrine of Christian
Science: that divine Love cannot be deprived of its
manifestation, or object; that joy cannot be turned into
sorrow, for sorrow is not the master of joy; that good can
never produce evil; that matter can never produce mind
nor life result in death. The perfect man — governed
by God, his perfect Principle — is sinless and eternal.

Harmony is produced by its Principle, is controlled
by it and abides with it. Divine Principle is the Life

Harmony natural

of man. Man's happiness is not, therefore, at
the disposal of physical sense. Truth is not
contaminated by error. Harmony in man is as beautiful
as in music, and discord is unnatural, unreal.

The science of music governs tones. If mortals caught
harmony through material sense, they would lose harmony, if time or accident robbed them of material sense.
To be master of chords and discords, the science of
music must be understood. Left to the decisions
of material sense, music is liable to be misappre-
hended and lost in confusion. Controlled by belief,
instead of understanding, music is, must be, imperfectly expressed. So man, not understanding the Science of being, — thrusting aside his divine Principle as
incomprehensible, — is abandoned to conjectures, left in

1   the hands of ignorance, placed at the disposal of illusions,
subjected to material sense which is discord. A discon-
3   tented, discordant mortal is no more a *man* than discord
is music.

    A picture in the camera or a face reflected in the mirror
6   is not the original, though resembling it. Man, in the
likeness of his Maker, reflects the central light   **Human**
of being, the invisible God. As there is no cor-   **reflection**
9   poreality in the mirrored form, which is but a reflection,
so man, like all things real, reflects God, his divine Principle, not in a mortal body.

12   Gender also is a quality, not of God, but a characteristic of mortal mind. The verity that God's image is not
a creator, though he reflects the creation of Mind, God,
15   constitutes the underlying reality of reflection. "Then
answered Jesus and said unto them: Verily, verily I say
unto you, the Son can do nothing of himself, but what he
18   seeth the Father do: for what things soever He doeth,
these also doeth the Son likewise."

    The inverted images presented by the senses, the de-
21   flections of matter as opposed to the Science of spiritual reflection, are all unlike Spirit, God. In   **Inverted**
the illusion of life that is here to-day and   **images**
24   gone to-morrow, man would be wholly mortal, were
it not that Love, the divine Principle that obtains in
divine Science, destroys all error and brings immor-
27   tality to light. Because man is the reflection of his
Maker, he is not subject to birth, growth, maturity, decay. These mortal dreams are of human origin, not
30   divine.

    The Sadducees reasoned falsely about the resurrec-
tion, but not so blindly as the Pharisees, who believed

error to be as immortal as Truth. The Pharisees thought   1
that they could raise the spiritual from the material. They

Jewish
traditions

would first make life result in death, and then   3
resort to death to reproduce spiritual life.
Jesus taught them how death was to be overcome by
spiritual Life, and demonstrated this beyond cavil.   6

Life demonstrates Life. The immortality of Soul makes
man immortal. If God, who is Life, were parted for a

Divinity not
childless

moment from His reflection, man, during that   9
moment there would be no divinity reflected.
The Ego would be unexpressed, and the Father would be
childless, — no Father.   12

If Life or Soul and its representative, man, unite for
a period and then are separated as by a law of divorce to
be brought together again at some uncertain future time   15
and in a manner unknown, — and this is the general
religious opinion of mankind, — we are left without a
rational proof of immortality. But man cannot be sep-   18
arated for an instant from God, if man reflects God.
Thus Science proves man's existence to be intact.

The myriad forms of mortal thought, made manifest   21
as matter, are not more distinct nor real to the mate-

Thought-
forms

rial senses than are the Soul-created forms
to spiritual sense, which cognizes Life as per-   24
manent. Undisturbed amid the jarring testimony of the
material senses, Science, still enthroned, is unfolding
to mortals the immutable, harmonious, divine Principle,   27
— is unfolding Life and the universe, ever present and
eternal.

God's man, spiritually created, is not material and   30
mortal.

The parent of all human discord was the Adam-dream,

the deep sleep, in which originated the delusion that life and intelligence proceeded from and passed into matter. This pantheistic error, or so-called *serpent*, insists still upon the opposite of Truth, saying, "Ye shall be as gods;" that is, I will make error as real and eternal as Truth.

The serpent's whisper

Evil still affirms itself to be mind, and declares that there is more than one intelligence or God. It says: "There shall be lords and gods many. I declare that God makes evil minds and evil spirits, and that I aid Him. Truth shall change sides and be unlike Spirit. I will put spirit into what I call matter, and matter shall seem to have life as much as God, Spirit, who *is* the only Life."

This error has proved itself to be error. Its life is found to be not Life, but only a transient, false sense of an existence which ends in death. Error charges its lie to Truth and says: "The Lord knows it. He has made man mortal and material, out of matter instead of Spirit." Thus error partakes of its own nature and utters its own falsities. If we regard matter as intelligent, and Mind as both good and evil, every sin or supposed material pain and pleasure seems normal, a part of God's creation, and so weighs against our course Spiritward.

Bad results from error

Truth has no beginning. The divine Mind is the Soul of man, and gives man dominion over all things. Man was not created from a material basis, nor bidden to obey material laws which Spirit never made; his province is in spiritual statutes, in the higher law of Mind.

Higher statutes

Above error's awful din, blackness, and chaos, the voice of Truth still calls: "Adam, where art thou? Conscious-

ness, where art thou? Art thou dwelling in the belief   1
that mind is in matter, and that evil is mind, or art thou

The great   in the living faith that there is and can be but   3
question   one God, and keeping His commandment?"

Until the lesson is learned that God is the only Mind governing man, mortal belief will be afraid as it was in the   6
beginning, and will hide from the demand, "Where art
thou?" This awful demand, "Adam, where art thou?"
is met by the admission from the head, heart, stomach,   9
blood, nerves, etc.: "Lo, here I am, looking for happiness
and life in the body, but finding only an illusion, a blending of false claims, false pleasure, pain, sin, sickness, and   12
death."

The Soul-inspired patriarchs heard the voice of Truth,
and talked with God as consciously as man talks with man.   15

Jacob was *alone*, wrestling with error, — struggling
with a mortal sense of life, substance, and intelligence

Wrestling   as existent in matter with its false pleasures   18
of Jacob   and pains, — when an angel, a message from
Truth and Love, appeared to him and smote the sinew,
or strength, of his error, till he saw its unreality; and   21
Truth, being thereby understood, gave him spiritual
strength in this Peniel of divine Science. Then said
the spiritual evangel: "Let me go, for the day breaketh;"   24
that is, the light of Truth and Love dawns upon thee.
But the patriarch, perceiving his error and his need
of help, did not loosen his hold upon this glorious light   27
until his nature was transformed. When Jacob was
asked, "What is thy name?" he straightway answered;
and then his name was changed to Israel, for "as a prince"   30
had he prevailed and had "power with God and with
men." Then Jacob questioned his deliverer, "Tell me,

1 I pray thee, *thy* name;" but this appellation was withheld, for the messenger was not a corporeal being, but a name-
3 less, incorporeal impartation of divine Love to man, which, to use the word of the Psalmist, *restored* his Soul, — gave him the spiritual sense of being and rebuked his material
6 sense.

The result of Jacob's struggle thus appeared. He had conquered material error with the understanding of Spirit
9 and of spiritual power. This changed the man. **Israel the**
He was no longer called Jacob, but Israel, — **new name**
a prince of God, or a soldier of God, who had fought
12 a good fight. He was to become the father of those, who through earnest striving followed his demonstration of the power of Spirit over the material senses; and the children
15 of earth who followed his example were to be called the children of Israel, until the Messiah should rename them. If these children should go astray, and forget that Life
18 is God, good, and that good is not in elements which are not spiritual, — thus losing the divine power which heals the sick and sinning, — they were to be brought back
21 through great tribulation, to be renamed in Christian Science and led to deny material sense, or mind in matter, even as the gospel teaches.
24 The Science of being shows it to be impossible for in-finite Spirit or Soul to be in a finite body or for man to have an intelligence separate from his Maker. **Life never**
27 It is a self-evident error to suppose that there **structural** can be such a reality as organic animal or vegetable life, when such so-called life always ends in death. Life is
30 never for a moment extinct. Therefore it is never struc-tural nor organic, and is never absorbed nor limited by its own formations.

Thought seen
as substance

The artist is not in his painting. The picture is the
artist's thought objectified. The human belief fancies
that it delineates thought on matter, but what
is matter? Did it exist prior to thought?
Matter is made up of supposititious mortal mind-force;
but all might is divine Mind. Thought will finally be
understood and seen in all form, substance, and color, but
without material accompaniments. The potter is not in
the clay; else the clay would have power over the potter.
God is His own infinite Mind, and expresses all.

Day may decline and shadows fall, but darkness flees
when the earth has again turned upon its axis. The sun

The central
intelligence

is not affected by the revolution of the earth.
So Science reveals Soul as God, untouched
by sin and death, — as the central Life and intelligence
around which circle harmoniously all things in the systems of Mind.

Soul changeth not. We are commonly taught that there
is a human soul which sins and is spiritually lost, — that

Soul
imperishable

soul may be lost, and yet be immortal. If
Soul could sin, Spirit, Soul, would be flesh instead of Spirit. It is the belief of the flesh and of material sense which sins. If Soul sinned, Soul would die.
Sin is the element of self-destruction, and spiritual death
is oblivion. If there was sin in Soul, the annihilation of
Spirit would be inevitable. The only Life is Spirit, and
if Spirit should lose Life as God, good, then Spirit, which
has no other existence, would be annihilated.

Mind is God, and God is not seen by material sense,
because Mind is Spirit, which material sense cannot discern. There is neither growth, maturity, nor decay in
Soul. These changes are the mutations of material sense,

1   the varying clouds of mortal belief, which hide the truth
of being.

3   What we term mortal mind or carnal mind, dependent
on matter for manifestation, is not Mind. God is Mind:
all that Mind, God, is, or hath made, is good, and He

6   made all. Hence evil is not made and is not real.

     Soul is immortal because it is Spirit, which has no ele-
ment of self-destruction. Is man lost spiritually? No,

9   he can only lose a sense material. All sin is   **Sin only of**
of the flesh. It cannot be spiritual. Sin exists   **the flesh**
here or hereafter only so long as the illusion of mind in

12   matter remains. It is a sense of sin, and not a sinful soul,
which is lost. Evil is destroyed by the sense of good.

     Through false estimates of soul as dwelling in sense

15   and of mind as dwelling in matter, belief strays into a
sense of temporary loss or absence of soul, spir-   **Soul**
itual truth. This state of error is the mortal   **impeccable**

18   dream of life and substance as existent in matter, and is
directly opposite to the immortal reality of being. So long
as we believe that soul can sin or that immortal Soul is in

21   mortal body, we can never understand the Science of being. When humanity does understand this Science, it
will become the law of Life to man, — even the higher law

24   of Soul, which prevails over material sense through harmony and immortality.

     The objects cognized by the physical senses have not

27   the reality of substance. They are only what mortal
belief calls them. Matter, sin, and mortality lose all
supposed consciousness or claim to life or existence, as

30   mortals lay off a false sense of life, substance, and intelligence. But the spiritual, eternal man is not touched by
these phases of mortality.

Sense-
dreams

How true it is that whatever is learned through material   1
sense must be lost because such so-called knowledge is
reversed by the spiritual facts of being in   3
Science. That which material sense calls
intangible, is found to be substance. What to material
sense seems substance, becomes nothingness, as the sense-   6
dream vanishes and reality appears.

The senses regard a corpse, not as man, but simply as
matter. People say, "Man is dead;" but this death is   9
the departure of a mortal's mind, not of matter. The
matter is still there. The belief of that mortal that he
must die occasioned his departure; yet you say that   12
matter has caused his death.

People go into ecstasies over the sense of a corporeal
Jehovah, though with scarcely a spark of love in their   15

Vain
ecstasies

hearts; yet God *is* Love, and without Love,
God, immortality cannot appear. Mortals try
to believe without understanding Truth; yet God *is*   18
Truth. Mortals claim that death is inevitable; but man's
eternal Principle is ever-present Life. Mortals believe in
a finite personal God; while God is infinite Love, which   21
must be unlimited.

Our theories are based on finite premises, which cannot penetrate beyond matter. A personal sense of God   24
and of man's capabilities necessarily limits

Man-made
theories

faith and hinders spiritual understanding. It
divides faith and understanding between matter and Spirit,   27
the finite and the infinite, and so turns away from the
intelligent and divine healing Principle to the inanimate
drug.   30

Jesus' spiritual origin and his demonstration of divine
Principle richly endowed him and entitled him to sonship

1   in Science. He was the son of a virgin. The term
Christ Jesus, or Jesus the Christ (to give the full and
3   proper translation of the Greek), may be rendered "Jesus the anointed," Jesus the God-
crowned or the divinely royal man, as it is said of him in
6   the first chapter of Hebrews: —

The one
anointed

> Therefore God, even thy God, hath anointed thee
> With the oil of gladness above thy fellows.

9   With this agrees another passage in the same chapter,
which refers to the Son as "the brightness of His [God's]
glory, and the express [expressed] image of His person
12   [infinite Mind]." It is noteworthy that the phrase "express image" in the Common Version is, in the Greek
Testament, *character.* Using this word in its higher mean-
15   ing, we may assume that the author of this remarkable
epistle regarded Christ as the Son of God, the royal
reflection of the infinite; and the cause given for the ex-
18   altation of Jesus, Mary's son, was that he "loved righteousness and hated iniquity." The passage is made
even clearer in the translation of the late George R.
21   Noyes, D.D.: "Who, being a brightness from His glory,
and an image of His being."

      Jesus of Nazareth was the most scientific man that
24   ever trod the globe. He plunged beneath the material
surface of things, and found the spiritual
cause. To accommodate himself to imma-

Jesus the
Scientist

27   ture ideas of spiritual power, — for spirituality was possessed only in a limited degree even by his disciples, —
Jesus called the body, which by spiritual power he
30   raised from the grave, "flesh and bones." To show
that the substance of himself was Spirit and the body

no more perfect because of death and no less material   1
until the ascension (his further spiritual exaltation),
Jesus waited until the mortal or fleshly sense had re-   3
linquished the belief of substance-matter, and spiritual
sense had quenched all earthly yearnings. Thus he found
the eternal Ego, and proved that he and the Father were   6
inseparable as God and His reflection or spiritual man.
Our Master gained the solution of being, demonstrating
the existence of but one Mind without a second or equal.   9

The Jews, who sought to kill this man of God, showed
plainly that their material views were the parents of their

wicked deeds. When Jesus spoke of repro-   12
ducing his body, — knowing, as he did, that
Mind was the builder, — and said, "Destroy this temple,
and in three days I will raise it up," they thought that he   15
meant their material temple instead of his body. To such
materialists, the real man seemed a spectre, unseen and
unfamiliar, and the body, which they laid in a sepulchre,   18
seemed to be substance. This materialism lost sight of
the true Jesus; but the faithful Mary saw him, and he
presented to her, more than ever before, the true idea of   21
Life and substance.

Because of mortals' material and sinful belief, the
spiritual Jesus was imperceptible to them. The higher   24

his demonstration of divine Science carried
the problem of being, and the more dis-
tinctly he uttered the demands of its divine Principle,   27
Truth and Love, the more odious he became to sinners
and to those who, depending on doctrines and material
laws to save them from sin and sickness, were submis-   30
sive to death as being in supposed accord with the
inevitable law of life. Jesus proved them wrong by

1　his resurrection, and said: "Whosoever liveth and believeth in me shall never die."

3　That saying of our Master, "I and my Father are one,"
separated him from the scholastic theology of the rabbis.
His better understanding of God was a rebuke

6　to them. He knew of but one Mind and laid
no claim to any other. He knew that the Ego was Mind
instead of body and that matter, sin, and evil were not

9　Mind; and his understanding of this divine Science
brought upon him the anathemas of the age.

The opposite and false views of the people hid from

12　their sense Christ's sonship with God. They could not
discern his spiritual existence. Their carnal
minds were at enmity with it. Their thoughts

15　were filled with mortal error, instead of with God's spiritual idea as presented by Christ Jesus. The likeness of
God we lose sight of through sin, which beclouds the spir-

18　itual sense of Truth; and we realize this likeness only
when we subdue sin and prove man's heritage, the liberty
of the sons of God.

21　Jesus' spiritual origin and understanding enabled him
to demonstrate the facts of being, — to prove irrefutably
how spiritual Truth destroys material error,

24　heals sickness, and overcomes death. The
divine conception of Jesus pointed to this truth and presented an illustration of creation. The history of Jesus

27　shows him to have been more spiritual than all other
earthly personalities.

Wearing in part a human form (that is, as it seemed

30　to mortal view), being conceived by a human mother,
Jesus was the mediator between Spirit and the flesh,
between Truth and error. Explaining and demonstrat-

ing the way of divine Science, he became the way of   1
salvation to all who accepted his word. From him mor-

tals may learn how to escape from evil. The   3
real man being linked by Science to his Maker,
mortals need only turn from sin and lose sight of mortal
selfhood to find Christ, the real man and his relation to   6
God, and to recognize the divine sonship. Christ, Truth,
was demonstrated through Jesus to prove the power of
Spirit over the flesh, — to show that Truth is made   9
manifest by its effects upon the human mind and body,
healing sickness and destroying sin.

Jesus represented Christ, the true idea of God. Hence   12
the warfare between this spiritual idea and perfunctory

religion, between spiritual clear-sightedness
and the blindness of popular belief, which led   15
to the conclusion that the spiritual idea could be killed
by crucifying the flesh. The Christ-idea, or the Christ-
man, rose higher to human view because of the crucifixion,   18
and thus proved that Truth was the master of death.
Christ presents the indestructible man, whom Spirit creates, constitutes, and governs. Christ illustrates that   21
blending with God, his divine Principle, which gives man
dominion over all the earth.

The spiritual idea of God, as presented by Jesus, was   24
scourged in person, and its Principle was rejected. That

man was accounted a criminal who could
prove God's divine power by healing the   27
sick, casting out evils, spiritualizing materialistic beliefs,
and raising the dead, — those dead in trespasses and
sins, satisfied with the flesh, resting on the basis of mat-   30
ter, blind to the possibilities of Spirit and its correla-
tive truth.

1   Jesus uttered things which had been "secret from the
foundation of the world," — since material knowledge
3   usurped the throne of the creative divine Principle, insisted
on the might of matter, the force of falsity, the insignificance of spirit, and proclaimed an anthropomorphic God.

6   Whosoever lives most the life of Jesus in this age
and declares best the power of Christian Science, will
drink of his Master's cup. Resistance to

            The cup
9   Truth will haunt his steps, and he will in-   *of Jesus*
cur the hatred of sinners, till "wisdom is justified of
her children." These blessed benedictions rest upon
12   Jesus' followers: "If the world hate you, ye know that
it hated me before it hated you;" "Lo, I am with you
alway," — that is, not only in all time, but in *all ways*
15   and conditions.

     The individuality of man is no less tangible because
it is spiritual and because his life is not at the mercy of
18   matter. The understanding of his spiritual individuality
makes man more real, more formidable in truth, and enables him to conquer sin, disease, and death. Our Lord
21   and Master presented himself to his disciples after his
resurrection from the grave, as the self-same Jesus whom
they had loved before the tragedy on Calvary.

24   To the materialistic Thomas, looking for the ideal
Saviour in matter instead of in Spirit and to the testimony of the material senses and the body,

            Material
27   more than to Soul, for an earnest of immor-   *skepticism*
tality, — to him Jesus furnished the proof that he was
unchanged by the crucifixion. To this dull and doubt-
30   ing disciple Jesus remained a fleshly reality, so long as
the Master remained an inhabitant of the earth. Nothing but a display of matter could make existence real

to Thomas. For him to believe in matter was no task,   1
but for him to conceive of the substantiality of Spirit —
to know that nothing can efface Mind and immortality, in   3
which Spirit reigns — was more difficult.

Corporeal senses define diseases as realities; but the
Scriptures declare that God made all, even while the cor-   6
poreal senses are saying that matter causes

**What
the senses
originate**

disease and the divine Mind cannot or will
not heal it. The material senses originate and   9
support all that is material, untrue, selfish, or debased.
They would put soul into soil, life into limbo, and doom
all things to decay. We must silence this lie of material   12
sense with the truth of spiritual sense. We must cause
the error to cease that brought the belief of sin and death
and would efface the pure sense of omnipotence.   15

Is the sick man sinful above all others? No! but
so far as he is discordant, he is not the image of God.

**Sickness
as discord**

Weary of their material beliefs, from which   18
comes so much suffering, invalids grow more
spiritual, as the error — or belief that life is in matter —
yields to the reality of spiritual Life.   21

The Science of Mind denies the error of sensation in
matter, and heals with Truth. Medical science treats
disease as though disease were real, therefore right, and   24
attempts to heal it with matter. If disease is right it is
wrong to heal it. Material methods are temporary, and
are not adapted to elevate mankind.   27

The governor is not subjected to the governed. In
Science man is governed by God, divine Principle, as
numbers are controlled and proved by His laws. Intelli-   30
gence does not originate in numbers, but is manifested
through them. The body does not include soul, but man-

1 ifests mortality, a false sense of soul. The delusion that
there is life in matter has no kinship with the Life supernal.

3 Science depicts disease as error, as matter *versus*
Mind, and error reversed as subserving the facts of
health. To calculate one's life-prospects
Unscientific
introspection
6 from a material basis, would infringe upon
spiritual law and misguide human hope. Having faith
in the divine Principle of health and spiritually under-
9 standing God, sustains man under all circumstances;
whereas the lower appeal to the general faith in material
means (commonly called nature) must yield to the all-
12 might of infinite Spirit.

Throughout the infinite cycles of eternal existence,
Spirit and matter neither concur in man nor in the universe.

15 The varied doctrines and theories which presuppose
life and intelligence to exist in matter are so many ancient
and modern mythologies. Mystery, miracle,
God the
only Mind
18 sin, and death will disappear when it becomes
fairly understood that the divine Mind controls man and
man has no Mind but God.

21 The divine Science taught in the original language
of the Bible came through inspiration, and needs inspiration to be understood. Hence the misappre-
Scriptures
misinterpreted
24 hension of the spiritual meaning of the Bible,
and the misinterpretation of the Word in
some instances by uninspired writers, who only wrote
27 down what an inspired teacher had said. A misplaced
word changes the sense and misstates the Science of
the Scriptures, as, for instance, to name Love as merely
30 an attribute of God; but we can by special and proper
capitalization speak of the love of Love, meaning by that
what the beloved disciple meant in one of his epistles,

when he said, "God is love." Likewise we can speak of   1
the truth of Truth and of the life of Life, for Christ plainly
declared, "I am the way, the truth, and the life."   3

Metaphors abound in the Bible, and names are often
expressive of spiritual ideas. The most distinguished

Interior
meaning

theologians in Europe and America agree that   6
the Scriptures have both a spiritual and literal meaning. In Smith's Bible Dictionary it is said:
"The spiritual interpretation of Scripture must rest   9
upon both the literal and moral;" and in the learned
article on Noah in the same work, the familiar text,
Genesis vi. 3, "And the Lord said, My spirit shall not   12
always strive with man, for that he also is flesh," is quoted
as follows, from the original Hebrew: "And Jehovah
said, My spirit shall not forever rule [or be humbled] in   15
men, seeing that they are [or, in their error they are]
but flesh." Here the original text declares plainly the
spiritual fact of being, even man's eternal and harmo-   18
nious existence as image, idea, instead of matter (however transcendental such a thought appears), and avers
that this fact is not forever to be humbled by the belief   21
that man is flesh and matter, for according to that error
man is mortal.

The one important interpretation of Scripture is the   24
spiritual. For example, the text, "In my flesh shall I
see God," gives a profound idea of the di-

Job, on the
resurrection

vine power to heal the ills of the flesh, and   27
encourages mortals to hope in Him who healeth all our
diseases; whereas this passage is continually quoted
as if Job intended to declare that even if disease and   30
worms destroyed his body, yet in the latter days he should
stand in celestial perfection before Elohim, still clad

1 in material flesh, — an interpretation which is just the opposite of the true, as may be seen by studying the book
3 of Job. As Paul says, in his first epistle to the Corinthians, "Flesh and blood cannot inherit the kingdom of
God."

6 The Hebrew Lawgiver, slow of speech, despaired of
making the people understand what should be revealed
to him. When, led by wisdom to cast down his

Fear of the
serpent
overcome

9 rod, he saw it become a serpent, Moses fled before it; but wisdom bade him come back and
handle the serpent, and then Moses' fear departed. In
12 this incident was seen the actuality of Science. Matter
was shown to be a belief only. The serpent, evil, under
wisdom's bidding, was destroyed through understanding
15 divine Science, and this proof was a staff upon which to
lean. The illusion of Moses lost its power to alarm him,
when he discovered that what he apparently saw was really
18 but a phase of mortal belief.

It was scientifically demonstrated that leprosy was a
creation of mortal mind and not a condition of matter,

Leprosy
healed

21 when Moses first put his hand into his bosom
and drew it forth white as snow with the dread
disease, and presently restored his hand to its natural con-
24 dition by the same simple process. God had lessened
Moses' fear by this proof in divine Science, and the inward voice became to him the voice of God, which said:
27 "It shall come to pass, if they will not believe thee, neither
hearken to the voice of the first sign, that they will believe
the voice of the latter sign." And so it was in the coming
30 centuries, when the Science of being was demonstrated
by Jesus, who showed his students the power of Mind by
changing water into wine, and taught them how to handle

serpents unharmed, to heal the sick and cast out evils in   1
proof of the supremacy of Mind.

When understanding changes the standpoints of life and   3
intelligence from a material to a spiritual basis, we shall
gain the reality of Life, the control of Soul over

Standpoints
changed

sense, and we shall perceive Christianity, or   6
Truth, in its divine Principle. This must be the climax
before harmonious and immortal man is obtained and his
capabilities revealed. It is highly important — in view   9
of the immense work to be accomplished before this recognition of divine Science can come — to turn our thoughts
towards divine Principle, that finite belief may be pre-   12
pared to relinquish its error.

Man's wisdom finds no satisfaction in sin, since God
has sentenced sin to suffer. The necromancy of yester-   15

Saving the
inebriate

day foreshadowed the mesmerism and hypnotism of to-day. The drunkard thinks he enjoys
drunkenness, and you cannot make the inebriate leave   18
his besottedness, until his physical sense of pleasure yields
to a higher sense. Then he turns from his cups, as
the startled dreamer who wakens from an incubus in-   21
curred through the pains of distorted sense. A man who
likes to do wrong — finding pleasure in it and refraining
from it only through fear of consequences — is neither   24
a temperate man nor a reliable religionist.

The sharp experiences of belief in the supposititious life
of matter, as well as our disappointments and ceaseless   27

Uses of
suffering

woes, turn us like tired children to the arms
of divine Love. Then we begin to learn Life
in divine Science. Without this process of weaning,   30
"Canst thou by searching find out God?" It is easier
to desire Truth than to rid one's self of error. Mortals

1   may seek the understanding of Christian Science, but they
will not be able to glean from Christian Science the facts
3   of being without striving for them. This strife consists
in the endeavor to forsake error of every kind and to possess no other consciousness but good.

6   Through the wholesome chastisements of Love, we
are helped onward in the march towards righteousness,
peace, and purity, which are the landmarks

A bright outlook

9   of Science. Beholding the infinite tasks of
truth, we pause, — wait on God. Then we push onward,
until boundless thought walks enraptured, and concep-
12   tion unconfined is winged to reach the divine glory.

        In order to apprehend more, we must put into prac-
tice what we already know. We must recollect that
15   Truth is demonstrable when understood, and
that good is not understood until demonstrated.

Need and supply

If "faithful over a few things," we shall be made rulers
18   over many; but the one unused talent decays and is lost.
When the sick or the sinning awake to realize their need
of what they have not, they will be receptive of divine
21   Science, which gravitates towards Soul and away from
material sense, removes thought from the body, and ele-
vates even mortal mind to the contemplation of some-
24   thing better than disease or sin. The true idea of God
gives the true understanding of Life and Love, robs the
grave of victory, takes away all sin and the delusion that
27   there are other minds, and destroys mortality.

        The effects of Christian Science are not so much seen
as felt. It is the "still, small voice" of Truth

Childlike receptivity

30   uttering itself. We are either turning away
from this utterance, or we are listening to it and going
up higher. Willingness to become as a little child and

to leave the old for the new, renders thought receptive of   1
the advanced idea. Gladness to leave the false landmarks
and joy to see them disappear, — this disposition helps   3
to precipitate the ultimate harmony. The purification
of sense and self is a proof of progress. "Blessed are the
pure in heart: for they shall see God."   6

Unless the harmony and immortality of man are becoming more apparent, we are not gaining the true idea

Narrow pathway
of God; and the body will reflect what gov-   9
erns it, whether it be Truth or error,
understanding or belief, Spirit or matter. Therefore
"acquaint now thyself with Him, and be at peace."   12
Be watchful, sober, and vigilant. The way is straight
and narrow, which leads to the understanding that God
is the only Life. It is a warfare with the flesh, in which   15
we must conquer sin, sickness, and death, either here
or hereafter, — certainly before we can reach the goal
of Spirit, or life in God.   18

Paul was not at first a disciple of Jesus but a persecutor of Jesus' followers. When the truth first appeared

Paul's enlightenment
to him in Science, Paul was made blind,   21
and his blindness was felt; but spiritual
light soon enabled him to follow the example and teachings of Jesus, healing the sick and preaching Christian-   24
ity throughout Asia Minor, Greece, and even in imperial
Rome.

Paul writes, "If Christ [Truth] be not risen, then is   27
our preaching vain." That is, if the idea of the supremacy of Spirit, which is the true conception of being,
come not to your thought, you cannot be benefited by   30
what I say.

Jesus said substantially, "He that believeth in me

1 shall not see death." That is, he who perceives the
true idea of Life loses his belief in death. He who has
3 the true idea of good loses all sense of evil,
and by reason of this is being ushered into the
undying realities of Spirit. Such a one abideth in Life, —
6 life obtained not of the body incapable of supporting life,
but of Truth, unfolding its own immortal idea. Jesus
gave the true idea of being, which results in infinite bless-
9 ings to mortals.

Abiding in Life

In Colossians (iii. 4) Paul writes: "When Christ, who
is our life, shall appear [be manifested], then shall ye also
12 appear [be manifested] with him in glory."
When spiritual being is understood in all its
perfection, continuity, and might, then shall man be found
15 in God's image. The absolute meaning of the apostolic
words is this: Then shall man be found, in His likeness,
perfect as the Father, indestructible in Life, "hid with
18 Christ in God," — with Truth in divine Love, where
human sense hath not seen man.

Indestructible being

Paul had a clear sense of the demands of Truth upon
mortals physically and spiritually, when he said: "Pre-
21 sent your bodies a living sacrifice, holy, acceptable unto God, which is your reasonable
service." But he, who is begotten of the beliefs of the
24 flesh and serves them, can never reach in this world the
divine heights of our Lord. The time cometh when
the spiritual origin of man, the divine Science which
27 ushered Jesus into human presence, will be understood
and demonstrated.

Consecration required

30 When first spoken in any age, Truth, like the light,
"shineth in darkness, and the darkness comprehended
it not." A false sense of life, substance, and mind

hides the divine possibilities, and conceals scientific   1
demonstration.

If we wish to follow Christ, Truth, it must be in the   3
way of God's appointing. Jesus said, "He that believeth
on me, the works that I do shall he do also."

He, who would reach the source and find the   6
divine remedy for every ill, must not try to climb the hill
of Science by some other road. All nature teaches God's
love to man, but man cannot love God supremely and set   9
his whole affections on spiritual things, while loving the
material or trusting in it more than in the spiritual.

We must forsake the foundation of material systems,   12
however time-honored, if we would gain the Christ as
our only Saviour. Not partially, but fully, the great
healer of mortal mind is the healer of the body.   15

The purpose and motive to live aright can be gained
now. This point won, you have started as you should.
You have begun at the numeration-table of Christian   18
Science, and nothing but wrong intention can hinder your
advancement. Working and praying with true motives,
your Father will open the way. "Who did hinder you,   21
that ye should not obey the truth?"

Saul of Tarsus beheld the way — the Christ, or Truth
— only when his uncertain sense of right yielded to a   24

spiritual sense, which is always right. Then
the man was changed. Thought assumed a
nobler outlook, and his life became more spiritual. He   27
learned the wrong that he had done in persecuting Christians, whose religion he had not understood, and in humility he took the new name of Paul. He beheld for the   30
first time the true idea of Love, and learned a lesson in
divine Science.

1   Reform comes by understanding that there is no abiding pleasure in evil, and also by gaining an affection for
3   good according to Science, which reveals the immortal
fact that neither pleasure nor pain, appetite nor passion,
can exist in or of matter, while divine Mind can and does
6   destroy the false beliefs of pleasure, pain, or fear and all
the sinful appetites of the human mind.

What a pitiful sight is malice, finding pleasure in re-
9   venge! Evil is sometimes a man's highest conception
of right, until his grasp on good grows stronger.   *Image of*
Then he loses pleasure in wickedness, and it   *the beast*
12   becomes his torment. The way to escape the misery of
sin is to cease sinning. There is no other way. Sin is
the image of the beast to be effaced by the sweat of agony.
15   It is a moral madness which rushes forth to clamor with
midnight and tempest.

To the physical senses, the strict demands of Christian
18   Science seem peremptory; but mortals are has-   *Peremptory*
tening to learn that Life is God, good, and that   *demands*
evil has in reality neither place nor power in the human or
21   the divine economy.

Fear of punishment never made man truly honest.
Moral courage is requisite to meet the wrong and to
24   proclaim the right. But how shall we re-   *Moral*
form the man who has more animal than   *courage*
moral courage, and who has not the true idea of good?
27   Through human consciousness, convince the mortal of
his mistake in seeking material means for gaining happiness. Reason is the most active human faculty. Let
30   that inform the sentiments and awaken the man's dormant sense of moral obligation, and by degrees he will
learn the nothingness of the pleasures of human sense

and the grandeur and bliss of a spiritual sense, which
silences the material or corporeal. Then he not only will
be saved, but *is* saved.

Mortals suppose that they can live without goodness,
when God is good and the only real Life. What is the

Final
destruction
of error

result? Understanding little about the divine
Principle which saves and heals, mortals get
rid of sin, sickness, and death only in belief. These errors
are not thus really destroyed, and must therefore cling
to mortals until, here or hereafter, they gain the true understanding of God in the Science which destroys human
delusions about Him and reveals the grand realities of
His allness.

This understanding of man's power, when he is
equipped by God, has sadly disappeared from Christian

Promise
perpetual

history. For centuries it has been dormant, a
lost element of Christianity. Our missionaries
carry the Bible to India, but can it be said that they
explain it practically, as Jesus did, when hundreds of
persons die there annually from serpent-bites? Understanding spiritual law and knowing that there is no material law, Jesus said: "These signs shall follow them that
believe, . . . they shall take up serpents, and if they
drink any deadly thing, it shall not hurt them. They
shall lay hands on the sick, and they shall recover." It
were well had Christendom believed and obeyed this
sacred saying.

Jesus' promise is perpetual. Had it been given only
to his immediate disciples, the Scriptural passage would
read *you,* not *they.* The purpose of his great life-work
extends through time and includes universal humanity.
Its Principle is infinite, reaching beyond the pale of a

single period or of a limited following. As time moves
on, the healing elements of pure Christianity will be fairly
dealt with; they will be sought and taught, and will glow
in all the grandeur of universal goodness.

A little leaven leavens the whole lump. A little understanding of Christian Science proves the truth of all that
I say of it. Because you cannot walk on the
water and raise the dead, you have no right to
question the great might of divine Science in these directions. Be thankful that Jesus, who was the true demonstrator of Science, did these things, and left his example for
us. In Science we can use only what we understand. We
must prove our faith by demonstration.

One should not tarry in the storm if the body is freezing, nor should he remain in the devouring flames. Until one is able to prevent bad results, he should avoid their
occasion. To be discouraged, is to resemble a pupil in
addition, who attempts to solve a problem of Euclid, and
denies the rule of the problem because he fails in his first
effort.

There is no hypocrisy in Science. Principle is imperative. You cannot mock it by human will. Science is a
divine demand, not a human. Always right,
its divine Principle never repents, but maintains the claim of Truth by quenching error.
The pardon of divine mercy is the destruction of error. If
men understood their real spiritual source to be all blessedness, they would struggle for recourse to the spiritual
and be at peace; but the deeper the error into which mortal mind is plunged, the more intense the opposition to
spirituality, till error yields to Truth.

Human resistance to divine Science weakens in pro-

Imitation of Jesus

Error destroyed, not pardoned

portion as mortals give up error for Truth and the un-   1
derstanding of being supersedes mere belief. Until the
The hopeful   author of this book learned the vastness of   3
outlook   Christian Science, the fixedness of mortal illusions, and the human hatred of Truth, she cherished
sanguine hopes that Christian Science would meet with   6
immediate and universal acceptance.

When the following platform is understood and the
letter and the spirit bear witness, the infallibility of divine   9
metaphysics will be demonstrated.

I. God is infinite, the only Life, substance, Spirit, or
Soul, the only intelligence of the universe, including man.   12
The deific   Eye hath neither seen God nor His image and
supremacy   likeness. Neither God nor the perfect man
can be discerned by the material senses. The individ-   15
uality of Spirit, or the infinite, is unknown, and thus a
knowledge of it is left either to human conjecture or to the
revelation of divine Science.   18

II. God is what the Scriptures declare Him to be, —
Life, Truth, Love. Spirit is divine Principle, and divine
The deific   Principle is Love, and Love is Mind, and   21
definitions   Mind is not both good and bad, for God is
Mind; therefore there is in reality one Mind only, be-
cause there is one God.   24

III. The notion that both evil and good are real is a
delusion of material sense, which Science annihilates.
Evil   Evil is nothing, no thing, mind, nor power.   27
obsolete   As manifested by mankind it stands for a lie,
nothing claiming to be something, — for lust, dishonesty,
selfishness, envy, hypocrisy, slander, hate, theft, adultery,   30
murder, dementia, insanity, inanity, devil, hell, with all
the etceteras that word includes.

1   IV. God is divine Life, and Life is no more confined
        to the forms which reflect it than substance is in its
3   shadow. If life were in mortal man or mate-   **Life the**
        rial things, it would be subject to their limi-   **creator**
        tations and would end in death. Life is Mind, the creator
6   reflected in His creations. If He dwelt within what He
        creates, God would not be reflected but absorbed, and the
        Science of being would be forever lost through a mortal
9   sense, which falsely testifies to a beginning and an
        end.
            V. The Scriptures imply that God is All-in-all. From
12   this it follows that nothing possesses reality nor existence
        except the divine Mind and His ideas. The   **Allness of**
        Scriptures also declare that God is Spirit.   **Spirit**
15   Therefore in Spirit all is harmony, and there can be no
        discord; all is Life, and there is no death. Everything
        in God's universe expresses Him.
18   VI. God is individual, incorporeal. He is divine Prin-
        ciple, Love, the universal cause, the only creator, and
        there is no other self-existence. He is all-   **The universal**
21   inclusive, and is reflected by all that is real   **cause**
        and eternal and by nothing else. He fills all space, and
        it is impossible to conceive of such omnipresence and in-
24   dividuality except as infinite Spirit or Mind. Hence all
        is Spirit and spiritual.
            VII. Life, Truth, and Love constitute the triune Person
27   called God, — that is, the triply divine Principle, Love.
        They represent a trinity in unity, three in   **Divine**
        one, — the same in essence, though multi-   **trinity**
30   form in office: God the Father-Mother; Christ the spirit-
        ual idea of sonship; divine Science or the Holy Comforter.
        These three express in divine Science the threefold, essen-

tial nature of the infinite. They also indicate the divine
Principle of scientific being, the intelligent relation of God
to man and the universe.

VIII. Father-Mother is the name for Deity, which indicates His tender relationship to His spiritual creation.

**Father-
Mother**

As the apostle expressed it in words which he
quoted with approbation from a classic poet:
"For we are also His offspring."

IX. Jesus was born of Mary. Christ is the true idea
voicing good, the divine message from God to men speak-

**The Son
of God**

ing to the human consciousness. The Christ
is incorporeal, spiritual, — yea, the divine
image and likeness, dispelling the illusions of the senses;
the Way, the Truth, and the Life, healing the sick and
casting out evils, destroying sin, disease, and death. As
Paul says: "There is one God, and one mediator between
God and men, the man Christ Jesus." The corporeal
man Jesus was human.

X. Jesus demonstrated Christ; he proved that Christ

**Holy Ghost
or Comforter**

is the divine idea of God — the Holy Ghost,
or Comforter, revealing the divine Principle,
Love, and leading into all truth.

XI. Jesus was the son of a virgin. He was appointed
to speak God's word and to appear to mortals in such

Christ Jesus

a form of humanity as they could understand
as well as perceive. Mary's conception of
him was spiritual, for only purity could reflect Truth
and Love, which were plainly incarnate in the good and
pure Christ Jesus. He expressed the highest type of
divinity, which a fleshly form could express in that age.
Into the real and ideal man the fleshly element cannot
enter. Thus it is that Christ illustrates the coincidence,

1   or spiritual agreement, between God and man in His
image.

3   XII. The word *Christ* is not properly a synonym for
Jesus, though it is commonly so used. Jesus was a human
name, which belonged to him in common with
6   other Hebrew boys and men, for it is identical
with the name Joshua, the renowned Hebrew leader. On
the other hand, Christ is not a name so much as the divine
9   title of Jesus. Christ expresses God's spiritual, eternal
nature. The name is synonymous with Messiah, and alludes to the spirituality which is taught, illustrated, and
12   demonstrated in the life of which Christ Jesus was the
embodiment. The proper name of our Master in the
Greek was Jesus the Christ; but Christ Jesus better sig-
15   nifies the Godlike.

Messiah or Christ

XIII. The advent of Jesus of Nazareth marked the
first century of the Christian era, but the Christ is
18   without beginning of years or end of days.
Throughout all generations both before and
after the Christian era, the Christ, as the spirit-
21   ual idea, — the reflection of God, — has come with some
measure of power and grace to all prepared to receive
Christ, Truth. Abraham, Jacob, Moses, and the prophets
24   caught glorious glimpses of the Messiah, or Christ, which
baptized these seers in the divine nature, the essence of
Love. The divine image, idea, or Christ was, is, and
27   ever will be inseparable from the divine Principle, God.
Jesus referred to this unity of his spiritual identity thus:
"Before Abraham was, I am;" "I and my Father are
30   one;" "My Father is greater than I." The one Spirit
includes all identities.

The divine Principle and idea

XIV. By these sayings Jesus meant, not that the hu-

man Jesus was or is eternal, but that the divine idea or
Christ was and is so and therefore antedated Abraham;

not that the corporeal Jesus was one with the
Father, but that the spiritual idea, Christ,
dwells forever in the bosom of the Father, God, from
which it illumines heaven and earth; not that the Father
is greater than Spirit, which is God, but greater, infinitely
greater, than the fleshly Jesus, whose earthly career was
brief.

XV. The invisible Christ was imperceptible to the
so-called personal senses, whereas Jesus appeared as a

bodily existence. This dual personality of the
unseen and the seen, the spiritual and material, the eternal Christ and the corporeal Jesus manifest
in flesh, continued until the Master's ascension, when
the human, material concept, or Jesus, disappeared,
while the spiritual self, or Christ, continues to exist in
the eternal order of divine Science, taking away the sins
of the world, as the Christ has always done, even before
the human Jesus was incarnate to mortal eyes.

XVI. This was "the Lamb slain from the foundation
of the world," — slain, that is, according to the testi-

mony of the corporeal senses, but undying in
the deific Mind. The Revelator represents the
Son of man as saying (Revelation i. 17, 18): "I am the
first and the last: I am he that liveth, and was dead
[not understood]; and, behold, I am alive for evermore,
[Science has explained me]." This is a mystical statement of the eternity of the Christ, and is also a reference
to the human sense of Jesus crucified.

XVII. Spirit being God, there is but one Spirit, for
there can be but one infinite and therefore one God.

1   There are neither spirits many nor gods many. There
    is no evil in Spirit, because God is Spirit. The theory,
3   that Spirit is distinct from matter but must   **Infinite**
    pass through it, or into it, to be individualized,   **Spirit**
    would reduce God to dependency on matter, and establish
6   a basis for pantheism.

        XVIII. Spirit, God, has created all in and of Him-
    self. Spirit never created matter. There is nothing in
9   Spirit out of which matter could be made,   **The only**
    for, as the Bible declares, without the Logos,   **substance**
    the Æon or Word of God, "was not anything made
12 that was made." Spirit is the only substance, the in-
    visible and indivisible infinite God. Things spiritual and
    eternal are substantial. Things material and temporal
15 are insubstantial.

        XIX. Soul and Spirit being one, God and Soul are
    one, and this one never included in a limited mind or a
18 limited body. Spirit is eternal, divine. Noth-   **Soul and**
    ing but Spirit, Soul, can evolve Life, for Spirit   **Spirit one**
    is more than all else. Because Soul is immortal, it does
21 not exist in mortality. Soul must be incorporeal to be
    Spirit, for Spirit is not finite. Only by losing the false
    sense of Soul can we gain the eternal unfolding of Life as
24 immortality brought to light.

        XX. Mind is the divine Principle, Love, and can pro-
    duce nothing unlike the eternal Father-Mother, God.
27 Reality is spiritual, harmonious, immutable,   **The one**
    immortal, divine, eternal. Nothing unspirit-   **divine Mind**
    ual can be real, harmonious, or eternal. Sin, sickness,
30 and mortality are the suppositional antipodes of Spirit,
    and must be contradictions of reality.

        XXI. The Ego is deathless and limitless, for limits

would imply and impose ignorance. Mind is the I AM, or infinity. Mind never enters the finite. Intelligence never passes into non-intelligence, or matter. Good never enters into evil, the unlimited into the limited, the eternal into the temporal, nor the immortal into mortality. The divine Ego, or individuality, is reflected in all spiritual individuality from the infinitesimal to the infinite.

The divine
Ego

XXII. Immortal man was and is God's image or idea, even the infinite expression of infinite Mind, and immortal man is coexistent and coeternal with that Mind. He has been forever in the eternal Mind, God; but infinite Mind can never be in man, but is reflected by man. The spiritual man's consciousness and individuality are reflections of God. They are the emanations of Him who is Life, Truth, and Love. Immortal man is not and never was material, but always spiritual and eternal.

The real
manhood

XXIII. God is indivisible. A portion of God could not enter man; neither could God's fulness be reflected by a single man, else God would be manifestly finite, lose the deific character, and become less than God. Allness is the measure of the infinite, and nothing less can express God.

Indivisibility
of the infinite

XXIV. God, the divine Principle of man, and man in God's likeness are inseparable, harmonious, and eternal. The Science of being furnishes the rule of perfection, and brings immortality to light. God and man are not the same, but in the order of divine Science, God and man coexist and are eternal. God is the parent Mind, and man is God's spiritual offspring.

God the
parent Mind

XXV. God is individual and personal in a scientific

sense, but not in any anthropomorphic sense. Therefore man, reflecting God, cannot lose his individuality; but as material sensation, or a soul in the body, blind mortals do lose sight of spiritual individuality. Material personality is not realism; it is not the reflection or likeness of Spirit, the perfect God. Sensualism is not bliss, but bondage. For true happiness, man must harmonize with his Principle, divine Love; the Son must be in accord with the Father, in conformity with Christ. According to divine Science, man is in a degree as perfect as the Mind that forms him. The truth of being makes man harmonious and immortal, while error is mortal and discordant.

Man reflects the perfect God

XXVI. Christian Science demonstrates that none but the pure in heart can see God, as the gospel teaches. In proportion to his purity is man perfect; and perfection is the order of celestial being which demonstrates Life in Christ, Life's spiritual ideal.

Purity the path to perfection

XXVII. The true idea of man, as the reflection of the invisible God, is as incomprehensible to the limited senses as is man's infinite Principle. The visible universe and material man are the poor counterfeits of the invisible universe and spiritual man. Eternal things (verities) are God's thoughts as they exist in the spiritual realm of the real. Temporal things are the thoughts of mortals and are the unreal, being the opposite of the real or the spiritual and eternal.

True idea of man

XXVIII. Subject sickness, sin, and death to the rule of health and holiness in Christian Science, and you ascertain that this Science is demonstrably true, for it heals the sick and sinning as no

Truth demonstrated

other system can. Christian Science, rightly under-   1
stood, leads to eternal harmony. It brings to light the
only living and true God and man as made in His like-   3
ness; whereas the opposite belief — that man originates
in matter and has beginning and end, that he is both
soul and body, both good and evil, both spiritual and   6
material — terminates in discord and mortality, in the
error which must be destroyed by Truth. The mortality
of material man proves that error has been ingrafted   9
into the premises and conclusions of material and mortal
humanity.

XXIX. The word *Adam* is from the Hebrew *adamah*,   12
signifying the *red color of the ground, dust, nothingness.*

Adam not   Divide the name Adam into two syllables,
ideal man   and it reads, *a dam,* or obstruction. This   15
suggests the thought of something fluid, of mortal mind
in solution. It further suggests the thought of that
"darkness . . . upon the face of the deep," when mat-   18
ter or dust was deemed the agent of Deity in creating
man, — when matter, as that which is accursed, stood
opposed to Spirit. Here *a dam* is not a mere play upon   21
words; it stands for obstruction, error, even the supposed separation of man from God, and the obstacle
which the serpent, sin, would impose between man and   24
his creator. The dissection and definition of words,
aside from their metaphysical derivation, is not scientific. Jehovah declared the ground was accursed; and   27
from this ground, or matter, sprang Adam, notwithstanding God had blessed the earth "for man's sake."
From this it follows that Adam was not the ideal man   30
for whom the earth was blessed. The ideal man was
revealed in due time, and was known as Christ Jesus.

1   XXX. The destruction of sin is the divine method of
pardon. Divine Life destroys death, Truth destroys
3 error, and Love destroys hate. Being destroyed, sin needs no other form of forgiveness.
Does not God's pardon, destroying any one sin, prophesy
6 and involve the final destruction of all sin?

Divine
pardon

    XXXI. Since God is All, there is no room for His
unlikeness. God, Spirit, alone created all, and called it
9 good. Therefore evil, being contrary to good,
is unreal, and cannot be the product of God.
A sinner can receive no encouragement from the fact that
12 Science demonstrates the unreality of evil, for the sinner
would make a reality of sin, — would make that real
which is unreal, and thus heap up "wrath against the
15 day of wrath." He is joining in a conspiracy against
himself, — against his own awakening to the awful unreality by which he has been deceived. Only those, who
18 repent of sin and forsake the unreal, can fully understand
the unreality of evil.

Evil not
produced
by God

    XXXII. As the mythology of pagan Rome has yielded
21 to a more spiritual idea of Deity, so will our material
theories yield to spiritual ideas, until the finite
gives place to the infinite, sickness to health,
24 sin to holiness, and God's kingdom comes "in
earth, as it is in heaven." The basis of all health, sinlessness, and immortality is the great fact that God is
27 the only Mind; and this Mind must be not merely believed, but it must be understood. To get rid of sin
through Science, is to divest sin of any supposed mind
30 or reality, and never to admit that sin can have intelligence or power, pain or pleasure. You conquer error by
denying its verity. Our various theories will never lose

Basis of
health and
immortality

their imaginary power for good or evil, until we lose our 1
faith in them and make life its own proof of harmony
and God. 3

This text in the book of Ecclesiastes conveys the
Christian Science thought, especially when the word
duty, which is not in the original, is omitted: "Let 6
us hear the conclusion of the whole matter: Fear God,
and keep His commandments: for this is the whole
duty of man." In other words: Let us hear the con- 9
clusion of the whole matter: love God and keep His
commandments: for this is the whole of man in His
image and likeness. Divine Love is infinite. Therefore 12
all that really exists is in and of God, and manifests His
love.

"Thou shalt have no other gods before me." (Exodus 15
xx. 3.) The First Commandment is my favorite text.
It demonstrates Christian Science. It inculcates the tri-
unity of God, Spirit, Mind; it signifies that man shall 18
have no other spirit or mind but God, eternal good, and
that all men shall have one Mind. The divine Principle
of the First Commandment bases the Science of being, by 21
which man demonstrates health, holiness, and life eternal.
One infinite God, good, unifies men and nations; constitutes the brotherhood of man; ends wars; fulfils the 24
Scripture, "Love thy neighbor as thyself;" annihilates
pagan and Christian idolatry, — whatever is wrong in
social, civil, criminal, political, and religious codes; 27
equalizes the sexes; annuls the curse on man, and leaves
nothing that can sin, suffer, be punished or destroyed.

Chapter 11

Some Objections Answered

And because I tell you the truth, ye believe me not.
Which of you convinceth me of sin?
And if I say the truth, why do ye not believe me? — JESUS.

But if the spirit of Him that raised up Jesus from the dead dwell in you,
He that raised up Christ from the dead shall also quicken
your mortal bodies by His spirit that dwelleth in you. — PAUL.

1   The strictures on this volume would condemn to
oblivion the truth, which is raising up thousands
3   from helplessness to strength and elevating them from
a theoretical to a practical Christianity. These criticisms
are generally based on detached sentences or clauses sep-
6   arated from their context. Even the Scriptures, which
grow in beauty and consistency from one grand root, appear contradictory when subjected to such usage. Jesus
9   said, "Blessed are the pure in heart: for they shall see
God" [Truth].

        In Christian Science mere opinion is valueless. Proof
12   is essential to a due estimate of this subject. Sneers at
the application of the word *Science* to Christianity cannot prevent that from being scien-

Supported
by facts

15   tific which is based on divine Principle, demonstrated according to a divine given rule, and subjected to proof.
The facts are so absolute and numerous in support of
18   Christian Science, that misrepresentation and denuncia-

341

tion cannot overthrow it. Paul alludes to "doubtful dis-   1
putations." The hour has struck when proof and demonstration, instead of opinion and dogma, are summoned to   3
the support of Christianity, "making wise the simple."

In the result of some unqualified condemnations of
scientific Mind-healing, one may see with sorrow the sad   6

Commands
of Jesus
effects on the sick of denying Truth. He that
decries this Science does it presumptuously,
in the face of Bible history and in defiance of the direct   9
command of Jesus, "Go ye into all the world, and preach
the gospel," to which command was added the promise
that his students should cast out evils and heal the sick.   12
He bade the seventy disciples, as well as the twelve,
heal the sick in any town where they should be hospitably
received.   15

If Christianity is not scientific, and Science is not of
God, then there is no invariable law, and truth becomes

Christianity
scientific
an accident. Shall it be denied that a system   18
which works according to the Scriptures has
Scriptural authority?

Christian Science awakens the sinner, reclaims the   21
infidel, and raises from the couch of pain the helpless

Argument of
good works
invalid. It speaks to the dumb the words of
Truth, and they answer with rejoicing. It   24
causes the deaf to hear, the lame to walk, and the blind
to see. Who would be the first to disown the Christli-
ness of good works, when our Master says, "By their   27
fruits ye shall know them"?

If Christian Scientists were teaching or practising
pharmacy or obstetrics according to the common theo-   30
ries, no denunciations would follow them, even if their
treatment resulted in the death of a patient. The people

are taught in such cases to say, Amen. Shall I then be
smitten for healing and for teaching Truth as the Principle of healing, and for proving my word by my deed?
James said: "Show me thy faith without thy works, and
I will show thee my faith by my works."

Is not finite mind ignorant of God's method? This
makes it doubly unfair to impugn and misrepresent the
facts, although, without this cross-bearing,   **Personal**
one might not be able to say with the apostle,   **experience**
"None of these things move me." The sick, the halt,
and the blind look up to Christian Science with blessings,
and Truth will not be forever hidden by unjust parody
from the quickened sense of the people.

Jesus strips all disguise from error, when his teachings
are fully understood. By parable and argument he explains the impossibility of good producing evil;   **Proof from**
and he also scientifically demonstrates this great   **miracles**
fact, proving by what are wrongly called miracles, that
sin, sickness, and death are beliefs — illusive errors —
which he could and did destroy.

It would sometimes seem as if truth were rejected because meekness and spirituality are the conditions of its
acceptance, while Christendom generally demands so
much less.

Anciently those apostles who were Jesus' students,
as well as Paul who was not one of his students, healed
the sick and reformed the sinner by their   **Example of**
religion. Hence the mistake which allows   **the disciples**
words, rather than works, to follow such examples!
Whoever is the first meekly and conscientiously to press
along the line of gospel-healing, is often accounted a
heretic.

It is objected to Christian Science that it claims God 1
as the only absolute Life and Soul, and man to be His

idea, — that is, His image. It should be 3
added that this is claimed to represent the
normal, healthful, and sinless condition of man in divine
Science, and that this claim is made because the Scrip- 6
tures say that God has created man in His own image
and after His likeness. Is it sacrilegious to assume that
God's likeness is not found in matter, sin, sickness, and 9
death?

Were it more fully understood that Truth heals and
that error causes disease, the opponents of a demonstrable 12

Science would perhaps mercifully withhold
their misrepresentations, which harm the sick;
and until the enemies of Christian Science test its efficacy 15
according to the rules which disclose its merits or de-
merits, it would be just to observe the Scriptural precept,
"Judge not." 18

There are various methods of treating disease, which
are not included in the commonly accepted systems; but

there is only one which should be presented 21
to the whole world, and that is the Christian
Science which Jesus preached and practised and left to us
as his rich legacy. 24

Why should one refuse to investigate this method
of treating disease? Why support the popular systems
of medicine, when the physician may perchance be an 27
infidel and may lose ninety-and-nine patients, while
Christian Science cures its hundred? Is it because
allopathy and homœopathy are more fashionable and 30
less spiritual?

In the Bible the word *Spirit* is so commonly applied

to Deity, that Spirit and God are often regarded as synonymous terms; and it is thus they are uniformly used and understood in Christian Science. As it is evident that the likeness of Spirit cannot be material, does it not follow that God cannot be in His unlikeness and work through drugs to heal the sick? When the omnipotence of God is preached and His absoluteness is set forth, Christian sermons will heal the sick.

Omnipotence set forth

It is sometimes said, in criticising Christian Science, that the mind which contradicts itself neither knows itself nor what it is saying. It is indeed no small matter to know one's self; but in this volume of mine there are no contradictory statements, — at least none which are apparent to those who understand its propositions well enough to pass judgment upon them. One who understands Christian Science can heal the sick on the divine Principle of Christian Science, and this practical proof is the only feasible evidence that one does understand this Science.

Contradictions not found

Anybody, who is able to perceive the incongruity between God's idea and poor humanity, ought to be able to discern the distinction (made by Christian Science) between God's man, made in His image, and the sinning race of Adam.

The apostle says: "For if a man think himself to be something, when he is nothing, he deceiveth himself." This thought of human, material nothingness, which Science inculcates, enrages the carnal mind and is the main cause of the carnal mind's antagonism.

It is not the purpose of Christian Science to "educate the idea of God, or treat it for disease," as is alleged

by one critic. I regret that such criticism confounds *man*   1
with Adam. When man is spoken of as made in God's

God's idea
the ideal man
image, it is not sinful and sickly mortal man   3
who is referred to, but the ideal man, reflecting
God's likeness.

It is sometimes said that Christian Science teaches the   6
nothingness of sin, sickness, and death, and then teaches

Nothingness
of error
how this nothingness is to be saved and healed.
The nothingness of nothing is plain; but we   9
need to understand that error *is* nothing, and that its
nothingness is not saved, but must be demonstrated in
order to prove the somethingness — yea, the allness —   12
of Truth. It is self-evident that we are harmonious only
as we cease to manifest evil or the belief that we suffer
from the sins of others. Disbelief in error destroys error,   15
and leads to the discernment of Truth. There are no
vacuums. How then can this demonstration be "fraught
with falsities painful to behold"?   18

We treat error through the understanding of Truth,
because Truth is error's antidote. If a dream ceases, it

Truth
antidotes error
is self-destroyed, and the terror is over. When   21
a sufferer is convinced that there is no reality
in his belief of pain, — because matter has no sensation,
hence pain in matter is a false belief, — how can he suffer   24
longer? Do you feel the pain of tooth-pulling, when you
believe that nitrous-oxide gas has made you unconscious?
Yet, in your concept, the tooth, the operation, and the   27
forceps are unchanged.

Material beliefs must be expelled to make room for

Serving
two masters
spiritual understanding. We cannot serve both   30
God and mammon at the same time; but is
not this what frail mortals are trying to do? Paul says:

1 "The flesh lusteth against the Spirit, and the Spirit against
the flesh." Who is ready to admit this?

3 It is said by one critic, that to verify this wonderful
philosophy Christian Science declares that whatever is
mortal or discordant has no origin, existence, nor real-

6 ness. Nothing really has Life but God, who is infinite
Life; hence all is Life, and death has no dominion. This
writer infers that if anything needs to be doctored, it

9 must be the one God, or Mind. Had he stated his syllogism correctly, the conclusion would be that there is nothing left to be doctored.

12 Critics should consider that the so-called mortal man
is not the reality of man. Then they would behold the
signs of Christ's coming. Christ, as the spir-

15 itual or true idea of God, comes now as of

Essential element of Christianity

old, preaching the gospel to the poor, healing the sick, and casting out evils. Is it error which

18 is restoring an essential element of Christianity, —
namely, apostolic, divine healing? No; it is the Science
of Christianity which is restoring it, and is the light

21 shining in darkness, which the darkness comprehends
not.

If Christian Science takes away the popular gods, —

24 sin, sickness, and death, — it is Christ, Truth, who destroys these evils, and so proves their nothingness.

The dream that matter and error are something

27 must yield to reason and revelation. Then mortals
will behold the nothingness of sickness and sin, and
sin and sickness will disappear from consciousness.

30 The harmonious will appear real, and the inharmonious unreal. These critics will then see that error
is indeed the nothingness, which they chide us for

naming nothing and which we desire neither to honor   1
nor to fear.

Medical theories virtually admit the nothingness of   3
hallucinations, even while treating them as disease; and
who objects to this? Ought we not, then, to approve
any cure, which is effected by making the disease appear   6
to be — what it really is — an illusion?

Here is the difficulty: it is not generally understood how
one disease can be just as much a delusion as another. It   9

**All disease
a delusion**

is a pity that the medical faculty and clergy
have not learned this, for Jesus established
this foundational fact, when devils, delusions, were cast   12
out and the dumb spake.

Are we irreverent towards sin, or imputing too much
power to God, when we ascribe to Him almighty Life   15

**Elimination
of sickness**

and Love? I deny His cooperation with evil,
because I desire to have no faith in evil or in
any power but God, good. Is it not well to eliminate from   18
so-called mortal mind that which, so long as it remains in
mortal mind, will show itself in forms of sin, sickness, and
death? Instead of tenaciously defending the supposed   21
rights of disease, while complaining of the suffering disease brings, would it not be well to abandon the defence,
especially when by so doing our own condition can be im-   24
proved and that of other persons as well?

I have never supposed the world would immediately
witness the full fruitage of Christian Science, or that sin,   27

**Full fruitage
yet to come**

disease, and death would not be believed for
an indefinite time; but this I do aver, that,
as a result of teaching Christian Science, ethics and   30
temperance have received an impulse, health has been
restored, and longevity increased. If such are the pres-

1 ent fruits, what will the harvest be, when this Science is
more generally understood?

3 As Paul asked of the unfaithful in ancient days, so
the rabbis of the present day ask concerning our healing and teaching, "Through breaking the law,

6 dishonorest thou God?" We have the gospel,
however, and our Master annulled material law by healing contrary to it. We propose to follow the Master's

9 example. We should subordinate material law to spiritual law. Two essential points of Christian Science are,
that neither Life nor man dies, and that God is not the

12 author of sickness.

Law and gospel

The chief difficulty in conveying the teachings of divine
Science accurately to human thought lies in this, that like

15 all other languages, English is inadequate to
the expression of spiritual conceptions and
propositions, because one is obliged to use material terms

18 in dealing with spiritual ideas. The elucidation of Christian Science lies in its spiritual sense, and this sense must
be gained by its disciples in order to grasp the meaning of

21 this Science. Out of this condition grew the prophecy
concerning the Christian apostles, "They shall speak with
new tongues."

Language inadequate

24 Speaking of the things of Spirit while dwelling on
a material plane, material terms must be generally employed. Mortal thought does not at once catch the

27 higher meaning, and can do so only as thought is educated up to spiritual apprehension. To a certain extent
this is equally true of all learning, even that which is

30 wholly material.

In Christian Science, substance is understood to be
Spirit, while the opponents of Christian Science believe

substance to be matter. They think of matter as some-   1
thing and almost the only thing, and of the things which

**Substance
spiritual**

pertain to Spirit as next to nothing, or as very   3
far removed from daily experience. Christian
Science takes exactly the opposite view.

To understand all our Master's sayings as recorded   6
in the New Testament, sayings infinitely important,

**Both words
and works**

his followers must grow into that stature of
manhood in Christ Jesus which enables them   9
to interpret his spiritual meaning. Then they know
how Truth casts out error and heals the sick. His
words were the offspring of his deeds, both of which   12
must be understood. Unless the works are comprehended which his words explained, the words are
blind.   15

The Master often refused to explain his words, because
it was difficult in a material age to apprehend spiritual
Truth. He said: "This people's heart is waxed gross,   18
and their ears are dull of hearing, and their eyes they
have closed; lest at any time they should see with their
eyes, and hear with their ears, and should understand   21
with their heart, and should be converted, and I should
heal them."

"The Word was made flesh." Divine Truth must be   24
known by its effects on the body as well as on the mind,

**The divine
life-link**

before the Science of being can be demonstrated. Hence its embodiment in the incar-   27
nate Jesus, — that life-link forming the connection through
which the real reaches the unreal, Soul rebukes sense, and
Truth destroys error.   30

In Jewish worship the Word was materially explained,
and the spiritual sense was scarcely perceived. The

religion which sprang from half-hidden Israelitish history
was pedantic and void of healing power. When we lose

faith in God's power to heal, we distrust the
divine Principle which demonstrates Christian
Science, and then we cannot heal the sick. Neither can
we heal through the help of Spirit, if we plant ourselves
on a material basis.

The author became a member of the orthodox Con-
gregational Church in early years. Later she learned
that her own prayers failed to heal her as did the prayers
of her devout parents and the church; but when the
spiritual sense of the creed was discerned in the Science
of Christianity, this spiritual sense was a *present help*. It
was the living, palpitating presence of Christ, Truth, which
healed the sick.

We cannot bring out the practical proof of Christianity,
which Jesus required, while error seems as potent and
real to us as Truth, and while we make a per-

sonal devil and an anthropomorphic God our
starting-points, — especially if we consider Satan as a
being coequal in power with Deity, if not superior to Him.
Because such starting-points are neither spiritual nor
scientific, they cannot work out the Spirit-rule of Christian
healing, which proves the nothingness of error, discord,
by demonstrating the all-inclusiveness of harmonious
Truth.

The Israelites centred their thoughts on the material
in their attempted worship of the spiritual. To them
matter was substance, and Spirit was shadow.

They thought to worship Spirit from a material standpoint, but this was impossible. They might
appeal to Jehovah, but their prayer brought down no

proof that it was heard, because they did not sufficiently 1
understand God to be able to demonstrate His power
to heal, — to make harmony the reality and discord the 3
unreality.

Our Master declared that his material body was not
spirit, evidently considering it a mortal and material be- 6

**Spirit the
tangible**

lief of flesh and bones, whereas the Jews took
a diametrically opposite view. To Jesus, not
materiality, but spirituality, was the reality of man's ex- 9
istence, while to the rabbis the spiritual was the intangible and uncertain, if not the unreal.

Would a mother say to her child, who is frightened at 12
imaginary ghosts and sick in consequence of the fear:

**Ghosts
not realities**

"I know that ghosts are real. They exist,
and are to be feared; but you must not be 15
afraid of them"?

Children, like adults, *ought* to fear a reality which
can harm them and which they do not understand, for 18
at any moment they may become its helpless victims;
but instead of increasing children's fears by declaring
ghosts to be real, merciless, and powerful, thus water- 21
ing the very roots of childish timidity, children should
be assured that their fears are groundless, that ghosts
are not realities, but traditional beliefs, erroneous and 24
man-made.

In short, children should be told not to believe in ghosts,
because there are no such things. If belief in their reality 27
is destroyed, terror of ghosts will depart and health be restored. The objects of alarm will then vanish into nothingness, no longer seeming worthy of fear or honor. To 30
accomplish a good result, it is certainly not irrational to
tell the truth about ghosts.

The Christianly scientific real is the sensuous unreal. Sin, disease, whatever seems real to material sense, is unreal in divine Science. The physical senses and Science have ever been antagonistic, and they will so continue, till the testimony of the physical senses yields entirely to Christian Science.

The real and the unreal

How can a Christian, having the stronger evidence of Truth which contradicts the evidence of error, think of the latter as real or true, either in the form of sickness or of sin? All must admit that Christ is "the way, the truth, and the life," and that omnipotent Truth certainly does destroy error.

The age has not wholly outlived the sense of ghostly beliefs. It still holds them more or less. Time has not yet reached eternity, immortality, complete reality. All the real is eternal. Perfection underlies reality. Without perfection, nothing is wholly real. All things will continue to disappear, until perfection appears and reality is reached. We must give up the spectral at all points. We must not continue to admit the somethingness of superstition, but we must yield up all belief in it and be wise. When we learn that error is not real, we shall be ready for progress, "forgetting those things which are behind."

Superstition obsolete

The grave does not banish the ghost of materiality. So long as there are supposed limits to Mind, and those limits are human, so long will ghosts seem to continue. Mind is limitless. It never was material. The true idea of being is spiritual and immortal, and from this it follows that whatever is laid off is the ghost, some unreal belief. Mortal beliefs can neither demonstrate Christianity nor apprehend the reality of Life.

Are the protests of Christian Science against the notion
that there can be material life, substance, or mind "utter
falsities and absurdities," as some aver? Why
then do Christians try to obey the Scriptures
and war against "the world, the flesh, and the devil"?
Why do they invoke the divine aid to enable them to leave
all for Christ, Truth? Why do they use this phraseology,
and yet deny Christian Science, when it teaches precisely
this thought? The words of divine Science find their
immortality in deeds, for their Principle heals the sick
and spiritualizes humanity.

On the other hand, the Christian opponents of Christian Science neither give nor offer any proofs that their
Master's religion can heal the sick. Surely
it is not enough to cleave to barren and desul-
tory dogmas, derived from the traditions of the elders who
thereunto have set their seals.

Consistency is seen in example more than in precept.
Inconsistency is shown by words without deeds, which
are like clouds without rain. If our words
fail to express our deeds, God will redeem that
weakness, and out of the mouth of babes He will perfect
praise. The night of materiality is far spent, and with
the dawn Truth will waken men spiritually to hear and
to speak the new tongue.

Sin should become unreal to every one. It is in itself
inconsistent, a divided kingdom. Its supposed realism
has no divine authority, and I rejoice in the apprehension
of this grand verity.

The opponents of divine Science must be
charitable, if they would be Christian. If the
letter of Christian Science appears inconsistent, they should

1 gain the spiritual meaning of Christian Science, and then
the ambiguity will vanish.

3 The charge of inconsistency in Christianly scientific
methods of dealing with sin and disease is met by something practical, — namely, the proof of the
6 utility of these methods; and proofs are better
than mere verbal arguments or prayers which evince no
spiritual power to heal.

Practical arguments

9 As for sin and disease, Christian Science says, in the
language of the Master, "Follow me; and let the dead
bury their dead." Let discord of every name and nature
12 be heard no more, and let the harmonious and true sense
of Life and being take possession of human consciousness.
What is the relative value of the two conflicting the-
15 ories regarding Christian healing? One, according to
the commands of our Master, heals the sick. The other,
popular religion, declines to admit that Christ's religion
18 has exercised any systematic healing power since the first
century.
The statement that the teachings of Christian Sci-
21 ence in this work are "absolutely false, and the most
egregious fallacies ever offered for acceptance," is an opinion wholly due to a misap-
24 prehension both of the divine Principle and practice of
Christian Science and to a consequent inability to demonstrate this Science. Without this understanding, no one
27 is capable of impartial or correct criticism, because demonstration and spiritual understanding are God's immortal
keynotes, proved to be such by our Master and evidenced
30 by the sick who are cured and by the sinners who are
reformed.
Strangely enough, we ask for material theories in sup-

Conditions of criticism

port of spiritual and eternal truths, when the two are so
antagonistic that the material thought must become spiritualized before the spiritual fact is attained.
So-called material existence affords no evidence
of spiritual existence and immortality. Sin,
sickness, and death do not prove man's entity or immortality. Discord can never establish the facts of harmony.
Matter is not the vestibule of Spirit.

Jesus reasoned on this subject practically, and controlled sickness, sin, and death on the basis of his spirituality. Understanding the nothingness of
material things, he spoke of flesh and Spirit
as the two opposites, — as error and Truth, not contrib-
uting in any way to each other's happiness and existence.
Jesus knew, "It is the spirit that quickeneth; the flesh
profiteth nothing."

There is neither a present nor an eternal copartnership between error and Truth, between flesh and Spirit.
God is as incapable of producing sin, sickness, and death as He is of experiencing these
errors. How then is it possible for Him to create man
subject to this triad of errors, — man who is made in the
divine likeness?

Does God create a material man out of Himself, Spirit?
Does evil proceed from good? Does divine Love commit a fraud on humanity by making man inclined to sin,
and then punishing him for it? Would any one call it
wise and good to create the primitive, and then punish its
derivative?

Does subsequent follow its antecedent? It does.
Was there original self-creative sin? Then there must
have been more than one creator, more than one God.

*Weakness
of material
theories*

*Irreconcilable
differences*

*Copartnership
impossible*

1

3

6

9

12

15

18

21

24

27

30

1   In common justice, we must admit that God will not
punish man for doing what He created man

Two infinite
creators
absurd

3   capable of doing, and knew from the outset
that man would do. God is "of purer eyes
than to behold evil." We sustain Truth, not by accept-

6   ing, but by rejecting a lie.

     Jesus said of personified evil, that it was "a liar, and
the father of it." Truth creates neither a lie, a capacity

9   to lie, nor a liar. If mankind would relinquish the belief
that God makes sickness, sin, and death, or makes man
capable of suffering on account of this malevolent triad,

12   the foundations of error would be sapped and error's destruction ensured; but if we theoretically endow mortals
with the creativeness and authority of Deity, how dare we

15   attempt to destroy what He hath made, or even to deny
that God made man evil and made evil good?

     History teaches that the popular and false notions

18   about the Divine Being and character have originated
in the human mind. As there is in reality but
one God, one Mind, wrong notions about God

Anthropo-
morphism

21   must have originated in a false supposition, not in immortal Truth, and they are fading out. They are false
claims, which will eventually disappear, according to the

24   vision of St. John in the Apocalypse.

     If what opposes God is real, there must be two
powers, and God is not supreme and infinite. Can

27   Deity be almighty, if another mighty and
self-creative cause exists and sways mankind? Has the Father "Life in Himself," as the Scrip-

One
supremacy

30   tures say, and, if so, can Life, or God, dwell in evil and
create it? Can matter drive Life, Spirit, hence, and so
defeat omnipotence?

Is the woodman's axe, which destroys a tree's so-called life, superior to omnipotence? Can a leaden bullet deprive a man of Life, — that is, of God, who is man's Life? If God is at the mercy of matter, then matter is omnipotent. Such doctrines are "confusion worse confounded." If two statements directly contradict each other and one is true, the other must be false. Is Science thus contradictory?

Matter impotent

Christian Science, understood, coincides with the Scriptures, and sustains logically and demonstratively every point it presents. Otherwise it would not be Science, and could not present its proofs. Christian Science is neither made up of contradictory aphorisms nor of the inventions of those who scoff at God. It presents the calm and clear verdict of Truth against error, uttered and illustrated by the prophets, by Jesus, by his apostles, as is recorded throughout the Scriptures.

Scientific and Biblical facts

Why are the words of Jesus more frequently cited for our instruction than are his remarkable works? Is it not because there are few who have gained a true knowledge of the great import to Christianity of those works?

Sometimes it is said: "Rest assured that whatever effect Christian Scientists may have on the sick, comes through rousing within the sick a belief that in the removal of disease these healers have wonderful power, derived from the Holy Ghost." Is it likely that church-members have more faith in some Christian Scientist, whom they have perhaps never seen and against whom they have been warned, than they have in their own accredited and orthodox

Personal confidence

1

3

6

9

12

15

18

21

24

27

30

1 pastors, whom they have seen and have been taught
to love and to trust?

3   Let any clergyman try to cure his friends by their
faith in him. Will that faith heal them? Yet Scientists will take the same cases, and cures will follow.

6 Is this because the patients have more faith in the Scientist than in their pastor? I have healed infidels whose
only objection to this method was, that I as a Chris-

9 tian Scientist believed in the Holy Spirit, while they, the
patients, did not.

    Even though you aver that the material senses are

12 indispensable to man's existence or entity, you must
change the human concept of life, and must at length
know yourself spiritually and scientifically. The evi-

15 dence of the existence of Spirit, Soul, is palpable only to
spiritual sense, and is not apparent to the material senses,
which cognize only that which is the opposite of Spirit.

18   True Christianity is to be honored wherever found,
but when shall we arrive at the goal which that word
implies? From Puritan parents, the discov-   **Author's**

21 erer of Christian Science early received her   **parentage**
religious education. In childhood, she often listened
with joy to these words, falling from the lips of her

24 saintly mother, "God is able to raise you up from sickness;" and she pondered the meaning of that Scripture
she so often quotes: "And these signs shall follow them

27 that believe; . . . they shall lay hands on the sick,
and they shall recover."

    A Christian Scientist and an opponent are like two

30 artists. One says: "I have spiritual ideals,   **Two different**
indestructible and glorious. When others see   **artists**
them as I do, in their true light and loveliness, — and

know that these ideals are real and eternal because drawn   1
from Truth, — they will find that nothing is lost, and all
is won, by a right estimate of what is real."   3

The other artist replies: "You wrong my experience.
I have no mind-ideals except those which are both mental
and material. It is true that materiality renders these   6
ideals imperfect and destructible; yet I would not exchange mine for thine, for mine give me such personal
pleasure, and they are not so shockingly transcendental.   9
They require less self-abnegation, and keep Soul well out
of sight. Moreover, I have no notion of losing my old
doctrines or human opinions."   12

Dear reader, which mind-picture or externalized thought
shall be real to you, — the material or the spiritual?

Choose ye
to-day

Both you cannot have. You are bringing out   15
your own ideal. This ideal is either temporal
or eternal. Either Spirit or matter is your model. If you
try to have two models, then you practically have none.   18
Like a pendulum in a clock, you will be thrown back and
forth, striking the ribs of matter and swinging between the
real and the unreal.   21

Hear the wisdom of Job, as given in the excellent translation of the late Rev. George R. Noyes, D.D.: —

Shall mortal man be more just than God?   24
Shall man be more pure than his Maker?
Behold, He putteth no trust in His ministering spirits,
And His angels He chargeth with frailty.   27

Of old, the Jews put to death the Galilean Prophet,
the best Christian on earth, for the truth he spoke and
demonstrated, while to-day, Jew and Christian can unite   30
in doctrine and denomination on the very basis of Jesus'
words and works. The Jew believes that the Messiah or

1   Christ has not yet come; the Christian believes that
Christ is God. Here Christian Science intervenes, ex-
3   plains these doctrinal points, cancels the disagreement,
and settles the question. Christ, as the true spiritual idea,
is the ideal of God now and forever, here and everywhere.
6   The Jew who believes in the First Commandment is a
monotheist; he has one omnipresent God. Thus the Jew
unites with the Christian's doctrine that God is come and
9   is present now and forever. The Christian who believes
in the First Commandment is a monotheist. Thus he
virtually unites with the Jew's belief in one God, and
12   recognizes that Jesus Christ is not God, as Jesus himself
declared, but is the Son of God. This declaration of
Jesus, understood, conflicts not at all with another of his
15   sayings: "I and my Father are one," — that is, one in
quality, not in quantity. As a drop of water is one with
the ocean, a ray of light one with the sun, even so God
18   and man, Father and son, are one in being. The Scripture reads: "For in Him we live, and move, and have
our being."
21   I have revised SCIENCE AND HEALTH only to give a
clearer and fuller expression of its original meaning. Spiritual ideas unfold as we advance. A human perception of
24   divine Science, however limited, must be correct in order
to be Science and subject to demonstration. A germ of infinite Truth, though least in the kingdom of heaven, is the
27   higher hope on earth, but it will be rejected and reviled
until God prepares the soil for the seed. That which
when sown bears immortal fruit, enriches mankind only
30   when it is understood, — hence the many readings given
the Scriptures, and the requisite revisions of SCIENCE AND
HEALTH WITH KEY TO THE SCRIPTURES.

Chapter 12

Christian Science Practice

Why art thou cast down, O my soul [sense]?
And why art thou disquieted within me?
Hope thou in God; for I shall yet praise Him,
Who is the health of my countenance and my God. — PSALMS.

And these signs shall follow them that believe:
In my name shall they cast out devils;
they shall speak with new tongues; they shall take up serpents;
and if they drink any deadly thing, it shall not hurt them;
they shall lay hands on the sick, and they shall recover. — JESUS.

A gospel narrative

It is related in the seventh chapter of Luke's Gospel 1
that Jesus was once the honored guest of a certain
Pharisee, by name Simon, though he was quite unlike 3
Simon the disciple. While they were at meat, an unusual
incident occurred, as if to interrupt the scene
of Oriental festivity. A "strange woman" 6
came in. Heedless of the fact that she was debarred from
such a place and such society, especially under the stern
rules of rabbinical law, as positively as if she were a Hin- 9
doo pariah intruding upon the household of a high-caste
Brahman, this woman (Mary Magdalene, as she has
since been called) approached Jesus. According to the 12
custom of those days, he reclined on a couch with his
head towards the table and his bare feet away from it.
It was therefore easy for the Magdalen to come behind 15

362

1 the couch and reach his feet. She bore an alabaster jar
containing costly and fragrant oil, — sandal oil perhaps,
3 which is in such common use in the East. Breaking
the sealed jar, she perfumed Jesus' feet with the oil,
wiping them with her long hair, which hung loosely
6 about her shoulders, as was customary with women of her
grade.

Did Jesus spurn the woman? Did he repel her adora-
9 tion? No! He regarded her compassionately. Nor was
this all. Knowing what those around him
were saying in their hearts, especially his host,

Parable of
the creditor

12 — that they were wondering why, being a prophet, the
exalted guest did not at once detect the woman's immoral
status and bid her depart, — knowing this, Jesus rebuked
15 them with a short story or parable. He described two
debtors, one for a large sum and one for a smaller, who
were released from their obligations by their common
18 creditor. "Which of them will love him most?" was the
Master's question to Simon the Pharisee; and Simon replied, "He to whom he forgave most." Jesus approved
21 the answer, and so brought home the lesson to all, following it with that remarkable declaration to the woman,
"Thy sins are forgiven."

24 Why did he thus summarize her debt to divine Love?
Had she repented and reformed, and did his insight
detect this unspoken moral uprising? She

Divine
insight

27 bathed his feet with her tears before she
anointed them with the oil. In the absence of other
proofs, was her grief sufficient evidence to warrant the
30 expectation of her repentance, reformation, and growth
in wisdom? Certainly there was encouragement in the
mere fact that she was showing her affection for a man

of undoubted goodness and purity, who has since been 1
rightfully regarded as the best man that ever trod this
planet. Her reverence was unfeigned, and it was mani- 3
fested towards one who was soon, though they knew it
not, to lay down his mortal existence in behalf of all
sinners, that through his word and works they might be 6
redeemed from sensuality and sin.

Which was the higher tribute to such ineffable affection, the hospitality of the Pharisee or the contrition of 9

Penitence or hospitality

the Magdalen? This query Jesus answered
by rebuking self-righteousness and declaring
the absolution of the penitent. He even said that this 12
poor woman had done what his rich entertainer had neglected to do, — wash and anoint his guest's feet, a special
sign of Oriental courtesy. 15

Here is suggested a solemn question, a question indicated by one of the needs of this age. Do Christian
Scientists seek Truth as Simon sought the Saviour, through 18
material conservatism and for personal homage? Jesus
told Simon that such seekers as he gave small reward
in return for the spiritual purgation which came through 21
the Messiah. If Christian Scientists are like Simon,
then it must be said of them also that they *love*
little. 24

On the other hand, do they show their regard for
Truth, or Christ, by their genuine repentance, by their

Genuine repentance

broken hearts, expressed by meekness and 27
human affection, as did this woman? If
so, then it may be said of them, as Jesus said of the
unwelcome visitor, that they indeed love much, because 30
much is forgiven them.

Did the careless doctor, the nurse, the cook, and the

brusque business visitor sympathetically know the thorns
they plant in the pillow of the sick and the heavenly

Compassion
requisite
homesick looking away from earth, — Oh, did
they know! — this knowledge would do much
more towards healing the sick and preparing their helpers
for the "midnight call," than all cries of "Lord, Lord!"
The benign thought of Jesus, finding utterance in such
words as "Take no thought for your life," would heal
the sick, and so enable them to rise above the supposed
necessity for physical thought-taking and doctoring;
but if the unselfish affections be lacking, and common
sense and common humanity are disregarded, what mental quality remains, with which to evoke healing from
the outstretched arm of righteousness?

If the Scientist reaches his patient through divine
Love, the healing work will be accomplished at one
visit, and the disease will vanish into its native

Speedy
healing
nothingness like dew before the morning sunshine. If the Scientist has enough Christly affection to
win his own pardon, and such commendation as the Magdalen gained from Jesus, then he is Christian enough to
practise scientifically and deal with his patients compassionately; and the result will correspond with the spiritual
intent.

If hypocrisy, stolidity, inhumanity, or vice finds its
way into the chambers of disease through the would-be

Truth
desecrated
healer, it would, if it were possible, convert
into a den of thieves the temple of the Holy
Ghost, — the patient's spiritual power to resuscitate himself. The unchristian practitioner is not giving to mind
or body the joy and strength of Truth. The poor suffering heart needs its rightful nutriment, such as peace,

patience in tribulation, and a priceless sense of the dear 1
Father's loving-kindness.

In order to cure his patient, the metaphysician 3
must first cast moral evils out of himself and thus

Moral evils
to be cast out
attain the spiritual freedom which will enable him to cast physical evils out of his 6
patient; but heal he cannot, while his own spiritual
barrenness debars him from giving drink to the thirsty
and hinders him from reaching his patient's thought, — 9
yea, while mental penury chills his faith and understanding.

The physician who lacks sympathy for his fellow- 12
being is deficient in human affection, and we have the

The true
physician
apostolic warrant for asking: "He that loveth
not his brother whom he hath seen, how can 15
he love God whom he hath not seen?" Not having this
spiritual affection, the physician lacks faith in the divine
Mind and has not that recognition of infinite Love which 18
alone confers the healing power. Such so-called Scientists will strain out gnats, while they swallow the camels
of bigoted pedantry. 21

The physician must also watch, lest he be over-
whelmed by a sense of the odiousness of sin and by the

Source of
calmness
unveiling of sin in his own thoughts. The 24
sick are terrified by their sick beliefs, and
sinners should be affrighted by their sinful beliefs; but
the Christian Scientist will be calm in the presence of 27
both sin and disease, knowing, as he does, that Life is
God and God is All.

If we would open their prison doors for the sick, we 30
must first learn to bind up the broken-hearted. If we
would heal by the Spirit, we must not hide the talent

of spiritual healing under the napkin of its form, nor
bury the *morale* of Christian Science in the grave-clothes
of its letter. The tender word and Christian
encouragement of an invalid, pitiful patience
with his fears and the removal of them, are better than
hecatombs of gushing theories, stereotyped borrowed
speeches, and the doling of arguments, which are but so
many parodies on legitimate Christian Science, aflame
with divine Love.

Genuine healing

This is what is meant by seeking Truth, Christ, not
"for the loaves and fishes," nor, like the Pharisee, with
the arrogance of rank and display of scholar-
ship, but like Mary Magdalene, from the summit of devout consecration, with the oil of gladness and
the perfume of *gratitude*, with tears of repentance and
with those hairs all numbered by the Father.

Gratitude and humility

A Christian Scientist occupies the place at this period
of which Jesus spoke to his disciples, when he said: "Ye
are the salt of the earth." "Ye are the light
of the world. A city that is set on an hill cannot be hid." Let us watch, work, and pray that this salt
lose not its saltness, and that this light be not hid, but
radiate and glow into noontide glory.

The salt of the earth

The infinite Truth of the Christ-cure has come to this
age through a "still, small voice," through silent utterances and divine anointing which quicken and increase
the beneficial effects of Christianity. I long to see the
consummation of my hope, namely, the student's higher
attainments in this line of light.

Because Truth is infinite, error should be known as
nothing. Because Truth is omnipotent in goodness,
error, Truth's opposite, has no might. Evil is but the

counterpoise of nothingness. The greatest wrong is

but a supposititious opposite of the highest right. The

confidence inspired by Science lies in the fact

that Truth is real and error is unreal. Error

is a coward before Truth. Divine Science insists that

time will prove all this. Both truth and error have come

nearer than ever before to the apprehension of mortals,

and truth will become still clearer as error is self-

destroyed.

Against the fatal beliefs that error is as real as Truth,

that evil is equal in power to good if not superior, and that

discord is as normal as harmony, even the hope

of freedom from the bondage of sickness and

sin has little inspiration to nerve endeavor. When we

come to have more faith in the truth of being than we have

in error, more faith in Spirit than in matter, more faith

in living than in dying, more faith in God than in man,

then no material suppositions can prevent us from healing

the sick and destroying error.

That Life is not contingent on bodily conditions is

proved, when we learn that life and man survive this

body. Neither evil, disease, nor death can be

spiritual, and the material belief in them dis-

appears in the ratio of one's spiritual growth. Because

matter has no consciousness or Ego, it cannot act; its

conditions are illusions, and these false conditions are the

source of all seeming sickness. Admit the existence of

matter, and you admit that mortality (and therefore dis-

ease) has a foundation in fact. Deny the existence of

matter, and you can destroy the belief in material con-

ditions. When fear disappears, the foundation of disease

is gone. Once let the mental physician believe in the

1   reality of matter, and he is liable to admit also the reality
    of all discordant conditions, and this hinders his de-
3   stroying them. Thus he is unfitted for the successful
    treatment of disease.

    In proportion as matter loses to human sense all en-
6   tity as man, in that proportion does man become its
    master. He enters into a diviner sense of the   **Man's entity**
    facts, and comprehends the theology of Jesus
9   as demonstrated in healing the sick, raising the dead,
    and walking over the wave. All these deeds manifested
    Jesus' control over the belief that matter is substance,
12 that it can be the arbiter of life or the constructor of any
    form of existence.

    We never read that Luke or Paul made a reality of
15 disease in order to discover some means of healing it.
    Jesus never asked if disease were acute or   **The Christ**
    chronic, and he never recommended atten-   **treatment**
18 tion to laws of health, never gave drugs, never prayed
    to know if God were willing that a man should live. He
    understood man, whose Life is God, to be immortal, and
21 knew that man has not two lives, one to be destroyed and
    the other to be made indestructible.

    The prophylactic and therapeutic (that is, the prevent-
24 ive and curative) arts belong emphatically to Christian
    Science, as would be readily seen, if psychology,   **Matter not**
    or the Science of Spirit, God, was understood.   **medicine**
27 Unscientific methods are finding their dead level. Lim-
    ited to matter by their own law, what have they of the
    advantages of Mind and immortality?

30 No man is physically healed in wilful error or by it,
    any more than he is morally saved in or by sin. It is
    error even to murmur or to be angry over sin. To be

every whit whole, man must be better spiritually as well   1
as physically. To be immortal, we must forsake the
mortal sense of things, turn from the lie of false   3
belief to Truth, and gather the facts of being
from the divine Mind. The body improves under the
same regimen which spiritualizes the thought; and if   6
health is not made manifest under this regimen, this
proves that fear is governing the body. This is the law
of cause and effect, or like producing like.   9

Homœopathy furnishes the evidence to the senses, that
symptoms, which might be produced by a certain drug,
are removed by using the same drug which   12
might cause the symptoms. This confirms
my theory that faith in the drug is the sole factor in the
cure. The effect, which mortal mind produces through   15
one belief, it removes through an opposite belief, but it
uses the same medicine in both cases.

The moral and spiritual facts of health, whispered   18
into thought, produce very direct and marked effects on
the body. A physical diagnosis of disease — since mortal mind must be the cause of disease — tends to induce   21
disease.

According to both medical testimony and individual
experience, a drug may eventually lose its supposed power   24
and do no more for the patient. Hygienic
treatment also loses its efficacy. Quackery
likewise fails at length to inspire the credulity   27
of the sick, and then they cease to improve. These lessons are useful. They should naturally and genuinely
change our basis from sensation to Christian Science,   30
from error to Truth, from matter to Spirit.

Physicians examine the pulse, tongue, lungs, to dis-

1   cover the condition of matter, when in fact all is
Mind. The body is the substratum of mortal mind,
3   and this so-called mind must finally yield   Diagnosis
to the mandate of immortal Mind.   of matter

Disquisitions on disease have a mental effect similar
6   to that produced on children by telling ghost-stories in
the dark. By those uninstructed in Christian   Ghost-stories
Science, nothing is really understood of material   inducing fear
9   existence. Mortals are believed to be here without their
consent and to be removed as involuntarily, not knowing
why nor when. As frightened children look everywhere
12   for the imaginary ghost, so sick humanity sees danger in
every direction, and looks for relief in all ways except the
right one. Darkness induces fear. The adult, in bond-
15   age to his beliefs, no more comprehends his real being
than does the child; and the adult must be taken out of
his darkness, before he can get rid of the illusive suffer-
18   ings which throng the gloaming. The way in divine
Science is the only way out of this condition.

I would not transform the infant at once into a
21   man, nor would I keep the suckling a lifelong babe.
No impossible thing do I ask when urging   Mind imparts
the claims of Christian Science; but because   purity, health,
                                                             and beauty
24   this teaching is in advance of the age, we
should not deny our need of its spiritual unfoldment.
Mankind will improve through Science and Christi-
27   anity. The necessity for uplifting the race is father to
the fact that Mind can do it; for Mind can impart
purity instead of impurity, strength instead of weak-
30   ness, and health instead of disease. Truth is an alterative in the entire system, and can make it "every whit
whole."

Remember, brain is not mind. Matter cannot be sick, and Mind is immortal. The mortal body is only an erroneous mortal belief of mind in matter. What you call matter was originally error in solution, elementary mortal mind, — likened by Milton to "chaos and old night." One theory about this mortal mind is, that its sensations can reproduce man, can form blood, flesh, and bones. The Science of being, in which all is divine Mind, or God and His idea, would be clearer in this age, but for the belief that matter is the medium of man, or that man can enter his own embodied thought, bind himself with his own beliefs, and then call his bonds material and name them divine law.

Brain not intelligent

When man demonstrates Christian Science absolutely, he will be perfect. He can neither sin, suffer, be subject to matter, nor disobey the law of God. Therefore he will be as the angels in heaven. Christian Science and Christianity are one. How, then, in Christianity any more than in Christian Science, can we believe in the reality and power of both Truth and error, Spirit and matter, and hope to succeed with contraries? Matter is not self-sustaining. Its false supports fail one after another. Matter succeeds for a period only by falsely parading in the vestments of law.

Veritable success

"Whosoever shall deny me before men, him will I also deny before my Father which is in heaven." In Christian Science, a denial of Truth is fatal, while a just acknowledgment of Truth and of what it has done for us is an effectual help. If pride, superstition, or any error prevents the honest recognition of benefits received, this will be a hindrance to the recovery of the sick and the success of the student.

Recognition of benefits

1   If we are Christians on all moral questions, but are in
darkness as to the physical exemption which Christian-

3   ity includes, then we must have more faith
in God on this subject and be more alive to
His promises. It is easier to cure the most

6   malignant disease than it is to cure sin. The author has
raised up the dying, partly because they were willing to
be restored, while she has struggled long, and perhaps in

9   vain, to lift a student out of a chronic sin. Under all
modes of pathological treatment, the sick recover more
rapidly from disease than does the sinner from his sin.

12   Healing is easier than teaching, if the teaching is faithfully
done.

Disease far more docile than iniquity

    The fear of disease and the love of sin are the sources

15   of man's enslavement. "The fear of the Lord
is the beginning of wisdom," but the Scriptures
also declare, through the exalted thought of John, that

18   "perfect Love casteth out fear."

Love frees from fear

    The fear occasioned by ignorance can be cured; but
to remove the effects of fear produced by sin, you must

21   rise above both fear and sin. Disease is expressed not
so much by the lips as in the functions of the body. Establish the scientific sense of health, and you relieve the

24   oppressed organ. The inflammation, decomposition, or
deposit will abate, and the disabled organ will resume its
healthy functions.

27   When the blood rushes madly through the veins or
languidly creeps along its frozen channels, we call these
conditions disease. This is a misconception.

30   Mortal mind is producing the propulsion or the
languor, and we prove this to be so when by mental means
the circulation is changed, and returns to that standard

Mind circulates blood

which mortal mind has decided upon as essential for   1
health. Anodynes, counter-irritants, and depletion never
reduce inflammation scientifically, but the truth of being,   3
whispered into the ear of mortal mind, will bring relief.

Hatred and its effects on the body are removed by
Love. Because mortal mind seems to be conscious, the   6

sick say: "How can my mind cause a disease
I never thought of and knew nothing about,
until it appeared on my body?" The author has an-   9
swered this question in her explanation of disease as originating in human belief before it is consciously apparent
on the body, which is in fact the objective state of mortal   12
mind, though it is called matter. This mortal blindness
and its sharp consequences show our need of divine metaphysics. Through immortal Mind, or Truth, we can   15
destroy all ills which proceed from mortal mind.

Ignorance of the cause or approach of disease is no
argument against the mental origin of disease. You con-   18
fess to ignorance of the future and incapacity to preserve
your own existence, and this belief helps rather than
hinders disease. Such a state of mind induces sickness.   21
It is like walking in darkness on the edge of a precipice.
You cannot forget the belief of danger, and your steps
are less firm because of your fear, and ignorance of mental   24
cause and effect.

Heat and cold are products of mortal mind. The body,
when bereft of mortal mind, at first cools, and after-   27

wards it is resolved into its primitive mortal
elements. Nothing that lives ever dies, and
vice versa. Mortal mind produces animal heat, and then   30
expels it through the abandonment of a belief, or increases it to the point of self-destruction. Hence it is

1   mortal mind, not matter, which says, "I die." Heat
would pass from the body as painlessly as gas dissipates
3   into the air when it evaporates but for the belief that inflammation and pain must accompany the separation of
heat from the body.

6   Chills and heat are often the form in which fever manifests itself. Change the mental state, and the chills and
fever disappear. The old-school physician

Science *versus* hypnotism

9   proves this when his patient says, "I am better,"
but the patient believes that matter, not mind,
has helped him. The Christian Scientist demonstrates
12   that divine Mind heals, while the hypnotist dispossesses
the patient of his individuality in order to control him.
No person is benefited by yielding his mentality to any
15   mental despotism or malpractice. All unscientific mental
practice is erroneous and powerless, and should be understood and so rendered fruitless. The genuine Christian
18   Scientist is adding to his patient's mental and moral power,
and is increasing his patient's spirituality while restoring
him physically through divine Love.

21   Palsy is a belief that matter governs mortals, and can
paralyze the body, making certain portions of
it motionless. Destroy the belief, show mortal

Cure for palsy

24   mind that muscles have no power to be lost, for Mind is
supreme, and you cure the palsy.

       Consumptive patients always show great hopeful-
27   ness and courage, even when they are supposed to be in
hopeless danger. This state of mind seems
anomalous except to the expert in Christian

Latent fear diagnosed

30   Science. This mental state is not understood, simply
because it is a stage of fear so excessive that it amounts
to fortitude. The belief in consumption presents to mor-

tal thought a hopeless state, an image more terrifying than
that of most other diseases. The patient turns involuntarily from the contemplation of it, but though unacknowledged, the latent fear and the despair of recovery remain
in thought.

Just so is it with the greatest sin. It is the most subtle,
and does its work almost self-deceived. The diseases

deemed dangerous sometimes come from the
most hidden, undefined, and insidious beliefs.
The pallid invalid, whom you declare to be wasting away
with consumption of the blood, should be told that blood
never gave life and can never take it away, — that Life is
Spirit, and that there is more life and immortality in one
good motive and act, than in all the blood which ever
flowed through mortal veins and simulated a corporeal
sense of life.

If the body is material, it cannot, for that very reason,
suffer with a fever. Because the so-called material body

is a mental concept and governed by mortal
mind, it manifests only what that so-called
mind expresses. Therefore the efficient remedy is to
destroy the patient's false belief by both silently and audibly arguing the true facts in regard to harmonious
being, — representing man as healthy instead of diseased,
and showing that it is impossible for matter to suffer, to
feel pain or heat, to be thirsty or sick. Destroy fear,
and you end fever. Some people, mistaught as to Mind-
science, inquire when it will be safe to check a fever.
Know that in Science you cannot check a fever after admitting that it must have its course. To fear and admit
the power of disease, is to paralyze mental and scientific
demonstration.

1   If your patient believes in taking cold, mentally convince him that matter cannot take cold, and that thought
3   governs this liability. If grief causes suffering, convince
the sufferer that affliction is often the source of joy, and
that he should rejoice always in ever-present Love.

6   Invalids flee to tropical climates in order to save their
lives, but they come back no better than when they went
away. Then is the time to cure them through   **Climate**
9   Christian Science, and prove that they can   **harmless**
be healthy in all climates, when their fear of climate is
exterminated.

12   Through different states of mind, the body becomes
suddenly weak or abnormally strong, showing mortal
mind to be the producer of strength or weak-   **Mind**
15   ness. A sudden joy or grief has caused what   **governs body**
is termed instantaneous death. Because a belief originates unseen, the mental state should be continually
18   watched that it may not produce blindly its bad effects.
The author never knew a patient who did not recover
when the belief of the disease had gone. Remove the
21   leading error or governing fear of this lower so-called mind,
and you remove the cause of all disease as well as the morbid or excited action of any organ. You also remove in
24   this way what are termed organic diseases as readily as
functional difficulties.

The cause of all so-called disease is mental, a mortal
27   fear, a mistaken belief or conviction of the necessity and
power of ill-health; also a fear that Mind is helpless to
defend the life of man and incompetent to control it. With-
30   out this ignorant human belief, any circumstance is of itself powerless to produce suffering. It is latent belief in
disease, as well as the fear of disease, which associates sick-

ness with certain circumstances and causes the two to   1
appear conjoined, even as poetry and music are reproduced in union by human memory. Disease has no in-   3
telligence. Unwittingly you sentence yourself to suffer.
The understanding of this will enable you to commute this
self-sentence, and meet every circumstance with truth.   6
Disease is less than mind, and Mind can control it.

Without the so-called human mind, there can be no
inflammatory nor torpid action of the system. Remove   9

**Latent
power**

the error, and you destroy its effects. By
looking a tiger fearlessly in the eye, Sir Charles
Napier sent it cowering back into the jungle. An ani-   12
mal may infuriate another by looking it in the eye, and
both will fight for nothing. A man's gaze, fastened
fearlessly on a ferocious beast, often causes the beast to   15
retreat in terror. This latter occurrence represents the
power of Truth over error, — the might of intelligence
exercised over mortal beliefs to destroy them; whereas   18
hypnotism and hygienic drilling and drugging, adopted
to cure matter, is represented by two material erroneous
bases.   21

Disease is not an intelligence to dispute the empire of
Mind or to dethrone Mind and take the government into

**Disease
powerless**

its own hands. Sickness is not a God-given,   24
nor a self-constituted material power, which
copes astutely with Mind and finally conquers it. God
never endowed matter with power to disable Life or to   27
chill harmony with a long and cold night of discord.
Such a power, without the divine permission, is incon-
ceivable; and if such a power could be divinely directed,   30
it would manifest less wisdom than we usually find displayed in human governments.

If disease can attack and control the body without
the consent of mortals, sin can do the same, for both
are errors, announced as partners in the beginning. The Christian Scientist finds only
effects, where the ordinary physician looks for causes.
The real jurisdiction of the world is in Mind, controlling
every effect and recognizing all causation as vested in
divine Mind.

Jurisdiction
of Mind

A felon, on whom certain English students experi-
mented, fancied himself bleeding to death, and died because of that belief, when only a stream of
warm water was trickling over his arm. Had
he known his sense of bleeding was an illusion, he would
have risen above the false belief. Let the despairing invalid, inspecting the hue of her blood on a cambric hand-
kerchief, think of the experiment of those Oxford boys,
who caused the death of a man, when not a drop of his
blood was shed. Then let her learn the opposite statement of Life as taught in Christian Science, and she will
understand that she is not dying on account of the state of
her blood, but is suffering from her belief that blood is
destroying her life. The so-called vital current does not
affect the invalid's health, but her belief produces the
very results she dreads.

Power of
imagination

Fevers are errors of various types. The quickened
pulse, coated tongue, febrile heat, dry skin, pain in the
head and limbs, are pictures drawn on the
body by a mortal mind. The images, held in
this disturbed mind, frighten conscious thought. Unless
the fever-picture, drawn by millions of mortals and imaged on the body through the belief that mind is in matter
and discord is as real as harmony, is destroyed through

Fevers the
effect of fear

Science, it may rest at length on some receptive thought, and become a fever case, which ends in a belief called death, which belief must be finally conquered by eternal Life. Truth is always the victor. Sickness and sin fall by their own weight. Truth is the rock of ages, the headstone of the corner, "but on whomsoever it shall fall, it will grind him to powder."

Misdirected contention

Contending for the evidence or indulging the demands of sin, disease, or death, we virtually contend against the control of Mind over body, and deny the power of Mind to heal. This false method is as though the defendant should argue for the plaintiff in favor of a decision which the defendant knows will be turned against himself.

Benefits of metaphysics

The physical effects of fear illustrate its illusion. Gazing at a chained lion, crouched for a spring, should not terrify a man. The body is affected only with the belief of disease produced by a so-called mind ignorant of the truth which chains disease. Nothing but the power of Truth can prevent the fear of error, and prove man's dominion over error.

A higher discovery

Many years ago the author made a spiritual discovery, the scientific evidence of which has accumulated to prove that the divine Mind produces in man health, harmony, and immortality. Gradually this evidence will gather momentum and clearness, until it reaches its culmination of scientific statement and proof. Nothing is more disheartening than to believe that there is a power opposite to God, or good, and that God endows this opposing power with strength to be used against Himself, against Life, health, harmony.

Every law of matter or the body, supposed to govern

1 man, is rendered null and void by the law of Life, God.
Ignorant of our God-given rights, we submit to unjust
3 decrees, and the bias of education enforces
this slavery. Be no more willing to suffer the
illusion that you are sick or that some disease is develop-
6 ing in the system, than you are to yield to a sinful temptation on the ground that sin has its necessities.

Ignorance of our rights

When infringing some supposed law, you say that
9 there is danger. This fear is the danger and induces the
physical effects. We cannot in reality suffer
from breaking anything except a moral or
12 spiritual law. The so-called laws of mortal belief are
destroyed by the understanding that Soul is immortal,
and that mortal mind cannot legislate the times, periods,
15 and types of disease, with which mortals die. God is the
lawmaker, but He is not the author of barbarous codes.
In infinite Life and Love there is no sickness, sin, nor
18 death, and the Scriptures declare that we live, move, and
have our being in the infinite God.

No laws of matter

Think less of the enactments of mortal mind, and you
21 will sooner grasp man's God-given dominion. You must
understand your way out of human theories
relating to health, or you will never believe
24 that you are quite free from some ailment. The harmony and immortality of man will never be reached
without the understanding that Mind is not in matter.
27 Let us banish sickness as an outlaw, and abide by the
rule of perpetual harmony, — God's law. It is man's
moral right to annul an unjust sentence, a sentence never
30 inflicted by divine authority.

God-given dominion

Christ Jesus overruled the error which would impose
penalties for transgressions of the physical laws of

health; he annulled supposed laws of matter, opposed
to the harmonies of Spirit, lacking divine authority and having only human approval for
their sanction.

If half the attention given to hygiene were given to the
study of Christian Science and to the spiritualization of
thought, this alone would usher in the millennium. Constant bathing and rubbing to alter
the secretions or to remove unhealthy exhalations from
the cuticle receive a useful rebuke from Jesus' precept,
"Take no thought . . . for the body." We must beware
of making clean merely the outside of the platter.

He, who is ignorant of what is termed hygienic law, is
more receptive of spiritual power and of faith in one
God, than is the devotee of supposed hygienic
law, who comes to teach the so-called ignorant one. Must we not then consider the so-called law
of matter a canon "more honored in the breach than
the observance"? A patient thoroughly booked in medical theories is more difficult to heal through Mind than
one who is not. This verifies the saying of our Master:
"Whosoever shall not receive the kingdom of God as a
little child, shall in no wise enter therein."

One whom I rescued from seeming spiritual oblivion,
in which the senses had engulfed him, wrote to me: "I
should have died, but for the glorious Principle you teach,
— supporting the power of Mind over the body and showing me the nothingness of the so-called pleasures and pains
of sense. The treatises I had read and the medicines I
had taken only abandoned me to more hopeless suffering
and despair. Adherence to hygiene was useless. Mortal
mind needed to be set right. The ailment was not bodily,

1

3

6

9

12

15

18

21

24

27

30

but mental, and I was cured when I learned my way in Christian Science."

We need a clean body and a clean mind, — a body rendered pure by Mind as well as washed by water. One says: "I take good care of my body." To do this, the pure and exalting influence of the divine Mind on the body is requisite, and the Christian Scientist takes the best care of his body when he leaves it most out of his thought, and, like the Apostle Paul, is "willing rather to be absent from the body, and to be present with the Lord."

A clean mind and body

A hint may be taken from the emigrant, whose filth does not affect his happiness, because mind and body rest on the same basis. To the mind equally gross, dirt gives no uneasiness. It is the native element of such a mind, which is symbolized, and not chafed, by its surroundings; but impurity and uncleanliness, which do not trouble the gross, could not be borne by the refined. This shows that the mind must be clean to keep the body in proper condition.

The tobacco-user, eating or smoking poison for half a century, sometimes tells you that the weed preserves his health, but does this make it so? Does his assertion prove the use of tobacco to be a salubrious habit, and man to be the better for it? Such instances only prove the illusive physical effect of a false belief, confirming the Scriptural conclusion concerning a man, "As he thinketh in his heart, so is he."

Beliefs illusive

The movement-cure — pinching and pounding the poor body, to make it sensibly well when it ought to be insensibly so — is another medical mistake, resulting from the common notion that health depends on inert matter

instead of on Mind. Can matter, or what is termed   1
matter, either feel or act without mind?

We should relieve our minds from the depressing thought   3
that we have transgressed a material law and must of

Corporeal
penalties
necessity pay the penalty. Let us reassure
ourselves with the law of Love. God never   6
punishes man for doing right, for honest labor, or for
deeds of kindness, though they expose him to fatigue,
cold, heat, contagion. If man seems to incur the penalty   9
through matter, this is but a belief of mortal mind, not
an enactment of wisdom, and man has only to enter his
protest against this belief in order to annul it. Through   12
this action of thought and its results upon the body, the
student will prove to himself, by small beginnings, the
grand verities of Christian Science.   15

If exposure to a draught of air while in a state of
perspiration is followed by chills, dry cough, influenza,

Not matter,
but Mind
congestive symptoms in the lungs, or hints of   18
inflammatory rheumatism, your Mind-remedy
is safe and sure. If you are a Christian Scientist, such
symptoms are not apt to follow exposure; but if you   21
believe in laws of matter and their fatal effects when
transgressed, you are not fit to conduct your own case or
to destroy the bad effects of your belief. When the fear   24
subsides and the conviction abides that you have broken
no law, neither rheumatism, consumption, nor any other
disease will ever result from exposure to the weather. In   27
Science this is an established fact which all the evidence
before the senses can never overrule.

Sickness, sin, and death must at length quail before   30
the divine rights of intelligence, and then the power
of Mind over the entire functions and organs of the

human system will be acknowledged. It is proverbial
that Florence Nightingale and other philanthropists engaged in humane labors have been able to
undergo without sinking fatigues and exposures which ordinary people could not endure. The explanation lies in the support which they derived from
the divine law, rising above the human. The spiritual
demand, quelling the material, supplies energy and endurance surpassing all other aids, and forestalls the
penalty which our beliefs would attach to our best
deeds. Let us remember that the eternal law of right,
though it can never annul the law which makes sin its
own executioner, exempts man from all penalties but
those due for wrong-doing.

Constant toil, deprivations, exposures, and all untow-
ard conditions, *if without sin,* can be experienced without suffering. Whatever it is your duty to do,
you can do without harm to yourself. If you
sprain the muscles or wound the flesh, your
remedy is at hand. Mind decides whether or not the
flesh shall be discolored, painful, swollen, and inflamed.

You say that you have not slept well or have overeaten.
You are a law unto yourself. Saying this and believing
it, you will suffer in proportion to your belief
and fear. Your sufferings are not the penalty
for having broken a law of matter, for it is a law of mortal
mind which you have disobeyed. You say or think, because you have partaken of salt fish, that you must be
thirsty, and you are thirsty accordingly, while the opposite belief would produce the opposite result.

Any supposed information, coming from the body or
from inert matter as if either were intelligent, is an illu-

Benefit of philanthropy

Honest toil has no penalty

Our sleep and food

sion of mortal mind, — one of its dreams. Realize that

**Doubtful
evidence**

the evidence of the senses is not to be accepted
in the case of sickness, any more than it is in
the case of sin.

Expose the body to certain temperatures, and belief
says that you may catch cold and have catarrh; but no

**Climate
and belief**

such result occurs without mind to demand
it and produce it. So long as mortals declare
that certain states of the atmosphere produce catarrh,
fever, rheumatism, or consumption, those effects will
follow, — not because of the climate, but on account of
the belief. The author has in too many instances healed
disease through the action of Truth on the minds of mortals, and the corresponding effects of Truth on the body,
not to know that this is so.

A blundering despatch, mistakenly announcing the
death of a friend, occasions the same grief that the friend's

**Erroneous
despatch**

real death would bring. You think that your
anguish is occasioned by your loss. Another
despatch, correcting the mistake, heals your grief, and
you learn that your suffering was merely the result of
your belief. Thus it is with all sorrow, sickness, and
death. You will learn at length that there is no cause
for grief, and divine wisdom will then be understood.
Error, not Truth, produces all the suffering on earth.

If a Christian Scientist had said, while you were laboring under the influence of the belief of grief, "Your sor-

**Mourning
causeless**

row is without cause," you would not have
understood him, although the correctness of
the assertion might afterwards be proved to you. So,
when our friends pass from our sight and we lament,
that lamentation is needless and causeless. We shall

1 perceive this to be true when we grow into the understanding of Life, and know that there is no death.

3 Because mortal mind is kept active, must it pay the
penalty in a softened brain? Who dares to say that actual
Mind can be overworked? When we reach

6 our limits of mental endurance, we conclude
that intellectual labor has been carried sufficiently far;
but when we realize that immortal Mind is ever active,

9 and that spiritual energies can neither wear out nor can
so-called material law trespass upon God-given powers
and resources, we are able to rest in Truth, refreshed by

12 the assurances of immortality, opposed to mortality.

Mind heals brain-disease

Our thinkers do not die early because they faithfully
perform the natural functions of being. If printers and

15 authors have the shortest span of earthly existence, it is not because they occupy the most
important posts and perform the most vital functions in

18 society. That man does not pay the severest penalty
who does the most good. By adhering to the realities of
eternal existence, — instead of reading disquisitions on

21 the inconsistent supposition that death comes in obedience
to the law of life, and that God punishes man for doing
good, — one cannot suffer as the result of any labor of

24 love, but grows stronger because of it. It is a law of so-
called mortal mind, misnamed matter, which causes all
things discordant.

Right never punishable

27 The history of Christianity furnishes sublime proofs
of the supporting influence and protecting power bestowed
on man by his heavenly Father, omnipotent

30 Mind, who gives man faith and understanding
whereby to defend himself, not only from temptation, but
from bodily suffering.

Christian history

The Christian martyrs were prophets of Christian
Science. Through the uplifting and consecrating power
of divine Truth, they obtained a victory over the corporeal senses, a victory which Science alone can explain.
Stolidity, which is a resisting state of mortal mind, suffers
less, only because it knows less of material law.

The Apostle John testified to the divine basis of Christian Science, when dire inflictions failed to destroy his
body. Idolaters, believing in more than one mind, had
"gods many," and thought that they could kill the body
with matter, independently of mind.

Admit the common hypothesis that food is the nutriment of life, and there follows the necessity for another
admission in the opposite direction, — that
food has power to destroy Life, God, through
a deficiency or an excess, a quality or a quantity. This
is a specimen of the ambiguous nature of all material
health-theories. They are self-contradictory and self-destructive, constituting a "kingdom divided against itself,"
which is "brought to desolation." If food was prepared
by Jesus for his disciples, it cannot destroy life.

The fact is, food does not affect the absolute Life of
man, and this becomes self-evident, when we learn that
God is our Life. Because sin and sickness are
not qualities of Soul, or Life, we have hope in
immortality; but it would be foolish to venture beyond
our present understanding, foolish to stop eating until
we gain perfection and a clear comprehension of the living
Spirit. In that perfect day of understanding, we shall
neither eat to live nor live to eat.

If mortals think that food disturbs the harmonious
functions of mind and body, either the food or this thought

Sustenance spiritual

God sustains man

1

3

6

9

12

15

18

21

24

27

30

must be dispensed with, for the penalty is coupled with
the belief. Which shall it be? If this decision be left
to Christian Science, it will be given in behalf
of the control of Mind over this belief and every
erroneous belief, or material condition. The less we
know or think about hygiene, the less we are predisposed
to sickness. Recollect that it is not the nerves, not matter, but mortal mind, which reports food as undigested.
Matter does not inform you of bodily derangements; it
is supposed to do so. This pseudo-mental testimony can
be destroyed only by the better results of Mind's opposite evidence.

Our dietetic theories first admit that food sustains the
life of man, and then discuss the certainty that food can
kill man. This false reasoning is rebuked in
Scripture by the metaphors about the fount
and stream, the tree and its fruit, and the kingdom divided against itself. If God has, as prevalent theories
maintain, instituted laws that food shall support human
life, He cannot annul these regulations by an opposite
law that food shall be inimical to existence.

Materialists contradict their own statements. Their
belief in material laws and in penalties for their infraction is the ancient error that there is fraternity
between pain and pleasure, good and evil, God
and Satan. This belief totters to its falling before the
battle-axe of Science.

A case of convulsions, produced by indigestion, came
under my observation. In her belief the woman had
chronic liver-complaint, and was then suffering from a
complication of symptoms connected with this belief. I
cured her in a few minutes. One instant she spoke de-

Margin notes:
Diet and digestion

Scripture rebukes

Ancient confusion

spairingly of herself. The next minute she said, "My   1
food is all digested, and I should like something more
to eat."   3

We cannot deny that Life is self-sustained, and we
should never deny the everlasting harmony of Soul, sim-

Ultimate harmony ply because, to the mortal senses, there is seem-   6
ing discord. It is our ignorance of God, the
divine Principle, which produces apparent discord, and
the right understanding of Him restores harmony. Truth   9
will at length compel us all to exchange the pleasures and
pains of sense for the joys of Soul.

When the first symptoms of disease appear, dispute the   12
testimony of the material senses with divine Science. Let

Unnecessary prostration your higher sense of justice destroy the false
process of mortal opinions which you name   15
law, and then you will not be confined to a sick-room nor
laid upon a bed of suffering in payment of the last farthing, the last penalty demanded by error. "Agree with   18
thine adversary quickly, whiles thou art in the way with
him." Suffer no claim of sin or of sickness to grow upon
the thought. Dismiss it with an abiding conviction that   21
it is illegitimate, because you know that God is no more
the author of sickness than He is of sin. You have no
law of His to support the necessity either of sin or sick-   24
ness, but you have divine authority for denying that necessity and healing the sick.

"Agree to disagree" with approaching symptoms of   27
chronic or acute disease, whether it is cancer, consump-

Treatment of disease tion, or smallpox. Meet the incipient stages
of disease with as powerful mental opposi-   30
tion as a legislator would employ to defeat the passage of
an inhuman law. Rise in the conscious strength of the

spirit of Truth to overthrow the plea of mortal mind, *alias* matter, arrayed against the supremacy of Spirit. Blot out the images of mortal thought and its beliefs in sickness and sin. Then, when thou art delivered to the judgment of Truth, Christ, the judge will say, "Thou art whole!"

Instead of blind and calm submission to the incipient or advanced stages of disease, rise in rebellion against them. Banish the belief that you can possibly entertain a single intruding pain which cannot be ruled out by the might of Mind, and in this way you can prevent the development of pain in the body. No law of God hinders this result. It is error to suffer for aught but your own sins. Christ, or Truth, will destroy all other supposed suffering, and real suffering for your own sins will cease in proportion as the sin ceases.

Righteous rebellion

Justice is the moral signification of law. Injustice declares the absence of law. When the body is supposed to say, "I am sick," never plead guilty. Since matter cannot talk, it must be mortal mind which speaks; therefore meet the intimation with a protest. If you say, "I am sick," you plead guilty. Then your adversary will deliver you to the judge (mortal mind), and the judge will sentence you. Disease has no intelligence to declare itself something and announce its name. Mortal mind alone sentences itself. Therefore make your own terms with sickness, and be just to yourself and to others.

Contradict error

Mentally contradict every complaint from the body, and rise to the true consciousness of Life as Love, — as all that is pure, and bearing the fruits of Spirit. Fear is the fountain of sickness,

Sin to be overcome

and you master fear and sin through divine Mind; hence   1
it is through divine Mind that you overcome disease.
Only while fear or sin remains can it bring forth death.   3
To cure a bodily ailment, every broken moral law should
be taken into account and the error be rebuked. Fear,
which is an element of all disease, must be cast out to   6
readjust the balance for God. Casting out evil and fear
enables truth to outweigh error. The only course is to
take antagonistic grounds against all that is opposed to   9
the health, holiness, and harmony of man, God's image.

The physical affirmation of disease should always be
met with the mental negation. Whatever benefit is pro-   12
duced on the body, must be expressed men-
tally, and thought should be held fast to this
ideal. If you believe in inflamed and weak nerves, you   15
are liable to an attack from that source. You will call it
neuralgia, but we call it a belief. If you think that consumption is hereditary in your family, you are liable to   18
the development of that thought in the form of what is
termed pulmonary disease, unless Science shows you
otherwise. If you decide that climate or atmosphere is   21
unhealthy, it will be so to you. Your decisions will master you, whichever direction they take.

Reverse the case. Stand porter at the door of thought.   24
Admitting only such conclusions as you wish realized in
bodily results, you will control yourself harmoniously. When the condition is present   27
which you say induces disease, whether it be air, exercise,
heredity, contagion, or accident, then perform your office
as porter and shut out these unhealthy thoughts and fears.   30
Exclude from mortal mind the offending errors; then the
body cannot suffer from them. The issues of pain or

Illusions about nerves

Guarding the door

pleasure must come through mind, and like a watchman
forsaking his post, we admit the intruding belief, forgetting that through divine help we can forbid this entrance.

The body seems to be self-acting, only because mortal
mind is ignorant of itself, of its own actions, and of their
results, — ignorant that the predisposing, re- **The strength of Spirit**
mote, and exciting cause of all bad effects is a
law of so-called mortal mind, not of matter. Mind is the
master of the corporeal senses, and can conquer sickness,
sin, and death. Exercise this God-given authority. Take
possession of your body, and govern its feeling and action.
Rise in the strength of Spirit to resist all that is unlike
good. God has made man capable of this, and nothing
can vitiate the ability and power divinely bestowed on
man.

Be firm in your understanding that the divine Mind
governs, and that in Science man reflects God's government. Have no fear that matter can ache, **No pain in matter**
swell, and be inflamed as the result of a law
of any kind, when it is self-evident that matter can have
no pain nor inflammation. Your body would suffer no
more from tension or wounds than the trunk of a tree
which you gash or the electric wire which you stretch,
were it not for mortal mind.

When Jesus declares that "the light of the body is the
eye," he certainly means that light depends upon Mind,
not upon the complex humors, lenses, muscles, the iris
and pupil, constituting the visual organism.

Man is never sick, for Mind is not sick and matter
cannot be. A false belief is both the tempter **No real disease**
and the tempted, the sin and the sinner, the
disease and its cause. It is well to be calm in sickness;

to be hopeful is still better; but to understand that sick-   1
ness is not real and that Truth can destroy its seeming
reality, is best of all, for this understanding is the uni-   3
versal and perfect remedy.

By conceding power to discord, a large majority of
doctors depress mental energy, which is the only real   6

Recuperation
mental

recuperative power. Knowledge that we
can accomplish the good we hope for, stimu-
lates the system to act in the direction which Mind points   9
out. The admission that any bodily condition is beyond
the control of Mind disarms man, prevents him from
helping himself, and enthrones matter through error. To   12
those struggling with sickness, such admissions are discouraging, — as much so as would be the advice to a man
who is down in the world, that he should not try to rise   15
above his difficulties.

Experience has proved to the author the fallacy of
material systems in general, — that their theories are   18
sometimes pernicious, and that their denials are better
than their affirmations. Will you bid a man let evils
overcome him, assuring him that all misfortunes are from   21
God, against whom mortals should not contend? Will
you tell the sick that their condition is hopeless, unless it
can be aided by a drug or climate? Are material means   24
the only refuge from fatal chances? Is there no divine
permission to conquer discord of every kind with harmony,
with Truth and Love?   27

We should remember that Life is God, and that God

Arguing
wrongly

is omnipotent. Not understanding Christian
Science, the sick usually have little faith in   30
it till they feel its beneficent influence. This shows
that faith is not the healer in such cases. The sick

1   unconsciously argue for suffering, instead of against it.
They admit its reality, whereas they should deny it.

3   They should plead in opposition to the testimony of the
deceitful senses, and maintain man's immortality and
eternal likeness to God.

6   Like the great Exemplar, the healer should speak to
disease as one having authority over it, leaving Soul to
master the false evidences of the corporeal

Divine authority

9   senses and to assert its claims over mortality and disease. The same Principle cures both sin and
sickness. When divine Science overcomes faith in a car-

12   nal mind, and faith in God destroys all faith in sin and in
material methods of healing, then sin, disease, and death
will disappear.

15   Prayers, in which God is not asked to heal but is besought to take the patient to Himself, do not benefit the
sick. An ill-tempered, complaining, or deceit-

Aids in sickness

18   ful person should not be a nurse. The nurse
should be cheerful, orderly, punctual, patient, full of
faith, — receptive to Truth and Love.

21   It is mental quackery to make disease a reality — to
hold it as something seen and felt — and then to attempt
its cure through Mind. It is no less erroneous

Mental quackery

24   to believe in the real existence of a tumor, a
cancer, or decayed lungs, while you argue against their
reality, than it is for your patient to feel these ills in

27   physical belief. Mental practice, which holds disease
as a reality, fastens disease on the patient, and it may
appear in a more alarming form.

30   The knowledge that brain-lobes cannot kill a man nor
affect the functions of mind would prevent the brain from
becoming diseased, though a moral offence is indeed the

worst of diseases. One should never hold in mind
the thought of disease, but should efface from
thought all forms and types of disease, both for
one's own sake and for that of the patient.

Avoid talking illness to the patient. Make no unnecessary inquiries relative to feelings or disease. Never
startle with a discouraging remark about recovery, nor draw attention to certain symptoms as unfavorable, avoid speaking aloud the name of
the disease. Never say beforehand how much you have
to contend with in a case, nor encourage in the patient's
thought the expectation of growing worse before a crisis
is passed.

The refutation of the testimony of material sense is
not a difficult task in view of the conceded falsity of this
testimony. The refutation becomes arduous,
not because the testimony of sin or disease is
true, but solely on account of the tenacity of belief in its
truth, due to the force of education and the overwhelming weight of opinions on the wrong side, — all teaching
that the body suffers, as if matter could have sensation.

At the right time explain to the sick the power which
their beliefs exercise over their bodies. Give them divine
and wholesome understanding, with which to
combat their erroneous sense, and so efface the
images of sickness from mortal mind. Keep distinctly in
thought that man is the offspring of God, not of man;
that man is spiritual, not material; that Soul is Spirit,
outside of matter, never in it, never giving the body life
and sensation. It breaks the dream of disease to understand that sickness is formed by the human mind, not by
matter nor by the divine Mind.

1   By not perceiving vital metaphysical points, not seeing
how mortal mind affects the body, — acting beneficially
3   or injuriously on the health, as well as on the
morals and the happiness of mortals, — we are
misled in our conclusions and methods. We throw the
6   mental influence on the wrong side, thereby actually injuring those whom we mean to bless.

Misleading
methods

Suffering is no less a mental condition than is enjoy-
9   ment. You cause bodily sufferings and increase them
by admitting their reality and continuance,
as directly as you enhance your joys by be-
12   lieving them to be real and continuous. When an accident happens, you think or exclaim, "I am hurt!"
Your thought is more powerful than your words, more
15   powerful than the accident itself, to make the injury
real.

Remedy for
accidents

Now reverse the process. Declare that you are not hurt
18   and understand the reason why, and you will find the
ensuing good effects to be in exact proportion to your
disbelief in physics, and your fidelity to divine meta-
21   physics, confidence in God as All, which the Scriptures
declare Him to be.

To heal the sick, one must be familiar with the great
24   verities of being. Mortals are no more material in their
waking hours than when they act, walk, see,
hear, enjoy, or suffer in dreams. We can
27   never treat mortal mind and matter separately, because
they combine as one. Give up the belief that mind
is, even temporarily, compressed within the skull, and
30   you will quickly become more manly or womanly. You
will understand yourself and your Maker better than
before.

Independent
mentality

**Naming
maladies**

Sometimes Jesus called a disease by name, as when he   1
said to the epileptic boy, "Thou dumb and deaf spirit, I
charge thee, come out of him, and enter no   3
more into him." It is added that "the spirit
[error] cried, and rent him sore and came out of him, and
he was as one dead," — clear evidence that the malady   6
was not material. These instances show the concessions
which Jesus was willing to make to the popular ignorance
of spiritual Life-laws. Often he gave no name to the   9
distemper he cured. To the synagogue ruler's daughter,
whom they called dead but of whom he said, "she is not
dead, but sleepeth," he simply said, "Damsel, I say unto   12
thee, arise!" To the sufferer with the withered hand
he said, "Stretch forth thine hand," and it "was restored
whole, like as the other."   15

**The action
of faith**

Homœopathic remedies, sometimes not containing a
particle of medicine, are known to relieve the symptoms
of disease. What produces the change? It is   18
the faith of the doctor and the patient, which
reduces self-inflicted sufferings and produces a new effect
upon the body. In like manner destroy the illusion of   21
pleasure in intoxication, and the desire for strong drink
is gone. Appetite and disease reside in mortal mind, not
in matter.   24

So also faith, cooperating with a belief in the healing
effects of time and medication, will soothe fear and change
the belief of disease to a belief of health. Even a blind   27
faith removes bodily ailments for a season, but hypnotism
changes such ills into new and more difficult forms of disease. The Science of Mind must come to the rescue,   30
to work a radical cure. Then we understand the process.
The great fact remains that evil is not mind. Evil has

no power, no intelligence, for God is good, and therefore good is infinite, is All.

You say that certain material combinations produce disease; but if the material body causes disease, can matter cure what matter has caused? Mortal mind prescribes the drug, and administers it. Mortal mind plans the exercise, and puts the body through certain motions. No gastric gas accumulates, not a secretion nor combination can operate, apart from the action of mortal thought, *alias* mortal mind.

So-called mortal mind sends its despatches over its body, but this so-called mind is both the service and message of this telegraphy. Nerves are unable to talk, and matter can return no answer to immortal Mind. If Mind is the only actor, how can mechanism be automatic? Mortal mind perpetuates its own thought. It constructs a machine, manages it, and then calls it material. A mill at work or the action of a water-wheel is but a derivative from, and continuation of, the primitive mortal mind. Without this force the body is devoid of action, and this deadness shows that so-called mortal life is mortal mind, not matter.

Scientifically speaking, there is no mortal mind out of which to make material beliefs, springing from illusion. This misnamed mind is not an entity. It is only a false sense of matter, since matter is not sensible. The one Mind, God, contains no mortal opinions. All that is real is included in this immortal Mind.

Our Master asked: "How can one enter into a strong man's house and spoil his goods, except he first bind the strong man?" In other words: How can I heal the body, without beginning with so-called

Corporeal combinations

Automatic mechanism

Mental strength

Confirmation in a parable

mortal mind, which directly controls the body? When   1
disease is once destroyed in this so-called mind, the fear
of disease is gone, and therefore the disease is thor-   3
oughly cured. Mortal mind is "the strong man," which
must be held in subjection before its influence upon health
and morals can be removed. This error conquered, we   6
can despoil "the strong man" of his goods, — namely, of
sin and disease.

Mortals obtain the harmony of health, only as they   9
forsake discord, acknowledge the supremacy of divine
Mind, and abandon their material beliefs.

Eradicate error from thought
Eradicate the image of disease from the per-   12
turbed thought before it has taken tangible
shape in conscious thought, *alias* the body, and you prevent the development of disease. This task becomes easy,   15
if you understand that every disease is an error, and has
no character nor type, except what mortal mind assigns to
it. By lifting thought above error, or disease, and con-   18
tending persistently for truth, you destroy error.

When we remove disease by addressing the disturbed
mind, giving no heed to the body, we prove that thought   21
alone creates the suffering. Mortal mind

Mortal mind controlled
rules all that is mortal. We see in the body
the images of this mind, even as in optics we see painted   24
on the retina the image which becomes visible to the
senses. The action of so-called mortal mind must be
destroyed by the divine Mind to bring out the harmony   27
of being. Without divine control there is discord, manifest as sin, sickness, and death.

The Scriptures plainly declare the baneful influence of   30
sinful thought on the body. Even our Master felt this.
It is recorded that in certain localities he did not many

mighty works "because of their unbelief" in Truth. Any
human error is its own enemy, and works against itself;
it does nothing in the right direction and much

Mortal mind
not a healer

in the wrong. If so-called mind is cherishing
evil passions and malicious purposes, it is not a healer,
but it engenders disease and death.

If faith in the truth of being, which you impart mentally while destroying error, causes chemicalization (as
when an alkali is destroying an acid), it is be-

Effect of
opposites

cause the truth of being must transform the
error to the end of producing a higher manifestation.
This fermentation should not aggravate the disease, but
should be as painless to man as to a fluid, since matter
has no sensation and mortal mind only feels and sees
materially.

What I term *chemicalization* is the upheaval produced
when immortal Truth is destroying erroneous mortal belief. Mental chemicalization brings sin and sickness to
the surface, forcing impurities to pass away, as is the case
with a fermenting fluid.

The only effect produced by medicine is dependent upon
mental action. If the mind were parted from the body,
could you produce any effect upon the brain

Medicine
and brain

or body by applying the drug to either? Would
the drug remove paralysis, affect organization, or restore
will and action to cerebrum and cerebellum?

Until the advancing age admits the efficacy and supremacy of Mind, it is better for Christian Scientists to leave
surgery and the adjustment of broken bones

Skilful
surgery

and dislocations to the fingers of a surgeon,
while the mental healer confines himself chiefly to mental
reconstruction and to the prevention of inflammation.

Christian Science is always the most skilful surgeon, but surgery is the branch of its healing which will be last acknowledged. However, it is but just to say that the author has already in her possession well-authenticated records of the cure, by herself and her students through mental surgery alone, of broken bones, dislocated joints, and spinal vertebræ.

Indestructible life of man

The time approaches when mortal mind will forsake its corporeal, structural, and material basis, when immortal Mind and its formations will be apprehended in Science, and material beliefs will not interfere with spiritual facts. Man is indestructible and eternal. Sometime it will be learned that mortal mind constructs the mortal body with this mind's own mortal materials. In Science, no breakage nor dislocation can really occur. You say that accidents, injuries, and disease kill man, but this is not true. The life of man is Mind. The material body manifests only what mortal mind believes, whether it be a broken bone, disease, or sin.

The evil of mesmerism

We say that one human mind can influence another and in this way affect the body, but we rarely remember that we govern our own bodies. The error, mesmerism — or hypnotism, to use the recent term — illustrates the fact just stated. The operator would make his subjects believe that they cannot act voluntarily and handle themselves as they should do. If they yield to this influence, it is because their belief is not better instructed by spiritual understanding. Hence the proof that hypnotism is not scientific; Science cannot produce both disorder and order. The involuntary pleasure or pain of the person under hypnotic control is proved to be a belief without a real cause.

1   So the sick through their beliefs have induced their own
diseased conditions. The great difference between vol-

3   untary and involuntary mesmerism is that voluntary mesmerism is induced consciously and
should and does cause the perpetrator to suffer, while self-

Wrong-doer
should suffer

6   mesmerism is induced unconsciously and by his mistake
a man is often instructed. In the first instance it is understood that the difficulty is a mental illusion, while in the

9   second it is believed that the misfortune is a material effect.
The human mind is employed to remove the illusion in
one case, but matter is appealed to in the other. In real-

12   ity, both have their origin in the human mind, and can be
healed only by the divine Mind.

     You command the situation if you understand that

15   mortal existence is a state of self-deception and not the
truth of being. Mortal mind is constantly
producing on mortal body the results of false

Error's power
imaginary

18   opinions; and it will continue to do so, until mortal
error is deprived of its imaginary powers by Truth,
which sweeps away the gossamer web of mortal illusion.

21   The most Christian state is one of rectitude and spiritual understanding, and this is best adapted for healing the sick. Never conjure up some new discovery from

24   dark forebodings regarding disease and then acquaint
your patient with it.

     The mortal so-called mind produces all that is unlike

27   the immortal Mind. The human mind determines the
nature of a case, and the practitioner improves
or injures the case in proportion to the truth

Disease-
production

30   or error which influences his conclusions. The mental
conception and development of disease are not understood by the patient, but the physician should be familiar

with mental action and its effect in order to judge the case   1
according to Christian Science.

If a man is an inebriate, a slave to tobacco, or the special   3
servant of any one of the myriad forms of sin, meet and
destroy these errors with the truth of being, —

by exhibiting to the wrong-doer the suffering   6
which his submission to such habits brings, and by convincing him that there is no real pleasure in false appetites. A corrupt mind is manifested in a corrupt body.   9
Lust, malice, and all sorts of evil are diseased beliefs, and
you can destroy them only by destroying the wicked
motives which produce them. If the evil is over in the   12
repentant mortal mind, while its effects still remain on the
individual, you can remove this disorder as God's law is
fulfilled and reformation cancels the crime. The healthy   15
sinner is the hardened sinner.

The temperance reform, felt all over our land, results
from metaphysical healing, which cuts down every tree   18
that brings not forth good fruit. This con-

viction, that there is no real pleasure in sin,
is one of the most important points in the theology of   21
Christian Science. Arouse the sinner to this new and
true view of sin, show him that sin confers no pleasure,
and this knowledge strengthens his moral courage and   24
increases his ability to master evil and to love good.

Healing the sick and reforming the sinner are one and
the same thing in Christian Science. Both cures require   27
the same method and are inseparable in Truth.

Hatred, envy, dishonesty, fear, and so forth,
make a man sick, and neither material medi-   30
cine nor Mind can help him permanently, even in body,
unless it makes him better mentally, and so delivers him

from his destroyers. The basic error is mortal mind.
Hatred inflames the brutal propensities. The indulgence
of evil motives and aims makes any man, who is above the
lowest type of manhood, a hopeless sufferer.

Christian Science commands man to master the propensities, — to hold hatred in abeyance with kindness,
to conquer lust with chastity, revenge with
charity, and to overcome deceit with honesty. Choke these errors in their early stages, if you
would not cherish an army of conspirators against
health, happiness, and success. They will deliver you
to the judge, the arbiter of truth against error. The
judge will deliver you to justice, and the sentence of
the moral law will be executed upon mortal mind and
body. Both will be manacled until the last farthing
is paid, — until you have balanced your account with
God. "Whatsoever a man soweth, that shall he also
reap." The good man finally can overcome his fear of
sin. This is sin's necessity, — to destroy itself. Immortal man demonstrates the government of God, good,
in which is no power to sin.

Mental conspirators

It were better to be exposed to every plague on earth
than to endure the cumulative effects of a guilty conscience. The abiding consciousness of wrong-
doing tends to destroy the ability to do right.
If sin is not regretted and is not lessening, then it is
hastening on to physical and moral doom. You are conquered by the moral penalties you incur and the ills they
bring. The pains of sinful sense are less harmful than its
pleasures. Belief in material suffering causes mortals to
retreat from their error, to flee from body to Spirit, and
to appeal to divine sources outside of themselves.

Cumulative repentance

The Bible contains the recipe for all healing. "The
leaves of the tree were for the healing of the nations."

Sin and sickness are both healed by the same
Principle. The tree is typical of man's divine
Principle, which is equal to every emergency, offering
full salvation from sin, sickness, and death. Sin will
submit to Christian Science when, in place of modes and
forms, the power of God is understood and demonstrated
in the healing of mortals, both mind and body. "Perfect Love casteth out fear."

The Science of being unveils the errors of sense, and
spiritual perception, aided by Science, reaches Truth.
Then error disappears. Sin and sickness will

abate and seem less real as we approach the
scientific period, in which mortal sense is subdued and
all that is unlike the true likeness disappears. The moral
man has no fear that he will commit a murder, and he
should be as fearless on the question of disease.

Resist evil — error of every sort — and it will flee from
you. Error is opposed to Life. We can, and ultimately

shall, so rise as to avail ourselves in every direction of the supremacy of Truth over error, Life
over death, and good over evil, and this growth will go
on until we arrive at the fulness of God's idea, and no
more fear that we shall be sick and die. Inharmony of
any kind involves weakness and suffering, — a loss of
control over the body.

The depraved appetite for alcoholic drinks, tobacco,
tea, coffee, opium, is destroyed only by Mind's mastery

of the body. This normal control is gained
through divine strength and understanding.
There is no enjoyment in getting drunk, in becoming a

fool or an object of loathing; but there is a very sharp
remembrance of it, a suffering inconceivably terrible to
man's self-respect. Puffing the obnoxious fumes of tobacco, or chewing a leaf naturally attractive to no creature except a loathsome worm, is at least disgusting.

Man's enslavement to the most relentless masters —
passion, selfishness, envy, hatred, and revenge — is conquered only by a mighty struggle. Every
hour of delay makes the struggle more severe.
If man is not victorious over the passions, they crush
out happiness, health, and manhood. Here Christian
Science is the sovereign panacea, giving strength to the
weakness of mortal mind, — strength from the immortal
and omnipotent Mind, — and lifting humanity above
itself into purer desires, even into spiritual power and
good-will to man.

Universal panacea

Let the slave of wrong desire learn the lessons of Christian Science, and he will get the better of that desire,
and ascend a degree in the scale of health, happiness,
and existence.

If delusion says, "I have lost my memory," contradict it. No faculty of Mind is lost. In Science, all
being is eternal, spiritual, perfect, harmonious in every action. Let the perfect model be
present in your thoughts instead of its demoralized opposite. This spiritualization of thought lets in the light,
and brings the divine Mind, Life not death, into your
consciousness.

Immortal memory

There are many species of insanity. All sin is insanity in different degrees. Sin is spared from
this classification, only because its method of
madness is in consonance with common mortal belief.

Sin a form of insanity

Every sort of sickness is error, — that is, sickness is   1
loss of harmony. This view is not altered by the fact
that sin is worse than sickness, and sickness is not ac-   3
knowledged nor discovered to be error by many who are
sick.

There is a universal insanity of so-called health, which   6
mistakes fable for fact throughout the entire round of the
material senses, but this general craze cannot, in a scientific diagnosis, shield the individual case from the special   9
name of insanity. Those unfortunate people who are
committed to insane asylums are only so many distinctly
defined instances of the baneful effects of illusion on mor-   12
tal minds and bodies.

The supposition that we can correct insanity by the use
of purgatives and narcotics is in itself a mild species of   15

Drugs and   insanity. Can drugs go of their own accord
brain-lobes to the brain and destroy the so-called inflammation of disordered functions, thus reaching mortal   18
mind through matter? Drugs do not affect a corpse, and
Truth does not distribute drugs through the blood, and
from them derive a supposed effect on intelligence and sen-   21
timent. A dislocation of the tarsal joint would produce
insanity as perceptibly as would congestion of the brain,
were it not that mortal mind thinks that the tarsal joint is   24
less intimately connected with the mind than is the brain.
Reverse the belief, and the results would be perceptibly
different.   27

The unconscious thought in the corporeal substratum of brain produces no effect, and that condition of

Matter and   the body which we call sensation in matter   30
animate error   is unreal. Mortal mind is ignorant of itself, — ignorant of the errors it includes and of their

effects. Intelligent matter is an impossibility. You may say: "But if disease obtains in matter, why do you insist that disease is formed by mortal mind and not by matter?" *Mortal mind* and body combine as one, and the nearer matter approaches its final statement, — animate error called nerves, brain, mind, — the more prolific it is likely to become in sin and disease-beliefs.

Unconscious mortal mind — *alias* matter, brain — cannot dictate terms to consciousness nor say, "I am sick." The belief, that the unconscious substratum of mortal mind, termed the body, suffers and reports disease independently of this so-called conscious mind, is the error which prevents mortals from knowing how to govern their bodies.

Dictation of error

The so-called conscious mortal mind is believed to be superior to its unconscious substratum, matter, and the stronger never yields to the weaker, except through fear or choice. The animate should be governed by God alone. The real man is spiritual and immortal, but the mortal and imperfect so-called "children of men" are counterfeits from the beginning, to be laid aside for the pure reality. This mortal is put off, and the new man or real man is put on, in proportion as mortals realize the Science of man and seek the true model.

So-called superiority

We have no right to say that life depends on matter now, but will not depend on it after death. We cannot spend our days here in ignorance of the Science of Life, and expect to find beyond the grave a reward for this ignorance. Death will not make us harmonious and immortal as a recompense for ignorance.

Death no benefactor

If here we give no heed to Christian Science, which is spiritual and eternal, we shall not be ready for spiritual Life hereafter.

"This is life eternal," says Jesus, — *is,* not *shall be;* and then he defines everlasting life as a present knowledge of his Father and of himself, — the knowledge of Love, Truth, and Life. "This is life eternal, that they might know Thee, the only true God, and Jesus Christ, whom Thou hast sent." The Scriptures say, "Man shall not live by bread *alone,* but by every word that proceedeth out of the mouth of God," showing that Truth is the actual life of man; but mankind objects to making this teaching practical.

Every trial of our faith in God makes us stronger. The more difficult seems the material condition to be overcome by Spirit, the stronger should be our faith and the purer our love. The Apostle John says: "There is no fear in Love, but perfect Love casteth out fear. . . . He that feareth is not made perfect in Love." Here is a definite and inspired proclamation of Christian Science.

MENTAL TREATMENT ILLUSTRATED

The Science of mental practice is susceptible of no misuse. Selfishness does not appear in the practice of Truth or Christian Science. If mental practice is abused or is used in any way except to promote right thinking and doing, the power to heal mentally will diminish, until the practitioner's healing ability is wholly lost. Christian scientific practice begins with Christ's keynote of harmony, "Be not afraid!"

Marginal headings:
Life eternal and present
Love casteth out fear
Be not afraid

1   Said Job: "The thing which I greatly feared is come upon me."

3   My first discovery in the student's practice was this: If the student silently called the disease by name, when he argued against it, as a general rule the body

6 would respond more quickly, — just as a person replies more readily when his name is spoken; but this was because the student was not perfectly attuned to

9 divine Science, and needed the arguments of truth for reminders. If Spirit or the power of divine Love bear witness to the truth, this is the ultimatum, the scientific

12 way, and the healing is instantaneous.

It is recorded that once Jesus asked the name of a disease, — a disease which moderns would call *dementia*.

15 The demon, or evil, replied that his name was Legion. Thereupon Jesus cast out the evil, and the insane man was changed and straightway be-

18 came whole. The Scripture seems to import that Jesus caused the evil to be self-seen and so destroyed.

The procuring cause and foundation of all sickness is

21 fear, ignorance, or sin. Disease is always induced by a false sense mentally entertained, not destroyed. Disease is an image of thought externalized.

24 The mental state is called a material state. Whatever is cherished in mortal mind as the physical condition is imaged forth on the body.

27 Always begin your treatment by allaying the fear of patients. Silently reassure them as to their exemption from disease and danger. Watch the re-

30 sult of this simple rule of Christian Science, and you will find that it alleviates the symptoms of every disease. If you succeed in wholly removing the fear,

Naming diseases

Evils cast out

Fear as the foundation

Unspoken pleading

your patient is healed. The great fact that God lovingly   1
governs all, never punishing aught but sin, is your standpoint, from which to advance and destroy the human fear   3
of sickness. Mentally and silently plead the case scientifically for Truth. You may vary the arguments to meet
the peculiar or general symptoms of the case you treat,   6
but be thoroughly persuaded in your own mind concerning the truth which you think or speak, and you will be
the victor.   9

You may call the disease by name when you mentally
deny it; but by naming it audibly, you are liable under

Eloquent
silence

some circumstances to impress it upon the   12
thought. The power of Christian Science and
divine Love is omnipotent. It is indeed adequate to un-
clasp the hold and to destroy disease, sin, and death.   15

To prevent disease or to cure it, the power of Truth,
of divine Spirit, must break the dream of the material

Insistence
requisite

senses. To heal by argument, find the type   18
of the ailment, get its name, and array your
mental plea against the physical. Argue at first mentally, not audibly, that the patient has no disease, and   21
conform the argument so as to destroy the evidence of
disease. Mentally insist that harmony is the fact, and
that sickness is a temporal dream. Realize the presence   24
of health and the fact of harmonious being, until the
body corresponds with the normal conditions of health
and harmony.   27

If the case is that of a young child or an infant, it needs
to be met mainly through the parent's thought, silently

The cure
of infants

or audibly on the aforesaid basis of Christian   30
Science. The Scientist knows that there can
be no hereditary disease, since matter is not intelligent

and cannot transmit good or evil intelligence to man, and
God, the only Mind, does not produce pain in matter.

The act of yielding one's thoughts to the undue contemplation of physical wants or conditions induces those very
conditions. A single requirement, beyond what is necessary to meet the simplest needs of the babe is harmful.
Mind regulates the condition of the stomach, bowels, and
food, the temperature of children and of men, and matter
does not. The wise or unwise views of parents and other
persons on these subjects produce good or bad effects on
the health of children.

The daily ablutions of an infant are no more natural
nor necessary than would be the process of taking a fish
out of water every day and covering it with dirt
in order to make it thrive more vigorously in its
own element. "Cleanliness is next to godliness," but
washing should be only for the purpose of keeping the
body clean, and this can be effected without scrubbing the
whole surface daily. Water is not the natural habitat of
humanity. I insist on bodily cleanliness within and without. I am not patient with a speck of dirt; but in caring
for an infant one need not wash his little body all over each
day in order to keep it sweet as the new-blown flower.

Ablutions for cleanliness

Giving drugs to infants, noticing every symptom of
flatulency, and constantly directing the mind to such
signs, — that mind being laden with illusions
about disease, health-laws, and death, — these
actions convey mental images to children's budding
thoughts, and often stamp them there, making it probable
at any time that such ills may be reproduced in the very
ailments feared. A child may have worms, if you say so,
or any other malady, timorously held in the beliefs con-

Juvenile ailments

cerning his body. Thus are laid the foundations of the　　1
belief in disease and death, and thus are children educated
into discord.　　3

The treatment of insanity is especially interesting.
However obstinate the case, it yields more readily than

do most diseases to the salutary action of　　6
truth, which counteracts error. The arguments to be used in curing insanity are the same as in
other diseases: namely, the impossibility that matter,　　9
brain, can control or derange mind, can suffer or cause
suffering; also the fact that truth and love will establish
a healthy state, guide and govern mortal mind or the　　12
thought of the patient, and destroy all error, whether it is
called dementia, hatred, or any other discord.

To fix truth steadfastly in your patients' thoughts, ex-　　15
plain Christian Science to them, but not too soon, — not
until your patients are prepared for the explanation, —
lest you array the sick against their own interests by troub-　　18
ling and perplexing their thought. The Christian Scientist's argument rests on the Christianly scientific basis of
being. The Scripture declares, "The Lord He is God　　21
[good]; there is none else beside Him." Even so, harmony
is universal, and discord is unreal. Christian Science declares that Mind is substance, also that matter neither　　24
feels, suffers, nor enjoys. Hold these points strongly in
view. Keep in mind the verity of being, — that man is
the image and likeness of God, in whom all being is　　27
painless and permanent. Remember that man's perfection is real and unimpeachable, whereas imperfection is
blameworthy, unreal, and is not brought about by divine　　30
Love.

Matter cannot be inflamed. Inflammation is fear, an

1 excited state of mortals which is not normal. Immortal Mind is the only cause; therefore disease is neither a
3 cause nor an effect. Mind in every case is the
eternal God, good. Sin, disease, and death
have no foundations in Truth. Inflammation as a mor-
6 tal belief quickens or impedes the action of the system,
because thought moves quickly or slowly, leaps or halts
when it contemplates unpleasant things, or when the in-
9 dividual looks upon some object which he dreads. Inflammation never appears in a part which mortal thought
does not reach. That is why opiates relieve inflammation.
12 They quiet the thought by inducing stupefaction and by
resorting to matter instead of to Mind. Opiates do not
remove the pain in any scientific sense. They only ren-
15 der mortal mind temporarily less fearful, till it can master
an erroneous belief.

Note how thought makes the face pallid. It either re-
18 tards the circulation or quickens it, causing a pale or
flushed cheek. In the same way thought increases or diminishes the secretions, the action
21 of the lungs, of the bowels, and of the heart. The muscles, moving quickly or slowly and impelled or palsied by
thought, represent the action of all the organs of the hu-
24 man system, including brain and viscera. To remove
the error producing disorder, you must calm and instruct
mortal mind with immortal Truth.

27 Etherization will apparently cause the body to disappear. Before the thoughts are fully at rest, the limbs
will vanish from consciousness. Indeed, the
30 whole frame will sink from sight along with
surrounding objects, leaving the pain standing forth as
distinctly as a mountain-peak, as if it were a separate

*Matter is
not inflamed*

*Truth calms
the thought*

*Effects of
etherization*

bodily member. At last the agony also vanishes. This
process shows the pain to be in the mind, for the inflammation is not suppressed; and the belief of pain will
presently return, unless the mental image occasioning
the pain be removed by recognizing the truth of being.

A hypodermic injection of morphine is administered
to a patient, and in twenty minutes the sufferer is qui-

Sedatives valueless
etly asleep. To him there is no longer any
pain. Yet any physician — allopathic, homœopathic, botanic, eclectic — will tell you that the troublesome material cause is unremoved, and that when the
soporific influence of the opium is exhausted, the patient will find himself in the same pain, unless the belief
which occasions the pain has meanwhile been changed.
Where is the pain while the patient sleeps?

The material body, which you call *me*, is mortal mind,
and this mind is material in sensation, even as the body,

The so-called physical ego
which has originated from this material sense
and been developed according to it, is material. This materialism of parent and child is only in
mortal mind, as the dead body proves; for when the
mortal has resigned his body to dust, the body is no
longer the parent, even in appearance.

The sick know nothing of the mental process by
which they are depleted, and next to nothing of the

Evil thought depletes
metaphysical method by which they can be
healed. If they ask about their disease, tell
them only what is best for them to know. Assure them
that they think too much about their ailments, and
have already heard too much on that subject. Turn
their thoughts away from their bodies to higher objects. Teach them that their being is sustained by

1 Spirit, not by matter, and that they find health, peace,
and harmony in God, divine Love.

3 Give sick people credit for sometimes knowing more
than their doctors. Always support their trust in the
power of Mind to sustain the body. Never

6 tell the sick that they have more courage
than strength. Tell them rather, that their strength
is in proportion to their courage. If you make the sick

9 realize this great truism, there will be no reaction from
over-exertion or from excited conditions. Maintain
the facts of Christian Science, — that Spirit is God, and

12 therefore cannot be sick; that what is termed matter
cannot be sick; that all causation is Mind, acting
through spiritual law. Then hold your ground with

15 the unshaken understanding of Truth and Love, and
you will win. When you silence the witness against your
plea, you destroy the evidence, for the disease disap-

18 pears. The evidence before the corporeal senses is not
the Science of immortal man.

To the Christian Science healer, sickness is a dream

21 from which the patient needs to be awakened. Disease should not appear real to the physician,
since it is demonstrable that the way to

24 cure the patient is to make disease unreal to him. To
do this, the physician must understand the unreality
of disease in Science.

27 Explain audibly to your patients, as soon as they can
bear it, the complete control which Mind holds over the
body. Show them how mortal mind seems to induce

30 disease by certain fears and false conclusions, and how
divine Mind can cure by opposite thoughts. Give your
patients an underlying understanding to support them

and to shield them from the baneful effects of their own   1
conclusions. Show them that the conquest over sickness,
as well as over sin, depends on mentally destroying all   3
belief in material pleasure or pain.

Stick to the truth of being in contradistinction to the
error that life, substance, or intelligence can be in matter.   6

Christian pleading

Plead with an honest conviction of truth and
a clear perception of the unchanging, unerr-
ing, and certain effect of divine Science. Then, if your   9
fidelity is half equal to the truth of your plea, you will
heal the sick.

It must be clear to you that sickness is no more   12
the reality of being than is sin. This mortal dream
of sickness, sin, and death should cease

Truthful arguments

through Christian Science. Then one dis-   15
ease would be as readily destroyed as another. Whatever the belief is, if arguments are used to destroy it,
the belief must be repudiated, and the negation must ex-   18
tend to the supposed disease and to whatever decides its
type and symptoms. Truth is affirmative, and confers
harmony. All metaphysical logic is inspired by this sim-   21
ple rule of Truth, which governs all reality. By the
truthful arguments you employ, and especially by the
spirit of Truth and Love which you entertain, you will   24
heal the sick.

Include moral as well as physical belief in your efforts
to destroy error. Cast out all manner of evil. "Preach   27

Morality required

the gospel to every creature." Speak the
truth to every form of error. Tumors, ulcers,
tubercles, inflammation, pain, deformed joints, are wak-   30
ing dream-shadows, dark images of mortal thought, which
flee before the light of Truth.

1   A moral question may hinder the recovery of the sick.
Lurking error, lust, envy, revenge, malice, or hate will
3 perpetuate or even create the belief in disease. Errors
of all sorts tend in this direction. Your true course is
to destroy the foe, and leave the field to God, Life, Truth,
6 and Love, remembering that God and His ideas alone
are real and harmonious.

    If your patient from any cause suffers a relapse, meet
9 the cause mentally and courageously, knowing that
there can be no reaction in Truth. Neither
             Relapse
disease itself, sin, nor fear has the power to
           unnecessary
12 cause disease or a relapse. Disease has no intelligence
with which to move itself about or to change itself from
one form to another. If disease moves, mind, not mat-
15 ter, moves it; therefore be sure that you move it off.
Meet every adverse circumstance as its master. Observe mind instead of body, lest aught unfit for develop-
18 ment enter thought. Think less of material conditions
and more of spiritual.

    Mind produces all action. If the action proceeds from
21 Truth, from immortal Mind, there is harmony; but mortal mind is liable to any phase of belief. A
           Conquer
relapse cannot in reality occur in mortals or
             beliefs
24 so-called mortal minds, for there is but one
          and fears
Mind, one God. Never fear the mental malpractitioner,
the mental assassin, who, in attempting to rule mankind,
27 tramples upon the divine Principle of metaphysics, for God
is the only power. To succeed in healing, you must conquer your own fears as well as those of your patients, and
30 rise into higher and holier consciousness.

    If it is found necessary to treat against relapse, know
that disease or its symptoms cannot change forms, nor

go from one part to another, for Truth destroys disease. 1
There is no metastasis, no stoppage of harmonious
True action, no paralysis. Truth not error, Love 3
government not hate, Spirit not matter, governs man. If
of man students do not readily heal themselves, they should
early call an experienced Christian Scientist to aid 6
them. If they are unwilling to do this for themselves,
they need only to know that error cannot produce this
unnatural reluctance. 9

Instruct the sick that they are not helpless victims,
for if they will only accept Truth, they can resist disease
Positive and ward it off, as positively as they can the 12
reassurance temptation to sin. This fact of Christian Science should be explained to invalids when they are in a
fit mood to receive it, — when they will not array them- 15
selves against it, but are ready to become receptive to the
new idea. The fact that Truth overcomes both disease
and sin reassures depressed hope. It imparts a healthy 18
stimulus to the body, and regulates the system. It increases or diminishes the action, as the case may require,
better than any drug, alterative, or tonic. 21

Mind is the natural stimulus of the body, but erroneous belief, taken at its best, is not promotive of health
Proper or happiness. Tell the sick that they can 24
stimulus meet disease fearlessly, if they only realize
that divine Love gives them all power over every physical
action and condition. 27

If it becomes necessary to startle mortal mind to break
its dream of suffering, vehemently tell your patient that
Awaken the he must awake. Turn his gaze from the false 30
patient evidence of the senses to the harmonious facts
of Soul and immortal being. Tell him that he suffers

only as the insane suffer, from false beliefs. The only
difference is, that insanity implies belief in a diseased
brain, while physical ailments (so-called) arise from the
belief that other portions of the body are deranged. Derangement, or *disarrangement,* is a word which conveys
the true definition of all human belief in ill-health, or disturbed harmony. Should you thus startle mortal mind
in order to remove its beliefs, afterwards make known
to the patient your motive for this shock, showing him
that it was to facilitate recovery.

If a crisis occurs in your treatment, you must treat
the patient less for the disease and more for the mental
disturbance or fermentation, and subdue the
symptoms by removing the belief that this
chemicalization produces pain or disease. Insist vehemently on the great fact which covers the whole ground,
that God, Spirit, is all, and that there is none beside
Him. There is *no disease.* When the supposed suffering is gone from mortal mind, there can be no pain; and
when the fear is destroyed, the inflammation will sub-
side. Calm the excitement sometimes induced by chemicalization, which is the alterative effect produced by
Truth upon error, and sometimes explain the symptoms
and their cause to the patient.

How to treat a crisis

It is no more Christianly scientific to see disease than
it is to experience it. If you would destroy the sense
of disease, you should not build it up by
wishing to see the forms it assumes or by
employing a single material application for
its relief. The perversion of Mind-science is like asserting that the products of eight multiplied by five, and
of seven by ten, are both forty, and that their combined

No perversion of Mind-science

sum is fifty, and then calling the process mathematics. 1
Wiser than his persecutors, Jesus said: "If I by Beelzebub cast out devils, by whom do your children cast them 3
out?"

If the reader of this book observes a great stir throughout his whole system, and certain moral and physical 6

**Effect of
this book**

symptoms seem aggravated, these indications
are favorable. Continue to read, and the book
will become the physician, allaying the tremor which 9
Truth often brings to error when destroying it.

Patients, unfamiliar with the cause of this commotion
and ignorant that it is a favorable omen, may be alarmed. 12

**Disease
neutralized**

If such be the case, explain to them the law
of this action. As when an acid and alkali
meet and bring out a third quality, so mental and moral 15
chemistry changes the material base of thought, giving
more spirituality to consciousness and causing it to depend
less on material evidence. These changes which go on 18
in mortal mind serve to reconstruct the body. Thus
Christian Science, by the alchemy of Spirit, destroys sin
and death. 21

Let us suppose two parallel cases of bone-disease, both
similarly produced and attended by the same symptoms.

**Bone-healing
by surgery**

A surgeon is employed in one case, and a 24
Christian Scientist in the other. The surgeon, holding that matter forms its own conditions and
renders them fatal at certain points, entertains fears and 27
doubts as to the ultimate outcome of the injury. Not
holding the reins of government in his own hands, he
believes that something stronger than Mind — namely, 30
matter — governs the case. His treatment is therefore
tentative. This mental state invites defeat. The belief

that he has met his master in matter and may not be able to mend the bone, increases his fear; yet this belief should not be communicated to the patient, either verbally or otherwise, for this fear greatly diminishes the tendency towards a favorable result. Remember that the unexpressed belief oftentimes affects a sensitive patient more strongly than the expressed thought.

The Christian Scientist, understanding scientifically that all is Mind, commences with mental causation, the truth of being, to destroy the error. This corrective is an alterative, reaching to every part of the human system. According to Scripture, it searches "the joints and marrow," and it restores the harmony of man.

Scientific corrective

The matter-physician deals with matter as both his foe and his remedy. He regards the ailment as weakened or strengthened according to the evidence which matter presents. The metaphysician, making Mind his basis of operation irrespective of matter and regarding the truth and harmony of being as superior to error and discord, has rendered himself strong, instead of weak, to cope with the case; and he proportionately strengthens his patient with the stimulus of courage and conscious power. Both Science and consciousness are now at work in the economy of being according to the law of Mind, which ultimately asserts its absolute supremacy.

Coping with difficulties

Ossification or any abnormal condition or derangement of the body is as directly the action of mortal mind as is dementia or insanity. Bones have only the substance of thought which forms them. They are only phenomena of the mind of mortals. The so-called substance of bone is formed first

Formation from thought

by the parent's mind, through self-division. Soon the   1
child becomes a separate, individualized mortal mind,
which takes possession of itself and its own thoughts of   3
bones.

Accidents are unknown to God, or immortal Mind,

and we must leave the mortal basis of belief   6
and unite with the one Mind, in order to
change the notion of chance to the proper sense
of God's unerring direction and thus bring out harmony.   9

Under divine Providence there can be no accidents,
since there is no room for imperfection in perfection.

In medical practice objections would be raised if one   12
doctor should administer a drug to counteract the work-

ing of a remedy prescribed by another doctor.
It is equally important in metaphysical prac-   15
tice that the *minds* which surround your patient should
not act against your influence by continually expressing
such opinions as may alarm or discourage, — either by   18
giving antagonistic advice or through unspoken thoughts
resting on your patient. While it is certain that the
divine Mind can remove any obstacle, still you need the   21
ear of your auditor. It is not more difficult to make yourself heard mentally while others are thinking about your
patients or conversing with them, if you understand   24
Christian Science — the oneness and the allness of divine
Love; but it is well to be alone with God and the sick
when treating disease.   27

To prevent or to cure scrofula and other so-called hereditary diseases, you must destroy the belief in these ills

and the faith in the possibility of their trans-   30
mission. The patient may tell you that he
has a humor in the blood, a scrofulous diathesis. His

parents or some of his progenitors farther back have so believed. Mortal mind, not matter, induces this conclusion and its results. You will have humors, just so long as you believe them to be safety-valves or to be ineradicable.

If the case to be mentally treated is consumption, take up the leading points included (according to belief) in this disease. Show that it is not inherited; **Nothing to consume** that inflammation, tubercles, hemorrhage, and decomposition are beliefs, images of mortal thought superimposed upon the body; that they are not the truth of man; that they should be treated as error and put out of thought. Then these ills will disappear.

If the body is diseased, this is but one of the beliefs of mortal mind. Mortal man will be less mortal, when he learns that matter never sustained existence **The lungs re-formed** and can never destroy God, who is man's Life. When this is understood, mankind will be more spiritual and know that there is nothing to consume, since Spirit, God, is All-in-all. What if the belief is consumption? God is more to a man than his belief, and the less we acknowledge matter or its laws, the more immortality we possess. Consciousness constructs a better body when faith in matter has been conquered. Correct material belief by spiritual understanding, and Spirit will form you anew. You will never fear again except to offend God, and you will never believe that heart or any portion of the body can destroy you.

If you have sound and capacious lungs and want them to remain so, be always ready with the **Soundness maintained** mental protest against the opposite belief in heredity. Discard all notions about lungs, tubercles, in-

herited consumption, or disease arising from any cir-   1
cumstance, and you will find that mortal mind, when
instructed by Truth, yields to divine power, which steers   3
the body into health.

The discoverer of Christian Science finds the path less
difficult when she has the high goal always before her   6

Our footsteps
heavenward
thoughts, than when she counts her footsteps
in endeavoring to reach it. When the desti-
nation is desirable, expectation speeds our progress. The   9
struggle for Truth makes one strong instead of weak,
resting instead of wearying one. If the belief in death
were obliterated, and the understanding obtained that   12
there is no death, this would be a "tree of life," known
by its fruits. Man should renew his energies and endeavors, and see the folly of hypocrisy, while also learn-   15
ing the necessity of working out his own salvation. When
it is learned that disease cannot destroy life, and that
mortals are not saved from sin or sickness by death, this   18
understanding will quicken into newness of life. It will
master either a desire to die or a dread of the grave,
and thus destroy the great fear that besets mortal   21
existence.

The relinquishment of all faith in death and also of
the fear of its sting would raise the standard of health   24

Christian
standard
and morals far beyond its present elevation,
and would enable us to hold the banner of
Christianity aloft with unflinching faith in God, in Life   27
eternal. Sin brought death, and death will disappear
with the disappearance of sin. Man is immortal, and
the body cannot die, because matter has no life to sur-   30
render. The human concepts named matter, death, disease, sickness, and sin are all that can be destroyed.

1   If it is true that man lives, this fact can never change
in Science to the opposite belief that man dies. Life is

3 the law of Soul, even the law of the spirit of

Life not
contingent
on matter

Truth, and Soul is never without its representative. Man's individual being can no more

6 die nor disappear in unconsciousness than can Soul, for
both are immortal. If man believes in death now, he
must disbelieve in it when learning that there is no reality

9 in death, since the truth of being is deathless. The belief that existence is contingent on matter must be met
and mastered by Science, before Life can be understood

12 and harmony obtained.

    Death is but another phase of the dream that exist-
ence can be material. Nothing can interfere with the

15 harmony of being nor end the existence of

Mortality
vanquished

man in Science. Man is the same after as
before a bone is broken or the body guillotined. If man

18 is never to overcome death, why do the Scriptures say,
"The last enemy that shall be destroyed is death"? The
tenor of the Word shows that we shall obtain the victory

21 over death in proportion as we overcome sin. The great
difficulty lies in ignorance of what God is. God, Life,
Truth, and Love make man undying. Immortal Mind,

24 governing all, must be acknowledged as supreme in the
physical realm, so-called, as well as in the spiritual.

    Called to the bed of death, what material remedy has

27 man when all such remedies have failed? Spirit is his
last resort, but it should have been his first

No death
nor inaction

and only resort. The dream of death must

30 be mastered by Mind here or hereafter. Thought
will waken from its own material declaration, "I am
dead," to catch this trumpet-word of Truth, "There

is no death, no inaction, diseased action, overaction, nor 1
reaction."

Life is real, and death is the illusion. A demonstra- 3
tion of the facts of Soul in Jesus' way resolves the dark

Vision opening

visions of material sense into harmony and
immortality. Man's privilege at this supreme 6
moment is to prove the words of our Master: "If a man
keep my saying, he shall never see death." To divest
thought of false trusts and material evidences in order 9
that the spiritual facts of being may appear, — this is
the great attainment by means of which we shall sweep
away the false and give place to the true. Thus we may 12
establish in truth the temple, or body, "whose builder
and maker is God."

We should consecrate existence, not "to the unknown 15
God" whom we "ignorantly worship," but to the eternal

Intelligent consecration

builder, the everlasting Father, to the Life
which mortal sense cannot impair nor mortal 18
belief destroy. We must realize the ability of mental
might to offset human misconceptions and to replace them
with the life which is spiritual, not material. 21

The great spiritual fact must be brought out that man
is, not *shall be*, perfect and immortal. We must hold

The present immortality

forever the consciousness of existence, and 24
sooner or later, through Christ and Christian
Science, we must master sin and death. The evidence
of man's immortality will become more apparent, as ma- 27
terial beliefs are given up and the immortal facts of being
are admitted.

The author has healed hopeless organic disease, and 30
raised the dying to life and health through the understanding of God as the only Life. It is a sin to believe

that aught can overpower omnipotent and eternal Life,
and this Life must be brought to light by the understanding that there is no death, as well as by other
graces of Spirit. We must begin, however,
with the more simple demonstrations of control, and
the sooner we begin the better. The final demonstration
takes time for its accomplishment. When walking, we
are guided by the eye. We look before our feet, and if
we are wise, we look beyond a single step in the line of
spiritual advancement.

Careful
guidance

The corpse, deserted by thought, is cold and decays,
but it never suffers. Science declares that man is subject to Mind. Mortal mind affirms that mind
is subordinate to the body, that the body is
dying, that it must be buried and decomposed
into dust; but mortal mind's affirmation is not true.
Mortals waken from the dream of death with bodies unseen by those who think that they bury the body.

Clay
replying to
the potter

If man did not exist before the material organization
began, he could not exist after the body is disintegrated.
If we live after death and are immortal, we
must have lived before birth, for if Life ever
had any beginning, it must also have an ending, even according to the calculations of natural science. Do you
believe this? No! Do you understand it? No! This
is why you doubt the statement and do not demonstrate
the facts it involves. We must have faith in all the sayings of our Master, though they are not included in the
teachings of the schools, and are not understood generally by our ethical instructors.

Continuity
of existence

Jesus said (John viii. 51), "If a man keep my saying,
he shall never see death." That statement is not con-

fined to spiritual life, but includes all the phenomena of
existence. Jesus demonstrated this, healing the dying

**Life
all-inclusive**
and raising the dead. Mortal mind must part
with error, must put off itself with its deeds,
and immortal manhood, the Christ ideal, will appear.
Faith should enlarge its borders and strengthen its base
by resting upon Spirit instead of matter. When man
gives up his belief in death, he will advance more rapidly
towards God, Life, and Love. Belief in sickness and
death, as certainly as belief in sin, tends to shut out the
true sense of Life and health. When will mankind wake
to this great fact in Science?

    I here present to my readers an allegory illustrative
of the law of divine Mind and of the supposed laws of matter and hygiene, an allegory in which the plea of Christian
Science heals the sick.

    Suppose a mental case to be on trial, as cases are tried
in court. A man is charged with having committed liver-

**A mental
court case**
complaint. The patient feels ill, ruminates,
and the trial commences. Personal Sense is
the plaintiff. Mortal Man is the defendant. False Belief
is the attorney for Personal Sense. Mortal Minds, Materia Medica, Anatomy, Physiology, Hypnotism, Envy,
Greed and Ingratitude, constitute the jury. The court-
room is filled with interested spectators, and Judge
Medicine is on the bench.

    The evidence for the prosecution being called for, a
witness testifies thus: —

    I represent Health-laws. I was present on certain nights
when the prisoner, or patient, watched with a sick friend.
Although I have the superintendence of human affairs, I
was personally abused on those occasions. I was told that

1   I must remain silent until called for at this trial, when I
would be allowed to testify in the case. Notwithstanding
3   my rules to the contrary, the prisoner watched with the sick
every night in the week. When the sick mortal was thirsty,
the prisoner gave him drink. During all this time the pris-
6   oner attended to his daily labors, partaking of food at ir-
regular intervals, sometimes going to sleep immediately
after a heavy meal. At last he committed liver-complaint,
9   which I considered criminal, inasmuch as this offence is
deemed punishable with death. Therefore I arrested Mortal Man in behalf of the state (namely, the body) and cast
12   him into prison.

At the time of the arrest the prisoner summoned Physiology, Materia Medica, and Hypnotism to prevent his pun-
15   ishment. The struggle on their part was long. Materia
Medica held out the longest, but at length all these assist-
ants resigned to me, Health-laws, and I succeeded in get-
18   ting Mortal Man into close confinement until I should
release him.

The next witness is called: —

21   I am Coated Tongue. I am covered with a foul fur,
placed on me the night of the liver-attack. Morbid Secretion hypnotized the prisoner and took control of his mind,
24   making him despondent.

Another witness takes the stand and testifies: —

I am Sallow Skin. I have been dry, hot, and chilled by
27   turns since the night of the liver-attack. I have lost my
healthy hue and become unsightly, although nothing on my
part has occasioned this change. I practise daily ablutions
30   and perform my functions as usual, but I am robbed of my
good looks.

The next witness testifies: —   1

I am Nerve, the State Commissioner for Mortal Man.
I am intimately acquainted with the plaintiff, Personal   3
Sense, and know him to be truthful and upright, whereas
Mortal Man, the prisoner at the bar, is capable of falsehood. I was witness to the crime of liver-complaint. I   6
knew the prisoner would commit it, for I convey messages
from my residence in matter, *alias* brain, to body.

Another witness is called for by the Court of Error   9
and says: —

I am Mortality, Governor of the Province of Body, in
which Mortal Man resides. In this province there is a stat-   12
ute regarding disease, — namely, that he upon whose person disease is found shall be treated as a criminal and
punished with death.   15

The Judge asks if by doing good to his neighbor, it is
possible for man to become diseased, transgress the laws,
and merit punishment, and Governor Mortality replies in   18
the affirmative.
Another witness takes the stand and testifies: —

I am Death. I was called for, shortly after the report of   21
the crime, by the officer of the Board of Health, who protested that the prisoner had abused him, and that my presence was required to confirm his testimony. One of the   24
prisoner's friends, Materia Medica, was present when I
arrived, endeavoring to assist the prisoner to escape from
the hands of justice, *alias* nature's so-called law; but my   27
appearance with a message from the Board of Health
changed the purpose of Materia Medica, and he decided at
once that the prisoner should die.   30

The testimony for the plaintiff, Personal Sense, being closed, Judge Medicine arises, and with great solemnity addresses the jury of Mortal Minds. He analyzes the offence, reviews the testimony, and explains the law relating to liver-complaint.

His conclusion is, that laws of nature render disease homicidal. In compliance with a stern duty, his Honor, Judge Medicine, urges the jury not to allow their judgment to be warped by the irrational, unchristian suggestions of Christian Science. The jury must regard in such cases only the evidence of Personal Sense against Mortal Man.

As the Judge proceeds, the prisoner grows restless. His sallow face blanches with fear, and a look of despair and death settles upon it. The case is given to the jury. A brief consultation ensues, and the jury returns a verdict of "Guilty of liver-complaint in the first degree."

Judge Medicine then proceeds to pronounce the solemn sentence of death upon the prisoner. Because he has loved his neighbor as himself, Mortal Man has been guilty of benevolence in the first degree, and this has led him into the commission of the second crime, liver-complaint, which material laws condemn as homicide. For this crime Mortal Man is sentenced to be tortured until he is dead. "May God have mercy on your soul," is the Judge's solemn peroration.

The prisoner is then remanded to his cell (sick-bed), and Scholastic Theology is sent for to prepare the frightened sense of Life, God, — which sense must be immortal, — for *death.*

Ah! but Christ, Truth, the spirit of Life and the friend of Mortal Man, can open wide those prison doors

and set the captive free. Swift on the wings of divine   1
Love, there comes a despatch: "Delay the execution;
the prisoner is not guilty." Consternation fills   3
the prison-yard. Some exclaim, "It is con-
trary to law and justice." Others say,
"The law of Christ supersedes *our* laws; let us follow   6
Christ."

After much debate and opposition, permission is obtained for a trial in the Court of Spirit, where Christian   9
Science is allowed to appear as counsel for
the unfortunate prisoner. Witnesses, judges,
and jurors, who were at the previous Court of Error,   12
are now summoned to appear before the bar of Justice
and eternal Truth.

When the case for Mortal Man *versus* Personal Sense   15
is opened, Mortal Man's counsel regards the prisoner
with the utmost tenderness. The counsel's earnest,
solemn eyes, kindling with hope and triumph, look up-   18
ward. Then Christian Science turns suddenly to the
supreme tribunal, and opens the argument for the
defence: —   21

The prisoner at the bar has been unjustly sentenced.
His trial was a tragedy, and is morally illegal. Mortal
Man has had no proper counsel in the case. All the testi-   24
mony has been on the side of Personal Sense, and we shall
unearth this foul conspiracy against the liberty and life of
Man. The only valid testimony in the case shows the   27
alleged crime never to have been committed. The prisoner is not proved "worthy of death, or of bonds."

Your Honor, the lower court has sentenced Mortal Man   30
to die, but God made Man immortal and amenable to
Spirit only. Denying justice to the body, that court com-

1   mended man's immortal Spirit to heavenly mercy, — Spirit
which is God Himself and Man's only lawgiver! Who or
3   what has sinned? Has the body or has Mortal Mind
committed a criminal deed? Counsellor False Belief has
argued that the body should die, while Reverend Theology
6   would console conscious Mortal Mind, which alone is capable of sin and suffering. The body committed no offence.
Mortal Man, in obedience to higher law, helped his fellow-
9   man, an act which should result in good to himself as well
as to others.

     The law of our Supreme Court decrees that whosoever
12   *sinneth* shall die; but good deeds are immortal, bringing
joy instead of grief, pleasure instead of pain, and life
instead of death. If liver-complaint was committed by
15   trampling on Laws of Health, this was a good deed, for the
agent of those laws is an outlaw, a destroyer of Mortal
Man's liberty and rights. Laws of Health should be sen-
18   tenced to die.

     Watching beside the couch of pain in the exercise of a
love that "is the fulfilling of the law," — doing "unto
21   others as ye would that they should do unto you," — this
is no infringement of law, for no demand, human or divine,
renders it just to punish a man for acting justly. If mor-
24   tals sin, our Supreme Judge in equity decides what penalty
is due for the sin, and Mortal Man can suffer only for his
sin. For naught else can he be punished, according to the
27   law of Spirit, God.

     Then what jurisdiction had his Honor, Judge Medicine,
in this case? To him I might say, in Bible language, "Sit-
30   test thou to judge . . . after the law, and commandest . . .
to be smitten contrary to the law?" The only jurisdiction
to which the prisoner can submit is that of Truth, Life, and
33   Love. If they condemn him not, neither shall Judge Medicine condemn him; and I ask that the prisoner be restored
to the liberty of which he has been unjustly deprived.

The principal witness (the officer of the Health-laws)
deposed that he was an eye-witness to the good deeds for
which Mortal Man is under sentence of death. After be-
traying him into the hands of your law, the Health-agent
disappeared, to reappear however at the trial as a witness
against Mortal Man and in the interest of Personal Sense,
a murderer. Your Supreme Court must find the prisoner on the night of the alleged offence to have been acting
within the limits of the divine law, and in obedience
thereto. Upon this statute hangs all the law and testimony.
Giving a cup of cold water in Christ's name, is a Christian
service. Laying down his life for a good deed, Mortal Man
should find it again. Such acts bear their own justification, and are under the protection of the Most High.

Prior to the night of his arrest, the prisoner summoned
two professed friends, Materia Medica and Physiology, to
prevent his committing liver-complaint, and thus save him
from arrest. But they brought with them Fear, the sheriff,
to precipitate the result which they were called to prevent.
It was Fear who handcuffed Mortal Man and would now
punish him. You have left Mortal Man no alternative.
He must obey your law, fear its consequences, and be punished for his fear. His friends struggled hard to rescue the
prisoner from the penalty they considered justly due, but
they were compelled to let him be taken into custody, tried,
and condemned. Thereupon Judge Medicine sat in judgment on the case, and substantially charged the jury, twelve
Mortal Minds, to find the prisoner guilty. His Honor sentenced Mortal Man to die for the very deeds which the divine law compels man to commit. Thus the Court of Error
construed obedience to the law of divine Love as disobedience to the law of Life. Claiming to protect Mortal Man
in right-doing, that court pronounced a sentence of death
for doing right.

One of the principal witnesses, Nerve, testified that he

1   was a ruler of Body, in which province Mortal Man resides.
He also testified that he was on intimate terms with the
3   plaintiff, and knew Personal Sense to be truthful; that he
knew Man, and that Man was made in the image of God,
but was a criminal. This is a foul aspersion on man's
6   Maker. It blots the fair escutcheon of omnipotence. It indicates malice aforethought, a determination to condemn
Man in the interest of Personal Sense. At the bar of Truth,
9   in the presence of divine Justice, before the Judge of our
higher tribunal, the Supreme Court of Spirit, and before
its jurors, the Spiritual Senses, I proclaim this witness,
12   Nerve, to be destitute of intelligence and truth and to be
a false witness.

     Man self-destroyed; the testimony of matter respected;
15   Spirit not allowed a hearing; Soul a criminal though
recommended to mercy; the helpless innocent body tortured, — these are the terrible records of your Court of
18   Error, and I ask that the Supreme Court of Spirit reverse
this decision.

     Here the opposing counsel, False Belief, called Chris-
21   tian Science to order for contempt of court. Various
notables — Materia Medica, Anatomy, Physiology, Scholastic Theology, and Jurisprudence — rose to the ques-
24   tion of expelling Christian Science from the bar, for such
high-handed illegality. They declared that Christian Science was overthrowing the judicial proceedings of a regu-
27   larly constituted court.

     But Judge Justice of the Supreme Court of Spirit over-
ruled their motions on the ground that unjust usages
30   were not allowed at the bar of Truth, which ranks above
the lower Court of Error.

     The attorney, Christian Science, then read from the
33   supreme statute-book, the Bible, certain extracts on the

Rights of Man, remarking that the Bible was better au- 1
thority than Blackstone: —

   Let us make man in our image, after our likeness; and 3
let them have dominion.
   Behold, I give unto you power . . . over all the power
of the enemy: and nothing shall by any means hurt you. 6
   If a man keep my saying, he shall never see death.

   Then Christian Science proved the witness, Nerve, to
be a perjurer. Instead of being a ruler in the Province 9
of Body, in which Mortal Man was reported to reside,
Nerve was an insubordinate citizen, putting in false
claims to office and bearing false witness against Man. 12
Turning suddenly to Personal Sense, by this time silent,
Christian Science continued: —

   I ask your arrest in the name of Almighty God on three 15
distinct charges of crime, to wit: perjury, treason, and conspiracy against the rights and life of man.

   Then Christian Science continued: — 18

   Another witness, equally inadequate, said that on the
night of the crime a garment of foul fur was spread over
him by Morbid Secretion, while the facts in the case show 21
that this fur is a foreign substance, imported by False Belief, the attorney for Personal Sense, who is in partnership
with Error and smuggles Error's goods into market with- 24
out the inspection of Soul's government officers. When
the Court of Truth summoned Furred Tongue for examination, he disappeared and was never heard of more. 27
   Morbid Secretion is not an importer or dealer in fur, but
we have heard Materia Medica explain how this fur is
manufactured, and we know Morbid Secretion to be on 30
friendly terms with the firm of Personal Sense, Error, &

1 Co., receiving pay from them and introducing their goods
into the market. Also, be it known that False Belief, the
3 counsel for the plaintiff, Personal Sense, is a buyer for this
firm. He manufactures for it, keeps a furnishing store,
and advertises largely for his employers.

6 Death testified that he was absent from the Province of
Body, when a message came from False Belief, commanding him to take part in the homicide. At this request
9 Death repaired to the spot where the liver-complaint was
in process, frightening away Materia Medica, who was then
manacling the prisoner in the attempt to save him. True,
12 Materia Medica was a misguided participant in the misdeed
for which the Health-officer had Mortal Man in custody,
though Mortal Man was innocent.

15 Christian Science turned from the abashed witnesses,
his words flashing as lightning in the perturbed faces
of these worthies, Scholastic Theology, Materia Medica,
18 Physiology, the blind Hypnotism, and the masked Personal Sense, and said: —

God will smite you, O whited walls, for injuring in your
21 ignorance the unfortunate Mortal Man who sought your
aid in his struggles against liver-complaint and Death.
You came to his rescue, only to fasten upon him an offence
24 of which he was innocent. You aided and abetted Fear
and Health-laws. You betrayed Mortal Man, meanwhile
declaring Disease to be God's servant and the righteous
27 executor of His laws. Our higher statutes declare you all,
witnesses, jurors, and judges, to be offenders, awaiting the
sentence which General Progress and Divine Love will
30 pronounce.

We send our best detectives to whatever locality is reported to be haunted by Disease, but on visiting the spot,
33 they learn that Disease was never there, for he could not

possibly elude their search. Your Material Court of Errors, 1
when it condemned Mortal Man on the ground of hygienic
disobedience, was manipulated by the oleaginous machina- 3
tions of the counsel, False Belief, whom Truth arraigns
before the supreme bar of Spirit to answer for his crime.
Morbid Secretion is taught how to make sleep befool reason 6
before sacrificing mortals to their false gods.

Mortal Minds were deceived by your attorney, False Belief, and were influenced to give a verdict delivering Mortal 9
Man to Death. Good deeds are transformed into crimes,
to which you attach penalties; but no warping of justice
can render disobedience to the so-called laws of Matter 12
disobedience to God, or an act of homicide. Even penal
law holds homicide, under stress of circumstances, to be
justifiable. Now what greater justification can any deed 15
have, than that it is for the good of one's neighbor? Wherefore, then, in the name of outraged justice, do you sentence
Mortal Man for ministering to the wants of his fellow-man 18
in obedience to divine law? You cannot trample upon the
decree of the Supreme Bench. Mortal Man has his appeal
to Spirit, God, who sentences only for sin. 21

The false and unjust beliefs of your human mental legis-
lators compel them to enact wicked laws of sickness and so
forth, and then render obedience to these laws punishable 24
as crime. In the presence of the Supreme Lawgiver, standing at the bar of Truth, and in accordance with the divine
statutes, I repudiate the false testimony of Personal Sense. 27
I ask that he be forbidden to enter against Mortal Man
any more suits to be tried at the Court of Material Error.
I appeal to the just and equitable decisions of divine Spirit 30
to restore to Mortal Man the rights of which he has been
deprived.

Here the counsel for the defence closed, and the Chief 33
Justice of the Supreme Court, with benign and imposing

Charge of the
Chief Justice

presence, comprehending and defining all law and evidence, explained from his statute-book, the
Bible, that any so-called law, which undertakes to punish aught but sin, is null and void.

He also decided that the plaintiff, Personal Sense, be
not permitted to enter any suits at the bar of Soul, but
be enjoined to keep perpetual silence, and in case of
temptation, to give heavy bonds for good behavior. He
concluded his charge thus: —

The plea of False Belief we deem unworthy of a hearing.
Let what False Belief utters, now and forever, fall into
oblivion, "unknelled, uncoffined, and unknown." According to our statute, Material Law is a liar who cannot bear
witness against Mortal Man, neither can Fear arrest Mortal
Man nor can Disease cast him into prison. Our law refuses
to recognize Man as sick or dying, but holds him to be forever in the image and likeness of his Maker. Reversing the
testimony of Personal Sense and the decrees of the Court of
Error in favor of Matter, Spirit decides in favor of Man
and against Matter. We further recommend that Materia
Medica adopt Christian Science and that Health-laws,
Mesmerism, Hypnotism, Oriental Witchcraft, and Esoteric
Magic be publicly executed at the hands of our sheriff,
Progress.

The Supreme Bench decides in favor of intelligence, that
no law outside of divine Mind can punish or reward Mortal
Man. Your personal jurors in the Court of Error are
myths. Your attorney, False Belief, is an impostor, per-
suading Mortal Minds to return a verdict contrary to law
and gospel. The plaintiff, Personal Sense, is recorded in
our Book of books as a liar. Our great Teacher of mental
jurisprudence speaks of him also as "a murderer from the
beginning." We have no trials for sickness before the tri-

bunal of divine Spirit. There, Man is adjudged innocent   1
of transgressing physical laws, because there are no such
laws. Our statute is spiritual, our Government is divine.   3
"Shall not the Judge of all the earth do right?"

The Jury of Spiritual Senses agreed at once upon a
verdict, and there resounded throughout the vast audience-   6
chamber of Spirit the cry, Not guilty. Then

Divine verdict

the prisoner rose up regenerated, strong, free.
We noticed, as he shook hands with his counsel, Chris-   9
tian Science, that all sallowness and debility had disappeared. His form was erect and commanding, his
countenance beaming with health and happiness. Divine   12
Love had cast out fear. Mortal Man, no longer sick
and in prison, walked forth, his feet "beautiful upon the
mountains," as of one "that bringeth good tidings."   15

Neither animal magnetism nor hypnotism enters into
the practice of Christian Science, in which truth cannot

Christ the great physician

be reversed, but the reverse of error is true.   18
An improved belief cannot retrograde. When
Christ changes a belief of sin or of sickness into
a better belief, then belief melts into spiritual understand-   21
ing, and sin, disease, and death disappear. Christ, Truth,
gives mortals temporary food and clothing until the material, transformed with the ideal, disappears, and man   24
is clothed and fed spiritually. St. Paul says, "Work
out your own salvation with fear and trembling: " Jesus
said, "Fear not, little flock; for it is your Father's good   27
pleasure to give you the kingdom." This truth is
Christian Science.

Christian Scientists, be a law to yourselves that mental   30
malpractice cannot harm you either when asleep or when
awake.

Chapter 13

Teaching
Christian Science

Give instruction to a wise man,
and he will be yet wiser:
teach a just man,
and he will increase in learning. — PROVERBS.

1   **W**hen the discoverer of Christian Science is consulted by her followers as to the propriety, advan-

Study of
medicine

3 tage, and consistency of systematic medical
study, she tries to show them that under ordinary circumstances a resort to faith in corporeal means

6 tends to deter those, who make such a compromise, from
entire confidence in omnipotent Mind as really possessing
all power. While a course of medical study is at times

9 severely condemned by some Scientists, she feels, as she
always has felt, that all are privileged to work out their
own salvation according to their light, and that our motto

12 should be the Master's counsel, "Judge not, that ye be
not judged."

    If patients fail to experience the healing power of

15 Christian Science, and think they can be benefited by
certain ordinary physical methods of medical
treatment, then the Mind-physician should

Failure's
lessons

18 give up such cases, and leave invalids free to resort to
whatever other systems they fancy will afford relief.
Thus such invalids may learn the value of the apostolic

21 precept: "Reprove, rebuke, exhort with all longsuffering
and doctrine." If the sick find these material expedients

unsatisfactory, and they receive no help from them, these   1
very failures may open their blind eyes. In some way,
sooner or later, all must rise superior to materiality, and   3
suffering is oft the divine agent in this elevation. "All
things work together for good to them that love God," is
the dictum of Scripture.   6

  If Christian Scientists ever fail to receive aid from
other Scientists, — their brethren upon whom they may

call, — God will still guide them into the right   9
use of temporary and eternal means. Step by
step will those who trust Him find that "God is our refuge
and strength, a very present help in trouble."   12

  Students are advised by the author to be charitable
and kind, not only towards differing forms of religion

and medicine, but to those who hold these dif-   15
fering opinions. Let us be faithful in pointing
the way through Christ, as we understand it,
but let us also be careful always to "judge righteous judg-   18
ment," and never to condemn rashly. "Whosoever shall
smite thee on thy right cheek, turn to him the other also."
That is, Fear not that he will smite thee again for thy for-   21
bearance. If ecclesiastical sects or medical schools turn
a deaf ear to the teachings of Christian Science, then part
from these opponents as did Abraham when he parted   24
from Lot, and say in thy heart: "Let there be no strife, I
pray thee, between me and thee, and between my herdmen and thy herdmen; for we be brethren." Immortals,   27
or God's children in divine Science, are one harmonious
family; but mortals, or the "children of men" in material
sense, are discordant and ofttimes false brethren.   30

  The teacher must make clear to students the Science
of healing, especially its ethics, — that all is Mind, and

that the Scientist must conform to God's requirements. Also the teacher must thoroughly fit his students to defend themselves against sin, and to guard against the attacks of the would-be *mental assassin,* who attempts to kill morally and physically. No hypothesis as to the existence of another power should interpose a doubt or fear to hinder the demonstration of Christian Science. Unfold the latent energies and capacities for good in your pupil. Teach the great possibilities of man endued with divine Science. Teach the dangerous possibility of dwarfing the spiritual understanding and demonstration of Truth by sin, or by recourse to material means for healing. Teach the meekness and might of life "hid with Christ in God," and there will be no desire for other healing methods. You render the divine law of healing obscure and void, when you weigh the human in the scale with the divine, or limit in any direction of thought the omnipresence and omnipotence of God.

Christian Science silences human will, quiets fear with Truth and Love, and illustrates the unlabored motion of the divine energy in healing the sick. Self-seeking, envy, passion, pride, hatred, and revenge are cast out by the divine Mind which heals disease. The human will which maketh and worketh a lie, hiding the divine Principle of harmony, is destructive to health, and is the cause of disease rather than its cure.

There is great danger in teaching Mind-healing indiscriminately, thus disregarding the morals of the student and caring only for the fees. Recalling Jefferson's words about slavery, "I tremble, when I remember that God is just," the author trembles whenever she sees a man, for the petty consideration of money,

Margin notes:

Conforming to explicit rules

Divine energy

Blight of avarice

teaching his slight knowledge of Mind-power, — per- 1
haps communicating his own bad morals, and in this way
dealing pitilessly with a community unprepared for self- 3
defence.

A thorough perusal of the author's publications heals
sickness. If patients sometimes seem worse while read- 6
ing this book, the change may either arise from the alarm
of the physician, or it may mark the crisis of the disease.
Perseverance in the perusal of the book has generally 9
completely healed such cases.

Whoever practises the Science the author teaches,
through which Mind pours light and healing upon this 12

Exclusion of malpractice generation, can practise on no one from sin-
ister or malicious motives without destroying

his own power to heal and his own health. Good must 15
dominate in the thoughts of the healer, or his demonstration is protracted, dangerous, and impossible in Science. A wrong motive involves defeat. In the Science 18
of Mind-healing, it is imperative to be honest, for victory
rests on the side of immutable right. To understand
God strengthens hope, enthrones faith in Truth, and 21
verifies Jesus' word: "Lo, I am with you alway, even
unto the end of the world."

Resisting evil, you overcome it and prove its nothing- 24
ness. Not human platitudes, but divine beatitudes, re-

Iniquity overcome flect the spiritual light and might which heal
the sick. The exercise of will brings on a 27
hypnotic state, detrimental to health and integrity of
thought. This must therefore be watched and guarded
against. Covering iniquity will prevent prosperity and the 30
ultimate triumph of any cause. Ignorance of the error
to be eradicated oftentimes subjects you to its abuse.

The heavenly law is broken by trespassing upon
man's individual right of self-government. We have no
authority in Christian Science and no moral
right to attempt to influence the thoughts of
others, except it be to benefit them. In mental practice you must not forget that erring human opinions, conflicting selfish motives, and ignorant attempts
to do good may render you incapable of knowing or
judging accurately the need of your fellow-men. Therefore the rule is, heal the sick when called upon for aid,
and save the victims of the mental assassins.

No trespass
on human
rights

Ignorance, subtlety, or false charity does not forever conceal error; evil will in time disclose and punish itself. The recuperative action of the
system, when mentally sustained by Truth,
goes on naturally. When sin or sickness —
the reverse of harmony — seems true to material sense,
impart without frightening or discouraging the patient the truth and spiritual understanding, which destroy disease. Expose and denounce the claims of
evil and disease in all their forms, but realize no
reality in them. A sinner is not reformed merely
by assuring him that he cannot be a sinner because
there is no sin. To put down the claim of sin,
you must detect it, remove the mask, point out the
illusion, and thus get the victory over sin and so prove
its unreality. The sick are not healed merely by
declaring there is no sickness, but by knowing that
there is none.

Expose sin
without
believing in it

A sinner is afraid to cast the first stone. He may
say, as a subterfuge, that evil is unreal, but to know it,
he must demonstrate his statement. To assume that

there are no claims of evil and yet to indulge them, is   1
a moral offence. Blindness and self-righteousness cling

Wicked
evasions

fast to iniquity. When the Publican's wail   3
went out to the great heart of Love, it won his
humble desire. Evil which obtains in the bodily senses,
but which the heart condemns, has no foundation; but if   6
evil is uncondemned, it is undenied and nurtured. Under
such circumstances, to say that there is no evil, is an evil
in itself. When needed tell the truth concerning the lie.   9
Evasion of Truth cripples integrity, and casts thee down
from the pinnacle.

Christian Science rises above the evidence of the cor-   12
poreal senses; but if you have not risen above sin your-

Truth's
grand results

self, do not congratulate yourself upon your
blindness to evil or upon the good you know   15
and *do* not. A dishonest position is far from Christianly
scientific. "He that covereth his sins shall not prosper:
but whoso confesseth and forsaketh them shall have   18
mercy." Try to leave on every student's mind the strong
impress of divine Science, a high sense of the moral and
spiritual qualifications requisite for healing, well knowing   21
it to be impossible for error, evil, and hate to accomplish
the grand results of Truth and Love. The reception or
pursuit of instructions opposite to absolute Christian   24
Science must always hinder scientific demonstration.

If the student adheres strictly to the teachings of Christian Science and ventures not to break its rules, he can-   27

Adherence to
righteousness

not fail of success in healing. It is Christian
Science to do right, and nothing short of right-
doing has any claim to the name. To talk the right and   30
live the wrong is foolish deceit, doing one's self the most
harm. Fettered by sin yourself, it is difficult to free

another from the fetters of disease. With your own wrists manacled, it is hard to break another's chains. A little leaven causes the whole mass to ferment. A grain of Christian Science does wonders for mortals, so omnipotent is Truth, but more of Christian Science must be gained in order to continue in well doing.

The wrong done another reacts most heavily against one's self. Right adjusts the balance sooner or later. Think it "easier for a camel to go through the eye of a needle," than for you to benefit yourself by injuring others. Man's moral mercury, rising or falling, registers his healing ability and fitness to teach. You should practise well what you know, and you will then advance in proportion to your honesty and fidelity, — qualities which insure success in this Science; but it requires a higher understanding to teach this subject properly and correctly than it does to heal the most difficult case.

Right adjusts the balance

The baneful effect of evil associates is less seen than felt. The inoculation of evil human thoughts ought to be understood and guarded against. The first impression, made on a mind which is attracted or repelled according to personal merit or demerit, is a good detective of individual character. Certain minds meet only to separate through simultaneous repulsion. They are enemies without the preliminary offence. The impure are at peace with the impure. Only virtue is a rebuke to vice. A proper teacher of Christian Science improves the health and the morals of his student if the student practises what he is taught, and unless this result follows, the teacher is a Scientist only in name.

Inoculation of thought

There is a large class of thinkers whose bigotry and   1
conceit twist every fact to suit themselves. Their creed

Three classes
of neophytes
teaches belief in a mysterious, supernatural   3
God, and in a natural, all-powerful devil. Another class, still more unfortunate, are so depraved that
they appear to be innocent. They utter a falsehood,   6
while looking you blandly in the face, and they never
fail to stab their benefactor in the back. A third class
of thinkers build with solid masonry. They are sincere,   9
generous, noble, and are therefore open to the approach
and recognition of Truth. To teach Christian Science
to such as these is no task. They do not incline long-   12
ingly to error, whine over the demands of Truth, nor
play the traitor for place and power.

Some people yield slowly to the touch of Truth. Few   15
yield without a struggle, and many are reluctant to ac-

Touchstone
of Science
knowledge that they have yielded; but unless this admission is made, evil will boast   18
itself above good. The Christian Scientist has enlisted
to lessen evil, disease, and death; and he will overcome
them by understanding their nothingness and the allness   21
of God, or good. Sickness to him is no less a temptation
than is sin, and he heals them both by understanding
God's power over them. The Christian Scientist knows   24
that they are errors of belief, which Truth can and will
destroy.

Who, that has felt the perilous beliefs in life, substance,   27
and intelligence separated from God, can say that there

False claims
annihilated
is no error of belief? Knowing the claim of
animal magnetism, that all evil combines in   30
the belief of life, substance, and intelligence in matter,
electricity, animal nature, and organic life, who will deny

that these are the errors which Truth must and will annihilate? Christian Scientists must live under the constant pressure of the apostolic command to come out from
the material world and be separate. They must re-
nounce aggression, oppression and the pride of power.
Christianity, with the crown of Love upon her brow,
must be their queen of life.

Students of Christian Science, who start with its letter
and think to succeed without the spirit, will either make
shipwreck of their faith or be turned sadly
awry. They must not only seek, but strive,
to enter the narrow path of Life, for "wide is the gate,
and broad is the way, that leadeth to destruction, and
many there be which go in thereat." Man walks in the
direction towards which he looks, and where his treasure
is, there will his heart be also. If our hopes and affections are spiritual, they come from above, not from beneath, and they bear as of old the fruits of the Spirit.

Every Christian Scientist, every conscientious teacher
of the Science of Mind-healing, knows that human will
is not Christian Science, and he must recognize this in order to defend himself from the
influence of human will. He feels morally obligated to
open the eyes of his students that they may perceive the
nature and methods of error of every sort, especially any
subtle degree of evil, deceived and deceiving. All mental
malpractice arises from ignorance or malice aforethought.
It is the injurious action of one mortal mind controlling
another from wrong motives, and it is practised either
with a mistaken or a wicked purpose.

Show your student that mental malpractice tends to
blast moral sense, health, and the human life. Instruct

*Treasure
in heaven*

*Obligations
of teachers*

him how to bar the door of his thought against this
seeming power, — a task not difficult, when one understands that evil has in reality no power.
Incorrect reasoning leads to practical error.
The wrong thought should be arrested before it has a
chance to manifest itself.

Indispensable defence

Walking in the light, we are accustomed to the light
and require it; we cannot see in darkness. But eyes accustomed to darkness are pained by the light.
When outgrowing the old, you should not fear
to put on the new. Your advancing course may pro-
voke envy, but it will also attract respect. When error
confronts you, withhold not the rebuke or the explanation which destroys error. Never breathe an immoral
atmosphere, unless in the attempt to purify it. Better is
the frugal intellectual repast with contentment and virtue,
than the luxury of learning with egotism and vice.

Egotistic darkness

Right is radical. The teacher must know the truth
himself. He must live it and love it, or he cannot impart
it to others. We soil our garments with conservatism, and afterwards we must wash them
clean. When the spiritual sense of Truth unfolds its
harmonies, you take no risks in the policy of error. Expect to heal simply by repeating the author's words, by
right talking and wrong acting, and you will be disap-
pointed. Such a practice does not demonstrate the
Science by which divine Mind heals the sick.

Unwarranted expectations

Acting from sinful motives destroys your power of
healing from the right motive. On the other hand, if
you had the inclination or power to practise
wrongly and then should adopt Christian
Science, the wrong power would be destroyed. You do

Reliable authority

1 not deny the mathematician's right to distinguish the correct from the incorrect among the examples on the black-
3 board, nor disbelieve the musician when he distinguishes
concord from discord. In like manner it should be granted
that the author understands what she is saying.

6 Right and wrong, truth and error, will be at strife in
the minds of students, until victory rests on the side of
invincible truth. Mental chemicalization fol-
9 lows the explanation of Truth, and a higher
basis is thus won; but with some individuals the morbid
moral or physical symptoms constantly reappear. I
12 have never witnessed so decided effects from the use of
material remedies as from the use of spiritual.

Winning the field

Teach your student that he must know himself be-
15 fore he can know others and minister to human needs.
Honesty is spiritual power. Dishonesty is
human weakness, which forfeits divine help.
18 You uncover sin, not in order to injure, but in order
to bless the corporeal man; and a right motive has
its reward. Hidden sin is spiritual wickedness in high
21 places. The masquerader in this Science thanks God
that there is no evil, yet serves evil in the name of
good.

Knowledge and honesty

24 You should treat sickness mentally just as you would
sin, except that you must not tell the patient that he is
sick nor give names to diseases, for such a
27 course increases fear, the foundation of disease, and impresses more deeply the wrong mind-picture.
A Christian Scientist's medicine is Mind, the divine Truth
30 that makes man free. A Christian Scientist never recom-
mends material hygiene, never manipulates. He does
not trespass on the rights of mind nor can he practise

Metaphysical treatment

animal magnetism or hypnotism. It need not be added   1
that the use of tobacco or intoxicating drinks is not in
harmony with Christian Science.   3

Teach your students the omnipotence of Truth, which
illustrates the impotence of error. The understanding,

Impotence
of hate

even in a degree, of the divine All-power de-   6
stroys fear, and plants the feet in the true path,
— the path which leads to the house built without hands
"eternal in the heavens." Human hate has no legiti-   9
mate mandate and no kingdom. Love is enthroned.
That evil or matter has neither intelligence nor power,
is the doctrine of absolute Christian Science, and this is 12
the great truth which strips all disguise from error.

He, who understands in a sufficient degree the Principle of Mind-healing, points out to his student error as   15

Love the
incentive

well as truth, the wrong as well as the right
practice. Love for God and man is the true
incentive in both healing and teaching. Love inspires,   18
illumines, designates, and leads the way. Right motives
give pinions to thought, and strength and freedom to
speech and action. Love is priestess at the altar of   21
Truth. Wait patiently for divine Love to move upon the
waters of mortal mind, and form the perfect concept.
Patience must "have her perfect work."   24

Do not dismiss students at the close of a class term,
feeling that you have no more to do for them. Let your

Continuity
of interest

loving care and counsel support all their feeble   27
footsteps, until your students tread firmly in
the straight and narrow way. The superiority of spiritual power over sensuous is the central point of Chris-   30
tian Science. Remember that the letter and mental
argument are only human auxiliaries to aid in bringing

1   thought into accord with the spirit of Truth and Love,
which heals the sick and the sinner.

3   A mental state of self-condemnation and guilt or a
faltering and doubting trust in Truth are unsuitable
conditions for healing the sick. Such mental
6   states indicate weakness instead of strength.

Weakness and guilt

Hence the necessity of being right yourself in order to
teach this Science of healing. You must utilize the moral
9   might of Mind in order to walk over the waves of error
and support your claims by demonstration. If you are
yourself lost in the belief and fear of disease or sin, and
12   if, knowing the remedy, you fail to use the energies of
Mind in your own behalf, you can exercise little or no
power for others' help. "First cast out the beam out
15   of thine own eye; and then shalt thou see clearly to cast
out the mote out of thy brother's eye."

      The student, who receives his knowledge of Christian
18   Science, or metaphysical healing, from a human teacher,
may be mistaken in judgment and demonstra-
tion, but God cannot mistake. God selects

The trust of the All-wise

21   for the highest service one who has grown into such a
fitness for it as renders any abuse of the mission an impossibility. The All-wise does not bestow His highest
24   trusts upon the unworthy. When He commissions a messenger, it is one who is spiritually near Himself. No person can misuse this mental power, if he is taught of God
27   to discern it.

      This strong point in Christian Science is not to be
overlooked, — that the same fountain cannot send forth
30   both sweet waters and bitter. The higher
your attainment in the Science of mental
healing and teaching, the more impossible it will be-

Integrity assured

come for you intentionally to influence mankind adverse   1
to its highest hope and achievement.

Teaching or practising in the name of Truth, but con-   3
trary to its spirit or rules, is most dangerous quackery.

Strict adherence to the divine Principle and
rules of the scientific method has secured   6
the only success of the students of Christian Science.
This alone entitles them to the high standing which
most of them hold in the community, a reputation ex-   9
perimentally justified by their efforts. Whoever affirms that there is more than one Principle and method
of demonstrating Christian Science greatly errs, igno-   12
rantly or intentionally, and separates himself from the
true conception of Christian Science healing and from
its possible demonstration.   15

Any dishonesty in your theory and practice betrays a
gross ignorance of the method of the Christ-cure. Science

makes no concessions to persons or opinions.   18
One must abide in the *morale* of truth or he
cannot demonstrate the divine Principle. So long as
matter is the basis of practice, illness cannot be effica-   21
ciously treated by the metaphysical process. Truth does
the work, and you must both understand and abide by the
divine Principle of your demonstration.   24

A Christian Scientist requires my work SCIENCE AND
HEALTH for his textbook, and so do all his students and

patients. Why? *First:* Because it is the voice   27
of Truth to this age, and contains the full
statement of Christian Science, or the Science of healing
through Mind. *Second:* Because it was the first book   30
known, containing a thorough statement of Christian
Science. Hence it gave the first rules for demonstrating

1   this Science, and registered the revealed Truth uncon-
taminated by human hypotheses. Other works, which
3   have borrowed from this book without giving it credit,
have adulterated the Science. *Third:* Because this book
has done more for teacher and student, for healer and
6   patient, than has been accomplished by other books.

Since the divine light of Christian Science first dawned
upon the author, she has never used this newly discovered
9   power in any direction which she fears to have

Purity of science

fairly understood. Her prime object, since
entering this field of labor, has been to prevent suffering,
12   not to produce it. That we cannot scientifically both
cure and cause disease is self-evident. In the legend of
the shield, which led to a quarrel between two knights
15   because each of them could see but one face of it, both
sides were beautiful according to their degree; but to
mental malpractice, prolific of evil, there is no good as-
18   pect, either silvern or golden.

Christian Science is not an exception to the general
rule, that there is no excellence without labor in a direct
21   line. One cannot scatter his fire, and at the

Backsliders and mistakes

same time hit the mark. To pursue other
vocations and advance rapidly in the demonstration of
24   this Science, is not possible. Departing from Christian
Science, some learners commend diet and hygiene.
They even practise these, intending thereby to initiate
27   the cure which they mean to complete with Mind, as if
the non-intelligent could aid Mind! The Scientist's
demonstration rests on one Principle, and there must
30   and can be no opposite rule. Let this Principle be applied to the cure of disease without exploiting other
means.

Mental
charlatanism

Mental quackery rests on the same platform as all   1
other quackery. The chief plank in this platform is the
doctrine that Science has two principles in   3
partnership, one good and the other evil, —
one spiritual, the other material, — and that these two
may be simultaneously at work on the sick. This   6
theory is supposed to favor practice from both a mental
and a material standpoint. Another plank in the platform is this, that error will finally have the same effect   9
as truth.

Divinity
ever ready

It is anything but scientifically Christian to think of
aiding the divine Principle of healing or of trying to sus-   12
tain the human body until the divine Mind
is ready to take the case. Divinity is always
ready. *Semper paratus* is Truth's motto. Having seen   15
so much suffering from quackery, the author desires to
keep it out of Christian Science. The two-edged sword
of Truth must turn in every direction to guard "the tree   18
of life."

The panoply
of wisdom

Sin makes deadly thrusts at the Christian Scientist as
ritualism and creed are summoned to give place to higher   21
law, but Science will ameliorate mortal malice.
The Christianly scientific man reflects the
divine law, thus becoming a law unto himself. He does   24
violence to no man. Neither is he a false accuser. The
Christian Scientist wisely shapes his course, and is honest and consistent in following the leadings of divine   27
Mind. He must prove, through living as well as healing and teaching, that Christ's way is the only one
by which mortals are radically saved from sin and   30
sickness.

Christianity causes men to turn naturally from matter

1 to Spirit, as the flower turns from darkness to light.
Man then appropriates those things which "eye hath
3 not seen nor ear heard." Paul and John

Advancement
by sacrifice

had a clear apprehension that, as mortal man
achieves no worldly honors except by sacrifice,
6 so he must gain heavenly riches by forsaking all worldli-
ness. Then he will have nothing in common with the
worldling's affections, motives, and aims. Judge not the
9 future advancement of Christian Science by the steps
already taken, lest you yourself be condemned for failing to take the first step.

12   Any attempt to heal mortals with erring mortal mind,
instead of resting on the omnipotence of the divine
Mind, must prove abortive. Committing the

Dangerous
knowledge

15 bare process of mental healing to frail mortals, untaught and unrestrained by Christian Science,
is like putting a sharp knife into the hands of a blind
18 man or a raging maniac, and turning him loose in
the crowded streets of a city. Whether animated by
malice or ignorance, a false practitioner will work mis-
21 chief, and ignorance is more harmful than wilful wickedness, when the latter is distrusted and thwarted in its
incipiency.

24   To mortal sense Christian Science seems abstract, but
the process is simple and the results are sure if the Science
is understood. The tree must be good, which

Certainty
of results

27 produces good fruit. Guided by divine Truth
and not guesswork, the *theologus* (that is, the student —
the Christian and scientific expounder — of the divine
30 law) treats disease with more certain results than any
other healer on the globe. The Christian Scientist should
understand and adhere strictly to the rules of divine meta-

physics as laid down in this work, and rest his demonstra- 1
tion on this sure basis.

Ontology is defined as "the science of the necessary 3
constituents and relations of all beings," and it underlies all metaphysical practice. Our system of

Ontology defined

Mind-healing rests on the apprehension of the 6
nature and essence of all being, — on the divine Mind
and Love's essential qualities. Its pharmacy is moral,
and its medicine is intellectual and spiritual, though used 9
for physical healing. Yet this most fundamental part of
metaphysics is the one most difficult to understand and
demonstrate, for to the material thought all is material, 12
till such thought is rectified by Spirit.

Sickness is neither imaginary nor unreal, — that is,
to the frightened, false sense of the patient. Sickness 15
is more than fancy; it is solid conviction. It

Mischievous imagination

is therefore to be dealt with through right apprehension of the truth of being. If Christian healing 18
is abused by mere smatterers in Science, it becomes a
tedious mischief-maker. Instead of scientifically effect-
ing a cure, it starts a petty crossfire over every cripple 21
and invalid, buffeting them with the superficial and cold
assertion, "Nothing ails you."

When the Science of Mind was a fresh revelation to 24
the author, she had to impart, while teaching its grand
facts, the hue of spiritual ideas from her own

Author's early instructions

spiritual condition, and she had to do this orally 27
through the meagre channel afforded by language and by
her manuscript circulated among the students. As former beliefs were gradually expelled from her thought, the 30
teaching became clearer, until finally the shadow of old
errors was no longer cast upon divine Science.

1   I do not maintain that anyone can exist in the flesh
without food and raiment; but I do believe that the

3   real man is immortal and that he lives in
Spirit, not matter. Christian Science must
be accepted at this period by induction. We admit the

Proof by induction

6   whole, because a part is proved and that part illustrates
and proves the entire Principle. Christian Science can
be taught only by those who are morally advanced and

9   spiritually endowed, for it is not superficial, nor is it
discerned from the standpoint of the human senses.
Only by the illumination of the spiritual sense, can

12   the light of understanding be thrown upon this Science,
because Science reverses the evidence before the material
senses and furnishes the eternal interpretation of God and

15   man.

    If you believe that you are sick, should you say, "I am
sick"? No, but you should tell your belief sometimes,

18   if this be requisite to protect others. If you commit a
crime, should you acknowledge to yourself that you are
a criminal? Yes. Your responses should differ because

21   of the different effects they produce. Usually to admit
that you are sick, renders your case less curable, while
to recognize your sin, aids in destroying it. Both sin and

24   sickness are error, and Truth is their remedy. The truth
regarding error is, that error is not true, hence it is unreal.
To prove scientifically the error or unreality of sin, you

27   must first see the claim of sin, and then destroy it.
Whereas, to prove scientifically the error or unreality of
disease, you must mentally unsee the disease; then you

30   will not feel it, and it is destroyed.

    Systematic teaching and the student's spiritual growth
and experience in practice are requisite for a thorough

comprehension of Christian Science. Some individu- 1
als assimilate truth more readily than others, but any

student, who adheres to the divine rules 3
of Christian Science and imbibes the spirit
of Christ, can demonstrate Christian Science, cast out
error, heal the sick, and add continually to his store of 6
spiritual understanding, potency, enlightenment, and
success.

If the student goes away to practise Truth's teach- 9
ings only in part, dividing his interests between God and

mammon and substituting his own views for
Truth, he will inevitably reap the error he sows. 12
Whoever would demonstrate the healing of Christian
Science must abide strictly by its rules, heed every statement, and advance from the rudiments laid down. There 15
is nothing difficult nor toilsome in this task, when the way
is pointed out; but self-denial, sincerity, Christianity, and
persistence alone win the prize, as they usually do in every 18
department of life.

Anatomy, when conceived of spiritually, is mental self-
knowledge, and consists in the dissection of thoughts to 21

discover their quality, quantity, and origin.
Are thoughts divine or human? That is the
important question. This branch of study is indispen- 24
sable to the excision of error. The anatomy of Christian
Science teaches when and how to probe the self-inflicted wounds of selfishness, malice, envy, and hate. It 27
teaches the control of mad ambition. It unfolds the
hallowed influences of unselfishness, philanthropy, spiritual love. It urges the government of the body both 30
in health and in sickness. The Christian Scientist,
through understanding mental anatomy, discerns and

1   deals with the real cause of disease. The material physician gropes among phenomena, which fluctuate every in-
3   stant under influences not embraced in his diagnosis, and
so he may stumble and fall in the darkness.

Teacher and student should also be familiar with the
6   obstetrics taught by this Science. To attend properly
the birth of the new child, or divine idea,   Scientific
you should so detach mortal thought from its   obstetrics
9   material conceptions, that the birth will be natural and
safe. Though gathering new energy, this idea cannot
injure its useful surroundings in the travail of spiritual
12   birth. A spiritual idea has not a single element of error,
and this truth removes properly whatever is offensive.
The new idea, conceived and born of Truth and Love, is
15   clad in white garments. Its beginning will be meek, its
growth sturdy, and its maturity undecaying. When
this new birth takes place, the Christian Science infant
18   is born of the Spirit, born of God, and can cause the
mother no more suffering. By this we know that Truth
is here and has fulfilled its perfect work.

21   To decide quickly as to the proper treatment of error —
whether error is manifested in forms of sickness, sin,
or death — is the first step towards destroy-   Unhesitating
24   ing error. Our Master treated error through   decision
Mind. He never enjoined obedience to the laws of nature,
if by these are meant laws of matter, nor did he use drugs.
27   There is a law of God applicable to healing, and it is a
spiritual law instead of material. The sick are not healed
by inanimate matter or drugs, as they believe that they
30   are. Such seeming medical effect or action is that of so-
called mortal mind.

It has been said to the author, "The world is bene-

fited by you, but it feels your influence without seeing   1
you. Why do you not make yourself more widely
known?" Could her friends know how little   3
time the author has had, in which to make
herself outwardly known except through her laborious
publications, — and how much time and toil are still re-   6
quired to establish the stately operations of Christian
Science, — they would understand why she is so secluded.
Others could not take her place, even if willing so to do.   9
She therefore remains unseen at her post, seeking no self-
aggrandizement but praying, watching, and working for
the redemption of mankind.   12

If from an injury or from any cause, a Christian Scientist were seized with pain so violent that he could not
treat himself mentally, — and the Scientists had failed   15
to relieve him, — the sufferer could call a surgeon, who
would give him a hypodermic injection, then, when the
belief of pain was lulled, he could handle his own case   18
mentally. Thus it is that we "prove all things; [and]
hold fast that which is good."

In founding a pathological system of Christianity, the   21
author has labored to expound divine Principle, and not

to exalt personality. The weapons of bigotry,
ignorance, envy, fall before an honest heart.   24
Adulterating Christian Science, makes it void.
Falsity has no foundation. "The hireling fleeth, because
he is an hireling, and careth not for the sheep." Neither   27
dishonesty nor ignorance ever founded, nor can they overthrow a scientific system of ethics.

Chapter 14

Recapitulation

For precept must be upon precept, precept upon precept;
line upon line, line upon line;
here a little, and there a little. — ISAIAH.

1   **T**his chapter is from the first edition of the author's
class-book, copyrighted in 1870. After much labor
3 and increased spiritual understanding, she revised that
treatise for this volume in 1875. Absolute Christian
Science pervades its statements, to elucidate scientific
6 metaphysics.

QUESTIONS AND ANSWERS

Question. — What is God?
9 *Answer.* — God is incorporeal, divine, supreme, infinite
Mind, Spirit, Soul, Principle, Life, Truth, Love.

Question. — Are these terms synonymous?
12 *Answer.* — They are. They refer to one absolute God.
They are also intended to express the nature, essence, and
wholeness of Deity. The attributes of God are justice,
15 mercy, wisdom, goodness, and so on.

Question. — Is there more than one God or Principle?
Answer. — There is not. Principle and its idea is one,
18 and this one is God, omnipotent, omniscient, and omni-

present Being, and His reflection is man and the universe.   1
Omni is adopted from the Latin adjective signifying *all.*
Hence God combines all-power or potency, all-science   3
or true knowledge, all-presence. The varied manifestations of Christian Science indicate Mind, never matter,
and have one Principle.   6

Question. — What are spirits and souls?
Answer. — To human belief, they are personalities
constituted of mind and matter, life and death, truth and   9
error, good and evil; but these contrasting

Real *versus* unreal

pairs of terms represent contraries, as Christian Science reveals, which neither dwell together nor   12
assimilate. Truth is immortal; error is mortal. Truth
is limitless; error is limited. Truth is intelligent; error
is non-intelligent. Moreover, Truth is real, and error is   15
unreal. This last statement contains the point you will
most reluctantly admit, although first and last it is the
most important to understand.   18

The term *souls* or *spirits* is as improper as the term
gods. Soul or Spirit signifies Deity and nothing else.

Mankind redeemed

There is no finite soul nor spirit. Soul or   21
Spirit means only one Mind, and cannot be
rendered in the plural. Heathen mythology and Jewish
theology have perpetuated the fallacy that intelligence,   24
soul, and life can be in matter; and idolatry and ritualism
are the outcome of all man-made beliefs. The Science
of Christianity comes with fan in hand to separate the   27
chaff from the wheat. Science will declare God aright,
and Christianity will demonstrate this declaration and
its divine Principle, making mankind better physically,   30
morally, and spiritually.

1 *Question.* — What are the demands of the Science of
Soul?

3 *Answer.* — The first demand of this Science is, "Thou
shalt have no other gods before me." This *me* is Spirit.
Therefore the command means this: Thou shalt
6 have no intelligence, no life, no substance, no
truth, no love, but that which is spiritual. The second
is like unto it, "Thou shalt love thy neighbor as thyself."
9 It should be thoroughly understood that all men have one
Mind, one God and Father, one Life, Truth, and Love.
Mankind will become perfect in proportion as this fact
12 becomes apparent, war will cease and the true brotherhood of man will be established. Having no other gods,
turning to no other but the one perfect Mind to guide
15 him, man is the likeness of God, pure and eternal, having that Mind which was also in Christ.

Science reveals Spirit, Soul, as not in the body, and
18 God as not in man but as reflected by man. The greater
cannot be in the lesser. The belief that the
greater can be in the lesser is an error that
21 works ill. This is a leading point in the Science of Soul,
that Principle is not in its idea. Spirit, Soul, is not
confined in man, and is never in matter. We reason im-
24 perfectly from effect to cause, when we conclude that
matter is the effect of Spirit; but *a priori* reasoning
shows material existence to be enigmatical. Spirit gives
27 the true mental idea. We cannot interpret Spirit, Mind,
through matter. Matter neither sees, hears, nor feels.

Reasoning from cause to effect in the Science of Mind,
30 we begin with Mind, which must be understood through the idea which expresses it and
cannot be learned from its opposite, matter. Thus we

*Two chief
commands*

*Soul
not confined
in body*

*Sinlessness of
Mind, Soul*

arrive at Truth, or intelligence, which evolves its own	1
unerring idea and never can be coordinate with human
illusions. If Soul sinned, it would be mortal, for sin is	3
mortality's self, because it kills itself. If Truth is immortal, error must be mortal, because error is unlike
Truth. Because Soul is immortal, Soul cannot sin, for	6
sin is not the eternal verity of being.

Question. — What is the scientific statement of being?
Answer. — There is no life, truth, intelligence, nor sub-	9
stance in matter. All is infinite Mind and its infinite
manifestation, for God is All-in-all. Spirit is immortal
Truth; matter is mortal error. Spirit is the real and	12
eternal; matter is the unreal and temporal. Spirit is
God, and man is His image and likeness. Therefore
man is not material; he is spiritual.	15

Question. — What is substance?
Answer. — Substance is that which is eternal and inca-
pable of discord and decay. Truth, Life, and Love are	18

**Spiritual
synonyms**

substance, as the Scriptures use this word in
Hebrews: "The substance of things hoped
for, the evidence of things not seen." Spirit, the synonym	21
of Mind, Soul, or God, is the only real substance. The
spiritual universe, including individual man, is a com-
pound idea, reflecting the divine substance of Spirit.	24

Question. — What is Life?
Answer. — Life is divine Principle, Mind, Soul, Spirit.

**Eternity
of Life**

Life is without beginning and without end.	27
Eternity, not time, expresses the thought of
Life, and time is no part of eternity. One ceases in
proportion as the other is recognized. Time is finite;	30

1 eternity is forever infinite. Life is neither in nor of matter. What is termed matter is unknown to Spirit, which
3 includes in itself all substance and is Life eternal. Matter is a human concept. Life is divine Mind. Life is not
limited. Death and finiteness are unknown to Life. If
6 Life ever had a beginning, it would also have an ending.

Question. — What is intelligence?
Answer. — Intelligence is omniscience, omnipresence,
9 and omnipotence. It is the primal and eternal quality
of infinite Mind, of the triune Principle, — Life, Truth,
and Love, — named God.

12 *Question.* — What is Mind?
Answer. — Mind is God. The exterminator of error
is the great truth that God, good, is the *only* Mind, and
15 that the supposititious opposite of infinite Mind   **True sense of**
— called *devil* or evil — is not Mind, is not   **infinitude**
Truth, but error, without intelligence or reality. There
18 can be but one Mind, because there is but one God; and
if mortals claimed no other Mind and accepted no other,
sin would be unknown. We can have but one Mind, if
21 that one is infinite. We bury the sense of infinitude,
when we admit that, although God is infinite, evil has a
place in this infinity, for evil can have no place, where all
24 space is filled with God.

We lose the high signification of omnipotence, when
after admitting that God, or good, is omnipresent and
27 has all-power, we still believe there is another   **The sole**
power, named *evil*. This belief that there   **governor**
is more than one mind is as pernicious to divine theology
30 as are ancient mythology and pagan idolatry. With

one Father, even God, the whole family of man would   1
be brethren; and with one Mind and that God, or good,
the brotherhood of man would consist of Love and Truth,   3
and have unity of Principle and spiritual power which
constitute divine Science. The supposed existence of
more than one mind was the basic error of idolatry. This   6
error assumed the loss of spiritual power, the loss of the
spiritual presence of Life as infinite Truth without an
unlikeness, and the loss of Love as ever present and   9
universal.

Divine Science explains the abstract statement that
there is one Mind by the following self-evident propo-   12
The divine   sition: If God, or good, is real, then evil, the
standard of   unlikeness of God, is unreal. And evil can
perfection   only seem to be real by giving reality to the   15
unreal. The children of God have but one Mind. How
can good lapse into evil, when God, the Mind of man,
never sins? The standard of perfection was originally   18
God and man. Has God taken down His own standard,
and has man fallen?

God is the creator of man, and, the divine Principle   21
of man remaining perfect, the divine idea or reflection,
man, remains perfect. Man is the expression
Indestructible   of God's being. If there ever was a moment   24
relationship   when man did not express the divine perfection, then there was a moment when man did not express
God, and consequently a time when Deity was unex-   27
pressed — that is, without entity. If man has lost perfection, then he has lost his perfect Principle, the divine
Mind. If man ever existed without this perfect Principle   30
or Mind, then man's existence was a myth.

The relations of God and man, divine Principle and

idea, are indestructible in Science; and Science knows
no lapse from nor return to harmony, but holds the divine
order or spiritual law, in which God and all that He creates are perfect and eternal, to have remained unchanged
in its eternal history.

The unlikeness of Truth, — named *error*, — the opposite of Science, and the evidence before the five corporeal senses, afford no indication of the grand
facts of being; even as these so-called senses
receive no intimation of the earth's motions or of the
science of astronomy, but yield assent to astronomical
propositions on the authority of natural science.

Celestial evidence

The facts of divine Science should be admitted, —
although the evidence as to these facts is not supported
by evil, by matter, or by material sense, — because the
evidence that God and man coexist is fully sustained by
spiritual sense. Man is, and forever has been, God's reflection. God is infinite, therefore ever present, and
there is no other power nor presence. Hence the spirituality of the universe is the only fact of creation. "Let
God be true, but every [material] man a liar."

Question. — Are doctrines and creeds a benefit to man?
Answer. — The author subscribed to an orthodox
creed in early youth, and tried to adhere to it until she
caught the first gleam of that which interprets God as above mortal sense. This
view rebuked human beliefs, and gave the spiritual import, expressed through Science, of all that proceeds
from the divine Mind. Since then her highest creed has
been divine Science, which, reduced to human apprehension, she has named Christian Science. This Science

The test of experience

teaches man that God is the only Life, and that this Life
is Truth and Love; that God is to be understood, adored,
and demonstrated; that divine Truth casts out suppositional error and heals the sick.

The way which leads to Christian Science is straight
and narrow. God has set His signet upon Science, making it coordinate with all that is real and only
with that which is harmonious and eternal.
Sickness, sin, and death, being inharmonious, do not
originate in God nor belong to His government. His
law, rightly understood, destroys them. Jesus furnished
proofs of these statements.

Question. — What is error?
Answer. — Error is a supposition that pleasure and
pain, that intelligence, substance, life, are existent in matter. Error is neither Mind nor one of Mind's
faculties. Error is the contradiction of Truth.
Error is a belief without understanding. Error is unreal
because untrue. It is that which seemeth to be and is not.
If error were true, its truth would be error, and we should
have a self-evident absurdity — namely, *erroneous truth.*
Thus we should continue to lose the standard of Truth.

Question. — Is there no sin?
Answer. — All reality is in God and His creation, harmonious and eternal. That which He creates is good,
and He makes all that is made. Therefore
the only reality of sin, sickness, or death is
the awful fact that unrealities seem real to human, erring
belief, until God strips off their disguise. They are not
true, because they are not of God. We learn in Christian

Marginal headings:

God's law
destroys evil

Evanescent
materiality

Unrealities
that seem real

Line numbers: 1, 3, 6, 9, 12, 15, 18, 21, 24, 27, 30

1 Science that all inharmony of mortal mind or body is illusion, possessing neither reality nor identity though seeming
3 to be real and identical.

The Science of Mind disposes of all evil. Truth, God,
is not the father of error. Sin, sickness, and death are
6 to be classified as effects of error. Christ
came to destroy the belief of sin. The God-
principle is omnipresent and omnipotent. God is every-
9 where, and nothing apart from Him is present or has
power. Christ is the ideal Truth, that comes to heal
sickness and sin through Christian Science, and attributes
12 all power to God. Jesus is the name of the man who,
more than all other men, has presented Christ, the true
idea of God, healing the sick and the sinning and destroy-
15 ing the power of death. Jesus is the human man, and
Christ is the divine idea; hence the duality of Jesus the
Christ.

18 In an age of ecclesiastical despotism, Jesus introduced
the teaching and practice of Christianity, affording the
proof of Christianity's truth and love; but to
21 reach his example and to test its unerring Science according to his rule, healing sickness, sin, and
death, a better understanding of God as divine Prin-
24 ciple, Love, rather than personality or the man Jesus, is
required.

Jesus established what he said by demonstration,
27 thus making his acts of higher importance than his
words. He proved what he taught. This
is the Science of Christianity. Jesus *proved*
30 the Principle, which heals the sick and casts out error,
to be divine. Few, however, except his students understood in the least his teachings and their glorious

*Christ the
ideal Truth*

*Jesus not
God*

*Jesus not
understood*

proofs, — namely, that Life, Truth, and Love (the Prin- 1
ciple of this unacknowledged Science) destroy all error,
evil, disease, and death. 3

The reception accorded to Truth in the early Christian era is repeated to-day. Whoever introduces the

Miracles
rejected

Science of Christianity will be scoffed at and 6
scourged with worse cords than those which
cut the flesh. To the ignorant age in which it first
appears, Science seems to be a mistake, — hence the 9
misinterpretation and consequent maltreatment which
it receives. Christian marvels (and *marvel* is the simple meaning of the Greek word rendered *miracle* in the 12
New Testament) will be misunderstood and misused
by many, until the glorious Principle of these marvels is
gained. 15

If sin, sickness, and death are as real as Life, Truth,
and Love, then they must all be from the same source;

Divine
fulfilment

God must be their author. Now Jesus came 18
to destroy sin, sickness, and death; yet the
Scriptures aver, "I am not come to destroy, but to fulfil."
Is it possible, then, to believe that the evils which Jesus 21
lived to destroy are real or the offspring of the divine
will?

Despite the hallowing influence of Truth in the de- 24
struction of error, must error still be immortal? Truth

Truth
destroys falsity

spares all that is true. If evil is real, Truth
must make it so; but error, not Truth, is 27
the author of the unreal, and the unreal vanishes,
while all that is real is eternal. The apostle says that
the mission of Christ is to "destroy the works of the 30
devil." Truth destroys falsity and error, for light and
darkness cannot dwell together. Light extinguishes the

1 darkness, and the Scripture declares that there is "no
night there." To Truth there is no error, — all is Truth.
3 To infinite Spirit there is no matter, — all is Spirit, divine
Principle and its idea.

Question. — What is man?
6 *Answer.* — Man is not matter; he is not made up of
brain, blood, bones, and other material elements. The
Scriptures inform us that man is made in **Fleshly**
9 the image and likeness of God. Matter is **factors unreal**
not that likeness. The likeness of Spirit cannot be so
unlike Spirit. Man is spiritual and perfect; and be-
12 cause he is spiritual and perfect, he must be so understood in Christian Science. Man is idea, the image, of
Love; he is not physique. He is the compound idea of
15 God, including all right ideas; the generic term for
all that reflects God's image and likeness; the conscious
identity of being as found in Science, in which man is
18 the reflection of God, or Mind, and therefore is eternal;
that which has no separate mind from God; that which
has not a single quality underived from Deity; that which
21 possesses no life, intelligence, nor creative power of his
own, but reflects spiritually all that belongs to his Maker.
And God said: "Let us make man in our image, after
24 our likeness; and let them have dominion over the fish
of the sea, and over the fowl of the air, and over the cattle,
and over all the earth, and over every creeping thing that
27 creepeth upon the earth."
Man is incapable of sin, sickness, and death. The
real man cannot depart from holiness, nor **Man**
30 can God, by whom man is evolved, engender **unfallen**
the capacity or freedom to sin. A mortal sinner is not

God's man. Mortals are the counterfeits of immortals.   1
They are the children of the wicked one, or the one evil,
which declares that man begins in dust or as a material   3
embryo. In divine Science, God and the real man are
inseparable as divine Principle and idea.

Error, urged to its final limits, is self-destroyed.   6
Error will cease to claim that soul is in body, that life
and intelligence are in matter, and that
Mortals are
not immortals
this matter is man. God is the Principle of   9
man, and man is the idea of God. Hence man is not
mortal nor material. Mortals will disappear, and immortals, or the children of God, will appear as the only   12
and eternal verities of man. Mortals are not fallen children of God. They never had a perfect state of being,
which may subsequently be regained. They were, from   15
the beginning of mortal history, "conceived in sin and
brought forth in iniquity." Mortality is finally swallowed
up in immortality. Sin, sickness, and death must dis-   18
appear to give place to the facts which belong to immortal
man.

Learn this, O mortal, and earnestly seek the spiritual   21
status of man, which is outside of all material selfhood.
Imperishable   Remember that the Scriptures say of mortal
identity
man: "As for man, his days are as grass: as   24
a flower of the field, so he flourisheth. For the wind
passeth over it, and it is gone; and the place thereof shall
know it no more."   27

When speaking of God's children, not the children of
men, Jesus said, "The kingdom of God is within you;"
The kingdom   that is, Truth and Love reign in the real   30
within
man, showing that man in God's image is
unfallen and eternal. Jesus beheld in Science the per-

1 fect man, who appeared to him where sinning mortal
man appears to mortals. In this perfect man the Saviour
3 saw God's own likeness, and this correct view of man
healed the sick. Thus Jesus taught that the kingdom
of God is intact, universal, and that man is pure and holy.
6 Man is not a material habitation for Soul; he is himself
spiritual. Soul, being Spirit, is seen in nothing imperfect
nor material.
9 Whatever is material is mortal. To the five corporeal
senses, man appears to be matter and mind united; but
Christian Science reveals man as the idea of
12 God, and declares the corporeal senses to be
mortal and erring illusions. Divine Science
shows it to be impossible that a material body, though
15 interwoven with matter's highest stratum, misnamed
mind, should be man, — the genuine and perfect man,
the immortal idea of being, indestructible and eternal.
18 Were it otherwise, man would be annihilated.

Material body never God's idea

Question. — What are body and Soul?
Answer. — Identity is the reflection of Spirit, the re-
21 flection in multifarious forms of the living Principle,
Love. Soul is the substance, Life, and intelligence of man, which is individualized, but not
24 in matter. Soul can never reflect anything inferior to
Spirit.

Reflection of Spirit

Man is the expression of Soul. The Indians caught
27 some glimpses of the underlying reality, when
they called a certain beautiful lake "the smile
of the Great Spirit." Separated from man,
30 who expresses Soul, Spirit would be a nonentity; man,
divorced from Spirit, would lose his entity. But there is,

Man inseparable from Spirit

there can be, no such division, for man is coexistent with   1
God.

What evidence of Soul or of immortality have you   3
within mortality? Even according to the teachings of
natural science, man has never beheld Spirit
or Soul leaving a body or entering it. What   6
basis is there for the theory of indwelling spirit, except
the claim of mortal belief? What would be thought of
the declaration that a house was inhabited, and by a cer-   9
tain class of persons, when no such persons were ever seen
to go into the house or to come out of it, nor were they
even visible through the windows? Who can see a soul   12
in the body?

Question. — Does brain think, and do nerves feel, and
is there intelligence in matter?   15
Answer. — No, not if God is true and mortal man a
liar. The assertion that there can be pain or pleasure
in matter is erroneous. That body is most   18
harmonious in which the discharge of the natural functions is least noticeable. How can intelligence
dwell in matter when matter is non-intelligent and   21
brain-lobes cannot think? Matter cannot perform the
functions of Mind. Error says, "I am man;" but this
belief is mortal and far from actual. From beginning   24
to end, whatever is mortal is composed of material human beliefs and of nothing else. That only is real which
reflects God. St. Paul said, "But when it pleased God,   27
who separated me from my mother's womb, and called me
by His grace, . . . I conferred not with flesh and blood."
Mortal man is really a self-contradictory phrase, for   30
man is not mortal, "neither indeed can be;" man is im-

1 mortal. If a child is the offspring of physical sense and
not of Soul, the child must have a material, not a spirit-
3 ual origin. With what truth, then, could the
Scriptural rejoicing be uttered by any mother,
"I have gotten a man from the Lord"? On the con-
6 trary, if aught comes from God, it cannot be mortal and
material; it must be immortal and spiritual.

Matter is neither self-existent nor a product of Spirit.
9 An image of mortal thought, reflected on the retina, is
all that the eye beholds. Matter cannot see,
feel, hear, taste, nor smell. It is not self-
12 cognizant, — cannot feel itself, see itself, nor
understand itself. Take away so-called mortal mind,
which constitutes matter's supposed selfhood, and matter
15 can take no cognizance of matter. Does that which we
call dead ever see, hear, feel, or use any of the physical
senses?

18 "In the beginning God created the heaven and the
earth. And the earth was without form, and void; and
darkness was upon the face of the deep."
21 (Genesis i. 1, 2.) In the vast forever, in the
Science and truth of being, the only facts are Spirit
and its innumerable creations. Darkness and chaos
24 are the imaginary opposites of light, understanding,
and eternal harmony, and they are the elements of
nothingness.

27 We admit that black is not a color, because it reflects
no light. So evil should be denied identity or power,
because it has none of the divine hues. Paul
30 says: "For the invisible things of Him, from
the creation of the world, are clearly seen, being understood by the things that are made." (Romans i. 20.)

When the substance of Spirit appears in Christian Science, the nothingness of matter is recognized. Where the spirit of God is, and there is no place where God is not, evil becomes nothing, — the opposite of the something of Spirit. If there is no spiritual reflection, then there remains only the darkness of vacuity and not a trace of heavenly tints.

Nerves are an element of the belief that there is sensation in matter, whereas matter is devoid of sensation. Consciousness, as well as action, is governed by Mind, — is in God, the origin and governor of all that Science reveals. Material sense has its realm apart from Science in the unreal. Harmonious action proceeds from Spirit, God. Inharmony has no Principle; its action is erroneous and presupposes man to be in matter. Inharmony would make matter the cause as well as the effect of intelligence, or Soul, thus attempting to separate Mind from God.

Man is not God, and God is not man. Again, God, or good, never made man capable of sin. It is the opposite of good — that is, evil — which seems to make men capable of wrong-doing. Hence, evil is but an illusion, and it has no real basis. Evil is a false belief. God is not its author. The supposititious parent of evil is a lie.

The Bible declares: "All things were made by Him [the divine Word]; and without Him was not anything made that was made." This is the eternal verity of divine Science. If sin, sickness, and death were understood as nothingness, they would disappear. As vapor melts before the sun, so evil would vanish before the reality of good. One must hide the

*Side notes:*
Harmony
from Spirit

Evil
non-existent

Vapor and
nothingness

Line numbers: 1 3 6 9 12 15 18 21 24 27 30

1 other. How important, then, to choose good as the
reality! Man is tributary to God, Spirit, and to nothing
3 else. God's being is infinity, freedom, harmony, and
boundless bliss. "Where the Spirit of the Lord is,
there is liberty." Like the archpriests of yore, man is
6 free "to enter into the holiest," — the realm of God.

  Material sense never helps mortals to understand
Spirit, God. Through spiritual sense only, man com-
9 prehends and loves Deity. The various con-   **The fruit**
tradictions of the Science of Mind by the ma-   **forbidden**
terial senses do not change the unseen Truth, which re-
12 mains forever intact. The forbidden fruit of knowledge,
against which wisdom warns man, is the testimony of
error, declaring existence to be at the mercy of death,
15 and good and evil to be capable of commingling. This
is the significance of the Scripture concerning this "tree
of the knowledge of good and evil," — this growth of
18 material belief, of which it is said: "In the day that thou
eatest thereof thou shalt surely die." Human hypotheses
first assume the reality of sickness, sin, and death, and
21 then assume the necessity of these evils because of their
admitted actuality. These human verdicts are the pro-
curers of all discord.

24 If Soul sins, it must be mortal. Sin has the elements
of self-destruction. It cannot sustain itself. If sin is
supported, God must uphold it, and this is   **Sense and**
27 impossible, since Truth cannot support error.   **pure Soul**
Soul is the divine Principle of man and never sins, —
hence the immortality of Soul. In Science we learn that
30 it is material sense, not Soul, which sins; and it will be
found that it is the sense of sin which is lost, and not a
sinful soul. When reading the Scriptures, the substitu-

tion of the word *sense* for *soul* gives the exact meaning in   1
a majority of cases.

Human thought has adulterated the meaning of the   3
word *soul* through the hypothesis that soul is both an evil
and a good intelligence, resident in matter.

Soul defined

The proper use of the word *soul* can always   6
be gained by substituting the word *God*, where the deific
meaning is required. In other cases, use the word *sense*,
and you will have the scientific signification. As used   9
in Christian Science, Soul is properly the synonym of
Spirit, or God; but out of Science, soul is identical with
sense, with material sensation.   12

Question. — Is it important to understand these explanations in order to heal the sick?

Answer. — It is, since Christ is "the way" and the   15
truth casting out all error. Jesus called himself "the
Son of man," but not the son of Joseph. As

Sonship of Jesus

woman is but a species of the genera, he was   18
literally the Son of Man. Jesus was the highest human
concept of the perfect man. He was inseparable from
Christ, the Messiah, — the divine idea of God outside   21
the flesh. This enabled Jesus to demonstrate his control over matter. Angels announced to the Wisemen of
old this dual appearing, and angels whisper it, through   24
faith, to the hungering heart in every age.

Sickness is part of the error which Truth casts out.
Error will not expel error. Christian Science is the law   27
of Truth, which heals the sick on the basis

Sickness erroneous

of the one Mind or God. It can heal in no
other way, since the human, mortal mind so-called is not   30
a healer, but causes the belief in disease.

1   Then comes the question, how do drugs, hygiene, and
animal magnetism heal? It may be affirmed that they
3 do not heal, but only relieve suffering temporarily, exchanging one disease for another.

True healing
transcendent

We classify disease as error, which nothing but Truth or
6 Mind can heal, and this Mind must be divine, not human.
Mind transcends all other power, and will ultimately supersede all other means in healing. In order to heal by
9 Science, you must not be ignorant of the moral and spiritual demands of Science nor disobey them. Moral ignorance or sin affects your demonstration, and hinders its
12 approach to the standard in Christian Science.

    After the author's sacred discovery, she affixed the
name "Science" to Christianity, the name "error" to
15 corporeal sense, and the name "substance" to
Mind. Science has called the world to battle
over this issue and its demonstration, which

Terms
adopted by
the author

18 heals the sick, destroys error, and reveals the universal
harmony. To those natural Christian Scientists, the ancient worthies, and to Christ Jesus, God certainly revealed
21 the spirit of Christian Science, if not the absolute letter.

    Because the Science of Mind seems to bring into dis-
honor the ordinary scientific schools, which wrestle with
24 material observations alone, this Science has
met with opposition; but if any system honors

Science
the way

God, it ought to receive aid, not opposition, from all think-
27 ing persons. And Christian Science does honor God as
no other theory honors Him, and it does this in the way
of His appointing, by doing many wonderful works
30 through the divine name and nature. One must fulfil
one's mission without timidity or dissimulation, for to be
well done, the work must be done unselfishly. Christianity

will never be based on a divine Principle and so found to   1
be unerring, until its absolute Science is reached. When
this is accomplished, neither pride, prejudice, bigotry,   3
nor envy can wash away its foundation, for it is built upon
the rock, Christ.

Question. — Does Christian Science, or metaphysical   6
healing, include medication, material hygiene, mesmerism, hypnotism, theosophy, or spiritualism?

Answer. — Not one of them is included in it. In di-   9
vine Science, the supposed laws of matter yield to the

**Mindless
methods**
law of Mind. What are termed natural
science and material laws are the objective   12
states of mortal mind. The physical universe expresses
the conscious and unconscious thoughts of mortals.
Physical force and mortal mind are one. Drugs and   15
hygiene oppose the supremacy of the divine Mind.
Drugs and inert matter are unconscious, mindless. Certain results, supposed to proceed from drugs, are really   18
caused by the faith in them which the false human consciousness is educated to feel.

Mesmerism is mortal, material illusion. Animal mag-   21
netism is the voluntary or involuntary action of error

**Animal
magnetism
error**
in all its forms; it is the human antipode
of divine Science. Science must triumph   24
over material sense, and Truth over error, thus putting
an end to the hypotheses involved in all false theories
and practices.   27

Question. — Is materiality the concomitant of spirituality, and is material sense a necessary preliminary to
the understanding and expression of Spirit?   30

1   *Answer.* — If error is necessary to define or to reveal
     Truth, the answer is yes; but not otherwise. *Material*

3   *sense* is an absurd phrase, for matter has no
     sensation. Science declares that Mind, not
     matter, sees, hears, feels, speaks. Whatever contradicts
6   this statement is the false sense, which ever betrays
     mortals into sickness, sin, and death. If the unimpor-
     tant and evil appear, only soon to disappear because
9   of their uselessness or their iniquity, then these ephem-
     eral views of error ought to be obliterated by Truth.
     Why malign Christian Science for instructing mortals how
12   to make sin, disease, and death appear more and more
     unreal?
         Emerge gently from matter into Spirit. Think not
15   to thwart the spiritual ultimate of all things, but come
     naturally into Spirit through better health and
     morals and as the result of spiritual growth.

18   Not death, but the understanding of Life, makes man im-
     mortal. The belief that life can be in matter or soul in
     body, and that man springs from dust or from an egg,
21   is the result of the mortal error which Christ, or Truth,
     destroys by fulfilling the spiritual law of being, in which
     man is perfect, even as the "Father which is in heaven
24   is perfect." If thought yields its dominion to other
     powers, it cannot outline on the body its own beautiful
     images, but it effaces them and delineates foreign agents,
27   called disease and sin.
         The heathen gods of mythology controlled war and
     agriculture as much as nerves control sensation or

30   muscles measure strength. To say that
     strength is in matter, is like saying that the
     power is in the lever. The notion of any life or intelli-

gence in matter is without foundation in fact, and you 1
can have no faith in falsehood when you have learned
falsehood's true nature. 3

Suppose one accident happens to the eye, another to
the ear, and so on, until every corporeal sense is quenched.

What is man's remedy? To die, that he may 6
regain these senses? Even then he must gain
spiritual understanding and spiritual sense in order to
possess immortal consciousness. Earth's preparatory 9
school must be improved to the utmost. In reality man
never dies. The belief that he dies will not establish his
scientific harmony. Death is not the result of Truth but 12
of error, and one error will not correct another.

Jesus proved by the prints of the nails, that his body
was the same immediately after death as before. If death 15

restores sight, sound, and strength to man,
then death is not an enemy but a better friend
than Life. Alas for the blindness of belief, which makes 18
harmony conditional upon death and matter, and yet
supposes Mind unable to produce harmony! So long
as this error of belief remains, mortals will continue mor- 21
tal in belief and subject to chance and change.

Sight, hearing, all the spiritual senses of man, are
eternal. They cannot be lost. Their reality and immor- 24

tality are in Spirit and understanding, not in
matter, — hence their permanence. If this
were not so, man would be speedily annihilated. If the 27
five corporeal senses were the medium through which
to understand God, then palsy, blindness, and deafness
would place man in a terrible situation, where he would 30
be like those "having no hope, and without God in the
world;" but as a matter of fact, these calamities often

1   drive mortals to seek and to find a higher sense of happiness and existence.

3   Life is deathless. Life is the origin and ultimate of
man, never attainable through death, but gained by walking in the pathway of Truth both before and

Exercise of Mind-faculties

6   after that which is called death. There is more
Christianity in seeing and hearing spiritually
than materially. There is more Science in the perpetual

9   exercise of the Mind-faculties than in their loss. Lost
they cannot be, while Mind remains. The apprehension
of this gave sight to the blind and hearing to the deaf cen-

12   turies ago, and it will repeat the wonder.

     Question. — You speak of belief. Who or what is it
that believes?

15   *Answer.* — Spirit is all-knowing; this precludes the
need of believing. Matter cannot believe, and Mind
understands. The body cannot believe. The

Understanding versus belief

18   believer and belief are one and are mortal.
Christian evidence is founded on Science or
demonstrable Truth, flowing from immortal Mind, and

21   there is in reality no such thing as *mortal* mind. Mere
belief is blindness without Principle from which to explain the reason of its hope. The belief that life is sen-

24   tient and intelligent matter is erroneous.
     The Apostle James said, "Show me thy faith without
thy works, and I will show thee my faith by my works."

27   The understanding that Life is God, Spirit, lengthens
our days by strengthening our trust in the deathless
reality of Life, its almightiness and immortality.

30   This faith relies upon an understood Principle. This
Principle makes whole the diseased, and brings out the

enduring and harmonious phases of things. The result   1
of our teachings is their sufficient confirmation. When,

Confirmation by healing

on the strength of these instructions, you are   3
able to banish a severe malady, the cure shows
that you understand this teaching, and therefore you receive the blessing of Truth.   6

The Hebrew and Greek words often translated *belief*
differ somewhat in meaning from that conveyed by the

Belief and firm trust

English verb *believe;* they have more the sig-   9
nificance of faith, understanding, trust, constancy, firmness. Hence the Scriptures often appear in
our common version to approve and endorse belief, when   12
they mean to enforce the necessity of understanding.

Question. — Do the five corporeal senses constitute
man?   15
Answer. — Christian Science sustains with immortal
proof the impossibility of any material sense, and defines

All faculties from Mind

these so-called senses as *mortal beliefs,* the   18
testimony of which cannot be true either of
man or of his Maker. The corporeal senses can take no
cognizance of spiritual reality and immortality. Nerves   21
have no more sensation, apart from what belief bestows upon them, than the fibres of a plant. Mind alone
possesses all faculties, perception, and comprehension.   24
Therefore mental endowments are not at the mercy of
organization and decomposition, — otherwise the very
worms could unfashion man. If it were possible for the   27
real senses of man to be injured, Soul could reproduce
them in all their perfection; but they cannot be disturbed nor destroyed, since they exist in immortal Mind,   30
not in matter.

1 The less mind there is manifested in matter the better. When the unthinking lobster loses its claw, the claw grows
3 again. If the Science of Life were understood, it would be found that the senses of Mind are never lost and that matter has no sensation. Then the
6 human limb would be replaced as readily as the lobster's claw, — not with an artificial limb, but with the genuine one. Any hypothesis which supposes life to be in matter
9 is an educated belief. In infancy this belief is not equal to guiding the hand to the mouth; and as consciousness develops, this belief goes out, — yields to the reality of
12 everlasting Life.

Possibilities
of Life

Corporeal sense defrauds and lies; it breaks all the commands of the Mosaic Decalogue to meet its own de-
15 mands. How then can this sense be the God-given channel to man of divine blessings or understanding? How can man, reflecting God, be de-
18 pendent on material means for knowing, hearing, seeing? Who dares to say that the senses of man can be at one time the medium for sinning against God, at another the me-
21 dium for obeying God? An affirmative reply would con-tradict the Scripture, for the same fountain sendeth not forth sweet waters and bitter.

Decalogue
disregarded

24 The corporeal senses are the only source of evil or error. Christian Science shows them to be false, be-cause matter has no sensation, and no organic
27 construction can give it hearing and sight nor make it the medium of Mind. Outside the material sense of things, all is harmony. A wrong sense
30 of God, man, and creation is *non-sense*, want of sense. Mortal belief would have the material senses sometimes good and sometimes bad. It assures mortals that there

Organic
construction
valueless

is real pleasure in sin; but the grand truths of Christian   1
Science dispute this error.

Will-power is but a product of belief, and this belief   3
commits depredations on harmony. Human will is an
animal propensity, not a faculty of Soul.

**Will-power
an animal
propensity**

Hence it cannot govern man aright. Chris-   6
tian Science reveals Truth and Love as the
motive-powers of man. Will — blind, stubborn, and headlong — cooperates with appetite and passion. From this   9
cooperation arises its evil. From this also comes its powerlessness, since all power belongs to God, good.

The Science of Mind needs to be understood. Until   12
it is understood, mortals are more or less deprived of
Truth. Human theories are helpless to make

**Theories
helpless**

man harmonious or immortal, since he is so   15
already, according to Christian Science. Our only need
is to know this and reduce to practice the real man's divine Principle, Love.   18

"Quench not the Spirit. Despise not prophesyings."
Human belief — or knowledge gained from the so-called

**True nature
and origin**

material senses — would, by fair logic, anni-   21
hilate man along with the dissolving elements
of clay. The scientifically Christian explanations of the
nature and origin of man destroy all material sense with   24
immortal testimony. This immortal testimony ushers
in the spiritual sense of being, which can be obtained
in no other way.   27

Sleep and mesmerism explain the mythical nature of
material sense. Sleep shows material sense as either

**Sleep
an illusion**

oblivion, nothingness, or an illusion or dream.   30
Under the mesmeric illusion of belief, a man
will think that he is freezing when he is warm, and that he

1   is swimming when he is on dry land. Needle-thrusts will
not hurt him. A delicious perfume will seem intolerable.
3   Animal magnetism thus uncovers material sense, and
shows it to be a belief without actual foundation or validity. Change the belief, and the sensation changes.
6   Destroy the belief, and the sensation disappears.

Material man is made up of involuntary and voluntary
error, of a negative right and a positive wrong, the latter
9   calling itself right. Man's spiritual individual-   **Man linked**
ity is never wrong. It is the likeness of man's   **with Spirit**
Maker. Matter cannot connect mortals with the true
12   origin and facts of being, in which all must end. It is only
by acknowledging the supremacy of Spirit, which annuls
the claims of matter, that mortals can lay off mortality and
15   find the indissoluble spiritual link which establishes man
forever in the divine likeness, inseparable from his creator.

The belief that matter and mind are one, — that mat-
18   ter is awake at one time and asleep at another, sometimes presenting no appearance of mind, —   **Material man**
this belief culminates in another belief, that   **as a dream**
21   man dies. Science reveals material man as never the real
being. The dream or belief goes on, whether our eyes are
closed or open. In sleep, memory and consciousness are
24   lost from the body, and they wander whither they will
apparently with their own separate embodiment. Personality is not the individuality of man. A wicked man
27   may have an attractive personality.

When we are awake, we dream of the pains and pleas-
ures of matter. Who will say, even though he   **Spiritual**
30   does not understand Christian Science, that   **existence the**
this dream — rather than the dreamer — may   **one fact**
not be mortal man? Who can rationally say otherwise,

when the dream leaves mortal man intact in body and   1
thought, although the so-called dreamer is unconscious?
For right reasoning there should be but one fact before   3
the thought, namely, spiritual existence. In reality there
is no other existence, since Life cannot be united to its
unlikeness, mortality.   6

Being is holiness, harmony, immortality. It is already
proved that a knowledge of this, even in small degree,

will uplift the physical and moral standard   9
of mortals, will increase longevity, will purify
and elevate character. Thus progress will finally destroy
all error, and bring immortality to light. We know that   12
a statement proved to be good must be correct. New
thoughts are constantly obtaining the floor. These two
contradictory theories — that matter is something, or   15
that all is Mind — will dispute the ground, until one is
acknowledged to be the victor. Discussing his cam-
paign, General Grant said: "I propose to fight it out on   18
this line, if it takes all summer." Science says: All is
Mind and Mind's idea. You must fight it out on this
line. Matter can afford you no aid.   21

The notion that mind and matter commingle in the
human illusion as to sin, sickness, and death must even-

tually submit to the Science of Mind, which   24
denies this notion. *God is Mind, and God is
infinite; hence all is Mind.* On this statement rests the
Science of being, and the Principle of this Science is di-   27
vine, demonstrating harmony and immortality.

The conservative theory, long believed, is that there
are two factors, matter and mind, uniting on some im-   30
possible basis. This theory would keep truth and error
always at war. Victory would perch on neither banner.

1   On the other hand, Christian Science speedily shows
     Truth to be triumphant. To corporeal sense, the sun
3   appears to rise and set, and the earth to stand
     still; but astronomical science contradicts this,

     and explains the solar system as working on a differ-
6   ent plan. All the evidence of physical sense and all the
     knowledge obtained from physical sense must yield to
     Science, to the immortal truth of all things.

9   *Question.* — Will you explain sickness and show how it
     is to be healed?
     Answer. — The method of Christian Science Mind-heal-
12   ing is touched upon in a previous chapter entitled Christian
     Science Practice. A full answer to the above
     question involves teaching, which enables the

15   healer to demonstrate and prove for himself the Principle
     and rule of Christian Science or metaphysical healing.
     Mind must be found superior to all the beliefs of the
18   five corporeal senses, and able to destroy all ills. Sick-
     ness is a belief, which must be annihilated by
     the divine Mind. Disease is an experience of

21   so-called mortal mind. It is fear made manifest on the
     body. Christian Science takes away this physical sense
     of discord, just as it removes any other sense of moral or
24   mental inharmony. That man is material, and that mat-
     ter suffers, — these propositions can only seem real and
     natural in illusion. Any sense of soul in matter is not the
27   reality of being.
     If Jesus awakened Lazarus from the dream, illusion, of
     death, this proved that the Christ could improve on a false
30   sense. Who dares to doubt this consummate test of the
     power and willingness of divine Mind to hold man forever

intact in his perfect state, and to govern man's entire   1
action? Jesus said: "Destroy this temple [body], and
in three days I [Mind] will raise it up;" and he did this   3
for tired humanity's reassurance.

Is it not a species of infidelity to believe that so great
a work as the Messiah's was done for himself or for God,   6
Inexhaustible divine Love who needed no help from Jesus' example to
preserve the eternal harmony? But mortals
did need this help, and Jesus pointed the way for them.   9
Divine Love always has met and always will meet every
human need. It is not well to imagine that Jesus demonstrated the divine power to heal only for a select number   12
or for a limited period of time, since to all mankind and
in every hour, divine Love supplies all good.

The miracle of grace is no miracle to Love. Jesus   15
demonstrated the inability of corporeality, as well as the
Reason and Science infinite ability of Spirit, thus helping erring
human sense to flee from its own convictions   18
and seek safety in divine Science. Reason, rightly directed, serves to correct the errors of corporeal sense; but
sin, sickness, and death will seem real (even as the ex-   21
periences of the sleeping dream seem real) until the Science of man's eternal harmony breaks their illusion with
the unbroken reality of scientific being.   24

Which of these two theories concerning man are you
ready to accept? One is the mortal testimony, changing,
dying, unreal. The other is the eternal and real evidence,   27
bearing Truth's signet, its lap piled high with immortal
fruits.

Our Master cast out devils (evils) and healed the sick.   30
It should be said of his followers also, that they cast fear
and all evil out of themselves and others and heal the sick.

1 God will heal the sick through man, whenever man is
governed by God. Truth casts out error now
3 as surely as it did nineteen centuries ago. All
of Truth is not understood; hence its healing power is not
fully demonstrated.

6 If sickness is true or the idea of Truth, you cannot
destroy sickness, and it would be absurd to try. Then
classify sickness and error as our Master did,
9 when he spoke of the sick, "whom Satan hath
bound," and find a sovereign antidote for error in the life-
giving power of Truth acting on human belief, a power
12 which opens the prison doors to such as are bound, and
sets the captive free physically and morally.

When the illusion of sickness or sin tempts you, cling
15 steadfastly to God and His idea. Allow nothing but His
likeness to abide in your thought. Let neither
fear nor doubt overshadow your clear sense and
18 calm trust, that the recognition of life harmonious — as
Life eternally is — can destroy any painful sense of, or
belief in, that which Life is not. Let Christian Science,
21 instead of corporeal sense, support your understanding of
being, and this understanding will supplant error with
Truth, replace mortality with immortality, and silence dis-
24 cord with harmony.

Question. — How can I progress most rapidly in the
understanding of Christian Science?
27 Answer. — Study thoroughly the letter and imbibe
the spirit. Adhere to the divine Principle of Christian Science and follow the behests of God,
30 abiding steadfastly in wisdom, Truth, and
Love. In the Science of Mind, you will soon ascertain

that error cannot destroy error. You will also learn   1
that in Science there is no transfer of evil suggestions
from one mortal to another, for there is but one Mind,   3
and this ever-present omnipotent Mind is reflected by
man and governs the entire universe. You will learn
that in Christian Science the first duty is to obey   6
God, to have one Mind, and to love another as
yourself.

We all must learn that Life is God. Ask yourself: 9
Am I living the life that approaches the supreme good?

Condition of progress Am I demonstrating the healing power of
Truth and Love? If so, then the way will   12
grow brighter "unto the perfect day." Your fruits
will prove what the understanding of God brings to man.
Hold perpetually this thought, — that it is the spiritual   15
idea, the Holy Ghost and Christ, which enables you to
demonstrate, with scientific certainty, the rule of healing,
based upon its divine Principle, Love, underlying, over-   18
lying, and encompassing all true being.

"The sting of death is sin; and the strength of sin is
the law," — the law of mortal belief, at war with the   21

Triumph over death facts of immortal Life, even with the spiritual
law which says to the grave, "Where is thy
victory?" But "when this corruptible shall have put   24
on incorruption, and this mortal shall have put on immortality, then shall be brought to pass the saying that
is written, Death is swallowed up in victory."   27

Question. — Have Christian Scientists any religious
creed?

Answer. — They have not, if by that term is meant   30
doctrinal beliefs. The following is a brief exposition of

1   the important points, or religious tenets, of Christian
Science: —

3   1. As adherents of Truth, we take the inspired Word
of the Bible as our sufficient guide to eternal Life.

    2. We acknowledge and adore one supreme and in-
6 finite God. We acknowledge His Son, one Christ; the
Holy Ghost or divine Comforter; and man in God's
image and likeness.

9   3. We acknowledge God's forgiveness of sin in the
destruction of sin and the spiritual understanding that
casts out evil as unreal. But the belief in sin is pun-
12 ished so long as the belief lasts.

    4. We acknowledge Jesus' atonement as the evi-
dence of divine, efficacious Love, unfolding man's unity
15 with God through Christ Jesus the Way-shower; and
we acknowledge that man is saved through Christ,
through Truth, Life, and Love as demonstrated by the
18 Galilean Prophet in healing the sick and overcoming
sin and death.

    5. We acknowledge that the crucifixion of Jesus and
21 his resurrection served to uplift faith to understand eternal Life, even the allness of Soul, Spirit, and the nothingness of matter.

24   6. And we solemnly promise to watch, and pray for
that Mind to be in us which was also in Christ Jesus; to
do unto others as we would have them do unto us; and
27 to be merciful, just, and pure.

Key to the Scriptures

These things saith He that is holy,
He that is true,
He that hath the key of David,
He that openeth, and no man shutteth;
and shutteth, and no man openeth;
I know thy works:
behold, I have set before thee an open door,
and no man can shut it. —REVELATION.

Genesis

And I appeared unto Abraham, unto Isaac,
and unto Jacob by the name of God Almighty;
but by My name Jehovah was I not known to them. — EXODUS.

All things were made by Him;
and without Him was not anything made that was made.
In Him was life; and the life was the light of men. — JOHN.

1   **S**cientific interpretation of the Scriptures properly starts with the beginning of the Old Testa-
3   ment, chiefly because the spiritual import of
the Word, in its earliest articulations, often
seems so smothered by the immediate context as to
6   require explication; whereas the New Testament narra-
tives are clearer and come nearer the heart. Jesus illumines them, showing the poverty of mortal existence,
9   but richly recompensing human want and woe with
spiritual gain. The incarnation of Truth, that amplifi-
cation of wonder and glory which angels could only
12   whisper and which God illustrated by light and harmony, is consonant with ever-present Love. So-called
mystery and miracle, which subserve the end of natural
15   good, are explained by that Love for whose rest the
weary ones sigh when needing something more native
to their immortal cravings than the history of perpetual
18   evil.

Spiritual interpretation

501

Spiritual
overture

A second necessity for beginning with Genesis is that	1
the living and real prelude of the older Scriptures is so
brief that it would almost seem, from the	3
preponderance of unreality in the entire narrative, as if reality did not predominate over unreality,
the light over the dark, the straight line of Spirit over	6
the mortal deviations and inverted images of the creator
and His creation.

Deflection
of being

Spiritually followed, the book of Genesis is the history	9
of the untrue image of God, named a sinful mortal. This
deflection of being, rightly viewed, serves to
suggest the proper reflection of God and the	12
spiritual actuality of man, as given in the first chapter
of Genesis. Even thus the crude forms of human thought
take on higher symbols and significations, when scien-	15
tifically Christian views of the universe appear, illuminat-
ing time with the glory of eternity.

In the following exegesis, each text is followed by its	18
spiritual interpretation according to the teachings of Christian Science.

EXEGESIS	21

Genesis i. 1. In the beginning God created the heaven
and the earth.

Ideas and
identities

The infinite has no beginning. This word *beginning*	24
is employed to signify *the only,* — that is, the eternal verity and unity of God and man, including
the universe. The creative Principle — Life,	27
Truth, and Love — is God. The universe reflects God.
There is but one creator and one creation. This crea-

1   tion consists of the unfolding of spiritual ideas and their
    identities, which are embraced in the infinite Mind and
3   forever reflected. These ideas range from the infini-
    tesimal to infinity, and the highest ideas are the sons
    and daughters of God.

6   *Genesis* i. 2. And the earth was without form, and void;
    and darkness was upon the face of the deep. And the
    spirit of God moved upon the face of the waters.

9   The divine Principle and idea constitute spiritual har-
    mony, — heaven and eternity. In the universe of Truth,
    matter is unknown. No supposition of error   **Spiritual**
12 enters there. Divine Science, the Word of   **harmony**
    God, saith to the darkness upon the face of error, "God
    is All-in-all," and the light of ever-present Love illumines
15 the universe. Hence the eternal wonder, — that infinite
    space is peopled with God's ideas, reflecting Him in
    countless spiritual forms.

18 *Genesis* i. 3. And God said, Let there be light: and
    there was light.

        Immortal and divine Mind presents the idea of God:
21 *first*, in light; *second*, in reflection; *third*, in spiritual and
    immortal forms of beauty and goodness. But   **Mind's idea**
    this Mind creates no element nor symbol of   **faultless**
24 discord and decay. God creates neither erring thought,
    mortal life, mutable truth, nor variable love.

    Genesis i. 4. And God saw the light, that it was good:
27 and God divided the light from the darkness.

        God, Spirit, dwelling in infinite light and harmony

from which emanates the true idea, is never reflected by   1
aught but the good.

Genesis i. 5. And God called the light Day, and the   3
darkness He called Night. And the evening and the morning were the first day.

All questions as to the divine creation being both   6
spiritual and material are answered in this passage, for

though solar beams are not yet included in
the record of creation, still there is light. This   9
light is not from the sun nor from volcanic flames, but it
is the revelation of Truth and of spiritual ideas. This
also shows that there is no place where God's light is not   12
seen, since Truth, Life, and Love fill immensity and are
ever-present. Was not this a revelation instead of a
creation?   15

The successive appearing of God's ideas is represented
as taking place on so many *evenings* and *mornings*, —

words which indicate, in the absence of solar   18
time, spiritually clearer views of Him, views
which are not implied by material darkness and dawn.
Here we have the explanation of another passage of   21
Scripture, that "one day is with the Lord as a thousand
years." The rays of infinite Truth, when gathered into
the focus of ideas, bring light instantaneously, whereas   24
a thousand years of human doctrines, hypotheses, and
vague conjectures emit no such effulgence.

Did infinite Mind create matter, and call it *light?*   27
Spirit is light, and the contradiction of Spirit is matter,

darkness, and darkness obscures light. Material sense is nothing but a supposition of the   30
absence of Spirit. No solar rays nor planetary revolutions

1 form the day of Spirit. Immortal Mind makes its own
record, but mortal mind, sleep, dreams, sin, disease, and
3 death have no record in the first chapter of Genesis.

Genesis i. 6. And God said, Let there be a firmament in
the midst of the waters, and let it divide the waters from
6 the waters.

Spiritual understanding, by which human conception,
material sense, is separated from Truth, is the firmament.
9 The divine Mind, not matter, creates all identities, and they are forms of Mind, the ideas of
Spirit apparent only as Mind, never as mindless matter
12 nor the so-called material senses.

Spiritual firmament

Genesis i. 7. And God made the firmament, and divided
the waters which were under the firmament from the waters
15 which were above the firmament: and it was so.

Spirit imparts the understanding which uplifts consciousness and leads into all truth. The Psalmist saith:
18 "The Lord on high is mightier than the noise
of many waters, yea, than the mighty waves of
the sea." Spiritual sense is the discernment of spiritual
21 good. Understanding is the line of demarcation between
the real and unreal. Spiritual understanding unfolds
Mind, — Life, Truth, and Love, — and demonstrates the
24 divine sense, giving the spiritual proof of the universe in
Christian Science.

Understanding imparted

This understanding is not intellectual, is not the result
27 of scholarly attainments; it is the reality of all things
brought to light. God's ideas reflect the immortal, unerring, and infinite. The mortal,
30 erring, and finite are human beliefs, which apportion to

Original reflected

themselves a task impossible for them, that of distinguish- 1
ing between the false and the true. Objects utterly unlike the original do not reflect that original. Therefore 3
matter, not being the reflection of Spirit, has no real entity. Understanding is a quality of God, a quality which
separates Christian Science from supposition and makes 6
Truth final.

Genesis i. 8. And God called the firmament Heaven.
And the evening and the morning were the second day. 9

**Exalted
thought**

Through divine Science, Spirit, God, unites understanding to eternal harmony. The calm and exalted
thought or spiritual apprehension is at peace. 12
Thus the dawn of ideas goes on, forming each
successive stage of progress.

Genesis i. 9. And God said, Let the waters under the 15
heaven be gathered together unto one place, and let the dry
land appear: and it was so.

**Unfolding
of thoughts**

Spirit, God, gathers unformed thoughts into their 18
proper channels, and unfolds these thoughts,
even as He opens the petals of a holy purpose
in order that the purpose may appear. 21

Genesis i. 10. And God called the dry land Earth; and
the gathering together of the waters called He Seas: and
God saw that it was good. 24

**Spirit names
and blesses**

Here the human concept and divine idea seem confused by the translator, but they are not so in the scientifically Christian meaning of the text. Upon 27
Adam devolved the pleasurable task of finding names for all material things, but Adam has not yet

1   appeared in the narrative. In metaphor, the *dry land*
    illustrates the absolute formations instituted by Mind,
3   while *water* symbolizes the elements of Mind. Spirit duly
    feeds and clothes every object, as it appears in the line
    of spiritual creation, thus tenderly expressing the father-
6   hood and motherhood of God. Spirit names and blesses
    all. Without natures particularly defined, objects and
    subjects would be obscure, and creation would be full of
9   nameless offspring, — wanderers from the parent Mind,
    strangers in a tangled wilderness.

    Genesis i. 11. And God said, Let the earth bring forth
12 grass, the herb yielding seed, and the fruit tree yielding
    fruit after his kind, whose seed is in itself, upon the earth:
    and it was so.

15   The universe of Spirit reflects the creative power of
    the divine Principle, or Life, which reproduces the multi-
    tudinous forms of Mind and governs the mul-
18 tiplication of the compound idea man. The   Divine
    tree and herb do not yield fruit because of any propagat-   propagation
    ing power of their own, but because they reflect the Mind
21 which includes all. A material world implies a mortal
    mind and man a creator. The scientific divine creation
    declares immortal Mind and the universe created by God.
24   Infinite Mind creates and governs all, from the men-
    tal molecule to infinity. This divine Principle of all
    expresses Science and art throughout His   Ever-
27 creation, and the immortality of man and the   appearing
    universe. Creation is ever appearing, and must ever con-   creation
    tinue to appear from the nature of its inexhaustible source.
30 Mortal sense inverts this appearing and calls ideas mate-
    rial. Thus misinterpreted, the divine idea seems to fall

to the level of a human or material belief, called mortal   1
man. But the seed is in itself, only as the divine Mind
is All and reproduces all — as Mind is the multiplier,   3
and Mind's infinite idea, man and the universe, is the
product. The only intelligence or substance of a thought,
a seed, or a flower is God, the creator of it. Mind is the   6
Soul of all. Mind is Life, Truth, and Love which governs all.

Genesis i. 12. And the earth brought forth grass, and   9
herb yielding seed after his kind, and the tree yielding
fruit, whose seed was in itself, after his kind: and God saw
that it was good.   12

God determines the gender of His own ideas. Gender is mental, not material. The seed within itself is
Mind's pure thought   the pure thought emanating from divine   15
Mind. The feminine gender is not yet ex-
pressed in the text. *Gender* means simply *kind* or *sort*,
and does not necessarily refer either to masculinity or   18
femininity. The word is not confined to sexuality, and
grammars always recognize a neuter gender, neither
male nor female. The Mind or intelligence of produc-   21
tion names the female gender last in the ascending order
of creation. The intelligent individual idea, be it male
or female, rising from the lesser to the greater, unfolds   24
the infinitude of Love.

Genesis i. 13. And the evening and the morning were
the third day.   27

The third stage in the order of Christian Science is an
important one to the human thought, letting in the light

1 of spiritual understanding. This period corresponds to
the resurrection, when Spirit is discerned to be the Life of
3 all, and the deathless Life, or Mind, dependent
upon no material organization. Our Master
reappeared to his students, — to their apprehension he
6 rose from the grave, — on the third day of his ascending
thought, and so presented to them the certain sense of
eternal Life.

*Rising to
the light*

9 *Genesis* i. 14. And God said, Let there be lights in the
firmament of the heaven, to divide the day from the night;
and let them be for signs, and for seasons, and for days,
12 and years.

Spirit creates no other than heavenly or celestial bodies,
but the stellar universe is no more celestial than our earth.
15 This text gives the idea of the rarefaction of
thought as it ascends higher. God forms and
peoples the universe. The light of spiritual understand-
18 ing gives gleams of the infinite only, even as nebulæ indicate the immensity of space.

*Rarefaction
of thought*

So-called mineral, vegetable, and animal substances
21 are no more contingent now on time or material structure than they were when "the morning stars
sang together." Mind made the "plant of
24 the field before it was in the earth." The periods of
spiritual ascension are the days and seasons of Mind's
creation, in which beauty, sublimity, purity, and holiness
27 — yea, the divine nature — appear in man and the universe never to disappear.

*Divine nature
appearing*

Knowing the Science of creation, in which all is Mind
30 and its ideas, Jesus rebuked the material thought of his
fellow-countrymen: "Ye can discern the face of the

sky; but can ye not discern the signs of the times?" 1
How much more should we seek to apprehend the spirit-

Spiritual ideas apprehended ual ideas of God, than to dwell on the objects 3
of sense! To discern the rhythm of Spirit
and to be holy, thought must be purely spiritual.

Genesis i. 15. And let them be for lights in the firma- 6
ment of the heaven, to give light upon the earth: and it
was so.

Truth and Love enlighten the understanding, in whose 9
"light shall we see light;" and this illumination is reflected spiritually by all who walk in the light and turn
away from a false material sense. 12

Genesis i. 16. And God made two great lights; the
greater light to rule the day, and the lesser light to rule the
night: He made the stars also. 15

The sun is a metaphorical representation of Soul outside the body, giving existence and intelligence to the

Geology a failure universe. Love alone can impart the limit- 18
less idea of infinite Mind. Geology has never
explained the earth's formations; it cannot explain them.
There is no Scriptural allusion to solar light until time has 21
been already divided into evening and morning; and the
allusion to fluids (Genesis i. 2) indicates a supposed formation of matter by the resolving of fluids into solids, 24
analogous to the suppositional resolving of thoughts into
material things.

Light is a symbol of Mind, of Life, Truth, and Love, 27

Spiritual subdivision and not a vitalizing property of matter. Science reveals only one Mind, and this one shin-
ing by its own light and governing the universe, including 30

1   man, in perfect harmony. This Mind forms ideas, its
       own images, subdivides and radiates their borrowed light,
3   intelligence, and so explains the Scripture phrase, "whose
       seed is in itself." Thus God's ideas "multiply and re-
       plenish the earth." The divine Mind supports the sub-
6   limity, magnitude, and infinitude of spiritual creation.

       Genesis i. 17, 18. And God set them in the firmament of
       the heaven, to give light upon the earth, and to rule over
9   the day and over the night, and to divide the light from the
       darkness: and God saw that it was good.

              In divine Science, which is the seal of Deity and has
12   the impress of heaven, God is revealed as in-   **Darkness**
       finite light. In the eternal Mind, no night is   **scattered**
       there.

15   *Genesis* i. 19. And the evening and the morning were
       the fourth day.

              The changing glow and full effulgence of God's infi-
18   nite ideas, images, mark the periods of progress.

       Genesis i. 20. And God said, Let the waters bring forth
       abundantly the moving creature that hath life, and fowl
21   that may fly above the earth in the open firmament of
       heaven.

              To mortal mind, the universe is liquid, solid, and aëri-
24   form. Spiritually interpreted, rocks and mountains stand
       for solid and grand ideas. Animals and mor-   **Soaring**
       tals metaphorically present the gradation of   **aspirations**
27   mortal thought, rising in the scale of intelligence, taking
       form in masculine, feminine, or neuter gender. The
       fowls, which fly above the earth in the open firmament

of heaven, correspond to aspirations soaring beyond and
above corporeality to the understanding of the incorporeal
and divine Principle, Love.

Genesis i. 21. And God created great whales, and every
living creature that moveth, which the waters brought forth
abundantly, after their kind, and every winged fowl after
his kind: and God saw that it was good.

**Seraphic
symbols**

Spirit is symbolized by strength, presence, and power,
and also by holy thoughts, winged with Love. These angels of His presence, which have the holiest
charge, abound in the spiritual atmosphere of
Mind, and consequently reproduce their own characteristics. Their individual forms we know not, but we do
know that their natures are allied to God's nature; and
spiritual blessings, thus typified, are the externalized, yet
subjective, states of faith and spiritual understanding.

Genesis i. 22. And God blessed them, saying, Be fruitful, and multiply, and fill the waters in the seas; and let
fowl multiply in the earth.

**Multiplication
of pure ideas**

Spirit blesses the multiplication of its own pure and
perfect ideas. From the infinite elements of the one
Mind emanate all form, color, quality, and
quantity, and these are mental, both primarily
and secondarily. Their spiritual nature is discerned only
through the spiritual senses. Mortal mind inverts the true
likeness, and confers animal names and natures upon its
own misconceptions. Ignorant of the origin and operations of mortal mind, — that is, ignorant of itself, — this
so-called mind puts forth its own qualities, and claims
God as their author; albeit God is ignorant of the ex-

1 istence of both this mortal mentality, so-called, and its
claim, for the claim usurps the deific prerogatives and is
3 an attempted infringement on infinity.

Genesis i. 23. And the evening and the morning were
the fifth day.

6 Advancing spiritual steps in the teeming universe of
Mind lead on to spiritual spheres and exalted beings. To
material sense, this divine universe is dim and
9 distant, gray in the sombre hues of twilight;
but anon the veil is lifted, and the scene shifts into light.
In the record, time is not yet measured by solar revolutions,
12 and the motions and reflections of deific power cannot be
apprehended until divine Science becomes the interpreter.

*Spiritual
spheres*

Genesis i. 24. And God said, Let the earth bring forth
15 the living creature after his kind, cattle, and creeping thing,
and beast of the earth after his kind: and it was so.

Spirit diversifies, classifies, and individualizes all
18 thoughts, which are as eternal as the Mind
conceiving them; but the intelligence, existence, and continuity of all individuality remain in God,
21 who is the divinely creative Principle thereof.

*Continuity
of thoughts*

Genesis i. 25. And God made the beast of the earth after
his kind, and cattle after their kind, and everything that
24 creepeth upon the earth after his kind: and God saw that
it was good.

God creates all forms of reality. His thoughts are
27 spiritual realities. So-called mortal mind — being non-
existent and consequently not within the range of im-

mortal existence — could not by simulating deific power
invert the divine creation, and afterwards recreate persons or things upon its own plane, since nothing exists beyond the range of all-inclusive
infinity, in which and of which God is the
sole creator. Mind, joyous in strength, dwells in the
realm of Mind. Mind's infinite ideas run and dis-
port themselves. In humility they climb the heights of
holiness.

Moral courage is "the lion of the tribe of Juda," the
king of the mental realm. Free and fearless it roams in
the forest. Undisturbed it lies in the open
field, or rests in "green pastures, . . . beside
the still waters." In the figurative transmission from the
divine thought to the human, diligence, promptness, and
perseverance are likened to "the cattle upon a thousand
hills." They carry the baggage of stern resolve, and
keep pace with highest purpose. Tenderness accompanies all the might imparted by Spirit. The individuality created by God is not carnivorous, as witness the
millennial estate pictured by Isaiah: —

> The wolf also shall dwell with the lamb,
> And the leopard shall lie down with the kid;
> And the calf and the young lion, and the fatling together;
> And a little child shall lead them.

Understanding the control which Love held over all,
Daniel felt safe in the lions' den, and Paul proved the
viper to be harmless. All of God's creatures,
moving in the harmony of Science, are harm-
less, useful, indestructible. A realization of this grand
verity was a source of strength to the ancient worthies.

1   It supports Christian healing, and enables its possessor
to emulate the example of Jesus. "And God saw that
3   it was good."

Patience is symbolized by the tireless worm, creeping
over lofty summits, persevering in its intent. The ser-
6   pent of God's creating is neither subtle nor   **The serpent**
poisonous, but is a wise idea, charming in its   **harmless**
adroitness, for Love's ideas are subject to the Mind which
9   forms them, — the power which changeth the serpent
into a staff.

Genesis i. 26. And God said, Let us make man in our
12   image, after our likeness; and let them have dominion over
the fish of the sea, and over the fowl of the air, and over
the cattle, and over all the earth, and over every creeping
15   thing that creepeth upon the earth.

The eternal Elohim includes the forever universe.
The name Elohim is in the plural, but this plurality of
18   Spirit does not imply more than one God, nor   **Elohistic**
does it imply three persons in one. It relates   **plurality**
to the oneness, the tri-unity of Life, Truth, and Love.
21   "Let *them* have dominion." Man is the family name
for all ideas, — the sons and daughters of God. All that
God imparts moves in accord with Him, reflecting good-
24   ness and power.

Your mirrored reflection is your own image or likeness. If you lift a weight, your reflection does this also.
27   If you speak, the lips of this likeness move in   **Reflected**
accord with yours. Now compare man before   **likeness**
the mirror to his divine Principle, God. Call the mirror
30   divine Science, and call man the reflection. Then note

how true, according to Christian Science, is the reflection	1
to its original. As the reflection of yourself appears in
the mirror, so you, being spiritual, are the reflection of	3
God. The substance, Life, intelligence, Truth, and Love,
which constitute Deity, are reflected by His creation;
and when we subordinate the false testimony of the	6
corporeal senses to the facts of Science, we shall see
this true likeness and reflection everywhere.

God fashions all things, after His own likeness. Life	9
is reflected in existence, Truth in truthfulness, God in
goodness, which impart their own peace and
Love imparts beauty	permanence. Love, redolent with unselfish-	12
ness, bathes all in beauty and light. The grass beneath
our feet silently exclaims, "The meek shall inherit the
earth." The modest arbutus sends her sweet breath to	15
heaven. The great rock gives shadow and shelter. The
sunlight glints from the church-dome, glances into the
prison-cell, glides into the sick-chamber, brightens the	18
flower, beautifies the landscape, blesses the earth. Man,
made in His likeness, possesses and reflects God's domin-
ion over all the earth. Man and woman as coexistent	21
and eternal with God forever reflect, in glorified quality,
the infinite Father-Mother God.

Genesis i. 27. So God created man in His own image,	24
in the image of God created He him; male and female
created He them.

To emphasize this momentous thought, it is repeated	27
that God made man in His own image, to reflect the
Ideal man and woman	divine Spirit. It follows that *man* is a generic
term. Masculine, feminine, and neuter gen-	30
ders are human concepts. In one of the ancient lan-

1   guages the word for *man* is used also as the synonym of
    mind. This definition has been weakened by anthropo-
3   morphism, or a humanization of Deity. The word *an-*
    thropomorphic, in such a phrase as "an anthropomorphic
    God," is derived from two Greek words, signifying *man*
6   and *form,* and may be defined as a mortally mental at-
    tempt to reduce Deity to corporeality. The life-giving
    quality of Mind is Spirit, not matter. The ideal man
9   corresponds to creation, to intelligence, and to Truth.
    The ideal woman corresponds to Life and to Love. In
    divine Science, we have not as much authority for con-
12 sidering God masculine, as we have for considering
    Him feminine, for Love imparts the clearest idea of
    Deity.

15   The world believes in many persons; but if God is per-
    sonal, there is but one person, because there is but one
    God. His personality can only be reflected,   Divine
18 not transmitted. God has countless ideas, and   personality
    they all have one Principle and parentage. The only
    proper symbol of God as person is Mind's infinite ideal.
21 What is this ideal? Who shall behold it? This ideal
    is God's own image, spiritual and infinite. Even eternity
    can never reveal the whole of God, since there is no limit
24 to infinitude or to its reflections.

    Genesis i. 28. And God blessed them, and God said unto
    them, Be fruitful, and multiply, and replenish the earth,
27 and subdue it; and have dominion over the fish of the sea,
    and over the fowl of the air, and over every living thing
    that moveth upon the earth.

30   Divine Love blesses its own ideas, and causes them to
    multiply, — to manifest His power. Man is not made

to till the soil. His birthright is dominion, not sub-   1
jection. He is lord of the belief in earth
and heaven, — himself subordinate alone to   3
his Maker. This is the Science of being.

Genesis i. 29, 30. And God said, Behold, I have given
you every herb bearing seed, which is upon the face of all   6
the earth, and every tree, in the which is the fruit of a tree
yielding seed; to you it shall be for meat. And to every
beast of the earth, and to every fowl of the air, and to   9
everything that creepeth upon the earth, wherein there is
life, I have given every green herb for meat: and it
was so.   12

God gives the lesser idea of Himself for a link to the
greater, and in return, the higher always protects the
lower. The rich in spirit help the poor in   15
one grand brotherhood, all having the same
Principle, or Father; and blessed is that man who seeth
his brother's need and supplieth it, seeking his own in   18
another's good. Love giveth to the least spiritual idea
might, immortality, and goodness, which shine through
all as the blossom shines through the bud. All the varied   21
expressions of God reflect health, holiness, immortality —
infinite Life, Truth, and Love.

Genesis i. 31. And God saw everything that He had   24
made, and, behold, it was very good. And the evening and
the morning were the sixth day.

The divine Principle, or Spirit, comprehends and ex-   27
presses all, and all must therefore be as perfect as the
divine Principle is perfect. Nothing is new to Spirit.

1 Nothing can be novel to eternal Mind, the author of all
things, who from all eternity knoweth His own ideas.

3 Deity was satisfied with His work. How could
He be otherwise, since the spiritual creation
was the outgrowth, the emanation, of His infinite self-

6 containment and immortal wisdom?

**Perfection
of creation**

Genesis ii. 1. Thus the heavens and the earth were
finished, and all the host of them.

9 Thus the ideas of God in universal being are complete
and forever expressed, for Science reveals infinity and
the fatherhood and motherhood of Love. Hu-

12 man capacity is slow to discern and to grasp
God's creation and the divine power and presence which
go with it, demonstrating its spiritual origin. Mortals

15 can never know the infinite, until they throw off the old
man and reach the spiritual image and likeness. What
can fathom infinity! How shall we declare Him, till,

18 in the language of the apostle, "we all come in the unity
of the faith, and of the knowledge of the Son of God, unto
a perfect man, unto the measure of the stature of the ful-

21 ness of Christ"?

**Infinity
measureless**

Genesis ii. 2. And on the seventh day God ended His
work which He had made; and He rested on the seventh

24 day from all His work which He had made.

God rests in action. Imparting has not impoverished,
can never impoverish, the divine Mind. No

27 exhaustion follows the action of this Mind,
according to the apprehension of divine Science. The

**Resting in
holy work**

highest and sweetest rest, even from a human standpoint, 	1
is in holy work.

Unfathomable Mind is expressed. The depth, breadth, 	3
height, might, majesty, and glory of infinite Love fill all

**Love and man
coexistent**

space. That is enough! Human language
can repeat only an infinitesimal part of what 	6
exists. The absolute ideal, man, is no more seen nor
comprehended by mortals, than is his infinite Principle,
Love. Principle and its idea, man, are coexistent and 	9
eternal. The numerals of infinity, called *seven days*, can
never be reckoned according to the calendar of time.
These days will appear as mortality disappears, and they 	12
will reveal eternity, newness of Life, in which all sense of
error forever disappears and thought accepts the divine
infinite calculus. 	15

Genesis ii. 4, 5. These are the generations of the heavens
and of the earth when they were created, in the day that the
Lord God [Jehovah] made the earth and the heavens, and 	18
every plant of the field before it was in the earth, and every
herb of the field before it grew: for the Lord God [Jehovah]
had not caused it to rain upon the earth, and there was not 	21
a man to till the ground.

Here is the emphatic declaration that God creates all
through Mind, not through matter, — that the plant 	24

**Growth is
from Mind**

grows, not because of seed or soil, but because
growth is the eternal mandate of Mind. Mor-
tal thought drops into the ground, but the immortal creat- 	27
ing thought is from above, not from beneath. Because
Mind makes all, there is nothing left to be made by a
lower power. Spirit acts through the Science of Mind, 	30
never causing man to till the ground, but making him

1 superior to the soil. Knowledge of this lifts man above
the sod, above earth and its environments, to conscious
3 spiritual harmony and eternal being.

Here the inspired record closes its narrative of being
that is without beginning or end. All that is made is
6 the work of God, and all is good. We leave
this brief, glorious history of spiritual creation
(as stated in the first chapter of Genesis) in the hands of
9 God, not of man, in the keeping of Spirit, not matter, —
joyfully acknowledging now and forever God's supremacy,
omnipotence, and omnipresence.

Spiritual
narrative

12 The harmony and immortality of man are intact. We
should look away from the opposite supposition that man
is created materially, and turn our gaze to the spiritual
15 record of creation, to that which should be engraved on
the understanding and heart "with the point of a diamond"
and the pen of an angel.

18 The reader will naturally ask if there is nothing more
about creation in the book of Genesis. Indeed there is,
but the continued account is mortal and material.

21 *Genesis* ii. 6. But there went up a mist from the earth,
and watered the whole face of the ground.

The Science and truth of the divine creation have been
24 presented in the verses already considered, and now the
opposite error, a material view of creation, is
to be set forth. The second chapter of Gene-
27 sis contains a statement of this material view of God and
the universe, a statement which is the exact opposite of
scientific truth as before recorded. The history of error
30 or matter, if veritable, would set aside the omnipotence

The story
of error

of Spirit; but it is the false history in contradistinction 1
to the true.

The Science of the first record proves the falsity of 3
the second. If one is true, the other is false, for they are
antagonistic. The first record assigns all

The two
records
might and government to God, and endows 6
man out of God's perfection and power. The second
record chronicles man as mutable and mortal, — as having broken away from Deity and as revolving in an orbit 9
of his own. Existence, separate from divinity, Science
explains as impossible.

This second record unmistakably gives the history of 12
error in its externalized forms, called life and intelligence in matter. It records pantheism, opposed to the
supremacy of divine Spirit; but this state of things is 15
declared to be temporary and this man to be mortal, —
dust returning to dust.

In this erroneous theory, matter takes the place of Spirit. 18
Matter is represented as the life-giving principle of the

Erroneous
representation
earth. Spirit is represented as entering matter in order to create man. God's glowing 21
denunciations of man when not found in His
image, the likeness of Spirit, convince reason and coincide
with revelation in declaring this material creation false. 24

This latter part of the second chapter of Genesis, which
portrays Spirit as supposedly cooperating with matter in

Hypothetical
reversal
constructing the universe, is based on some 27
hypothesis of error, for the Scripture just pre-
ceding declares God's work to be finished. Does Life,
Truth, and Love produce death, error, and hatred? Does 30
the creator condemn His own creation? Does the unerring Principle of divine law change or repent? It can-

1 not be so. Yet one might so judge from an unintelligent perusal of the Scriptural account now under comment.

3 Because of its false basis, the mist of obscurity evolved by error deepens the false claim, and finally declares that God knows error and that error can improve

6 His creation. Although presenting the exact opposite of Truth, the lie claims to be truth. The creations of matter arise from a mist or false claim, or from

9 mystification, and not from the firmament, or understanding, which God erects between the true and false. In error everything comes from beneath, not from above.

12 All is material myth, instead of the reflection of Spirit.

It may be worth while here to remark that, according

15 to the best scholars, there are clear evidences of two distinct documents in the early part of the book of Genesis. One is called the Elohistic, because

18 the Supreme Being is therein called Elohim. The other document is called the Jehovistic, because Deity therein is always called Jehovah, — or Lord God, as our common

21 version translates it.

Throughout the first chapter of Genesis and in three verses of the second, — in what we understand to be the

24 spiritually scientific account of creation, — it is Elohim (God) who creates. From the fourth verse of chapter two to chapter five, the creator is called

27 Jehovah, or the Lord. The different accounts become more and more closely intertwined to the end of chapter twelve, after which the distinction is not definitely trace-

30 able. In the historic parts of the Old Testament, it is usually Jehovah, peculiarly the divine sovereign of the Hebrew people, who is referred to.

Mist, or false claim

Distinct documents

Jehovah or Elohim

The idolatry which followed this material mythology is
seen in the Phœnician worship of Baal, in the Moabitish
god Chemosh, in the Moloch of the Amorites,
in the Hindoo Vishnu, in the Greek Aphro-
dite, and in a thousand other so-called deities.

Gods of the heathen

It was also found among the Israelites, who constantly
went after "strange gods." They called the Supreme
Being by the national name of Jehovah. In
that name of Jehovah, the true idea of God
seems almost lost. God becomes "a man of war," a
tribal god to be worshipped, rather than Love, the divine
Principle to be lived and loved.

Jehovah a tribal deity

Genesis ii. 7. And the Lord God [Jehovah] formed man
of the dust of the ground, and breathed into his nostrils
the breath of life; and man became a living soul.

Did the divine and infinite Principle become a finite
deity, that He should now be called Jehovah? With
a single command, Mind had made man,
both male and female. How then could a
material organization become the basis of man? How
could the non-intelligent become the medium of Mind,
and error be the enunciator of Truth? Matter is not
the reflection of Spirit, yet God is reflected in all His
creation. Is this addition to His creation real or unreal? Is it the truth, or is it a lie concerning man and
God?

Creation reversed

It must be a lie, for God presently curses the ground.
Could Spirit evolve its opposite, matter, and give matter
ability to sin and suffer? Is Spirit, God, injected into
dust, and eventually ejected at the demand of matter?
Does Spirit enter dust, and lose therein the divine nature

1   and omnipotence? Does Mind, God, enter matter to be-
     come there a mortal sinner, animated by the breath of
3   God? In this narrative, the validity of matter is opposed,
     not the validity of Spirit or Spirit's creations. Man re-
     flects God; *mankind* represents the Adamic race, and is
6   a human, not a divine, creation.

     The following are some of the equivalents of the term
     man in different languages. In the Saxon, *mankind, a*
9   *woman, any one*; in the Welsh, *that which rises*   **Definitions**
     up, — the primary sense being *image, form*; in   **of man**
     the Hebrew, *image, similitude*; in the Icelandic, *mind*.
12   The following translation is from the Icelandic: —

     And God said, Let us make man after our mind and
     our likeness; and God shaped man after His mind; after
15   God's mind shaped He him; and He shaped them male and
     female.

     In the Gospel of John, it is declared that all things were
18   made through the Word of God, "and without Him [the
     logos, or *word*] was not anything made that   **No baneful**
     was made." Everything good or worthy, God   **creation**
21   made. Whatever is valueless or baneful, He did not
     make, — hence its unreality. In the Science of Genesis
     we read that He saw everything which He had made,
24   "and, behold, it was very good." The corporeal senses
     declare otherwise; and if we give the same heed to the
     history of error as to the records of truth, the Scriptural
27   record of sin and death favors the false conclusion of the
     material senses. Sin, sickness, and death must be deemed
     as devoid of reality as they are of good, God.

30   *Genesis* ii. 9. And out of the ground made the Lord God
     [Jehovah] to grow every tree that is pleasant to the sight,

and good for food; the tree of life also, in the midst of the   1
garden, and the tree of knowledge of good and evil.

The previous and more scientific record of creation   3
declares that God made "every plant of the field before it was in the earth." This opposite
**Contradicting
first creation**
declaration, this statement that life issues   6
from matter, contradicts the teaching of the first chapter, — namely, that all Life is God. Belief is less than
understanding. Belief involves theories of material hear-   9
ing, sight, touch, taste, and smell, termed the five senses.
The appetites and passions, sin, sickness, and death,
follow in the train of this error of a belief in intelligent   12
matter.

The first mention of evil is in the legendary Scriptural
text in the second chapter of Genesis. God pronounced   15
**Record of
error**
good all that He created, and the Scriptures
declare that He created all. The "tree of
life" stands for the idea of Truth, and the sword which   18
guards it is the type of divine Science. The "tree of
knowledge" stands for the erroneous doctrine that the
knowledge of evil is as real, hence as God-bestowed, as   21
the knowledge of good. Was evil instituted through God,
Love? Did He create this fruit-bearer of sin in contradiction of the first creation? This second biblical account   24
is a picture of error throughout.

Genesis ii. 15. And the Lord God [Jehovah] took the
man, and put him into the garden of Eden, to dress it and   27
to keep it.

The name Eden, according to Cruden, means *pleasure,
delight*. In this text Eden stands for the mortal, mate-   30

1 rial body. God could not put Mind into matter nor infinite Spirit into finite form to dress it and

3 keep it, — to make it beautiful or to cause it
to live and grow. Man is God's reflection, needing no
cultivation, but ever beautiful and complete.

6 *Genesis* ii. 16, 17. And the Lord God [Jehovah] commanded the man, saying, Of every tree of the garden thou
mayest freely eat: but of the tree of the knowledge of good

9 and evil, thou shalt not eat of it: for in the day that thou
eatest thereof thou shalt surely die.

Here the metaphor represents God, Love, as tempting

12 man, but the Apostle James says: "God cannot be
tempted with evil, neither tempteth He any
man." It is true that a knowledge of evil would

15 make man mortal. It is plain also that material perception, gathered from the corporeal senses, constitutes evil and mortal knowledge. But is it true that God,

18 good, made "the tree of life" to be the tree of death to His
own creation? Has evil the reality of good? Evil is unreal because it is a lie, — false in every statement.

21 *Genesis* ii. 19. And out of the ground the Lord God
[Jehovah] formed every beast of the field, and every fowl
of the air; and brought them unto Adam to see what he

24 would call them: and whatsoever Adam called every living
creature, that was the name thereof.

Here the lie represents God as repeating creation, but

27 doing so materially, not spiritually, and asking a prospective sinner to help Him. Is the
Supreme Being retrograding, and is man giving up his

30 dignity? Was it requisite for the formation of man

that dust should become sentient, when all being is the
reflection of the eternal Mind, and the record declares
that God has already created man, both male and
female? That Adam gave the name and nature of
animals, is solely mythological and material. It cannot be true that man was ordered to create man anew
in partnership with God; this supposition was a dream,
a myth.

Genesis ii. 21, 22. And the Lord God [Jehovah, Yawah]
caused a deep sleep to fall upon Adam, and he slept: and
He took one of his ribs, and closed up the flesh instead
thereof; and the rib, which the Lord God [Jehovah] had
taken from man, made He a woman, and brought her unto
the man.

Here falsity, error, credits Truth, God, with inducing
a sleep or hypnotic state in Adam in order to perform a

Hypnotic surgery surgical operation on him and thereby create
woman. This is the first record of magnet-
ism. Beginning creation with darkness instead of light,
— materially rather than spiritually, — error now simulates the work of Truth, mocking Love and declaring what great things error has done. Beholding the
creations of his own dream and calling them real and
God-given, Adam — *alias* error — gives them names.
Afterwards he is supposed to become the basis of the
creation of woman and of his own kind, calling them
mankind, — that is, a kind of man.

But according to this narrative, surgery was first per-

Mental midwifery formed mentally and without instruments;
and this may be a useful hint to the medical
faculty. Later in human history, when the forbidden

1   fruit was bringing forth fruit of its own kind, there
came a suggestion of change in the *modus operandi*, —

3   that man should be born of woman, not woman again
taken from man. It came about, also, that instruments
were needed to assist the birth of mortals. The first

6   system of suggestive obstetrics has changed. Another
change will come as to the nature and origin of man,
and this revelation will destroy the *dream* of existence,

9   reinstate reality, usher in Science and the glorious fact
of creation, that both man and woman proceed from
God and are His eternal children, belonging to no lesser

12   parent.

    Genesis iii. 1–3. Now the serpent was more subtle than
any beast of the field which the Lord God [Jehovah] had

15   made. And he said unto the woman, Yea, hath God said,
Ye shall not eat of every tree of the garden? And the
woman said unto the serpent, We may eat of the fruit of

18   the trees of the garden: but of the fruit of the tree which is
in the midst of the garden, God hath said, Ye shall not eat
of it, neither shall ye touch it, lest ye die.

21   Whence comes a talking, lying serpent to tempt the
children of divine Love? The serpent enters into the
metaphor only as evil. We have nothing in the

              Mythical

24   animal kingdom which represents the species   *serpent*
described, — a talking serpent, — and should rejoice that
evil, by whatever figure presented, contradicts itself and

27   has neither origin nor support in Truth and good. Seeing
this, we should have faith to fight all claims of evil, because we know that they are worthless and unreal.

30   Adam, the synonym for error, stands for a belief of
material mind. He begins his reign over man some-

what mildly, but he increases in falsehood and his days   1
become shorter. In this development, the immortal, spiritual law of Truth is made manifest   3
as forever opposed to mortal, material sense.

In divine Science, man is sustained by God, the divine
Principle of being. The earth, at God's command, brings   6

forth food for man's use. Knowing this, Jesus
once said, "Take no thought for your life,
what ye shall eat, or what ye shall drink," — presuming   9
not on the prerogative of his creator, but recognizing God,
the Father and Mother of all, as able to feed and clothe
man as He doth the lilies.   12

Genesis iii. 4, 5. And the serpent said unto the woman,
Ye shall not surely die: for God doth know that in the day
ye eat thereof, then your eyes shall be opened; and ye shall   15
be as gods, knowing good and evil.

This myth represents error as always asserting its superiority over truth, giving the lie to divine Science and   18

saying, through the material senses: "I can
open your eyes. I can do what God has not
done for you. Bow down to me and have another god.   21
Only admit that I am real, that sin and sense are more
pleasant to the eyes than spiritual Life, more to be desired than Truth, and I shall know you, and you will be   24
mine." Thus Spirit and flesh war.

The history of error is a dream-narrative. The dream
has no reality, no intelligence, no mind; therefore the   27

dreamer and dream are one, for neither is
true nor real. *First*, this narrative supposes
that something springs from nothing, that matter pre-   30
cedes mind. *Second*, it supposes that mind enters matter,

1   and matter becomes living, substantial, and intelligent.
The order of this allegory — the belief that everything
3   springs from dust instead of from Deity — has been maintained in all the subsequent forms of belief. This is the
error, — that mortal man starts materially, that non-
6   intelligence becomes intelligence, that mind and soul are
both right and wrong.

It is well that the upper portions of the brain represent
9   the higher moral sentiments, as if hope were ever prophe-
sying thus: The human mind will sometime
rise above all material and physical sense, ex-

Higher
hope

12   changing it for spiritual perception, and exchanging human concepts for the divine consciousness. Then man
will recognize his God-given dominion and being.

15   If, in the beginning, man's body originated in non-
intelligent dust, and mind was afterwards put into body
by the creator, why is not this divine order

Biological
inventions

18   still maintained by God in perpetuating the
species? Who will say that minerals, vegetables, and
animals have a propagating property of their own?
21   Who dares to say either that God is in matter or that
matter exists without God? Has man sought out other
creative inventions, and so changed the method of his
24   Maker?

Which institutes Life, — matter or Mind? Does Life
begin with Mind or with matter? Is Life sustained by
27   matter or by Spirit? Certainly not by both, since flesh
wars against Spirit and the corporeal senses can take no
cognizance of Spirit. The mythologic theory of mate-
30   rial life at no point resembles the scientifically Christian
record of man as created by Mind in the image and likeness of God and having dominion over all the earth. Did

God at first create one man unaided, — that is, Adam, —   1
but afterwards require the union of the two sexes in order
to create the rest of the human family? No! God makes   3
and governs all.

All human knowledge and material sense must be
gained from the five corporeal senses. Is this knowledge   6

**Progeny
cursed**

safe, when eating its first fruits brought death?
"In the day that thou eatest thereof thou shalt
surely die," was the prediction in the story under consid-   9
eration. Adam and his progeny were cursed, not blessed;
and this indicates that the divine Spirit, or Father, condemns material man and remands him to dust.   12

Genesis iii. 9, 10. And the Lord God [Jehovah] called
unto Adam, and said unto him, Where art thou? And he
said, I heard Thy voice in the garden, and I was afraid,   15
because I was naked; and I hid myself.

Knowledge and pleasure, evolved through material
sense, produced the immediate fruits of fear and shame.   18

**Shame the
effect of sin**

Ashamed before Truth, error shrank abashed
from the divine voice calling out to the corporeal senses. Its summons may be thus paraphrased: 21
"Where art thou, man? Is Mind in matter? Is Mind
capable of error as well as of truth, of evil as well as of
good, when God is All and He is Mind and there is but   24
one God, hence one Mind?"

Fear was the first manifestation of the error of material sense. Thus error began and will end the dream of   27

**Fear comes
of error**

matter. In the allegory the body had been
naked, and Adam knew it not; but now error
demands that *mind* shall see and feel through matter, the   30
five senses. The first impression material man had of

1   himself was one of nakedness and shame. Had he lost
     man's rich inheritance and God's behest, dominion over
3   all the earth? No! This had never been bestowed on
     Adam.

     Genesis iii. 11, 12. And He said, Who told thee that
6   thou wast naked? Hast thou eaten of the tree, whereof I
     commanded thee that thou shouldst not eat? And the man
     said, The woman whom Thou gavest to be with me, she gave
9   me of the tree, and I did eat.

     Here there is an attempt to trace all human errors
     directly or indirectly to God, or good, as if He were the
12   creator of evil. The allegory shows that the
     snake-talker utters the first voluble lie, which
     beguiles the woman and demoralizes the man. Adam,
15   *alias mortal error*, charges God and woman with his own
     dereliction, saying, "The woman, whom Thou gavest
     me, is responsible." According to this belief, the rib taken
18   from Adam's side has grown into an evil mind, named
     woman, who aids man to make sinners more rapidly than
     he can alone. Is this an help meet for man?
21   Materiality, so obnoxious to God, is already found in the
     rapid deterioration of the bone and flesh which came from
     Adam to form Eve. The belief in material life and in-
24   telligence is growing worse at every step, but error has its
     suppositional day and multiplies until the end thereof.
          Truth, cross-questioning man as to his knowledge of
27   error, finds woman the first to confess her fault. She
     says, "The serpent beguiled me, and I did
     eat;" as much as to say in meek penitence,
30   "Neither man nor God shall father my fault." She has
     already learned that corporeal sense is the serpent. Hence

*The beguiling
first lie*

*False
womanhood*

she is first to abandon the belief in the material origin of   1
man and to discern spiritual creation. This hereafter
enabled woman to be the mother of Jesus and to behold   3
at the sepulchre the risen Saviour, who was soon to manifest the deathless man of God's creating. This enabled
woman to be first to interpret the Scriptures in their true   6
sense, which reveals the spiritual origin of man.

Genesis iii. 14, 15. And the Lord God [Jehovah] said
unto the serpent, . . . I will put enmity between thee and   9
the woman, and between thy seed and her seed; it shall
bruise thy head, and thou shalt bruise his heel.

This prophecy has been fulfilled. The Son of the Virgin-   12
mother unfolded the remedy for Adam, or error; and the

**Spirit and
flesh**

Apostle Paul explains this warfare between the
idea of divine power, which Jesus presented,   15
and mythological material intelligence called *energy* and
opposed to Spirit.

Paul says in his epistle to the Romans: "The carnal   18
mind is enmity against God; for it is not subject to the
law of God, neither indeed can be. So then they that
are in the flesh cannot please God. But ye are not in the   21
flesh, but in the Spirit, if so be that the spirit of God dwell
in you."

There will be greater mental opposition to the spirit-   24
ual, scientific meaning of the Scriptures than there has

**Bruising
sin's head**

ever been since the Christian era began. The
serpent, material sense, will bite the heel of   27
the woman, — will struggle to destroy the spiritual idea
of Love; and the woman, this idea, will bruise the head
of lust. The spiritual idea has given the understanding   30

1   a foothold in Christian Science. The seed of Truth and
the seed of error, of belief and of understanding, — yea,
3   the seed of Spirit and the seed of matter, — are the wheat
and tares which time will separate, the one to be burned,
the other to be garnered into heavenly places.

6   *Genesis* iii. 16. Unto the woman He said, I will greatly
multiply thy sorrow and thy conception: in sorrow thou
shalt bring forth children; and thy desire shall be to thy
9   husband, and he shall rule over thee.

Divine Science deals its chief blow at the supposed material foundations of life and intelligence. It dooms idol-
12   atry. A belief in other gods, other creators,   **Judgment**
and other creations must go down before Chris-   **on error**
tian Science. It unveils the results of sin as shown in
15   sickness and death. When will man pass through the
open gate of Christian Science into the heaven of Soul,
into the heritage of the first born among men? Truth is
18   indeed "the way."

Genesis iii. 17–19. And unto Adam He said, Because
thou hast hearkened unto the voice of thy wife, and hast
21   eaten of the tree of which I commanded thee, saying, Thou
shalt not eat of it: cursed is the ground for thy sake; in
sorrow shalt thou eat of it all the days of thy life: thorns
also and thistles shall it bring forth to thee; and thou shalt
24   eat the herb of the field: in the sweat of thy face shalt thou
eat bread, till thou return unto the ground; for out of it
wast thou taken: for dust thou art, and unto dust shalt
27   thou return.

In the first chapter of Genesis we read: "And God
called the dry land Earth; and the gathering together

of the waters called He Seas." In the Apocalypse it is   1
written: "And I saw a new heaven and a new earth: for

New earth   the first heaven and the first earth were passed   3
and no more   away; and there was no more sea." In St.
sea   John's vision, heaven and earth stand for spiritual ideas, and the sea, as a symbol of tempest-tossed   6
human concepts advancing and receding, is represented
as having passed away. The divine understanding reigns,
is *all*, and there is no other consciousness.   9

The way of error is awful to contemplate. The illusion of sin is without hope or God. If man's spiritual

The fall   gravitation and attraction to one Father, in   12
of error   whom we "live, and move, and have our being," should be lost, and if man should be governed by
corporeality instead of divine Principle, by body instead   15
of by Soul, man would be annihilated. Created by flesh
instead of by Spirit, starting from matter instead of from
God, mortal man would be governed by himself. The   18
blind leading the blind, both would fall.

Passions and appetites must end in pain. They are
"of few days, and full of trouble." Their supposed joys   21
are cheats. Their narrow limits belittle their gratifica-
tions, and hedge about their achievements with thorns.

Mortal mind accepts the erroneous, material concep-   24
tion of life and joy, but the true idea is gained from the

True   immortal side. Through toil, struggle, and sor-
attainment   row, what do mortals attain? They give up   27
their belief in perishable life and happiness; the mortal
and material return to dust, and the immortal is reached.

Genesis iii. 22–24. And the Lord God [Jehovah] said,   30
Behold, the man is become as one of us, to know good

1 and evil: and now, lest he put forth his hand, and take
also of the tree of life, and eat, and live forever; therefore
3 the Lord God [Jehovah] sent him forth from the garden
of Eden, to till the ground from whence he was taken.
So He drove out the man: and He placed at the east
6 of the garden of Eden Cherubims, and a flaming sword
which turned every way, to keep the way of the tree of
life.

9 A knowledge of evil was never the essence of divinity or manhood. In the first chapter of Genesis, evil
has no local habitation nor name. Crea-

Justice and recompense

12 tion is there represented as spiritual, entire,
and good. "Whatsoever a man soweth, that shall he
also reap." Error excludes itself from harmony. Sin
15 is its own punishment. Truth guards the gateway
to harmony. Error tills its own barren soil and buries
itself in the ground, since ground and dust stand for
18 nothingness.

No one can reasonably doubt that the purpose of this
allegory — this second account in Genesis — is to depict
21 the falsity of error and the effects of error.

Inspired interpretation

Subsequent Bible revelation is coordinate
with the Science of creation recorded in the
24 first chapter of Genesis. Inspired writers interpret the
Word spiritually, while the ordinary historian interprets
it literally. Literally taken, the text is made to appear
27 contradictory in some places, and divine Love, which
blessed the earth and gave it to man for a possession, is
represented as changeable. The literal meaning would
30 imply that God withheld from man the opportunity to
reform, lest man should improve it and become better;
but this is not the nature of God, who is Love always, —

Love infinitely wise and altogether lovely, who "seeketh   1
not her own."

Truth should, and does, drive error out of all selfhood.   3
Truth is a two-edged sword, guarding and guiding.

Spiritual gateway   Truth places the cherub wisdom at the gate
of understanding to note the proper guests.   6
Radiant with mercy and justice, the sword of Truth
gleams afar and indicates the infinite distance between
Truth and error, between the material and spiritual, —   9
the unreal and the real.

The sun, giving light and heat to the earth, is a figure
of divine Life and Love, enlightening and sustaining the   12

Contrasted testimony   universe. The "tree of life" is significant of
eternal reality or being. The "tree of knowl-
edge" typifies unreality. The testimony of the serpent is   15
significant of the illusion of error, of the false claims that
misrepresent God, good. Sin, sickness, and death have
no record in the Elohistic introduction of Genesis, in which   18
God creates the heavens, earth, and man. Until that
which contradicts the truth of being enters into the arena,
evil has no history, and evil is brought into view only as   21
the unreal in contradistinction to the real and eternal.

Genesis iv. 1. And Adam knew Eve his wife; and she
conceived, and bare Cain, and said, I have gotten a man   24
from the Lord [Jehovah].

This account is given, not of immortal man, but of mortal man, and of sin which is temporal. As both mortal   27

Erroneous conception   man and sin have a beginning, they must
consequently have an end, while the sinless,
real man is eternal. Eve's declaration, "I have gotten   30
a man from the Lord," supposes God to be the author

1   of sin and sin's progeny. This false sense of existence
is fratricidal. In the words of Jesus, it (evil, devil) is
3   "a murderer from the beginning." Error begins by
reckoning life as separate from Spirit, thus sapping the
foundations of immortality, as if life and immortality
6   were something which matter can both give and take
away.

     What can be the standard of good, of Spirit, of Life,
9   or of Truth, if they produce their opposites, such as evil,
matter, error, and death? God could never
impart an element of evil, and man possesses

Only one
standard

12   nothing which he has not derived from God. How then
has man a basis for wrong-doing? Whence does he
obtain the propensity or power to do evil? Has Spirit
15   resigned to matter the government of the universe?

     The Scriptures declare that God condemned this lie as
to man's origin and character by condemning its symbol,
18   the serpent, to grovel beneath all the beasts
of the field. It is false to say that Truth and
error commingle in creation. In parable and argument,

A type of
falsehood

21   this falsity is exposed by our Master as self-evidently
wrong. Disputing these points with the Pharisees and
arguing for the Science of creation, Jesus said: "Do men
24   gather grapes of thorns?" Paul asked: "What communion hath light with darkness? And what concord
hath Christ with Belial?"

27   The divine origin of Jesus gave him more than human
power to expound the facts of creation, and demonstrate
the one Mind which makes and governs man

Scientific
offspring

30   and the universe. The Science of creation,
so conspicuous in the birth of Jesus, inspired his wisest
and least-understood sayings, and was the basis of his

marvellous demonstrations. Christ is the offspring of   1
Spirit, and spiritual existence shows that Spirit creates
neither a wicked nor a mortal man, lapsing into sin, sick-   3
ness, and death.

In Isaiah we read: "I make peace, and create evil. I
the Lord do all these things;" but the prophet referred to   6

Cleansing upheaval

divine law as stirring up the belief in evil to its
utmost, when bringing it to the surface and reducing it to its common denominator, nothingness. The   9
muddy river-bed must be stirred in order to purify the
stream. In moral chemicalization, when the symptoms
of evil, illusion, are aggravated, we may think in our igno-   12
rance that the Lord hath wrought an evil; but we ought
to know that God's law uncovers so-called sin and its
effects, only that Truth may annihilate all sense of evil   15
and all power to sin.

Science renders "unto Cæsar the things which are
Cæsar's; and unto God the things that are God's." It   18

Allegiance to Spirit

saith to the human sense of sin, sickness, and
death, "God never made you, and you are a
false sense which hath no knowledge of God." The pur-   21
pose of the Hebrew allegory, representing error as assum-
ing a divine character, is to teach mortals never to believe
a lie.   24

Genesis iv. 3, 4. Cain brought of the fruit of the ground
an offering unto the Lord [Jehovah]. And Abel, he also
brought of the firstlings of his flock, and of the fat thereof. 27

Cain is the type of mortal and material man, conceived
in sin and "shapen in iniquity;" he is not the

Spiritual and material

type of Truth and Love. Material in origin   30
and sense, he brings a material offering to God. Abel

1 takes his offering from the firstlings of the flock. A lamb
is a more animate form of existence, and more nearly re-
3 sembles a mind-offering than does Cain's fruit. Jealous
of his brother's gift, Cain seeks Abel's life, instead of making his own gift a higher tribute to the Most High.

6 *Genesis* iv. 4, 5. And the Lord [Jehovah] had respect
unto Abel, and to his offering: but unto Cain, and to his
offering, He had not respect.

9 Had God more respect for the homage bestowed through
a gentle animal than for the worship expressed by Cain's
fruit? No; but the lamb was a more spiritual type of
12 even the human concept of Love than the herbs of the
ground could be.

Genesis iv. 8. Cain rose up against Abel his brother, and
15 slew him.

The erroneous belief that life, substance, and intelligence can be material ruptures the life and brotherhood
18 of man at the very outset.

Genesis iv. 9. And the Lord [Jehovah] said unto Cain,
Where is Abel thy brother? And he said, I know not: Am
21 I my brother's keeper?

Here the serpentine lie invents new forms. At first it
usurps divine power. It is supposed to say **Brotherhood**
24 in the first instance, "Ye shall be as gods." **repudiated**
Now it repudiates even the human duty of man towards
his brother.

27 *Genesis* iv. 10, 11. And He [Jehovah] said, . . . The
voice of thy brother's blood crieth unto Me from the ground.
And now art thou cursed from the earth.

The belief of life in matter sins at every step. It in-   1
curs divine displeasure, and it would kill Jesus that it

Murder brings its curse   might be rid of troublesome Truth. Material   3
beliefs would slay the spiritual idea when-
ever and wherever it appears. Though error hides
behind a lie and excuses guilt, error cannot forever be   6
concealed. Truth, through her eternal laws, unveils
error. Truth causes sin to betray itself, and sets upon
error the mark of the beast. Even the disposition to   9
excuse guilt or to conceal it is punished. The avoidance
of justice and the denial of truth tend to perpetuate sin,
invoke crime, jeopardize self-control, and mock divine   12
mercy.

Genesis iv. 15. And the Lord [Jehovah] said unto him,
Therefore whosoever slayeth Cain, vengeance shall be taken   15
on him sevenfold. And the Lord [Jehovah] set a mark
upon Cain, lest any finding him should kill him.

"They that take the sword shall perish with the   18
sword." Let Truth uncover and destroy error in God's

Retribution and remorse   own way, and let human justice pattern the
divine. Sin will receive its full penalty, both   21
for what it is and for what it does. Justice marks
the sinner, and teaches mortals not to remove the
waymarks of God. To envy's own hell, justice con-   24
signs the lie which, to advance itself, breaks God's
commandments.

Genesis iv. 16. And Cain went out from the presence of   27
the Lord [Jehovah], and dwelt in the land of Nod.

The sinful misconception of Life as something less

1 than God, having no truth to support it, falls back upon
itself. This error, after reaching the climax of suffering,

3 yields to Truth and returns to dust; but it
is only mortal man and not the real man,
who dies. The image of Spirit cannot be effaced, since it

6 is the idea of Truth and changes not, but becomes more
beautifully apparent at error's demise.

Climax of
suffering

    In divine Science, the material man is shut out from

9 the presence of God. The five corporeal senses cannot
take cognizance of Spirit. They cannot come
into His presence, and must dwell in dream-

12 land, until mortals arrive at the understanding that material life, with all its sin, sickness, and death, is an illusion, against which divine Science is engaged in a warfare

15 of extermination. The great verities of existence are
never excluded by falsity.

Dwelling in
dreamland

    All error proceeds from the evidence before the mate-

18 rial senses. If man is material and originates in an
egg, who shall say that he is not primarily
dust? May not Darwin be right in think-

21 ing that apehood preceded mortal manhood? Minerals
and vegetables are found, according to divine Science,
to be the creations of erroneous thought, not of matter.

Man springs
from Mind

24 Did man, whom God created with a word, originate
in an egg? When Spirit made all, did it leave aught
for matter to create? Ideas of Truth alone are reflected

27 in the myriad manifestations of Life, and thus it is
seen that man springs solely from Mind. The belief
that matter supports life would make Life, or God,

30 mortal.

    The text, "In the day that the Lord God [Jehovah
God] made the earth and the heavens," introduces the

record of a material creation which followed the spiritual,   1
— a creation so wholly apart from God's, that Spirit
had no participation in it. In God's creation   3

Material inception

ideas became productive, obedient to Mind.
There was no rain and "not a man to till the ground."
Mind, instead of matter, being the producer, Life was   6
self-sustained. Birth, decay, and death arise from the
material sense of things, not from the spiritual, for in
the latter Life consisteth not of the things which a man   9
eateth. Matter cannot change the eternal fact that
man exists because God exists. Nothing is new to the
infinite Mind.   12

In Science, Mind neither produces matter nor does
matter produce mind. No mortal mind has the might

First evil suggestion

or right or wisdom to create or to destroy.   15
All is under the control of the one Mind,
even God. The first statement about evil, — the first
suggestion of more than the one Mind, — is in the fable   18
of the serpent. The facts of creation, as previously recorded, include nothing of the kind.

The serpent is supposed to say, "Ye shall be as gods,"   21
but these gods must be evolved from materiality and be

Material personality

the very antipodes of immortal and spiritual
being. Man is the likeness of Spirit, but a   24
material personality is not this likeness. Therefore man,
in this allegory, is neither a lesser god nor the image and
likeness of the one God.   27

Material, erroneous belief reverses understanding and
truth. It declares mind to be in and of matter, so-called
mortal life to be Life, infinity to enter man's nostrils   30
so that matter becomes spiritual. Error begins with
corporeality as the producer instead of divine Prin-

1 ciple, and explains Deity through mortal and finite conceptions.

3 "Behold, the man is become as one of us." This could
not be the utterance of Truth or Science, for according
to the record, material man was fast degenerating and
6 never had been divinely conceived.

The condemnation of mortals to till the ground means
this, — that mortals should so improve material belief
9 by thought tending spiritually upward as to *Mental tillage*
destroy materiality. Man, created by God,
was given dominion over the whole earth. The notion
12 of a material universe is utterly opposed to the theory
of man as evolved from Mind. Such fundamental errors
send falsity into all human doctrines and conclusions,
15 and do not accord infinity to Deity. Error tills the
whole ground in this material theory, which is entirely a
false view, destructive to existence and happiness. Out-
18 side of Christian Science all is vague and hypothetical, the
opposite of Truth; yet this opposite, in its false view of
God and man, impudently demands a blessing.

21 The translators of this record of scientific creation
entertained a false sense of being. They believed in
the existence of matter, its propagation and *Erroneous standpoint*
24 power. From that standpoint of error, they
could not apprehend the nature and operation of Spirit.
Hence the seeming contradiction in that Scripture, which
27 is so glorious in its spiritual signification. Truth has
but one reply to all error, — to sin, sickness, and death:
"Dust [nothingness] thou art, and unto dust [nothingness]
30 shalt thou return."

"As in Adam [error] all die, even so in Christ [Truth]
shall all be made alive." The mortality of man is a

myth, for man is immortal. The false belief that spirit is

now submerged in matter, at some future time to be eman-

Mortality mythical

cipated from it, — this belief alone is mortal.

Spirit, God, never germinates, but is "the same

yesterday, and to-day, and forever." If Mind, God, cre-

ates error, that error must exist in the divine Mind, and

this assumption of error would dethrone the perfection

of Deity.

Is Christian Science contradictory? Is the divine

Principle of creation misstated? Has God no Science to

No truth from a material basis

declare Mind, while matter is governed by un-

erring intelligence? "There went up a mist

from the earth." This represents error as

starting from an idea of good on a material basis. It

supposes God and man to be manifested only through

the corporeal senses, although the material senses can

take no cognizance of Spirit or the spiritual idea.

Genesis and the Apocalypse seem more obscure than

other portions of the Scripture, because they cannot

possibly be interpreted from a material standpoint. To

the author, they are transparent, for they contain the deep

divinity of the Bible.

Christian Science is dawning upon a material age.

The great spiritual facts of being, like rays of light, shine

Dawning of spiritual facts

in the darkness, though the darkness, com-

prehending them not, may deny their reality.

The proof that the system stated in this book is Chris-

tianly scientific resides in the good this system accom-

plishes, for it cures on a divine demonstrable Principle

which all may understand.

If mathematics should present a thousand different

examples of one rule, the proving of one example would

authenticate all the others. A simple statement of Christian Science, if demonstrated by healing, contains the
proof of all here said of Christian Science. If
one of the statements in this book is true, every
one must be true, for not one departs from the stated system and rule. You can prove for yourself, dear reader,
the Science of healing, and so ascertain if the author has
given you the correct interpretation of Scripture.

Proof given
in healing

The late Louis Agassiz, by his microscopic examination
of a vulture's ovum, strengthens the thinker's conclusions
as to the scientific theory of creation. Agassiz
was able to see in the egg the earth's atmosphere, the gathering clouds, the moon and stars, while the
germinating speck of so-called embryonic life seemed a
small sun. In its history of mortality, Darwin's theory
of evolution from a material basis is more consistent than
most theories. Briefly, this is Darwin's theory, — that
Mind produces its opposite, matter, and endues matter
with power to recreate the universe, including man. Material evolution implies that the great First Cause must
become material, and afterwards must either return to
Mind or go down into dust and nothingness.

Embryonic
evolution

The Scriptures are very sacred. Our aim must be to
have them understood spiritually, for only by this understanding can truth be gained. The true theory of the universe, including man, is not in
material history but in spiritual development.
Inspired thought relinquishes a material, sensual, and
mortal theory of the universe, and adopts the spiritual and
immortal.

True theory
of the
universe

It is this spiritual perception of Scripture, which lifts
humanity out of disease and death and inspires faith.

Scriptural
perception

"The Spirit and the bride say, Come! . . . and whoso-   1
ever will, let him take the water of life freely." Christian
Science separates error from truth, and breathes   3
through the sacred pages the spiritual sense of
life, substance, and intelligence. In this Science, we discover man in the image and likeness of God. We see that   6
man has never lost his spiritual estate and his eternal
harmony.

How little light or heat reach our earth when clouds   9
cover the sun's face! So Christian Science can be seen
only as the clouds of corporeal sense roll away.

The clouds
dissolving

Earth has little light or joy for mortals before   12
Life is spiritually learned. Every agony of mortal error
helps error to destroy error, and so aids the apprehension
of immortal Truth. This is the new birth going on   15
hourly, by which men may entertain angels, the true
ideas of God, the spiritual sense of being.

Speaking of the origin of mortals, a famous naturalist   18
says: "It is very possible that many general statements
now current, about birth and generation, will

Prediction of
a naturalist

be changed with the progress of information."   21
Had the naturalist, through his tireless researches, gained
the diviner side in Christian Science, — so far apart from
his material sense of animal growth and organization, —   24
he would have blessed the human race more abundantly.

Natural history is richly endowed by the labors and
genius of great men. Modern discoveries have brought   27
to light important facts in regard to so-called

Methods of
reproduction

embryonic life. Agassiz declares ("Methods
of Study in Natural History," page 275): "Certain ani-   30
mals, besides the ordinary process of generation, also
increase their numbers naturally and constantly by self-

division." This discovery is corroborative of the Science
of Mind, for this discovery shows that the multiplication
of certain animals takes place apart from sexual conditions. The supposition that life germinates in eggs and
must decay after it has grown to maturity, if not before,
is shown by divine metaphysics to be a mistake, — a
blunder which will finally give place to higher theories
and demonstrations.

Creatures of lower forms of organism are supposed
to have, as classes, three different methods of reproduction and to multiply their species sometimes
through eggs, sometimes through buds, and
sometimes through self-division. According to recent
lore, successive generations do not begin with the *birth* of
new individuals, or personalities, but with the formation
of the nucleus, or egg, from which one or more individualities subsequently emerge; and we must therefore look
upon the simple ovum as the germ, the starting-point, of
the most complicated corporeal structures, including those
which we call human. Here these material researches
culminate in such vague hypotheses as must necessarily
attend false systems, which rely upon physics and are devoid of metaphysics.

The three
processes

In one instance a celebrated naturalist, Agassiz, dis-
covers the pathway leading to divine Science, and beards
the lion of materialism in its den. At that
point, however, even this great observer mistakes nature, forsakes Spirit as the divine origin of
creative Truth, and allows matter and material law to
usurp the prerogatives of omnipotence. He absolutely
drops from his summit, coming down to a belief in the
material origin of man, for he virtually affirms that

Deference to
material law

the germ of humanity is in a circumscribed and non-intelligent egg.

If this be so, whence cometh Life, or Mind, to the human race? Matter surely does not possess Mind.

Deep-reaching
interrogations

God is the Life, or intelligence, which forms and preserves the individuality and identity of animals as well as of men. God cannot become finite, and be limited within material bounds. Spirit cannot become matter, nor can Spirit be developed through its opposite. Of what avail is it to investigate what is miscalled material life, which ends, even as it begins, in nameless nothingness? The true sense of being and its eternal perfection should appear now, even as it will hereafter.

Error of thought is reflected in error of action. The continual contemplation of existence as material and corporeal — as beginning and ending, and with

Stages of
existence

birth, decay, and dissolution as its component stages — hides the true and spiritual Life, and causes our standard to trail in the dust. If Life has any starting-point whatsoever, then the great I AM is a myth. If Life is God, as the Scriptures imply, then Life is not embryonic, it is infinite. An egg is an impossible enclosure for Deity.

Embryology supplies no instance of one species producing its opposite. A serpent never begets a bird, nor does a lion bring forth a lamb. Amalgamation is deemed monstrous and is seldom fruitful, but it is not so hideous and absurd as the supposition that Spirit — the pure and holy, the immutable and immortal — can originate the impure and mortal and dwell in it. As Christian Science repudiates self-evident impossibilities, the material senses

1   must father these absurdities, for both the material senses
and their reports are unnatural, impossible, and unreal.

3   Either Mind produces, or it is produced. If Mind is
first, it cannot produce its opposite in quality and quantity,
called matter. If matter is first, it cannot pro-

6   duce Mind. Like produces like. In natural
history, the bird is not the product of a beast. In spiritual
history, matter is not the progenitor of Mind.

9   One distinguished naturalist argues that mortals spring
from eggs and in races. Mr. Darwin admits this, but he
adds that mankind has ascended through all

12   the lower grades of existence. Evolution describes the gradations of human belief, but it does not
acknowledge the method of divine Mind, nor see that ma-

15   terial methods are impossible in divine Science and that
all Science is of God, not of man.

Naturalists ask: "What can there be, of a material

18   nature, transmitted through these bodies called eggs, —
themselves composed of the simplest material
elements, — by which all peculiarities of an-

21   cestry, belonging to either sex, are brought down from
generation to generation?" The question of the naturalist amounts to this: How can matter originate or trans-

24   mit mind? We answer that it cannot. Darkness and
doubt encompass thought, so long as it bases creation on
materiality. From a material standpoint, "Canst thou

27   by searching find out God?" All must be Mind, or
else all must be matter. Neither can produce the other.
Mind is immortal; but error declares that the material

30   seed must decay in order to propagate its species, and
the resulting germ is doomed to the same routine.

The ancient and hypothetical question, Which is first,

the egg or the bird? is answered, if the egg produces the parent. But we cannot stop here. Another question

Causation not in matter

follows: Who or what produces the parent of the egg? That the earth was hatched from the "egg of night" was once an accepted theory. Heathen philosophy, modern geology, and all other material hypotheses deal with causation as contingent on matter and as necessarily apparent to the corporeal senses, even where the proof requisite to sustain this assumption is undiscovered. Mortal theories make friends of sin, sickness, and death; whereas the spiritual scientific facts of existence include no member of this dolorous and fatal triad.

Human experience in mortal life, which starts from an egg, corresponds with that of Job, when he says, "Man

Emergence of mortals

that is born of a woman is of few days, and full of trouble." Mortals must emerge from this notion of material life as all-in-all. They must peck open their shells with Christian Science, and look outward and upward. But thought, loosened from a material basis but not yet instructed by Science, may become wild with freedom and so be self-contradictory.

From a material source flows no remedy for sorrow, sin, and death, for the redeeming power, from the ills

Persistence of species

they occasion, is not in egg nor in dust. The blending tints of leaf and flower show the order of matter to be the order of mortal mind. The intermixture of different species, urged to its utmost limits, results in a return to the original species. Thus it is learned that matter is a manifestation of mortal mind, and that matter always surrenders its claims when the perfect and eternal Mind is understood.

Naturalists describe the origin of mortal and material

1 existence in the various forms of embryology, and accompany their descriptions with important observations,
3 which should awaken thought to a higher and
purer contemplation of man's origin. This
clearer consciousness must precede an under-
6 standing of the harmony of being. Mortal thought must
obtain a better basis, get nearer the truth of being, or
health will never be universal, and harmony will never
9 become the standard of man.

Better basis
than
embryology

One of our ablest naturalists has said: "We have no
right to assume that individuals have grown or been
12 formed under circumstances which made material conditions essential to their maintenance and reproduction,
or important to their origin and first introduction."
15 Why, then, is the naturalist's basis so materialistic,
and why are his deductions generally material?

Adam was created before Eve. In this instance, it is
18 seen that the maternal egg never brought forth Adam.
Eve was formed from Adam's rib, not from a
fœtal ovum. Whatever theory may be adopted
21 by general mortal thought to account for human origin,
that theory is sure to become the signal for the appearance of its method in finite forms and operations. If con-
24 sentaneous human belief agrees upon an ovum as the
point of emergence for the human race, this potent belief
will immediately supersede the more ancient supersti-
27 tion about the creation from dust or from the rib of our
primeval father.

All nativity
in thought

You may say that mortals are formed before they
30 think or know aught of their origin, and you
may also ask how belief can affect a result
which precedes the development of that belief. It can

Being is
immortal

only be replied, that Christian Science reveals what "eye
hath not seen," — even the cause of all that exists, — for
the universe, inclusive of man, is as eternal as God, who
is its divine immortal Principle. There is no such thing
as mortality, nor are there properly any mortal beings,
because being is immortal, like Deity, — or, rather, being
and Deity are inseparable.

Error is always error. It is *no thing*. Any statement
of life, following from a misconception of life, is errone-

**Our conscious
development**

ous, because it is destitute of any knowledge
of the so-called selfhood of life, destitute of
any knowledge of its origin or existence. The mortal
is unconscious of his fœtal and infantile existence; but
as he grows up into another false claim, that of self-con-
scious matter, he learns to say, "I am somebody; but
who made me?" Error replies, "God made you." The
first effort of error has been and is to impute to God the
creation of whatever is sinful and mortal; but infinite
Mind sets at naught such a mistaken belief.

Jesus defined this opposite of God and His creation
better than we can, when he said, "He is a liar, and the

**Mendacity
of error**

father of it." Jesus also said, "Have not I
chosen you twelve, and one of you is a devil?"
This he said of Judas, one of Adam's race. Jesus never
intimated that God made a devil, but he did say, "Ye
are of your father, the devil." All these sayings were to
show that mind in matter is the author of itself, and is
simply a falsity and illusion.

It is the general belief that the lower animals are less

**Ailments
of animals**

sickly than those possessing higher organizations, especially those of the human form.
This would indicate that there is less disease in propor-

1

3

6

9

12

15

18

21

24

27

30

1 tion as the force of mortal mind is less pungent or sensitive, and that health attends the absence of mortal mind.
3 A fair conclusion from this might be, that it is the human
belief, and not the divine arbitrament, which brings the
physical organism under the yoke of disease.
6 An inquirer once said to the discoverer of Christian
Science: "I like your explanations of truth, but I do
not comprehend what you say about error."

Ignorance the
sign of error

9 This is the nature of error. The mark of ignorance is on its forehead, for it neither understands nor
can be understood. Error would have itself received as
12 mind, as if it were as real and God-created as truth; but
Christian Science attributes to error neither entity nor
power, because error is neither mind nor the outcome of
15 Mind.

Searching for the origin of man, who is the reflection
of God, is like inquiring into the origin of God, the self-
18 existent and eternal. Only impotent error
would seek to unite Spirit with matter, good
with evil, immortality with mortality, and call this

The origin
of divinity

21 sham unity *man,* as if man were the offspring of both
Mind and matter, of both Deity and humanity. Creation rests on a spiritual basis. We lose our standard of
24 perfection and set aside the proper conception of Deity,
when we admit that the perfect is the author of aught
that can become imperfect, that God bestows the power
27 to sin, or that Truth confers the ability to err. Our
great example, Jesus, could restore the individualized
manifestation of existence, which seemed to vanish in
30 death. Knowing that God was the Life of man, Jesus
was able to present himself unchanged after the crucifixion. Truth fosters the idea of Truth, and not the be-

lief in illusion or error. That which is real, is sustained   1
by Spirit.

Vertebrata, articulata, mollusca, and radiata are mor-   3
tal and material concepts classified, and are supposed to

possess life and mind. These false beliefs
will disappear, when the radiation of Spirit   6
destroys forever all belief in intelligent matter. Then
will the new heaven and new earth appear, for the former things will have passed away.   9

Mortal belief infolds the conditions of sin. Mortal
belief dies to live again in renewed forms, only to go out

at last forever; for life everlasting is not to be   12
gained by dying. Christian Science may ab-
sorb the attention of sage and philosopher, but
the Christian alone can fathom it. It is made known   15
most fully to him who understands best the divine Life.
Did the origin and the enlightenment of the race come
from the deep sleep which fell upon Adam? Sleep is   18
darkness, but God's creative mandate was, "Let there be
light." In sleep, cause and effect are mere illusions.
They seem to be something, but are not. Oblivion and   21
dreams, not realities, come with sleep. Even so goes on
the Adam-belief, of which mortal and material life is the
dream.   24

Ontology receives less attention than physiology. Why?

Because mortal mind must waken to spiritual
life before it cares to solve the problem of   27
being, hence the author's experience; but when
that awakening comes, existence will be on a new standpoint.   30

It is related that a father plunged his infant babe, only
a few hours old, into the water for several minutes, and

1   repeated this operation daily, until the child could remain
     under water twenty minutes, moving and playing with-
3   out harm, like a fish. Parents should remember this,
     and learn how to develop their children properly on dry
     land.

6   Mind controls the birth-throes in the lower realms of
     nature, where parturition is without suffering. Vege-
     tables, minerals, and many animals suffer no   **The curse**
9   pain in multiplying; but human propagation   **removed**
     has its suffering because it is a false belief. Christian Sci-
     ence reveals harmony as proportionately increasing as the
12   line of creation rises towards spiritual man, — towards
     enlarged understanding and intelligence; but in the line
     of the corporeal senses, the less a mortal knows of sin,
15   disease, and mortality, the better for him, — the less pain
     and sorrow are his. When the mist of mortal mind evap-
     orates, the curse will be removed which says to woman,
18   "In sorrow thou shalt bring forth children." Divine
     Science rolls back the clouds of error with the light of
     Truth, and lifts the curtain on man as never born and as
21   never dying, but as coexistent with his creator.

         Popular theology takes up the history of man as if he
     began materially right, but immediately fell into mental
24   sin; whereas revealed religion proclaims the Science of
     Mind and its formations as being in accordance with
     the first chapter of the Old Testament, when God, Mind,
27   spake and it was done.

Chapter 16

The Apocalypse

Blessed is he that readeth,
and they that hear the words of this prophecy,
and keep those things which are written therein:
for the time is at hand. — REVELATION.

Great is the Lord,
and greatly to be praised in the city of our God,
in the mountain of His holiness. — PSALMS.

S t. John writes, in the tenth chapter of his book of   1
Revelation: —

And I saw another mighty angel come down from heaven,   3
clothed with a cloud: and a rainbow was upon his head, and
his face was as it were the sun, and his feet as pillars of
fire: and he had in his hand a little book open: and he   6
set his right foot upon the sea, and his left foot on the
earth.

This angel or message which comes from God, clothed   9
with a cloud, prefigures divine Science. To mortal sense
Science seems at first obscure, abstract, and

The new
Evangel

dark; but a bright promise crowns its brow.   12
When understood, it is Truth's prism and praise. When
you look it fairly in the face, you can heal by its means,
and it has for you a light above the sun, for God "is the   15
light thereof." Its feet are pillars of fire, foundations
of Truth and Love. It brings the baptism of the Holy
Ghost, whose flames of Truth were prophetically de-   18
scribed by John the Baptist as consuming error.

1 This angel had in his hand "a little book," open for
all to read and understand. Did this same book contain
3 the revelation of divine Science, the "right
foot" or dominant power of which was upon
the sea, — upon elementary, latent error, the source of
6 all error's visible forms? The angel's left foot was upon
the earth; that is, a secondary power was exercised upon
visible error and audible sin. The "still, small voice"
9 of scientific thought reaches over continent and ocean
to the globe's remotest bound. The inaudible voice of
Truth is, to the human mind, "as when a lion roareth."
12 It is heard in the desert and in dark places of fear. It
arouses the "seven thunders" of evil, and stirs their latent
forces to utter the full diapason of secret tones. Then is
15 the power of Truth demonstrated, — made manifest in
the destruction of error. Then will a voice from harmony
cry: "Go and take the little book. . . . Take it, and eat
18 it up; and it shall make thy belly bitter, but it shall be in
thy mouth sweet as honey." Mortals, obey the heavenly
evangel. Take divine Science. Read this book from
21 beginning to end. Study it, ponder it. It will be indeed
sweet at its first taste, when it heals you; but murmur not
over Truth, if you find its digestion bitter. When you
24 approach nearer and nearer to this divine Principle, when
you eat the divine body of this Principle, — thus partaking of the nature, or primal elements, of Truth and Love,
27 — do not be surprised nor discontented because you must
share the hemlock cup and eat the bitter herbs; for the
Israelites of old at the Paschal meal thus prefigured this
30 perilous passage out of bondage into the El Dorado of faith
and hope.

The twelfth chapter of the Apocalypse, or Revela-

Truth's volume

tion of St. John, has a special suggestiveness in connec-   1
tion with the nineteenth century. In the opening of the
sixth seal, typical of six thousand years since   3
Adam, the distinctive feature has reference
to the present age.

Revelation xii. 1. And there appeared a great wonder in   6
heaven; a woman clothed with the sun, and the moon
under her feet, and upon her head a crown of twelve
stars.   9

Heaven represents harmony, and divine Science interprets the Principle of heavenly harmony. The great
miracle, to human sense, is divine Love, and   12
the grand necessity of existence is to gain the
true idea of what constitutes the kingdom of
heaven in man. This goal is never reached while we   15
hate our neighbor or entertain a false estimate of anyone whom God has appointed to voice His Word. Again,
without a correct sense of its highest visible idea, we can   18
never understand the divine Principle. The botanist must
know the genus and species of a plant in order to classify
it correctly. As it is with things, so is it with persons.   21
Abuse of the motives and religion of St. Paul hid from
view the apostle's character, which made him equal to

his great mission. Persecution of all who have   24
spoken something new and better of God has
not only obscured the light of the ages, but has been fatal
to the persecutors. Why? Because it has hid from   27
them the true idea which has been presented. To misunderstand Paul, was to be ignorant of the divine idea he
taught. Ignorance of the divine idea betrays at once a   30
greater ignorance of the divine Principle of the idea — igno-

1   rance of Truth and Love. The understanding of Truth
and Love, the Principle which works out the ends of eternal
3   good and destroys both faith in evil and the practice of
evil, leads to the discernment of the divine idea.

Agassiz, through his microscope, saw the sun in an
6   egg at a point of so-called embryonic life. Because of
his more spiritual vision, St. John saw an   **Espousals**
"angel standing in the sun." The Revelator   **supernal**
9   beheld the spiritual idea from the mount of vision.
Purity was the symbol of Life and Love. The Revelator
saw also the spiritual ideal as a woman clothed in light, a
12   bride coming down from heaven, wedded to the Lamb
of Love. To John, "the bride" and "the Lamb" represented the correlation of divine Principle and spiritual idea,
15   God and His Christ, bringing harmony to earth.

John saw the human and divine coincidence, shown in
the man Jesus, as divinity embracing humanity in Life
18   and its demonstration, — reducing to human   **Divinity and**
perception and understanding the Life which   **humanity**
is God. In divine revelation, material and corporeal self-
21   hood disappear, and the spiritual idea is understood.

The woman in the Apocalypse symbolizes generic man,
the spiritual idea of God; she illustrates the coincidence
24   of God and man as the divine Principle and   **Spiritual**
divine idea. The Revelator symbolizes Spirit   **sunlight**
by the sun. The spiritual idea is clad with the radiance
27   of spiritual Truth, and matter is put under her feet. The
light portrayed is really neither solar nor lunar, but spiritual Life, which is "the light of men." In the first chapter
30   of the Fourth Gospel it is written, "There was a man sent
from God . . . to bear witness of that Light."

John the Baptist prophesied the coming of the im-

maculate Jesus, and John saw in those days the spiritual   1
idea as the Messiah, who would baptize with the Holy

Spiritual idea revealed

Ghost, — divine Science. As Elias presented   3
the idea of the fatherhood of God, which Jesus
afterwards manifested, so the Revelator completed this
figure with woman, typifying the spiritual idea of God's   6
motherhood. The moon is under her feet. This idea
reveals the universe as secondary and tributary to Spirit,
from which the universe borrows its reflected light, sub-   9
stance, life, and intelligence.

The spiritual idea is crowned with twelve stars. The
twelve tribes of Israel with all mortals, — separated by   12

Spiritual idea crowned

belief from man's divine origin and the true
idea, — will through much tribulation yield to
the activities of the divine Principle of man in the har-   15
mony of Science. These are the stars in the crown of
rejoicing. They are the lamps in the spiritual heavens
of the age, which show the workings of the spiritual idea   18
by healing the sick and the sinning, and by manifesting
the light which shines "unto the perfect day" as the night
of materialism wanes.   21

Revelation xii. 2. And she being with child cried, travail-
ing in birth, and pained to be delivered.

Also the spiritual idea is typified by a woman in trav-   24
ail, waiting to be delivered of her sweet promise, but re-

Travail and joy

membering no more her sorrow for joy that
the birth goes on; for great is the idea, and the   27
travail portentous.

Revelation xii. 3. And there appeared another wonder in
heaven; and behold a great red dragon, having seven heads   30
and ten horns, and seven crowns upon his heads.

1   Human sense may well marvel at discord, while, to a
diviner sense, harmony is the real and discord the unreal.

3   We may well be astonished at sin, sickness, and
death. We may well be perplexed at human
fear; and still more astounded at hatred, which lifts

6   its hydra head, showing its horns in the many inventions
of evil. But why should we stand aghast at nothingness?
The great red dragon symbolizes a lie, — the belief

9   that substance, life, and intelligence can be material.
This dragon stands for the sum total of human error.
The ten horns of the dragon typify the belief that mat-

12 ter has power of its own, and that by means of an
evil mind in matter the Ten Commandments can be
broken.

15   The Revelator lifts the veil from this embodiment of
all evil, and beholds its awful character; but he also
sees the nothingness of evil and the allness of

18 God. The Revelator sees that old serpent,
whose name is devil or evil, holding untiring watch, that
he may bite the heel of truth and seemingly impede the

21 offspring of the spiritual idea, which is prolific in health,
holiness, and immortality.

Revelation xii. 4. And his tail drew the third part of the

24 stars of heaven, and did cast them to the earth: and the
dragon stood before the woman which was ready to be
delivered, for to devour her child as soon as it was born.

27   The serpentine form stands for subtlety, winding its
way amidst all evil, but doing this in the name of good.
Its sting is spoken of by Paul, when he refers

30 to "spiritual wickedness in high places." It
is the animal instinct in mortals, which would impel

Marginal headings:

The dragon as a type

The sting of the serpent

Animal tendency

them to devour each other and cast out devils through   1
Beelzebub.

As of old, evil still charges the spiritual idea with error's   3
own nature and methods. This malicious animal instinct, of which the dragon is the type, incites mortals to
kill morally and physically even their fellow-mortals, and   6
worse still, to charge the innocent with the crime. This
last infirmity of sin will sink its perpetrator into a night
without a star.   9

The author is convinced that the accusations against
Jesus of Nazareth and even his crucifixion were instigated

**Malicious
barbarity**

by the criminal instinct here described. The   12
Revelator speaks of Jesus as the Lamb of God
and of the dragon as warring against innocence. Since Jesus
must have been tempted in all points, he, the immaculate,   15
met and conquered sin in every form. The brutal barbarity of his foes could emanate from no source except the
highest degree of human depravity. Jesus *opened not*   18
his mouth. Until the majesty of Truth should be demonstrated in divine Science, the spiritual idea was arraigned
before the tribunal of so-called mortal mind, which was   21
unloosed in order that the false claim of mind in matter
might uncover its own crime of defying immortal Mind.

From Genesis to the Apocalypse, sin, sickness, and   24
death, envy, hatred, and revenge, — all evil, — are typi-

**Doom of
the dragon**

fied by a serpent, or animal subtlety. Jesus
said, quoting a line from the Psalms, "They   27
hated me without a cause." The serpent is perpetually
close upon the heel of harmony. From the beginning
to the end, the serpent pursues with hatred the spiritual   30
idea. In Genesis, this allegorical, talking serpent typifies mortal mind, "more subtle than any beast of the

1   field." In the Apocalypse, when nearing its doom, this
evil increases and becomes the great red dragon, swollen
3   with sin, inflamed with war against spirituality, and ripe
for destruction. It is full of lust and hate, loathing the
brightness of divine glory.

6   *Revelation* xii. 5. And she brought forth a man child,
who was to rule all nations with a rod of iron: and her
child was caught up unto God, and to His throne.

9   Led on by the grossest element of mortal mind, Herod
decreed the death of every male child in order that the
man Jesus, the masculine representative of the   **The conflict**
12   spiritual idea, might never hold sway and de-   **with purity**
prive Herod of his crown. The impersonation of the
spiritual idea had a brief history in the earthly life of our
15   Master; but "of his kingdom there shall be no end,"
for Christ, God's idea, will eventually rule all nations
and peoples — imperatively, absolutely, finally — with di-
18   vine Science. This immaculate idea, represented first
by man and, according to the Revelator, last by woman,
will baptize with fire; and the fiery baptism will burn up
21   the chaff of error with the fervent heat of Truth and Love,
melting and purifying even the gold of human character.
After the stars sang together and all was primeval har-
24   mony, the material lie made war upon the spiritual idea;
but this only impelled the idea to rise to the zenith of
demonstration, destroying sin, sickness, and death, and
27   to be caught up unto God, — to be found in its divine
Principle.

Revelation xii. 6. And the woman fled into the wilder-
30   ness, where she hath a place prepared of God.

As the children of Israel were guided triumphantly
through the Red Sea, the dark ebbing and flowing tides
of human fear, — as they were led through the
wilderness, walking wearily through the great
desert of human hopes, and anticipating the promised
joy, — so shall the spiritual idea guide all right desires
in their passage from sense to Soul, from a material sense
of existence to the spiritual, up to the glory prepared for
them who love God. Stately Science pauses not, but
moves before them, a pillar of cloud by day and of fire
by night, leading to divine heights.

If we remember the beautiful description which Sir
Walter Scott puts into the mouth of Rebecca the Jewess
in the story of Ivanhoe, —

> When Israel, of the Lord beloved,
> Out of the land of bondage came,
> Her fathers' God before her moved,
> An awful guide, in smoke and flame, —

we may also offer the prayer which concludes the same
hymn, —

> And oh, when stoops on Judah's path
> In shade and storm the frequent night,
> Be Thou, longsuffering, slow to wrath,
> A burning and a shining light!

Revelation xii. 7, 8. And there was war in heaven:
Michael and his angels fought against the dragon; and the
dragon fought, and his angels, and prevailed not; neither
was their place found any more in heaven.

The Old Testament assigns to the angels, God's divine
messages, different offices. Michael's characteristic is spiritual strength. He leads the
hosts of heaven against the power of sin, Satan, and

1   fights the holy wars. Gabriel has the more quiet task
of imparting a sense of the ever-presence of ministering
3   Love. These angels deliver us from the depths. Truth
and Love come nearer in the hour of woe, when strong
faith or spiritual strength wrestles and prevails through
6   the understanding of God. The Gabriel of His presence
has no contests. To infinite, ever-present Love, all is
Love, and there is no error, no sin, sickness, nor death.
9   Against Love, the dragon warreth not long, for he is
killed by the divine Principle. Truth and Love prevail
against the dragon because the dragon cannot war with
12   them. Thus endeth the conflict between the flesh and
Spirit.

Revelation xii. 9. And the great dragon was cast out,
15   that old serpent, called the devil, and Satan, which deceiveth the whole world: he was cast out into the earth, and his
angels were cast out with him.

18   That false claim — that ancient belief, that old serpent
whose name is devil (evil), claiming that there is intelligence in matter either to benefit or to injure
21   men — is pure delusion, the red dragon; and
it is cast out by Christ, Truth, the spiritual
idea, and so proved to be powerless. The words "cast
24   unto the earth" show the dragon to be nothingness, dust
to dust; and therefore, in his pretence of being a talker,
he must be a lie from the beginning. His angels, or mes-
27   sages, are cast out with their author. The beast and the
false prophets are lust and hypocrisy. These wolves in
sheep's clothing are detected and killed by innocence, the
30   Lamb of Love.
     Divine Science shows how the Lamb slays the wolf.

Dragon cast down to earth

Innocence and Truth overcome guilt and error. Ever   1
since the foundation of the world, ever since error would
establish material belief, evil has tried to slay   3

the Lamb; but Science is able to destroy this
lie, called evil. The twelfth chapter of the Apocalypse
typifies the divine method of warfare in Science, and the   6
glorious results of this warfare. The following chapters
depict the fatal effects of trying to meet error with error.
The narrative follows the order used in Genesis. In   9
Genesis, first the true method of creation is set forth and
then the false. Here, also, the Revelator first exhibits
the true warfare and then the false.   12

Revelation xii. 10–12. And I heard a loud voice saying
in heaven, Now is come salvation, and strength, and the
kingdom of our God, and the power of His Christ: for the   15
accuser of our brethren is cast down, which accused them
before our God day and night. And they overcame him by
the blood of the Lamb, and by the word of their testimony;   18
and they loved not their lives unto the death. Therefore
rejoice, ye heavens, and ye that dwell in them. Woe to the
inhabiters of the earth and of the sea! for the devil is   21
come down unto you, having great wrath, because he
knoweth that he hath but a short time.

For victory over a single sin, we give thanks and mag-   24
nify the Lord of Hosts. What shall we say of the mighty

conquest over all sin? A louder song, sweeter
than has ever before reached high heaven,   27
now rises clearer and nearer to the great heart of Christ;
for the accuser is not there, and Love sends forth her
primal and everlasting strain. Self-abnegation, by which   30
we lay down all for Truth, or Christ, in our warfare against
error, is a rule in Christian Science. This rule clearly

1   interprets God as divine Principle, — as Life, represented
by the Father; as Truth, represented by the Son; as Love,
3   represented by the Mother. Every mortal at some period,
here or hereafter, must grapple with and overcome the
mortal belief in a power opposed to God.

6   The Scripture, "Thou hast been faithful over a few
things, I will make thee ruler over many," is literally fulfilled, when we are conscious of the supremacy

**The robe
of Science**

9   of Truth, by which the nothingness of error
is seen; and we know that the nothingness of error is in
proportion to its wickedness. He that touches the hem
12 of Christ's robe and masters his mortal beliefs, animality,
and hate, rejoices in the proof of healing, — in a sweet
and certain sense that God is Love. Alas for those who
15 break faith with divine Science and fail to strangle the
serpent of sin as well as of sickness! They are dwellers
still in the deep darkness of belief. They are in the surg-
18 ing sea of error, not struggling to lift their heads above the
drowning wave.

What must the end be? They must eventually expi-
21 ate their sin through suffering. The sin, which one has
made his bosom companion, comes back to him
at last with accelerated force, for the devil

**Expiation by
suffering**

24 knoweth his time is short. Here the Scriptures declare
that evil is temporal, not eternal. The dragon is at last
stung to death by his own malice; but how many periods
27 of torture it may take to remove all sin, must depend upon
sin's obduracy.

Revelation xii. 13. And when the dragon saw that he
30 was cast unto the earth, he persecuted the woman which
brought forth the man child.

Apathy to
occultism

The march of mind and of honest investigation will
bring the hour when the people will chain, with fetters of
some sort, the growing occultism of this period.
The present apathy as to the tendency of
certain active yet unseen mental agencies will finally be
shocked into another extreme mortal mood, — into human
indignation; for one extreme follows another.

Revelation xii. 15, 16. And the serpent cast out of his
mouth water as a flood, after the woman, that he might
cause her to be carried away of the flood. And the earth
helped the woman, and the earth opened her mouth, and
swallowed up the flood which the dragon cast out of his
mouth.

Receptive
hearts

Millions of unprejudiced minds — simple seekers for
Truth, weary wanderers, athirst in the desert — are waiting and watching for rest and drink. Give
them a cup of cold water in Christ's name,
and never fear the consequences. What if the old dragon
should send forth a new flood to drown the Christ-idea?
He can neither drown your voice with its roar, nor again
sink the world into the deep waters of chaos and old night.
In this age the earth will help the woman; the spiritual
idea will be understood. Those ready for the blessing
you impart will give thanks. The waters will be paci-
fied, and Christ will command the wave.

Hidden ways
of iniquity

When God heals the sick or the sinning, they should
know the great benefit which Mind has wrought. They
should also know the great delusion of mortal mind, when it makes them sick or sinful.
Many are willing to open the eyes of the people to the
power of good resident in divine Mind, but they are

1

3

6

9

12

15

18

21

24

27

30

1   not so willing to point out the evil in human thought,
and expose evil's hidden mental ways of accomplishing
3   iniquity.

Why this backwardness, since exposure is necessary
to ensure the avoidance of the evil? Because people like
6   you better when you tell them their virtues *Christly warning*
than when you tell them their vices. It re-
quires the spirit of our blessed Master to tell a man his
9   faults, and so risk human displeasure for the sake of doing
right and benefiting our race. Who is telling mankind
of the foe in ambush? Is the informer one who sees the
12   foe? If so, listen and be wise. Escape from evil, and
designate those as unfaithful stewards who have seen the
danger and yet have given no warning.

15   At all times and under all circumstances, overcome
evil with good. Know thyself, and God will supply
the wisdom and the occasion for a victory *The armor of divinity*
18   over evil. Clad in the panoply of Love,
human hatred cannot reach you. The cement of a
higher humanity will unite all interests in the one
21   divinity.

Through trope and metaphor, the Revelator, immortal
scribe of Spirit and of a true idealism, furnishes the
24   mirror in which mortals may see their own *Pure religion enthroned*
image. In significant figures he depicts the
thoughts which he beholds in mortal mind. Thus he
27   rebukes the conceit of sin, and foreshadows its doom.
With his spiritual strength, he has opened wide the gates
of glory, and illumined the night of paganism with the
30   sublime grandeur of divine Science, outshining sin, sorcery,
lust, and hypocrisy. He takes away mitre and sceptre.
He enthrones pure and undefiled religion, and lifts on

high only those who have washed their robes white in   1
obedience and suffering.

Thus we see, in both the first and last books of the   3
Bible, — in Genesis and in the Apocalypse, — that sin
is to be Christianly and scientifically reduced

Native
nothingness
of sin

to its native nothingness. "Love one an-   6
other" (I John, iii. 23), is the most simple and profound
counsel of the inspired writer. In Science we are children of God; but whatever is of material sense, or mor-   9
tal, belongs not to His children, for materiality is the
inverted image of spirituality.

Love fulfils the law of Christian Science, and nothing   12
short of this divine Principle, understood and demonstrated, can ever furnish the vision of the

Fulfilment
of the Law

Apocalypse, open the seven seals of error with   15
Truth, or uncover the myriad illusions of sin, sickness,
and death. Under the supremacy of Spirit, it will be seen
and acknowledged that matter must disappear.   18

In Revelation xxi. 1 we read: —

And I saw a new heaven and a new earth: for the first
heaven and the first earth were passed away; and there was   21
no more sea.

The Revelator had not yet passed the transitional
stage in human experience called death, but he already   24
saw a new heaven and a new earth. Through

Man's present
possibilities

what sense came this vision to St. John? Not
through the material visual organs for seeing, for optics   27
are inadequate to take in so wonderful a scene. Were this
new heaven and new earth terrestrial or celestial, mate-

1   rial or spiritual? They could not be the former, for the
human sense of space is unable to grasp such a view.
3   The Revelator was on our plane of existence, while yet
beholding what the eye cannot see, — that which is invisible to the uninspired thought. This testimony of Holy
6   Writ sustains the fact in Science, that the heavens and
earth to one human consciousness, that consciousness
which God bestows, are spiritual, while to another, the
9   unillumined human mind, the vision is material. This
shows unmistakably that what the human mind terms
matter and spirit indicates states and stages of con-
12   sciousness.

Accompanying this scientific consciousness was another revelation, even the declaration from heaven, su-
15   preme harmony, that God, the divine Principle   **Nearness
of harmony, is ever with men, and they are   of Deity**
His people. Thus man was no longer regarded as a mis-
18   erable sinner, but as the blessed child of God. Why?
Because St. John's corporeal sense of the heavens and
earth had vanished, and in place of this false sense was
21   the spiritual sense, the subjective state by which he could
see the new heaven and new earth, which involve the
spiritual idea and consciousness of reality. This is Scrip-
24   tural authority for concluding that such a recognition of
being is, and has been, possible to men in this present
state of existence, — that we can become conscious,
27   here and now, of a cessation of death, sorrow, and pain.
This is indeed a foretaste of absolute Christian Science.
Take heart, dear sufferer, for this reality of being will
30   surely appear sometime and in some way. There will
be no more pain, and all tears will be wiped away. When
you read this, remember Jesus' words, "The kingdom of

God is within you." This spiritual consciousness is   1
therefore a present possibility.

The Revelator also takes in another view, adapted to   3
console the weary pilgrim, journeying "uphill all the way."

He writes, in Revelation xxi. 9: —

And there came unto me one of the seven angels which   6
had the seven vials full of the seven last plagues, and talked
with me, saying, Come hither, I will show thee the bride,
the Lamb's wife.   9

This ministry of Truth, this message from divine Love,
carried John away in spirit. It exalted him till he be-

**Vials of
wrath and
consolation**
came conscious of the spiritual facts of being   12
and the "New Jerusalem, coming down from
God, out of heaven," — the spiritual outpour-
ing of bliss and glory, which he describes as the city   15
which "lieth foursquare." The beauty of this text is,
that the sum total of human misery, represented by
the seven angelic vials full of seven plagues, has full   18
compensation in the law of Love. Note this, — that the
very message, or swift-winged thought, which poured
forth hatred and torment, brought also the experience   21
which at last lifted the seer to behold the great city, the
four equal sides of which were heaven-bestowed and
heaven-bestowing.   24
Think of this, dear reader, for it will lift the sack-
cloth from your eyes, and you will behold the soft-

**Spiritual
wedlock**
winged dove descending upon you. The very   27
circumstance, which your suffering sense
deems wrathful and afflictive, Love can make an angel
entertained unawares. Then thought gently whispers: 30

1   "Come hither! Arise from your false consciousness
    into the true sense of Love, and behold the Lamb's
3   wife, — Love wedded to its own spiritual idea." Then
    cometh the marriage feast, for this revelation will de-
    stroy forever the physical plagues imposed by material
6   sense.

    This sacred city, described in the Apocalypse (xxi. 16)
    as one that "lieth foursquare" and cometh "down from
9   God, out of heaven," represents the light and   The city
    glory of divine Science. The builder and   foursquare
    maker of this New Jerusalem is God, as we read in the
12 book of Hebrews; and it is "a city which hath founda-
    tions." The description is metaphoric. Spiritual teach-
    ing must always be by symbols. Did not Jesus illustrate
15 the truths he taught by the mustard-seed and the prodi-
    gal? Taken in its allegorical sense, the description of
    the city as foursquare has a profound meaning. The
18 four sides of our city are the Word, Christ, Christianity,
    and divine Science; "and the gates of it shall not be shut
    at all by day: for there shall be no night there." This
21 city is wholly spiritual, as its four sides indicate.

    As the Psalmist saith, "Beautiful for situation, the
    joy of the whole earth, is mount Zion, on the sides of
24 the north, the city of the great King." It is   The royally
    indeed a city of the Spirit, fair, royal, and   divine gates
    square. Northward, its gates open to the North Star,
27 the Word, the polar magnet of Revelation; eastward,
    to the star seen by the Wisemen of the Orient, who fol-
    lowed it to the manger of Jesus; southward, to the
30 genial tropics, with the Southern Cross in the skies,
    — the Cross of Calvary, which binds human society
    into solemn union; westward, to the grand realization

of the Golden Shore of Love and the Peaceful Sea of   1
Harmony.

This heavenly city, lighted by the Sun of Righteous-   3
ness, — this New Jerusalem, this infinite All, which to

us seems hidden in the mist of remoteness, —
reached St. John's vision while yet he taber-   6
nacled with mortals.

In Revelation xxi. 22, further describing this holy city,
the beloved Disciple writes: —   9

And I saw no temple therein: for the Lord God Almighty
and the Lamb are the temple of it.

There was no temple, — that is, no material structure   12
in which to worship God, for He must be worshipped

in spirit and in love. The word *temple* also
means *body*. The Revelator was familiar   15
with Jesus' use of this word, as when Jesus spoke of his
material body as the temple to be temporarily rebuilt
(John ii. 21). What further indication need we of the   18
real man's incorporeality than this, that John saw
heaven and earth with "no temple [body] therein"?
This kingdom of God "is within you," — is within   21
reach of man's consciousness here, and the spiritual
idea reveals it. In divine Science, man possesses this
recognition of harmony consciously in proportion to his   24
understanding of God.

The term Lord, as used in our version of the Old
Testament, is often synonymous with Jehovah, and ex-   27

presses the Jewish concept, not yet elevated
to deific apprehension through spiritual trans-
figuration. Yet the word gradually approaches a higher   30
meaning. This human sense of Deity yields to the divine

1   sense, even as the material sense of personality yields
    to the incorporeal sense of God and man as the infinite
3   Principle and infinite idea, — as one Father with His uni-
    versal family, held in the gospel of Love. The Lamb's
    wife presents the unity of male and female as no longer
6   two wedded individuals, but as two individual natures
    in one; and this compounded spiritual individuality re-
    flects God as Father-Mother, not as a corporeal being.
9   In this divinely united spiritual consciousness, there is no
    impediment to eternal bliss, — to the perfectibility of
    God's creation.
12   This spiritual, holy habitation has no boundary
    nor limit, but its four cardinal points are: first, the
    Word of Life, Truth, and Love; second,   **The city of
                                                                   our God**
15 the Christ, the spiritual idea of God; third,
    Christianity, which is the outcome of the divine Prin-
    ciple of the Christ-idea in Christian history; fourth,
18 Christian Science, which to-day and forever interprets
    this great example and the great Exemplar. This city
    of our God has no need of sun or satellite, for Love
21 is the light of it, and divine Mind is its own interpreter.
    All who are saved must walk in this light. Mighty
    potentates and dynasties will lay down their honors
24 within the heavenly city. Its gates open towards light
    and glory both within and without, for all is good, and
    nothing can enter that city, which "defileth, . . . or
27 maketh a lie."
        The writer's present feeble sense of Christian Science
    closes with St. John's Revelation as recorded by the
30 great apostle, for his vision is the acme of this Science
    as the Bible reveals it.
        In the following Psalm one word shows, though faintly,

the light which Christian Science throws on the Scriptures   1
by substituting for the corporeal sense, the incorporeal
or spiritual sense of Deity: —   3

PSALM XXIII

[DIVINE LOVE] is my shepherd; I shall not want.

[LOVE] maketh me to lie down in green pastures: 6
[LOVE] leadeth me beside the still waters.

[LOVE] restoreth my soul [spiritual sense]: [LOVE] leadeth me in the paths of righteousness for His name's sake.   9

Yea, though I walk through the valley of the shadow of
death, I will fear no evil: for [LOVE] is with me; [LOVE's]
rod and [LOVE's] staff they comfort me.   12

[LOVE] prepareth a table before me in the presence of
mine enemies: [LOVE] anointeth my head with oil; my cup
runneth over.   15

Surely goodness and mercy shall follow me all the days of
my life; and I will dwell in the house [the consciousness]
of [LOVE] for ever.   18

Chapter 17

Glossary

These things saith He that is holy, He that is true,
He that hath the key of David,
He that openeth, and no man shutteth;
and shutteth, and no man openeth;
I know thy works:
behold, I have set before thee an open door,
and no man can shut it. — REVELATION.

1   In Christian Science we learn that the substitution of
the spiritual for the material definition of a Scrip-
3   tural word often elucidates the meaning of the inspired
writer. On this account this chapter is added. It contains the metaphysical interpretation of Bible terms,
6   giving their spiritual sense, which is also their original
meaning.

ABEL. Watchfulness; self-offering; surrendering to
9   the creator the early fruits of experience.

ABRAHAM. Fidelity; faith in the divine Life and in the
eternal Principle of being.
12   This patriarch illustrated the purpose of Love to create
trust in good, and showed the life-preserving power of
spiritual understanding.

15   ADAM. Error; a falsity; the belief in "original sin,"
sickness, and death; evil; the opposite of good, — of God
and His creation; a curse; a belief in intelligent matter,

finiteness, and mortality; "dust to dust;" red sand- 1
stone; nothingness; the first god of mythology; not
God's man, who represents the one God and is His own 3
image and likeness; the opposite of Spirit and His creations; that which is not the image and likeness of good,
but a material belief, opposed to the one Mind, or Spirit; 6
a so-called finite mind, producing other minds, thus making "gods many and lords many" (I Corinthians viii. 5);
a product of nothing as the mimicry of something; an 9
unreality as opposed to the great reality of spiritual existence and creation; a so-called man, whose origin,
substance, and mind are found to be the antipode of 12
God, or Spirit; an inverted image of Spirit; the image
and likeness of what God has not created, namely, matter, sin, sickness, and death; the opposer of Truth, 15
termed error; Life's counterfeit, which ultimates in
death; the opposite of Love, called hate; the usurper
of Spirit's creation, called self-creative matter; immor- 18
tality's opposite, mortality; that of which wisdom saith,
"Thou shalt surely die."

The name Adam represents the false supposition that 21
Life is not eternal, but has beginning and end; that the
infinite enters the finite, that intelligence passes into non-
intelligence, and that Soul dwells in material sense; that 24
immortal Mind results in matter, and matter in mortal
mind; that the one God and creator entered what He created, and then disappeared in the atheism of matter. 27

ADVERSARY. An adversary is one who opposes, denies,
disputes, not one who constructs and sustains reality and
Truth. Jesus said of the devil, "He was a murderer from 30
the beginning, . . . he is a liar and the father of it."

1 This view of Satan is confirmed by the name often conferred upon him in Scripture, the "adversary."

3 ALMIGHTY. All-power; infinity; omnipotence.

ANGELS. God's thoughts passing to man; spiritual
intuitions, pure and perfect; the inspiration of goodness,
6 purity, and immortality, counteracting all evil, sensuality,
and mortality.

ARK. Safety; the idea, or reflection, of Truth, proved
9 to be as immortal as its Principle; the understanding of
Spirit, destroying belief in matter.
God and man coexistent and eternal; Science show-
12 ing that the spiritual realities of all things are created
by Him and exist forever. The ark indicates temptation
overcome and followed by exaltation.

15 ASHER (Jacob's son). Hope and faith; spiritual compensation; the ills of the flesh rebuked.

BABEL. Self-destroying error; a kingdom divided
18 against itself, which cannot stand; material knowledge.
The higher false knowledge builds on the basis of evidence obtained from the five corporeal senses, the more
21 confusion ensues, and the more certain is the downfall
of its structure.

BAPTISM. Purification by Spirit; submergence in
24 Spirit.
We are "willing rather to be absent from the body,
and to be present with the Lord." (II Corinthians v. 8.)

BELIEVING. Firmness and constancy; not a faltering nor a blind faith, but the perception of spiritual Truth. Mortal thoughts, illusion.

BENJAMIN (Jacob's son). A physical belief as to life, substance, and mind; human knowledge, or so-called mortal mind, devoted to matter; pride; envy; fame; illusion; a false belief; error masquerading as the possessor of life, strength, animation, and power to act.

Renewal of affections; self-offering; an improved state of mortal mind; the introduction of a more spiritual origin; a gleam of the infinite idea of the infinite Principle; a spiritual type; that which comforts, consoles, and supports.

BRIDE. Purity and innocence, conceiving man in the idea of God; a sense of Soul, which has spiritual bliss and enjoys but cannot suffer.

BRIDEGROOM. Spiritual understanding; the pure consciousness that God, the divine Principle, creates man as His own spiritual idea, and that God is the only creative power.

BURIAL. Corporeality and physical sense put out of sight and hearing; annihilation. Submergence in Spirit; immortality brought to light.

CANAAN (the son of Ham). A sensuous belief; the testimony of what is termed material sense; the error which would make man mortal and would make mortal mind a slave to the body.

CHILDREN. The spiritual thoughts and representatives of Life, Truth, and Love.

1   Sensual and mortal beliefs; counterfeits of creation, whose better originals are God's thoughts, not in em-

3   bryo, but in maturity; material suppositions of life, substance, and intelligence, opposed to the Science of being.

    CHILDREN OF ISRAEL. The representatives of Soul, not

6   corporeal sense; the offspring of Spirit, who, having wrestled with error, sin, and sense, are governed by divine Science; some of the ideas of God beheld as men, casting

9   out error and healing the sick; Christ's offspring.

    CHRIST. The divine manifestation of God, which comes to the flesh to destroy incarnate error.

12   **CHURCH.** The structure of Truth and Love; whatever rests upon and proceeds from divine Principle.
    The Church is that institution, which affords proof of

15   its utility and is found elevating the race, rousing the dormant understanding from material beliefs to the apprehension of spiritual ideas and the demonstration of

18   divine Science, thereby casting out devils, or error, and healing the sick.

    CREATOR. Spirit; Mind; intelligence; the animating

21   divine Principle of all that is real and good; self-existent Life, Truth, and Love; that which is perfect and eternal; the opposite of matter and evil, which have no Prin-

24   ciple; God, who made all that was made and could not create an atom or an element the opposite of Himself.

    DAN (Jacob's son). Animal magnetism; so-called mor-

27   tal mind controlling mortal mind; error, working out the designs of error; one belief preying upon another.

DAY. The irradiance of Life; light, the spiritual idea   1
of Truth and Love.

"And the evening and the morning were the first day."   3
(Genesis i. 5.) The objects of time and sense disappear
in the illumination of spiritual understanding, and Mind
measures time according to the good that is unfolded.   6
This unfolding is God's day, and "there shall be no night
there."

DEATH. An illusion, the lie of life in matter; the un-   9
real and untrue; the opposite of Life.

Matter has no life, hence it has no real existence. Mind
is immortal. The flesh, warring against Spirit; that   12
which frets itself free from one belief only to be fettered
by another, until every belief of life where Life is not
yields to eternal Life. Any material evidence of death is   15
false, for it contradicts the spiritual facts of being.

DEVIL. Evil; a lie; error; neither corporeality nor
mind; the opposite of Truth; a belief in sin, sickness,   18
and death; animal magnetism or hypnotism; the lust of
the flesh, which saith: "I am life and intelligence in
matter. There is more than one mind, for I am mind, —   21
a wicked mind, self-made or created by a tribal god and
put into the opposite of mind, termed matter, thence to
reproduce a mortal universe, including man, not after the   24
image and likeness of Spirit, but after its own image."

DOVE. A symbol of divine Science; purity and peace;
hope and faith.   27

DUST. Nothingness; the absence of substance, life, or
intelligence.

1 **EARS.** Not organs of the so-called corporeal senses, but spiritual understanding.

3 Jesus said, referring to spiritual perception, "Having ears, hear ye not?" (Mark viii. 18.)

EARTH. A sphere; a type of eternity and immortality, which are likewise without beginning or end.

6 To material sense, earth is matter; to spiritual sense, it is a compound idea.

9 **ELIAS.** Prophecy; spiritual evidence opposed to material sense; Christian Science, with which can be discerned the spiritual fact of whatever the material senses behold; the basis of immortality.

12 "Elias truly shall first come and restore all things." (Matthew xvii. 11.)

15 **ERROR.** See chapter on Recapitulation, page 472.

EUPHRATES (river). Divine Science encompassing the universe and man; the true idea of God; a type of the glory which is to come; metaphysics taking the place of physics; the reign of righteousness. The atmosphere of human belief before it accepts sin, sickness, or death; a state of mortal thought, the only error of which is limitation; finity; the opposite of infinity.

18

21

EVE. A beginning; mortality; that which does not last forever; a finite belief concerning life, substance, and intelligence in matter; error; the belief that the human race originated materially instead of spiritually, — that man started first from dust, second from a rib, and third from an egg.

24

27

EVENING. Mistiness of mortal thought; weariness of mortal mind; obscured views; peace and rest.

EYES. Spiritual discernment, — not material but mental.

Jesus said, thinking of the outward vision, "Having eyes, see ye not?" (Mark viii. 18.)

FAN. Separator of fable from fact; that which gives action to thought.

FATHER. Eternal Life; the one Mind; the divine Principle, commonly called God.

FEAR. Heat; inflammation; anxiety; ignorance; error; desire; caution.

FIRE. Fear; remorse; lust; hatred; destruction; affliction purifying and elevating man.

FIRMAMENT. Spiritual understanding; the scientific line of demarcation between Truth and error, between Spirit and so-called matter.

FLESH. An error of physical belief; a supposition that life, substance, and intelligence are in matter; an illusion; a belief that matter has sensation.

GAD (Jacob's son). Science; spiritual being understood; haste towards harmony.

GETHSEMANE. Patient woe; the human yielding to the divine; love meeting no response, but still remaining love.

GHOST. An illusion; a belief that mind is outlined and limited; a supposition that spirit is finite.

GIHON (river). The rights of woman acknowledged morally, civilly, and socially.

GOD. The great I AM; the all-knowing, all-seeing, all-acting, all-wise, all-loving, and eternal; Principle; Mind; Soul; Spirit; Life; Truth; Love; all substance; intelligence.

GODS. Mythology; a belief that life, substance, and intelligence are both mental and material; a supposition of sentient physicality; the belief that infinite Mind is in finite forms; the various theories that hold mind to be a material sense, existing in brain, nerve, matter; supposititious minds, or souls, going in and out of matter, erring and mortal; the serpents of error, which say, "Ye shall be as gods."

God is one God, infinite and perfect, and cannot become finite and imperfect.

GOOD. God; Spirit; omnipotence; omniscience; omnipresence; omni-action.

HAM (Noah's son). Corporeal belief; sensuality; slavery; tyranny.

HEART. Mortal feelings, motives, affections, joys, and sorrows.

HEAVEN. Harmony; the reign of Spirit; government by divine Principle; spirituality; bliss; the atmosphere of Soul.

HELL. Mortal belief; error; lust; remorse; hatred;   1
revenge; sin; sickness; death; suffering and self-destruction; self-imposed agony; effects of sin; that which   3
"worketh abomination or maketh a lie."

HIDDEKEL (river). Divine Science understood and
acknowledged.   6

HOLY GHOST. Divine Science; the development of
eternal Life, Truth, and Love.

I, or EGO. Divine Principle; Spirit; Soul; incor-   9
poreal, unerring, immortal, and eternal Mind.
    There is but one I, or Us, but one divine Principle, or
Mind, governing all existence; man and woman un-   12
changed forever in their individual characters, even as
numbers which never blend with each other, though they
are governed by one Principle. All the objects of God's   15
creation reflect one Mind, and whatever reflects not this
one Mind, is false and erroneous, even the belief that
life, substance, and intelligence are both mental and   18
material.

I AM. God; incorporeal and eternal Mind; divine
Principle; the only Ego.   21

IN. A term obsolete in Science if used with reference
to Spirit, or Deity.

INTELLIGENCE. Substance; self-existent and eternal   24
Mind; that which is never unconscious nor limited.
    See chapter on Recapitulation, page 469.

ISSACHAR (Jacob's son). A corporeal belief; the offspring of error; envy; hatred; selfishness; self-will; lust.

JACOB. A corporeal mortal embracing duplicity, repentance, sensualism. Inspiration; the revelation of Science, in which the so-called material senses yield to the spiritual sense of Life and Love.

JAPHET (Noah's son). A type of spiritual peace, flowing from the understanding that God is the divine Principle of all existence, and that man is His idea, the child of His care.

JERUSALEM. Mortal belief and knowledge obtained from the five corporeal senses; the pride of power and the power of pride; sensuality; envy; oppression; tyranny. Home, heaven.

JESUS. The highest human corporeal concept of the divine idea, rebuking and destroying error and bringing to light man's immortality.

JOSEPH. A corporeal mortal; a higher sense of Truth rebuking mortal belief, or error, and showing the immortality and supremacy of Truth; pure affection blessing its enemies.

JUDAH. A corporeal material belief progressing and disappearing; the spiritual understanding of God and man appearing.

KINGDOM OF HEAVEN. The reign of harmony in divine   1
Science; the realm of unerring, eternal, and omnipotent
Mind; the atmosphere of Spirit, where Soul is supreme.   3

KNOWLEDGE. Evidence obtained from the five corporeal senses; mortality; beliefs and opinions; human
theories, doctrines, hypotheses; that which is not divine   6
and is the origin of sin, sickness, and death; the opposite of spiritual Truth and understanding.

LAMB OF GOD. The spiritual idea of Love; self-im-   9
molation; innocence and purity; sacrifice.

LEVI (Jacob's son). A corporeal and sensual belief;
mortal man; denial of the fulness of God's creation;   12
ecclesiastical despotism.

LIFE. See chapter on Recapitulation, page 468.

LORD. In the Hebrew, this term is sometimes em-   15
ployed as a title, which has the inferior sense of master,
or ruler. In the Greek, the word *kurios* almost always
has this lower sense, unless specially coupled with the   18
name God. Its higher signification is Supreme Ruler.

LORD GOD. Jehovah.
    This double term is not used in the first chapter of   21
Genesis, the record of spiritual creation. It is introduced in the second and following chapters, when the
spiritual sense of God and of infinity is disappearing   24
from the recorder's thought, — when the true scientific
statements of the Scriptures become clouded through a

1   physical sense of God as finite and corporeal. From this
       follow idolatry and mythology, — belief in many gods, or
3   material intelligences, as the opposite of the one Spirit,
       or intelligence, named Elohim, or God.

       MAN. The compound idea of infinite Spirit; the spirit-
6   ual image and likeness of God; the full representation of
       Mind.

       MATTER. Mythology; mortality; another name for
9   mortal mind; illusion; intelligence, substance, and life
       in non-intelligence and mortality; life resulting in death,
       and death in life; sensation in the sensationless; mind
12   originating in matter; the opposite of Truth; the oppo-
       site of Spirit; the opposite of God; that of which immortal
       Mind takes no cognizance; that which mortal mind sees,
15   feels, hears, tastes, and smells only in belief.

       MIND. The only I, or Us; the only Spirit, Soul, divine
       Principle, substance, Life, Truth, Love; the one God;
18   not that which is *in* man, but the divine Principle, or God,
       of whom man is the full and perfect expression; Deity,
       which outlines but is not outlined.

21

       MIRACLE. That which is divinely natural, but must
       be learned humanly; a phenomenon of Science.

       MORNING. Light; symbol of Truth; revelation and
24   progress.

       MORTAL MIND. Nothing claiming to be something,
27   for Mind is immortal; mythology; error creating other
       errors; a suppositional material sense, *alias* the belief

that sensation is in matter, which is sensationless; a be-   1
lief that life, substance, and intelligence are in and of
matter; the opposite of Spirit, and therefore the opposite   3
of God, or good; the belief that life has a beginning
and therefore an end; the belief that man is the offspring of mortals; the belief that there can be more than   6
one creator; idolatry; the subjective states of error;
material senses; that which neither exists in Science nor
can be recognized by the spiritual sense; sin; sickness;   9
death.

MOSES. A corporeal mortal; moral courage; a type
of moral law and the demonstration thereof; the proof   12
that, without the gospel, — the union of justice and affection, — there is something spiritually lacking, since justice
demands penalties under the law.   15

MOTHER. God; divine and eternal Principle; Life,
Truth, and Love.

NEW JERUSALEM. Divine Science; the spiritual facts   18
and harmony of the universe; the kingdom of heaven,
or reign of harmony.

NIGHT. Darkness; doubt; fear.   21

NOAH. A corporeal mortal; knowledge of the nothingness of material things and of the immortality of all
that is spiritual.   24

OIL. Consecration; charity; gentleness; prayer; heavenly inspiration.

PHARISEE. Corporeal and sensuous belief; self-right-   27
eousness; vanity; hypocrisy.

1   **PISON** (river). The love of the good and beautiful, and their immortality.

3   **PRINCIPLE.** See chapter on Recapitulation, page 465.

PROPHET. A spiritual seer; disappearance of material sense before the conscious facts of spiritual Truth.

6   **PURSE.** Laying up treasures in matter; error.

RED DRAGON. Error; fear; inflammation; sensuality; subtlety; animal magnetism; envy; revenge.

9   **RESURRECTION.** Spiritualization of thought; a new and higher idea of immortality, or spiritual existence; material belief yielding to spiritual understanding.

12   **REUBEN** (Jacob's son). Corporeality; sensuality; delusion; mortality; error.

RIVER. Channel of thought.

15   When smooth and unobstructed, it typifies the course of Truth; but muddy, foaming, and dashing, it is a type of error.

18   **ROCK.** Spiritual foundation; Truth. Coldness and stubbornness.

SALVATION. Life, Truth, and Love understood and
21   demonstrated as supreme over all; sin, sickness, and death destroyed.

SEAL. The signet of error revealed by Truth.

SERPENT (*ophis*, in Greek; *nacash*, in Hebrew). 1
Subtlety; a lie; the opposite of Truth, named error;
the first statement of mythology and idolatry; the belief 3
in more than one God; animal magnetism; the first lie
of limitation; finity; the first claim that there is an opposite of Spirit, or good, termed matter, or evil; the first 6
delusion that error exists as fact; the first claim that sin,
sickness, and death are the realities of life. The first
audible claim that God was not omnipotent and that 9
there was another power, named *evil*, which was as real
and eternal as God, good.

SHEEP. Innocence; inoffensiveness; those who follow 12
their leader.

SHEM (Noah's son). A corporeal mortal; kindly affection; love rebuking error; reproof of sensualism. 15

SON. The Son of God, the Messiah or Christ. The
son of man, the offspring of the flesh. "Son of a year."

SOULS. See chapter on Recapitulation, page 466. 18

SPIRIT. Divine substance; Mind; divine Principle;
all that is good; God; that only which is perfect, everlasting, omnipresent, omnipotent, infinite. 21

SPIRITS. Mortal beliefs; corporeality; evil minds;
supposed intelligences, or gods; the opposites of God;
errors; hallucinations. (See page 466.) 24

SUBSTANCE. See chapter on Recapitulation, page
468.

1 **SUN.** The symbol of Soul governing man, — of Truth, Life, and Love.

3 **SWORD.** The idea of Truth; justice. Revenge; anger.

TARES. Mortality; error; sin; sickness; disease;
6 death.

TEMPLE. Body; the idea of Life, substance, and intelligence; the superstructure of Truth; the shrine of
9 Love; a material superstructure, where mortals congregate for worship.

THUMMIM. Perfection; the eternal demand of divine
12 Science.
     The Urim and Thummim, which were to be on Aaron's breast when he went before Jehovah, were holiness and
15 purification of thought and deed, which alone can fit us for the office of spiritual teaching.

TIME. Mortal measurements; limits, in which are
18 summed up all human acts, thoughts, beliefs, opinions, knowledge; matter; error; that which begins before, and continues after, what is termed death, until the mortal
21 disappears and spiritual perfection appears.

TITHE. Contribution; tenth part; homage; gratitude. A sacrifice to the gods.

24 **UNCLEANLINESS.** Impure thoughts; error; sin; dirt.

UNGODLINESS. Opposition to the divine Principle and its spiritual idea.

UNKNOWN. That which spiritual sense alone compre-　1
hends, and which is unknown to the material senses.

　　Paganism and agnosticism may define Deity as "the　3
great unknowable;" but Christian Science brings God
much nearer to man, and makes Him better known as
the All-in-all, forever near.　6

　　Paul saw in Athens an altar dedicated "to the unknown
God." Referring to it, he said to the Athenians: "Whom
therefore ye ignorantly worship, Him declare I unto you."　9
(Acts xvii. 23.)

URIM. Light.

　　The rabbins believed that the stones in the breast-　12
plate of the high-priest had supernatural illumination,
but Christian Science reveals Spirit, not matter, as the
illuminator of all. The illuminations of Science give us　15
a sense of the nothingness of error, and they show the
spiritual inspiration of Love and Truth to be the only fit
preparation for admission to the presence and power of　18
the Most High.

VALLEY. Depression; meekness; darkness.

　　"Though I walk through the valley of the shadow of　21
death, I will fear no evil." (Psalm xxiii. 4.)

　　Though the way is dark in mortal sense, divine Life
and Love illumine it, destroy the unrest of mortal thought,　24
the fear of death, and the supposed reality of error. Christian Science, contradicting sense, maketh the valley to bud
and blossom as the rose.　27

VEIL. A cover; concealment; hiding; hypocrisy.

　　The Jewish women wore veils over their faces in token

1 of reverence and submission and in accordance with
Pharisaical notions.

3 The Judaic religion consisted mostly of rites and ceremonies. The motives and affections of a man were of
little value, if only he appeared unto men to fast. The

6 great Nazarene, as meek as he was mighty, rebuked the
hypocrisy, which offered long petitions for blessings upon
material methods, but cloaked the crime, latent in thought,

9 which was ready to spring into action and crucify God's
anointed. The martyrdom of Jesus was the culminating
sin of Pharisaism. It rent the veil of the temple. It re-

12 vealed the false foundations and superstructures of superficial religion, tore from bigotry and superstition their
coverings, and opened the sepulchre with divine Science,

15 — immortality and Love.

WILDERNESS. Loneliness; doubt; darkness. Spon-
taneity of thought and idea; the vestibule in which a

18 material sense of things disappears, and spiritual sense
unfolds the great facts of existence.

WILL. The motive-power of error; mortal belief; ani-

21 mal power. The might and wisdom of God.
"For this is the will of God." (I Thessalonians
iv. 3.)

24 Will, as a quality of so-called mortal mind, is a wrong-
doer; hence it should not be confounded with the term
as applied to Mind or to one of God's qualities.

27 WIND. That which indicates the might of omnipotence and the movements of God's spiritual government,
encompassing all things. Destruction; anger; mortal

30 passions.

The Greek word for *wind (pneuma)* is used also for   1
spirit, as in the passage in John's Gospel, the third chapter, where we read: "The wind [*pneuma*] bloweth where   3
it listeth. . . . So is every one that is born of the Spirit
[*pneuma*]." Here the original word is the same in both
cases, yet it has received different translations, as in other   6
passages in this same chapter and elsewhere in the New
Testament. This shows how our Master had constantly
to employ words of material significance in order to unfold   9
spiritual thoughts. In the record of Jesus' supposed
death, we read: "He bowed his head, and gave up the
ghost;" but this word *ghost* is *pneuma*. It might be trans-   12
lated *wind* or *air,* and the phrase is equivalent to our
common statement, "He breathed his last." What
Jesus gave up was indeed air, an etherealized form of   15
matter, for never did he give up Spirit, or Soul.

WINE. Inspiration; understanding. Error; fornication; temptation; passion.   18

YEAR. A solar measurement of time; mortality;
space for repentance.
"One day is with the Lord as a thousand years."   21
(II Peter iii. 8.)
One moment of divine consciousness, or the spiritual
understanding of Life and Love, is a foretaste of eternity.   24
This exalted view, obtained and retained when the Science of being is understood, would bridge over with life
discerned spiritually the interval of death, and man   27
would be in the full consciousness of his immortality and
eternal harmony, where sin, sickness, and death are unknown. Time is a mortal thought, the divisor of which   30

1   is the solar year. Eternity is God's measurement of Soul-filled years.

3   **YOU.** As applied to corporeality, a mortal; finity.

      ZEAL. The reflected animation of Life, Truth, and Love. Blind enthusiasm; mortal will.

6   **ZION.** Spiritual foundation and superstructure; inspiration; spiritual strength. Emptiness; unfaithfulness; desolation.

Fruitage

Wherefore by their fruits ye shall know them. — JESUS.

That ye might walk worthy of the Lord unto all pleasing,
being fruitful in every good work,
and increasing in the knowledge of God. — PAUL.

Let us get up early to the vineyards;
let us see if the vine flourish, whether the tender grape appear,
and the pomegranates bud forth. — SOLOMON'S SONG.

T housands of letters could be presented in testimony of the healing efficacy of Christian Science and particularly concerning the vast number of people who have been reformed and healed through the perusal or study of this book.

For the assurance and encouragement of the reader, a few of these letters are here republished from THE CHRISTIAN SCIENCE JOURNAL and CHRISTIAN SCIENCE SENTINEL. The originals are in the possession of the Editor, who can authenticate the testimonials which follow.

RHEUMATISM HEALED

I was a great sufferer from a serious form of rheumatic trouble, my hands being affected to such an extent that it was impossible for me even to dress without assistance. The trouble finally reached the knees, and I became very lame and had to be assisted in and out of bed. I went to the different health resorts for the benefit I hoped to derive from the baths and waters that were prescribed by physicians, but found no permanent relief. I was placed under an X-ray examination, and was told that the joints were becoming ossified. I then consulted a celebrated specialist, who after a thorough examination said my condition would continue to grow worse and that I would become completely helpless.

At that time a copy of "Science and Health with Key to the Scriptures" by Mrs. Eddy was loaned me. I read it more from curiosity than with the thought of any physical benefit. As the truth was unfolded to me, I realized that the mental condition was what needed correcting, and that the Spirit of truth which inspired this book was my physician. My healing is complete, and the liberation in thought is manifest in a life of active usefulness rather than the bondage of helpless invalidism and suffering. I owe to our beloved Leader, Mrs. Eddy, gratitude which words cannot express. Her revelation of the practical rather than the merely theoretical application of Jesus' words, "Ye shall know the truth, and the truth shall make you free," proved to be my redeemer. I did not even have to apply to a practitioner, but am most grateful for the helpful words of loving friends. — E. B. B., Pasadena, Cal.

ASTIGMATISM AND HERNIA HEALED

It is nearly five years since I bought my first copy of Science and Health, the reading of which cured me of chronic constipation, nervous headache, astigmatism, and hernia, in less than four months.

Where would I be now, had not this blessed truth been brought to me by much persuasion of a very dear friend?

I certainly should have been deep in the slough of despond, if not in the grave. Am I truly thankful for all the good that has come to me and mine? I try to let my works testify of that; but to those whom I do not meet in person, I can truly say, Yes; I am indeed more thankful than words can express for the glorious healing that has come to me, both physical, mental, and moral, and I also convey herein, my song of gratitude to the dear Leader who has through her fidelity to Truth enabled me to touch at least the hem of Christ's garment. — B. S. J., Sioux City, Iowa.

SUBSTANCE OF LUNGS RESTORED

It was about fifteen years ago that Christian Science first came to my notice. At that time I had been a chronic invalid for a good many years. I had acute bowel trouble, bronchitis, and a number of other troubles. One physician had told me that my lungs were like wet paper, ready to tear at any time, and I was filled with fear, as my mother, two brothers, and a sister had been victims of consumption. I tried many physicians and every material remedy that promised help, but no help came until I found a copy of Mrs. Eddy's book, Science and Health. The book was placed in my hands by one who did not then appreciate it, and I was told that it would be hard for me to understand it. I commenced reading it with this thought, but I caught beautiful glimpses of Truth, which took away my fear and healed me of all those diseases, and they have never returned.

I would also like to tell how I was healed of a sprained

ankle. The accident occurred in the morning, and all
that day and during the night I gave myself Christian
Science treatment, as best I could. The next morning
it seemed to be no better, being very sore, badly swollen,
and much discolored. Feeling that I had done all I could,
I decided to stop thinking about it. I took my copy of
Science and Health and began reading. Very soon I
became so absorbed in the book that I forgot all about
my ankle; it went entirely out of my thought, for I had
a glimpse of all God's creation as spiritual, and for the
time being lost sight of my material selfhood. After two
hours I laid the book down and walked into another room.
When next I thought of my ankle, I found it was not hurt-
ing me. The swelling had gone down, the black and blue
appearance had nearly vanished, and it was perfectly well.
It was healed while I was "absent from the body" and
"present with the Lord." This experience was worth
a great deal to me, for it showed me how the healing is
done. — C. H., Portland, Ore.

FIBROID TUMOR HEALED IN A FEW DAYS

My gratitude for Christian Science is boundless. I
was afflicted with a fibroid tumor which weighed not
less than fifty pounds, attended by a continuous hemorrhage for eleven years. The tumor was a growth of
eighteen years.

I lived in Fort Worth, Tex., and I had never heard
of Christian Science before leaving there for Chicago
in the year 1887. I had tried to live near to God, and
I feel sure He guided me in all my steps to this healing and saving truth. After being there several weeks

I received letters from a Texas lady who had herself been healed, and who wrote urging me to try Christian Science.

Changing my boarding-place, I met a lady who owned a copy of Science and Health, and in speaking to her of having seen the book, she informed me she had one, and she got it and told me I could read it. The revelation was marvellous and brought a great spiritual awakening. This awakened sense never left me, and one day when walking alone it came to me very suddenly that I was healed, and I walked the faster declaring every step that I was healed. When I reached my boarding-place, I found my hostess and told her I was healed. She looked the picture of amazement. The tumor began to disappear at once, the hemorrhage ceased, and perfect strength was manifest.

There was no joy ever greater than mine for this Christ-cure, for I was very weary and heavy laden. I thought very little of either sleeping or eating, and my heart was filled with gratitude, since I knew I had touched the hem of his garment.

I must add that the reading of Science and Health, and that alone, healed me, and it was the second copy I ever saw. — S. L., Fort Worth, Tex.

SPINAL TROUBLE AND INDIGESTION HEALED

For many years I have relied wholly upon Christian Science for healing; and I am glad to acknowledge the spiritual help and many other benefits received from following its teachings. I have great cause to be grateful to God and to our revered Leader, Mrs. Eddy, for these blessings, which her discovery and love for

humanity made possible. I had read but a few pages
in our textbook, "Science and Health with Key to
the Scriptures," when I saw that it was the truth, and
that it contained something I had thought could never
be found in this existence. Proofs of healing came
immediately, and I was able to do much useful work
without a sense of burden or fatigue.

As time went on I learned the nothingness of discouragement, and understood in a measure that God is
my Life and that all action is in divine Mind. I was
healed of spinal trouble; and nervousness and weakness
faded away and were replaced by health and strength.
A larger sense of joy and gratitude did much towards
overcoming indigestion, which had caused suffering for a
number of years. A sprained ankle was cured in a few
hours by applying what I understood of Christian
Science, and by holding steadfastly to the statement
our Leader makes on page 384 of Science and Health,
that "God never punishes man for doing right, for
honest labor, or for deeds of kindness." The following
day I walked two miles with no sense of discomfort.
Beliefs of heredity and lack have been overcome, and
self-will, self-love, and pride are less in evidence. —
Miss G. W., Brookline, Mass.

A CASE OF MENTAL SURGERY

I have felt for some time I should give my experience
in mental surgery. In May, 1902, going home for
lunch, on a bicycle, and while riding down a hill at a
rapid gait, I was thrown from the wheel, and falling
on my left side with my arm under my head, the bone
was broken about half-way between the shoulder and

elbow. While the pain was intense, I lay still in the dust, declaring the truth and denying that there could be a break or accident in the realm of divine Love, until a gentleman came to assist me, saying, he thought I had been stunned. I was only two and a half blocks from home, so I mounted my wheel again and managed to reach it. On arriving there I lay down and asked my little boy to bring me our textbook. He immediately brought Science and Health, which I read for about ten minutes, when all pain left.

I said nothing to my family of the accident, but attended to some duties and was about half an hour late in returning to the office, this being my only loss of time from work. My friends claimed that the arm had not been broken, as it would have been impossible for me to continue my work without having it set, and carrying it in a sling until the bone knit together. Their insistence almost persuaded me that I might have been mistaken, until one of my friends invited me to visit a physician's office where they were experimenting with an X-ray machine. The physician was asked to examine my left arm to see if it differed from the ordinary. On looking through it, he said, "Yes, it has been broken, but whoever set it made a perfect job of it, and you will never have any further trouble from that break." My friend then asked the doctor to show how he could tell where the break had been. The doctor pointed out the place as being slightly thicker at that part, like a piece of steel that had been welded. This was the first of several cases of mental surgery that have come under my notice, and it made a deep impression on me.

For the benefit of others who may have something
similar to meet, I will say that I have overcome almost
constant attacks of sick headaches, extending back
to my earliest recollection. — L. C. S., Salt Lake City,
Utah.

CATARACT QUICKLY CURED

I wish to add my testimony to those of others, and
hope that it may be the means of bringing some poor
sufferer to health, to happiness, and to God. I was
healed through simply reading this wonderful book,
Science and Health. I had been troubled periodically
for many years with sore eyes, and had been to many
doctors, who called the disease iritis and cataract. They
told me that my eyes would always give me trouble, and
that I would eventually lose my sight if I remained in
an office, and advised me to go under an operation. Later
on I had to wear glasses at my work, also out of doors
as I could not bear the winds, and my eyes were gradually
becoming worse. I could not read for longer than a few
minutes at a time, otherwise they would smart severely.
I had to rest my eyes each evening to enable me to use
them the next day; in fact gas-light was getting unbearable
because of the pain, and I made home miserable. A
dear brother told me about Christian Science, and said
that if I would read Science and Health it would help
me. He procured for me the loan of the book. The
first night I read it, it so interested me I quite forgot
all about my eyes until my wife remarked that it was
eleven o'clock. I found that I had been reading this
book for nearly four hours, and I remarked immediately
after, "I believe my eyes are cured," which was really

the case. The next day, on looking at my eyes, my wife noticed that the cataract had disappeared. I put away my outdoor glasses, which I have not required since, and through the understanding gained by studying Christian Science I have been able to do away with my indoor glasses also, and have had no return of pain in my eyes since. This is now a year and a half ago. — G. F. S., Liverpool, England.

VALVULAR HEART DISEASE HEALED

Fourteen years ago my heart awoke to gratitude to God and the dear Leader at the same time. After a patient and persistent effort of three months' duration, to procure a copy of Science and Health (during which time I had visited every bookstore, and many of the second-hand bookstores in the city of St. Paul), and had failed to find it, I at last remembered that the stranger who told me I might be healed, had mentioned a name, and McVicker's Theatre Building in Chicago as being in some way connected with the work. I sent there for information regarding a book called Health and Science, and the return mail brought me the book, Science and Health, and in it I at once found sure promise of deliverance from valvular heart disease, with all the accompaniments, such as extreme nervousness, weakness, dyspepsia, and insomnia. I had suffered from these all my life, finding no permanent relief, even, in material remedies, and no hope of cure at any time. Only those who have been held in such bondage and have been liberated by the same means, can know the eager joy of the first perusal of that wonderful book.

Half a day's reading convinced me that I had found the way to holiness and health. I read on, thinking only of the spiritual enlightenment, content to wait until I should be led to some person who would heal me; but old things had passed away, and all things had become new. I was completely healed before I had met a Scientist, or one who knew anything about Christian Science, and before I had read a line of any other Christian Science literature except one leaf of a tract; so it is absolutely certain that the healing was entirely impersonal, as was also the teaching, which enabled me to begin at once demonstrating the power of Truth to destroy all forms of error. — E. J. W., North Yakima, Wash.

THE TRUE PHYSICIAN FOUND

It is with a deep sense of gratitude that I send the particulars of my healing through Christian Science. While visiting friends in the southwestern part of Ontario, about three years ago, my attention was called to Christian Science and the wonderful healing it was doing. I had lived in New York for twenty-five years, but had never heard of Christian Science before, to my recollection.

Up to that time, for seventeen years, I had suffered with indigestion and gastritis in the worst form, often being overcome from a seeming pressure against the heart. I had asthma for four years, also had worn glasses for four years. It seemed to me that I had swallowed every known medicine to relieve my indigestion, but they only gave me temporary benefit. I purchased a copy of Science and Health, and simply from the reading of that

grand book I was completely healed of all my physical
ailments in two weeks' time. I have used no medicine from that day to this, and with God's help, and
the wonderful light revealed to me through the reading
of Mrs. Eddy's book, I never expect to again. I used
to smoke eight or ten cigars a day, and also took an
occasional drink, but the desire for these has gone, — I
feel forever. I travel on the road, and am constantly
being invited to indulge, but it is no effort to abstain,
and in many instances I find that my refusal helps
others.

While I fully appreciate the release from my physical
troubles, this pales into insignificance in comparison with
the spiritual uplifting Christian Science has brought me.
I had not been inside a church for more than ten years,
to attend regular services, until I entered a Christian
Science church. What I saw and realized there, seemed
so genuine that I loved Christian Science from the very
start. I have never taken a treatment, — every inch
of the way has been through study and practical demonstration, and I know that all can do the same thing if they
will try.

Since I have been in Science I have overcome a case of
ulcerated tooth in one night through the reading of Science
and Health; also a severe attack of grip in thirty-six hours
by obeying the Scripture saying, "Physician, heal thyself." — B. H. N., New York, N. Y.

CANCER AND CONSUMPTION HEALED

I was a great sufferer for many years from internal
cancer and consumption. I was treated by the best of

physicians in New York, Minneapolis, and Duluth, and was finally given up as incurable, when I heard of Christian Science. A neighbor who had been healed of consumption, kindly loaned me Science and Health by Mrs. Eddy, which I read and became interested in. In three months' time, I was healed, the truth conveyed to me by this book being the healer, and not only of these diseases, but I was made whole mentally as well. I have not been in bed one day since, or rather in eleven years. I have had many good demonstrations during this time, have passed through many a "fiery trial," but this blessed truth has caused me to stand, at times seemingly alone, and God was with me.

I will mention a demonstration of painless childbirth which I have had since coming to Idaho. Perhaps it may help some sister who is looking through the *Journal* for a demonstration of this kind, as I was before my baby came. Good help being scarce here, I did my housework up to the time I was confined, and was in perfect health. I awoke my husband one morning at five o'clock, and at half past five baby was born, no one being present but my husband and myself. It was quite a surprise to the rest of the family to see me sitting by the fire with a new baby on my lap. My son got the breakfast, of which I ate heartily; at noon I joined the family in the dining-room. I was out on the porch the second day, around the yard the third day, and have been perfectly well ever since, which has been now over three years. To one who had previously passed through agony untold, with a physician in attendance, this seemed wonderful. I hope this will interest some one who is seeking the truth, and I wish to express my sincere love for our beloved

Leader, who has given us the "Key to the Scriptures." —
E. C. C., Lewiston, Idaho.

A REMARKABLE CASE

Nine years ago my only child was hovering between
life and death. Some of the best physicians in Boston
had pronounced his case incurable, saying that if he
lived he would always be an invalid and a cripple. One
of the diseases was gastric catarrh. He was allowed
to eat but very few things, and even after taking every
precaution, he suffered to the extent that he would
lie in spasms for half a day. He also had rickets; physicians saying that there was not a natural bone in his
body.

It was while he was in what seemed to be his greatest
agony, and when I was in the darkest despair, that I
first heard of Christian Science. The bearer of the joyful
tidings could only tell me to come and hear of the wonderful things that Christian Science was doing. I accepted
the invitation, for I was willing to try anything to save
my child, and the following Friday evening I attended
my first meeting, which was in The Mother Church of
Christ, Scientist. Long before the service began every
seat was filled, which was amazing to me, being an ordinary weekly meeting, and that night I realized from the
testimonies given that Christian Science was the religion
for which I had been searching for years. The next
day I went to find a practitioner, but was unable to get
the one who had been recommended, he being too busy.
On my way home I thought of some of the testimonies
which I had heard the night before, — of people being

healed by simply reading Science and Health. I resolved
at once to borrow a copy, and not dreaming of the
sacrifice that my friend would make by conferring such
a favor, I went and asked her for a loan of Science
and Health. I never saw any one part so reluctantly
with a book as my friend did with her copy of the
textbook.

I read it silently and audibly, day and night, in my
home, and although I could not seem to understand
it, yet the healing commenced to take place at once.
The little mouth which had been twisted by spasms
grew natural and the child was soon able to be up,
playing and romping about the house as any child
should. About this time we decided to move to the
far West.

I was young in Science at the time, and my husband
greatly feared that the journey would cause a relapse
for the child, but instead, he continued to improve. I
constantly read the Bible, Science and Health, and Miscellaneous Writings, the two weeks we traveled, and we
were the only ones in our car who, throughout the journey,
did not get train sick. The child's limbs grew perfectly
straight, he ate anything he wanted, and for years he has
been a natural, healthy child in every way. He has passed
through some of the worst forms of contagion untouched
and unharmed.

I had been reading Science and Health several months,
before I gave any thought to myself and my numerous
complaints. I had never been very strong, and some of
my ailments were supposed to be hereditary and chronic,
hence I dragged through many tedious years with a belief
in medical laws and hereditary laws resting upon me.

Just before I commenced reading Science and Health
I spent a half day in having my eyes examined by one
of the leading oculists in Boston. His verdict was that
my eyes were in a dreadful condition, and that I would
always need to wear glasses. In the meantime I commenced to read Science and Health, and when I thought
of my eyes, I had no need for glasses. The years that
I have been in Science I have used my eyes incessantly,
night as well as day, doing all kinds of trying work and
without requiring the aid of glasses. I was healed of
all my complaints whilst seeking the truth for my child,
and many of them have never returned. Those that
appeared simply came to the surface to be destroyed.
Teeth have been restored and facial blemishes removed, unconsciously, simply by reading Science and
Health. All of this is, however, nothing to compare
with the spiritual uplifting which I have received, and
I have everything to be thankful for. — M. T. W., Los
Angeles, Cal.

INTENSE SUFFERING OVERCOME

For about five years I was afflicted with sciatic rheumatism, in such a severe form that my body was drawn
out of shape. When able to be around, I walked with
the assistance of a cane. The attacks were periodical,
recurring every few months; any exposure to rain or
dampness would bring one. At one time I was in bed
eleven weeks, suffering intensely all the time except when
relieved by hypodermic injections. When I had these
attacks, my regular physician was always in attendance.
My daughter consulted another physician, who said there

would have to be an operation which would include the exposing and scraping of the sciatic nerve. There was also another physician who, knowing of the case, examined my heart and claimed that it was weak and that I was liable to pass on at any time from heart trouble.

After suffering three years I heard of Christian Science, but did not avail myself of it for two years, when I decided to give up all other means and rely wholly upon it. It was not convenient to call a practitioner, so I took Science and Health and applied its teachings as best I could. In three days the trouble completely left me and there has never been the slightest return. My health has been good ever since, and I am at present in perfect physical health. I have been benefited in every way by Christian Science, physically, mentally, and spiritually, and would not be without my understanding of it for anything. — Mrs. E. A. K., Billings, Mont.

HEALED OF RHEUMATISM AND BRIGHT'S DISEASE

I am very thankful to God for what He has done for me. I was suddenly left alone, with many troubles and trials, and I took up the study of the Bible. I was trying to understand it, prior to joining some church, as it seemed to me this would be expected. I had attended all sorts of churches from my childhood up, but never could find any that met my need. As time passed on, my condition became very alarming. Sciatic rheumatism, that had troubled me for some years, became so severe I could scarcely do anything.

Then there appeared some complications, so distressing that I was unable to walk far, and had to sit down frequently by the way. I thought I had Bright's disease, — such excruciating pains, no tongue could tell my sufferings. With all these things upon me, death seemed very near. I had never joined any church, and I thought it now too late, as I would have to wait six months on probation, and I would be dead before that.

About this time I made some inquiries of my sister in reference to Christian Science, as she had already turned to that faith, and I soon found that it was just what I had been looking for. I saw at once that it declared the truth and nothing but the truth. I commenced reading Science and Health, also the New Testament. I wanted to find out what Jesus said, as I did not expect then to live long. I did not go to the meetings, nor did I read Science and Health to be cured, — not thinking of that, — but to be saved from an everlasting hell hereafter. My sister urged me to have a practitioner, but I kept on reading, and praying to God in silence, and what happened? Where had the diseases gone? I persisted in reading Science and Health, together with the Bible, with the knowledge that God as revealed by Christ Jesus can do everything, that He made everything that was made, that He can and does heal the afflicted. He has healed me, thanks to His most holy name. — G. J. H., Charleston, Ill.

GRATEFUL FOR MANY BLESSINGS

In the year 1901, Christian Science found me a hopeless invalid. I had suffered for seven years previous with a very painful back, the result of an operation. I could get no rest or sleep at night, as I could not lie down, but had to sit propped in a chair with pillows around me. Only those who have suffered as I did can know the full misery of it. I had come to the end of material means and never hoped to get well. One day, however, while out walking, it was my good fortune to come to a Christian Scientist's house, and there the teaching was explained to me. I was advised to buy Science and Health, which I did, and the study of this book has healed my back entirely. Christian Science has also cured me of long-standing catarrh of the throat, and neuralgia with which I had been afflicted from childhood. Before coming into Science I had doctored with three of the best physicians in Seattle, but none could give me relief.

I am no longer a sufferer, but rejoice exceedingly in Christian Science. God's promise has been fulfilled to me, "But unto you that fear my name shall the Sun of righteousness arise with healing in his wings." — E. O., Georgetown, Wash.

FREED FROM NEURASTHENIC AND OTHER TROUBLES

Christian Science found in me a minister's son who had failed to profit by continuous teaching in the old thought. Some years ago I was pronounced by a professor of *materia medica*, whose works are in general use, a neurasthenic. I had been in this condition more or less for eight years, and up to two years ago, when Christian Science was first brought to my attention (thanks to Almighty God) through a kind friend, I was almost constantly taking medicine and had in all eleven physicians who undoubtedly did their best, but without avail, notwithstanding almost all known drugs were prescribed, and further I had tried very many patent medicines. I was also put through forms of hygienic treatment and other things that offered inducements. At the time of coming into Science I was taking three times daily forty minims of cod-liver oil and three of creosote, also three drops of Fowler's solution of arsenic, and on the month or so previous had bought eighteen dollars' worth of patent medicine. I was restricted to the simplest means of diet, — all stews, fries, sweets, berries, and tomatoes I had not touched for two years.

I started to read Science and Health, and before I had half finished the book once I was eating everything that any one does. I read the book eleven times straight ahead and many times skipping about. The book has done the work and I am a well man. — C. E. M., Philadelphia, Pa.

MANY ILLS OVERCOME

I have received much help, spiritually and physically, through Christian Science. I had what the doctors diagnosed as muscular rheumatism, dropsy, and constipation of thirty years' standing. A dear friend whom I had known as an invalid had been healed by Christian Science and advised me to read Science and Health. I did so, having a desire to know the truth. One of my troubles was that I could not sleep. I began reading the Bible and the Christian Science textbook, and troubles of every kind disappeared before I had read Science and Health through. The thought came, What about the old remedies? but truth prevailed, and I took all the

material remedies I had and threw them away. That
was seven years ago, and I have not had any use for them
since. My husband was healed of the tobacco habit
of fifty years' standing, also of kidney trouble, by reading Science and Health. I have not words to express
the gratitude I feel to-day for the many blessings that
have come to our home. — Mrs. M. K. O., Seattle,
Wash.

A HELPFUL HEALING

I became interested in Christian Science about eleven
years ago, and was healed of neuralgia of the stomach,
from which I had suffered from a child. As I grew older,
the spells became more frequent and more severe; the
only relief physicians could give me was by hypodermic
injections of morphine. Finally, after each spell, I would
be prostrated for a day or two with the after-effect of the
morphine. I was entirely healed of this trouble through
the study of Science and Health. I think I never realized
what fear meant until I began to try and put into practice
my understanding of Christian Science for my children.
I have proved, however, many times, that fear can
neither help nor hinder in our demonstration of truth.
The first time I realized this was in the overcoming of
a severe case of croup for my little boy. I was
awakened one night by the sound that seems to bring
terror to every mother's heart, and found the little
fellow sitting up in bed, gasping for breath. I got up,
took him in my arms, and went into the next room.
My first thought was, "O if only there was another
Christian Scientist in town!" But there was not, and
the work must be done and done quickly. I tried

to treat him, but was so frightened I could not think;
so I picked up Science and Health, which lay on the
table beside me, and began reading aloud. I had read
but a few lines when these words came to me as though
a voice spoke, "The word of God is quick, and powerful,
and sharper than any two-edged sword." Almost immediately after, the little one said, "Mamma, sing 'Shepherd,' " — our Leader's hymn, that both the big and
the little children love. I began singing, and commenc-
ing with the second line, the little voice joined me. I
shall never forget the feeling of joy and peace that came
over me, when I realized how quickly God's word, through
Science and Health and the beautiful hymn, had accomplished the healing work. This is only one of many
instances in which the power of God's word to heal has
been demonstrated in our home. — A. J. G., River-
side, Cal.

RELIEF FROM MANY ILLS

Paul said, "Be ye transformed by the renewing of your
mind." In my own case deafness has been overcome by
an enlarged understanding of God's word, as explained
by Mrs. Eddy in Science and Health. Many times I
have been enabled to turn to God, to know it was His
will to help in trouble, and obtained the needed benefit.
Catarrh has disappeared; tonsilitis, which very frequently
laid me aside from duties in the schoolroom and home,
is no longer manifest. When temptation comes (for
Christian Science is both preventive and curative), I turn
to that wonderful book, Science and Health, and my
precious Bible, grown dearer since read in the new light

of spiritual understanding, until I know that my mind is renewed, because the action is changed and the inflammation has abated.

Thus in my experience in Christian Science, I have seen the transformation begun, and Truth is able to perfect that which is begun in me so gloriously. — Mrs. C. A. McL., Brooklyn, Nova Scotia.

HEALTH AND PEACE ATTAINED

For fifteen years I was a great sufferer physically and mentally. Eminent physicians treated me for hereditary consumption, torpid liver, and many other diseases. I sought relief at famous springs, the ozone of Florida, and the pure air of Colorado, but in vain. My life was one ceaseless torture.

During all this time, however, I was an earnest seeker after Truth. I examined every religious teaching with a calm and unprejudiced attention. From an orthodox Protestant I became a skeptic, and a follower of Voltaire, Tom Paine, and Ingersoll; yet all the while I retained faith in a supreme intelligent Being who made all. Sick, weary, doubting, and despairing, I accidentally went into a Christian Science church in New York City, on a Wednesday evening, not knowing what kind of a place it was. Seeing a large number of people going into the building, I followed, supposing that a marriage ceremony had attracted the crowd. Being informed it was their regular Wednesday evening service, I inquired as to the denomination. I concluded that it was another new fad, but after investigation I procured a copy of Science and Health, promising I would read it carefully. I began reading the book on Tuesday and finished on Friday of the same week. I was still in the dark. I laid the book down, involuntarily closed my eyes, and silently prayed to God.

I remained in that attitude a few moments, when I felt like the mariner who had been tossed for days upon a boisterous sea, the clouds bending low, the billows rolling high, all nature wrapped in darkness; in his despair he kneels and commits his soul to God, when he suddenly beholds the North Star breaking through the clouds, enabling him to guide his ship to the shores of safety. Many things were made plain to me. I saw that there is one Fatherhood of God and one brotherhood of man; that though "once I was blind, now I see;" that there was no more pain, nor aches, no fear, nor indigestion. I slept that night like a babe and awoke next morning refreshed. There are now no traces whatever of my former complaint and I feel like a new being. — L. P., New York, N. Y.

HEALTH AND PEACE GAINED

About nine years ago I was drawn to Christian Science by a relative whose many afflictions had given place to health and harmony, and whose loving gratitude was reflected in every word and deed. The thought came to me, God indeed healeth all our diseases.

My first reading of Science and Health was without understanding. I was full of darkness and gloom, and it was laid aside for a time. The good seed had been sown, however, and erelong the reading was resumed, and with such interest that my afflictions disappeared "like mist before the morning sun." Asthma (thought to be hereditary), neuralgia in an aggravated form, and besides these, the tobacco and liquor habit of many years' standing left me. Bless the Lord, "He sent his word" and healed me, — for the reading of Science and Health brought to my consciousness the truth that makes free. — S., Shellman, Ga.

CONSUMPTION QUICKLY CURED

I became interested in Christian Science nearly five years ago through the healing of my wife of what the doctors called consumption in its last stages. I had tried everything that I could get in the way of *materia medica*, and every doctor would tell me nearly the same story about the case. At last they recommended for her only a higher, drier climate, and when she would be at her worst to give her something to quiet her.

I tried different climates, but she was no better, indeed worse. At last she struggled along until the first of March, 1899. She had taken to her bed again. For two days and nights she suffered, and I called a physician. He came and diagnosed the case, and said that he could do nothing for her but give her some morphine tablets to make her rest. I gave her two of them according to direction, and just before the time to give her the third, she called me to her bedside, and said, "Don't give me any more of that stuff, for it does me more harm than good," so I turned and placed them in the fire, though I did not then know anything about Christian Science. We had heard of it, but that was all. I gave her the last tablet at eight o'clock that night, and about nine o'clock the next day a lady who had been healed in Christian Science visited her, and introduced her to this great truth. She accepted it and thought she would try it. The lady loaned her Science and Health. She got the book about ten o'clock that day and read it until dinner was called. She ate a hearty dinner, the first in about three days, and that same evening she dressed herself, walked into the dining-room, ate a hearty supper and enjoyed it. She slept well that night. She borrowed this lady's copy of Science and Health two hours each day for eight days, and was healed. The first day that she read Science and Health she weighed about ninety-five pounds. Three months later she weighed one hundred and thirty-five pounds. — A. J. D., Houston, Tex.

A PROFITABLE STUDY

It may help others to know that some one was really healed of severe illness through Christian Science. It is over nine years since we first became interested in the Science, and it would be hard to find a healthier person than I am now. I can go all day, from morning till night, upheld by the thought that "they that wait upon the Lord shall renew their strength." I can truly say that I scarcely know what physical weariness is any more. Before I came into Science the physicians said that one lung was gone, and that the other was affected with tuberculosis; so, from their standpoint, there was little left for me to hope for. We had tried every remedy that they had suggested. I had

gone to the mountains, but could not stay there on account
of the altitude; and when they did not know what else
to do, they said we would better go to England — that
the ocean air would be beneficial. So we spent three
months in the British Isles, and when I came back I
seemed much better, but this only lasted a short time.
In little more than a month I was worse than ever, and
my mother was told that I had but a few weeks, or at
most months, to live.

At that time, a lady, a stranger to us, suggested that
we try Christian Science. There was no prejudice against
it, as we did not even know what it was. We knew of
no Scientists in the Western town where we were living,
and when we were told that we could send to Kansas City
for absent treatment, we thought it was absurd. We were
then told that many people had been healed through the
reading of the Christian Science textbook, Science and
Health, and to us this seemed a little worse than the
absent treatment, but as we had tried everything we
had heard of up to that time, my mother sent for the
book.

It came in the middle of October and we began to read
it together. It seemed to me from the first that it was
something I had always believed, but did not know how
to express — it seemed such a natural thing. My improvement was very gradual, but I felt I was recovering.
After the Christmas holidays I started in at school and
went the whole term without missing a day, — something I had never done before. I finished my school
course without missing a day — in fact, I have not spent
a day in bed since that time. I feel absolutely certain
that I have two sound, healthy lungs now. The hollows

in my chest have filled out, and I breathe perfectly on both sides; rarely have a cold to meet, and have not a sign of a cough.

People sometimes say, "Oh, well, maybe you never had consumption." Well, I had all the symptoms, and they are every one gone through the reading of Science and Health. — E. L. B., Chicago, Ill.

HEALED OF INFIDELITY AND MANY PHYSICAL ILLS

I feel compelled to write my testimony and hope that I may be accepted as one more witness to the Truth as contained in Science and Health with Key to the Scriptures.

In the year 1883 I first heard of Christian Science. I was sitting in a saloon in Leadville, Col., reading a daily paper of that place. My eyes lighted upon an article which spoke of some peculiar people in Boston who claimed to have discovered how to heal as Jesus healed. I do not remember much of the article, but those words stayed with me.

I had drifted out to Colorado from New York City (my home), where I had been under the treatment of many leading physicians. The last one, who was too honest to take my money knowing that he could not cure me, advised me to keep away from doctors and quit taking medicine, as nothing but death could cure me. My trouble was pronounced by some to be Bright's disease, by others gravel on the kidneys with very acute inflammation of the bladder and prostate gland.

In the spring of 1888 my wife and myself were spending the evening at the house of a gentleman whose wife had been healed in the East by Christian Science. The gentleman took a book from its bookcase saying, "Here is a work on Christian Science." It proved to be Science and Health. I knew as soon as I had read the title-page that this was the very book we wanted. We immediately sent for the book, and when it arrived we obeyed the angel and feasted on it. I was very much prejudiced against the Bible, and my first demonstration over self was to consent to read the four Gospels. My wife bought me a New Testament and I began to read it. What a change came over me! All my prejudice was gone in an instant! When I read the Master's words, I caught his meaning and the lesson he tried to convey. It was not difficult for me to accept the whole Bible, for I could not help myself, I was just captured. The disease with which I had been troubled for years tormented me worse than ever for about six months, as if trying to turn me aside; but I lost all fear of it.

I kept up my study of Science and Health and the disease disappeared. I can honestly say that Science and Health was my only healer, and it has been my only teacher. — R. A. C., Los Angeles, Cal.

DISEASED EYES CURED

Christian Science came to me when I was a wreck, my body being completely covered with sores. My eyes were very bad, so that I sat in a darkened room for weeks together, most of the time in bed under opiates. The home doctor and a specialist said the disease of the eyes could not be cured, though they might help me for a while. I had one operation, and the doctor said if I took cold I would become totally blind. My suffering was beyond telling.

A clergyman called almost every day, and sat by my bed and wept, and my good, kind doctor shed tears many times. Finally, after a year of this terrible suffering, I was sent to Indiana, to a sister who had been healed of lung trouble by Christian Science. The first day I was there she read to me from the Bible and from "Science and Health with Key to the Scriptures" by Mrs. Eddy, and I was healed. I knew that God was no respecter of persons, and when I saw what had been done for my sister, who was changed from being a mere frame to a strong, robust, healthy, rosy-cheeked woman, the cough all gone, I said, "God has as much for me, if I will accept it." I was healed instantaneously by Christian Science, and am thankful to God for giving us this understanding through Mrs. Eddy, our beloved Leader. I am now in perfect health. — Mrs. F. S., Laurel, Miss.

THE TEXTBOOK HEALED ME

For twelve years previous to the fall of 1897 I had been under the care of a physician much of the time. Different opinions were given by them, as to the nature of the trouble, some diagnosing it as an abnormal growth, etc. I was healed through reading "Science and Health with Key to the Scriptures" by Mrs. Eddy. It was a clear case of transformation of the body by the renewal of the mind. I am perfectly well at the present time. — J. M. H., Omaha, Neb.

OBSTINATE STOMACH TROUBLE HEALED

There is no doubt that by far the greater number come to Christian Science by the way of physical healing, but there are those to whom this does not particularly appeal. In the hope that it may be of benefit to some such, and in gratitude for help received, I submit my own experience. Three years ago I knew nothing of Christian Science, aside from the knowledge gathered from the daily papers and current literature. When I thought of the subject at all, it was to class Christian Science with various human theories with which I could not be in sympathy, for they seemed to rely upon both good and evil. I had never known of a case of healing, had never read the textbook or heard of the *Journal* or *Sentinel*, but I would sometimes see people going into the Christian Science church. I was tired of trying to find anything satisfactory in religious belief, for it seemed as if God either could not or would not bring into harmony the terrible conditions existing in human society. I had quit using any form of prayer except the Lord's Prayer, and even then omitted the words "lead us not into temptation." How I longed to know just a little of the "why?" and "wherefore?" of it all.

Here is where Christian Science found me. I was thrown in contact with a dear friend of whom I had seen very little for a year or more, a thoroughly educated woman and a thinker. She told me she had taken some treatments in Christian Science for a physical trouble, and had become very much interested in the study of "Science and Health with Key to the Scriptures" by Mrs. Eddy. She asked me if I would like to look at the book, and I said I would be glad to do so. The first chapter, "Prayer," appealed to me from the first, and when I came to Mrs. Eddy's spiritual sense of the Lord's Prayer (Science and Health, p. 17), my interest was fully aroused. I knew that in a dim way I was learning what it means to "pray without ceasing." Very soon I bought a book of my own, and with the help of our Lesson-Sermons, as given in the *Quarterly*, I began in earnest the study of Science and Health, in connection with the Bible.

I stood very much in need of physical healing at this time, having suffered for several years from an obstinate form of stomach trouble. So far as I know, I gave no thought to the benefits I might derive physically from the study, but I did believe this Science held the truth of things, and I was so absorbed in getting an understanding of the Principle that I thought very little of myself. After about three or four months' study I realized that the stomach trouble was gone, and with it went other physical troubles, which have never returned. This healing was brought about by the earnest, conscientious seeking for the truth, as contained in the Bible and interpreted by our Leader in our textbook, Science and Health. I have since learned more of the Science of healing and have been able in a small way to help others in need. I have also learned that in living and loving is healing realized, and in reflecting divine Love I have the "signs following."

When we think of the pure, loving, unselfish life Mrs. Eddy must have lived in order to become conscious of this truth and give it to us, words are a poor medium through which to express the gratitude which her followers feel for her. It is best expressed by obediently following her, even as she is following Christ. — H. T., Omaha, Neb.

DYSPEPSIA QUICKLY HEALED

It has occurred to me that I have had ample time to meditate on the many blessings which I have received through Christian Science, as it is now more than six years since I was entirely healed of dyspepsia as well as constipation in its worst form by the reading of Science and Health. So aggravated were the conditions that for three years or more I was unable to drink a glass of cold water. Everything that I drank had to be hot, and my only means of relief from the bowel trouble was hot water injections, for a period of more than three years.

I can truthfully say that I was permanently, and I might say instantly, healed of those two ailments by reading Science and Health as before stated, and in fact I do not think I had read more than thirty pages of this book when I ignored entirely the most rigid kind of diet. I ate and drank everything I wished without a single harmful effect from that time to this date, and there has not been a drop of medicine in our home for more than six years, in a family of five.

I have also seen the power of Truth manifested in our home by having our youngest child relieved of the most excruciating pain, and changed to his most playful mood, immediately upon notifying one of the faithful practitioners of this city. For all this I am endeavoring to be thankful to God and to our faithful Leader, Mrs. Eddy, whose pure and undefiled life enabled her to discover this precious truth for the benefit of all mankind. — M. C. McK., Denver, Col.

AFTER TWENTY YEARS' SUFFERING

From early girlhood I was considered an invalid, having been injured by a hard fall while playing. The pain was intense for some time and for several hours I was unable to walk or stand alone. Later, a growing weakness of the back accompanied with sharp pains alarmed my parents, who called a physician, and he pronounced it spinal trouble. Then followed nearly twenty years of increased suffering, at times very severe. As years went by and I became a wife and mother, my suffering increased. Everything that medical skill could do was done, but finding no lasting benefit from anything, I lost hope of recovery.

When Christian Science found me I was under the doctor's sentence that if I lived the week through I would become entirely helpless, not able to move hand or foot. My husband was a travelling man, and being urgently called home, he met an old friend on the train who asked why we did not try Christian Science. The reply, We know nothing of it, was followed by a brief explanation of its healing power and the benefit his family had received. This inspired my husband with new hope, and on his arrival at home he called on a practitioner, who recommended our getting Science and Health, which we did, but ignorance and the prejudice of old education produced such fear that I hid the book under the covers of the bed whenever the children came into the room, fearing that it was not of God and would injure them. God's dear love was, however, more potent than these foolish fears, and the first day I read from its sacred pages I was convinced its teachings were the same truths as Jesus Christ had taught centuries ago. When I had read a few pages, I reached out and threw my medicine from the open window at the head of my bed. I then turned back to the book and began reading again, when, lo, the Christ-idea dawned upon me, and I was healed instantaneously.

I first noticed the spot in my back cooling, and soon
I got out of bed. I continued to read eagerly; I felt as
if I wanted to devour the healing truth, and drank it in
as a thirsty plant does the gentle rain. When dinner was
prepared, I walked out and ate a hearty meal with the
family, to the amazement of all. We shall never forget
what a joyful meal this was. How we did thank God
for Christian Science!

As year after year has gone by, till twenty years have
passed and the healing has remained perfect, I have
grown to thank God with deeper sincerity that one brave
woman was found pure enough to bring forth this Christ-
healing again, to remain forever among men and to save
suffering humanity from all disease and sin. — Mrs.
P. L. H., Fairmont, Minn.

FROM DESPAIR TO HOPE AND JOY

I have often had a desire to make public what Christian Science has done for me, but I never could tell of
all my blessings, they are so many. From childhood
I was always sick, never knew one hour of rest, and was
under the doctor's care most of the time. I was living in
the East at that time, and was advised to try change of
climate, which I did. I came West with my family in
the spring of the year, but instead of growing better I
grew steadily worse, until at last I was obliged to keep
my bed for nearly three years, — a great sufferer. My
ailments were, it seemed, all that flesh is heir to, and
were called incurable by the doctors; viz., Bright's disease, and many others, — in the last stages. My case was
known among physicians, many of whom were prominent

specialists, as a most extreme one. Many, upon looking at me, would turn away with a wise shake of the head and say, "What keeps her alive?" My physicians, who were exceedingly kind and did all that lay within their power for me, gave me up and the death sentence was pronounced on me by all who attended me.

It was then I realized that "man's extremity is God's opportunity." The "little book" was handed me at this hour of great need. I read it, not thinking it would heal me, but, like a drowning man, I grasped at it. I read it, read it again, and soon found myself growing stronger; then I kept on reading and was perfectly healed of all the supposedly incurable diseases. — L. B., Austin, Minn.

TRUTH MAKES FREE

As the son of a physician, a graduate in pharmacy, and an ex-druggist, I had a perfect contempt for what I thought Christian Science to be. About six and a half years ago, however, having exhausted all material means at my command, — *materia medica*, electricity, gymnastics, cycling, and so on, — and being in a hopeless state, the study of Christian Science was taken up. I had been a sufferer from catarrh and sore throat for over thirty years, and in the last five were added several others, including dyspepsia, and bronchitis, and a loss in flesh of sixty pounds. I was completely healed, and regained health, strength, and flesh through the spiritual understanding of Christian Science, the result of about six weeks' study. This good and perfect gift came to me through the careful and prayerful study of Christian Science, as revealed to the world to-day through Science and Health. The promise of Christ Jesus, "the truth shall make you free," was fulfilled, and the past six years of health and harmony have been spent in striving to "hold fast that which is good."

While most grateful for the physical healing, my gratitude for the mental and spiritual regeneration is beyond expression. When I learned that Jesus' mission of healing sickness as well as sin did not end with his short stay upon earth, but is practical in all ages, my joy was unbounded. Having spent thousands in the old way, it seemed wonderful to be healed at such small cost as the price of the "little book" and a few weeks' study. Every thought of prejudice immediately vanished before the proofs that Christian Science is indeed the elucidation and practical application of Jesus' teachings, which are demonstrable truth, "The same yesterday, and to-day, and forever." — C. N. C., Memphis, Tenn.

DEAF EARS UNSTOPPED

As a mother of a family my heart goes out in love and gratitude to that good woman we are privileged to call our Leader, for all she has done through her book for me and mine.

Ten years ago I was healed of hereditary deafness and catarrh of the head, simply through reading the book, Science and Health. For years previous I had consulted and taken treatment from some of the best specialists for the ear and throat, both in England and America, but grew worse all the time. I was then urged by a lady who had been healed through Christian Science to buy this book and study it. I did so very reluctantly, but

had not read fifty pages before I felt I had indeed found
the truth which makes free, and can truly say, from that
time I have never had a return of the ailment.

That for which I am, however, most grateful, is the
daily help it is to me in my household of young children. I am sure if mothers only knew what Christian
Science truly means they would give all they possess
to know it. We have seen croup, measles, fever, and
various other children's complaints, so-called, disappear
like dew before the morning sun, through the application of Christian Science, — the understanding of God
as ever-present and omnipotent. It has been proven
to me without a doubt that God is a very present help in
trouble, and what a blessed help this wonderful truth is
in the training of our children, and how quickly the child
grasps it.

Some time ago my little girl, then three years old,
dislocated her shoulder. I was alone in the house at
the time. The pain was so intense that she became
faint. I treated her the best I knew how, but kept
holding the thought that just as soon as some one came
I would run for help. She seemed to grow worse and
cried very much. I undressed her and tried to twist
the arm into place, but it caused such suffering that I
began to get afraid. Then like a flash came the thought,
What would you do if you were out of the reach of a practitioner? Now is your time to prove God's power and
presence. With these thoughts came such a sense of
calm and trustfulness that I lost all fear. I then asked
the child if I should read to her; she said "Yes, mamma,
read the truth-book." I began reading aloud to her
from Science and Health. In about half an hour I noticed

she tried to lift the arm but screamed and became very pale. I continued to read aloud and again she made an effort to put some candy into her mouth. This time I noticed with joy that she almost reached her mouth before she felt the pain. I kept reading aloud to her until my sister and two boys came in, when she jumped off her bed, so delighted to see her brothers that she forgot her arm. She then began to tell her aunt that she had broken her arm and mamma treated it with the truthbook. When this happened, it was about 10.30 A. M. and by 3 P. M. she was playing out doors as though nothing had ever happened. — Mrs. M. G., Winnipeg, Man.

SAVED FROM INSANITY AND SUICIDE

A few years ago, while under a sense of darkness and despair caused by ill health and an unhappy home, Science and Health was loaned me with a request that I should read it.

At that time my daughter was given up by *materia medica* to die of lingering consumption, supposed to have been inherited. My own condition seemed even more alarming, as insanity was being manifested, and rather than go to an insane asylum, it seemed to me the only thing to do was to commit suicide. Heart trouble, kidney complaint, and continual headaches caused from female trouble were some of the many ailments I had to contend with. My doctor tried to persuade me to undergo an operation as a means of relief, but I had submitted to a severe operation ten years previous, and found only additional suffering as a result, so I would not consent.

When I began with Science and Health, I read the chapter on "Prayer" first, and at that time did not suppose it possible for me to remember anything I read, but felt a sweet sense of God's protection and power, and a hope that I should at last find Him to be what I so much needed, — a present help in time of trouble. Before that chapter on "Prayer" was finished, my daughter was downstairs eating three meals a day, and daily growing stronger. Before I had finished reading the textbook she was well, but never having heard that the reading of Science and Health healed any one, it was several months before I gave God the glory.

One by one my many ailments left me, all but the headaches; they were less frequent, until at the end of three years the fear of them was entirely overcome.

Neither myself nor my daughter have ever received treatments, but the study of the Bible and Science and Health, the Christian Science textbook by Mrs. Eddy, has healed us and keeps us well.

While Christian Science was very new to me, I attended an experience meeting in First Church of Christ, Scientist, Chicago. A gentleman told of an unhappy woman who was about to separate from her husband. This gentleman had asked her if she did not love her husband. She replied, "No; when I married him I did, but not now." He told her God made man in His image and likeness, and that He is perfect. He said to her, "Go home and see only God's perfect man; you don't need to love a sinful mortal such as you have been looking upon." The lady followed his advice, as he told her there is no separation in divine Mind. In a short time peace and harmony were in her home, and both husband and wife became members of a Christian Science church.

This testimony was like a message from heaven to me. I had received many benefits from the study of Science and Health, but it had never dawned upon my darkened consciousness till then how wonderful our God is. I knew what had taken place in that home could take place in my unhappy home where there was neither rest nor peace.

I hopefully took up my cross, and step by step my burden grew lighter, as I journeyed along, realizing the presence of the Christ, Truth, that indeed makes us free. Not all at once did any outward change appear, but at the end of three years all was peace, all the members of the family attending church together and realizing that there is but one Mind. — E. J. B., Superior, Wis.

STOMACH TROUBLE HEALED

I was healed of stomach trouble of many years' standing by reading Science and Health. My condition had reached the stage in which I had periodical attacks, that came on with greater frequency. I was a travelling salesman, and it was a common occurrence for me to have to call a physician to my hotel to administer morphine for an acute form of this disease. This became a regular thing at certain places, and these attacks always left me worse than before. As a result of the last one I lost a great deal in weight. I had tried many physicians and most of the usual remedies during these years of suffering, without any good result. Finally, as a last resort, I decided to try Christian Science, and I was healed by reading "Science and Health with Key to the Scriptures" by Mrs. Eddy.

My health has been of the best since I was healed, now six years ago. In the family we have depended entirely on Christian Science for our healing, and have ever found it efficacious. We consider the physical healing, however, only incidental to the understanding of God and His goodness. This, together with our increased love for the Bible, is proving most valuable to us. We are humbly trying to live the lives that will prove our gratitude to God, and to our beloved Leader, Mrs. Eddy. — Charles E. Peck, St. Johnsbury, Vt.

FREED FROM MANY YEARS OF SUFFERING

In the spring of 1880 I was taken down with a severe attack of stomach trouble, was bedfast for three months, and not able to drive out for nearly six months. During this time I had three good doctors treating me. I gained a little in strength, but had very little relief from the stomach trouble. I was recommended to try mineral springs and did so, but with the same disappointment. I went to a sanitarium, but yet the stomach trouble prevailed. I had some friends who recommended patent medicines, but no healing came.

I worried along in this way for several years. Finally I read medicine nearly two years with a good doctor friend, especially for my own benefit, and during this time I had a severe attack of bladder trouble, and for fifteen years I suffered so severely at times that I thought life was not really worth living. In connection with these troubles I suffered every winter with rheumatism and the grip. I also had a growth coming on both eyes called cataract, which caused my eyes to be inflamed nearly all the time, and this growth had made such progress that it was causing my vision to be very dim when reading. Corns were not forgotten, as I was reminded of them very frequently, and for all these troubles I had tried every remedy I heard of that I was able to get, specialists included, without relief.

Thanks to a friend who took me in this hopeless, discouraged condition and led me to the light that never knows darkness, I got a copy of Science and Health by Mrs. Eddy and was healed in a short time by reading this work. — D. W. L., Anderson, Ind.

RELIEF FROM INTENSE SUFFERING

I became interested in Christian Science in 1901. For four or five years I had suffered with severe attacks which nothing but an opiate seemed to relieve. After one which I think was the worst I ever had, I consulted our family physician, who diagnosed my case as a dangerous kidney disease and said that no medicine could help me but that I must undergo a surgical operation. I continued to grow worse and went to see the physician again, and he advised me to consult a doctor who was connected with the city hospital of Augusta. This doctor made an examination and diagnosed the difficulty as something different but quite as serious. Meanwhile a friend offered me a copy of Science and Health. I said I did not care to read the book, but she was so urgent that I finally promised to do so. I received the book on Saturday, and on Sunday morning I sat down to read it. When I reached the place where Mrs. Eddy says she found this truth in the Bible, I began comparing the two books. I read passages which looked very reasonable to me, and said to myself, This is nearer to the truth than anything I have ever seen. I continued to read all day, stopping only long enough to eat my dinner. As I read on, everything became clearer to me, and I felt that I was healed. During the evening a neighbor came in, and I said, "I am healed, and that book has healed me." I read on and was certainly healed. Eight days after my healing I did my own washing. This occurred in February, 1901. About six weeks after, I was called to care for my mother, who was under the care of my former physician. I again let him examine my side, as he wished to see if the trouble was still there. He said, "It is certainly gone." I said to him, "Doctor, you told me I would never be a well woman unless I was operated upon; what has healed me?" He replied, "God has healed you." — S. H. L., North Pittston, Me.

GRATEFUL FOR MANY BLESSINGS

It is with sincere gratitude for the many blessings Christian Science has brought me, that I give this testimony. I first heard of Christian Science about fifteen years ago. A friend of mine was taking treatment for physical troubles, and was reading the textbook of Christian Science, Science and Health with Key to the Scriptures. The title of the book appealed to me very strongly. I said to my friend, "If that is a Key to the Scriptures, I must have it."

I had long been a member of a Bible class in an orthodox Sabbath school, but I never felt satisfied with
that which was taught; there was something lacking,
I did not understand then what it was. I purchased a
copy of Science and Health and began to study it. I
wish I could express in words what that book brought
me. It illumined the Bible with a glorious light and I
began to understand some of the Master's sayings, and
tried to apply them.

I had had a longing to live a better Christian life for
many years, and often wondered why I failed so utterly
to understand the Bible. Now I knew; it was lack of
spiritual apprehension.

I did not know at first that people were healed of disease and sin by simply reading Science and Health,
but found after a while that such was the case. At
that time I had many physical troubles, and one after
another of these ills simply disappeared and I found
that I had no disease, — I was perfectly free. The
spiritual uplifting was glorious, too, and as I go on in the
study of this blessed Science, I find I am gaining surely
an understanding that helps me to overcome both sin and
disease in myself and in others. My faith in good is increased and I know I am losing my belief in evil as a power
equal to good. The pathway is not wearisome, because
each victory over self gives stronger faith and a more
earnest desire to press on. — E. J. R., Toledo, Ohio.

GRATEFUL FOR MORAL AND SPIRITUAL AWAKENING

About four years ago, after I had tried different ways
and means to be relieved from bodily suffering, a faith-

ful friend called my attention to the teaching of Christian Science. After some opposition, I decided to investigate it, with the thought that if this teaching would be helpful, it was meant for me as well as for others; if it did not afford any help, I could put it aside again, but that I would find out and be convinced.

After I had read Mrs. Eddy's work, Science and Health, a few days, I found that my ailments had disappeared, and a rest had come to me which I had never before known. I had smoked almost incessantly, although I had often determined to use my will power and never smoke again, but had always failed. This desire as well as the desire for drink simply disappeared, and I wish to say here, that I received all these benefits before I had gained much understanding of what I was reading. Like a prisoner, who had been in chains for years, I was suddenly set free. I did not then know how the chain had been removed, but I had to acknowledge that it came through the reading of this book. I then felt an ardent desire to read more, and to know what this power was that had freed me in a few days of that which I had been trying for years to shake off and had failed. It then became clear to me that this was the truth which Jesus Christ taught and preached to free humanity almost two thousand years ago. It did not, however, occur to me to apply it in my business affairs; on the contrary, I first thought that if I continued in my study I would have to retire from business.

This did not happen, however, for I gradually found that the little understanding of this wonderful teaching which I had acquired became a great help to me in my business. I became more friendly, more honest, more loving to my fellow-men; and I also acquired better judgment and was able to do the right thing at the right time. As a natural result my business improved. Before I knew anything of Christian Science my business had often been a burden to me, fear and worry deprived me of my rest. How different it is now! Through the study of the Bible, which now possesses unmeasurable treasures for me, and of our textbook, Science and Health, and the other works of our Leader, I receive peace and confidence in God and that insight into character which is necessary for the correct management of any business. — W. H. H., Bloomfield, Neb.

HEREDITARY DISEASE OF THE LUNGS CURED

For a long time I have been impelled to contribute a testimony of the healing power of Truth. As I read other testimonies and rejoice in them, some one may rejoice in mine. I was healed by reading Science and Health. By applying it, I found it to be the truth that Jesus taught, — the truth that sets free.

From childhood I had never known a well day. I was healed of lung trouble of long standing. Consumption was hereditary in our family, my mother and three brothers having passed on with it. The law of *materia medica* said that in a short time I must follow them. I also had severe stomach trouble of over eight years' standing, during which time I always retired without supper, as the fear of suffering from my food was so great that I denied myself food when hungry. For over twenty years I had ovarian trouble, which was almost unbearable at times. It dated from the birth of my first child, and at one time necessitated an operation. I suffered with about all the ills that flesh is heir to: I had trouble with my eyes from a child; wore glasses for fourteen years, several oculists saying I would go blind, one declaring I would be blind in less than a year if I did not submit to an operation, which I refused to do.

But thanks be to God whose Truth reached me through the study of our textbook. Words fail to express what Christian Science has done for me in various ways, for my children, my home, my all. The physical healing is but a small part; the spiritual unfolding and uplifting is the "pearl of great price," the half that has never been told. — Mrs. J. P. M., Kansas City, Mo.

TEXTBOOK APPRECIATED

It has been my privilege to have interviews with representatives of more than sixty per cent of the nations of this earth, under their own vine and fig-tree. I had never heard a principle understandingly advanced that would enable mankind to obey the apostolic command, "prove all things," until Science and Health with Key to the Scriptures was placed in my hands. I believe that the honest study of this book in connection with the Bible will enable one to "prove all things."

I make this unqualified statement because of what my eyes have seen and my ears heard from my fellow-men of unquestioned integrity, and the positive proofs I have gained by the study of these books. Many supposed material laws that had been rooted and

grounded in my mentality from youth have been overcome. It required some time for me to wake up to
our Leader's words in Miscellaneous Writings, p. 206:
"The advancing stages of Christian Science are gained
through growth, not accretion." I had many disappointments and falls before I was willing to do the scientific
work required to prove this statement; yet notwithstanding
the cost to ourselves, I am convinced that we cannot do
much credit to the cause we profess to love until we place
ourselves in a position to prove God as He really is to us
individually, and our relation to Him, by scientific work.

I wish to express loving gratitude to our Leader for
the new edition of Science and Health. In studying
this new edition one cannot help seeing the wisdom,
love, and careful and prayerful thought expressed in
the revision. Often the changing of a single word in
a sentence makes the scientific thought not only more
lucid to him who is familiar with the book, but also to
those just coming into the blessed light. All honor to
that God-loving, God-fearing woman, Mary Baker G.
Eddy, whose only work is the work of love in the helping
of mankind to help themselves; who has placed before her
fellow-men understandingly, what man's divine rights are,
and what God really is. — H. W. B., Hartford, Conn.

RUPTURE AND OTHER SERIOUS ILLS HEALED

When I took up the study of Christian Science
nearly three years ago, I was suffering from a very
bad rupture of thirty-two years' standing. Sometimes
the pain was so severe that it seemed as if I could not
endure it. These spells would last four or five hours,

and while everything was done for me that could be done, no permanent relief came to me until I commenced reading Science and Health with Key to the Scriptures. After I had once looked into it I wanted to read all the time. I was so absorbed in the study of the "little book" that I hardly realized when the healing came, but I was healed, not only of the rupture, but also of other troubles, — inflammatory rheumatism, catarrh, corns, and bunions.

I would never part with the book if I could not get another. I am seventy-seven years old, and am enjoying very good health. — Mrs. M. E. P., St. Johnsbury, Vt.

MOTHER AND DAUGHTER HEALED

When Christian Science came to me, I had been taking medicine every day for twenty years, on account of constipation. I had been treated by doctors and specialists; had taken magnetic treatments and osteopathy; had tried change of climate; had an operation in a hospital, and when I came out was worse than before. I was so discouraged, after I had tried everything I ever heard of, and was no better but rather grew worse, that it seemed as though I must give up trying to get well, when a friend suggested that I try Christian Science. I had heard that Christian Scientists healed by prayer, and I thought this must be the way Jesus had healed. I felt that this was all there was left for me to try. I sent for the book, Science and Health, and commenced to read it out of curiosity, not thinking or knowing that I could be helped by the reading, but thinking I must still take medicine and that I must also have treatment by a Scientist. I, however, dropped my medicine and read for three days; then a light began to shine in the darkness. I was healed of the trouble and have never had to take medicine since. I have studied Science and Health faithfully ever since, and other ailments have disappeared. My little daughter has also been healed and has learned to use this knowledge in her school work. — Mrs. O. R., Leadville, Col.

LIVER COMPLAINT HEALED

As my thoughts go back to the time when I believed I had nothing to live for, and when each morning's awaking from sleep brought a sense of disappointment to find myself still among the living (for I had hoped each night that I closed my eyes in sleep that it would be the last time), my heart overflows with love and gratitude to God for our dear Leader who discovered this blessed truth and to the dear ones who have helped me so lovingly and patiently over many rough places.

Twelve years ago, I consulted a physician because I had noticed some odd-looking spots on one of my arms. He said they were liver spots, but that it was not worth while prescribing for those few, that I should wait until I was covered with them. About three months later, with the exception of my face and hands, I was covered with them. Then I became alarmed and called on another physician who prescribed for me, but he finally said he could do no more for me. Other physicians were consulted with no better results. Six years ago, friends advised me to see their family physician, and when I called on him he said he was positive he could cure me, so I asked him to prescribe for me. At the

end of two years, after prescribing steadily, he said I
was so full of medicine that he was afraid to have me
take any more, and advised a rest. After having paid
out a small fortune, I was no better, and very much
discouraged.

Two years ago, having failed in business, I applied to
one of my patrons for a furnished room where I could
meet the few I still had left. This lady, who is a Christian
Scientist, loaned me Science and Health, and because
she asked me so often how I was getting on with the
book, I began reading it. I also attended the Wednesday evening meetings which I found very interesting.
After hearing the testimonies at the meetings, I decided
to speak to some practitioner about these spots, but
not until I had at least a hundred dollars on hand, because I thought I would require that amount for treatments, as I had been accustomed to paying high prices.
I had not inquired about prices, and in fact did not speak
to any one about my intentions, because I felt sensitive
on this subject. When I had read about half of Science
and Health, I missed the spots, and upon searching
could find no trace of them. They had entirely disappeared without treatment. In a few weeks the reading of that book had accomplished what *materia medica*
had failed to accomplish in ten years. It is impossible
to express the feeling of relief and happiness which came
over me then. — C. K., Astoria, N. Y.

A CONVINCING INVESTIGATION

While I have testified to those around me and in many
localities, of my healing in Christian Science, I feel that

it is high time I put the candle in the candlestick where all who will may see. My earliest recollection was a day of suffering, — a physical inheritance from my mother, which gave simple interest for a time until years advanced and compound interest was added. My father was a physician, and material remedies were used for my mother without avail, consequently his confidence in them for me was shaken, — in fact he often told me it was better to suffer without medicine than become a chronic doser, without pain.

I began teaching in early life and continued for more than twenty years, and during that time not a day passed without pain, or fear of pain, and only for my innate love of life it would have become an intolerable burden. For five years oatmeal was my chief food and I became almost as attached to it as Kaspar Hauser to his crust. I was early taught to have faith in God, and many times was relieved of pain only to have it appear again in an aggravated form.

At last my heart cried out for the living God, and the answer came by one of His messengers, who told me of Christian Science. I replied that I believed God could heal, but that I had no faith in the healing of Christian Science, but would like to investigate its theology, as it might aid in giving me some clue to the meaning of life. For three years I had searched the works of the most scientific writers to find the origin of life; many times I would think I had traced it to the beginning, but it would elude my grasp every time. One day in talking with my friend, she said she would like to loan me the textbook, Science and Health, which I very willingly accepted. Not long afterward I felt a severe attack of suffering. I opened the book for the first time and found a paragraph near the middle which attracted my attention. I read the same paragraph over and over for nearly two hours. When the tea bell rang I closed the book and I shall never forget my perception of the new heaven and the new earth, — everything in nature that I could see seemed to have been washed and made clean. The flowers that I have always loved so much, and that from childhood had told me such sweet stories, now spoke to me of the All-in-all, the hearts of my friends seemed kinder, — I had touched the hem of the garment of healing.

I ate my supper that evening forgetful of the preparations I had made for suffering, and when the next day began I was more zealous of good work than ever before. Since closing Science and Health at my first reading I have never been able to find the paragraph which I had read so many times over, the words seemed to have slipped away from me, but my joy knew no bounds at having found the pearl of great price. By the continued reading of the book I was entirely healed, and for fourteen years I have not seen a day of physical suffering. — Miss L. M., Rome, N. Y.

DEAFNESS AND DROPSY HEALED

I had been deaf from childhood. I suffered intensely after eating, and dropsy was another of my complaints. This, with consumption, caused one doctor to say, "It puzzles me; I have never seen such a case before as yours."

I met a friend who had been cured in Christian

Science, and she said, "Try Christian Science." I got
a copy of Science and Health and in three weeks I
was entirely cured. I felt uplifted. It seemed as if
God's arms were around and about me. I felt as if
heaven had come down to earth for me. After five
years of suffering can any one wonder at my unspeakable gratitude? — A. B., Pittsburgh, Pa.

GRATEFUL FOR MANY BLESSINGS

In 1894 I began the study of Christian Science. At
that time I was greatly in need of its healing truth.
For a number of years previous I had been a semi-
invalid with no hope of ever being well and strong
again. Several years before this time I had undergone
an operation which resulted in peritonitis. For three
years previous to my study of Science and Health
by Mrs. Eddy, I was scarcely ever free from headache
caused by the weakened and diseased condition of the
internal organs. At the time I began the study of
Christian Science I was taking five kinds of medicine.

I began to read Science and Health, and did not
take treatment, for I thought, "If this is truth, I shall
be healed; if it is not, I shall be able to detect it,
and will have nothing to do with it." I became a
devoted student and gradually my bodily diseases left
me, — I was free, and since that time, nearly ten
years ago, neither my two children nor myself have
taken any medicine; and our understanding of truth
has been able to meet and overcome any suggestion of
illness.

I was a devoted member of an orthodox church,

but as I grew older I began to question my beliefs, and to my questions I could find no satisfactory answer. I became dissatisfied and finally ceased attending church. I could not accept the idea of God taught there, and at last my friends looked sadly upon me as an atheist. There I stood until I learned to know God as revealed in Science and Health, and then all my questionings were answered. In my girlhood I had always prayed to the God I held in mind, and when the shadows of sickness, pain, and death came to my family, I prayed as only those can who know that if He helps not, there is none; but my prayers were unanswered. Then I closed my Bible, saying, "There is a mistake somewhere, perhaps some time I may know."

Only those who know the attitude of mind that I was in can understand the joy that came to me as I began to learn of God in Christian Science, and of my relation to Him.

Many proofs of the healing power of Truth and of His protecting care throng my thoughts. Seven years ago, when we were in a far distant country, where Christian Science was then unknown, my little daughter came in one morning from her school, saying, "Mother, I have measles; twenty of the girls are sick in bed and I am afraid they will put me there also." Her face, hands, and chest were covered with a deep red rash, throat sore, and eyes inflamed. We began immediately to do our work in Science and at night, when I left her at the door of the college, her face was clear, her eyes bright, and all fear destroyed. That was the end of the disease. — F. M. P., Boston, Mass.

A JOYFUL EXPERIENCE

In love and gratitude to God, and to Mrs. Eddy, the interpreter of Jesus' beautiful teachings, I wish to tell of some of the benefits which I have received from Christian Science. It is a little over a year since Science found me in a deplorable condition, physically as well as mentally. I had ailments of many years' standing, — chronic stomach trouble, severe eye trouble, made almost unbearable from the constant fear of losing my sight (a fate which had befallen my mother), also a painful rupture of twenty-five years' standing. These ailments, combined with unhappy conditions in my home, made me very despondent. I had entirely lost my belief in an all-merciful God, and I did not know where to turn for help. At that time Christian Science was brought to my notice, and I shall never forget the sublime moment when I perceived that an all-loving Father is always with me. Forgotten was all sorrow and worry, and after four weeks' reading in Science and Health all my ailments had disappeared. I am to-day a healthy, contented woman.

All this has come to pass in one short year, and my earnest desire is to be more and more worthy to be called a child of God. This is in loving gratitude for an understanding of this glorious truth. — Mrs. R. J., Chicago, Ill.

AN EVER-PRESENT HELP

It is a year since I began to read Science and Health, and I will now try to outline what a knowledge of its teachings has done for me.

My condition was then very trying; my eyes, which had caused me much trouble since childhood, were very painful. For these I had been treated by some of the best specialists in my native land, and after coming to the United States I had been doctored much and had worn glasses for four years. I also had catarrh, for which I had taken much medicine without being relieved. In addition to this I was an excessive smoker, using tobacco in some form almost constantly. I had contracted a smoker's heart, and used liquors freely.

The one who brought to me that which I now prize so highly, was a book agent. I told him that I should be forced to leave my trade on account of my eyes. He then told me of having been healed of a cancer, through Christian Science treatment. He showed me a copy of Science and Health, which had the signs of much use, and after being assured that if I did my part I would be healed of all my diseases, I sent for a copy of the book.

My recovery was very rapid, for after reading the book only three weeks I was completely healed of the tobacco habit. I will say, in regard to this healing, that it did not require even as much as a resolution on my part. I was smoking a cigar, while reading Science and Health, when all the desire to continue smoking left me, and I have never had a desire to use tobacco in any form since then. My eyes were the next to manifest the influence of the new knowledge gained, and had soon so far recovered that I could go about my work with ease, and I have had no more use for glasses. To-day my heart is normal, the catarrh has totally disappeared, and I am not addicted to the use of liquor.

Christian Science has proved to be an ever-present help, not only in overcoming physical ailments, but in business and daily life. It has also overcome a great sense of fear. The Bible, which I regarded with suspicion, has become my guide, and Christianity has become a sweet reality, because the Christian Science textbook has indeed been a "Key to the Scriptures" and has breathed through the Gospel pages a sweet sense of harmony. — A. F., Sioux City, Iowa.

SEVERE EYE TROUBLE OVERCOME

After hearing Christian Science lightly spoken of, from a Christian pulpit, I decided to go to one of the services and hear for myself. From infancy I had been devoted to my church, and as soon as I was old enough I was ever active in the work. Feeling it to be my duty to attend every service held in my own church, I took advantage of the Wednesday evening meetings. My first visit was not my last, I am thankful to say, for I saw immediately that these people not only preached Christianity, but practised and lived it. At that time I was wearing glasses and had worn them for sixteen years. At times I suffered the most intense pain, and for this phase of the trouble, one specialist after another had been consulted. All gave me very much the same advice; each one urged extreme carefulness and gave me glasses that seemed to relieve for a time. None of them held out any hope that my sight would ever be restored, saying that the

defect had existed since infancy, and that in time I should
be blind.

The thought of blindness was very distressing to me,
but I tried to bear it with Christian resignation, since
I thought that God had seen fit to afflict me; but since
I have learned that He is a loving Father, who gives
only good, I regret that I ever charged Him with my
affliction. I had no treatment, but I read Science and
Health, and my eyes were healed and glasses laid aside.
I can never find words to express my thanks to our dear
Leader, through whose teachings my sight has been regained. I can truthfully say that "whereas I was blind,
now I see" — through an understanding of Truth I
have found my sight perfect as God gave it. — Miss
B. S., Wilmington, N. C.

A TESTIMONY FROM IRELAND

It is with a heart full of love and gratitude to God,
and to our dear Leader, that I send this testimony to
the Field. I had never been a strong girl; had always
been subject to colds and chills, and suffered all my
life from a delicate throat. Seven years ago I had a
very severe attack of rheumatic fever and subsequently
two less severe ones. These left all sorts of evils behind them, — debility, chronic constipation, and several
others, so that with these ills my life was often a
burden to me and I used to think I never should receive relief or health. I had also lost all love for
God and faith in Him. I could not accept a God who,
as I then believed, visited sickness and sorrow upon
His children as a means for drawing them to Him.

I was in this state of mind and body when Christian Science found me. A dear friend, seeing my suffering, presented the truth to me, and though at first I did not believe that there could be healing for me, the Christian Scientists' God seemed to be the one I had been looking for all my life. I began to read Science and Health, and shall never forget my joy at finding that I could love and trust God. I took to studying the Bible, and read nothing but Science and Health and other Christian Science literature for a year. After studying the "little book" for about six weeks, I one day realized that I was a well woman, that I had taken no medicine for three weeks, and that my body was perfectly harmonious. The reading of Science and Health had healed me. The wonderful joy and spiritual uplifting which came to me then no words of mine can describe. I had also suffered from astigmatism and had for several years been obliged to use special glasses when reading or working, and could never use my eyes for more than half an hour; but from the first reading of Science and Health I found that I could read in any light and for any length of time without the slightest discomfort. I am not only grateful for the physical healing but for the mental regeneration. I rejoice that I am now able to help others who are sick and sorrowing. — E. E. L., Curragh Camp, County Kildare, Ireland.

THE TEXTBOOK MAKES OPERATION UNNECESSARY

In the early part of the year 1895 my physician said I must undergo a surgical operation in order ever to be well.

While in great fear, and dreading the operation, a kind neighbor called, and after telling me of Christian Science gave me a copy of Science and Health. She said I must put aside all medicine, and by reading faithfully she knew I could be healed. The book became my constant companion, and in a short time I was healed. Besides the relief from an operation, I was completely healed of severe headaches and stomach trouble. Physicians could give me no help for either of these ailments. For ten years I have not used medicine of any kind, and have not missed a Christian Science service on account of sickness during this period. I am perfectly well. To say that I am grateful to God for all this does not express my feelings. The physical healing was wonderful, but the understanding given me of God, and the ability to help others outweigh all else. I also love our dear Leader. — Mrs. V. I. B., Concord, N. H.

KIDNEY DISEASE AND EYE TROUBLE HEALED

Early in 1904 I was teaching in a private boarding-school. I was a very unhappy, discontented woman; I had kidney disease, besides sore eyes, and my general health was very bad. The doctor said that the climate did not suit me, and that I certainly should have a change. The best thing, he said, was to go back to France (my own country); but I did not like to leave the school, so I struggled on until July, when we went travelling for a month, but I came home worse than ever. I had a lot of worry, one disappointment after another, and I often thought that life was not worth living. In September, 1904, we heard for the first time of Christian Science through a girl who was attending our boarding-school, and who was healed through Christian Science treatment. We bought the textbook, "Science and Health with Key to the Scriptures" by Mrs. Eddy, and what a revelation it was and is to us; it is indeed the fountain of Truth. I had read Science and Health but a very short time when I took off my glasses, began to sleep well, and soon found myself well in mind and body. Besides this, it has brought harmony into our school, where there had been discord, and everything is changed for the better. I cannot describe the happiness that has come to me through Christian Science; I can only exclaim with the psalmist: "Bless the Lord, O my soul;" and may God bless Mrs. Eddy.

My one aim now is to live Christian Science, not in words only, but in deeds; loving God more and my neighbor as myself, and following meekly and obediently all our Leader's teachings. Words cannot express my gratitude to Mrs. Eddy for Christian Science. — S. A. K., Vancouver, B. C.

DISEASE OF BOWELS HEALED

When I first heard of Christian Science I had been afflicted for nine years with a very painful disease of the bowels, which four physicians failed even to diagnose, all giving different causes for the dreadful sufferings I endured. The last physician advised me to take no more medicine for these attacks, as drugs would not reach the cause, or do any good. About this time I heard of Christian Science, and had the opportunity of reading "Science and Health with Key to the Scriptures" by Mrs. Eddy, a few minutes every day for about a week, and I was thereby healed. In looking back I found I had not suffered in the least from the time I began reading this book. It has been nearly seventeen years since this wonderful healing, and I have had no return of the disease. My gratitude is endless and can be best expressed by striving mightily to walk in the path our Leader has so lovingly shown us in Science and Health. — Mrs. J. W. C., Scranton, Pa.

HEALED BY READING THE TEXTBOOK

After doctoring about a year, I was obliged to give up school and was under medical care for two years; but grew worse instead of better. I was then taken to specialists, who pronounced my case incurable, saying I was in the last stages of kidney disease and could live only a short time. Shortly afterward my uncle gave me a copy of "Science and Health with Key to the Scriptures," and asked me to study it. After studying a short time I was able to walk a distance of several miles, which I had not been able to do for three years. I also laid aside glasses which I had worn seven years, having been told I would become blind if my eyes did not receive proper care. It is over a year since I received God's blessing, and I am now enjoying perfect health and happiness. I have never had my glasses on since I first began reading Science and Health, and I have not used any medicine. — L. R., Spring Valley, Minn.

A TESTIMONY FROM SCOTLAND

I came to Christian Science purely for physical healing. I was very ill and unhappy; very cynical and disbelieving in regard to what I heard of God and religion.

I tried to live my life in my own way and put religion aside. I was a great believer in fate and in will-power, and thought to put them in the place of God, with the consequence that I was led to do many rash and foolish things. I am now thankful to say that my outlook on life is entirely changed; I have proved God's wisdom and goodness so often that I am willing and thankful to know my future is in His hands and that all things must work out for the best. I have found a God whom I can love and worship with my whole heart, and I now read my Bible with interest and understanding.

I was healed of very bad rheumatism simply by reading Science and Health. I had tried many medicines, also massage, with no result, and the doctors told me that I would always suffer from this disease, as it was inherited, and also because I had rheumatic fever when a child. I suffered day and night, and nothing relieved me until Science proved to me the falseness of this belief by removing it. I gave up all the medicines I was taking and have never touched any since, and that is more than two years ago. Before this I had often tried to do without a medicine that I had taken every day for ten years, but was always ill and had to return to it, until I found out that one Mind is the only medicine, and then I was freed from the suffering.

I had also suffered constantly from bilious attacks, colds, and a weak chest, and had been warned not to be out in wet weather, etc., but now, I am glad to say, I am quite free from all those material laws and go out in all sorts of weather. — R. D. F., Edinburgh, Scotland.

CURING BETTER THAN ENDURING

For eight years I was a great sufferer from weak lungs and after being treated by ten different physicians, in the States of Illinois, Missouri, and Colorado, I was told there was no hope of my recovery from what they pronounced tuberculosis, which was hereditary, my father having been afflicted with it. I was greatly emaciated and hardly able to be about. My general condition was aggravated by what the doctors said was paralysis of the bowels. Three physicians so diagnosed it at different times, and assured my husband that I could never get more than temporary relief. This indeed I found difficult to obtain, in spite of my almost frantic efforts. At times I was nearly insane from suffering, and after eight years of doctoring I found myself steadily growing worse. For four years I did not have a normal action of the bowels, and it was only by extreme effort and by resort to powerful drugs or mechanical means, with resultant suffering, that any action whatever could be brought about.

I had heard nothing of the curative power of Christian Science, and only to oblige a friend I went one night, about three years ago, to one of their mid-week testimonial meetings, in Boulder, Colorado. I was much impressed by what I heard there, and determined at once to investigate this strange religion, in the hope that it might have something good for me. I bought the textbook, Science and Health, and from the first I found myself growing stronger and better, both physically and mentally, as I acquired a better understanding and endeavored to put into practice what I learned. In one week

I was able to get along better without drugs than I had for years with them, and before three months had passed I was better than I had been any time in my life, for I had always suffered more or less from bowel trouble. Since that time I have taken no medicine whatever, and rely wholly upon Christian Science. My lungs are now sound, my bowels normally active, my general health excellent, and I am able to endure without fatigue tasks that before would have prostrated me. The study of our textbook was the sole means of my healing. — L. M. St. C., Matachin, Canal Zone, Panama.

SEVERE ECZEMA DESTROYED

It is only two years since I came from darkness into the light of Christian Science, and to me the spiritual uplifting has been wonderful, to say nothing of the physical healing. Words cannot express my gratitude for benefits I have received in that time. For five years I suffered with that dreaded disease, eczema, all over my body. Five doctors said there was no help for me. The suffering seemed as terrible as the hell fire that I had been taught to believe in. When Christian Science came to me two years ago through a dear friend, she gave me a copy of Science and Health and asked me to read it. I told her that I would, for I was like a drowning man grasping at a straw. I had been a Bible student for twenty-eight years, but when I commenced reading Science and Health with the Bible I was healed in less than a week. I never had a treatment. A case of measles was also destroyed in twenty-four hours after it appeared. — Mrs. M. B. G., Vermilion, Ohio.

SCIENCE AND HEALTH A PRICELESS BOON

I am a willing witness to the healing power of Christian Science, having had a lifetime's battle with disease and medical experiments. Various doctors finally admitted that they had exhausted their resources, and could only offer me palliatives, saying that a cure was impossible. I had paralysis of the bowels, frequent sick headaches with unutterable agony, and my mortal career was nearly brought to an end by a malignant type of yellow fever. Many were the attending evils of this physical inharmony, but God confounds the wisdom of men, for while studying Science and Health two years ago, the veil of ignorance was lifted and perfect health was shown to me to be my real condition, and to such there is no relapse. The constant use of glasses, which were apparently a necessity to me for years, was proven needless, and they were laid aside. Mrs. Eddy has made Scripture reading a never-failing well of comfort to me. By her interpretation "the way of the Lord" is made straight to me and mine. It aids us in our daily overcoming of the tyranny of the flesh and its rebellion against the blessed leading of Christ, Truth. The daily study of the Bible and our textbook is bringing more and more into our consciousness the power of God unto salvation. — J. C., Manatee, Fla.

A CRITIC CONVINCED

With gratitude to God I acknowledge my lifelong debt to Christian Science. In 1895 I attended my first

Christian Science meeting, and was deeply impressed
with the earnestness of the people and the love reflected, but as for the spiritual healing of the physical
body, I did not believe such a thing to be possible.
I bought Science and Health and studied it to be
able to dispute intelligently with the supposedly deluded followers of Christian Science. I pursued the
study carefully and thoroughly, and I have had abundant reason since to be glad that I did, for through this
study, and the resultant understanding of my relation to God, I was healed of a disease with which I
had been afflicted since childhood and for which there
was no known remedy. Surely my experience has
been the fulfilling in part of the Scripture: "He sent
His Word and healed them, and delivered them from
their destructions." I believe that Science and Health
reveals the Word referred to by David. — C. A. B. B.,
Kansas City, Mo.

BORN AGAIN

It was in April, 1904, that I first heard the "still,
small voice" of the Christ and received healing through
Christian Science; and the blessings have been so
many since, that it would take too much space to
name them. Reared from childhood in an intellectual
atmosphere, my paternal grandfather having been an
orthodox minister of the old school for forty years,
and my father a deep student, ever seeking for the
truth of all things, I began early to ponder and to
study into the meaning of life, and came to the conclusion before I was twenty that though God probably

existed in some remote place, still it was impossible to connect Him with my present living. My highest creed, therefore, became, "Do right because it *is* right and not for fear of being punished." Then began the suffering. Sorrow after sorrow followed each other in rapid succession; for ten long years there was no rest, the road was indeed long and hard and had no turning, until finally the one thing that had stood by me all through the trials, namely, my health, gave way, and with that went my last hope. But the last hour of the night had come, the dawn of day was at hand; a dear friend left Science and Health upon my piano one day, saying that I would gain much good by reading it.

Glad to get away from my own poor thoughts, I opened the "little book" and began to read. I had read only a short time when such a wonderful transformation took place! I was renewed; born again. Mere words cannot tell the story of the mighty uplifting that carried me to the very gates of heaven. When I began to read the book, life was a burden, but before I had finished reading it the first time, I was doing all my housework and doing it easily; and since that glorious day I have been a well woman. My health is splendid, and I am striving to let my light so shine that others may be led to the truth. There have been some mighty struggles with error, and I have learned that we cannot reach heaven with one long stride or easily drift inside the gate, but that the "asking" and the "seeking" and the "knocking" must be earnest and persistent.

For a long time I was always looking back to see if

the error had gone, until one day when I realized
that to catch a glimpse of what spiritual sense means
I must put corporeal sense behind me. I then set to
work in earnest to find the true way. I opened
Science and Health and these words were before me,
"If God were understood, instead of being merely believed, this understanding would establish health" (p. 203).
I saw that I must get the right understanding of God!
I closed the book and with head bowed in prayer I
waited with longing intensity for some answer. How
long I waited I do not know, but suddenly, like a wonderful burst of sunlight after a storm, came clearly
this thought, "Be still, and know that I am God." I
held my breath — deep into my hungering thought
sank the infinite meaning of that "I." All self-
conceit, egotism, selfishness, everything that constitutes
the mortal "I," sank abashed out of sight. I trod, as
it were, on holy ground. Words are inadequate to convey the fulness of that spiritual uplifting, but others
who have had similar experiences will understand.

From that hour I have had an intelligent consciousness
of the ever-presence of an infinite God who is only good.
— C. B. G., Hudson, Mass.

A RESTLESS SENSE OF EXISTENCE DESTROYED

Through reading Science and Health and the illumination which followed, I was healed of ulceration of
the stomach and kindred troubles, a restless sense of
existence, agnosticism, etc. The torture I endured with
the stomach trouble I will not attempt to describe. The
attending physician declared that I could live but a short

time, and I felt there would be a limit to my endurance of the torture, but the disease was dissipated into
nothingness through Christian Science, which brought
me peace.

Like many others I had been seemingly lost in the
sea of error, without a compass, yet earnestly and honestly seeking a haven. I had investigated all kinds of
religions and philosophies that came under my notice,
with the exception of Christian Science, which was
not then deemed worthy of inquiry, and yet it held
the very truth I was searching for — the light which
"shineth in the darkness; and the darkness comprehended it not." Three years of stubborn resistance to Truth, with increasing suffering, followed —
then the light came, and with it a new experience.
Now, after nine years of Christian Science experience,
under severe tests, it can be truthfully said that it
has not failed me in any hour of need. — J. F. J.,
Cincinnati, Ohio.

MORALLY AND PHYSICALLY HEALED

I did not accept Christian Science on account of any
healing of my own, but after seeing my mother, who was
fast drifting toward helplessness with rheumatism, restored
to perfect health with only a few treatments in Christian
Science, I thought surely this must be the truth as Jesus
taught and practised it, and if so it was what I had been
longing for.

This was about ten years ago and was the first I had
ever heard of Christian Science. We soon got a copy
of Science and Health and I began in the right way to

see if Christian Science were the truth. I had no thought of studying it for bodily healing; in fact, I did not think I needed it for that, but my soul cried out for something I had not yet found. This book was indeed a key to the Scriptures.

It was not long after I began reading before I discovered that my eyes were good and strong, I could read as much as I wished, and at any time, which was something I could not do before, as my eyes had always been weak. The doctors said they never would be very strong, and that if I did not wear glasses, I might lose my sight altogether. I never gave up to wearing glasses, and now, thanks to Christian Science, I do not need them, my work for the past two years as a railway mail clerk being a good test. At the same time my eyes were healed, I also noticed that I was entirely healed of another ailment which had been with me all my life, and which was believed to be inherited. Since that time my growth has seemed to me slow, yet when I look back and view myself as I was before Christian Science found me, and compare it with my life as it now is, I can only close my eyes to the picture and rejoice that I have been "born again" and that I have daily been putting off "the old man with his deeds," and putting on "the new man."

Some of the many things that have been overcome through the study of Science and Health, and through realizing and practising the truth it teaches, are profanity, the use of tobacco, a very quick temper, which made both myself and those around me at times very miserable, and such thoughts as malice, revenge, etc. — O. L. R., Fort Worth, Tex.

HEALTH AND UNDERSTANDING GAINED

Most of my boyhood days were spent in the hands of physicians. From birth I was considered a very weakly child, but my mother was brave, and being much devoted to me did everything within her knowledge and power for my comfort. Sickness and medicine were continually before me, and by the time I reached my teens I thought I knew a material remedy for every ill. I continued in my delusion, because I was never told the real cause of my trouble. Besides being under a leading specialist for two years, I was also an outdoor patient at a noted hospital, but I was not healed. It is wonderful how the "little ones" are cared for in the face of all these seeming difficulties. I always used the prayers that I had been taught, and as I grew older I began to ask for wisdom. Little by little I gained a desire for freedom, and my prayers finally led me to the truth. The first week that I heard of Christian Science, I visited the home of dear Christian Science friends, and was at once refreshed by their purity of thought and example. I bought a copy of Science and Health, and, after studying it a little while with the Bible, I saw that if the Bible was true, Science and Health must also be true. I began to demonstrate over my physical and mental condition, and as soon as the fear and pain began to leave me I felt encouraged to go on. I was healed, and stopped complaining. I kept on studying our textbook, and when I got an understanding in a small degree of the Science of Mind, my first thought was to help others. I was guided where I could pro-

gress in Science, and was no longer "carried about with
every wind of doctrine," but held to Principle as closely
as possible. From the time the healing came into my
consciousness, the desire for material remedies left me,
because Christian Science at once pointed out the way to
get at the cause of discord and disease. All that I had to
give up were the false beliefs of mortal mind. Christian
Science then taught me to love the church, and to appreciate what it had already done for mankind. I often
thought of the old adage, "Charity begins at home,"
and after three years' preparation I felt able to take Christian Science to my home, where it found, in due time,
ready acceptance and willing disciples. This gave me
even greater joy than my own healing. The more good
I saw accomplished, the more love I had for the truth.
Christian Science changed my course from the first, and
gave me a nobler aim and purpose in life. I was not
so easily influenced by other people's shortcomings,
when I learned that evil has neither personality nor place.
I was not so ready to take offence, when I found out the
way to work unselfishly for the upbuilding of the Cause.
— A. E. J., Toledo, Ohio.

AN EVER-PRESENT HELP FOUND

On the 23rd of March, 1900, I received from one of my
daughters a copy of Science and Health on my seventy-first
birthday. Although a constant reader of all kinds of papers
and books, I had never heard anything of Christian Science, except a short notice that spring in a San Francisco
newspaper, from an orthodox clergyman, referring to the
Christian Science people in not very complimentary style.

In Mrs. Eddy's book I came across a great deal of
thought that was not readily understood at the first reading, but by continued and careful study, and a good deal
of help from my knowledge of chemistry and natural philosophy, I soon shook off the belief of sensation
in matter, — the so-called elementary substance. One
afternoon I put the belt on my circular saw to cut blocks
of firewood and also to split a small stick of frame tim-
ber. In doing this the stick closed and pinched the saw.
I picked up a small wooden wedge and tried to drive
it into the saw kerf, but a bit of ice let the stick on to the
back of the saw and instantly it flew, with heavy force,
into my face, and bouncing off my left cheek fell about
twenty feet off on the snow. The blood spattered on the
snow next the saw table, and on feeling with my hand
there were two wounds, one on the lock of the jaw and
another forward, as big as a dollar, on the cheek bone.
"Now," I thought to myself, "there is a case of surgery
for you," and without further ceremony, I began to
treat the case to the best of my knowledge, with the
result that the bleeding stopped almost instantly, and
so did a thumping pain, which had commenced. I
paid no more attention to the matter, but finished my
work, and then went to supper. When I washed my
face, I felt a big lump on the jawbone where the block
of wood struck, but after my usual reading I went to
bed and slept all night until near daylight, when a pain
on the right side awoke me. On feeling with my hand
there was another big lump on the right side, but I
treated it and went to sleep again. I never lost an
hour from the hurt, although I found out that my jaw
was broken. There is no scar, only a little red spot on

the cheek, and the lumps on the bone have long since disappeared.

In summing up the benefits I have received from the reading of Science and Health, I can but refer to a condition of sickness dating back to the war (1862), when chronic and malignant diarrhœa came near making an end of my material existence. My hearing, also, was seriously impaired from the effect of cannon firing at Shiloh, but it has come back to me, and where I formerly dared not eat an orange, or grapes, I can now eat anything without being hurt. My peace of mind is giving me a rest which I never experienced before during my life, and I have ceased to look away off for the divine presence that was always near, though I did not know it. — L. B., Baldy, N. M.

MANY PHYSICAL AND MENTAL TROUBLES OVERCOME

Less than a year ago, when nothing but trouble seemed to encompass me, I was led to Christian Science. My mother's copy of Science and Health was always lying on the table, but I scarcely ever read it. One day, however, the mental conflict was so great I commenced reading in the hope of obtaining peace. Every day since then my companions have been the Bible and Science and Health. At that time I had a very serious eruption on my face, which had been there two years. We had consulted several physicians, and used every remedy suggested to eradicate it, but they proved useless. I had given up all hopes of its ever being healed, as the physician we last consulted pronounced it tuberculosis of the skin and incurable. A few weeks after I commenced reading, I was amazed to see it almost healed over, and to-day my cheek is perfectly smooth, while the scar is disappearing.

In April my baby was born with only the practitioner and a woman friend present. I suffered little pain, and the third day I went down-stairs. I am able to nurse him, — a privilege of which I was deprived with my first child. He is a picture of health, having never been sick a day since he was born. — K. E. W. L., Mt. Dora, Fla.

A NEW LIFE GAINED

Leaving home when a young man, I carried with me a protection against the temptation of a great city, — a mother's prayers and a small Bible. For a time I read the Bible and prayed, but without understanding. This did not suffice, and evil seemed to gain the victory. I soon omitted to read my Bible; forgot to go to God in prayer for guidance and help, and looked to the world for that which it never has and never can give, — health, peace, and joy.

Thus, years later, when Christian Science came into my home, it found me prayerless, churchless, godless; a home discordant, and with no thought or knowledge of spiritual things. Up to this time, my wife had for years been seeking health through the physicians, but without success, and as a last resort had been sent to Christian Science. The help received was so wonderful that I commenced the study of Science and Health. The first effect which I realized from the reading of our textbook, was a great love for the Bible and a desire to read it, something which I had not done

for years. I went in silent prayer to God, that I might
see the light and truth which would enable me to become a better man. "Ye must be born again." Thus
again, and as a child, was I taught to pray "the effectual
fervent prayer" which "availeth much." In a few
weeks' study of Science and Health together with the
Bible, and without other help, I was healed of a desire
for liquor, of years' standing, and of the use of tobacco.
Ten years have passed and these appetites have never
returned. I have never used either liquor or tobacco
in any form from that time to the present. Surely this
Scripture is fulfilled in our home: "Old things are passed
away; behold, all things are become new." How can
we estimate the value of a book, the study of which brings
such transformation and regeneration? Only as we
endeavor to live, and strive to practise what it teaches,
can we begin to pay our debt to God, and to her whom
He has sent to make plain to human understanding the
life and teaching of Christ Jesus. — W. H. P., Boston,
Mass.

A VOICE FROM ENGLAND

For a number of years I was a weary woman, not ill
enough in health to be called an invalid, but suffering
more than could be told with fatigue and weakness.
Feeling that this was God's will, I did not ask to be healed,
although I was constantly doctoring. I suffered with dyspepsia, congestion of the liver, and many other things,
including weak eyesight. With all the medicine, and
with different changes for rest, I never regained health,
and thought I never should, so I prayed for grace to bear
my cross patiently for others' sake. One day, while

lying on my couch exhausted, which had become a frequent experience, the words came to me, "Whatsoever ye shall ask in prayer, believing, ye shall receive." I rose, knelt down and said, O God, make me well. I was telling a friend this and she kindly gave me a *Sentinel.* Imagine my joy when I saw the testimonies of healing! I believed them, remembering our Lord's words, "Blessed are they that have not seen, and yet have believed." I obtained a copy of Science and Health and before a week had passed I realized that if God was my all I needed no glasses. My eyes were healed in a few days, and since then I have never thought of glasses. I was also cured of dyspepsia, and nothing that I have eaten has hurt me since then. The belief in health laws was next destroyed, by knowing that our heavenly Father did not make them, and from this has come the beautiful experience of the overcoming of fatigue.

For this alone I can never be thankful enough. True indeed are the words, "They shall run, and not be weary." This was more than a year ago, and I can say that not once have I felt inclined to lie on the couch, nor have I had a headache, although I am doing more work than ever before. Fear has also been overcome in many ways. — A. L., Chelmsford, England.

DEPRAVED APPETITES OVERCOME

When Christian Science first came to me, or rather, when I first came to Christian Science, I did not have a very bad opinion of myself. I thought I was a pretty good fellow. I had no religious views. I seemed to be getting along as well as, if not better than, some who

professed Christianity. So I drifted along until I was
led to investigate Christian Science.

As I progressed in the understanding as gained from
the study of both Science and Health and the Bible,
and commenced to know myself, I found that a great
change had been wrought in me. For fifteen years I
had used tobacco, both chewing and smoking; for ten
years I had been a victim of the drink habit, sometimes
to excess; I was also addicted to profanity. Christian
Science removed these appetites. A stomach trouble
and other lesser ills, such as headache, a bad temper, an
inordinate love of money, etc., disappeared under the
same benign influence. Those things that seemed to be
pleasure do not give me pleasure now. They were not
real pleasure. I have lost nothing, I have sacrificed
nothing; but I have gained everything, and not yet the
whole, for I can see plenty yet to be done.

The condition of mind before investigating and after
is as different as black and white. As Mrs. Eddy
says, "Not matter, but Mind, satisfieth." — G. B. P.,
Henry, S. D.

CATARRH OF THE STOMACH HEALED

I should like to express my gratitude for the many
benefits I have received through Christian Science, and
to mention the great joy brought to me in the thought
that man is not the helpless victim of sin, disease, and
death. Through its teachings I have been able to overcome many errors.

When Christian Science found me, one year ago
last April, in Chicago, I was suffering from catarrh

of the stomach, which had been very persistent, and I had been a slave to the cigarette habit for eighteen years. Pain and weakness had robbed me of all that one holds dear. The first symptoms of the disease appeared about five years ago in the form of severe cramps of the stomach, which finally developed into other symptoms of that painful disease. I doctored continually, my diet daily becoming more rigid, until three slices of toast became my daily allowance of food.

In this condition I left the East for my home in Chicago, hoping that a change of climate might benefit me. After spending six weeks there and finding no relief, I concluded to return East. The Sunday morning before leaving I picked up a Sunday paper, and glancing through the religious items my eyes fell on the notices of Christian Science church services. Curiosity led me to a service and I shall never forget that morning or the surprise and joy it gave me to find that beautiful church, and to know that so great a number actually believed that God does heal the sick to-day. This brought a first ray of hope. The evening service found me there again. Among the notices read was that of a reading room, giving the location and time of opening. Monday morning found me there promptly, and the first book I picked up was Science and Health which opened a new world to me.

I had dieted so long and suffered so much that I had a morbid fear of food. When I had reached and read "neither food nor the stomach, without the consent of mortal mind, can make one suffer" (Science and Health, p. 221), I left the reading room for something to eat. I found a bakery near by, and bought a bag of cakes which I ate, and shortly after I had a hearty dinner without the least complaint from my stomach.

From that time until now I have eaten anything that I wished, and the craving for cigarettes, which I had for many years, has entirely vanished. The understanding of Truth, which entirely relieved the diseased stomach, healed also the morbid appetite for smoking. After coming back East, I bought a copy of Science and Health, which I have read daily, and find it a continual help in all the affairs of life.

In my home and at work I find this Science a comfort and source of strength. I have had many difficulties in the way, but it has helped me out of them all. — W. E. B., New Britain, Conn.

SPINAL DISEASE HEALED

When I first heard of Christian Science, seven years ago, I supposed that it was some old fad under a new name. In the little Texas town where we then lived there were two or three Christian Scientists who met at the home of one of their number to read the Lesson-Sermon. Meeting one of them one day, I asked if unbelievers could come to their meetings. She said that they could if they wanted to. I went, expecting them to do something that I could laugh at when telling my friends about it. How surprised I was to find out that they didn't do anything but read the Bible and another book which they called Science and Health. I still thought it all foolishness, but resolved to go to their meetings until I found out all they believed. I continued to go until I began to understand a little of what they knew,

not what they believed; and instead of spending my
time telling others what a silly thing Christian Science
is, I am now trying to find words to tell what a great
and wonderful thing it is. I have been healed of so-
called incurable spinal disease of ten years' standing
by studying the Bible and Science and Health. Science
and Health has been my only teacher, and I wish to send
my thanks to our dear Leader.

There are no other Scientists near where we now live,
but I have the *Quarterly* and study the lessons by myself.
I have five small children, and Christian Science is in-
valuable to me in controlling them, and in overcoming
their common ills. They often help themselves and
each other to destroy their little hurts and fears. — Mrs.
M. H., Oleta, Okla.

MANY TROUBLES OVERCOME

In the second chapter of First Peter, ninth verse, I
read "that ye should show forth the praises of him who
hath called you out of darkness into his marvellous
light." The periodicals so wisely established by our
Leader give us one means of showing forth the praises
of Truth.

From the darkness of physical pain and weariness into
the light of wholeness and joyousness in work and
living, — from the darkness of a clouded sight into the
light of clearer vision, — from the darkness of doubt
and discord into the marvellous light of the reality of
good, — this is what a reading of the Christian Science
textbook has done for me.

At the time the book was lent to me, I was teach-

ing in the public schools of Chicago, and absences from
my work on account of illness were of frequent occurrence.
For five weeks I had been under the care of a specialist
for an organic trouble, and he said I would have to come
as many more months before a cure could be effected.
At this time, Science and Health was brought to my
notice. I never thought of such a thing as being healed
by the reading of the book, but my thought was so changed
that I was healed, not only of the organic trouble, but of
blurred eyesight, fatigue, and a train of other discordant
manifestations. I did not go back to the physician
until four months later to pay my bill (which, by the
way, was more than five times the price of the Science
and Health I had purchased). From the time I read
the book I taught steadily without losing time from my
work. I was helped, too, with my work in many other
ways.

Through reading the textbook I learned that God has
given us strength to do all we have to do, and that it is
the things we do not have to do (the envying, strife, emu-
lating, vainglorying, and so on) that leave in their wake
fatigue and discord.

Gratitude to our beloved Leader, Mrs. Eddy, and
to her faithful students, with whom I afterwards became associated, can be expressed only by daily efforts
to put into practice what has been taught. — T. H. A.,
Madison, Wis.

PREJUDICE OVERCOME

I became interested in Christian Science somewhat
over three years ago when in much need of help. I
had never been strong, and as I grew older I grew

weaker and at last became so ill that life was a burden to me. Science and Health by Mrs. Eddy was sent to me, in answer to prayer, as I thought. I was a little afraid of all these new fads, as I thought them, but I had not read far before I felt that I had found the truth which makes us free. I was healed of stomach trouble, inward weakness, and bilious attacks.

One physician said I might have to undergo an operation before I could get well, but, thanks to this Truth, I have found that the only operation needed was the regeneration of this so-called human mind by learning to know God. In many cases I have been able to help myself and others.

Words cannot express my thanks to Mrs. Eddy, and to all who are bringing these great truths to the help of the whole world. — E. E. M., Huntington, W. Va.

A CONVINCING TESTIMONY

I became interested in Christian Science some five years ago, the practical nature of its statements appealing to me, and I must say, at the outset, that with my little experience I have found it all and more than I ever dreamt of realizing on this plane of existence. I am satisfied that I have found Truth. God is indeed to me an ever-present help.

My little girl, some ten months old, was afflicted with constipation. It was so severe I dreaded to go out anywhere with her, as I knew not when she would be taken with a convulsion. I had tried all the usual remedies in such cases, but it seemed to grow more obstinate. There was a Christian Scientist living in

the same house with us, a Scientist who let her light
shine, and while she said little, I felt the reflection of
Love. I had no knowledge of the teachings of Christian Science, save that God was the physician at all
times. In my own way I believed He was all-powerful, and I said to my husband one day, "I am through
with medicine for baby. I am just going to leave her
in God's care and see what He will do. I have done
all I can." I did as I said, laid my burden at God's
feet, and did not pick it up again. In two days the
child was perfectly natural, and has since been free
from the trouble. She is now six years of age. Some
months later a second test came. She woke up at nine
o'clock at night crying and holding her ear. There
was to sense a gathering. I was alone. I took up my
Science and Health and Bible, but the more I worked
the louder she screamed. Error kept suggesting material remedies, but I said firmly: "No; I shall not go
back to error. God will help me." Just then I thought
of my own fear, how excessive it was, and a conversation
I had with the Scientist who first voiced the truth to me,
came to mind. She said she always found it helpful
to treat herself and cast out her own fear before treating a patient. I put baby down and again took up
my Science and Health, and these were the words I
read: —

"Every trial of our faith in God makes us stronger.
The more difficult seems the material condition to be
overcome by Spirit, the stronger should be our faith
and the purer our love. The Apostle John says: 'There
is no fear in Love, but perfect Love casteth out fear' "
(Science and Health, p. 410). I looked up, the crying

had ceased, the child was smiling, and in a few minutes asked to be put to bed. There has been no further trouble of that kind.

I have since seen the power of Truth overcome error of many forms, including croup, whooping-cough, tonsilitis, etc. I am thankful for all these proofs, but far more grateful am I for the spiritual teaching to love, to forgive, to curb my tongue, and cease my criticism. — M. A. H., Brockton, Mass.

HEALED PHYSICALLY AND SPIRITUALLY

I had been taking medicine continually for many years. Finally I was taken suddenly ill and could not leave my room for about two months, then I went away for three months, thinking that I should come back and be able to continue my work. I improved very much, but the fear of quick consumption was with my doctor and my family and friends, and I was warned about the coming winter. Only too soon the fear manifested itself. I had worked just three weeks when all the pains and aches returned, and I had to go to bed as soon as I got home, so there was no pleasure in living. My employer advised me to see my physician, and said perhaps I should not work that winter. I then and there turned to Christian Science. I could not afford to give up work and live away from home, neither did I want to depend on doctors and medicine any longer. I took the book and read it on my way to work, and at noon I lay down on a couch instead of going out for luncheon and fell asleep. When I awoke I was a different person, all pains and aches had gone, and I was free. I was so

happy I could hardly contain myself; to material
sense it was wonderful. As I walked I kept saying,
"Wonderful, wonderful, wonderful," and tried to understand "the scientific statement of being" by repeating portions at a time, then pondering over them. I
read the book four times in succession, and every
time I found more and more to aid in the understanding.

This healing was in October, 1901, with no other
help than Science and Health, and soon I was relieved
of other chronic ailments. In February I was able to
put away eyeglasses, which I had worn ten years and
a half for astigmatism. Oculists told me I would always
have to wear them. A month later my father asked
me to help him, as he was suffering so much from constipation, dyspepsia, and neuralgia. He had been sub-
sisting on bran, nearly starving himself until he was most
miserable, and his limbs seemed so cold that they were
kept wrapped in blankets. I felt very humble as he
asked me, and told him I would have a practitioner help
him, as I had never treated any one; but he would not
consent to have any one but myself, and I finally told
him I would try, but that he must not hold Science responsible if he were not benefited, for my lack of understanding, and not Science, would be at fault. At my request
he read Science and Health, ate whatever he wanted,
and used no medicine in any form. After two treatments I received word from him that he was healed
of that bondage of thirty years' standing. In view of
all these signs which followed my acceptance of Christian Science, I knew it must be true. — R. L. A.,
Chicago, Ill.

A VOICE FROM THE SOUTH

I was delicate from childhood, and my parents did not think it was possible for me to live more than a few years. I lived, however, although there was not much improvement in my health. Travel and change of climate brought only temporary relief, and the physicians gave me no hope that I would ever be well.

As a last resort I began the study of Science and Health, and before I had finished reading the book I realized that its author was divinely commissioned to bring this spiritual message to a waiting world. Through this reading my health was restored, and I was healed of one disease that has been called incurable by all physicians.

For this, together with the greater and higher blessing of having the spiritual fact of being unfolded to me, I am most grateful.

What shall be rendered for such benefits received and made possible by the consecrated life of our revered Leader? Only by following the teachings of our textbook, and by loving obedience to her gentle and timely admonitions can we show our true sense of gratitude. — F. H. D., De Funiak Springs, Fla.

HEALED AFTER MUCH SUFFERING

A testimony given in the *Journal* led me to investigate Christian Science, and I hope in return to be the means of leading some one else to see the beauty of this saving truth, and to learn to know God aright and man's relationship to Him. I know from experience that it is prejudice and misapprehension of what Christian Science is, that keeps many from enjoying the blessings it bestows.

I had been taking patent medicines for several years, and had been to one of the best sanitariums in this country, but was not healed, although I received some benefit, for which I shall always feel grateful, for I know the physicians did all they could for me. I sometimes thought I had exhausted all remedies, but did not give up, for I felt there must be something to heal me if I could find it.

When in this state of mind Christian Science came to my notice, and after reading several *Journals,* I purchased a copy of Science and Health. I read for several days at odd times. I commenced to improve, and in about a week I was healed of most of my ills, among which were dyspepsia and nervous debility.

Although I had heard about Christian Science before, I had never heard that the reading of the Christian Science textbook had ever effected the healing of anybody. I commenced reading to find out what Christian Science was, but was surprised to find myself improving, and was soon assured that it was the theology of Science and Health that healed me, just as it was the theology of Jesus that healed the sick.

It has also proved to me that there can be no Christian Science Church that does not heal the sick and sinful, for healing follows as the natural result of the teaching of Christian Science. The Bible has become a new revelation to me, and I can read it much more understandingly by the light received through the reading of Science and Health. — A. F. M., Fairmont, Minn.

THROUGH GREAT TRIBULATIONS

When I attempt to make plain what Christian Science has done for me, words fail me. For twenty years I was a constant sufferer, my spine having been injured when I was very young. As a little child I suffered so much that I would look up to the stars and beg God, who I thought might be up there somewhere, to take me away from the earth, — I was so tired. A great wall of pain seemed to separate me from the pleasures enjoyed by others, and I could not explain how I felt, because no one could understand. Years passed, and I saw my earthly happiness swept away; my heart was broken and I did not know what to do. I cried for help, day after day and night after night, although I was not sure what God was, nor where He was. I only knew that I suffered, and was in need of help, and that there was no earthly help for either mind or body. I loved purity, truth, and right always, and this made evil seem a most terrible reality. I was unable to cope with it, and so found myself in despair. This was my condition when I commenced reading Science and Health. I was ready for its message, and in about ten days there came a wonderful insight into the truth which heals the sick and binds up the broken-hearted. All pain left me, I had a glimpse of the new heavens and the new earth, and was beginning to be fed by Love divine.

I had suffered for years with insomnia. That night I rested like a child, and awoke the next morning well and happy. A flood of light daily illumined the pages of the "little book," and the revelation it holds for all came to my waiting heart. "The peace which passeth all understanding" rested upon me, and joy too deep for words transformed my life. My prayers were answered, for I had found God in Christian Science.

The Bible, which I knew very little about, became my constant study, my joy, and my guide. The copy which I bought at the time of my healing is marked from Genesis to Revelation. It was so constantly in my hands for three years that the cover became worn and the leaves loose, so it has been laid away for a new one. Two and three o'clock in the morning often found me poring over its pages, which grew more and more sacred to me every day, and the help I received therefrom was wonderful, for which I can find no words to express my gratitude. — I. L., Los Angeles, Cal.

A HELPFUL TESTIMONY

Words cannot express my gratitude to God for Christian Science. When I first read Science and Health, I had tried every remedy I had ever heard of. I felt no change in mind or body that I was conscious of until I read page 16 of the chapter on "Prayer," in Science and Health. The first words of the "spiritual sense of the Lord's Prayer," telling of our Father-Mother God, gave me a glimpse of heavenly light. I stopped and reasoned, and remembered the teachings of Jesus. The truth of man's spiritual being dawned on my consciousness. I realized I was not subject to mortal laws, as I had been taught all my life. I could not explain how I knew this, but I knew it. Through Christian Science, Mrs. Eddy had given me what

I had longed for all my life, — a Mother, a perfect
"Father-Mother God." I had known there was a
great lack, and at that time I believe the orthodox
world had but half of the truth which Jesus came to
establish. When I read, "Give us this day our daily
bread," and its spiritual interpretation, my tears began
to flow; all the years of bitterness, hate, and fear melted
away. I knew then, as I know now, that nothing satisfies
but Love. That day began the outward and inward
conscious healing, — mental and physical. There never
came a doubt! I absolutely knew that Christian Science
was and is the truth. Money, friends, materiality, are
nothing beside the conscious knowledge of God, man,
and the universe.

I did not need treatment from any one, — Science
and Health was so clear and beautiful. I could not
understand the Bible before, but I found it illumined
now that I had a little understanding of Christian
Science. For ten years I have not had to lie down in
the daytime from any sickness. I am now, and have
been all these years, the picture of perfect health.
When I first read Science and Health I weighed one
hundred and four pounds; I now weigh over one hundred and sixty. This physical health is not to be com-
pared to my happiness, — my harmony that nothing
can take away, — because it is the gift of God. Nothing
has shown me the perversity of the human mind more
than in its conclusions in regard to my healing. Even
when I felt and knew that I was healed, people constantly said, because I was thin and delicate looking,
"You are not well, any one could look at you and know
it." Now that I am fleshy, they say, "You don't look

as if you ever had a pain in all your life. You could not have had consumption."

When I think what my life was before I had Christian Science, of the six years of colds, suffering, and coughing, not to mention the unhappiness, I want to "work, watch, and pray" for the Mind of Christ, that I may work rightly in God's vineyard, and to know that in truth, what belongs to one belongs to all, — that one God, one Life, Truth, and Love is all. — A. C. L., Kansas City, Kans.

DESIRE FOR LIQUOR AND TOBACCO DISAPPEARED

I first heard of Christian Science four years ago. At that time drinking and smoking were my comforters. I had no other companionship. I had lived almost constantly from childhood in an evil atmosphere. Though I was far from being satisfied with my condition, I failed to see how to better it until I read Science and Health. I used occasionally to listen to a sermon, but sermons did not give me any more comfort than I derived from my pipe, hence I concluded that church-going could not satisfy me and I preferred drinking and smoking. When I began to read Science and Health, I saw it offered something substantial. After a few months' study all desire for drinking and smoking disappeared. I did not give them up; I made no sacrifices, I simply found something better. I might mention that I had smoked ever since I can remember. I used to smoke years before I left school, and, like most Englishmen, loved my pipe, and would almost prefer to miss a meal rather than to go without my smoke. I used to think it gave me comfort.

During my four years' study of Christian Science I

have not spent a cent for doctors or medicine, neither
have I lost a day from my work on account of sickness,
which compares wonderfully with the previous four years.
I take a great interest and pleasure in reading the Bible
and studying the lessons in the *Quarterly*. The Bible
used to be a most mysterious book to me, but Science
and Health makes it a most precious book, making its
meaning clearer, plainer, and simpler.

I take this opportunity to express my gratitude to Mrs.
Eddy and to the friend who invited me to attend the service held in the Auditorium years ago. I also wish to
acknowledge the benefit I have had from the *Journal*
and the *Sentinel*. They have helped me wonderfully. If
the value of Science and Health and these publications
were measured as business men value things, by the
results or benefits they bring, they certainly would be
priceless to me. It would be impossible to measure
their value, as I have got something from Science and
Health that all the money in the world could not buy. —
H. P. H., Chicago, Ill.

AN EXPRESSION OF LOVING GRATITUDE

In the spring of 1893, while studying for the ministry, Science and Health was placed in my hands, and
the truth contained therein at once became to me the
pearl of great price. I literally devoured the book,
reading it about eighteen hours a day. Its originality
was startling, upsetting my preconceived opinions of
God, man, and creation. Two sentences especially
appealed to me: "The foundation of mortal discord is a
false sense of man's origin" (p. 262), and, "For right

reasoning, there should be but one fact before the thought, namely, spiritual existence" (p. 492). I had found the keynote to the Science of being as taught in this marvellous book, and persevered until a glimpse of the new heavens and new earth came, for the old were passing away. With this spiritual uplifting came also physical health.

All my life had been spent in semi-invalidism, and I seemed destined to a life of suffering. In three weeks after beginning Science and Health, to my joyful surprise I found myself a well man, sound physically, and uplifted spiritually. Life was being lived from a new basis, the old things of personal sense were passing away and all things becoming new. I learned that the infinite good is the one Friend upon whom we can call at all times, an all-powerful, ever-present help in every time of trouble; that His children are really governed in peace and harmony by spiritual law, and as the right understanding of it is gained, the other things soon follow, bringing a peace the human concept can never know.

For the last twelve years my whole time has been devoted to Christian Science practice, and I have seen nearly every so-called incurable disease healed by its beneficent influence. God bless our dear Leader! She has set before us an open door, which no man can shut, and it is but a question of time when the world will know her better and love her more. — E. E. N., Washington, D. C.

HEALED OF BRIGHT'S DISEASE

August 18, 1902, I was taken down with what three doctors pronounced Bright's disease, and they stated that I would not live a year, or if I did succeed in living longer, I would be mentally unbalanced. On December 6, 1902, my wife presented me with Science and Health as a birthday gift, and it was indeed the best present I ever received. Since that time I have been reading it and attending Second Church here. I have not used any medicine since, nor has any one in our home. I am in the finest of health and have lost all my bad habits. This truth has brought a great spiritual uplifting to all of us, and words cannot express my gratitude to Mrs. Eddy and to all who have helped me to the same. — T. V., Chicago, Ill.

FIBROID TUMOR DESTROYED

When quite young I was impressed that the Bible was not properly interpreted by the preachers, for I could not conceive of a God of wrath who was unjust enough to allow His little ones to suffer pain, misery, and death. I had hope, however, that some day the truth would be revealed to an awakening world, but little did I dream that even then there was one of God's noble women who reflected sufficient purity and holiness to entertain the "angel of his presence," and commune with the true God.

I was believed to be predisposed to scrofula, so that I was not a strong or attractive child, and my girlhood and womanhood were scarcely ever free from dread of the laws of matter and lack of strength. The climax was reached when a physician informed me, after weeks of treatment, that I had a fibroid tumor, which required an operation. The conditions were most trying and I

was heartsick and discouraged when, in January, 1893,
I heard of Christian Science through a letter from a dear
sister who had been greatly benefited thereby, and I resolved to go at once to a practitioner, for I believed it
to be the long-lost truth that would make me free. It
meant a great effort and sacrifice for me to go to Chicago
at that time, but divine Love opened the way and I reached
there in March. I had been in my sister's home but
a few days, reading Science and Health almost constantly, when I asked her if I had not better have
treatment for the tumor, which had given me so much
trouble. She said to me, "You feel well, do you not?"
I assured her that I never had felt so well as I had since
reaching there. "Well," she said with decision, "your
tumor is gone, for God never made it," and her statements
were true, for it has never been heard of from that day.
Since then I have been healed of chronic sore throat,
hay fever, and other troubles, and I know that Christian
Science is the truth. — B. W. S., Coldwater, Mich.

LIGHT OUT OF DARKNESS

I have received so much benefit from the testimonies
in the *Sentinel* and *Journal* that I send mine, hoping
it may cheer some struggling heart. I was reared by
kind and loving Christian parents and was a member
of an orthodox church for over twenty years, but I was
never satisfied. I was filled with fear and bound down
by the false gods of this world, — sin, disease, and poverty; consequently every way I turned, and in everything
I attempted to do, I was met with disappointment and
failure; but God was leading me into a different life.

My interest was first awakened to Christian Science about thirteen years ago, and I have been a willing disciple ever since. Through the reading of Science and Health I was healed of chronic catarrh and laryngitis, and it also enabled me to lay off my glasses. Christian Science has not only helped me mentally, morally, and physically, but the greatest blessing of all is the spiritual uplifting which enabled me to know that God is both able and willing to care for His children, if we are but willing to do our part and bear the cross which, though it seems heavy at times, always brings a sure reward. Christian Science has not only helped me, but it has enabled me to help others.

The Bible is a new book to me. I now see what Jesus meant when he said, "Come unto me, all ye that labor and are heavy laden, and I will give you rest."

My heart goes out in gratitude to Mrs. Eddy for the work she has done and is still doing for the world, and to God I am most grateful that He has guided me into the truth, that I may have life, and have it more abundantly. — Mrs. M. M., Chicago, Ill.

A GRATEFUL TESTIMONY

"Thy word is a lamp unto my feet, and a light unto my path."

This has been proven to me in every way. When Christian Science came to me, I was a wreck, physically, mentally, and financially; but since the reading of Science and Health turned my thought toward the light, I have found that, as far as I am willing to receive the word and live it, all comforts are supplied me. I am especially grateful for the spiritual help. I know that things which I did and thought last year I would not do or think this year, and am satisfied. Through the careful and prayerful study of Science and Health I have been lifted from sickness to health, from sorrow to peace, from lack to plenty, and, the most beautiful of all, from darkness to light. — Mrs. H. S. C., Seattle, Wash.

HEALED OF CONSUMPTION AND ASTHMA

It is a pleasure to acknowledge the great benefits which have come to me through Christian Science. It is nearly ten years since I began the investigation of the subject by borrowing a copy of Science and Health. I had become a hopeless sufferer from asthma, — the disease being so aggravated at times as to make breathing almost impossible. I was also a victim of that dread disease, consumption. It was hereditary, nearly all my family on both sides having passed away with it. I took up Christian Science very much as a drowning man catches at a straw. However, I was much interested as soon as I began to understand it, and having read the book nearly all my waking hours for a few weeks, I became so much better and so convinced of its truth, that myself and wife destroyed all the medicines in the home, and have never since used any remedy except Christian Science. I continued to study and to put into practice the teaching as best I knew, and was restored to health in a few months.

Prior to my investigation of Christian Science I had been from boyhood an outspoken infidel, had read that class of literature extensively, and had no desire for anything of a religious nature, — the orthodox teaching never having appealed to me as a rational exposition of an all-wise God. I now have no more doubt of the truth of the teaching of the great Way-shower, Jesus of Nazareth, than I doubt the correctness of the basic law of mathematics or music. I have no doubt whatever that Christian Science saved me from the grave, and thus proved a most practicable and efficient help in time of greatest need. However great my physical suffering has been, I can but feel glad that through it the door of consciousness was opened to let in the light of Truth. Thus I have progressed a little way in the knowledge of God, good, as revealed in Christian Science. — C. B., Webb City, Mo.

Word Index

Word Index

T he following index provides a convenient listing of many key words found in this book. It is not exhaustive, but simply offers an introduction to the ideas of the author. For more comprehensive research a complete concordance is helpful. This is available, in print or computerized form, from the publisher.

This book has been prepared to be used with the aid of a concordance. The column of line numbers on each page, together with the page number, establishes a system to help readers find specific passages quickly.

Spelling of key words is consistent with that found in the text, even though in some cases this differs from modern American spelling. Special capitalization appears throughout the text for words that refer to God: Mind, Spirit, Soul, Principle, Life, Truth, Love. These synonyms for Deity are included in the index.

Page citations referring to marginal headings are enclosed in brackets.

Word Index

ability, abilities: 128, 260, 393.

Abraham: *definition* 579.

accident(s): 397, 424.

action: 166; higher plane of 256, 265, 384; voluntary and involuntary 187, 239.

Adam: *definition* 579-580; 214, 338, 345.

adultery (infidelity): 56, 106.

adversary: *definition* 580-581; *see also* **devil**.

affection(s): 8, 57, 58, 60, 239, 451.

affirmation(s): 219, 392.

Agassiz, Louis: 104, 547.

age: 244-246.

agnosticism: 596.

alcoholic drinks: 406; *see also* **appetites, drugs**.

All-in-all (God): 275, 331, 468; *see also* **God**.

anatomy: 160, 173; as dissection of thoughts 462.

angels: *definition* 581; 298-299; Gabriel and Michael 566-567; *see also* **thought(s)**.

animal magnetism: Chapter 5 "Animal Magnetism Unmasked" (100-106); 484; *see also* **hypnotism**.

animals: 550; *see also* **creatures**.

anxiety: *See* **fear**.

Apocalypse, the: Chapter 16 "The Apocalypse" (558-578); *see also* **Bible**.

appetite(s): 398, 490; depraved 188, 406; *see also* **alcoholic drinks, food**.

ark: *definition* 581.

ascension: of Jesus 46, 292; spiritual 509.

astronomy: 119, 188, 195; astronomer 125.

atonement: Chapter 2 "Atonement and Eucharist" (18-55); 497.

authority: 134, 342, 381, 390, 395, 573.

baptism: *definition* 581; with fire 565; of the Holy Ghost 558; spiritual 241-242; *see also* **sacrament**.

beauty, beautiful: 57, 246-248.

Beethoven, Ludwig von: 213.

being: Chapter 10 "Science of Being" (268-340); 191, 207, 249, 309, 518; facts of 228, 479; in God 108, 381; harmony of 6; scientific statement of 468; true conception of 260; *see also* **existence, Science**.

belief(s): 43, 77, 428, 488; effects of 219, 377, 386; improved 296; and understanding 203, 251, 289, 297, 425.

Bible: authority 126; central fact of 131; guide 497; misinterpretation of spiritual meaning 319; Science and 146; *see also* **Apocalypse, Genesis, glossary of selected Bible terms, Scriptures, Sermon on the Mount, Word**.

birth: 463; of Jesus 30, 539.

birthright: 518.

blessings: vii, 3, 4, 10, 15, 325.

blood: of Jesus 25; and life 376; *see also* **circulation**.

body: 14, 62, 119, 125, 162, 477; consciousness and 425; scientific government of 167; Soul/Spirit (God) and 93, 223; thought and 208, 260-261, 383, 400, 485; *see also* **thought(s)**.

bones: broken 401-402.

brain: 191, 372, 478.

brotherhood (of man): 340, 467, 470, 518.

cause, causation: and effect 114, 207, 275; is mental 187, 377; and Mind (God) 195, 208, 262, 379, 415, 467; spiritual 170; universal 331.

Word Index

chance: 424, 486.

chaos: 255, 479.

character: 4, 60, 357, 492; nurseries of 235.

charity: xii, 270, 444.

chastity: 57, 405.

child, children: *definition* 582-583; 62, 130, 236, 237; of God 444, 476, 573; health of 413; of Israel 583; *see also* **parent(s)**.

Christ: *definition* 583; atonement of 18; coming of 118, 230; divinity of 25, 26; dual nature of Jesus and 333, 334, 473, 482; healing 143, 332; idea of God 29, 54, 316, 347; *see also* **Jesus, Messiah**.

Christian(s): 15, 21, 138, 242; duties 31, 37; healers 146; warfare 29.

Christianity: 138, 142, 210, 232, 271, 322, 341, 342, 466.

Christian Science: Chapter 12 "Christian Science Practice" (362-442), Chapter 13 "Teaching Christian Science" (443-464); discovery 107-109; doctrine 304, 454; mission 150; platform 330-340; system of healing 123; tenets of 497; *see also* **Science**.

church: *definition* 583; built upon the rock 137-138; healing and 136; uniting with 35.

circulation: 373, 415; *see also* **blood**.

clairvoyance: *See* **mind-reading**.

clergy: 235-236; *see also* **preaching**.

Comforter: 55, 127, 271; *see also* **Holy Ghost**.

commandment(s): 4, 19, 340.

communion: *See* **Eucharist, sacrament**.

consciousness: 14, 302, 355, 391, 425, 480, 573; divine 531, 598.

consecration: 3, 28, 262, 428.

contagion, contagious: 153-154, 176, 220, 392.

control: 392; of body 167, 228; Mind's (God's) 125, 169, 171.

courage: *See* **moral(s)**.

creation: Chapter 9 "Creation" (255-267), Chapter 15 "Genesis" (501-557); *see also* **creator**.

creator: *definition* 583; 263, 507-508; *see also* **creation**.

creatures: 514; *see also* **animals**.

crime: 61, 97, 104-105, 404.

cross: 50, 224; take the 15, 34, 254.

crucifixion: 27, 45-46, 137, 497.

cup (of Jesus): 10, 26, 33-34; *see also* **Eucharist**.

Darwin, Charles: *See* **evolution**.

day: *definition* 584.

death: *definition* 584; 289-291, 426-430.

demonstration: 99, 112-113, 147, 547.

desire: for holiness 11; as prayer 1, 2, 4, 13.

despair: 8, 170, 174.

develop, development: 128, 258, 419, 547.

devil: *definition* 584; *see also* **adversary, evil**.

diet: *See* **food**.

disciple(s): 21, 271; and healing 328, 342.

disease: 176, 411; cause of 174, 178, 230, 377; contagious 154; cure of 180, 412; as error 483; as illusion 168, 348; *see also* **fear, healing, sickness, treatment**.

dishonesty: 453.

divinity and humanity: 2, 561.

doctor: *See* **physician**.

dream: 14, 188, 249-250, 491-492, 530; of death 427, 429.

drugs: and brain 408; faith in 146, 155, 160, 169, 484; not used by Jesus 143, 157, 185; *see also* **alcoholic drinks, homeopathy, medicine, narcotics, tobacco**.

duty: 37, 385, 496.

ears: *definition* 585; 213; *see also* **hearing**.

earth: *definition* 585; 96.

Eddy, Mary Baker: author vii, x, 460, 463-464; Bible as guide 126; discovery of Christian Science 107-109; early years 351, 359, 471; experiments in medicine 152-153; healings 156, 184-185, 192-193, 382, 389.

Word Index

education (academics): 62, 195, 235.

Ego (God): *definition* 588; 216, 335-336; *see also* **God.**

energy: divine 249, 445; material 534.

error: 472.

eternity: 468-469, 598-599.

Eucharist: 32, 35; *see also* **cup (of Jesus), sacrament.**

Eve: *definition* 585; 533.

evidence: 356, 380.

evil: 16, 71, 92, 103, 207; *see also* **devil.**

evolution: [172], 547, 551; spiritual 135.

exercise: 165, 174, 198-199, 232.

existence: 110, 167, 246, 331, 427, 492; mortal 70, 188, 403; *see also* **being.**

eyes: *definition* 586; *see also* **sight.**

---

faith: 23, 297, 319; blind 398; in drugs 146, 155, 169, 484; and works 145-146.

family, families: 103, 444, 470, 515; human 202, 234; universal 577.

fasting: 220, 221.

Father (God): *definition* 586; *see also* **God.**

Father-Mother (God): 16, 331-332, 516; *see also* **God.**

fatigue: 217-219, 384, 385.

fear: *definition* 586; of death 426; and disease 188, 376, 377, 411, 493; effects of 159; and fever 376; and inflammation 421; and Love (God) 373, 410, 578; *see also* **disease.**

fever: 375-376.

flesh: 241, 274, 316, 320, 350, 385.

food: 197, 221-222, 388-389; *see also* **appetites.**

force(s): 96, 124, 192, 293.

forgiven, forgiveness, forgives: 5, 6, 7, 339, 497; *see also* **sin.**

form(s): 263-264, 281, 306, 503.

freedom: 225-228, 242, 454; moral 58.

---

gender (feminine, masculine): 508, 516; *see also* **man.**

Genesis: Chapter 15 "Genesis" (501-557); *see also* **Bible.**

ghost(s): *definition* 587; as images of thought 86; imaginary 352-353, 371.

glory: 262, 323, 566.

glossary of selected Bible terms: Chapter 17, "Glossary" (579-599); *see also* **Bible.**

God: *definition* 587; 465-466; Elohim 515, 523; *see also* **All-in-all, Ego, Father, Father-Mother, I AM, Life, Love, Mind, Mother, Principle, Soul, Spirit, Supreme Being, Truth.**

gods: *definition* 587; 280, 535.

goodness: 213, 246, 260, 277, 304, 518.

grace: 4, 67, 134, 247, 333, 494.

Graham, Sylvester: 170, 221.

gratitude: 3, 4, 26.

grief: 386; *see also* **sorrow.**

growth: of Christian character 291; spiritual 91, 243, 260, 485.

guilt, guilty: 455, 568.

---

happiness: 57, 60, 232, 304, 337.

harmony: 134, 242, 338.

hatred: 404-405, 571.

healer: [169], 395, 417, 446, 493.

healing: viii, xi, 31, 41, 44, 145, 367, 404, 419; Bible and 146, 406; Jesus and 55, 271; *see also* **disease.**

health: 69, 79, 120, 166, 241, 339, 381-382.

hearing: 214, 486-487; *see also* **ears.**

heart: *definition* 587; honest 8, 272, 464; pure in 241, 337; valves of 187.

heaven: *definition* 587; 6, 36, 242, 266, 291; *see also* **kingdom of heaven.**

hell: *definition* 588; 35, 266.

heredity: 178, 228, 425.

Word Index

Word Index

Mother (God): *definition* 592; 256, 332, 530; *see also* **God.**

motive(s): 2, 15, 104-105, 326, 446, 454.

movement(s): 90, 283.

Mozart, Wolfgang Amadeus: 213.

muscle(s): 160, 198-199, 217.

music: 213, 255, 304-305.

narcotics: 157, [230]; *see also* **drugs, medicine.**

need(s): 13, 16, 323, 494, 518.

neighbor: 9, 55, 239, 340.

nerve(s): 211-212, 392, 478-480.

Nightingale, Florence: 385.

nurse(s): 155, 364, 395.

obedience, obey: 25, 182, 183, 239, 242, 253.

obstetrics: 463.

omnipotence, omnipotent: 17, 182, 206, 228, 345, 412; *see also* **power.**

ontology: 129, 460, 556.

oppression: 225-227.

pain: 153, 212, 346, 393, 415-416, 464.

pantheism: 27, 129, 294.

parent(s): 62, 236, [336]; *see also* **child.**

path(s): 254, 265, 426, 454.

patience: 242, 254, 367, 454.

patient(s): 149, 179, 365, 411.

Paul (Apostle): 324-326.

peace: 264, 265, 323, 329, 506.

penalty: 384-385, 387.

perfection: 168, 233, 253-254, 325, 414, 470.

persecution: 28-29, 238, 560.

personality: 40, 285, 337.

Peter (Simon): 137-138.

pharmacy: 460.

philosophy: 269; *see also* **Socrates.**

physician(s): 144, 151, 180, 235, 422.

physiology: Chapter 7 "Physiology" (165-200).

power: 192, 228, 264, 270, 276, 490; *see also* **omnipotence.**

practice of Christian Science: Chapter 12 "Christian Science Practice" (362-442).

prayer: Chapter 1 "Prayer" (1-17); *see also* **Lord's Prayer.**

preaching: 201, 241; *see also* **clergy.**

Principle (God): 3, 13, 272, 465; *see also* **God.**

problem (of being): 44, 254, 262, 273.

progress: 224, 239, 240, 256, 296, 426.

prophet(s): *definition* 593; 84, 98, 214, 243, 270, 333.

Psalm 23: 578.

Ptolemy: 122.

punishment: 230, 340, 384, 387, 497.

purity: 241, 337.

purpose: 8, 326, 506.

questions and answers: Chapter 14 "Recapitulation" (465-497).

reality: 207, 275, 335, 353.

red dragon: *definition* 593; 562-565.

reflection: 259, 515-516.

reform, reformation: 5, 19, 22, 139, 285, 327.

regeneration: 242.

repentance: 19, 242.

rest: 217, 387, 519.

resurrection: *definition* 593; 34, 42, 45, 317.

Revelation: *See* **Apocalypse.**

rights: 63, 225-227, 253, 381.

Word Index

sacrament: 32, 34; *see also* **baptism, Eucharist.**

sacrifice: 11, 16, 459; of Jesus 26, 54.

salvation: *definition* 593; 22, 39, 45, 51, 285, 291, 316; saved 328, 497.

Satan: *See* **adversary, devil.**

Saviour: *See* **Christ, Jesus.**

Science: Chapter sub-section 107-131; demands of 467; *see also* **being, Christian Science.**

Science and Health (book): Chapter 11 "Some Objections Answered" (341-361); x, 456-457; first edition x; required textbook 456-457; revisions of 361; strictures and criticisms 110.

Scriptures: 241, 319-320, 501, 547-548; "Key to the Scriptures" 499-599; *see also* **Bible, Word.**

seeker, seeking: x, xii, 10, 518.

self: 324.

selfhood: 68, 91, 294, 316.

self-knowledge: 462.

self-love: 242.

senses: 488-493; material/physical 120, 122, 284, 293, 543; spiritual 209, 272, 298, 498, 505.

separate(d): 91, 303, 306, 522.

Sermon on the Mount: 174, 271; *see also* **Bible.**

serpent: *definition* 594; 92, 269, 529-534.

Shakespeare, William: iii, 66, 244.

sickness: 166, 188, 208, 390, 411, 417, 460; *see also* **disease.**

sight: 84, 214, 247, 486, 489; *see also* **eyes.**

sin: 253, 311, 339, 404, 447, 472-475, 497, 568; sinner 6, 22-23, 475-476; *see also* **forgiveness.**

slavery: 68, 224-228, 381.

smoking: *See* **tobacco.**

Socrates: 66, 215; *see also* **philosophy.**

sorrow: 66, 304; wrong-doing 5; *see also* **grief.**

Soul (God): 119-120, 467, 477-478, 481-482; *see also* **God.**

Spirit (God): *definition* 594; viii, 173, 192, 223, 275, 278, 335; *see also* **God.**

spirits: *definition* 594; 206-207.

spiritualism: Chapter 4 "Christian Science versus Spiritualism" (70-99).

spirituality: 99, 484-487; spiritualization 96, 158, 407, 593.

steps: 213, 242, 429, 444, 513.

stomach: 220-222, 413.

strength: [79], 80, 183, 192, 219, 377.

substance: *definition* 468; 90, 278, 508.

suffering: 270, 365, 377, 385, 394-395.

sun: 188-189, 209, 246, 250.

supernatural: xi, 83, 111, 134.

superstition: 4, 288, 353.

Supreme Being: 93, 117, 285; *see also* **God.**

surgery: 401-402.

symptoms: 194, 390, 411.

testimonials of healing: Chapter 18 "Fruitage" (600-700).

theology: Chapter sub-section 131-142; and anatomy 148; and healing 145.

thought(s): 86, 125, 199, 248, 259, 261, 284, 310, 506; dissection of 462; evil 234; God's 286, 513-514; *see also* **angels, body.**

time: *definition* 595; 468, 584, 598-599.

tobacco: 383, 404, 406-407, 454; *see also* **drugs.**

treatment (mental): vii-viii, 126, 410, 425; *see also* **disease.**

trust: 299, 417, 488, 495.

Truth (God): viii, 126, 230, 287-288, 288-289, 466, 495; *see also* **God.**

understanding: 462, 505-506.

universe: 114, 121, 264, 289, 295, 300, 337, 468.

Word Index

MARY BAKER EDDY

Thinker, Healer, Author

Mary Baker Eddy spent many years searching for practical, permanent solutions to the many challenges that threatened her life and happiness. She discovered a method of spiritual healing that enabled her to gain control of her life and triumph over obstacles such as divorce, homelessness, family rejection, and chronic poor health.

Eddy devoted her life to sharing with others this scientific, spiritual system of healing based on an understanding of God as both all powerful and completely good. In addition to healing thousands, teaching others to heal, and giving public talks, she wrote and published many books and articles explaining these revolutionary ideas.

Her primary work, *Science and Health with Key to the Scriptures*, has sold over 9 million copies worldwide. In addition to English, it is available in French, German, Spanish, Portuguese, 12 other bilingual editions, and Braille.

TITLES BY THIS AUTHOR

SCIENCE AND HEALTH WITH KEY TO THE SCRIPTURES

One of the first books to set forth the mind/body connection, *Science and Health* answers questions about spirituality and how spiritual healing works. Includes over 100 pages of reader testimonials.

700 pages. Paperback, $9.95.
ISBN 0-87952-259-3
Hardcover, $24.
ISBN 0-87952-260-7

RETROSPECTION AND INTROSPECTION

This is Mary Baker Eddy's own story. She writes about her youth, publication of *Science and Health with Key to the Scriptures,* and experiences as a healer and author.

95 pages. Paperback, $10.
ISBN 0-87952-044-2

MISCELLANEOUS WRITINGS 1883-1896

Includes addresses, letters, poems, and articles on topics such as mental healing, forgiveness, angels, and marriage. Offers inspiring insights and practical ideas that support personal growth and mental and physical well-being. Includes letters from people healed by reading *Science and Health with Key to the Scriptures*.

471 pages. Paperback, $16.
ISBN 0-87952-040-X

RUDIMENTAL DIVINE SCIENCE

Answers some of the most commonly asked questions about Christian Science and how it heals.

17 pages. Booklet, $5.
ISBN 0-87952-059-0

THE PEOPLE'S IDEA OF GOD — ITS
EFFECT ON HEALTH AND CHRISTIANITY

Looks at how individuals' lives are influenced by their views of God, and the life-transforming effect of spiritual ideals.

14 pages. Booklet, $5.
ISBN 0-87952-235-6

CHRISTIAN HEALING

Explains how the healings performed by Christ Jesus and his early followers are possible today.

20 pages. Booklet, $5.
ISBN 0-87952-058-2

NO AND YES

A thought-provoking look at Christian Science in relation to other Christian faith traditions.

46 pages. Booklet, $5.
ISBN 0-87952-237-2

UNITY OF GOOD

Shows how a better understanding of God as completely good can bring healing to your life. Includes "The Ego," "Soul," "The Deep Things of God," and other articles.

64 pages. Booklet, $5.
ISBN 0-87952-053-1

ALSO BY MARY BAKER EDDY

POEMS

CHRIST AND CHRISTMAS

CHRISTIAN SCIENCE VERSUS PANTHEISM

PULPIT AND PRESS

THE FIRST CHURCH OF CHRIST, SCIENTIST, AND MISCELLANY

MANUAL OF THE MOTHER CHURCH

MESSAGE TO THE MOTHER CHURCH FOR 1900

MESSAGE TO THE MOTHER CHURCH FOR 1901

MESSAGE TO THE MOTHER CHURCH FOR 1902

To order in the U.S. and Canada, call 1-800-877-8400.

In other countries call 1-617-450-2790. Prices listed are in US dollars. VISA®, MasterCard®, American Express®, Discover®, and checks accepted. Prices subject to change. Minimum order US$10.

Or write for more information: Publisher, The Writings of Mary Baker Eddy, P.O. Box 174, Boston, MA 02117-0174 USA.

Mary Baker Eddy's writings are also available at Christian Science Reading Rooms worldwide.

For an on-line companion to *Science and Health*, browse www.scienceandhealth.com

EN0600SHHC

SCIENCE AND HEALTH
WITH KEY TO THE SCRIPTURES

MARY BAKER EDDY

How I first found out about this book:

○ Found in bookstore, name: _____
○ Advertisement–Newspaper/Magazine, name: _____
○ Word of mouth   ○ Catalog
○ Advertisement/Show–T.V.   ○ Gift
○ Advertisement/Show–Radio   ○ Other

Benefits I received from reading this book: _____

_____

Other comments: _____

_____

Number of books on this subject I purchase a year:

○ 1   ○ 2-5   ○ 6-10   ○ more than 10

How I got started reading this type of book:
○ Personal growth   ○ Quest for meaning of life
○ Improving mental outlook   ○ Professional enhancement
○ Staying healthy/healing   ○ Other _____
○ Religious reasons

I would like more information about:

○ The author   ○ Talking with others who
○ The author's other titles   read this book

Browse **www.scienceandhealth.com** *to learn more about the author, connect with other readers and explore practical spirituality.*

I would recommend this book to others: ○ Yes   ○ No

Name: _____   **Business Title:** _____
Address: ○ Home ○ Work/Co. **Name:** _____
Street/Suite#: _____
City/State/Zip: _____   **Country:** _____
E-Mail: _____

○ Please include me in your ongoing mailing list.

SH0600HC

Exploring Practical Spirituality